FREE MOVEMENT OF PERSONS WITHIN THE EUROPEAN COMMUNITY

This book explores the extent to which European Community law confers upon individuals the right to gain access to public services in other Member States. Are European citizens and third country nationals who have moved to other Member States entitled to claim minimum subsistence benefits, to receive medical care or to be admitted to education? Does Community law provide for a freedom of movement for patients, students and persons in need of social welfare benefits? If so, to what extent does Community law have regard for the Member States' fears for, and concerns about, welfare tourism? Besides addressing numerous detailed questions on the precise degree to which Community law allows for cross-border access to public services, the author analyses how Community law, and the Court of Justice in particular, have sought to reconcile the Community's objectives of realising freedom of movement and ensuring equality of treatment with the need to develop and maintain adequate social services within the Community. In addition, the book contains a detailed analysis of United States constitutional law on cross-border access to public services, exploring the question whether the European Community can possibly learn from the American experience.

Free Movement of Persons Within the European Community
Cross-Border Access to Public Benefits

A.P. VAN DER MEI

·HART·
PUBLISHING

OXFORD – PORTLAND OREGON
2003

Published in North America (US and Canada) by
Hart Publishing c/o
International Specialized Book Services
5804 NE Hassalo Street
Portland, Oregon
97213-3644
USA

Hart Publishing is a specialist legal publisher based in Oxford, England.
To order further copies of this book or to request a list of other
publications please write to:

Hart Publishing, Salter's Boatyard, Folly Bridge,
Abingdon Road, Oxford OX1 4LB
Telephone: +44 (0)1865 245533 or Fax: +44 (0)1865 794882
e-mail: mail@hartpub.co.uk
WEBSITE: http//www.hartpub.co.uk

British Library Cataloguing in Publication Data
Data Available
ISBN 1–84113–288–8 (hardback)

Typeset by Hope Services (Abingdon) Ltd.
Printed and bound in Great Britain on acid-free paper by
Biddles Ltd, *www.biddles.co.uk*

For Aba Atta and Baaba Atta

Contents

1

Introduction

This book examines the rules of European Community law governing cross-border access to public benefits. More specifically, the book aims to explore the extent to which the Community's rules on freedom of movement and non-discrimination confer upon individuals the right to obtain minimum subsistence benefits, health care and education in other Member States.

Lurking beneath virtually all questions on cross-border access to public services[1] lies a potential conflict between, on the one hand, the Community's goal of realising a free movement of persons and, on the other hand, the need to develop and maintain public services within the Community. Whatever its precise meaning and scope, a right to freedom of movement, which is relevant and practical, would seem to require that beneficiaries are able to gain access to certain public benefits while staying or residing in the territory of other Member States. For instance, beneficiaries might be discouraged from exercising their free movement rights if these did not encompass a right to claim medical assistance, a right to be admitted to schools and universities or if cross-border movement were to lead to a loss of social benefits. Further, on a broad construction, the free movement objective could be interpreted as to include a right to freedom of movement for students, patients and persons in need of social benefits, which entitles beneficiaries to go to other Member States for the sole purpose of obtaining welfare state services.

A too broadly interpreted free movement of persons, however, might affect public services within the European Community. An unconditional and unlimited freedom of movement for patients, students and 'needy' persons could possibly jeopardise the funding and infrastructure of welfare state facilities. To some degree, the Member States ability to develop and maintain public services would seem to depend on the capacity to exclude nationals and/or residents of other States.

Besides addressing numerous concrete questions regarding cross-border access to public services, this book seeks to establish how European Community

---

[1] The terms 'public benefits' and 'public services' will be used interchangeably in this book. The title of the book refers to public benefits in order to avoid any possible confusion with the public service exception contained in Art 39(4) EC.

law has sought to reconcile the potentially conflicting interests of promoting freedom of movement and preserving public benefit systems.

2 FREE MOVEMENT OF PERSONS VERSUS THE PROTECTION OF
PUBLIC BENEFIT SYSTEMS

2.1 Public Benefits

In order to gain some insight into the subject of cross-border access to public benefits it is worth taking a closer look at public services. Even though it would have been appropriate, no attempt is made here to define the term 'public benefits' or 'public services.' Public benefits are too diverse.[2] They include facilities such as education, public roads and transport facilities, social insurance for risks such as unemployment, disability and old-age, public parks and libraries, police and fire services as well as subsidies for cultural activities, housing subsidies and programmes, social assistance and child benefit schemes, court and legal aid systems, health care and insurance, national defence, etc. Moreover, public services are organised, financed and administered in different ways. Public benefit programmes can be initiated by governments at municipal, provincial, state and/or federal level and they may be publicly provided or merely publicly funded. Public services can be funded from various sources, such as taxes, premiums and contributions of beneficiaries[3] and they are administered by public, semi-public and/or private bodies. The range of public benefit schemes is so vast that it is virtually impossible to include them all in a single definition that would have much analytical or other additional value.

For the purposes of this book, it is more useful to categorise public benefits. Although the lines of demarcation are fluid, three groups of public benefits can be distinguished. A first group consists of benefits such as defence, police and fire protection, court systems and other 'facilities' that are primarily aimed at ensuring public security or safeguarding law and order. These benefits may be seen as products of the classical 'night-watch state.' A second group of benefits can be attributed to the role that governments play in the 'industrial welfare state.' These services include public roads and transport facilities, tax benefits for companies, telecommunications facilities, etc. By offering such public facilities governments provide individuals and companies with the basic tools and facilities needed to operate in the private market. Minimum subsistence benefits, education and health care fall primarily within the last group of benefits with which governments seek to modify or correct market outcomes. This concerns 'welfare state benefits.'

---

[2] Cp Clermonts *et al*, *Verblijfsrecht en Gebruik van Collectieve Voorzieningen door Immigranten* (1991) 52–7.

[3] Eg, own contributions for medical care, tuition and enrolment fees for public schools or the price of membership cards for public libraries.

Among the numerous and diverse welfare state benefits two further distinctions can be made. First, such benefits may come in the form of 'benefits in kind' or in the form of 'cash benefits.' The former include health care, public housing and educational facilities. In economic terms, such services can be seen as 'commodities' which could in principle be provided by private 'actors.' For various reasons, however, governments have often withdrawn such 'products' from the private market and taken it upon themselves to provide such services in kind, and often largely free of charge, to the population. Cash benefits, such as social assistance benefits and child allowances, consist of payments that enable beneficiaries to purchase 'commodities' on the private market. Secondly, within the scheme of welfare state benefits, contributory and non-contributory benefit schemes can be distinguished. The former are insurance-based programmes which usually oblige the insured to pay premiums and entitle them to, most often cash, benefits when the insured risk (unemployment, sickness, disability, retirement, etc) occurs. Non-contributory benefits are funded out of tax-revenues. Usually, enjoyment of, or entitlement to, such benefits is not linked to or conditional upon the actual payment of tax-contributions.

2.2 Welfare State Benefits: Solidarity, Territoriality and Nationality

Welfare state services, which this book is primarily concerned with, may come in multiple forms, but they do share a number of common features. These may be defined by three concepts: solidarity, territoriality and nationality.

The first two concepts relate to, and result from, the very essence of the welfare state. The notion of the 'welfare state' defies precise definition,[4] but, highly simplified, it may be viewed as a state or other political community whose 'members' have collectively decided to set, and to work towards, a number of social objectives[5] that the private market is unable to

---

[4] See, eg: Barr, *The Economics of the Welfare State* (1993) 6.

[5] Besides objectives of social justice, public intervention in the private market is motivated by reasons of efficiency. See, eg: Barr (1993) n 4 above, ch 4 and Kleinman and Piachaud, 'European Social Policy: Conceptions and Choices' (1993) *JESP* 1–19, 3–5. In economic terms, efficiency implies that resources are used over a given period of time in such a way as to make it impossible to increase the well being of any one person without reducing the well being of any other person (Pareto-optimality). See, eg: Hyman, *Public Finance—A Contemporary Application of Theory to Policy* (1999) 53. Markets can only be (Pareto-)efficient when a number of assumptions hold true: perfect information (ie, consumers and firms are well-informed about the nature, quality and prices of products), perfect competition (ie, economic agents of equal power are able to determine the price they are willing to pay) and the absence of market failures (which may arise in the form of public goods, external effects or increasing returns to scale). When all standard assumptions are present, the market is considered Pareto-efficient; no State intervention is necessary. When one of the assumptions fails, intervention in the market is required. Government intervention can take different forms: regulation (eg, rules concerning the quality of products or mandatory affiliation to social insurance schemes), finance (eg, subsidies or taxes which influence the price of certain products), income transfers (social benefits such as pensions) and public production (State provision of certain goods such as education or medical care).

achieve.[6] In the private marketplace individuals are responsible for their own financial well-being. They are supposed to gain the means needed to meet the costs of living by pursuing economic activities. Not all individuals, however, are able to generate sufficient private income. Incomes may be too low to cover the often high costs of housing, medical care or education and due to illness, disability, dismissal, retirement, pregnancy or lack of jobs, individuals may be faced with drastic reductions in income or even be deprived of any financial means. Social justice, as it is commonly understood in European countries, demands that all members of society have the minimum means at their disposal to meet the basic costs of living (food, clothing, shelter) and that they are all to some extent protected against sudden or drastic reductions in income caused by disability, involuntary unemployment and other reasons beyond their control. Furthermore, social justice requires that all members of society, regardless of economic status or place of residence within the national territory, have access to essential facilities such as education, medical care and housing. In order to meet these objectives the private market rule of distribution of resources in accordance with individual economic performance must be partly

---

[6] The disparities among the welfare states which have developed in post-war Europe are considerable. Some States have invested far more in the development of welfare state facilities than others (see, eg: Olssen, 'Welfare State Research Inc—The Growth of a Crises Industry' (1987) *AS* 371–8) and the ways in which they have organised the welfare state varies. These disparities have inspired some authors to develop typologies of welfare states.

One of the most well known is the one offered by Titmuss. Looking at the specific features of social services and rights, he distinguishes three types of welfare states: (*i*) a 'residual welfare model' in which the State assumes responsibility for not much more than social assistance schemes; (*ii*) an 'industrial achievement-performance model' in which social rights are largely based on merit and investment and (*iii*) an 'institutional redistributive model' in which social benefits are made available on the basis of need rather than merit. See Titmuss, *Social Policy* (1974) 30 *et seq*.

Another classification is made by Esping-Andersen who looks inter alia at the degree to which social rights decrease dependency of beneficiaries on the market ('decommodification'). He distinguishes: (*i*) 'liberal welfare states' which stress the predominance of the private market and only provide for minimal and means-tested welfare benefits; (*ii*) 'conservative-corporatistic welfare states' in which States play a significant role in society and primarily intend to protect status and the family and (*iii*) 'social-democratic welfare states' which are characterised by universal benefits and a high degree of 'decommodification'. See Espings-Andersen, *Three Worlds of Welfare Capitalism* (1990) 26–8. See also: van der Veen, 'De Wankele Verzorgingsstaat—Een Vergelijkende Analyse van Verzorgingsstaten in het Licht van Internationaliseringsprocessen' in Engbersen *et al* (eds), *Zorgen in het Europese Huis—De Grenzen van Nationale Verzorgingsstaaten* (1994) 59–88, 69–74.

Bertola *et al* have classified the Community's Member States in four groups. The first comprises the Nordic States and the Netherlands. These countries come from a tradition of universal welfare provision. They have the highest levels of social expenditure, a high share of benefits offered in kind and a very low level of income inequality. The second group consist of countries which have a Bismarckian tradition such as Austria, Belgium, France and Germany. Income inequality is modest in these countries which have relatively high minimum wages, high unemployment benefits and quite strict employment protection. The Anglo–Saxon countries constitute a third group. They are closer to the Beveredgian tradition. Social assistance plays a comparatively important role, unemployment benefit levels are rather low and employment is less well protected. The last group comprises the southern Member States. Welfare states in Greece, Italy, Spain and Portugal have been developed more recently. Social expenditure is relatively low; income inequality is considerable. See also: Bertola *et al*, 'EU Welfare Systems and Labor Markets: Diverse in the Past, Integrated in the Future?' in Bertola *et al Welfare and Employment in a United Europe* (2000) 23–122, 50–3.

replaced by some form of redistribution in accordance with principles of 'human need,' 'solidarity' and 'mutual aid.'[7]

The territoriality of the welfare state and its public benefit schemes implies mainly two things. First, public benefits are preserved for persons residing or working within the state territory to the exclusion of those living or working outside the state borders.[8] The aforementioned redistributing and solidarity cannot be achieved on a voluntary basis. They need to be organised by governments that have the power to take the necessary measures, to make affiliation to public benefits systems compulsory for the majority of the population and to enforce duties to pay taxes or premiums. Welfare states are based on a notion of 'membership' which not only entails rights[9] to enjoy or claim benefits, but also duties to contribute to the financing of benefit systems.[10]

In the case of social insurance, this link between rights and duties is imposed at the level of the individual beneficiary. As a rule, benefits can only be enjoyed by individuals who(se employers) have paid, or who(se employers) can be required to pay, premiums. Individual enjoyment of tax-funded benefits is not linked to actual payment of, or duties to pay, taxes, but this link does exist at 'group level.' An efficient supply of tax-funded benefits requires that the group consuming the benefits largely coincides with the group that can be required to contribute to the financing of these benefits.[11] Governments lack effective

---

[7] See, eg: Freeman, 'Migration and the Political Economy of the Welfare State' (1986) *Annals AAPSS* 51–63, 52.

[8] Welfare states are often described as territorially closed systems. The 'idea of redistributive justice presupposes a bounded world; a group of people committed to dividing, exchanging and sharing social goods, first of all among themselves'. Walzer, *Spheres of Justice* (1983) 31. See also: Bauböck, *Transnational Citizenship—Membership and Rights in International Migration* (1994) 19; Entzinger, 'De Andere Grenzen van de Verzorgingsstaat—Migratiestromen en Migratiebeleid'in Engbersen *et al* (eds), *Zorgen in het Europese Huis—De Grenzen van Nationale Verzorgingsstaaten* (1994) 142–72, 142 and Freeman (1986) n 7 above.

It is often argued that the afore mentioned commitment depends on some kind of 'identification with a particular group' (Kleinman and Piachaud (1993) n 5 above, 7), 'kinship' (Freeman (1986) n 7 above, 52), 'a sense of common bonds' (Carens, 'Immigration and the Welfare State' in Gutmann (ed), *Democracy and the Welfare State* (1991) 207–30, 209) or a 'fellow feeling' which 'facilitates cooperation on common projects and makes redistribution within the polity more acceptable' (Barry, 'Self-Government Revisited' in Miller and Siedentrop, *The Nature of Political Theory* (1983) 141). On the impact of ethno-linguistic diversity on the social role of the state see, eg: Banting, 'Looking in Three Directions—Migration and European Welfare State in Comparative Perspective' in Bommes and Geddes (eds), *Immigration and Welfare—Challenging the Borders of the Welfare State* (2000) 13–33.

[9] Welfare states and public benefit systems entail more than just private or public charity. The 'essence of the welfare state is government protected minimum standards of income, nutrition, health, housing, and education assured to every citizen as a political right, not as charity'. Wilensky, *The Welfare State and Equality: Structural and Ideological Roots of Public Expenditures* (1975) 1. See also: Schuyt, 'Het Rechtskarakter van de Verzorgingsstaat' in van Doorn and Schuyt, *De Stagnerende Verzorgingsstaat* (1982) 73–96.

[10] See also: Altmaier, 'Europäisches Koordinierendes Sozialrecht—Ende des Territorialitätsprinzip?' in Eichenhofer and Zuleeg, *Die Rechtsprechung des Europäischen Gerichtshof zum Arbeits- und Sozialrecht im Streit* (1995) 71–91, 73–4.

[11] Public finance theories of fiscal federalism teach that in federal political settings public benefits can only be efficiently provided for at local level if the persons who make the collective choices are also the ones who finance and consume the benefits. Bertola *et al* (2000) n 6 above, 90 and Scholsem,

powers to collect tax-contributions from those residing outside the State territory and such persons therefore cannot claim enjoyment of benefits as 'equal members.'

Secondly, territoriality implies that welfare state benefits must be consumed within the State borders. Public benefits such as education, housing or health care often can only be effectively provided and consumed in the State territory and for many cash benefits territoriality basically implies that they cannot be transferred abroad. Among the numerous reasons that account for the non-exportability of cash benefits are the fact that movement to other States is interpreted as giving up membership and, hence, entitlement to benefits and the fact that governments lack sufficient powers to effectively supervise and enforce conditions of eligibility[12] in other States.[13]

The third common feature concerns, as said, the notion of nationality. The logic of the welfare state would seem to imply a membership status, which is defined in terms of residence or employment in the State territory. As a rule, nationality is an immaterial factor as regards duties to make tax or premium contributions and one might expect the same to hold true for rights to enjoy public benefits. Welfare states, however, have been developed by, and within the legal-political framework of, nation States that have a specific bond with, and hold a specific responsibility towards, their own nationals. National laws may contain provisions that make entitlement to, in particular non-contributory,[14] benefits conditional upon the nationality of the State or that impose additional eligibility criteria on non-nationals. Further, and most prominently, the distinction between nationals and non-nationals is reflected in the States' immigration policies. International law obliges States to admit their nationals to their territory,[15] and nationals who actually establish residence there are usually offered access to public benefit schemes, provided they meet substantive eligibility criteria. In

'A Propos de la Circulation des Etudiants: Vers un Federalisme Financier Européen?' (1989) *CDE* 306–23, 309–10.

[12] Eg, the duty to actively seek new employment for entitlement to unemployment benefits or, as regards means-tested benefits, the possibility to establish the resources of beneficiaries. See eg: ch 3, s 5 (exportability of minimum subsistence benefits), ch 4, s 2.4 (right to sickness benefits for persons staying or residing in other states) and ch 5, ss 3 and 4 (right to claim study grants for studies outside the state of residence).

[13] A third, for the moment less relevant, aspect of the territoriality principle is that national rules only allow facts that occur, or have occurred, within the atate borders to be taken into account. For instance, death grants may be limited to the family members of persons who have died within the state borders and child benefits may be preserved for persons whose children are also residing in the State concerned.

[14] See, eg: von Maydel, 'Treatment of Third Country Nationals in the Member States of the European Union and the European Economic Area in Terms of Social Law' in *Commission of the European Communities/Departemento de Relações Internacionais e Convenções de Segurança Social, Social Security in Europe—Equality Between Nationals and Non-Nationals* (1995) 137–54, 148–50.

[15] Staples, *The Legal Status of Third Country Nationals Resident in the European Union* (1999) 24 and Goodwin-Gill, *International Law and the Movement of Persons between States* (1978) 136–7.

principle, however, States are free to deny and regulate the access of non-nationals to their territories,[16] labour markets and welfare state benefit systems.

2.3 Immigration Policy and the Welfare State

Welfare states are thus territorially operating systems based on some kind of membership which implies both rights to enjoy, and duties to contribute to the financing of, public services. In a world where cross-border trade and migration have always been factual realities, States have recognised that they need to regulate and control this welfare state membership. The required balance between revenue and expenditure could not be maintained if taxpaying members were to respond to any increase of tax- or premium-duties by moving to other States with a more favourable 'tax climate' or if States were to allow non-nationals unconditional access to their territory and public services.

For the purposes of this book, it is useful to briefly consider how States have traditionally regulated the admission of non-nationals to their territories and welfare state services. Immigration policies and policies concerning access of non-nationals to public benefit systems have usually been linked to each other.[17] In determining whether, under which conditions and for how long non-nationals will be admitted to the national territory States consider whether, or to what extent, non-nationals are, or are expected to become, in need of public benefits[18] and the specific immigration status conferred upon non-nationals constitutes one of the main criteria for entitlement to public benefits.[19]

---

[16] International law provides for only two exceptions: (*i*) the right to family life (eg, European Convention on Fundamental Freedoms, Art 8) can found a claim to reside in a State of which individuals do not hold the nationality and (*ii*) persons are entitled to remain in another territory if the only alternative is to return to a place or State where they fear inhuman treatment (eg, UN Convention on the Status of Refugees of 1951 and the Protocol of 1967). Guild, *European Community Law from a Migrant's Perspective* (2000) 1.

[17] Indeed, the origin of current migration policies can be linked to the rise of social welfare states. See, eg: Lucassen, 'The Great War and the Origins of Migration Control in Western Europe and the United States (1880–1920)' in Böcker *et al* (eds), *Regulation of Migration—International Experiences* (1998) 45–72.

[18] The question whether non-nationals will be net-contributors to or net-beneficiaries of the welfare state is in practice of course quite difficult to answer. Zolberg, 'Contemporary Transnational Migrations in Historical Perspective: Patterns and Dilemmas' in Kritz (ed), *U.S. Immigration and Refugee Policy* (1983) 36 *et seq*.

[19] In reverse, policies concerning eligibility for public benefits have been used to deter and regulate migration. See, eg: Minderhoud, 'Regulation of Migration—Introduction' in Böcker *et al* (eds), *Regulation of Migration—International Experiences* (1998) 7–24. On the relationship between immigration status and access to social benefits see, eg Brubaker, 'Membership without Citizenship: The Economic and Social Rights of Non-citizens' in Brubaker, *Immigration and the Politics of Citizenship in Europe and North America* (1989) 145–62 and Vermeylen, 'Elementen van het Juridisch Statuut van de Vreemdeling in Europa' in Deslé *et al* (eds), *Denken over Migranten in Europa* (1983) 211–28.

States' policies can be best described as a form of gate keeping.[20] At the first gate, States decide on the grant of visas that entitle tourists, business people or other foreign 'visitors' to enter the national territory and to stay there for a brief period of time. Usually, States do not engage in an in-depth analysis of the possible access to, or need for access to, welfare state benefits because non-residents, as a rule, are only offered limited access to public services. Generally, non-resident foreigners can only benefit from services which *de facto* cannot be denied or whose financing is not seriously affected by an increase in the numbers of beneficiaries, such as street-lightning, public roads and parks,[21] or services which cannot be denied for humanitarian reasons, such as emergency care and police protection. As a rule, foreign visitors have no right to services as non-emergency care, student grants and other social benefits. Entitlement to such benefits is made conditional upon residence or employment in and/or nationality of the State.

At the second gate, States apply rules concerning admission for temporary residence. In deciding on the grant of temporary residence permits to, for instance, seasonal, posted and temporary workers and students, States usually consider the purpose of residence as well as the question whether or not non-nationals are, or are likely to become, in need of public benefits. Foreign students can be required to demonstrate that they have sufficient health insurance and/or that they are able to provide for themselves, whilst workers may have to prove that their job entitles them to a wage not falling below the minimum subsistence level. As temporary residents, non-nationals can be required to pay taxes or pay social security premiums and they may be entitled to take advantage of certain public benefits such as housing programmes, child support systems or public education.[22] Access to benefits such as non-emergency medical care, student grant systems and certain social benefit schemes, however, is often denied by rules which make enjoyment of these benefits conditional upon a minimum period of residence, permanent residence, employment and/or nationality. For temporary residents, lack of sufficient financial means may even lead to the loss of the residence permit and be a ground for expulsion.[23]

---

[20] Hammar, *Democracy and the Nation State: Aliens, Denizens and Citizens in a World of International Migration* (1990) 9–26; Hammar, 'Legal Time of Residence and the Status of Immigrants' in Bauböck, *From Aliens to Citizens—Redefining the Status of Immigrants in Europe* (1994) 187–97 and Sørensen, *The Exclusive European Citizenship—The Case for Refugees and Immigrants in the European Union* (1996) ch 3.

[21] In economic theories such benefits are classed as public goods which are characterised by absence of rivalry in consumption, ie increases in the number of beneficiaries or users do not increase costs, and non-excludability, ie people cannot be prevented from using the good. Barr (1993) n 4 above, 81–2. National defence and street lighting are typical examples of 'pure' public goods; public parks and roads can be classed as 'congestible' public goods, ie, goods of which the marginal costs of additional beneficiaries may be minimal but not wholly zero. Hyman (1999) n 5 above, 139.

[22] Various international human rights instruments have strengthened the legal status of migrant workers. For an overview see, eg: Madra, *Migrant Workers and International Law* (1986) and, in particular, Cholewinski, *Migrant Workers in International Human Rights Law—Their Protection in Countries of Employment* (1997).

[23] See also: ch 3, s 2.2.

The third gate concerns admission for permanent resident status. As a rule, it concerns non-nationals who have passed the second gate and who thus already have lived, worked and paid taxes in the State for a number of years.[24] In deciding on the grant of permanent residence, States usually consider the past, current and the expected future employment status of the non-nationals and they may include in their considerations whether, or to what extent, they have been, are or are expected to become a burden on the 'public purse.' Once admitted for permanent residency, non-nationals can be required to pay an equal share in the financing of public benefits and they are offered access to these benefits under the same conditions as the nationals of the host State. Their residence status is not, or is no longer, affected by their possible use or need of public services.

States' immigration policies are tailed at a fourth gate at which States apply rules and procedures for acquiring their nationality.[25] Usually, non-nationals must have passed the third gate of permanent residence status before they can apply for the host State's nationality. Non-nationals may be required to demonstrate their 'good moral character,' that they have sufficient knowledge of the host State's language, and/or that they have integrated into the State's society. Questions concerning their need of public benefits are not addressed at this stage. As a rule, acquisition of nationality or citizenship does not imply a significant extension of social rights, but it does entitle the persons concerned to political rights that enable them to participate in the decision-making process concerning the welfare state.

In more general terms, States' admission policies can be viewed in terms of granting of membership status. Non-nationals who have been allowed to pass the first gate of entry to the State territory are not offered any membership status. Foreign visitors cannot be required to contribute equally to and, hence, are in principle denied access to welfare state benefits. They are supposed to be members of the welfare state of the State where they reside. Non-nationals who have passed the second gate are granted a partial or conditional membership status. Temporary residents have not paid contributions for long enough to acquire 'full' membership status of the welfare state. That status is only granted

[24] In many states the period of previous residence required for obtaining permanent resident status is about five years. In some states. however, permanent residence status can be acquired after a short period of two up to four years of previous, whilst other states require considerably longer periods of 10 or even 20 years. Groenendijk and Guild, 'Converging Criteria: Creating an Area of Security of Residence for Europe's Third Country Nationals' (2001) *EJML* 37–59, 42; Cholewinski (1997) n 22 above, 384 and Thomas, 'Summing Up and Points of Comparison' in Thomas (ed), *Immigrant Workers in Europe: Their Legal Status, A Comparative Study* (1982) 211 *et seq*, 221–2.

[25] In some states non-nationals are given a right to naturalisation when certain conditions are met, whilst in others the grant of nationality is merely a privilege which governments may but do not have to give. See, eg: Brubaker, 'Citizenship and Naturalization: Policies and Politics' in Brubaker (ed), *Immigration and the Politics of Citizenship in Europe and North America* (1989) 99–125. On the laws concerning the attribution and acquisition of nationality in the Member States of the European Community see especially de Groot, *Staatsangehörigkeit im Wandel—Eine rechtsvergleichende Studie zu den Erwerb- und Verlustgründen der Staatsangehörigkeit* (1989) (with numerous references to other literature).

at the third gate. The non-nationals who have been allowed to pass this gate can be classed as 'denizens,' a concept that has been used to describe the status of non-nationals who have acquired a secure or permanent resident status and who enjoy the same rights as nationals with the exception of political rights such as the right to vote and stand as a candidate in elections.[26] At the fourth gate this 'denizenship' can be transformed into (nominal) citizenship. Non-nationals may become nationals, which implies that they are not offered 'membership' of the welfare state but also membership of the nation State.

2.4 Free Movement of Persons and Cross-Border Access to Welfare State Benefits

In the late 1950s, when the European Economic Community was established and the foundations for the current welfare states were laid, States in western Europe made full use of their powers to regulate the admission of non-nationals to their territories, labour markets and welfare states. Generally, States' policies were restrictive and self-serving. Non-nationals were only admitted in order to fill job vacancies for which no national workers were available and residence permits were restricted to the duration of employment. During their stay foreign workers were required to pay taxes and premiums, but they were only offered access to a few welfare state benefits. Foreign guest workers had been invited to fuel the economy of the host State; they were not to become a burden on the welfare state.[27] At the time, migration was not so much seen as a threat to the welfare state. Rather, by strictly regulating it, migration was regarded and served as a means for developing and strengthening welfare state regimes.

Against this background, it may come as no surprise that the 1957 Treaty of Rome imposed few limits on the States' powers to regulate access to their welfare states. Member States had committed themselves to an integration of their private economic markets, but they had not given up their powers in the public fields of social security, education and health care.[28] National welfare states were not intended to be supplemented by, or to be transformed into, a 'European welfare state.' Furthermore, free movement of persons was only foreseen for workers (Article 48 EEC; now, after amendment, Article 39 EC) and self-employed persons (Article 52 EEC; now Article 43 EC) who were expected to be able to provide for themselves. The Treaty did not contain any specific

---

[26] Hammar (1990) fn 20 above, 12–13; Layton-Henry, 'Citizenship or Denizenship for Migrant Workers' in Layton-Henry (ed), *The Political Rights of Migrant Workers in Western Europe* (1990) 186–95, 188 and Brubaker (1989) n 25 above.

[27] See, eg: Böhning, 'The Migration of Workers in the United Kingdom and the European Community' (1972) and Garth, 'Migrant Workers and Rights of Mobility in the European Community and the United States: A Study of Law, Community and Citizenship in the Welfare State' in Cappelletti *et al*, *Integration Through Law—Europe and the American Federal Experience* (1986) vol 1, 85–163, 90–6.

[28] See also: ch 3, s 2 (social benefit schemes), ch 4, s 2 (health care) and ch 5, s 2 (education).

provision entitling employed and self-employed persons to social benefits, to be admitted to educational institutions or to claim health care services.

To be sure, those drafting the Treaty had recognised that the realisation of free movement of persons would require the grant of certain social rights to workers who due to illness, disability, unemployment or retirement were no longer able to generate a sufficient income.[29] The 1957 Treaty of Rome entrusted the Council with the task of adopting 'measures in the field of social security as are necessary to provide freedom of movement for workers' (Article 51 EEC; now, after amendment, Article 42 EC). The transfer of these social security powers, however, did not seem to have far-reaching implications for the Member States. The measures to be adopted were intended to be based on a number of bi- and multi-lateral social security conventions that the States had already voluntarily signed in the pre-Community period and that only offered social security rights in as far as this did not affect the interests of States with comparatively better developed benefit systems. In addition, the social security measures that were envisaged could only be adopted, and amended, by a unanimous decision of the Council. By joining the European Community the Member States had agreed to open the doors to their national labour markets for each others nationals,[30] but the same did not hold true for the doors to their welfare states. Access to public benefits would remain regulated by national law and/or Community rules that all Member States had voluntarily agreed to.

Over the years, however, the Community rules on the free movement of persons have undergone a significant evolution during which the Member States' powers to control and regulate access to their territories and admission to their welfare states have increasingly been curtailed. First, the Community legislator has been willing to confer upon workers a number of rights that are not expressly mentioned in Article 39. It has developed a comprehensive system for the co-ordination of social security schemes and it has included students, pensioners and even all Community citizens in the free movement regime.[31] Secondly, the European Court of Justice has assumed a very active role in promoting a genuine free movement of persons which is relevant and practical. In hundreds of judgements decided under the Community's social security rules, the Court has given quite a broad interpretation of many provisions and concepts. It has imposed on Member States obligations which they had not foreseen and/or agreed to, when they, as members of the Council, adopted the regulations.[32] In addition, the Court

---

[29] Cp Leibfried, 'Multitiered Institutions and the Making of Social Policy' in Leibfried and Pierson, *European Social Policy—Between Fragmentation and Integration* (1995) 43–77, 52 and Romero, 'Migration as an Issue in European Interdependence and Integration: The Case of Italy' in Milward *et al* (eds), *The Frontier of National Sovereignty 1945–1992: History and Theory* (1993) 33–58.

[30] But see: ch 2, s 2.1.

[31] See also: ch 2, s 3.

[32] Occasionally, the court has not hesitated to overrule the Council by invalidating certain provisions of the regulations as being incompatible with the Treaty. See, eg: Case 41/84 *Pinna* [1986] ECR 1.

has given a particularly broad interpretation of the general Community provisions governing, or relevant to, the free movement of persons such as Article 39 EC, secondary legislation and 12(1) EC, which prohibits 'within the scope of application' of the Treaty 'any discrimination on grounds of nationality.'

As a result of the various legislative and judicial initiatives, the conflict between the goal of promoting freedom of movement, on the one hand, and the need to develop and maintain adequate welfare state benefits, on the other hand, has gradually come to the surface. The Community institutions, and the Court of Justice in particular, have been faced with delicate and fundamental questions. For instance, those drafting the original EEC Treaty had assumed that Article 39 would only apply to full-time workers. In light of more recent developments in the labour markets, however, it could very well be argued that part-time workers should also be able to benefit from Article 39 EC. States have resisted and claimed that such workers may often earn an income falling below the minimum subsistence level and that they are likely to become a burden on their social assistance schemes. The financing of these schemes could be affected if all 'foreign' part-timers were to be given supplementary social benefits. Should Member States be obliged, then, to admit part-time workers to their territory and/or benefits schemes or are their financial concerns of sufficient weight to deny such workers residence and/or social benefits?

Further, Community citizens may be deterred from taking up employment in another Member State if the unforeseen loss of employment would lead to a loss of the right to reside and/or enjoyment of public benefits. States have claimed, however, that unemployed workers must have worked and paid taxes for a given period of time before they, as 'members of the welfare state,' can become eligible for unemployment benefits, social assistance benefits or access to retraining programmes. Can such unemployed workers claim rights under Article 39 EC and, if so, is the length of employment or residence of any relevance in this regard? Further, questions arise as regards frontier workers. Often such workers will be taxable in the State of residence. Does this imply that the State of employment can consider, and treat, frontier workers as 'non-members' who do not contribute to and, hence, can be denied access to public benefits? Should any distinction be made in this regard between tax-funded benefits and social insurance programmes and between schemes that have been developed for workers and residents respectively?

Furthermore, freedom of movement would be deprived of much significance if family members could not join workers. Member States have always insisted that the number of family members entitled to accompany workers should be limited and that these members should not be offered benefits aimed at covering living or maintenance costs such as study grants or social assistance benefits. Who should take financial responsibility for the family members: the host State or the workers themselves?

Member States have expressed even stronger objections as regards the access of economically inactive nationals of other Member States. The efforts of

Community institutions, and the Commission and the European Parliament in particular, to realise a general non-economically determined right of residence[33] have been impeded by fears of Member States that large influxes of non-nationals solely moving to their territories for the purpose of obtaining public benefits would undermine the capacity to maintain such public services. Are Member States indeed obliged to admit such non-economically active nationals of other States to their territories? If so, are such persons to be treated as 'members of the welfare state' or can they be viewed as 'non-members' or 'partial members' who can be denied public benefits or be expelled when they become in need of social assistance benefits or apply for study grants? In answering these questions, is it of any relevance whether, or to what extent, 'welfare tourism' actually occurs?

Even more controversial issues may arise as regards Community citizens who merely wish to visit other Member States. Does Community law confer upon individuals the right to travel to other States, and if, so, are the beneficiaries of this right also entitled to gain access to public benefit systems during their stay? Do Community citizens have the right to travel to other States for the sole purpose of collecting public benefits? From the perspective of individual Community citizens, affirmative answers would seem in order. Such rights would enable them to gain access to educational courses that are not offered in the State of their residence or to avoid waiting lists for medical treatment. States, however, may, and often indeed do, claim that their systems should remain closed for non-residents who do not, and cannot be required, to contribute their equal share of the financing of public benefits. A free movement of students could lead to overcrowded classrooms, affect teacher-student ratios or limit the housing facilities for the States 'own' students. Upon graduation, students may often decide to return to, and work in, their own State and use the acquired knowledge and skills in, and to the benefit of the economies of, this State. Spillover effects might even incite States to lower investments in education in the hope that free-riders will move to other States. Similarly, a large influx of foreign patients could lead to an increase in health care expenditure or cause waiting-lists, whilst a net-outflow of patients may cause problems of under-utilisation which may force States to eliminate certain facilities or to close down hospital clinics.

More examples could be given, but the above may suffice to demonstrate that a broadly interpreted freedom of movement may indeed conflict with, and have implications for, the States' policies concerning access to their territories and public benefits systems and their ability to maintain these systems. This book seeks to explore how Community law has sought to settle the conflict between the competing claims of promoting freedom of movement and protecting the welfare state benefit systems.

---

[33] See also: ch 2, s 3.

3.1 Economic Residents, Non-Economic Residents, Non-Residents and Third Country Nationals

Having introduced the subject of cross-border access to public benefits within the European Community, the precise scope and aim of this book need to be defined. Some choices have to be made. The first concerns the categories of the beneficiaries whose free movement and cross-border welfare rights will be studied.

Over the years, the personal scope of the free movement of persons has been expanded and increasingly fragmented. Where the original Treaty of Rome merely conferred free movement and equal treatment rights upon (full-time) workers, the self-employed beneficiaries of the right of establishment and providers of services, Community law on the free movement of persons today also grants rights to work-seekers,[34] part-time workers,[35] unemployed workers,[36] 'student-workers,'[37] retired workers,[38] posted workers,[39] recipients of economic services[40] (such as students, patients,[41] business persons and tourists), pensioners,[42] 'travellers,'[43] Union citizens[44] and, regardless of their nationality,[45] family members of the various categories.[46]

For the purpose of this book there is no need to discuss and analyse the cross-border welfare rights of each of these categories separately. Formally, the legal status of the various categories may be based on, and governed by, different provisions, but the case law of the Court of Justice reveals a convergence of the principles governing the status of the various categories. More than once, the Court has indicated that the provisions concerning the free movement of workers, the right to establishment and the free movement of services are based on, and to be interpreted in accordance with, the same principles as regards both the free movement and the equal treatment rights.[47] Further, the Court has increasingly referred to a general class of persons[48] covered by the free movement

---

[34] See, eg: C–292/89 *Antonissen* [1991] ECR I–745.
[35] See, eg: Case 53/81 *Levin* [1983] ECR 1035.
[36] See, eg: Case C–57/96 *Meints* [1997] ECR I–6689.
[37] See, eg: Case 39/86 *Lair* [1988] ECR 3161.
[38] See, eg: Reg 1251/70.
[39] See, eg: Case C–113/89 *Rush Portuguesa* [1990] ECR I–1417.
[40] See, eg: Joined Cases 286/82 and 36/83 *Luisi and Carbone* [1984] ECR 377.
[41] See, eg: Case C–158/96 *Kohll* [1998] ECR I–1931.
[42] See, eg: Dir 90/365.
[43] See, eg: Case C–378/97 *Wijsenbeek* [1999] ECR I–6207.
[44] See, eg: Case C–85/96 *Martínez Sala* [1998] ECR I–2691.
[45] Case C–94/84 *Deak* [1985] ECR I–1873.
[46] See, eg: Case C–337/97 *Meeusen* [1999] ECR I–3289.
[47] See, eg: Case 48/75 *Royer* [1976] ECR 497, 12 and Case 118/75 *Watson* [1976] ECR 1185, 9.
[48] Handoll, 'Free Movement of Persons in the EU' (1995) 61.

regime using terms as 'persons enjoying the protection of Community law,'[49] 'persons to whom Community law gives the right to equal treatment'[50] or nationals of the Member States 'lawfully residing in the territory of another Member State.'[51] The formal fragmentation of the personal scope of the free movement of persons has gone hand in hand with a 'defragmentation' of the substantive principles governing the legal status of the various categories.[52]

This process of defragmentation, however, has not gone so far as to render distinctions among the various categories wholly superfluous. For the purpose of this book, four groups are distinguished.[53] The first category whose cross-border welfare rights will be discussed consists of Community citizens who have acquired[54] the right to stay or the right to reside in other Member States under Articles 39 or 43 of the EC Treaty. This category may be labelled the 'economic residents.' The prime focus will be on the rules and principles governing the rights of workers and their family members, the basic assumption being that the self-employed and their family members enjoy the same social, educational and health care rights.

The second category of beneficiaries to be studied comprises 'non-economic residents.' It concerns Community citizens whose right to reside in other Member States is not governed by Article(s) 39 (and 43) EC, but by the Directives No 93/96, No 90/365 and No 90/364. More specifically, the non-economic residents include students, pensioners and the residual category of the 'other' Community citizens. The conditions under which these three categories can establish residence in other Member States differ from the ones to be met by the economic residents. Their legal status raises some specific questions that do not arise as regards the beneficiaries of Article(s) 39 and (43) EC.

The third category comprises 'non-residents' or 'travellers.' It concerns Community citizens who only go to other States for a limited period of time

---

[49] Case 8/77 *Sagulo* [1977] ECR 1495, 8.

[50] Case C–43/95 *Data Delecta* [1996] ECR I–4671, 12.

[51] Case C–85/96 *Martínez Sala* [1998] ECR I–2691, 61.

[52] This de-fragmentation is of particular interest for the subject of the cross-border access to public benefits. For instance, the main reason why Community law makes a distinction between employed and self-employed persons is that the legal obstacles to cross-border pursuit of economic activities by the two categories have traditionally differed. These differences in the 'economic' obstacles, however, are of much less, if any, relevance for the rights concerning the access to 'welfare state benefits' of these 'economic beneficiaries'.

[53] For more precise definitions, and the main rules and principles governing the legal status, of the four categories of beneficiaries, see ch 2. For Community citizens, the distinction between the various categories is not always critical. Cp Peers, 'Aliens, Workers, Citizens or Humans? Models for Community Immigration Law' in Guild and Harlow (eds), *Implementing Amsterdam, Immigration and Asylum Rights in EC Law* (2001) 291–318, 293. Community citizens may switch from one category to another (eg, students may take up employment and subsequently claim rights as workers) and they may enjoy rights in more than one capacity (eg, self-employed persons may claim economic and social rights as self-employed persons and enjoy voting rights in their capacity as union citizens).

[54] For the purposes of this study, the category of economic residents also includes, in principle, frontier workers or other (self-) employed persons who have acquired under Art 39 or Art 43 EC the right to reside but have decided not to make use of this right.

without relocating their economic base or private residence. As follows from the brief discussion in section 2, questions concerning the cross-border access of this category differ profoundly from the ones arising as regards the economic and the non-economic residents. As regards the non-residents the core question is not whether, or to what extent, they can become 'members' of the host State's welfare state, but rather whether, as 'non-members,' they can benefit from public benefit schemes to which they cannot be required to contribute.

The last category consists of third country nationals. As will be demonstrated,[55] this category is in principle still excluded from the free movement regime. This is not to say, however, that Community law has nothing to offer to them in the fields of social, health care and educational policy. The Community and its Member States have concluded various association and co-operation agreements with third States under which the nationals of these States are offered free movement and/or equal treatment rights.[56] This book mainly discusses the rights guaranteed by the Agreement on the European Economic Area, the Association Agreement with Turkey and the agreements which have been concluded with the Maghreb countries Morocco, Algeria and Tunisia.

3.2 Minimum Subsistence Benefits, Health Care and Education

A second choice to be made concerns the benefits to be included in the book. As stated in section 1, three benefits have been selected for analysis: social assistance and other minimum subsistence[57] benefits, health care and education. These benefits have been chosen for two separate, albeit related, reasons. The first is that the conflict between the Community's goal to realise a free movement of persons and the Member States' 'welfare state interest' arises as regards each of these benefits. The three benefits are all of vital significance for (the beneficiaries of) the free movement of persons. Community citizens might actually be deterred from moving elsewhere if this did not include a right to obtain medical treatment, to gain access to education or lead to a loss of the basic

---

[55] See especially: ch 2, s 5.

[56] Currently, there are some thirty international agreements that have been signed by the Community and the Member States, on the one hand, and third countries, on the other hand, which confer upon nationals of the latter States residing within one of the Member States free movement or equal treatment rights. Besides the agreements that are discussed in this book, these include the EC-Switzerland Agreement on free movement of persons (See, eg: Peers, 'The EC-Switzerland Agreement on Free Movement of Persons: Overview and Analysis' (2000) *EJML* 127–42), Euro-Mediterranean agreements concluded with Jordan and Israel, the Europe Agreements and Partnership and Co-operation Agreements with Central and European Countries and States of the former Soviet Union and the Lomé and Cotonou agreements concluded with African, Caribbean and Pacific States. For an overview see Hedemann-Robinson, 'An Overview of Recent Legal Developments at Community Level in Relation to Third Country Nationals Resident within the European Union, with Particular Reference to the Case Law of the European Court of Justice' (2001) *CMLRev* 525–86.

[57] For a further clarification of the notions of 'social assistance' and 'minimum subsistence benefits' see ch 3, s 2.1.

means of subsistence. Indeed, Community citizens might attach so much importance to these benefits that they might move to other States for the sole purpose of obtaining these benefits. At the same time, social assistance, education and health care are all public benefits that are vulnerable to increases in the number of beneficiaries. An influx of non-nationals or non-residents claiming such benefits could affect the States' ability to develop and maintain the systems. The second reason is that Community institutions, and the Court of Justice in particular, have frequently been faced with questions concerning cross-border access to minimum subsistence benefits, education and health care. The number of Court judgments and legislative measures is large enough to engage in a useful and systematic analysis of the way in which Community law has sought to settle the previously mentioned conflict.

3.3 The United States of America

The subject of cross-border access to public services within the European Community has only come to the surface in the last two decades. In spite of an increasing number of Court judgments and legislative initiatives, the Community is still quite inexperienced in settling the conflict between promoting freedom of movement and the need to preserve adequate public benefit systems. The Community can still learn, or draw inspiration, from the experiences of other 'multi-level systems of government' with cross-border access to public services. This book explores whether, and if so, what, lessons can be learnt from the United States of America.

Of course, one has to be careful in comparing European Community law and American constitutional law, and this particularly holds true for the free movement of persons.[58] The historical, political, socio-economic and legal backgrounds against which the subject of the free movement of persons and cross-border access to public benefits must be placed differ profoundly on both sides of the Atlantic. In the United States a free movement of persons never had to be created and this freedom has never been seen as functional, or subordinate, to the process of economic integration.[59] From the nation's inception more than two hundred years ago, the right to travel, as the notion of a free movement of persons is commonly known,[60] has been assumed to exist as a fundamental right for all United States citizens. Furthermore, American views on the welfare state and social policy differ profoundly from the European perceptions. In the United States there is greater emphasis on the private market; by comparison

---

[58] Cp Varat, 'Economic Integration and Interregional Migration in the United States Federal System' in Tushnet (ed), *Comparative Constitutional Federalism—Europe and America (1990)* 21–66, 49 and Rosberg, 'Free Movement of Persons in the United States' in Sandalow and Stein (eds), *Courts and Free Markets—Perspectives from the United States and Europe (1982)* 275–362, 276–8.

[59] See ch 2, s 8.

[60] See Rosberg (1982) n 58 above, 275.

with most European States, governments in the United States have assumed a rather limited welfare responsibility *vis-à-vis* their populations.

Nonetheless, the above and other differences do not imply that no meaningful comparisons can be made. The core questions and issues raised by the subject of cross-border access to public benefits are quite similar. In brief, both the United States and the European Community may be regarded as multi-level governmental entities in which (*i*) the public task of developing welfare state services is primarily carried out at State or local level and (*ii*) in which a right to freedom of movement is 'constitutionally' protected. Just as are the Member States of the European Community, the individual American States are faced with problems concerning the access of 'outsiders' to their public benefit systems. Both European Community law and American constitutional law[61] have to settle the potential conflict between the 'free movement interest' and the interest of maintaining adequate 'welfare systems.'

3.4 Aims of the Book

The main goal of this book is to examine the degree to which European Community law confers upon individuals the right to gain access to minimum subsistence benefit schemes, public health care and public education and to establish how Community law has settled the potential conflict between the goal of promoting freedom of movement, on the one hand, and the need to develop and maintain adequate public benefit schemes, on the other hand. In addition, the book investigates whether, and if so, how, Community law governing access to these three types of public benefits, as it stands today, can, or may have to, be adjusted or improved and whether in doing so, some lessons can be drawn from American constitutional, and where applicable federal, law.

3.5 Structure of the Book

This book consists of six chapters. After this introductory chapter, the book commences in chapter 2 with a general introduction to the free movement of persons within the European Community and the United States. The chapter aims to put the subject of cross-border access to public benefits in its proper legal-historical context by describing how the main rules and principles on the free movement of persons have been developed over the years and what they entail, in the context of the present state of European Community law and American constitutional law. Chapter 2 may serve as a guide for readers throughout the course of the book. The subsequent three chapters analyse the degree to which European Community law and American constitutional law

---

[61] Cp Varat, "State Citizenship' and Interstate Equality' (1981) *ChicLRev* 487 *et seq.*

entitle individuals to move to and to claim access to minimum subsistence benefits schemes, health care systems and education systems respectively in other Member States. The structure of chapters 3, 4 and 5 is quite similar. After an introduction, each of the three chapters first puts the subject in its proper context by describing the main features of the national benefits systems under consideration, the ways in which the Member States have traditionally regulated access to these systems and the activities of the Community institutions in the respective fields which are not directly related to the free movement of persons. The subsequent sections consider in further detail the degree to which Community law entitles the four categories of economic residents, non-economic residents, non-residents and third country nationals to move to and/or to claim access to the respective benefit schemes. After a brief summary and evaluation, chapters 3, 4 and 5 then proceed with a description of the degree to which American constitutional law entitles individuals to move to and to claim in other States access to minimum subsistence benefits schemes, health care and public education. After having compared the degree to which individuals enjoy cross-border 'welfare rights' on both sides of the Atlantic, the three chapters are rounded off with a section in which the findings are summarised and evaluated. In the final sections the question is addressed whether European Community law on cross-border access to the benefits in question can possibly be improved or adjusted and whether, and if so, how, the American experiences can be of help in this regard. In chapter 6 the findings of this book are summarised. Some 'horizontal' comparisons will be drawn with a view to establishing the more general principles governing cross-border access to public benefits.

2

Free Movement of Persons Within the European Community and the United States: History, Legal Framework and Basic Principles

1 INTRODUCTION

This chapter aims to put the subject of cross-border access to public benefits in its proper legal-historical context. As noted in the introductory chapter, questions concerning access to public benefits in other Member States have only gradually come up. In the view of those drafting the original EEC Treaty free movement rights would only be granted in order to facilitate the free pursuit of economic activities across inter-State borders. The rights to move and reside freely were preserved for employed and self-employed persons and the right to equal treatment would, in principle, be limited to matters related to work and income. Since the Community's inception, however, the free movement of persons has developed in a way and direction that the drafters had probably never foreseen. Over the years, many more categories of persons have become entitled to free movement rights and the material scope of the right to equal treatment has been extended to include many rights and benefits which are not related to the pursuit of, or involvement in, economic activities. During this development, many questions and problems regarding the right to gain access to public benefits have arisen. In some cases the Community institutions have responded by adopting specific legislative measures, but most questions on cross-border access to public benefits have been, and must be, answered (by the Court of Justice) on the basis of the general provisions on the free movement of persons. In this respect European Community law parallels American constitutional law. The history of, and the main rules and principles governing, the so-called right to travel differ, but specific legislative measures governing access to public benefits in other States have not, or hardly, been taken in the United States. Issues regarding cross-border access to public benefits have mainly been, and must be, settled (by the Supreme Court) on the basis of clauses contained in the American Constitution.

This chapter analyses the way in which the main rules and principles governing the rights to freedom of movement and equality of treatment of the various categories of beneficiaries have been shaped over the years. In addition, this chapter looks at what they entail in the light of current European Community and American law. For the purpose of this book, there is no need to describe all relevant rules and principles in detail.[1] In particular, this chapter does not intend to set out the precise conditions under which employed and self-employed persons may pursue economic activities in other Member States. The focus will be on the rules and principles that are directly or indirectly relevant to the cross-border access to public benefits.

2 ECONOMIC RESIDENTS

For the purpose of this book four categories of beneficiaries of free movement of persons within the European Community have been identified: economic residents, non-economic residents, non-residents and third country nationals.[2] This section examines the category of economic residents which consists of those Community citizens who stay or have acquired the right to reside in other Member States on the basis of Articles 39 or 43 of the EC Treaty. The discussion primarily focuses on the rules and principles governing the rights of Community workers and their family members.

2.1 Free Movement of Workers: a Brief History

For a proper understanding of the Community rules governing freedom of movement of workers, it is necessary to establish why Community law provides for this freedom. It is generally claimed that Article 48 (now 39) was included in the original EEC Treaty with a view to realising freedom of movement for the production factor labour.[3] In support of this view, reference is often made to the

---

[1] For more extensive descriptions of Community law on the free movement of persons see, eg: Dollat, *Libre Circulation des Personnes et Citoyenneté européenne: Enjeux et Perspectives* (1998); Schulz, *Freizügigkeit für Unionsbürger* (1997); Wapenaar, *Personenverkeer binnen de Europese Unie—Het Communautaire Recht inzake Personenverkeer, met Bijzondere Aandacht voor de Positie van Derdelanders* (1997); Jørgensen, *Union Citizens—Free Movement and Non-Discrimination* (1996); Martin and Guild, *Free Movement of Persons* (1996); O'Leary, *The Evolving Concept of Community Citizenship—From the Free Movement of Persons to Union Citizenship* (1996); Garrone, *La Libre Circulation des Personnes—Liberté de Mouvement, Egalité, Liberté économique—Etude de Droit communautaire et suisse* (1995); Handoll, *Free Movement of Persons under EC Law* (1995); Schermers *et al* (eds), *Free Movement of Persons in Europe* (1993) and Hartley, 'Free Movement of Persons', in Green *et al*, *The Legal Foundations of the Single European Market* (1991) chs 8–13.

[2] For a brief description of the various categories see ch 1, s 3.1.

[3] See, eg: Wohlfahrt *et al*, Die Europäische Wirtschaftgemeinschaft—Kommentar zum Vertrag (1960) 150–1; Plender, 'An Incipient Form of European Citizenship' in Jacobs (ed), *European Law and the Individual* (1976) 39–53, 39; Holloway, *Social Policy Harmonisation in the European Community* (1981) 235; Verschueren, *Internationale Arbeidsmigratie* (1990) at 236–7; Vonk, *De Coördinatie van Bestaansminimumuitkeringen in de Europese Gemeenschap* (1991) 248 and Evans, 'Union Citizenship and the Constitutionalization of Equality in EU Law' in La Torre, *European Citizenship: An Institutional Challenge* (1998) 267–91, 270.

Spaak-report. This report was based on macroeconomic theories that demon-strated that integration of national markets could best be achieved if both products (goods, services) and production factors (labour, capital) could move freely across inter-State borders.[4] The Spaak-report, however, merely served as the basis for the 1956-1957 Treaty negotiations[5] and during the deliberations in Val Duchesse most States expressed objections to the introduction of free labour mobility. At the time, western European countries had virtually full control over immigration and admission to their labour markets. Most countries regulated migration in accordance with the needs of their national labour mar-kets.[6] Foreign workers were invited merely to fill the job vacancies for which no national workers were available; they were not entitled to bring their family mem-bers and after the 'job had been done' the workers were supposed to return to their country of origin. During their 'visit' foreign workers did not enjoy a strongly protected legal status. The guest workers from abroad had been invited to fuel the economy of the host State; they were not supposed to benefit from, or to become a burden,on the welfare state.[7] The States feared free labour mobility; a liberalisa-tion of labour market admission rules ran counter to the interests of most States.[8] Among the States present in Val Duchesse only Italy had a concrete

---

[4] The realisation of a free movement of goods, services and producers was expected to lead to a restructuring and relocation of the production process. In order to avoid unemployment in certain regions and to provide producers with the labour they needed, workers should have the possibility of moving to places where their labour was required. *Rapport des Chefs de Délégation aux Ministres des Affaires etrangères* (1956) 17–18; Braeutigam, 'Das Problem des 'gemeinsamen' Marktes unter sozialem Aspekt' (1956) *Aussenwirtschaft* 170–89; Driver, *Die Integration des europäischen Arbeitsmarktes* (1962) 170–89 and Verschueren (1990) n 3 above, 236–7.

[5] It must be noted, however, that the theoretical justifications for freedom of movement of the production factor labour were not widely accepted. See, eg: Boni, *Freizügigkeit und Integration—Struktur und integrationspolitike Bedeutung der Arbeitsmarktverflechtung zwischen den Mitgliedstaaten der Europäischen Wirtschaftsgemeinschaft* (1976) 221. Also the drafters of the Spaak-report had doubts: 'On ne doit pas surestimer l'ampleur des mouvements de main-d'oeuvre qui se produiraient dans un marché commun entièrement libre. On connaît la rétitence aux change-ments de métier ou de résidence, fût-ce à l'intérieur d'un meme pays. . . . En outre, on reconnaît de plus en plus que l'émigration ne constitue pas une solution économique pour un pays surpeuplé, car elle risque de proter essentiellement sur la population active, et conséquent, d'accroître la propor-tion de la population á charge. Pour toutes ces raisons, la tendance la plus récente est aux efforts de développement et de création d'emploi sur place'. *Rapport des Chefs de Délégation aux Ministres des Affaires etrangères* (1956) 88.

[6] Foreign workers were only admitted upon the grant of a labour permit and a residence permit. For further details see, eg: International Labour Office, *Analysis of the Immigration Laws and Regulations of Selected Countries* (1954); Hampel, *Einwanderungsgesetzgebung und innereu-ropäische Wanderung—Die rechtlichen Regelungen der Zulassung ausländischer Arbeitnehmer in Fünfzehn europäischen Staaten* (1957) and Reisner, 'National Regulation of the Movement of Workers in the European Community' (1964) *AJCL* 360–84.

[7] On the notion of 'guestworker' see especially: Böhning, *The Migration of Workers in the United Kingdom and the European Community* (1972) and Garth, 'Migrant Workers and Rights of Mobility in the European Community and the United States: A Study of Law, Community and Citizenship in the Welfare State' in Cappelletti *et al, Integration Through Law—Europe and the American Federal Experience* (1986) vol 1, 85–163, 90–6.

[8] Prior to the negotiations on the EEC Treaty, various attempts to liberalise labour market admission rules in Western Europe had already been made within the context of international organisations such as the OECD and the Council of Europe. See, eg: Delperee, 'De

interest in introducing a free movement for workers, seeing the introduction of a free labour mobility as a means to solving its unemployment problem.[9]

In the end the Member States did agree 'to bring about, by progressive stages, freedom of movement.'[10] The wording of Article 39 EC, however, suggests that this provision has never been included in the Treaty with a view to actually realising free labour mobility. Two examples illustrate the point. First, if the Member States had really wanted free factor mobility, Article 39 should have provided for free movement rights for all workers established in the Member States regardless of their nationality.[11] Article 39 merely speaks of 'workers of the Member States,' but the absence of an explicit reference to Member State nationality does not imply that the drafters wished to leave room to include third country nationals in the free movement regime. The omission of a reference to Member State nationality is explained by the fact that the Member States did not wish to include all nationals, and especially those from the overseas territories, in the free movement regime.[12] Secondly, a free mobility of the production

Gemeenschappelijke Arbeidsmarkt en het Vrije Arbeidskrachtenverkeer' (1956) *Arbbl* 177–205; Lannes, 'International Mobility of Manpower in Western Europe: II' (1956) *ILRev* 135–49; Hanekuijck, *Het Recht op Vrijheid van Migratie* (1957); Schieffer, *De Europese Arbeidsmarkt. Het Vrije Verkeer en de Migratie van Werknemers* (1961); Driver (1962) n 4 above; Schmidt, *Die arbeitsrechtliche und sozialversicherungsrechtliche Stellung der europäischen Wanderarbeiter im Rahmen der europäischen Wirtschaftsgemeinschaft* (1963); Schulz, *Freier Arbeitsmarkt und Niederlassungsfreiheit in der Europäischen Wirtschaftsgemeinschaft—Unter besonderer Berücksichtigung der Grenz- und Gastarbeitnehmer* (1967); Troclet, *Europees Sociaal Recht— Institutioneel Kader, Rechtsinstrumenten, Sociale Problemen en hun Oplossing* (1970) and Boni (1976) n 5 above.

[9] It was also Italy which took most of the initiatives during the Treaty negotiations as regards the free movement of workers. On the role of Italy see, eg: Romero, 'Migration as an Issue in European Interdependence and Integration: the Case of Italy' in Milward *et al* (eds), *The Frontier of National Sovereignty—History and Theory 1945–1992* (1993) 33–58. This is not to say that all other States objected to the free movement of workers. The Netherlands, for instance, did favour such a freedom of movement. On the position that the various Member States' delegations took during the negotiations see also Renardel de Lavalette, 'Facetten van het Vrij Verkeer van Werknemers in de Europese Gemeenschappen' (1983) *SMA* 213–27.

[10] Art 40 (formerly 49) E(E)C.

[11] Cp Hoogenboom, 'Free Movement and Integration of Non-EC nationals and the Logic of the Internal Market' in Schermers *et al* (eds), *Free Movement of Persons in Europe* (1993) 497–511 and Hedemann-Robinson, 'Third Country Nationals, European Union Citizenship and Free Movement of Persons: A Time for Bridges Rather than Division' (1997) *YEL* 321–62.

[12] The drafters of the Spaak-report had intended to include third country nationals established within the Community in the scope of the free movement of workers. *Rapport des Chefs de Délégation aux Ministres des Affaires etrangères* (1956) 88–91. Residence in the Community rather than the nationality of a Member State would determine who could benefit from this freedom of movement. Verschueren (1990) n 3 above, 302–3. By analogy with the free movement of goods and services a common policy for all workers in the Community, irrespective of their nationality, would have been envisaged. See, eg: Plender, *International Migration Law* (1988) 197–8 and Plender, 'Competence, European Community Law and Nationals of Non-Member States' (1990) *ICLQ* 599 *et seq*. See also:Lanfranchi, *Droit communautaire et Travailleurs migrants des Etats tiers—Entrée et Circulation dans la Communauté européenne* (1994) 20–33. The reports of the Treaty negotiations in Val Duchessse (hereinafter referred to by their MAE-numbering (Ministres des Affaires Etrangères)) strongly suggest, however, that the Member States' delegations did not support the views of the drafters of the Spaak-report. All the drafts for the article(s) on the free movement of workers which were presented during the negotiations spoke of a free movement of 'travailleurs

factor labour that was practical and relevant would have required a right for individuals to look for work in other Member States. The grant of such a right was discussed during the negotiations,[13] but in the end it was rejected. Article 39(3) EC merely speaks of a right to move to other States 'in order to accept offers of employment actually made.' Presumably, the majority of the States held to the view that labour mobility should continue to be determined by the needs of national labour markets.[14]

Thus, it does not seem very likely that the Member States which signed and ratified the EEC Treaty ever intended to translate the theoretical notion of a free factor mobility into practical reality. In fact, when they included Article 39 in the Treaty, the six States did not seem to have had any theoretical notion in mind. Probably, Article 39 was not much more than the product of a political compromise, which implied that 'the five' would gradually soak up the Italian labour surplus during a transitional period of twelve years.[15]

Community law on the free movement of workers took shape, and was only given a more defined objective, during the 1958–1970 transitional period. The 1960s were the heyday of the guest worker system and the prospects for implementing Article 39 in time through measures based on Article 40 (formerly 49) E(E)C did not seem too promising.[16] Nonetheless, the Community institutions

nationaux'. See, eg: MAE 175/56 and MAE 437/56. In a footnote in MAE 88 f/57 dvl it was stated that the extent to which the term 'travailleurs nationaux' should be altered should be considered in order to deal with some problems concerning the overseas countries and territories. In MAE 653/57 it was further held that a general provision should be drafted with a view to defining the term. It was only in the last draft that the term 'travailleurs nationaux' was replaced by the term 'travailleurs des Etats membres'. MAE 776 f/57 mts. Art 135 (now 186) was inserted which provides that freedom of movement for workers from overseas countries and territories shall be governed by agreements to be concluded with the unanimous approval of Member States. On the basis of the above mentioned texts of the documents no definite conclusions can be drawn as to the precise motives of the Member States delegations, but the documents do suggest that the term 'workers of the Member States' was used in order to leave the option open to exclude some nationals of the Member States from the oversees countries and territories from the free movement of workers. Cp also van der Mei, 'The Bosman Case and the Legal Status of Third Country Nationals under European Community Law', (1996) *ASICL Proceedings of the 8th Annual Conference* 144–58, 153.

13 See, eg: MAE 437f/56 and MAE 474f/56.

14 A third indication that the drafters were not driven by the goal to realise a free mobility for the production factor labour can be found in Art 39(3)d EC which states that workers shall have the right to remain in the territory of a Member State after having been employed in that State under conditions to be determined by the European Commission. Cp Groenendijk, 'De Betekenis van Artikel 39 EG-Verdrag voor Werknemers uit Landen buiten de Europese Unie' in Fernhout (ed), *Dertig Jaar Vrij Verkeer van Werknemers* (1999) 35–49, 38.

15 Cp Romero (1993) n 9 above, 54.

16 And indeed, the negotiations in the Council proved to be difficult. The free movement of workers was realised in three stages. Reg 15/61 (OJ 1961 1073), Reg 38/64 (OJ 1964 965) and Reg 1612/68 (OJ 1968 L 257). For descriptions of the realisation of the free movement of workers during the 1960s see inter alia Heynig, 'Freizügigkeit in der Europäischen Wirtschaftgemeinschaft Endgültig Hergestellt' (1968) *BB* 337–9; Miller, 'Völlige Freizügigkeit der Arbeitskräfte in den Europäischen Gemeinschaften' (1968) *BArbBl* 590–4; Miller, 'Freizügigkeit in der EWG' (1968) *der Landskreis* 56–8; Flath, 'Noch Einmal: Freizügigkeit in der EWG' (1968) *der Landskreis* 342–4; Di Stefano, *La Libre Circulation des Travailleurs dans la Communauté économique européenne* (1968); Lyon-Caen, 'La Libre Circulation des Travailleurs (Règlement et Directive des

managed to realise the free movement of workers two years before the end of the transitional period when they adopted Regulation No 1612/68 and Directive No 68/360. In addition, the institutions were able to give this freedom a much broader meaning than the Member States had in mind in the late 1950s. Many factors may account for this progress, but the most important is that Article 39 EC was implemented during a time of virtual full employment. In the course of the 1960s, economic growth had largely solved the Italian unemployment problem. Italy had gradually become a labour-importing country itself; like the other Member States, it started to recruit workers from 'third' countries. Labour mobility between Member States and third countries increased considerably, whilst labour mobility of European workers between the Member States virtually came to a standstill. As a result, Member States no longer had strong motives for obstructing or delaying the realisation of free movement of workers provided third country nationals[17] and workers from overseas territories[18] would not be included in the free movement regime. The mobility of European workers was no longer socially and politically dangerous.[19] This development in the labour market paved the way for the European Commission which, through its right of initiative, could take the lead in the legislative process. From the beginning the Commission had rejected the view that the free movement of workers should be conceived in macroeconomic terms of a free movement of the production factor labour. Possible problems of unemployment should not be solved by promoting labour mobility, but rather through other means such as the free movement of capital and a regional policy. Work should be brought to the unemployed and not the other way round.[20] In the

---

Communautés européennes du 15 octobre 1969)' (1969) *Juris-Classeur Periodique* nr.2222; Macheret, *L'Immigration étrangère en Suisse a l'Heure de l'Integration Européenne* (1969); Maertens, *De Geografische Mobiliteit van Werknemers in de Europese Gemeenschap* (1969); Pabon, 'Het Vrije Verkeer van Werknemers' (1969) *SMA* 83–95; van Look, 'Het Vrije Verkeer van Werknemers in de EEG nu een Realiteit' (1969) *SEW* 274–88; Charalambis, *Die Arbeitnehmer im EWG-Recht* (1970) and Brüggemann, *Die Freizügigkeit der Arbeitnehmer im Bereich der Europäischen Gemeinschaften* (1973).

[17] Arts 1(1) and 7(1) of Reg 1612/68 which, unlike Art 39 of the Treaty, explicitly state that only nationals of the Member States have the right to work in other Member States. See also: van der Mei (1996) n 12 above, 152–4. The creation of a genuine common labour market in which third country nationals could also move freely would have required the establishment of a common policy regarding the admission of third country workers. Such a common market and common policy was never (seriously) considered during the 1960s. As regards workers, only a free trade area was envisaged. Hartley, 'The International Scope of the Community Provisions Concerning Free Movement of Workers' in Jacobs (ed), *European Law and the Individual* (1976) 19–37, 33.

[18] The agreements referred to in Art 186 EC (the former 135 E(E)C—see n 12 above) have never been concluded. See also Art 42(3) of Reg 1612/68 where it is stated that workers from the overseas countries and territories cannot benefit from the free movement of workers. Quite difficult questions arise as to when nationals of the Member States must be regarded as workers from the overseas territories. See, eg: Verschueren (1990) n 3 above, 309–10; Mortelmans and Temmink, 'Het Vrije Personenverkeer tussen de Nederlandse Antillen en Aruba en de Europese Gemeenschap' (1992) *Justicia—TvAR* Vol 1 and Hartley, *EEC Immigration Law* (1978) 77–80.

[19] Romero (1993) n 9 above, 55.

[20] Commission Recommendation and Opinion of 7 July 1965 (OJ 1965 2293).

Commission's view another role was envisaged for the free movement of persons. Freedom of movement should be seen as a personal freedom, a fundamental individual right for European citizens to choose the place where they wish to work.[21] With less opposition from the Member States, the Commission was able to have the free movement of workers realised by the Council and to give it an interpretation which went beyond the strict wording of Article 39 EC. In the preamble to Regulation No 1612/68 freedom of movement was referred to as a fundamental right for workers which may be exercised in 'freedom and dignity' and which includes the elimination of all obstacles to 'the worker's right to be joined by his family and the conditions for the integration of that family into the host country.'[22] A right to look for work was (informally) recognised[23] and workers were granted a right to equal treatment as regards vocational training,[24] social advantages,[25] trade union rights[26] and public housing.[27] In addition, family members were given the right to reside with the worker in the host State[28] and children were granted the right to gain access to education.[29]

Shortly after the adoption of Regulation No 1612/68 and Directive No 68/360 the vice-president of the European Commission referred to the free movement of workers as an 'embryonic form of European Citizenship.'[30] This notion of citizenship was vague and ill-defined but it did reflect two factors which have been decisive for the realisation of the free movement of workers during the 1960s and have influenced the development of this freedom of movement ever since. First, the use of the term 'citizenship' underlines that the free movement of workers is not to be conceived in macroeconomic terms of a free movement

---

[21] Evans, 'European Citizenship' (1982) *MLRev* 497–515, 498–500.

[22] See the fifth indent of the preamble to Reg 1612/68.

[23] The right to look for work was not mentioned in the Reg itself; it was only recognised in the minutes of the Council meeting of 15 October 1968 at which Reg 1612/68 was adopted. The minutes contained a Declaration in which it was stated that: 'Nationals of a Member State as referred to in article 1 (of Dir 68/360) who move to another Member State in order to seek work there shall be allowed a minimum period of three months for the purpose; in the event of their not having found employment by the end of that period, their residence in the territory of this second State may be brought to an end. However, if the above-mentioned persons should be taken charge of by national assistance (social welfare) in the second State during the aforesaid period they may be invited to leave the territory of this second State'. The conditions laid down in this declaration were subsequently implemented in the legislation of many Member States. Vonk (1991) n 3 above, 272 and Hartley(1978) n 18 above, 193.

[24] Art 7(3) of the Reg 1612/68.

[25] Art 7(2) of Reg 1612/68.

[26] Art 8 of Reg 1612/68.

[27] Art 9 of Reg 1612/68.

[28] Art 10 of Reg 1612/68.

[29] Art 12 of Reg 1612/68.

[30] Levi-Sandri, 'Free Movement of Workers in the European Community' (1968) *Bull.EC* 11, 5. See also Plender (1976) n 3 above, 40. The reference to European Citizenship was not wholly new. In 1961 the European Commission had already held that the right to work in other Member States granted by Art 39 EC was to be regarded as 'le premier aspect d'une citoyenneté européenne'. Debs. EP no.48, 135, 22 November 1961.

for the production factor labour. Rather, it is seen as a fundamental individual right to work in other Member States for all nationals of the Member States. The Court of Justice, which has largely been responsible for the further development of the free movement of workers since the early 1970s, has frequently stressed the fundamental nature of this individual freedom and therefore interpreted Article 39 EC and provisions of secondary legislation broadly. Secondly, the fact that reference was made to an 'European' citizenship underlines the position of third country workers. The main concern of the Member States in the 1960s was to secure their power to regulate the immigration of guest workers from third countries. The free movement of workers could only be realised because third country nationals were excluded from the benefits of free movement of workers and ever since no formal steps have been taken to bring them into the scope of the free movement regime.[31]

2.2 Community Workers

2.2.1 Right to Work

The main purpose of Article 39 EC is to enable Community citizens to take up and to pursue economic activities as employed persons throughout the Community.[32] This right to work in other[33] Member States[34] has been interpreted broadly by the Court. The right is legally enforceable[35] and, notwithstanding the text of Article 39(3) EC, it encompasses a Treaty-based right to look

---

[31] See also: s 5.

[32] Cp Case 143/87 *Stanton* [1988] ECR I–3877, 13; Case C–415/93 *Bosman* [1995] ECR I–4921, 94 and Case C–18/95 *Terhoeve* [1999] ECR I–345, 37.

[33] Art 39 EC only grants Community citizens the right to take up employment in *other* Member States. Community law does not apply to 'purely internal situations' which have been defined as cases in which the activities 'are confined in all respects within a single Member State'. See, eg: Case C–41/90 *Höfner* [1991] ECR I–1979, 37 and Case C–332/90 *Steen* [1992] ECR I–341, 9. Community citizens can only invoke Art 39 EC against their own Member States after they have made use of the right to move to other States. See, eg: Case C–419/92 *Scholtz* [1994] ECR I–505; Case C–370/89 *Singh* [1992] ECR I–4625, 21 and Case C–107/94 *Asscher* [1996] ECR I–3089, 34. The requirement of an 'interstate element' may lead to so-called reverse discrimination which occurs when Member States treat their own nationals less favourably than nationals of other Member States. See also s 7.4 of this chapter.

[34] The territorial scope of the free movement of workers is in principle limited to the territory of the Member States. Art 299 EC (formerly 227). See also:Martin and Guild (1996) n 1 above, 48–9 and Hartley (1976) n 17 above. This does not imply, however, that Art 39 EC cannot have effect outside the Community. It is settled case law that Community law may apply to activities pursued outside the territory of the Community as long as the employment relationship retains a 'sufficiently close link with the Community'. See Case 237/83 *Prodest* [1984] ECR 3153, 63 and Case C–214/94 *Boukhalfa* [1995] ECR I–2253, 15. On this requirement of a 'sufficiently close link' see, eg: Lhoest, 'Annotation *Boukhalfa*' (1998) *CMLRev* 247–67.

[35] Art 39 has direct effect. Case 41/74 *Van Duyn* [1974] ECR 1337, 6–7.

for work in other Member States.[36] In seeking[37] and accepting employment, Community citizens must be treated equally by governmental institutions, private bodies such as the bar[38] and sports associations[39] which regulate certain economic activities in a collective manner, and individual[40] employers.[41] Once employed in another State, Community citizens must be treated equally as national workers in all matters related to employment.[42] Both direct

[36] Community citizens are entitled to stay in other Member States for 'a reasonable period of time' in order to apprise themselves of offers of employment and to take the necessary steps in order to be engaged. Case C–292/89 *Antonissen* [1991] ECR I–745, 21. See also Case C–271/91 *Tsiotras* [1993] ECR I–2925 and Case C–344/95 *Commission v Belgium* [1997] ECR I–1035. The duration of the right to stay is extended for as long as job seekers provide evidence that they are still seeking employment *and* that they have genuine chances of finding employment. Case C–292/89 *Antonissen* [1991] ECR I–745, 21. In *Antonissen* the Court held that the declaration which the Council had adopted in 1968 (see s 2.1, n 23 above) had no legal significance and that the three-month period mentioned in the declaration therefore could not be decisive. Case C–292/89 *Antonissen* [1991] ECR I–745, 18. On this judgment and the right to look for work see, eg: Verschueren, 'Vrij Verkeer van Werkzoekenden' (1992) *MR* 15–19 and Badoux, 'Dertig Jaar Vrij Verkeer van Personen' Fernhout (ed), *Dertig Jaar Vrij Verkeer van Werknemers* (1999) 13–24, 14–16.

[37] Community citizens enjoy equality of treatment with nationals of the host State in all matters related to looking for work. In particular, they enjoy the same assistance from employment offices. See Art 5 of Reg 1612/68. Unemployment benefits, however, fall outside the field of access to employment in the strict sense. Case C–278/94 *Commission v Belgium* [1996] ECR I–4307, 39.

[38] See, eg: Case 71/76 *Thieffry* [1977] ECR 765.

[39] See, eg: Case 36/74 *Walrave* [1974] ECR 1405 and Case C–415/93 *Bosman* [1995] ECR I–4291.

[40] Case C–281/98 *Angonese* [2000] ECR I–4139, 36. See also Lengauer, 'Drittwirkung von Grundfreiheiten—Eine Besprechung der Rs C–281/98, *Angonese*' (2001) *ZfRV* 57–65 and van der Steen, 'Horizontale Werking van de Vier Vrijheden en van het Discriminatieverbod van Artikel 12 EG' (2001) *NTER* 4–9. Prior to *Angonese* the horizontal effect of Art 39 EC was still quite controversial. See, eg: Zuleeg, in Groeben *et al* (eds), *Kommentar zum EWG-Vertrag* (1991) 170 *et seq* and Durand in Mégret *et al* (eds), *Commentaire Mégret Le Droit de la CEE* (1992) at 60 *et seq*.

[41] The prohibition of discrimination on grounds of nationality does not only apply to rules or provisions which wholly exclude non-nationals from certain activities but also to rules which reserve a certain number of positions to nationals of the host State. Cp the French Seamen case in which the Court held that a French rule which reserved 75% of the jobs on board French fishing boats to French nationals was contrary to Art 39 EC. Case 167/73 *Commission v France* [1974] ECR 359. Further, the prohibition does not only apply to legislative rules but also to administrative practices. Case C–185/96 *Commission v Greece* [1998] ECR I–1095, 24. Equality of treatment must further be guaranteed in, or by, collective agreements concluded between social partners. Discriminatory clauses in such agreements are null and void. See Art 7(4) of Reg 1612/68 and Case C–15/96 *Schöning-Kougebetopoulou* [1998] ECR I–47. Finally, Art 39 EC can also be invoked by employers. Case C–350/96 *Clean Car* [1998] ECR I–2521, 19.

[42] Art 7(1) specifies that the right to equal treatment applies to remuneration, dismissal and in case of unemployment, reinstatement and re-employment. See also, Case 15/69 *Ugliola* [1969] ECR 363 (disadvantages resulting from obligations to fulfil military service); Case 44/72 *Marsman* [1972] ECR 1243 (protection against dismissal); Case 152/73 *Sotgiu* [1974] ECR 153 (seperation allowances); Case 225/85 *Commission v Italy* [1987] ECR 2625 (protection and aspects of job security like the duration and extension of labour contracts); Case 33/88 *Allué* [1989] ECR 1591 (employment contracts of limited duration); Joined Cases C–259/91, C–331/91 and C–332/91 *Allué II* [1993] ECR I–4309 (idem); Case C–272/92 *Spotti* [1993] I–5185 (idem); Case C–90/96 *Petrie* [1997] ECR I–6843 (fulfilment of specific tasks) and Case C–35/97 *Commission v France* [1998] ECR I–5325 (supplementary pension rights in cases of early retirement). Member States cannot discriminate against nationals of other Member States with regard to conditions of work by invoking Art 39(4). Furthermore, Art 8 of the Reg provides for a right to equal treatment as regards membership of trade unions and the exercise of trade union rights (see, eg: Case C–213/90 *ASTI* [1991] ECR I–3507) and vocational training (Art 7(3) of Reg 1612/68).

and indirect[43] discrimination on grounds of nationality is prohibited. Even nationality-neutral rules which hamper the right to work in other Member States may be caught by Article 39.[44] The public service exception contained in Article 39(4) EC has been interpreted narrowly to allow Member States to exclude nationals of other Member States only from certain posts in the public service.[45]

2.2.2 Right to Reside

Community citizens who have made use of their right to take up employment in another Member State may become entitled to a whole set of corollary rights. The first is a right to establish residence in the Member State concerned. The right of residence is based on Article 39(3) EC; the details concerning the exercise of the right, and the administrative formalities to be fulfilled, are set out in Directive No 68/360.[46] The right to reside may be temporary or permanent in nature. Workers who are employed for less than a year have the right to reside in the host State for the duration of the employment.[47] Community workers

---

[43] On the concepts of direct and indirect discrimination on grounds of nationality see ss 7.1 and 7.2 of this chapter.

[44] See, eg: Case C–415/93 *Bosman* [1995] ECR I–4291 and Case C–18/95 *Terhoeve* [1999] ECR I–345. See also: s 7.3.

[45] Once Community citizens have been appointed to public service posts in another Member State, they can be classed as workers and enjoy the right to equal treatment. The very fact that nationals of another Member State have been appointed shows that the interests which may have justified an exception to the free movement of workers and the principle of non-discrimination are presumably not present. Case 152/73 *Sotgiu* [1974] ECR 153 4. On the status of Community workers employed in the public sector see, eg: van der Steen, 'Vrij Verkeer van Overheidswerknemers en CAO's in de Publieke Sector' (1998) *SMA* 484–6. See also: s 7.

[46] The right is evidenced by a document entitled 'Residence Permit for a National of a Member State of the EEC'. Art 4 of Dir 68/360. This residence card only has declaratory effect; the right to reside itself follows directly from the Treaty. Case 48/75 *Royer* [1976] ECR 497, 31–3; Case 8/77 *Sagulo* [1977] ECR 1495, 8 and Case 157/79 *Pieck* [1980] ECR 2171, 13. In order to become entitled to the residence card workers must produce a valid passport or identity card and a document proving that they have found employment. See Art 4(3) of Dir 68/360. The passport or identity card must be valid (Case C–68/89 *Commission v the Netherlands* [1991] ECR I–2637, 15), but it is not required that the passport or identity card entitles holders to leave the territory of the issuing Member State (Case C–376/89 *Giagounidis* [1991] ECR I–1069 15, 19). The residence card is valid throughout the territory of the host State. Art 6(1) of Dir 68/360. According to Art 9, the residence card can be obtained or renewed free of charge or on payment of an amount not exceeding the dues and taxes charged for the issue of identity cards to nationals. Completion of the formalities for obtaining the residence card does not hinder the right to start employment. Art 5. Member States are entitled to require from nationals of other Member States to report their presence to the competent authorities in order to obtain knowledge of population movements in their territory. Art 8(2) and Case 118/75 *Watson* [1976] ECR 1185, 18–19. A period of three days is too short though. Case C–265/88 *Messner* [1989] ECR 4209, 9–12. Member States are entitled within certain limits to impose penalties for non-fulfilment of administrative formalities. Case 118/75 *Watson* [1976] ECR 1185; Case 8/77 *Sagulo* [1977] ECR 1495; Case 157/79 *Pieck* [1980] ECR 2171; Case C–265/88 *Messner* [1989] ECR 4209; Case C–363/89 *Roux* [1992] ECR I–273 and Case C–24/97 *Commission v Germany* [1998] ECR I–2133.

[47] Dir 68/360 makes a distinction between workers who have found employment that is not expected to exceed three months and workers who have an employment contract for more than three months but less than one year. Just as frontier workers and seasonal workers working for less than three months, the former may work without having to obtain the residence card referred to in the previous footnote. Art 8 of Dir 68/360. Workers who have found employment for a period

who have found work which is expected to last for more than a year obtain the right to reside in the Member State of employment for five years. If after five years workers are still in employment, they obtain the right to reside in the host State permanently.[48] Workers who voluntarily give up employment lose the right to reside in the host State;[49] involuntary unemployment does not end the right of residence.[50] Community workers who definitively have ended their working-career either because of permanent incapacity or retirement formally lose the right to reside in the host State as a Community worker, although they may become entitled to the so-called 'right to remain.'[51]

2.2.3 *Right to Equal Treatment in Matters not Related to Employment*

In addition to a right of residence, employment in another Member State may entitle Community citizens to equal treatment rights in areas which are not or are only tenuously related to the employment issues expressly mentioned in Article 39(2) EC. Regulation No 1612/68 provides for equality of treatment as

---

between three and twelve months are entitled to a residence card which may be limited to the duration of the expected period of employment. Art 6(3).

[48] The right to reside may not depend on possession of a residence card (n 46 above), but the wording and objective of Dir 68/360 suggest that the right to reside will not be lost as long as workers hold such a card. The residence card referred to in the previous footnotes must be valid for five years and be automatically renewable. Art 6(1)b of Dir 68/360. The residence card, and with that the right to reside, remains valid when workers become involuntarily unemployed. Art 7(1). Thus, workers who have found employment for more than one year and who become unemployed against their will, remain entitled to reside as workers in the host State for at least five years. After the expiration of this period the residence card is in principle automatically renewable. Where workers have been unemployed for twelve consecutive months at the moment of renewal of their card, the new residence card may be limited to a period of twelve months. Art 7(2). Basically, workers who have found employment in another Member State for more than one year, are ensured of a right to reside in that Member State for at least six years. The workers become entitled to reside permanently in the host State if at the end of the sixth year they are (still) in employment.

[49] Art 7(1) and (2) of Dir 68/360 (*a contrario*). This is different as regards workers who have voluntarily given up employment with a view to taking up studies that are in some way linked to the previous employment. Case 39/86 *Lair* [1988] ECR 3161; Case 197/86 *Brown* [1988] ECR 3205; Case C–357/89 *Raulin* [1992] ECR I–1027 and Case C–3/90 *Bernini* [1992] ECR I–1071. On this category see especially ch 5, s 3.2.3.

[50] Art 7(1) and (2) of Dir 68/360.

[51] Art 39(3)d EC as worked out in further detail in Reg 1251/70 (OJ Sp.Ed. 1970 L 142). The right to remain may be regarded as the prolongation of the right to reside and can, according to Art 2(1)a of the Reg, be obtained by persons who at the time they stop working (*i*) have reached the age laid down by the law of the host Member State for entitlement to an old-age pension, (*ii*) have been employed in the host Member State for at least twelve months and (*iii*) who have resided in the host Member State for more than three years. The right may also be obtained by persons who have become unemployed as a result of a permanent incapacity to work and have resided continuously in the territory of the host Member State for more than two years. The latter condition does not apply if the incapacity is the result of an accident at work or an occupational disease entitling him to a pension for which an institution of that State is (entirely or partially) responsible. See Art 2(1)b Reg 1251/70.

regards public housing (Article 9),[52] fiscal advantages[53] and social advantages (Article 7(2)).[54] Most important, the Court has given a very broad interpretation of the concept of 'social advantages.' The concept covers all rights or benefits which:

> 'whether or not linked to a contract of employment, are generally granted to national workers primarily because of their objective status as workers or by virtue of the mere fact of their residence on the national territory and whose extension to workers who are nationals of other Member States therefore seems likely to facilitate the mobility of such workers within the Community.'[55]

[52] On this provision see Case C–305/87 *Commission v Greece* [1989] ECR 1461. Equality of treatment as regards housing also extends to public loans or public rent allowances. Case 63/86 *Commission v Italy* [1988] ECR 29. The latter case concerned self-employed persons and the judgment was based on Art 52 EC (now 43). The *rationale* of the judgment, however, applies *mutatis mutandis* to Community workers. See also: Hartley (1991) n 1 above, 149–50 and Jørgensen (1996) n 1 above, 235–8.

[53] In recent years the Court has increasingly been confronted with cases concerning the right to equal treatment of employed and self-employed persons in fiscal matters. Most of these cases were not decided on the basis of Art 7(2) of Reg 1612/68, but on the provisons of the Treaty itself. See, eg: Case C–175/88 *Biehl* [1990] ECR I–1779; Case C–204/90 *Bachmann* [1992] ECR I–249; Case C–112/91 *Werner* [1993] ECR I–4017; Case C–279/93 *Schumacker* [1995] ECR I–225; Case C–80/94 *Wielockx* [1995] ECR I–2493; Case C–107/94 *Asscher* [1996] ECR I–3089; Case C–336/96 *Gilly* [1998] I–2793; Case C–251/98 *Baars* [2000] ECR I–2787 and Case C–87/99 *Zurstrassen* [2000] ECR I–3337.

On this case law see, eg: van Thiel, *Free Movement of Persons and Income Tax Law: The European Court in Search of Principles—An Investigation into the Compatibility of Income Tax Laws and Tax Treaties of the Member States and the Potential Consequences of the Court's Income Tax Case Law* (2001); Rossi, 'The Taxation Aspects of the Free Movement of Persons' in Carlier and Verwilghen, *Thirty Years of Free Movement of Workers in Europe* (2000) 127–42; van der Woude, *Belastingen Begrensd: De Doorwerking van het Discriminatieverbod en de Richtlijnen van de EG op Nationale Belastingen* (2000); Vanistendael, 'The Consequences of Schumacker and Wielockx: The Steps Forward in the Tax Procession of Echternach' (1996) *CMLRev* 255–69; Buys, *Met het EG-Recht Strijdige Belastingstelsels en de Rechtsbescherming van de Burger* (1994) and Wouters, 'The Case-Law of the European Court of Justice on Direct Taxes: Variations Upon a Theme' (1994) *MJ* 179–220.

[54] Reg 1612/68 implements, and determines the scope of, Art 39 EC. The reg does not create any 'new' rights. Cp Case 48/75 *Royer* [1976] ECR 4875, 23–4.

[55] Case 207/78 *Even* [1979] ECR 2019, 22; Case C–249/83 *Hoeckx* [1985] ECR 973, 20 and Case C–122/84 *Scrivner* [1985] ECR 1027, 24. Initially, the Court interpreted the concept of social advantages so as to apply only to benefits connected with employment. Case 76/72 *Michel S.* [1973] ECR 457, 9. Two years later, however, the Court gave a much broader meaning to Art 7(2) which was extended to cover all social advantages 'whether or not attached to the contract of employment'. Case 32/75 *Cristini* [1975] ECR 1085, 12–13. This interpretation of the concept of Art 7(2) was very far-reaching. It even suggested that the scope of the right to equal treatment would be unlimited: *all* aspects whether or *not* connected to the contract of employment seemed to be covered by the concept. This left room for the conclusion that Community workers could also enjoy equality of treatment as regards political rights such as the right to vote and stand as a candidate in elections. In *Even*, however, the Court took a small step backwards. The concept of 'social advantages' does not include rights or benefits that are political in nature and closely linked to the nationality of a State.

In applying this definition, the Court has classed numerous social security(-like) benefits,[56] student grants,[57] benefits to cover funeral expenses,[58] the right to live together in the host State with an unmarried partner[59] and the right to use one's own language in Court[60] as 'social advantages.'[61] Virtually all social and economic benefits are covered.[62] The fact that many of the rights or benefits

---

[56] These include eg: childbirth loans (Case 65/81 *Reina* [1982] ECR 33, 13), minimum income benefits for old people (Case 261/83 *Castelli* [1984] ECR 3199, 11), social assistance(-like) benefits (Case 249/83 *Hoeckx* [1985] ECR 973, 22 and Case 122/84 *Scrivner* [1985] ECR 1027, 26), special old-age allowances (Case 157/84 *Frascogna* [1985] ECR 1739, 21–2), unemployment benefits (Case 94/84 *Deak* [1985] ECR 1873, 21–2; Case 57/96 *Meints* [1998] ECR I–6689 and Case C–278/94 *Commission v Belgium* [1996] ECR I–4307) and family benefits (Case C–85/96 *Martínez Sala* [1998] ECR I–2691, 28).

[57] Case 39/86 *Lair* [1988] ECR 3161, 22–3.

[58] Case C–237/94 *O'Flynn* [1996] ECR I–2617, 14.

[59] Case 59/85 *Reed* [1986] ECR 1283, 28.

[60] Case 137/84 *Mutsch* [1985] ECR 2681, 17.

[61] For an overview of the case law see, eg: O'Keeffe, 'Equal Rights for Migrants: The Concept of Social Advantages in Article 7(2), Regulation 1612/68' (1986) *YEL* 93–123; Jørgensen (1996) n 1 above, ch 7; Lippert, *Gleichbehandlung bei sozialen Vergünstigungen und Arbeitnehmerfreizügigkeit in der Europäischen Gemeinschaft—Eine Analyse von Art.7 II (EWG) Nr.1612/68 auf der Basis der Rechtsprechung des Europäischen Gerichtshofes* (1993) and Allen, 'Equal Treatment, Social Advantages and Obstacles: In Search of Coherence in Freedom and Dignity' in Guild (ed), *The Legal Framework and Social Consequences of Free Movement of Persons in the European Union* (1999) 31–48.

[62] The conclusion that a given benefit does not constitute a social advantage does not necessarily imply that workers cannot claim equality of treatment. First, they may possibly rely on Art 39 EC. In *Commission v France* the Court held that this provision guarantees equality of treatment as regards rights or benefits which are essential to the workers' well-being and can be regarded as a corollary of the right to freedom of movement. Case C–334/94 *Commission v France* [1996] ECR I–1307, 21. The case concerned French legislation that preserved the right to register maritime pleasure boats to French nationals. In the view of Adv Gen Fennelly this right could not be regarded as a social advantage for the purposes of Art 7(2). He argued, however, that Reg 1612/68 does not provide for an enumerative lists of rights to equality of treatment and that workers may rely on Art39 of the Treaty in order to claim rights or benefits which are essential to their well-being and which can be regarded as a corollary to the right to freedom of movement. The Adv Gen concluded that the right to register maritime pleasure boats, and more generally opportunities for social and leisure activities, must be regarded as a corollary to the right to freedom of movement. Case C–334/94 *Commission v France* [1996] ECR I–1307, 41–4 (AG Fennelly). The Court seemed to support this line of reasoning. Access to leisure activities such as the registration of leisure crafts are a corollary to the right to freedom of movement and thus covered by the Community provisions relating to freedom of movement. Case C–334/94 *Commission v France* [1996] ECR I–1307, 21–2. See also: Case C–151/96 *Commission v Ireland* [1997] ECR I–3327, 8–11.

Further, Community workers may rely on Art 12(1) EC in order to claim equal treatment in cases where no social advantages are asked for. See, eg: Case C–411/98 *Ferlini* [2000] ECR I–8081. *Ferlini* concerned a Community worker who was working for the European Commission in Luxembourg. Mr Ferlini challenged the legality of the fees for the care given at his wife's confinement and for her stay in a maternity unit of a Luxembourg hospital. At first glance, one might have expected that the Court, following the suggestion of the Advocate General (at 59), would have decided the case under Art 7(2) of Reg 1612/68. Cp Martin, 'Annotation *Ferlini*' (2001) EJML 257–70, 258–9. The Court, however, held that Mr Ferlini was not claiming entitlement to a social advantage which consisted of a payment of a flat rate. The Court concluded, however, that the application to Community citizens who are not affiliated to a national insurance scheme of scales of fees for medical and hospital care, which are higher than those applied to persons who are affiliated to such a scheme, is in breach of Art 12(1) EC and it answered the question under the heading of Art 12(1) EC. Case C–411/98 *Ferlini* [2000] ECR I–8081, 62.

covered by Article 7(2) of Regulation No 1612/68 fall under, or derive from, policy areas which have not as such been brought within the ambit of the Treaty has never been a reason for the Court to deny the application of the right to equal treatment. In determining the scope of this right a functional criterion must be applied;[63] equal treatment is guaranteed as regards rights or benefits which may facilitate the right to work in other Member States or promote the integration of the worker into the host State's society.

The right to equal treatment may be broad but it is limited. Political rights such as the rights to vote and to stand as a candidate in elections as well as certain rights linked to the performance of military service[64] fall outside the scope of the provisions on free movement of workers.[65] In sum, both as workers and residents of the host State,[66] Community workers have the right to be treated equally with the nationals of the host State,[67] but Community law does not require that they must be treated as though they actually were nationals of the host State.

2.2.4 *Status of Community Worker*

All Community citizens have the right to move to other Member States in order to take up employment. However, not all Community citizens who exercise this right are entitled to establish residence or to claim benefits under Article 7(2) of

---

[63] See, eg: Case 9/74 *Casagrande* [1974] ECR 773, 12 and Case C–18/95 *Terhoeve* [1999] ECR I–345, 33–35 and USZ 1999/67 (with annotation van der Mei). See also De Witte, 'The Scope of Community Powers in Education and Culture in the Light of Subsequent Practice' in Bieber and Ress (eds), *Die Dynamik des Europäischen Gemeinschaftsrechts* (1987) 261–81.

[64] See, eg: Case 207/78 *Even* [1979] ECR 2019 (the right of war veterans to early retirement on full pension) and Case C–315/94 *de Vos* [1996] ECR I–1417 (pension contributions concerning military service).

[65] Such political-like rights are not covered by Art 7(2) and cannot, as one may assume, be regarded as a corollary to the right to freedom of movement (n 62 above). The notion of corollary rights to the right to freedom of movement is rather vague. In *Commission v France* Adv Gen Fennelly suggested that the bounds of these rights have to be defined 'by reference to the essential human as well as economic needs of those who avail themselves of the primary Treaty right'. Case C–334/94 *Commission v France* [1996] ECR I–1307, 42 (Adv Gen Fennelly). Under Art 19 of the Treaty, however, Community workers have, as citizens of the Union, the right to vote and to stand as a candidate in municipal elections (Art 19(1)) *juncto* Council Dir 94/80—OJ 1994 L 368/38) and elections for the European Parliament (Art 19(2) *juncto* Council Dir93/109—OJ 1993 L 329/34). Community law does not provide for voting rights in elections for national parliaments. See also O'Leary: (1996) n 1 above, ch 6.

[66] The rights covered by Art 7(2) do not necessarily have to be enjoyed in the State of employment. For instance, a Member State which gives national workers the opportunity of pursuing vocational training in another Member State by making student financial aid available, must grant such aid under the same conditions to Community workers domiciled in its territory. Case 235/87 *Matteucci* [1988] ECR 5589, 16. Further, temporary employment outside the territory of the host State does not necessarily imply that a worker cannot invoke Art 7(2). Case 237/83 *Prodest* [1984] ECR 3153, 10.

[67] O'Keeffe (1986) n 62 above, 105.

Regulation No 1612/68. In order to become entitled to the full panoply of rights discussed in this section, Community citizens must possess the status of Community worker. In order to avoid Member States excluding certain Community citizens from the provisions on the free movement of workers and the rights provided there under,[68] the Court has consistently held that the concept of Community worker may not be defined by reference to national laws. The concept has a Community meaning.[69] From the case law, and the rulings in *Levin* (1982)[70] and *Lawrie-Blum* (1986)[71] in particular, it follows that the status of Community worker[72] can be obtained by nationals[73] of the Member States[74] who are pursuing effective and genuine economic activities under the direction of an employer established in another Member State and who, in return for their

---

[68] Case 53/81 *Levin* [1982] ECR 1035, 11.

[69] Case 75/63 *Unger* [1964] ECR 177, 22–4 and Case C–27/91 *Le Manoir* [1991] ECR I–5531, 7. By stating that the concept has a Community meaning the Court conferred upon itself a 'hermeneutic monopoly' to counteract possible unilateral restrictions on the application of rules relating to the free movement of workers by the Member States. Mancini, 'The Free Movement of Workers in the Case-Law of the European Court of Justice' in Curtin and O'Keeffe, *Constitutional Adjudication in European Community and National Law* (1992) 67–77, 68.

[70] Case 53/81 *Levin* [1982] ECR 1035.

[71] Case 66/85 *Lawrie-Blum* [1986] ECR 2121.

[72] See also Vilá Costa, 'The General Concept of Worker' in Carlier and Verwilghen, *Thirty Years of Free Movement of Workers in Europe* (2000) 69–77.

[73] The concept of Community worker has a Community meaning, but the question who must be regarded as a national must be answered by reference to national law. Case C–360/90 *Micheletti* [1992] ECR I–4239. See also Declaration No 2 on nationality of a Member State annexed to the Final Act of the Treaty on European Union which states that the question 'whether aṇ individual possesses the nationality of a Member State shall be settled solely by reference to the national law of the Member State concerned'. In *Micheletti* the Court also held, however, that in applying their nationality laws, Member States must give due regard to the requirements of Community law. Case C–360/90 *Micheletti* [1992] ECR I–4239, 10. On this rather ambiguous observation, the judgment in *Micheletti* and/or, more generally, the difficult relationship between Community law and nationality law see, eg: Jesserun d'Oliveira, 'Nationality and the European Union after Amsterdam' in O'Keeffe amd Twomey (eds), *Legal Issues of the Amsterdam Treaty* (1999) 395–412; O'Leary (1996) n 1 above, ch 2; Closa, 'Citizenship of the Union and Nationality of Member States' (1995) *CMLRev* 487–519; Hall, *Nationality, Migration and Citizenship of the Union* (1995) ch 3; Evans, 'Nationality Law and European Integration' (1992) ELRev 190–215; O'Leary, 'Nationality Law and Community Citizenship: A Tale of Two Uneasy Bedfellows' (1992) *YEL* 353 *et seq*; Evans and Jesserun d'Oliveira, 'Nationality and Citizenship' in Cassese *et al* (eds), *Human Rights and the European Community: Methods of Protection* (1991) 298–345 and Greenwood, 'Nationality and the Limits of the Free Movement of Persons in Community Law' (1987) *YEL* 7 *et seq*. Germany and the United Kingdom have adopted unilateral declarations in which they define the term 'nationals' for the purposes of Community law, and the free movement of persons in particular. In *Kaur* (2001) the Court accepted the validity of the United Kingdom's definitions because (*i*) the other Member States were fully aware of the content of the British declaration and (*ii*) the declaration did not have the effect of depriving any person of rights guaranteed by Community law. Case C–192/99 *Kaur* [2001] ECR I–0000, 23–7. See also: Shah, 'British Nationals under Community Law: The Kaur Case' (2001) *EJML* 271–8 and Staples, 'Vrij Verkeer van Personen—Wie is Burger van de Unie?' (2001) *NTER* 109–11.

[74] Community workers must be nationals of one of the Member States. A national who died before his country acceded to the Community does not hold the status of worker. Case C–131/96 *Romero* [1997] ECR I–3659, 17.

activities, receive a remuneration.[75] The Court's definition is quite broad. The nature of the work,[76] the specific features of the employment relationship[77] and the context[78] or the sector[79] in which work is performed are all irrelevant in principle for obtaining the status of Community worker. Furthermore, the Court has given due regard to the growing importance of part-time work and rejected the view that only full-time workers may obtain the status of Community worker.[80]

The concept of Community worker, however, is not unlimitedly broad. Not all part-time workers can claim to be a Community worker. In order to obtain this status a Community citizen must perform 'effective and genuine' activities. Activities that are on such a small scale that they have to be regarded as 'purely marginal and ancillary' do not suffice for acquiring the status of Community worker.[81] What precisely must be understood by 'effective and genuine' work is hard to say, but, roughly speaking, one could say that a Community citizen must work at least half of the normal working-hours in a given sector in order to be

[75] The requirements of work, subordination and remuneration were laid down by the Court in *Lawrie-Blum*. Case 66/85 *Lawrie-Blum* [1986] ECR 2121, 17. The additional requirement that the work or the economic activities must also be 'effective and genuine' was introduced in *Levin*. Case 53/81 *Levin* [1982] ECR 1035, 17. In *Lawrie-Blum* the Court also held that Community workers must pursue economic activities 'for a certain period of time'. The phrase does not seem to have a substantive meaning. Community law does not require that employment contracts must be concluded for a minimum period of time or that a certain period of occupational activity must be completed before a person can invoke the status of worker. On the latter point see Case 39/86 *Lair* [1988] ECR 3161, 42 and Case 197/86 *Brown* [1988] ECR 3205, 22. The facts that activities are only pursued for a short period of time or that they are perhaps of a non-recurring character relate to the amount of work performed by a person and must be taken into account when establishing the 'effective and genuine' or 'marginal and ancillary' nature of activities. Case C–357/89 *Raulin* [1992] ECR I–1027, 14.

[76] Prostitution, for instance, can be classed as an economic activity. See Joined Cases 115 and 116/81 *Adoui and Cornaille* [1982] ECR 1665 and in particular the Opinion of Adv Gen Capotorti. See also: Verschueren (1990) n 3 above, 288.

[77] Joined Cases 389/87 and 390/87 *Echternach* [1989] ECR 723, 11(employment for international organisations); Case C–357/89 *Raulin* [1992] ECR I–1027, 11 ('on-call contracts') and Case C–337/97 *Meeusen* [1999] ECR I–3289, 15–16 (spouse of director and sole shareholder of undertaking).

[78] See, eg: *Steymann* in which the Court held that the mere fact that activities are performed in the context of a community based on religion (*in casu* the Bagwhan community) does not preclude the possibility that employees can be classed as Community workers. Case 196/87 *Steymann* [1988] ECR 6159, 14.

[79] Professional sports people, for instance, can obtain the status of Community worker. Case 36/74 *Walrave & Koch* [1974] ECR 1405; Case 13/76 *Doná* [1976] ECR 1333; Case 222/86 *Heylens* [1987] ECR 4097; Case C–118/91 *Bosman* [1995] ECR I–4291; Joined Cases C–51/96 and C–191/97 *Deliège* [2000] I–6511 and Case C–176/96 *Lehtonen* [2000] ECR I–2681. See also Parret, 'EG-Recht en Sport: Is Sport Anders' (2001) *SEW* 53–61 and Misson, 'The Sporting Side of Community Law' in Carlier and Verwilghen, Thirty Years of Free Movement of Workers in Europe (2000) 79–87.

[80] Case 53/81 *Levin* [1982] ECR 1035, 16 and Case C–106/91 *Ramrath* [1992] ECR I–3351, 25.

[81] Case 53/81 *Levin* [1982] ECR 1035, 17.

classed as a Community worker.[82] Community citizens who do not meet this minimum requirement are entitled to pursue 'marginal and ancillary' activities in other Member States, and they must be treated equally as regards all employment-related issues. Yet, they do not enjoy the right to reside under Article 39 EC and they cannot rely on Article 7(2) of Regulation No 1612/68 with a view to claiming social advantages.

Community citizens do not in all circumstances have to continue to meet the criteria developed in *Levin* and *Lawrie-Blum* in order to retain the status of

---

[82] Jørgensen (1996) n 1 above, 31. The Court has never laid down clear criteria for determining how much work has to be done or how many hours must be worked. In *Lawrie-Blum* and *Kempf* the Court seems to have accepted that the work of teachers who gave 11 or 12 lessons a week could be classed as 'effective and genuine'. Case 66/85 *Lawrie-Blum* [1986] ECR 2121 and Case 139/85 *Kempf* [1986] ECR 1741. Including the time teachers need for preparing classes, one could therefore conclude that 50% of the normal working-hours in a given sector suffices. See also Opinion of Adv Gen Slynn in Case 139/85 *Kempf* [1986] ECR 1741, 1743. In determining whether 'effective and genuine' activities are pursued, only the activities performed in the host Member State can be considered. Activities pursued in other Member States cannot be taken into account. Case C–357/89 *Raulin* [1992] ECR I–1027, 17–19. In every individual case the number of working hours must be considered and compared to the normal working hours in the particular sector under consideration. Case 139/86 *Kempf* [1986] ECR 1741, 1743 (Adv Gen Slynn).

The requirement of 'effective and genuine' work does not only have implications for the amount of work or the number of working hours, but also for the nature of the work. A typical example concerns *Bettray* (1989). The case concerned the Dutch Social Employment Law that intended to provide work for persons who could not work under normal conditions due to physical and mental illness. Special jobs were created in undertakings or associations solely set up for the retraining and rehabilitation of such persons. The law sought to promote reintegration of the persons into the normal work process. Although the Court admitted that the basic criteria were fulfilled in case of employment under the Social Employment Law, it denied that the persons concerned could be regarded as workers for the purposes of Community law. In the Court's view the activities carried out under such a scheme were merely a means of rehabilitation or reintegration and could therefore not be regarded as 'effective and genuine' activities. The social and therapeutic nature of the activities was predominant and the activities therefore could not be regarded as 'effective and genuine' economic activities. Case 344/87 *Bettray* [1989] ECR 1621, 17–19. For criticism on this judgment see especially O'Leary (1996) n 1 above, 93–8. *Bettray* must, however, be interpreted in light of the particular characteristics of the employment scheme at issue. Not all sheltered forms of employment are excluded from Art 39 EC. Cp Case C–1/97 *Birden* [1998] ECR I–7747, 31.

The mere fact that part-time workers often earn less than the minimum subsistence level in the host State, does not prevent them from being classed as a Community worker. An income must be earned, but this may be supplemented by private resources, earnings of an accompanying family member (Case 53/81 *Levin* [1982] ECR 1035, 16) or even social assistance benefits (Case 139/85 *Kempf* [1986] 1741, 14—see ch 3, s 3.1.). Remuneration must be received, but the Court has never indicated what the minimum level should be. Logically, purely symbolic payments do not suffice, but a general and uniform minimum level of remuneration applicable throughout the Community cannot be given. The least one could say is that the remuneration must be a real *quid pro quo* for the pursuit of 'effective and genuine' activities. In other words, an 'effective and genuine' remuneration is required. It is not required that the compensation from the employer for the work has to be paid out in money. This compensation can also consist of eg, board and lodging. Case 196/87 *Steymann* [1988] ECR 6159, 12 and 14. Further, the fact that the payment depends on the productivity of the workers or of the group in which they are working is immaterial with respect to the status of worker. Case C–3/87 *Agegate* [1989] ECR 4459, 36–7. The fact that the remuneration is largely provided by subsidies from the public funds is of no significance. Case 344/87 *Bettray* [1991] ECR 1621, 15.

Community worker. Unemployment[83] does lead, in principle, to the loss of the status of worker, but, as the Court held in *Martínez Sala* (1998), this status 'may produce effects after the employment relationship has ended.'[84] The Court has never fully explained what these effects are, but, arguably, a distinction must be made between involuntary unemployment and voluntary unemployment. Community citizens who have voluntarily given up employment lose the right to reside as a worker in the host State[85] and, in matters not related to former employment, the equal treatment rights which Community law confers upon workers.[86] The involuntary unemployed, however, may retain the right of residence or, in the case of retirement or permanent incapacity, acquire the right to remain. In both cases the persons concerned can still benefit from the equal treatment rights discussed in Section 2.2.3.[87] For as long as they continue to live in the host State by virtue of either the right to reside or the right to remain,[88] the involuntary unemployed remain entitled to the rights they initially enjoyed as Community workers. For the purposes of this book this category will be dealt with as though they were still holding the status of Community worker.[89]

---

[83] The loss of nationality does not necessarily imply the loss of the status of worker or the right and benefits linked to it. Various situations may be distinguished. A first one concerns Community citizens who have moved to another Member State, acquired that State's nationality and lost the nationality of the State of origin. Such Community citizens have exercised their right to freedom of movement and may rely on the provisions for free movement of workers against the State of which they (now) hold the nationality. A so-called 'internal situation' (n 33 above) is not present. Cp Case C–419/92 *Scholz* [1994] ECR I–505. A second situation relates to Community citizens who have acquired the status of workers in another Member State and subsequently lose their nationality and are left only with the nationality of a non-Member State. Strictly speaking, such 'third country nationals' do no meet the criteria for the status of Community worker, but by analogy with the judgment in *Scholz* it may be assumed that the loss of nationality will not affect their status under Community law in the host State. Cp de Groot, 'The Relationship between the Nationality Legislation of the Member States of the European Union and European Citizenship' in La Torre, *European Citizenship—An Institutional Challenge* (1998) 115–47.

[84] Case C–85/96 *Martínez Sala* [1998] ECR I–2691, 32.

[85] s 2.2.2. above.

[86] This may be different for Community workers who have given up work with a view to commencing studying. Provided the studies concerned are linked to the previous employment, such Community citizens retain the right to rely on Art 7(2) in order to claim equal treatment as regards 'social advantages'. See Case 39/86 *Lair* [1988] ECR 3161; Case 197/86 *Brown* [1988] ECR 3205; Case C–357/89 *Raulin* [1992] ECR I–1027; Case C–3/90 *Bernini* [1992] ECR I–1071 and Case C–184/99 *Grzelczyk* [2001] ECR I–6193. See also: ch 5, s 3.2.3.

[87] As regards the beneficiaries of the right to remain this is explicitly provided for in Art 7 of Reg 1251/70. As regards the other category, it could either be argued that for as long as Community citizens enjoy the residence rights regulated by Dir 68/360, they retain the rights to equal treatment guaranteed by Reg 1612/68, and Art 7(2) in particular, or that they enjoy these rights under Art 12 of the Treaty. All rights and benefits covered by the equal treatment provisions of Reg 1612/68 also fall within the ambit of Art 12 EC. Case C–85/96 *Martínez Sala* [1998] ECR I–2691, 57 and s 3 below.

[88] The right to equal treatment guaranteed by Art 7(2) of Reg 1612/68 does not extend to workers who, after ceasing to exercise occupational activities in the host state, decide to return to the state of origin. Case C–33/99 *Fahmi* [2001] ECR I–2415, 47. This right can only be retained in special circumstances. Case C–57/96 *Meints* [1997] ECR I–6689.

[89] Cp Wapenaar (1997) n 1 above, 41. In the literature a distinction has been made between a core concept and an extended concept of workers. See, eg: Jørgensen (1996) n 1 above, 36 and Hartley

2.3 Family Members

When the Community institutions implemented Article 48 (now 39) E(E)C during the 1960s, they recognised that a genuine free movement of workers could not be realised without eliminating the obstacles to 'the worker's right to be joined by his family and the conditions for the integration of that family into the host country.'[90] Article 10 of Regulation No 1612/68 entitles the worker's spouse,[91] their (grand)children who are under the age of 21 years or dependent[92]

(1991) n 1 above, 93–5. The former concept would cover all Community citizens who at a given moment fulfil all the criteria for the status of Community worker. This category would enjoy all rights provided for by the provisions for the free movement of workers. The extended concept of workers would consist of Community citizens who do derive rights from Art 39 but who do not yet, or no longer, meet the standard criteria for the concept of Community worker. Some of the 'extended-workers' would enjoy only some of the rights granted to workers (eg, work-seekers—see Case C–85/96 *Martínez Sala* [1998] ECR I–2691, 32), whilst others would qualify for all rights granted to Community workers (eg, the beneficiaries of the right to remain). This chapter does not use this distinction between a core concept and an extended concept. For the purposes of this chapter, Community workers are all EC nationals who are pursuing effective and genuine economic activities under the direction of an employer established in another Member State and who, in return for their activities, receive a remuneration as well as those who after the involuntary loss of employment still hold the right to reside in the host state under Art 39.

[90] See the fifth indent of the preamble to Reg 1612/68 and Case C–356/98 *Kaba* [2000] ECR I–2623. On the status of the family members see also: Sewandono, *Werknemersverkeer en Gezinsleven* (1998) and Lundström, 'Family Life and the Freedom of Movement of Workers in the European Union' (1996) *IJLPF* 250–80.

[91] The concept of spouse doest have a Community meaning. It only refers to the marital relationship as defined by national law. See, eg: Case 267/83 *Diatta* [1985] ECR 567 and Case 58/85 *Reed* (1986) ECR 1283. Community law doest require that spouses live together under the same roof: 'the marital relationship cannot be regarded as dissolved so long as it hast been terminated by the competent authority. It is dissolved merely because the spouses live separately, even where they intend to divorce at a later date'. Case 267/83 *Diatta* [1985] ECR 567, 20. For the purposes of Art 10 cohabitees dot have to be treated as spouses. Case 59/85 *Reed* [1986] ECR 1283, 11–13. Yet, residence rights for unmarried partners can be classed as a social advantage in the sense of Art 7(2) of Reg 1612/68. Case 59/85 *Reed* (1986) ECR 1283, 22 and 28.

[92] The Court has never specified what exactly should be understood by 'dependence' or 'dependent family member'. The mere fact that a family member applies for a social assistance benefit doest prevent a family member from being regarded as a dependent family member. Case 316/85 *Lebon* [1987] ECR 2811, 20. See also: ch 3, s 3.2. In *Lebon* the Court further held that the status of dependent family member 'is the result of a factual situation. The person having that status is a member of the family who is supported by the worker and there is need to determine the reasons for recourse to the worker's support or to raise the question whether the person concerned is able to support himself by taking up paid employment'. Case 316/85 *Lebon* [1987] ECR 2811, 22. On a very strict interpretation of the Reg one could reason that family members who exercise the right to work granted by Art 11 of the Reg can longer be regarded as dependent on the Community worker. Yet, if this were actually the case Art 11 would be deprived of all useful effect. Oliver, 'Non-Community Nationals and the Treaty of Rome' (1985) *YEL* 57–92, 74; Verschueren (1990) n 3 above, 320 and van der Mei, 'Kinderen van EG-werknemers' (1995) *NTOR* 211–17, 213.

and their dependent (grand)parents to reside[93] with the worker in the host State.[94] The nationality of the family members is of no relevance.[95]

The right of family members to reside[96] in the host State derives from the right of residence of the worker himself. As a result, family members can in principle only take up residence if the worker himself does so and they will lose their right at the moment that the worker gives up or loses his residence.[97] In order to promote the integration of the worker's family into the host State, Article 11 entitles family members to work in that State[98] and Article 12 confers upon the children of Community workers the right to be admitted to educational institutions under the same conditions as the nationals of the host State.[99] The rights granted by Articles 11 and 12 do not suffice for a full and effective integration of the family member in the host State. The Court has recognised this. In *Cristini*

---

[93] The formalities to be fulfilled regarding the right to reside (as laid down in Dir 68/360 and Reg 1251/70) are essentially the same as those applicable to the workers. s 2.2.2. Some special provisions apply to family members, however. Next to a valid passport or identity card, family members can be required to present a document issued by the State of origin proving their relationship with the worker and, where applicable, a document testifying that they are dependent on the worker or that they live(d) under the roof of the worker in the State whence they came. Art 4(3) Dir 68/360. Furthermore, as regards family members who do not hold the nationality of one of the Member States, the authorities of the host state may demand the presentation of an entry visa or an equivalent document. Art 3(2) of Dir 68/360.

[94] Art 10(2) further states that the Member States shall 'facilitate the admission' of other family members who are dependent on the worker or who were living in the Member State of origin under the same roof. These other family members do not have a legally enforceable right to reside in the state of employment. Hartley (1978) n 18 above, 132.

[95] See, eg: Case 94/84 *Deak* [1985] ECR 1874 and Case C–243/91 *Taghavi* [1992] ECR I–4401.

[96] The right of family members to reside is subject to the condition that the worker must have available for his family housing 'considered as normal for national workers in the region where the worker is employed'. Art 10(3) of Reg 1612/68. The condition only applies, however, at the moment the family members wish to install themselves with the worker. If, later on, the housing can for some reason no longer be considered 'normal' the right to reside is not affected. Case 249/86 *Commission v Germany* [1989] ECR 1290, 11.

[97] In some cases, however, family members can retain their right to reside. For instance, under certain circumstances they may keep their right in order to complete studies. See, eg: Joined Cases 389 and 390/87 *Echternach* [1989] ECR 723. On this judgment see ch 5, s 3.3.3. Furthermore, family members may become entitled to the right to remain (permanently) in the host state when (*i*) the worker has become entitled to the right to remain himself (Art 3(1) of Reg 1251/70) or (*ii*) where the worker dies before having acquired the right to remain provided the worker had resided continuously in the host state for at least two years, his death resulted from an accident at work or an occupational disease or the surviving spouse is a national of the host state or lost nationality of this state by marriage to the worker (Art 3(2)).

[98] In practice, Art 11 is only relevant for family members who do not hold the nationality of one of the Member States. Case C–413/99 *Baumbast*, pending, 40 (Adv Gen Geelhoed). Family members who possess such nationality can directly invoke Art 39 EC. The right to work granted by Art11 is limited to the territory of the State where the worker is employed. Family members must possess the professional qualifications required by the national rules of the host State and they must observe the specific rules governing the pursuit of occupations. Case 131/85 *Gül* (1986) ECR 1573, 15 and Case 292/86 *Gullung* [1988] ECR 111, 29. Dependent (grand)parents and grandchildren are not mentioned in Art 11. Yet, the right to work no doubt contributes to the integration of such family members in the host State and can probably be classed as a 'social advantage' in the sense of Art 7(2) of the Reg. Oliver (1985) n 92 above, 74.

[99] On Art 12 see ch 5, s 3.3.

(1976) it held that family members can rely on Article 7(2) in order to claim equality of treatment as regards 'social advantages.'[100] In *Lebon* (1987) the Court specified, however, that family members qualify only indirectly for the equal treatment granted by Article 7(2). They may only rely on this provision as regards benefits which can be regarded as social advantages for the worker himself and this seems to imply that the right to claim benefits under Article 7(2) is preserved for family members who are dependent on the worker.[101]

2.4 Self-Employed Persons and their Family Members

The category of economic residents also includes the self-employed beneficiaries of the right of establishment guaranteed by Article 43 (formerly 52) EC and their family members. The rights of the self-employed are governed by different provisions, but the Court has frequently held that Articles 43 and 39 EC are based on the same principles.[102] Thus, Community citizens may move to other Member States in order to set up a business and in so doing they are protected against any rule or measure which treats them less favourably than the nationals of the host State. Even nondiscriminatory rules that hamper the right of establishment may be prohibited.[103] The self-employed who have established themselves in another Member State obtain a right to reside there, which is governed by provisions that are very similar to the ones applicable to workers[104] and they

---

[100] Case 32/75 *Cristini* [1975] ECR 1085, 15. Initially, the Court interpreted Art 7(2) rather restrictively by holding that this provision can only be invoked by workers in matters connected with employment. Family members were expressly excluded by the Court from the equal enjoyment of social advantages. Case 76/72 *Michel S* [1972] ECR 457, 9–10.

[101] Case 316/85 *Lebon* [1987] ECR 2811 at 2. In *Lebon* itself, for instance, the Court ruled that Art 7(2) could not be applied to a child who was no longer dependent on the worker. The social benefit at issue (social assistance benefit) could not be classed as a 'social advantage' for the worker himself. Once it is established that a benefit also favours the worker, family members can enforce the right to equal treatment in the national courts themselves. Case C–3/90 *Bernini* [1993] ECR I–1071, 29. Art 7(2) can be applied to all family members falling within the scope of Art 10 of the Reg (Case 261/83 *Castelli* [1984] ECR 3199, 9–10 and Case 316/85 *Lebon* [1987] ECR 2811, 12) including family members who do not possess an EC-nationality (Case 94/84 *Deak* [1985] ECR 1873 26). Art 7(2) can also be invoked by family members who do not, or no longer, reside with the worker in the host State. Art 7(2) does not contain a residence requirement. Case C–3/90 *Bernini* [1993] ECR I–1071, 29. It could be argued, however, that the 'independent' family members can claim social advantages under Art 12 EC. See, eg: Case C–85/96 *Martínez Sala* [1998] ECR I–2691; Fries and Shaw, 'Citizenship of the Union: First Steps in the European Court of Justice' (1998) *EPL* 533–59, 550 and ch 3, s 3.2 of this study.

[102] See, eg: Case 48/75 *Royer* [1976] ECR 497, 12; Case 118/75 *Watson* [1976] ECR 1185, 9; Case C–363/89 *Roux* [1991] ECR I–273, 23; Case C–106/91 *Ramrath* [1992] ECR I–3351, 17 and Case C–24/97 *Commission v Germany* [1998] ECR I–2133, 11. See also: Voogsgeerd, *Interstatelijkheid— De Aard en de Intensiteit van het Grensoverschrijdend Element in de Rechtspraak van het Hof van Justitie van de EG met Betrekking tot de Vier Vrijheden* (2000) 233–5.

[103] Cp Case C–55/94 *Gebhard* [1995] ECR I–4165. See also: Reich, *Bürgerrechte in der Europäischen Union* (1999) 181–8.

[104] Dir 73/148 (OJ 1973 L 172—right to reside) and 75/34 (OJ 1975 L 14—right to remain).

are entitled to equality of treatment in many matters which are not or barely related to the pursuit of economic activities. A 'self-employed' equivalent of Regulation No 1612/68 has never been adopted, but the self-employed may rely on Article 43 EC in order to claim the various social rights which Community workers enjoy under Regulation No 1612/68. Such social rights and advantages may be regarded as a corollary of the right of establishment.[105] As noted in the introductory chapter,[106] this book is based on the assumption that the rules and principles governing, or relevant for, cross-border access to public benefits of the self-employed are in principle the same as the ones applicable to workers and for this reason the legal status of the self-employed will not be discussed separately.

2.5 Conclusions

Looking back, one must conclude that Community law on the free movement of workers has undergone significant changes since the coming into force of the EEC Treaty. The drafters of the Treaty had only agreed to a rather limited freedom of movement, which would not include much more than a right to accept offers of employment in other States made and a right to equal treatment in employment-related matters. Today, however, the right to work in other Member States is regarded as a fundamental right for European citizens which includes a firmly protected right of residence, a right to be treated equally in virtually all social and economic aspects and a right to be joined by family members who also enjoy a far-reaching right to equal treatment in the host State. In order to become entitled to the full panoply of rights, however, the Court has laid down a threshold requirement. The status of Community worker, and thus all the rights linked to that status, can be obtained only when 'effective and genuine' employed activities are performed in another Member State. Community citizens who do not meet this minimum requirement do have the right to work in other Member States, but they cannot rely on Article 39 EC and the secondary legislation adopted on the basis of Article 40 EC in order to claim residence rights and equality of treatment in matters not related to employment. They can only claim such rights in their capacity as non-economic residents.[107]

---

[105] Cp Opinion of Adv Gen Fennelly in Case C–334/94 *Commission v France* [1996] ECR I–1307, 41–4. See also: Case 197/84 *Steinhauser* [1985] ECR 1819; Case 63/86 *Commission v Italy* [1989] ECR 29; Case C–151/96 *Commission v Ireland* [1997] ECR I–3327 and Case C–337/97 *Meeusen* [1999] ECR I–3289. On this point see also: van der Steen, 'Studiefinanciering ook voor Kinderen van Grensarbeiders' (1999) *NTER* 210–15; Craig and De Búrca, *EU Law—Text, Cases & Materials* (1998) 754 and Jørgensen (1996) n 1 above, 278–87.

[106] Ch 1, s 3.1.

[107] The fact that the legal foundations for freedom of movement have been laid does not imply that freedom of movement for workers has increased in practice. Carlier, 'Proportionality and Citizenship in Relation to the Free Movement of Workers' in Carlier and Verwilghen, *Thirty Years of Free Movement of Workers in Europe* (2000) 41–57, 42–3. For an overview of research and literature on migration patterns within the Community see O'Leary, 'The Free Movement of Persons and Services' in Craig and de Búrca, *The Evolution of EU Law* (1999) 377–415, 386–92.

3 NON-ECONOMIC RESIDENTS

The second category of beneficiaries of free movement of persons whose legal status will be examined in this book consists of 'non-economic residents.'[108] It concerns Community citizens whose right to reside in other Member States is based on Articles 18(1) or 12(1) EC and regulated by Directives No 93/96, No 90/365 and No 90/364. More specifically, the non-economic residents include students, pensioners and the residual category of the 'other' Community citizens.' It is worthwhile beginning the discussion of the legal status of non-economic residents with a brief history.

3.1 Towards a General Right of Residence: A Brief History

In 1968 the vice-president of the Commission referred to the free movement of workers in terms of a European citizenship.[109] This citizenship was still limited in scope. At the time, it did not entail much more than the right to choose the place of work within the Community.[110] Over the years, Community provisions on the free movement of workers have been construed broadly, but up until today the enjoyment of the rights guaranteed by Article 39 EC has been conditional upon the pursuit of economic activities in other Member States. For this reason, the free movement of workers has aptly been described in terms of a market citizenship.[111]

From the early 1970s, however, the political Community institutions have taken several initiatives to transform this market citizenship into a genuine European citizenship.[112] As members of the European Community, nationals of

---

[108] The beneficiaries of the three residence directives of 1990 are often referred to as 'non-economically active'. The term is appropriate in that it indicates that the residence rights of the persons concerned are not linked to or conditional upon the pursuit of economic activities. The term is somewhat misleading as far as it suggests that these persons do not perform economic activities. This may very well be the case. For instance, Community citizens who have taken up relatively small jobs which must be classed as 'marginal and ancillary' do not become entitled to the residence right which Art 39 EC confers upon Community workers. Such Community citizens are economically active but, as far as the right to reside in the state of employment is concerned, they have to rely on one of the 1990 residence directives and/or possibly Art 18(1) EC.

[109] s 2.1.

[110] Evans (1982) n 21 above, 501.

[111] The term was first introduced by Ipsen. Ipsen, 'Europäisches Gemeinschaftsrecht' (1964) NJW 340 (n 2). See also: Grabitz, Europäisches Bürgerrecht zwischen Marktbürgerschaft und Staatsbürgerschaft (1970); Everling, 'Von der Freizügigkeit der Arbeitnehmer zum Europäisches Bürgerrecht?' (1990) EuR Beiheft I 81–103, 81; Verschueren (1990) n 3 above, 448–50 and Everson, 'The Legacy of the Market Citizen' in Shaw and More (eds), New Legal Dynamics of European Union (1995) 73–90.

[112] The european citizen should be brought 'into the construction of Europe' by establishing a 'European Citizenship which would be in addition to the citizenship which the inhabitants' of the Member States already possess. Bull.EC 11–1972, 37. See also: O'Leary (1996) n 1 above, 17–20.

the Member States would be granted a number of 'special' rights'[113] including a general right of residence. The right to establish residence in other Member States would no longer be subordinate to, or dependent on, the pursuit of economic activities; it would be granted as an independent right which nationals of Member States could enjoy simply in their capacity as European citizen. In furtherance of this policy objective, the European Commission submitted to the Council in 1979 a proposal for a directive on a 'right of residence for nationals of the member States in the territory of another Member State.'[114] The draft directive was based on Articles 308 (formerly 235) and 46(2) (formerly 56(2)) E(E)C which implied that the Council should be unanimous in order to adopt the directive. The directive was intended to supplement the existing free movement provisions; the right of residence would have to be granted to all nationals of the Member States and their family members who did not already enjoy such a right under Articles 39 or 43 EEC.

In recognition of the fear of many Member States that they might be faced with an influx of 'needy' citizens from other Member States moving for the sole purpose of collecting comparatively high social benefits, the Commission proposed that Member States could require citizens 'to provide proof of sufficient resources for their own needs and the dependent members of their family.'[115] Because of this financial means requirement, one might have expected that the directive would be adopted relatively easy, but this did not turn out to be the case. On the contrary, negotiations in the Council proved to be very difficult. The fear of 'social tourism' was too strong. After some years the European Commission had to conclude that the likelihood of the Council reaching a unanimous decision had been reduced to virtually zero.[116]

In 1985, however, the Commission received unexpected support from the Court of Justice. In *Gravier* the Court ruled that Community citizens could

---

[113] In 1974 the Heads of States and Governments assigned the European Commission the task of studying the conditions under which nationals of Member States could be given 'special rights' with a view to developing a 'Citizens' Europe'. The right to reside in other Member States was regarded as one of these special rights. Bull.EC 12–1974, 1104 and Bull.EC, Suppl.7/75, 25. See also the chapter 'Towards a Europe of Citizens' of the Tindemans report (Bull.EC 8–1975); the Scelba Report (PE Doc.346/77) and European Parliament, *Proceedings of the Round Table on Special Rights and a Charter of the Rights of the Citizens of the European Community* (1979).

[114] OJ 1979 C 204; COM(79) 215 final.

[115] Art 4(2) of the 1979 draft directive.

[116] More specifically, during the negotiations the Member States could not reach agreement on the definition of family members who would be given the right to join the principal beneficiaries and on the question of whether students should have to prove that they possess adequate financial means. On the Council negotiations on the 1979 draft directive see, eg: Schulz, *Freizügigkeit für Unionsbürger* (1997) 53–64; O'Leary (1996) n 1 above, 109–18; Bolly, 'Droit d'Entrée et de Sejour des Ressortissants communautaire: Développements récents' (1990) *ActduDr* 735–48; Taschner, 'Free Movement of Students, Retired Persons and other European Citizens—A Difficult Legislative Process' in Schermers *et al* (eds), *Free Movement of Persons in Europe* (1993) 427–36 and van Nuffel, 'Een Bijna Algemeen Verblijfsrecht in de Europese Gemeenschap—Commentaar op de Verblijfsrecht-richtlijnen van 28 juni 1990' (1990) *SEW* 887–903.

invoke Article 12 EC (at the time 7 EEC) in order to get access to vocational training in other Member States.[117] In the Commission's view the judicially created right to study in other Member States necessarily encompassed a right to reside in those States.[118] There was no longer a need to grant students a right of residence and the Commission subsequently decided to exclude students from the original draft directive.[119] The Council, however, was still not willing to adopt the proposal and this urged the Commission to alter its strategy. In 1989 the Commission withdrew its proposal and replaced it with three new proposals for specific directives for rights of residence for students,[120] pensioners[121] and 'all other Community citizens.'[122] The 'splitting-up' of the 1979 proposal enabled the Commission to give due regard to the Member States diverse objections to residence rights for the various categories of beneficiaries[123] and to base two of its proposals on Treaty provisions which allow for decision-making by a qualified majority within the Council.[124] The Commission's new strategy proved successful. In June 1990 the Council adopted the three directives which had to be implemented by 30 June 1992.[125]

By adopting the directives the Council had contributed to a strengthening of the notion of European citizenship, but this contribution was still quite modest. The citizens who could benefit from 'non-economic residence rights' were often persons who in many cases would already have been entitled to reside in other Member States on the basis of national law.[126] For Community citizens who were not able to provide for themselves not much progress had been made; they still did not enjoy the right to establish residence in other Member States.

---

[117] Case 293/83 *Gravier* [1985] ECR 593. See also: ch 5, s 4. In the same year the Commission also received support from the Adonnino Committee which stressed that a general right of residence was essential for a 'People's Europe'. Bull.EC Suppl.7/85 12.

[118] This conclusion has later been confirmed by the Court in Case C–357/89 *Raulin* [1992] ECR I–1027, 34. See also: ch 5, ss 4.1 and 4.4.

[119] OJ 1985 C 171; COM(85) 292 final.

[120] OJ 1989 C 191.

[121] *Ibid.*

[122] *Ibid.*

[123] Taschner (1993) n 116 above, 433.

[124] The draft directive for students was based on EEC Treaty Art 7(2) (now Art 12(2) EC) (qualified majority) and the proposal for the pensioners directive was based on Arts 49 (now 40) and 54 (now 54) of the Treaty (qualified majority). The directive for the residual category of 'other Community citizens' was based on Art 100 (now 94) of the Treaty (unanimity).

[125] Dir 90/366/EEC (students—OJ 1990 L 180); Dir 90/365/EEC (pensioners—OJ 1990 L 180) and Dir 90/364 ('other' Community citizens—OJ 1990 L 180). The Council did not base the directives on the proposed legal bases but on Art 235 EC(now 308). The European Parliament objected and claimed that the student directive should have been based solely on EEC Treaty Art 7(2). It started a procedure under Art 173 EC (now 230) asking the Court to annul Dir 90/366 on the ground of an improper legal basis. The Court concluded that the residence directive should indeed have been based on EEC Treaty Art 7(2) alone. Case C–295/90 *Parliament v Council* [1992] ECR I–4193, 18. Subsequently, the original Dir 90/366 was replaced by Dir 93/96 which, qua substance, was virtually identical to the directive of 1990. OJ 1993 L 317. See also: ch 5 s 4.4. On the (non)implementation of the directives see C–96/95 *Commission v Germany* [1997] ECR I–1653.

[126] O'Leary (1996) n 1 above, 119–20.

During the 1990-1991 Intergovernmental Conferences, which ultimately led to the Treaty on European Union, some Member States proposed that the planned political and economic union should be accompanied by a strengthened European citizenship. This would entail a number of 'political' rights among which an unlimited general right to freedom of movement that would be included in the Treaty itself.[127] Ultimately, Member States could reach agreement on formally introducing a Citizenship of the Union (Article 8 EC; since 'Amsterdam': Article 17 EC)[128] which encompasses rights to vote and stand for election in European and municipal elections[129] and a right for all Union citizens to move and reside freely among the Member States (Article 8a EC; now Article 18 EC). The Member States could not agree, however, on extending free movement rights. Article 18 EC explicitly provides that free movement rights are subject 'to the limitations and conditions laid down in this Treaty and by the measures adopted to give it effect.'[130] By inserting Article 18 EC the Member States did not intend to do more than codify the *acquis communautaire* in the field of the free movement of persons. In their view, progress was to be made by the Council which, according to Article 18(2) EC, was granted the power to adopt by unanimity provisions aimed at facilitating the exercise of the free movement rights mentioned in Article 18(1) EC.

3.2 Right to Reside

The limitations and conditions upon the right to reside of students, pensioners and the remaining Union citizens, are set out in the three directives of 1990. In

[127] Agence Europe, 11 May 1990, 3. In a memorandum which was presented during the Intergovernmental Conference the Spanish Government had proposed to grant Community citizens an unlimited right to move and reside freely and to adopt legislation which would lay down 'provisions to ensure a fair distribution of the resulting burden on the Member States, particularly in the area of social protection'. 'Spanish Memorandum on European Citizenship' in Cornett, *The Treaty of Maastricht* (1993) 156. On the negotiations during the Intergovernmental Conference see also: O'Leary (1996) n 1 above, 23–30.

[128] On the notion of union citizenship see, eg: O'Keeffe, 'Union Citizenship' in O'Keeffe and Twomey (eds), *Legal Issues of the Maastricht Treaty* (1994) 87–107; Closa, 'The Concept of Citizenship of the European Union' (1992) *CMLRev* 1137–70; Covar and Simon, 'La Citoyenetté de l'Union' (1993) *CDE* 285–316 and Constantinesco, 'La Citoyenetté de l'Union' in Schwarze (ed), *Vom Binnenmarkt zur Europäischen Union* (1993) 25 *et seq.*

[129] Art 19 EC. See also: Dollat (1998) n 1 above, 467–504; Marias, 'European Citizenship in Action: From Maastricht to the Intergovernmental Conference' in La Torre (ed), *European Citizenship—An Institutional Challenge* (1998) 293–316; O'Leary (1996) n 1 above, chs 6 and 7 and Degen, 'Die Unionsbürgerschaft nach dem Vertrag über die Europäische Union unter besonderer Berücksichtigung des Wahlrechts' (1993) *DöV* 749–58. See also: Case C–323/97 *Commission v Belgium* [1998] ECR I–4281.

[130] Thus, as Community law stands at present, the rights of Community citizens in other Member States are not unconditional. Case C–356/98 *Kaba* [2000] ECR I–2623, 30.

the preambles to the directives it is stipulated that beneficiaries must not become an unreasonable burden on the public finances of the host Member State. This financial safeguard for Member States is specified in Article 1 of each of the directives. Pensioners shall be granted the right of residence[131] when they receive invalidity, early retirement or other pensions or old age benefits of an amount sufficient to avoid becoming a burden on the social security system of the host State. The residual class of 'other Community citizens' must have sufficient means to provide for themselves and their family members.[132] Pensions and resources are deemed sufficient where they are higher than the level at which Member States grant social assistance benefits to its nationals.[133] Students only have to assure the relevant national authority that they have resources sufficient to avoid becoming a 'public burden.' Directive No 93/96 does not require resources of any specific amount, nor that they be evidenced by specific documents.[134] In order to avoid beneficiaries becoming a financial burden on the host State, beneficiaries must also be covered by sickness insurance in respect of all risks.[135] As regards pensioners and the category of 'other' Community citizens,' the right to reside is also granted to the spouse and the dependent (grand)children and (grand)parents of pensioners and 'other Community citizens.' Students are only entitled to be joined by their spouse and their dependent children. In each of the three directives it is stated that the right of residence exists only for as long as beneficiaries fulfill the financial means and health insurance requirements. Quite recently, however, the Court concluded in *Grzelczyk* (2001) that Directives No 93/96, 90/365 and 90/364 embody a 'certain degree of financial solidarity' between Community citizens. The right of residence will only be

[131] The directive for pensioners applies to persons who wish to reside in a Member State other than the one in which they have worked (or the state of their nationality). Community citizens who have worked in other Member States and who wish to remain there afterwards are covered by Reg 1251/70 (or, in case of the self-employed, Dir 73/41). See also: s 2.2.2.

[132] As in the case of Community workers, the right of residence shall be evidenced by a 'Residence Permit for a National of a Member State of the EEC'. The validity of this permit may be limited to five years on a renewable basis. See also: Art 2 of both Directives. In applying the financial means requirements contained in Dir 90/364 and 90/365, Member States enjoy a certain discretion which implies that they do not, at least in as far as applied to family members, have to phrase and apply the requirements identically to the various categories. Case C–424/98 *Commission v Italy* [2000] ECR I–4001, 26.

[133] Where this requirement cannot be applied in a Member State, the resources are deemed sufficient when they are higher than the level of the minimum social security pension paid by the host Member State. Art 1(1), third para of both directives. The pensioner directive requires that the pension or the benefit, which is received, must be 'sufficient'. This could imply that a Community citizen who receives a pension that is relatively low and falls under the minimum subsistence level in other Member States, cannot rely on Dir 90/365. Such a pensioner, however, may possess other financial resources which together with the pension would be 'sufficient'. In such cases the pensioner may rely on Dir 90/364. Martin and Guild (1996) n 1 above, 220.

[134] Case C–184/99 *Grzelczyk* [2001] ECR I–6193, 40. On the right of residence of students see ch 5, s 4.4.

[135] For further details on this requirement see ch 4 s 3.3.3.

lost when beneficiaries become an 'unreasonable burden' on the host State's public finances.[136]

3.3 Right to Equal Treatment

Community citizens who have exercised their non-economic right of residence are entitled to be treated equally with the nationals of the host State. In as far as the pursuit of economic activities is concerned, equality of treatment is guaranteed by Community provisions on free movement for employed and self-employed persons. In non-economic matters, Article 12(1) EC, which prohibits 'within the scope of application' of the Treaty 'any discrimination on grounds of nationality,' must be relied on. The number of cases decided under Article 12 EC is still relatively small and until recently the scope of the right to equal treatment of the non-economic residents was uncertain. In the first cases in which it had to determine the scope of Article 12 EC, the Court considered the degree to which the powers in a given policy area had been transferred to the Community in order to determine whether or not a given right, opportunity or matter is covered by the Treaty. Thus, in *Gravier* (1985), after having referred to various measures Member States and Community institutions had taken in the field of vocational training, the Court concluded that access to such training falls within the scope of the Treaty.[137] Following a comparable line of reasoning, the Court concluded in *Lair* (1988), however, that Article 12 EC (then 7 EEC) does not in principle cover student financial aid. Student grants were considered matters of educational and social policy, which as such had not yet been brought within the competence of the Community.[138]

From an educational perspective these two judgments were no doubt revolutionary. The Court read into Article 7 EEC (read together with Article 128 EEC) much more than the drafters of the Treaty had envisaged.[139] Nonetheless, the 'transfer-of-power-approach' also seemed rather restrictive because it basically implied that Article 12(1) EC could not be invoked by Community citizens in the

---

[136] 136 Case C–184/99 *Grzelczyk* [2001] ECR I–6193, 44. Pursuant to Art 5 of each of the three directives, Member States had to implement the Directives by 30 June 1992. Most Member States did not meet the deadline. The Commission subsequently started infringement procedures for non-transposition, which were terminated the moment the state in question adopted the required implementation measures. The procedure against Germany was not ended and was finally referred to the Court. The Court ruled against Germany for not adopting measures implementing Dir 90/364 and 90/365 and it rejected Germany's argument that there were no grounds for the action because beneficiaries could rely on the Directive itself. Case C–96/95 *Commission v Germany* [1997] ECR I–1653. The Commission also started various procedures against Member States that had not transposed the directives correctly. Upon proper transposition, most proceedings were terminated. Only the procedure against Italy was continued. Case C–424/98 *Commission v Italy* [2000] ECR I–4001.

[137] Case 293/83 *Gravier* [1985] ECR 293, 19–25.

[138] Case 39/86 *Lair* [1988] ECR 3161, 14–15.

[139] On this point see also: ch 5, s 4.1.

numerous policy areas (still) falling within the domain of the Member States. Furthermore, the approach followed in *Gravier* and *Lair* differed from the case law on the free movement of workers in which the Court had rejected the view that the scope of the right to equal treatment would depend on the degree to which powers in substantive policy areas have been transferred to the Community. In interpreting the scope of Article 39 EC and Article 7(2) of Regulation No 1612/68 the Court has taken a functional approach. Equality of treatment must be ensured in all matters facilitating freedom of movement and the integration of the worker and his family in the host State's society.

In various cases concerning the right to equal treatment of non-residents under Article 12(1) EC the Court had already adopted a comparable approach.[140] The judgments in *Martínez Sala* (1998) and *Grzelczyk* (2001) demonstrate that the scope of Article 12 is, also in relation to non-economic residents, to be determined by the same criteria as the ones the Court has applied in the context of the free movement of workers. Mrs Martínez Sala was a Spanish national who lived and received a social assistance benefit in Germany. After the birth of her daughter she applied for a child-raising allowance, but this benefit was refused because she did not hold German nationality and could not produce a residence permit. In determining whether the child-raising allowance fell within the scope of Article 12, the Court referred to its judgment in *Hoever* (1996) in which it had already held that the allowance in question constituted a social advantage in the sense of Article 7(2) of Regulation No 1612/68.[141] The Court concluded that the allowance therefore 'indisputably' fell within the scope of Community law and that Mrs Martínez Sala could as a 'national of a Member State lawfully residing in the territory of another Member State' rely on Article 12 EC in claiming the allowance.[142]

The observations of the Court on this point were rather short, but they did already suggest that the scope of Article 12 EC has to be determined by the same criteria as the ones which have been applied under the provisions on the free movement of workers. This conclusion is confirmed by *Grzelczyk*, in which the Court was asked whether Community students could claim social assistance benefits under Article 12(1) EC. The Court held that they may indeed have such a right reasoning that Community citizens, lawfully resident in the territory of another Member State, can rely on Article 12(1) EC in all situations which fall within the scope *ratione materiae* of Community including those in which

---

[140] See below s 4.2.

[141] Joined Cases C–245/94 and C–312/94 *Hoever* [1996] ECR I–4895.

[142] Case C–85/96 *Martínez Sala* [1998] ECR I–2691, 57–61. On *Martínez Sala* see, eg: Tomuschat, 'Annotation *Martínez Sala*' (2000) *CMLRev* 449–57; Becker, 'Freizügigkeit in der EU—Auf dem Weg vom Begleitrecht zur Bürgerfreiheit' (1999) *EuR* 522–33; O'Leary, 'Putting Flesh on the Bones of European Union Citizenship' (1999) *ELRev* 68–79; Fries and Shaw, 'Citizenship of the Union: First Steps in the European Court of Justice' (1998) *EPL* 533–59; Schrauwen, 'Annotatie *Martínez Sala*' (1999) *SEW* 426–30; Denys, 'Het Burgerschap: Meer dan een Schim?' (1998) *NTER* 210–13 and van der Steen, 'De Europese Burger Krijgt Handen en Voeten' (1998) NTER 163–6.

Community citizens have exercised the right to freedom of movement as guaranteed by Article 18 EC.[143]

Like economic residents, non-economic residents thus enjoy a right to equal treatment in virtually all social and economic matters. This right to national treatment, however, is not protected as securely as the equivalent right of Community workers. Community law still allows Member States to end legal residence when beneficiaries of the general right of residence become in need of social assistance and an 'unreasonable burden' on the public finances of the host State.

4 NON-RESIDENTS

The third category of beneficiaries of free movement of persons whose legal status under Community law will be examined in this book consists of 'non-residents'. It concerns Community citizens who go to other States for a limited period of time without relocating their private residence or place of economic establishment. The legal status of these 'Community travellers' is mainly governed by Articles 49, 18 and 12 EC.[144]

4.1 Right to Travel Freely within the Community

Under the original EEC Treaty, the right to travel to other Member States was a functional right granted only in order to enable self-employed persons to provide services in Member States other than the one in which they are established. From the early years, however, Community institutions have recognised that the right to cross the inter-Member State borders could not be confined to providers of services. In particular, the institutions took the view that a genuine free movement of services required that the recipients of services should also have the right to move to other Member States.[145] In the absence of a specific reference in the Treaty to a right to travel for service recipients the issue remained in dis-

---

[143] Case C–184/99 *Grzelczyk* [2001] ECR I–6193, 32.

[144] For the purposes of this study, the category of non-residents does not include Community citizens who through the pursuit of 'effective and genuine' work have acquired the status of Community worker, but who have decided not to exercise their right to reside as a worker in the state of employment. The legal status of frontier workers is governed by Art 39 EC, not by Arts 49, 18 and 12 EC.

[145] A right to move to other Member States for the purpose of receiving services had already been recognised in secondary legislation. See, eg: *Title II of the General Program for the Abolition of restrictions on Freedom to Provide Services* (OJ Spec.Ed. (2nd Series) IX, 3, Art 1 of Dir 64/221 and Art 1 Dir 73/148. Probably, even the authors of the Treaty were of the opinion that recipients of services would be covered. Everling, 'Vertragsverhandlungen 1957 und Vertragspraxis 1987 dargestellt an den Kapiteln Niederlassungsrecht und Dienstleistungen des EWG-Vertrages' in *Festschrift für von der Groeben* (1987) 111–30, 121. In the Spaak-report reference had already been made to the hotel sector as one of the areas in which the free movement of services would be of particular significance. *Rapport des Chefs de Délégations* (1956) n 12 above, 40.

pute for quite some time.¹⁴⁶ In *Luisi and Carbone* (1984), however, the Court confirmed that the Treaty provisions on the free movement of services indeed also guarantee a right to move to other Member States in order to receive services. The latter right was said to be a corollary of the former right.¹⁴⁷ Strictly speaking, the right of service recipients to go to other States was still economically determined in the sense that the right was solely recognised in order to make the right to provide economic services effective. The practical effect of *Luisi and Carbone*, however, reached much further. In a 'sweeping statement'¹⁴⁸ the Court added that tourists, patients, business travellers and students could be regarded as recipients of services.¹⁴⁹ This basically implied that virtually all Community citizens enjoy the right to travel freely throughout the Community. This conclusion was confirmed in *Commission v. the Netherlands* (1991) where the Court held that Community nationals are generally to be considered beneficiaries of the right to enter other Member States, and as recipients of services in particular, and that, in order to cross the borders of the Member States, they only have to produce a valid passport or identity card.¹⁵⁰ In practice, all Community citizens enjoy a right to travel freely across the intra-Community borders under the Treaty.¹⁵¹ This case law now seems codified in Article 18 EC.

¹⁴⁶ In his Opinion in *Watson* Adv Gen Trabucchi claimed that the practical effect of the inclusion of recipients of services would be an extension of the right of freedom of movement to all EC-nationals since everyone is actually or potentially a recipient of services. This would not accord with the wording of Art 59 EC (now 49) and would be inconsistent with the structure of the Treaty which only provides for a freedom of movement for specific categories of persons. See the Opinion of Adv Gen Trabucchi in Case 118/75 *Watson* [1976] ECR 1185 at 1201.

¹⁴⁷ Joined Cases 286/82 and 36/83 *Luisi and Carbone* (1984) ECR 377, 16. See also: Case C–224/97 *Ciola* [1999] ECR I–2517, 11. Cp also *GB-INNO-BM* where the Court held that the free movement of goods 'requires, particularly in frontier areas, that consumers resident in one Member State may travel freely to the territory of another Member State to shop under the same conditions as the local population'. Case C–362/88 *GB-INNO-BM* [1990] ECR I–667, 8. The Treaty provisions on the free movement of services may cover four situations. Next to cases where the (*i*) provider or the (*ii*) recipient moves from one Member States to another, these are situations in which (*iii*) both the provider and recipient cross the inter-State borders and cases in which (*iv*) neither the provider or the recipient but solely the service itself crosses the borders. An example of the third situation concerns travel agencies that organise holidays in other states. See, eg: the Tourist Guide cases (Case C–154/89 *Commission v France* [1991] ECR I–569; Case C–180/89 *Commission v Italy* [1991] ECR I–709 and Case C–198/89 *Commission v Greece* [1991] ECR I–4221) and Case C–55/98 *Vestergaard* [1999] ECR I–7641. The fourth type of cases concerns eg financial and telecommunication services. See, eg: Case C–353/89 *Commission v the Netherlands* [1991] ECR I–4069; Case C–76/90 *Säger* [1991] ECR I–4421 and Case C–384/93 *Alpine Investments* [1995] ECR I–1141.

¹⁴⁸ Timmermans, 'Annotation *Luisi and Carbone*' (1984) *SEW* 753–79, 755.

¹⁴⁹ Joined Cases 286/82 and 36/83 *Luisi and Carbone* (1984) ECR 377, 16.

¹⁵⁰ The purpose of the travel was held to be irrelevant. According to the Court, immigration officers are not even entitled to ask questions as to the purpose and duration of the stay in the territory of the State concerned. Case C–68/89 *Commission v the Netherlands* [1991] ECR I–2637, 13.

¹⁵¹ Cp also the judgment in *Bickel* in which the Court held that Art 49 EC covers all Community citizens 'who, independently of other freedoms guaranteed by the Treaty, visit another Member State where they intend or are *likely* to receive services' (*ital.*: APvdM). Case C–274/96 *Bickel* [1998] ECR I–7637, 15.

The right to enter another State logically includes the right to stay in the territory of that State for a certain period of time. The duration of this right to stay is limited (Case 196/87 *Steymann* [1989] ECR 6159, 17), but so far no clear criteria have been developed as to the precise duration of the right. The

The right to move freely within the Community facilitates the provision or receipt of services in other States, but no longer seems granted solely for this purpose. The right to move freely within the Community may be regarded as a non-economic right which nationals of the Member States enjoy as citizens of the Union.[152]

4.2 Right to Equal Treatment

In the territory of the Member State they visit, Union citizens have the right to provide and receive services under the same conditions as the nationals of the host State. Article 49 prohibits the application of all national rules which directly or indirectly discriminate against nationals or residents[153] of other Member States as well as nondiscriminatory rules which impinge on the rights to provide and receive services.[154] The concept of services, however, is limited. Article 50 (formerly 60) EC stipulates that services shall be considered 'services' when they are 'normally provided for remuneration.' Public services which are mainly funded out of public funds are not services for the purposes of Articles 49 *et seq.*[155] This is not to say, however, that Community travellers can never rely on Community law in order to claim such public benefits. They may do so under Article 12 EC. Consider *Cowan* (1989).[156] The case concerned a British tourist who was assaulted at a metro station in Paris. Mr Cowan sought financial compensation for his injuries under a French compensation scheme for victims of crime. His request was rejected on the ground that he was neither a French national nor a resident of France. It was beyond doubt that the benefit Mr Cowan applied for could not be regarded as a service, but he argued that, as a recipient of touristic services, he fell within the personal scope of the Treaty and that he therefore was entitled to rely on Article 7 EEC (now Article 12 EC) in order to claim the desired benefit. The French government objected by arguing that the national rules Mr Cowan challenged did not in any relevant way impinge on freedom of movement. The Court did not agree. Whenever:

most one could say is that the duration of the right to stay is of 'equal duration with the period during which the services are provided' (Art 4(1) of Dir 73/148).

[152] There is, however, no absolute certainty. In *Wijsenbeek*, for instance, the Court avoided the question whether the right to travel is now actually based on Art 18 EC. Case C–378/97 *Wijsenbeek* [1999] ECR I–6207, 43. Cp Toner, 'Passport Controls at Borders between Member States' (2000) *ELRev* 415–24, 420 and Bulterman, 'Annotation *Bickel*' (1999) *CMLRev* 1325–34, 1333–4.

[153] National rules which make the right to provide services conditional upon residence in the host State are prohibited since they would deprive the right to provide services in other Member States of all useful effect. Case 33/74 *van Binsbergen* [1974] ECR 1299, 11.

[154] See, eg: Case C–55/94 *Gebhard* [1995] ECR I–4165, 37 and Case C–19/92 *Kraus* [1993] ECR I–1663, 32.

[155] Case 263/86 *Humbel* [1988] ECR 5365, 17–18 and Case C–109/92 *Wirth* [1993] ECR I–6447, 19.

[156] Case 186/87 *Cowan* [1989] ECR 195. On *Cowan* see Weatherill, 'Annotation *Cowan*' (1989) *CMLRev* 563–88.

'Community law guarantees a natural person the freedom to go to another Member State the protection of that person from harm in the Member State in question, on the same basis as that of nationals residing there, is a corollary of that freedom of movement.'[157]

The French Government had also argued that Mr Cowan could not rely on Article 7 EEC because the compensation rules in question were part of criminal law and procedure, areas falling within the competence of the Member States. The Court refused to follow such a 'transfer-of-powers-approach' in determining the material scope of Article 7 EEC. Criminal law and procedure are indeed matters for which Member States are responsible, but Community law does impose certain limits on the powers of the Member States. Member States, the Court concluded, 'may not discriminate against persons to whom Community law gives the right to equal treatment or restrict the fundamental freedoms guaranteed by Community law.'[158]

In later cases the Court followed a similar line of reasoning as regards the rights to visit public museums,[159] to get access to courts[160] and to use minority languages in court proceedings.[161] The case law thus indicates that in determining the material scope of the right to equal treatment there is no need to determine whether or to what extent the powers in the policy area concerned have been transferred to the Community. A functional criterion must be applied. Equality of treatment is ensured as regards rights or benefits which may be regarded as a corollary, or which may enhance the exercise of, the right to move to other Member States. The judgments in *Martínez Sala* and, in particular, *Grzelczyk* suggest that the scope of travellers' right to equal treatment is not even restricted by the notion of a corollary of the right to travel. The Court held in *Grzelcyk* that Article 12 must be read in conjunction with Articles 17 and 18[162] and the judgment leaves room for the suggestion that the scope of the travellers' right to equal treatment is as broad as the scope of the right to equal treatment of economic and non-economic residents.

5 THIRD COUNTRY NATIONALS

5.1 Introduction

The Community provisions on the free movement of persons apply in principle only to Community citizens.[163] Article 39 EC merely speaks of 'workers of the

---

[157] Case 186/87 *Cowan* [1989] ECR 195, 17.

[158] *Ibid*, 19.

[159] Cp Case C–45/93 *Commission v Spain* [1994] ECR I–911 (implicitly).

[160] Case C–43/95 *Data Delecta* [1996] ECR I–4661, 12–14; Case C–323/95 *Hayes* [1997] ECR I–1711, 13 and Case C–122/96 *Saldanha* [1997] ECR I–5325, 17.

[161] Case C–274/96 *Bickel* [1998] ECR I–7637.

[162] Case C–184/99 *Grzelczyk* [2001] ECR I–6193, 30 and 37.

[163] Persons who hold the nationality of a Member State and the nationality of a third country are Community citizens for the purposes of Community law. See, eg: Case C–360/90 *Micheletti* [1992] ECR I–4239, 15 and Case C–122/96 *Saldanha* [1997] ECR I–5325, 15.

Member States,' but the omission of an explicit reference to a nationality of one of the Member States was never intended,[164] and does not mean,[165] that workers from third countries are included in the free movement regime. Third country nationals had also not been considered as possible beneficiaries of the general, non-economic, right of residence. From the early 1970s, this right was planned to be a right which nationals of the Member States would enjoy as citizens of the European Community. Article 18 EC as well as the three 1990 residence directives specifically state that the right of residence is conferred upon nationals of the Member States. As regards the right to move or travel among the Member States, the position of third country nationals has been more controversial, but up until today the required harmonisation of national immigration, visa and asylum policies has not been realised.[166] Community law does not

---

[164] s 2.1 above.

[165] See, eg: Art 7(1) of Reg 1612/68. The judgment in *Meade* (Case 283/83 [1984] ECR 2631) suggested (see, eg: Staples, *The Legal Status of Third Country Nationals Resident in the European Union* (1999) at 34–5; Arnull, *The General principles of EEC Law and the Individual* (1990) 10; Greenwood (1987) n 73 above, 205–6; Oliver (1985) n 92 above, 62 and the Opinion of Adv Gen Jacobs in Joined Cases C–95/99, C–98/99 and C–180/99 *Khalil*, pending, 19), but did not compel the conclusion (see, eg: Verschueren (1990) n 3 above, 303 and van der Mei (1996) n 12 above, 156) that third country nationals are excluded from Art 39. EC The more recent judgment in *Awoyemi* (1998), however, confirms this exclusion. The case concerned a Nigerian national who was living in Belgium and who was charged with driving a motor vehicle on the public highway in Belgium without being in possession of a valid driving licence. The Court ruled that Mr. Awoyemi could not invoke the Community provisions on the free movement of persons in order to challenge the imposed penalty because these provisions would only apply to nationals of the Member States. Case C–230/97 *Awoyemi* [1998] ECR I–6781, 29–30.

[166] Art 14 EC (formerly 7a) EEC) speaks of the internal market as an area 'without internal frontiers' in which a free movement of persons is ensured. The European Commission and the European Parliament have interpreted this provision so as to require the elimination of all border controls for 'all persons, irrespective of their nationality'. COM (97) 230, 4. This view, however, was contested by various Member States that insisted on retaining powers as regards the immigration of third country nationals. Due to the uncertainties about the meaning of Art 14 EC and the powers of the Community to abolish border controls (see, eg: Timmermans, 'Free Movement of Persons and the Division of Powers between the Community and its Member States—Why Do It the Intergovernmental Way?' in Schermers *et al* (eds), *Free Movement of Persons in Europe* (1993) 352–88 and the Opinion of Adv Gen Cosmas in Case C–378/97 *Wijsenbeek* [1999] ECR I–6207, 37–42), most of the initiatives as regards the abolition of border controls were taken outside the framework of the Community in the context of the Schengen Treaty (see, eg: Meijers *et al* (eds), *Schengen—Internationalisation of Central Chapters of the Law on Aliens, Refugees Privacy, Security and Police* (1992); O'Keeffe, 'The Schengen Convention: A Suitable Model for European Integration' (1991) *YEL* 185 *et seq*; Schutte, 'Schengen: Its Meaning for the Free Movement of Persons in Europe' (1991) *CMLRev* 549 *et seq* and Donner, 'De Ontwikkeling van het Vrije Verkeer van Personen binnen de Europese Gemeenschappen en de Overeenkomst ter Uitvoering van het Akkoord van Schengen' (1990) *SEW* 766 *et seq*) and, later, the third pillar of the Treaty on European Union on 'Justice and Home Affairs' (see, eg: O'Keeffe, 'Recasting the Third Pillar' (1995) *CMLRev* 893–920 and Peers, *Justice and Home Affairs in Europe* (1999)). The Treaty of Amsterdam has brought virtually all issues concerning immigration and the abolition of border controls under the first pillar of the Treaty on European Union comprising inter alia the EC Treaty. In the new Art 61 the goal is to progressively establish 'an area of freedom, security and justice' and Art 62 provides that the Council shall, within a period of five years after the entry into force of Treaty of Amsterdam, adopt measures 'with a view of ensuring ... the absence of any controls on persons, be they citizens of the Union or nationals of third countries'. See also the various contributions in Guild and Harlow (eds), *Implementing Amsterdam—Immigration and Asylum Rights in EC Law* (2001); Guild, *European Community Law From a Migrant's Perspective* (2000) and Staples (1999) n 165 above, ch 5.

yet provide for a border control free Community in which third country nationals are also entitled to move freely.[167]

The non-Community citizens from third countries only enjoy rights under the free movement regime when, or in as far as, these rights facilitate freedom of movement for Community citizens. In particular, third country nationals can only enjoy rights in their capacity as family members of one of the categories of principal beneficiaries.[168]

The Community provisions on the free movement of persons, as described so far in this chapter, however, do not present the whole picture. The Community and its Member States have concluded various association and cooperation agreements with third States under which the nationals of these States are offered free movement and/or equal treatment rights. The provisions of the agreements, and the various measures adopted there under, form an integral part of Community law[169] and, having regard to their wording and the purpose of and nature of the agreement, they may have direct effect.[170] As noted in the introductory chapter, this book will discuss the rights which third country nationals enjoy under the Agreement on the European Economic Area, the Association Agreement with Turkey and the agreements which have been concluded with the Maghreb countries Morocco, Algeria and Tunisia.[171]

---

[167] Cp Case C–378/97 *Wijsenbeek* [1999] ECR I–6207, 39–40.

[168] In addition, third country nationals may, as employees of providers of services, enjoy certain benefits from the provisions on the free movement of services. Case C–113/89 *Rush Portuguesa* [1990] ECR I–1417 (where the Court held that providers of services may move with their employees to other Member States) as interpreted by the Court in Case C–43/93 *van der Elst* [1994] ECR 3803 (where it was held that the nationality of the employees is of no significance). See also: Dir 97/71 on the posting of workers in the framework of the provision of services (OJ 1997 L 18). See also: Case C–376/96 *Arblade* [1999] ECR I–8453; Onslow-Cole, 'The Right of Establishment and Provision of Services: Community Employers and Third Country Nationals' in Guild (ed), *The Legal Framework and Social Consequences of Free Movement of Persons in the European Union* (1999) 63–71; Jorens, *De Rechtspositie van Niet-EU-Onderdanen in het Europees Socialezekerheidsrecht* (1997) 357–67 and Voogsgeerd, 'Aspecten van Grensoverschrijdende Tewerkstelling' in Pennings, *Tewerkstelling over de Grenzen* (1996) 129–63.

[169] Case 12/86 *Demirel* [1987] ECR 3719, 7 and Case 30/88 *Commission v Greece* [1989] ECR 3711, 12–13.

[170] Case C–192/89 *Sevince* [1990] ECR I–3461, 15 and Case C–18/90 *Kziber* [1991] ECR I–199, 15. See also: Jorens, 'Non-European Union Nationals and the Co-ordination of European Social Security Law: The International Agreements Concluded by the European Union with Third Countries and Conflict Rules in European Social Security Law' in Jorens and Schulte, *European Social Security Law and Third Country Nationals* (1998) 1–110, 25–59.

[171] On the legal status of third country nationals under Community law see, eg: Hedemann-Robinson, 'An Overview of Recent Legal Developments at Community level in relation to Third Country Nationals Resident within the European Union, with Particular Reference to the Case Law of the European Court of Justice' (2001) *CMLRev* 525–86; Groenendijk, 'The Growing Relevance of Article 39 (ex 48) EC Treaty for Third Country Immigrants' in Carlier and Verwilghen, *Thirty Years of Free Movement of Workers in Europe* (2000) 207–23; Vilá Costa, 'The Quest for a Consistent Set of Rules Governing the Status of non-Community Nationals' in Alston (ed), *The EU and Human Rights* (1999) 411–46; Cremona, 'Citizens of Third Countries: Movement and Employment of Migrant Workers within the European Union' (1996) *LIEI* 87–113; Peers, 'Towards Equality: Actual and Potential Rights of Third-Country Nationals in the European Union' (1996) *CMLRev* 7–50; Sørensen, *The Exclusive European Citizenship—The Case for Refugees and Immigrants in the European Union* (1996); Alexander, 'Free Movement of non-EC nationals: A Review of the Case Law

5.2 EEA Nationals

In 1992 the then twelve EC Member States concluded with the then seven EFTA States the agreement on the European Economic Area (EEA).[172] After the refusal of Switzerland to ratify the agreement, and the accession of Austria, Finland and Sweden to the European Union, the EEA Agreement now governs the relationship between the EC Member States and Norway, Iceland and Liechtenstein. The aim of the agreement is to 'promote a continuous and balanced strengthening of trade and economic relations' between the contracting parties with a view to creating a 'homogeneous European Economic Area' which entails *inter alia* a free movement of goods, persons, services, and capital.[173] The rules governing the free movement of persons are set out in Articles 28 up to 35 EEA. Article 28 EEA provides that a free movement of workers shall be secured among the EC Member States and the three EFTA States. The wording of the Article largely coincides with Article 39 EC and the main measures of secondary legislation adopted under Article 40 EC. Regulation No 1612/68 and Directive No 68/360 have been extended, for example, in order to apply, with a small number of adjustments, to the free movement of workers within the entire European Economic Area.[174] Even though some of the provisions may have to be interpreted differently in the context of the EEA Agreement,[175] it may be assumed that the legal status of EEA workers and their family members is governed by the same principles as the status of Community workers and their family members. Basically, the EEA agreement has extended Community law on the free movement of workers, as described in section 2 of this chapter, to the territory and the nationals of Norway, Iceland and Liechtenstein. The same holds true for the Community provisions on the free

---

of the Court of Justice' in Schermers *et al* (eds), *Free Movement of Persons in Europe* (1993) 485–502; Evans, 'Third Country Nationals and the Treaty on European Union' (1994) *EJIL* 199 *et seq*; Hailbronner and Polakiewicz, 'Non-EC Nationals in the European Community: The Need for a Co-ordinated Approach' (1992) *Duke JICL* 49 *et seq*; Hoogenboom, 'Integration into Society and Free Movement of non-EC Nationals' (1992) *EJIL* 36 *et seq*; Ketelsen, 'Einreise, Aufenthalt und Ausweisung von Ausländern aus Drittstaaten' (1991) *ZfRV* 115–27; Plender, 'Competence, European Community Law and Nationals of non-Member States' (1990) *ICLQ* 599–610; Hilf, 'Europäisches Gemeinschaftsrecht und Drittstaatsangehörige' in Hailbronner *et al* (eds), *Staat und Völkerrechtordnung—Festschrift für Karl Doehring* (1989) 339–64 and Oliver (1985) n 92 above, at 57–92.

[172] OJ 1995 L 86. For general descriptions of the EEA Agreement see, eg: Norberg, 'The Agreement on a EEA' (1992) *CMLRev* at 1171 *et seq*; O'Keeffe, 'The Agreement on the European Economic Area' LIEI (1992) 1 *et seq* and Stuijck and Looijetijn-Clearie, *The European Economic Area EC-EFTA* (1993). For a description of the EEA provisions on the free movement of persons see also: Sakslin, 'The Agreements on the European Economic Area' in Jorens and Schulte, *European Social Security Law and Third Country Nationals* (1998) 1–110, at 399–417.

[173] Art 1 of the EEA Agreement (EEA).

[174] Art 28(5) EEA *juncto* Annex v. to the Agreement.

[175] Cp Opinion 1/91 on the Draft Agreement Relating to the Creation of the European Economic Area [1991] ECR 6079 at 6102. Further, under certain circumstances Iceland and Liechtenstein may take safeguard measures. See also: Handoll (1995) n 1 above, at 319.

movement of services (Article 36–39 EEA).[176] As a result, EEA nationals enjoy the right to move to other States in order to receive services and, following the judgments of the Court of Justice in *Luisi and Carbone* and *Commission v. the Netherlands*, all EEA nationals can, as tourists, business persons or patients, cross the internal 'EEA-borders' simply upon the production of a valid passport. In addition, the three 1990 residence directives for students, pensioners and 'other' Community citizens have been extended to EEA-nationals. EEA-nationals, however, do not hold the right to travel and the non-economic right to residence by virtue of the fact that they possess Norwegian, Icelandic or Liechtenstein nationality. The EEA Agreement does not provide for equivalents of Articles 17 (Union citizenship) and 18 (general right to freedom of movement) EC.[177]

5.3 Turkish Nationals

In 1963 the Community and its Member States concluded in Ankara an Association Agreement with Turkey which was designed to promote 'the continuous and balanced strengthening of trade and economic relations between the parties' and to prepare Turkey for an eventual accession to the Community.[178] Among other things,[179] the contracting partners agreed to be 'guided' by Articles 48–50 EEC (now 39–41 EC) for the purpose of progressively securing freedom of movement for workers between them.[180] Article 36 of the Additional Protocol of 1970[181] entrusted the EEC-Turkey Association Council with the task of adopting measures necessary for securing, in three consecutive

---

[176] See also: Arts 31–5 EEA as regards the right of establishment.

[177] Cp Sakslin (1998) n 172 above, at 409.

[178] Art 2 of the Agreement establishing an Association between the European Economic Community and Turkey. OJ 1963 C 113. Prior to this agreement the Community and its Member States had already concluded a comparable association agreement with Greece. See also: Papastamkos, *Die Erweiterung der EG-Freizügigkeit auf griechische Arbeitnehmer* (1983).

[179] The EEC Treaty has served as a model for the gradual integration of Turkey to the Community. The planned free movement of workers was supposed to supplement the establishment of a customs union which would in time have to develop into an economic union. See also: Alanat, 'Freizügigkeit als Prüfstein der Assoziation EWG-Türkei—General Framework of the Association' in Lichtenberg *et al* (eds), *Gastarbeiter—Einwanderer—Bürger? Die Rechtstellung der türkischen Arbeitnehmer in der Europäischen Union* (1996) 17–26, at 17 and Gümrükcü, 'EU-Türkei-Beziehungen im Spannungsfeld zwischen Assoziation und Vollmitgliedschaft—Werdegang einer ungleichen Partnerschaft' in Lichtenberg *et al* (eds) *Gatsarbeiter—Einwanderer—Bürger? Die Rechtstellung der türkisher Arbeitnehmer in der Europäischen Union* (1996) 27–60, at 30–41.

[180] Art 12 of the Ankara Agreement. All contracting parties seemed to have agreed with this objective. At the time, the EC Member States were in need of foreign labour and had already recruited large numbers of Turkish workers, whilst Turkey saw the progressive realisation of a free movement of workers as a means to solve its social problems which included considerable unemployment. See also: Sayari, 'Migration Policies of Sending Countries: Perspectives on the Turkish Experience' in Heisler and Schmitter-Heisler (eds), *From Foreign Workers to Settlers? Transnational Migration and the Emergence of New Minorities—Annals AAPSS* (1986) 86–97.

[181] OJ 1973 L 293.

stages, the free movement of workers no later than 1 December 1986. In furtherance of this task, the Association Council adopted Decisions No 2/76 and No 1/80,[182] but a third decision which would govern the third and final stage in which the free movement for workers would finally be realised, was never adopted.[183] As a result, Turkish nationals do not have the right to move to the Community's Member States in order to take up employment. It is up to the Member States to determine the conditions under which Turkish nationals are admitted to their territory and labour market.[184]

Once admitted, however, Turkish workers enjoy a number of rights under Decision No 1/80. As regards conditions of work and remuneration, Turkish workers must be treated equally with the nationals of the host State[185] and, by virtue of Article 6(1) of Decision No 1/80,[186] Turkish workers are given the right to gradually integrate into the labour force of the host member States. After one year of legal employment[187] Turkish workers are entitled to renewal of their work permit for the same employer;[188] after three years of employment they

---

[182] Council of Association Decision 1/80 (Council Doc 8795/1/80). Decision 1/80 replaced Decision 2/76 which is no longer of significance. Cp Case C–434/93 *Bozkurt* [1995] ECR I–1475, 14.

[183] See also: Jansen, 'Vrij Verkeer van Turkse Werknemers in de EG?' (1986) *MR* 261–63. The fact that the Association Council did not fulfil its obligation to realise a free movement for Turkish workers by 1 December 1986 implies that Turkish workers have no legally enforceable right to freedom of movement. As with Art 12 of the 1963 Agreement, Art 36 of the Additional Protocol is of a programmatic character. The provision is not precise and unconditional enough to be directly effective. Case 12/86 *Demirel* [1987] ECR 3719, 23. See also: Hailbronner, 'Die Entscheidung des EuGH zur Freizügigkeit türkischer Arbeitnehmer' (1988) *NVwZ* 220–4; Joris, Het Hof van Justitie van de Europese Gemeenschappen en het Vrije verkeer van Turkse Werknemers: De Zaak Demirel, in: *TvV* (1988) 3–20 and Dimakopoulos, Wanderarbeitnehmer aus der Türkei in der Europäischen Gemeinschaft—Zur Zukunft der Gastarbeiterfrage in Europa, in: InfAuslR (1988) 309–15.

[184] Case C–237/91 *Kus* [1992] ECR I–6781, 25; Case C–351/95 *Kadiman* [1997] ECR I–2133, 31 and Case C–36/96 *Günayadin* [1997] ECR I–5159, 22.

[185] Art 37 of the Additional Protocol and Art 10 of Decision 1/80.

[186] In order to benefit from the rights granted by Art 6(1) a Turkish worker must be 'duly registered as belonging to the labour force' of the Member State concerned. On this requirement see Case C–434/93 *Bozkurt* [1995] ECR I–1475, 22–3 (the requirement demands that the employment relationship can be located within the territory of a Member State or retains a sufficiently close link with that territory); Case C–171/95 *Tetik* [1997] ECR I–329 (concluding that a Turkish worker who after eight years of employment in a Member State, voluntarily gives up employment, still belongs to that State's labour force, provided he is genuinely seeking new employment) and Case C–1/97 *Birden* [1998] ECR I–7747, 51 (holding that the requirement cannot be interpreted as applying to the labour market in general as opposed to a specific market with a social objective supported by public authorities).

[187] The legality of employment presupposes a stable and secure situation as a member of the labour force of a Member State. Case C–192/89 *Sevince* [1990] ECR I–3461 at 30; Case C–237/91 *Kus* [1992] ECR I–6781, 12; Case C–285/95 *Kol* [1997] ECR I–3069, 27 and Case C–1/97 *Birden* [1998] ECR I–7747, 55–69.

[188] Art 6(1), first indent, merely aims to ensure continuity of employment with the same employer. Case C–355/93 *Eroglu* [1994] ECR I–5113, 13. The provision cannot be relied upon by Turkish workers who in the first year of employment, with the permission of the national authorities, have worked for different employers and who wish to continue employment with their last employer (Case C–386/95 *Eker* [1997] ECR I–2697). The same holds true for workers who have worked for an employer for more than one year and who, after having worked for almost one year for another, wish to continue employment with the first employer. Case C–355/93 *Eroglu* [1994] ECR I–5113, 15.

may take up another offer of employment in the same occupation and after four years of employment Turkish workers enjoy free access to any paid employment in the State concerned. Furthermore, after three years of legal residence in the host State,[189] family members of Turkish workers enjoy the right to respond to any offer of employment subject to priority being given to Community nationals under Article 7 of the Decision No 1/80; after five years of legal residence they have free access to any paid employment of their choice.[190] In addition, Turkish children must be admitted to courses of general education, apprenticeship and vocational training under the same educational entry qualifications as the children of nationals of that Member State (Article 9).[191]

In interpreting Articles 6(1) and 7, the Court has drawn inspiration from the principles developed in its case law on the free movement of workers within the Community.[192] Both Article 6(1) and 7 produce direct effect.[193] Employment rights guaranteed by these provisions encompass a right of residence in the host State[194] and the concept of worker covers persons who perform on behalf of and at the direction of another person, genuine and effective economic activities in return for which they receive a remuneration.[195] The Court, however, has only transposed principles governing Article 39 EC to the rights conferred by Decision No 1/80 'as far as possible.'[196] Decision No 1/80 merely governs the

---

[189] Art 7 is designed to create conditions conducive to family unity in the host State. Therefore, Member States may require that the family members live together with the worker uninterruptedly for three years in the host State, even though there may be objective reasons to justify the family member concerned living apart from the Turkish migrant worker. Case C–351/95 *Kadiman* [1997] ECR I–2180. See also: Case C–329/97 *Ergat* [2000] ECR I–1487, 38–9.

[190] Children of Turkish workers who have completed a course of vocational training in the host State may respond to any offer of employment there, irrespective of the length of time they have been resident in that State, provided one of the parents has been legally employed in the Member State concerned for at least three years. Art 7, para 2. Art 7 does not require that the Turkish parent is still working or residing in the host State at the time when the child wishes to gain access to the employment market. Case C–210/97 *Akman* [1998] ECR I–7519, 51.

[191] Case C–210/97 *Akman* [1998] ECR I–7519. See also: Peers, 'Annotation *Akman*' CMLRev (1999) 1027–42.

[192] See also: O'Leary, 'Employment and Residence for Turkish Workers and their Families: Analogies with the Case Law of the Court of Justice on Article 48 EC' in Scritti, *Onore di Giuseppe Federico Mancini—Volume II Diritto Dell'Unione Europea* (1998) 731–67.

[193] Case C–192/89 *Sevince* [1990] ECR I–3461, 26; Case C–355/93 *Eroglu* [1994] ECR I–5113, 11; Case C–351/95 *Kadiman* [1997] ECR I–213, 28 and Case C–36/96 *Günayadin* [1997] ECR I–5159, 24.

[194] Case C–171/95 *Tetik* [1997] ECR I–329, 24; Case C–237/91 *Kus* [1992] ECR I–6781, 27–36 and Case C–355/93 *Eroglu* [1994] ECR I–5113, 20 and 23. These residence rights are based on Arts 6 or 7; administrative documents concerning this right of residence only have declaratory effect. Case C–434/93 *Bozkurt* [1995] ECR–I1475, 30.

[195] Case C–98/96 *Ertanir* [1997] ECR I–5193, 43; Case C–36/96 *Günayadin* [1997] ECR I–5159, 31 and in particular Case C–1/97 *Birden* [1998] ECR I–7747, 23–32 (which held that a Turkish worker who had a job sponsored by the State with public funds and which was meant to enable him to enter or re-enter 'real' working life could be classed as a worker for the purposes of Art 6(1) of Decision 1/80).

[196] The main principles governing the public policy exception (s 7.1) are by analogy to be applied to the similarly phrased provisions contained in Decision 1/80. See Case C–340/97 *Nazli* [2000] ECR I–957, 56. See also: *Demirel* (1987) in which the Court considered whether Art 8 of the European Convention on Human Rights (right to family life) had any bearing on the question whether family members enjoy free movement rights under the Ankara Agreement. The Court recognised that it is

second stage of the free movement of workers during which Turkish workers who have been admitted by a Member State to employment for the first time, are after one year given the right to gradually integrate into the host State's labour force. The absence, in the Decision of a provision comparable to Article 7(2) of Regulation No 1612/68, has limited the Court's power to strengthen the legal status outside the employment context and to promote the integration of workers and their families into the host State's society as it has done as regards Community workers and their family members.[197]

5.4 Maghreb Nationals

In 1976 the Community and its Member States concluded cooperation agreements with Algeria,[198] Morocco[199] and Tunisia.[200] The Agreements, which came into force on 1 November 1978, aimed to promote overall cooperation between the contracting parties with a view to contributing to the economic and social development of the respective Maghreb country. More recently, the agreements with Tunisia and Morocco have been replaced by Euro-Mediterranean agreements which have established associations between the Community and its Member States, on the one hand, and Tunisia and Morocco, on the other hand.[201] The Maghreb Agreements do not provide, nor do they envisage, a freedom of movement for workers (or persons) between these North-African countries and the EC Member States or a freedom of movement for Maghreb nationals among the Member States. It is up to Member States to determine whether Algerian, Moroccan or Tunisian nationals are admitted to their national labour markets and territories. Further, neither Maghreb workers nor their family members are offered a right to gradually integrate the labour market of the host Member State. Maghreb nationals merely enjoy a right to equal treatment as regards working conditions, remuneration and, so far as Tunisian and Moroccan nationals are concerned,

---

its duty to ensure observance of fundamental rights in the field of Community law, but it held that it did not have the power to examine whether a national law or regulation is compatible with the European Convention. In the absence of Community provisions defining the free movement rights of family members of Turkish workers established in the Community, the Member States did not have to implement Community law and this implied, according to the Court, that it had no jurisdiction to determine whether national rules were compatible with the principles enshrined in the Convention. Case 12/86 *Demirel* [1987] ECR 3719, 28. For a critique see: Weiler, "Thou Shall Not Oppress a Stranger' (Ex.23:9): On the Judicial Protection of Human Rights of Non-EC Nationals' in Schermers *et al* (eds), *Free Movement of Persons in Europe* (1993) 248–71.

[197] On the legal status of Turkish workers and nationals see also: Staples, 'De Associatieovereenkomst EEG-Turkije—Een Leidraad voor de Rechtshulp' (1999) MR 179–88 and Guttmann, *Die Assoziationsfreizügigkeit Türkischer Angehöriger* (1999).

[198] OJ 1978 L 263.

[199] OJ 1978 L 264.

[200] OJ 1978 L 265.

[201] OJ 1998 L 97 (Tunisia) and OJ 2000 L 70 (Morocco).

dismissal.[202] In interpreting the provisions of Maghreb agreements the Court has shown more restraint than it has as regards the agreement and decisions regarding Turkey.[203] The principles developed in the case law on the rules governing the EEC-Turkey association cannot be applied by analogy to the Maghreb agreements. In particular, employment in one of the Member States does not guarantee Maghreb nationals a right to reside there.[204]

6 COORDINATION OF SOCIAL SECURITY SCHEMES: EC REGULATIONS NO 1408/71 AND NO 574/72

For a proper understanding of the numerous issues involved in the subject of cross-border access to public services, some discussion of social security Regulations No 1408/71 and No 574/72 is necessary.[205] Within the European

---

[202] For Morocco see Art 40 of the 1976 agreement and Art 64 of the association agreement; for Tunisia see Arts 39 and 64 respectively and for Algeria Art 38 of the 1976 agreement. The afore mentioned provisions are all sufficiently clear and unconditional in order to have direct effect. Martin and Guild (1996) n 1 above, at 14.12. See also: Eicke, 'The Third Country Agreements: The Right to Work and Reside in the First Generation Agreements' in Guild (ed), *The Legal Framework and Social Consequences of Free Movement of Persons in the European Union* (1999) 89–103.

[203] By comparison with the 1976 co-operation agreements, the new association agreements with Tunisia and Morocco foresee a strengthening of the relationship between the contracting parties and this may have consequences for the interpretation of provisions of the agreements. Martin and Guild (1996) n 1 above at 14.3.

[204] Consider *El-Yassini* (1999). Mr El-Yassini was a Moroccan national who through marriage with a British national had obtained the right to reside and work in the United Kingdom. He separated from his wife and, while still lawfully employed, he applied for an extension of his right to reside in the United Kingdom. El-Yassini claimed that Art 40 of the EEC-Morocco Agreement, which guarantees equality of treatment as regards working conditions and remunerations, should by analogy with the case-law on the EEC–Turkey association be interpreted as to encompass a residence right for the duration of employment. The Court accepted that Art 40 could be relied upon in court (Case C–416/96 *El-Yassini* (1999) ECR I–1209, 32), but rejected El-Yassini's substantive claim. Provisions of the various agreements the Community concludes with third States must be interpreted in light of both their object and context. Unlike the Turkey agreement, however, the agreement with Morocco is not intended to progressively secure freedom of movement for workers and since there are no implementation measures comparable to the Decision adopted by the Turkey Association Council, the Court concluded, that the principles developed in the case-law on the rules governing the EEC–Turkey association cannot be applied by analogy to the Morocco agreement. Member States are under no obligation to extend the residence permit of Moroccan nationals where the initial reason for the grant of such a permit (*in casu* marriage to a British national) no longer exists. The fact that persons as Mr El-Yassini would be forced to terminate his employment relationship could not alter this conclusion. The situation would according to the Court only have been different if Mr El-Yassini had been granted specific rights in relation to employment which were more extensive than the granted residence rights and that would only have been the case where the duration of the work permit would exceed the duration of the initial residence permit. Case C–416/96 *El-Yassini* (1999) ECR I–1209, 64–6. On *El-Yassini* see Bulterman, 'Annotation *El-Yassini*' (1999) *CMLRev* 1357–64 and van der Steen, 'Verbod van Nationaliteitsdiscriminatie op het Gebied van Arbeidsvoorwaarden: Gevolgen voor het Verblijfsrecht' (1999) *NTER* 137–9.

[205] For general descriptions of the co-ordination mechanism established by the two Regulations see eg: Keunen, *Schets van het Europees Socialezekerheidsrecht—Europese Coördinatieregels inzake Sociale Zekerheid* (2001); Pennings, *Grondslagen van het Europese Sociale Zekerheidsrecht* (2000); Voogsgeerd, *Vrij Verkeer en Sociale Zekerheid* (1999); White, *EC Social Security Law* (1999); Pennings, *Introduction to European Social Security Law* (1998); Jorens, *Wegwijs in het*

Community it has never been disputed that it is for the Member States to organise, administer and finance social security schemes.[206] A harmonisation of national social security systems[207] or the establishment of a common social security system has never been seriously considered. However, it has always been recognised that the existence of different territorially organised social security systems could have a deterrent effect on the exercise of free movement rights guaranteed by Community law. If it were left to national law alone,[208] movement to other Member States could lead to a loss of social security rights. Rights acquired in the Member State of origin may not be transferable abroad and in the host State workers may not be eligible for social benefits because they have not worked, resided or been insured there long enough. In order to overcome the various obstacles resulting from the territoriality principle, Article 42 (formerly 51) EC empowers the Council to adopt measures necessary for securing a free movement of workers in the field of social security. In furtherance of this goal, in 1958 the Council adopted Regulations No 3 and No 4, which established a coordination mechanism aimed at preventing a loss of social security

Europees Sociaal Zekerheidsrecht (1995) and van Raepenbusch, *La Securité sociale des Personnes qui Circulent a l'Intérieur de la Communauté économique européenne* (1991).

[206] See, eg: Case C–18/95 *Terhoeve* [1999] ECR I–345, 33; Case C–70/95 *Sodemare* [1996] ECR I–3422, 27 and Case 238/82 *Duphar* [1984] ECR 523, 16.

[207] To be sure, from the early years discussions have been held regarding a possible harmonisation of social security systems. For some of the earliest debates see, eg: Meinhold, 'Notwendigkeit und Möglichkeit der Harmonisierung von Sozialleistungen im EWG-Raum' (1964) *DVZ* 1–4; Heise, 'Les Possibilités d'une Harmonisation social des Régimes d'Assurance sociale dans les Etats Membres de la Communauté Economique Européenne' (1966) *DS* 580–9 and Holloway, *Social Policy Harmonization in the European Community* (1981). For more recent discussions (which have primarily been motivated by the fear of 'social dumping' after '1992') see Pieters, 'Brengt '1992' Coördinatie en Harmonisatie van de Sociale Zekerheid?' (1989) *NJB* 831 *et seq*; Pieters, *Sociale Zekerheid na 1992: Eén over Twaalf* (1989) and Schulte, 'Social Security Legislation in the European Communities: Co-ordination, Harmonization and Convergence' in Pieters, *Social Security in Europe* (1991) 153–68. Generally, harmonisation of social security is not (or no longer) considered to be desirable or feasible; discussions have shifted in the direction of (stimulating) a 'spontaneous'convergence of the national systems. See, eg: Council Recommendation 92/442 of 27 July 1992 (OJ 1992 L 245).

[208] To be sure, next to the Community measures discussed in this Section, numerous bi- and multilateral treaties (eg, the European Interim Agreements concluded within the framework of the Council of Europe and the various conventions adopted by the International Labour Conference) have been concluded which intend to offer migrants social security protection. For an overview see, eg: Eichenhofer, *Internationales Sozialrecht* (1994). In order to avoid possible conflicts with the rules laid down in these international instruments, Art 6 of Reg 1408/71 stipulates, in brief, that the regulation replaces other social security conventions which bind two or more Member States. Reg 1408/71 prevails even if the application of international conventions would be more advantageous to migrant workers. This may only differ in cases where the persons concerned had already acquired social security rights under an international convention prior to the coming into force of the social security regulation. Case 82/72 *Walder* [1973] ECR 599, 6–8; Case C–227/89 *Rönfeldt* [1991] ECR I–323, 26–9; Case C–475/93 *Thevenon* [1995] ECR I–3813, 27 and Case C–95/99 *Thelen* [2000] ECR I–0000. See also: Jorens, 'Non-European Union Nationals and the Co-ordination of European Social Security Law: The International Agreements Concluded by the European Union with Third Countries and Conflict Rules in European Social Security Law' in Jorens and Schulte (eds), *European Social Security Law and Third Country Nationals* (1998) 1–110, 68–110.

rights caused by the exercise of free movement of workers.[209] In response to the Court of Justice case law and developments in the national social security systems, the two regulations were replaced in 1971 by Regulations Nos 1408/71[210] and 574/72.[211] The former regulation sets out the rights which migrants enjoy; the latter contains the administrative rules for the implementation of these rights.

The two regulations aim to promote freedom of movement by co-ordinating the national social security systems in such a way that beneficiaries enjoy 'constant social security protection.'[212] The regulations are based on four basic principles. The first is laid down in Article 3(1) of Regulation No 1408/71. The provision stipulates that beneficiaries 'shall be subject to the same obligations and enjoy the same benefits under the legislation of a Member State as nationals of that State.' Equality of treatment is the Regulation's starting; nationality should not play a role as regards the social security status of migrants. The second principle implies that migrants can only be compulsorily affiliated to the social security system of one Member State. In the absence of any rules, in moving to another Member State migrants might not have access to any social security system or they might be required to pay social insurance contributions (and be entitled to obtain benefits) in more than one Member State. Articles 13 to 17 of Regulation No 1408/71 contain rules determining the applicable national legislation.[213] The starting-point is that beneficiaries are insured in the State of employment.[214] The third principle is that of aggregation. It implies that the competent national authorities whose legislation makes the enjoyment of social security rights conditional upon the completion of periods of insurance,

---

[209] For a brief description of Reg 3 and 4 see, eg: Troclet, *Europees Sociaal Recht—Institutioneel Kader, Rechtsinstrumenten, Sociale Problemen en hun Oplossing* (1971) 282 *et seq.*

[210] OJ 1971 L 149. For the consolidated version see OJ 1997 L 28.

[211] OJ 1972 L 74.

[212] Watson, 'Social Security Law of the European Communities' (1980) 249.

[213] The conflict rules have exclusive and binding effect. Exclusive effect is relevant for situations in which, on the basis of national laws, more than one piece of legislation would be applicable (positive conflict of laws). The conflict rules determine which legislation is exclusively applicable. The 'other' legislation is overruled by the conflict rule. See, eg: Case 92/63 *Nonnenmacher* [1964] ECR 583 and Case 302/84 *Ten Holder* [1986] ECR 1821. Binding effect is relevant in case, on the basis of national laws, no legislation would be applicable (negative conflict of laws). In such a case, the legislation must be applied. See, eg: Case 276/81 *Kuijpers* [1982] ECR 3027 and Case C–196/90 *De Paep* [1991] ECR 4815.

[214] The choice for the State of employment is explained by the fact that the original Member States all had (Bismarckian) social security schemes based on the pursuit of economic activities. The costs of social security benefits must be borne by the State where workers pay their contributions. Chardon, 'Principles of Co-ordination' in Jorens and Schulte, *Co-ordination of Social Security Schemes in Connection with the Accession of Central and Eastern European States—'The Riga Conference'* (1999) 43–79, 67. Many states which later joined the Community (as well as the EEA States), however, have social benefits systems which are based on residence. Debates have started as to whether the current principle of being insured in the state of employment should be replaced by the principle of insurance in the state of residence. See, eg: Christensen and Malmstedt, 'Lex Loci Laboris versus Lex Loci Domicilii—An Inquiry into the Normative Foundations of European Social Security Law' (2000) *EJSS* 69 *et seq.*

employment or residence in the host state, must take such periods completed in other Member States into account as if they had been completed under their own legislation.[215] The fourth[216] principle concerns the exportability of benefits. The payment of benefits to which a worker is entitled cannot be made conditional upon residence in the State responsible for paying the benefit. The coordination system de-territorialises the national systems in order to ensure that migrants are entitled to benefits on the basis of their own insurance record.[217]

The material scope of Regulation No 1408/71 is defined in Article 4. According to Article 4(1), the regulation applies to legislation[218] concerning sickness and maternity benefits, invalidity benefits, old age benefits, survivors' benefits, benefits in respect of accidents at work and occupational diseases, death grants, unemployment benefits and family benefits.[219] Article 4(4), how-

---

[215] Reg 1408/71 contains aggregation rules for various types of benefits. See, eg: Art 18 (sickness and maternity benefits), Art 67 (unemployment benefits) and Art 72 (family benefits). This rule is not applied as regards long-term benefits such as invalidity, survivors' and old-age pensions. See also Pennings (1998) n 205 above, 133–4. In some cases a duty to take into account periods of insurance or employment fulfilled in other Member States can directly follow from Arts 48 and 51 of the Treaty. See, eg: Case C–443/93 *Vougioukas* [1995] I–4033. Indeed, aggregation can be analysed as an extended form of equal treatment. Lyon-Caen, 'Social Security and the Principle of Equal Treatment in the EC Treaty and Regulation 1408/71' in *Commission of the European Communities/Departemento de Relações Internaçionais e Convenções de Segurança Social, Social Security in Europe—Equality Between Nationals and Non-Nationals* (1995) 45–73, 52.

[216] In its case law the Court has in fact developed a fifth principle according to which migrant workers should not lose autonomous rights they have acquired under national law. See, eg: Case 24/75 *Petroni* [1975] ECR 1149.

[217] Migrants should be able to receive benefits anywhere within the Community irrespective of the Member State where the insurance contributions are paid. Arnull (1990) n 165 above, 130. The general export provision contained in Art 10 of Reg 1408/71 aims to promote the free movement of persons by ensuring that individuals retain their right to benefits if they move to another Member State. Case 139/82 *Piscitello* [1983] ECR 1427, 15 and Case C–73/99 *Movrin* [2000] ECR I–5625, 33. For unemployment benefits exportability is limited to a maximum period of three months. Art 69 of Reg 1408/71 and Case 139/78 *Coccioli* [1979] ECR 991.

[218] The regulation only applies to statutory social security schemes. In principle, it does not apply to schemes set up by industrial or collective agreements. Art 4(1) *juncto* Art 1(j).

[219] The list contained in Art 4(1) is exhaustive. See, eg: Case C–66/92 *Acciardi* [1993] ECR I–4567 and Case 122/84 *Scrivner* [1985] ECR 1029, 19. The social security benefits covered by the Regulation can also be classed as 'social advantages' for the purposes of Art 7(2) of Reg 1612/68. For quite some time it was not entirely clear whether both regulations could be applied to a given benefit simultaneously or whether the regulations would mutually exclude each other. See Gouloussis, 'Equality of Treatment and the Relationship between Regulations 1612/68 and 1408/71' in *Commission of the European Communities/Departemento de Relações Internaçionais e Convenções de Segurança Social, Social Security in Europe—Equality between Nationals and Non-Nationals* (1995) 75–88. The issue could be particularly relevant because the personal scope of the two Regulations is not identical. Martin and Guild (1996) n 1 above, 136. In some cases the Court made 'procedural preference' to Reg 1408/71 (Vonk (1990) n 3 above, 354 and O'Keeffe (1986) n 62 above, 97) which implied that the Court first established whether a benefit fell under Reg 1408/71 and that in case of an affirmative answer, Art 7(2) of Reg 1612/68 was deemed not to be applicable. See, eg: Case 1/72 *Frilli* [1972] ECR 457, 4 and Case 122/84 *Scrivner* [1985] ECR 1027, 16. In case a benefit did not fall within the scope of Reg 1408/71, Art 7(2) could be applied as a 'safety net-clause'. See, eg: Case 249/83 *Hoeckx* [1985] ECR 982. In other cases the Court held that both Regulations could be applied. See, eg: Case 94/84 *Deak* [1985] ECR 1873; Case 147/87 *Zaoui* [1987] ECR 5511 and Case C–111/91 *Commission v Luxembourg* [1993] I–817 21. Recently, the Court concluded that

ever, excludes 'social and medical assistance, benefits schemes for victims of war or its consequences'[220] from the scope of the regulation's application.[221]

The personal scope of Regulation No 1408/71 has been expanded over the years. Initially, the Regulation only applied to workers holding the nationality of one of the Member States[222] and who are or have been subject to the legislation of one or more Member States. Subsequent amendments have brought the self-employed[223] and students[224] within the scope of the Regulation and

---

since 'Regulation 1612/68 is of general application regarding the free movement of workers, Article 7(2) thereof may be applied to social advantages which at the same time fall specifically within the scope of Regulation 1408/71'. Case C–85/96 *Martínez Sala* [1998] ECR I–2691, 27. The simultaneous application of both regulations may not, however, be justified in all cases. See, eg: the Opinion of Adv Gen in Case C–160/96 *Molenaar* [1998] ECR I–843 point 99–100. In case application of the rules of Reg 1612/68 would run counter to the specific rules of Reg 1408/71, the rules of the latter regulation must be applied as the *lex specialis*. Art 42(3) of Reg 1612/68 which provides that this 'Regulation shall not affect measures taken in accordance with Article 51 (now 42: APvdM) of the Treaty'.

In 1998 a special directive was adopted for supplementary pension rights. Dir 98/49 (OJ 1998 L 209). See also: Schulte, 'Pensions and Social Security' in Carlier and Verwilghen, *Thirty Years of Free Movement of Workers in Europe* (2000) 143–58 and Wienk, *Europese Coördinatie van Aanvullende Pensioenen* (1999).

[220] Until recently, Art 4(4) also excluded 'special schemes for civil servants and persons treated as such' from the scope of application of the Regulation. In response to the judgment of the Court in *Vougioukas* (Case C–443/93 [1995] ECR I–4033) special schemes for civil servants have been brought within the scope of the Regulation. OJ 1998 L 209. See also: Vilaras, 'Freedom of Movement in the Public Sector—Developments and Prospects' Carlier and Verwilghen, *Thirty Years of Free Movement of Workers in Europe* (2000) 89–104 and van der Steen, 'Vrij Verkeer en Sociale Zekerheid van Ambtenaren' (1996) *NTER* 53–6.

[221] A given benefit (scheme) falls within the scope of the regulation when (*i*) the legislation under which the benefit is granted place claimants in a legally defined position as a result of which they have an absolute right to benefit (Case 1/72 *Frilli* [1972] ECR 457, 18 and Case 139/82 *Piscitello* [1983] ECR 1471, 11) and when (*ii*) the benefit covers one of the risks enumerated in Art 4(1) (Case 249/83 *Hoeckx* [1985] ECR 982, 12 and Case 122/84 *Scrivner* [1985] ECR 1029, 19). Occasionally, the Court has applied a third criterion according to which a benefit only falls within the scope of the Regulation when the recipient has been subject to the social security system of the State under whose legislation the benefit is made available. Case C–356/89 *Newton* [1991] ECR I–3017, 19. Generally, the Court seems to favour a broad interpretation of the material scope of Reg 1408/71, but this is not to say that all benefits are covered. See, eg: Case C–25/95 *Otte* [1996] ECR I–3745.

[222] Art 2 of the Reg. The fact that third country nationals are in principle excluded is explained by the fact that the Regulation is aimed at facilitating the exercise of free movement rights which are preserved for nationals of the Member States. On the question whether or when a person must be considered as a national of one of the Member States for the purposes of Reg 1408/71 see Case 10/78 *Belhouab* [1978] ECR 1915 and Case C–105/89 *Buhari Haji* [1990] ECR 4211. Stateless persons and refugees, however, are covered by Reg 1408/71. In *Khalil* the Court concluded that stateless persons and refugees are indeed covered by the Regulation even though they do not enjoy the right to freedom of movement. Joined Cases C–95 to 98/99, and Case 99 *Khalil* [2001] ECR1–88

[223] Reg 1390/81 (OJ 1981 L 143). Prior to Reg 1390/81 the Court had already held that self-employed persons could under certain conditions fall within the scope of the Regulation. See, eg: Case 19/68 *De Cicco* [1968] ECR 475; Case 23/71 *Janssen* [1971] ECR 859 and Case 17/76 *Brack* [1976] ECR 1429. The Court accepted the extension of the regulation to self-employed persons in Case 300/84 *Van Roosmalen* [1986] ECR 3097.

[224] Reg 307/1999 (OJ 1999 L 38) has extended the personal scope of Reg 1408/71 in its entirety to students. Art 2 of Reg 1408/71 was amended and now provides that in addition to employed and self-employed persons, students who are or have been subject to the legislation of one or more Member States also fall within the scope of the Regulation.

proposals have been made to include all insured Union citizens.[225] The concept of 'worker' for the purposes of the Regulation does not coincide with the notion of 'worker' in Article 39 EC. Article 1 of Regulation No 1408/71 indicates that a 'worker' is any EC national who is insured under a social security scheme for employed and self-employed persons. Thus, also Community citizens who do not perform 'effective and genuine' activities may be classed as a 'worker' for the purposes of Regulation No 1408/71.[226] Also, family members of workers may benefit from the Regulation, but their status under the Regulation has been rather ambiguous. Since family members derive their rights from workers, discussions have taken place as to whether they can rely on Regulation 1408/71 only with respect to rights or benefits which they enjoy in their capacity as family members or whether they could enjoy benefits in their own right. In *Kermaschek* (1976) the Court chose the first option[227] which seemed to imply that family members can only rely on the Regulation as regards benefits payable to family members such as survivors' benefits, death grants or sickness benefits for which the family members are coinsured. For a long time the Court clung to the rather restrictive rule laid down in *Kermaschek*.[228] In *Cabanis-Issarte* (1996), however, the Court largely abandoned the distinction between derived rights and rights which may be enjoyed 'in person.' The Court held that being unable to claim rights that may not be regarded as derived rights could adversely affect the free movement of workers. The judgment in *Cabanis-Issarte* seems to imply that family members can rely on all provisions of Regulation No 1408/71 except for those that apply to benefits to which only workers are entitled such as unemployment benefits.[229]

---

[225] COM(1998) 779 final. Art 1 of the proposed new social security regulation provides that all 'persons who are or have been subject to the social security legislation of one or more Member States' shall be covered. Even third country nationals are proposed to be included even though they do not enjoy independent free movement rights. On the Commission's proposal, which aims at a simplication of the entire regulation, see Eichenhofer, 'How to Simplify the Co-ordination of Social Security' (2000) *EJSS* 231–40; Pennings and Essers, 'Het Voorstel van de Europese Commissie tot Vereenvoudiging van Verordening 1408/71' (2000) *SMA* 512–25 and Sakslin, 'Social Security—Adapting to Change' (2000) *EJSS* 169–87.

[226] See, eg: Case 2/89 *Kits van Heijningen* [1990] ECR 1755.

[227] The Court held that the Regulation: 'refers to two clearly distinct categories: workers on the one hand, and the members of their family and their survivors on the other. . . . Whereas the persons belonging to the first category can claim rights to benefits covered by the regulation as rights of their own, the persons belonging to the second category can only claim derived rights, acquired through their status as a member of the family or survivor of a worker'. Case 40/76 *Kermaschek* [1976] ECR 1669, 7.

[228] See, eg: Case 157/84 *Frascogna* [1985] ECR 1739; Case 94/84 *Deak* [1985] ECR 1873 and Case C–243/91 *Taghavi* [1992] ECR I–4401. The Court, however, has not applied the rule following from *Kermaschek* unequivocally. This is particularly true in as far as mixed benefits for disabled persons are concerned. See, eg: Case 7/75 *Mr and Mrs F* [1975] ECR 679 and Case 63/76 *Inzirillo* [1976] ECR 2057.

[229] Case C–87/94 *Cabanis-Issarte* [1996] ECR I–2097, 30–44. See also: Moore, 'Annotation *Cabanis*', (1997) *CMLRev* 727–39; Peers, 'Equality, Free Movement and Social Security' (1997) *ELRev* 342–51 and van der Steen, 'Annotatie *Cabanis*' (1997) *SEW* 207 *et seq.*

In principle, third country nationals are excluded from the coordination mechanism set up by the two social security regulations. Some of them, however, may enjoy social security rights under the agreements which the Community and its Member States have concluded with the country of which they hold the nationality or measures that have been adopted within the framework of these agreements. EEA nationals enjoy the most extensive social security protection. Article 29 EEA repeats the wording of Article 42 EC and, by virtue of Annex VI to the EEA Agreement, Regulations Nos 1408/71 and 574/72 have been extended to the territories and nationals of Liechtenstein, Iceland and Norway.[230] Turkish workers are offered social security protection by Decision No 3/80 which the EEC-Turkey Association Council has adopted in furtherance of Article 39 of the Additional Protocol of 1970.[231] Decision No 3/80 largely resembles Regulation No 1408/71.[232] Albeit with deviations and exceptions, the Decision has extended the principles of equality of treatment,[233] aggregation and exportability[234] as well as the rules determining the applicable legislation to Turkish workers.[235] Finally, Maghreb nationals enjoy various rights in the field of social security by virtue of the agreements which Morocco, Tunisia and Algeria have concluded with the Community and its Member States. These include *inter alia* a directly enforceable right to equal treatment and a right to aggregation as regards periods of insurance, employment and residence fulfilled in other Member States.[236]

[230] See also: Sakslin (1998) n 172 above.

[231] s 5.3 above.

[232] For more extensive descriptions see Centel, 'The Social Security of the Turkish Workers in Europe within the Framework of the Association Agreement' in Jorens and Schulte (eds), *European Social Security Law and Third Country Nationals* (1998) 281–97 and Hänlein, 'Problems Concerning Decision 3/80 of the Council of Association—A Point of View from a EU Perspective' in Jorens and Schulte (eds), *European Social Security Law and Third Country Nationals* (1998) 299–322.

[233] Art 3 of Dec 3/80. Art 3 only provides for a right to equal treatment under national social security law. It does not imply that Turkish workers can claim all the benefits of Reg 1408/71 under the same conditions as the nationals of the host state. Jorens (1998) n 208 above, 9–10.

[234] Turkish workers can export benefits to Turkey or another Member State (Art 39(4) of the Additional Protocol and Art 6 of Decision 3/80), but the application of the aggregation rules is only possible for Turkish workers moving within the Community. Cp Hänlein (1998) n 232 above, 302.

[235] As will be explained later in this book, the practical significance of Decision 3/80 is still limited by the fact that it is not accompanied by an implementing decision which, like Reg 574/72, contains the administrative rules necessary for implementing social security rights. See especially: ch 3, s 6.3.

[236] See also: Roberts, 'The Rulings of the European Court of Justice on the Association and Co-operation Agreements in Matters Concerning Social Security' in Jorens and Schulte (eds), *European Social Security Law and Third Country Nationals* (1998) 209–34 and Gacon-Estrada, 'The Co-operation Agreements Concluded Between the European Community and the Maghreb Countries' in Jorens and Schulte (eds), *European Social Security Law and Third Country Nationals* (1998) 323–31.

7 JUDICIAL REVIEW OF NATIONAL RULES AND MEASURES UNDER THE
COMMUNITY PROVISIONS ON THE FREE MOVEMENT OF PERSONS

Community citizens and, to a lesser extent, third country nationals have acquired an increasing number of rights under Community law over the years. These rights have imposed significant limitations on the powers of Member States to regulate access of non-nationals and/or non-residents to their territory, (employment) markets and welfare systems. The Community provisions, however, do not guarantee that beneficiaries can in all cases enter, reside and work in other Member States or enjoy social, economic or political rights there. Community law has not taken from the Member States the power to lay down the conditions under which economic and social rights may be enjoyed. Community law merely prohibits rules or measures which discriminate against non-nationals or non-residents, or which hamper the free movement of persons. In addition, Member States are entitled, under certain conditions, to derogate from and to impose limitations on the free movement rights. This section sets out the rules, principles and tests that must be applied (by courts) in order to determine whether or not a given national provision or measure is compatible with Community law.[237] A distinction is made between national provisions or measures which directly discriminate against nationals of other Member States, measures that affect non-nationals only indirectly and nationality-neutral rules which hamper freedom of movement.[238]

---

[237] Member States that wish to derogate from or impose restrictions on the free movement rights, are bound to observe fundamental human rights such as those enshrined in the European Convention on Human Rights. See eg: Case 36/75 *Rutili* [1975] ECR 1219 and Case C–368/95 *Familiapress* [1997] ECR I–3869. The Charter of Fundamental Rights, as proclaimed at the recent summit in Nice, may enhance human rights' protection in future (see, eg: the Editorial Comments in *CMLRev* (2001) 1–6), but the precise degree to which fundamental rights must be observed by the Member States is, at present, still quite uncertain. For this reason, the issue will not be discussed separately in this section. On the role of human rights in the European Union see, eg: Alston (ed), *The EU and Human Rights* (1999); Betten and Grief, *EU Law and Human Rights* (1999); De Witte, 'The Past and Future Role of the European Court of Justice in the Protection of Human Rights' in Alston (1999) above, at 859–97; Neuwahl, 'The Treaty on European Union: A Step Forward in the Protection of Human Rights?' in Neuwahl and Rosas, *The European Union and Human Rights* (1995) 1 *et seq*; Clapham, 'Human Rights and the European Community: A Critical Overview' in Cassese *et al* (1991) above 29–61; Weiler, 'Methods of Protection: Towards a Second and Third Generation of Protection' in Cassese *et al* (1991) above, at 575–620 and Mendelsohn, 'The European Court of Justice and Human Rights' (1981) *YEL* 125 *et seq*.

[238] In reviewing national rules courts will usually have to take two steps. The first concerns the question whether a national rule or practice directly or indirectly discriminates against non-nationals or whether it may hamper freedom of movement. This prima facie relevance test seeks to establish whether the rule in question is caught, in principle, by the prohibitions of Community law. When this first test has been passed, courts will have to take the second step concerning the possible justification of the rule in question. Voogsgeerd (2000) n 102 above, at 417–18.

7.1 Direct Discrimination on Grounds of Nationality

Article 12(1) EC and the various specific non-discrimination provisions[239] order the elimination[240] of discrimination based on nationality.[241] The prohibition covers direct (or overt) discrimination which occurs where differential treatment of two (groups of) persons by a single legal subject is based on the criterion of nationality. It concerns national provisions or practices[242] which make the enjoyment of, or eligibility for, a certain right, benefit or opportunity explicitly conditional upon the nationality of the host State or upon conditions which only

[239] Art 12 EC applies independently only in cases where none of the more specific provisions guaranteeing equality of treatment is applicable. Case C–55/98 *Vestergaard* [1999] ECR I–7641, 16; Case C–22/98 *Becu* [1999] ECR I–5665, 32; Case C–193/94 *Skanavi* [1996] ECR I–929, 20; Case C–18/93 *Corsica Ferries* [1994] ECR I–1783, 19 and Case C–176/96 *Lehtonen* [2000] ECR I–2681, 37. More generally, the relationship between the various equal treatment provisions is governed by the principle of *lex specialis derogat lex generalis*. This first implies that a national provision that violates a specific equal treatment provision is by definition also contrary to the more general provision that the specific provision implements. Thus, a national provision which is contrary to eg, Art 7(2) of Reg No 1612/68 also violates Art 39(2) EC (and Art 12(1) EC). In order to claim equality of treatment reliance on Art 7(2) of the Regulation suffices; a Community worker may, but does not have to, invoke Art 39 EC (or Art 12 EC). Furthermore, discriminatory treatment which is permitted by a specific provision is also compatible with the general equal treatment provision. Thus, a Community citizen who has been refused access to a post in the public service on the basis of Art 39(4) EC cannot claim access to such a post by relying on Art 12 EC. Cp the Opinion of Adv Gen Jacobs in Joined Cases C–92/92 and C–326/92 *Collins* [1993] ECR I–5145, 14. Where the specific provisions do not apply, beneficiaries can invoke the general non-discrimination provision of Art 12(1) EC. See, eg: Case C–411/98 *Ferlini* [2000] ECR I–8081 and Case 152/82 *Forcheri* [1983] ECR 2323. Art 12 serves the purpose of closing off the system of non-discrimination and enables any lacunae in the Community legal order to be bridged. Guild (2000) n 166 above, 39–40 (citing Opinion of Adv Gen La Pergola in Case C–43/95 *Data Delecta* [1996] ECR I–4671).

[240] Following its case law in the field of of sex discrimination, the Court has held that so long as national rules are not adapted to the non-discrimination principle, Member States must apply the more favourable rules applicable to their own nationals to non-nationals. Case C–15/96 *Schöning-Kougebetopoulou* [1998] ECR I–47. On this 'only valid point of reference case law' see also: Wouters, 'The Principle of Non-Discrimination in European Community Law' (1999) *ECTaxRev* 98–106, at 106.

[241] The prohibition of discrimination on grounds of nationality is a 'specific enunciation' of the general principle of equality, which is one of the 'fundamental principles' (Joined Cases 117/76 and 16/77 *Ruckdeschel* [1977] ECR 1769) underlying Community law. According to this principle, similar situations should be treated equally and dissimilar situations unequally unless there is an objective justification for the (dis)similar treatment. See, eg: Case 13/63 *Italy v Commission* ('Italian Refrigarators') [1963] ECR 165 and Case C–217/91 *Brandy* [1993] ECR I–3923. A distinction is often made between formal and material discrimination. The former concerns the unequal treatment of equal cases, whilst the latter involves the equal treatment of unequal cases. In order to determine whether a given rule or measure violates the non-discrimination principle it has first to be established whether or not two cases are similar or comparable and after that the question of a possible justification of the (in)comparable situations may (have to) be addressed. The notions of formal and material discrimination, however, are rarely used under Community law. Community law merely prohibits discrimination on specific grounds such as nationality and gender and one generally speaks of direct (or overt) and indirect (or covert) discrimination. Especially in cases concerning nationality-based discrimination, the Court rarely engages in a comparability test. Within the scope of Community law nationals of the various Member States are presumed to be in a comparable situation. See also: Wouters (1999) n 240 above.

[242] See, eg: Case C–185/96 *Commission v Greece* [1998] ECR I–1095, 24.

nationals of other Member States have to meet.[243] Nationality requirements are by their very nature at odds with the objectives of the Community. The common market could never have been realised, and could never operate effectively, if Member States were free to exclude nationals of other Member States from their territory and labour markets. The concept of a common European citizenship could never have been introduced, and would not develop any further, if Community citizens could be discriminated against for reason of their national-ity. From the perspective of Community law, nationality requirements are 'sus-pect' and the basic assumption is that such requirements cannot be validly applied. Yet, as broad as the Community's objectives may be, they are limited. The Community is not a State, it is not expected to be transformed into one and Union citizenship is not intended to replace Member State nationality.[244] The Community consists of a number of nation States which have, or are based on, a special bond with their own nationals. Community law does not aim to abolish all State discriminations against nationals of other Member States in favour of its own nationals. Two situations must be distinguished.

The first concerns rights such as the right to vote and stand as a candidate in national elections, benefits linked to the pursuit of military service and access to employment in the public service (Article 39(4) EC).[245] These 'political' rights fall outside the scope of Community law and the non-discrimination principle. Member States are entitled to make the enjoyment of these rights conditional upon 'their' nationality. They are under no obligation to justify discrimination against non-nationals. Community law, however, does impose significant restric-tions on the freedom of Member States to determine whether or when a given right, benefit or opportunity falls outside the scope of the non-discrimination principle.[246] This is particularly true for the public service exception. On the face of it, Article 39(4) EC seems to allow Member States to exclude non-nationals from their public service altogether. Yet, the Court has consistently held that the provision, as an exception to the free movement of workers, should be interpreted strictly. Member States can only rely on Article 39(4) as regards specific posts or functions 'which involve direct or indirect participation in the exercise of the

---

[243] See, eg: Case 249/83 *Hoeckx* [1985] ECR 982 and Case 39/86 *Lair* [1988] ECR 3161 (both con-cerning requirements of a minimum period of residence or employment in the host State which only non-nationals were required to satisfy).

[244] Cp the Preamble to Decision 95/553 regarding protection of citizens of the European Union by diplomats and consular representatives (OJ 1995 L 314—Union citizenship 'is different from and in no way a substitute for the concept of national citizenship').

[245] National rules or measures cannot be regarded as exempt from the application of Community law solely because they have been adopted for reasons of demographic policy. Case 65/81 *Reina* [1982] ECR 33, 15 and Case C–185/96 *Commission v Greece* [1998] ECR I–1095, 34.

[246] Cp also the rulings in *Even* (Case 207/78 [1979] ECR 2019) and *De Vos* (Case C–315/94 [1996] ECR I–1417) in which the Court concluded that certain social benefits granted as compensation for the consequences of their obligation to perform military service could not be regarded as a social advantage for the purposes of Art 7(2) of Reg 1612/68, with the judgment in *Ugliola* (Case 15/69 [1970] ECR 363) in which the non-discrimination principle was held not to apply to a national rule under which a worker's security of employment was protected by having periods of military service taken into account in calculating the length of employment.

powers conferred by public law and duties to safeguard the general interests of the state or other public authorities' and which 'presume on the part of those occupying them the existence of a special relationship of allegiance to the State and reciprocity of rights and duties which form the foundation of the bond of nationality' for their own nationals.[247] The case law indicates that the Court carefully supervises Member States' use of Article 39(4) EC for its proper purpose and that it ensures that they do not 'in times of high unemployment' rely on the public service 'as a convenient reservoir of posts.'[248]

The second situation in which non-nationals may be directly discriminated against concerns rights that do fall within the scope of Community law. In principle,[249] these rights can only be denied to non-nationals when and in as far as

[247] Case 149/79 *Commission v Belgium* [1980] ECR 3881, 10 and Case C–4/91 *Bleis* [1991] ECR I–562, 7. The Court has thus opted for a functional test and rejected an institutional test under which the scope of the exception would be determined by reference to the organisation of the public service in the Member State or the national legal status (public or private?) of a post. Verschueren (1990) n 3 above, at 399–404. In applying this test the Court has ruled that Art 39(4) EC does not apply to railway workers, gardeners, painters (Case 149/79 *Commission v Belgium* [1982] ECR 1845), primary school teachers (Case C–473/93 *Commission v Luxembourg* [1996] ECR I–3207), secondary school teachers (Case C–4/91 *Bleis* [1991] ECR I–5627), trainee teachers (Case 66/85 *Lawrie Blum* [1986] ECR 2121) and nurses (Case 307/84 *Commission v France* [1986] ECR 1725). The Article does cover posts in the judiciary, tax authorities and the diplomatic corps as well as certain supervisory or security functions, the position of municipal architect (Case 149/79 *Commission v Belgium* [1982] ECR 1845) and certain research positions (Case 225/85 *Commission v Italy* [1987] ECR 2625). See also: Case 147/86 *Commission v Greece* [1988] ECR 1637;Case C–290/94 *Commission v Greece* [1996] ECR I–3285 and Case C–273/94 *Commission v Belgium* [1996] ECR I–3265.

In the literature Art 39(4) and the case law have been discussed extensively. See, eg: Beenen, *Citizenship, Nationality and Access to Public Services Employment—The Impact of European Community Law* (2001); Vilaras (2000) n 220 above; Denys, 'Grote Schoonmaak in de Overheidssector' (1996) *NTER* 221–4; O'Keeffe, 'Judicial Interpretation of the Public Service Exception to the Free Movement of Workers' in Curtin and O'Keeffe (eds), *Constitutional Adjudication in European Community and National Law* (1992) at 89 *et seq*; Eschmann, *Die Freizügigkeit der EG-Bürger und der Zugang zur öffentlichen Verwaltung* (1992); Verschueren, 'De Toegang tot de Openbare Dienst voor EG-onderdanen—Macht en Onmacht van het Europese Gemeenschapsrecht' (1991) *MR* 211–20; Verschueren (1990) n 3 above, at 399–417; Everling, 'Zur Rechtsprechung des Europäischen Gerichtshofs über die Beschäftigung von EG-Ausländern in der öffentlichen Verwaltung' (1990) *DVBl* 225–31; Lenz, 'The Public Service in Article 48(4) EEC with Special Reference to the Law in England and the Federal Republic of Germany' (1989) *LIEI* 75–122 and Handoll, 'Article 48(4) and Non-National Access to Public Employment' (1988) *ELRev* 223–42. It has been argued that the introduction of Union citizenship and the grant of voting rights in municipal elections could (or should) affect the scope of the public service (see, eg: O'Keeffe (1992) 89 *et seq* above), but so far the case law does not provide for any examples actually supporting this argument.

[248] Opinion of Adv Gen Mancini in Case 307/84 *Commission v France* [1986] ECR 1725.

[249] Case 15/69 *Ugliola* [1970] ECR 363, 6; Case 352/85 *Bond van Adverteerders* [1988] ECR 2085, 32–3 and Case C–484/93 *Svensson and Gustavsson* [1995] ECR I–3955, 15. There are some exceptions to this rule. For instance, the exercise of free movement rights can be made subject to fulfillment of certain administrative formalities. See, eg: s 2.2.2 above. Further, the Court has occasionally left room for some 'unwritten' exemptions. The first, and the most well known, example concerns the composition of sports teams. In *Donà* (1976) and *Bosman* (1995) the Court accepted that Community law does not prohibit rules or practices which exclude non-national players from certain matches which are not of an economic nature but rather of a sporting interest. These include matches between national teams (Case 13/76 *Donà* [1976] ECR 1333, 14–15), but not matches in national leagues between club teams (Case C–415/93 *Bosman* [1995] ECR I–4291, 127). A second unwritten exception was applied in *Gilly* in which the Court accepted that in the absence of any

this is necessary for the protection of 'public policy, public security or public health.'[250] Unlike the public service exception, the public policy proviso does not relate to, and does not entitle States to exclude non-nationals from, certain activities. The proviso is concerned with the behaviour or specific characteristics of non-nationals[251] and allows derogation from migration rights.[252] Both the Community legislator and the Court of Justice have limited the power of Member States to invoke the proviso. According to Article 4 of Directive No

unifying or harmonising Community measures, Member States are competent to define the criteria including nationality to be used for allocating fiscal powers in bilateral conventions aimed at eliminating double taxation. Case C–336/96 *Gilly* [1998] ECR I–2793, 30. Van der Hurk, 'The European Court of Justice Knows its Limits' (1999) *EC Tax Rev* 211–23; Vanistendael, 'Annotation *Gilly*' (2000) *CMLRev* 167–79; Hinnekens, 'Compatability of Bilateral Tax Treaties with European Community law—The Rules' (1994) *EC Tax Rev* 146 and Harmaeckers, 'Fiscal Sovereignty and Tax Harmonization in the EC' (1991) *EurTax* 173 *et seq.*

One cannot entirely exclude the possibility that the Court will accept more unwritten exceptions to the prohibition of direct discriminations on grounds of nationality. Yet, in light of the 'suspect' nature of nationality requirements the utmost restraint is to be exercised. In spite of judgments as *Donà*, *Bosman* and *Gilly*, the basic assumption still must be that within the scope of Community law discrimination by reason of nationality can only be justified where these can be brought within the realm of the public policy proviso.

[250] Art 39(3) EC (Community workers and their family members), Art 46(1) EC (self-employed persons and recipients of services); Arts 2(2) of the three 1990 residence directives (non-economic residents); Art 28(3) and 33 EEA (EEA nationals) and Art 14 of Decision 1/80 (Turkish workers and their family members).

The literature has dealt with the public policy exception extensively. See, eg: Duarte, 'Rights of Residence of Community Workers and Derogations: Reflections on the Meaning of "Worker-Citizen"' in Carlier and Verwilghen, *Thirty Years of Free Movement of Workers in Europe* (2000) 177–90; Hartley (1991) n 1 above, ch 10; Verschueren (1990) n 3 above, 389–94; Wood, '"Public Policy" Discrimination in the EEC: A Proposal for Assuring the Free Movement of Workers' (1985) *FordILJ* 447–78; O'Keeffe, 'Practical Difficulties in the Application of Article 48 of the EEC Treaty' (1982) *CMLRev* 35–60; Hartley (1978) n 23 above, ch 5; Weber, 'Die Rechtsprechung des EuGH zum Vorbehalt der öffentlichen Ordnung und Sicherheit im Bereich der Freizügigkeit' (1978) *EuGRZ* 157–60; Boonk, *Openbare Orde als Grens aan het Vrij Verkeer van Goederen, Personen en Diensten in de E.E.G.* (1977); Singer, 'Free Movement of Workers in the European Economic Community: The Public Policy Exception' (1977) *StanfLRev* 1283–97; Bongen, *Schranken der Freizügigkeit aus Gründen der öffentlichen Ordnung und Sicherheit im Recht der Europäischen Wirtschaftsgemeinschaft* (1975) and Selmer, 'Die öffentlichen Sicherheit und Ordnung als Schranke der Arbeitnehmer-Freizügigkeit gemäss Art.48 Abs.3 EWG-Vertrag' (1967) *DöV* 328–34. The wording of the various public policy provisions is not identical, but there is no doubt that, at least in as far as Community citizens are concerned, the provisions applicable to the various categories must be interpreted in the same way. Arnull (1990) n 165 above, at 93. The Commission has proposed to include a new provision in Dir 68/360 (workers) which states that in applying the public policy Member States shall take into account the degree to which the person concerned has been integrated into their territory. COM(1998) 394 def.

[251] Craig and De Búrca (1998) n 105 above, at 787. The right of Member States to restrict freedom of movement on public health grounds, for instance, is not intended to permit the States to exclude the public health sector as a sector of economic activity from the free movement rules, but merely to allow the States to refuse access to or residence in their territory to persons whose presence would in itself constitute a danger to public health. Case 131/85 *Gül* [1986] ECR 1573, 17.

[252] The Community provisions suggest that the public policy proviso primarily allows for derogation from migration rights, but the exercise of the right to work (Case 44/72 *Marsman* [1974] ECR 1243, 4) and the rights to provide and receive services (Case C–157/99 *Geraets-Smits* [2001] ECR I–5473, 74 and Case C–158/96 *Kohll* [1998] ECR I–1931 at 50–1) may also be limited on public policy, security or health grounds.

64/221,[253] entry to or residence in the territory of another Member State can only be refused on public health grounds as regards contagious diseases or disabilities which are listed in an Annex to Directive No 64/221.[254] The concepts of public policy and public security are nowhere defined in the directive. It is in principle up to individual Member States to determine when a threat to public policy or security exists with the result that the circumstances in which migration rights may be restricted may vary from Member State to Member State and from time to time.[255] Article 3(1) of Directive No 64/221 provides, however, that measures taken on grounds of public policy or public security must be based on the personal conduct of the person concerned;[256] Article 3(2) adds that previous criminal convictions do not in themselves constitute a valid ground for refusing entrance or residence or expulsion. The Court has interpreted the two provisions strictly. The public policy ground may only be invoked where the presence or the individual behaviour of a non-national constitutes a genuine and sufficiently serious threat to fundamental interests of society.[257] More generally,

[253] OJ 1963/1964 Spec.Ed. 117. For the Commission's recent views on the interpretation of this directive see European Commission, *Communication to the Council and the European Parliament on the Special Measures Concerning the Movement and Residence of Citizens of the Union which are Justified on Grounds of Public Policy, Public Security and Public Health*.

[254] Art 4(1) of Dir 64/221. If a disease or disability manifests itself after a first residence permit has been granted it cannot justify expulsion or a refusal to renew the said permit. Art 4(2) of Dir 64/221. The diseases are listed under two headings. The first concerns the contagious diseases which are listed in International Health Regulation No 2 of the World Health Organisation as being subject to quarantine (tuberculosis of the respiratory system in an active state or showing a tendency to develop; syphilis; other infectious diseases or contagious parasitic diseases if they are the subject of provisions for the protection of nationals of the host country); the second category consists of diseases and disabilities which can justify exclusion or expulsion on the grounds of public policy or public security (drug addiction, profound mental disturbance; manifest conditions of psychotic disturbance with agitation, delirium, hallucinations or confusion).

In the literature it has been debated whether Member States are entitled to restrict the free movement rights of persons infected by the HIV-virus or suffering from AIDS. See, eg: Hendriks, 'The Right to Freedom of Movement and the (Un)lawfulness of Aids/HIV Specific Travel Restrictions from a European Perspective' (1990) *NJIL* 86 *et seq*; Pais Macedo van Overbeek, 'AIDS/HIV Infection and the Free Movement of Persons within the European Community' (1990) *CMLRev* 791–824 and Dworkin and Steyger, 'Aids Victims in the European Community and the United States: Are They Protected from Unjustified Discrimination? (1989) *Texas ILJ* 295–329.

[255] Case 41/74 *Van Duyn* [1974] ECR 1337, 18.

[256] See, eg: Case 67/74 *Bonsignore* [1975] ECR 297 (where it was held that the public policy exception cannot be relied upon for reasons of a 'general preventive nature'). On specific circumstances in which preventive measures may be justified as regards gatherings attended by large numbers of people such as in the case of sport events, see, eg: Council Recommendation of 22 April 1996 on guidelines for preventing and restraining disorder connected with football matches, OJ 1996 C 131.

[257] Case 67/74 *Bouchereau* [1975] ECR 1999, 35 and Case C–348/96 *Calfa* [1999] ECR I–11, 25. Logically, failures to comply with immigration formalities do not suffice for constituting a threat to public order. Case 48/75 *Royer* [1976] ECR 497, 38–9. In relying on the proviso Member States must observe the principle of proportionality (see also: Arnull (1990) n 165 above, at 99) as well as fundamental rights such as those enshrined in the European Convention (see, eg: Case C–260/89 *Tileorassi* [1991] ECR I–2925; Case 36/75 *Rutili* [1975] ECR 1219 and Hall, 'The ECHR and Public Policy Exceptions to the Free Movement of Workers under the EEC Treaty' (1991) *ELRev* 466 *et seq*). In relying on the public policy exception the principle of proportionality is to be observed and this would seem to imply that States have to take into consideration the length of residence and the

the case law suggests that in combating crime and the inherent threats to public policy and security, Member States must first rely on their powers under criminal law and procedure. In principle, immigration powers may only be used in last resort.[258] Furthermore, Article 2 of Directive No 64/221 states that the public policy exception may not be invoked for economic ends. Member States cannot limit the free movement rights of nationals of other Member States in order to safeguard the employment opportunities of its own nationals[259] or to secure the financing of public advertising funds.[260] The mere fact, however, that as well as objective reasons based on public security or public health, economic objectives are strived for does not necessarily exclude the possibility of relying on the exception.[261]

7.2 Indirect Discrimination on Grounds of Nationality

Besides direct (or overt) discrimination, Community provisions on the free movement of persons prohibit indirect (or covert) discrimination on grounds of nationality. These concern cases in which Member States apply other criteria of differentiation that lead in fact to the same result as nationality criteria.[262] The *rationale* behind the concept and prohibition of indirect discrimination is not hard to find. If Community law were merely to prohibit nationality requirements, the right to equal treatment of Community citizens would be deprived of

degree to which the persons concerned have integrated into their society. Cp also the Commission proposal for amending Dir 68/360 (COM(1998) 394 fin).

[258] Consider *Calfa*. The case involved an Italian national who was charged with possession and use of prohibited drugs while staying as a tourist in Greece. The Court held that a Member State may consider that the use of drugs constitutes a danger for society and that such a State may take 'special measures' against foreign nationals. However, an expulsion order against a Community citizen as Ms Calfa can only be made if, besides her having committed an offence under drug laws, her personal conduct creates 'a genuine and sufficiently serious threat affecting one of the fundamental interests of society'. Case C–348/96 *Calfa* [1999] ECR I–11, 25. In some cases, however, Member States seem entitled to refuse entry or residence to a national of another Member State even if it does not criminalise certain activities. See, eg: Case 41/74 *Van Duyn* [1974] ECR 1337 (which held that a non-national who wished to work for the Church of Scientology could be refused entry to the United Kingdom even though the undesirable and harmful practice of scientology was not prohibited in this Member State).

[259] Craig and de Búrca (1998) n 105 above, at 787.

[260] Case C–352/85 *Bond van Adverteerders* [1988] ECR 2124, 24.

[261] Cp Case 72/83 *Campus Oil* [1984] ECR 2727, 36 and Case C–158/96 *Kohll* [1998] ECR I–1931, 50–1. See also: Ch 4 S 4. Arts 6–9 of Dir 64/221 contain several procedural provisions which require that each Member State grants to nationals of other Member States the possibility of challenging administrative measures concerning restrictions on the exercise of the free movement rights. On these provisions see Case C–357/98 *Yiadom* [2000] ECR I–9265; Joined Cases C–65/95 *Shingara* [1997] ECR I–3343; Case C–175/94 *Gallagher* [1995] ECR I–4523; Case C–197/89 *Dzodzi* [1990] ECR I–3763; Joined Cases 115/81 and 116/81 *Adoui* [1982] ECR 1665; Case 131/79 *Regina* [1980] ECR 1585 and Case 98/79 *Pescataing* [1980] ECR 691.

[262] Case 152/73 *Sotgiu* [1974] ECR 153, 10 and Case C–237/94 *O'Flynn* [1996] ECR I–2617, 17. On the notion of indirect discrimination see especially: Garrone, 'La Discrimination indirecte en Droit communautaire: Vers une Théorie générale' (1994) *RTDE* 425–49.

much of its practical effect. Member States could circumvent the prohibition of discrimination on grounds of nationality by making the enjoyment of rights conditional upon language,[263] diploma[264] or other requirements which non-nationals are often unable to meet.

Over the years, the Court has interpreted the notion of indirect discrimination quite broadly. It is of no relevance whether a Member State has the intent to discriminate against non-nationals. The effect of the application of a given criterion is decisive. The notion applies to national rules containing criteria that can be more easily satisfied by nationals[265] or which essentially affect non-nationals.[266] Even the mere risk that a certain requirement 'may operate to the particular detriment' of non-nationals may suffice for it to be classified as indirect discrimination.[267] Besides language and diploma requirements, the concept of indirect discrimination on grounds of nationality, may extend to residence[268] requirements.[269]

The prohibition of indirect discrimination is not as strict as the prohibition of direct discrimination. National provisions that mainly affect non-nationals often serve wholly legitimate interests which deserve protection under Community law. For instance, nobody would seriously question the validity of a national rule that requires national language teachers in primary and high schools to have an adequate knowledge of that language, even though such a rule would mainly work to the benefit of nationals. Similarly, virtually anybody would agree that Member States cannot be required to grant social assistance benefits to residents and non-residents alike. Residence requirements for such benefits will generally work to the disadvantage of non-nationals but they would appear necessary for maintaining social assistance benefit schemes. Language, residence and other indirect discriminatory requirements are simply not as 'suspect' as nationality requirements are. The Court has recognised this

---

[263] See, eg: Case 379/87 *Groener* [1989] ECR 3967.

[264] See, eg: Case 222/86 *Heylens* [1987] ECR 4097 and Case C–340/89 *Vlassopoulou* [1991] ECR I–3257.

[265] Case C–349/87 *Paraschi* [1991] ECR I–4501, 23.

[266] Case 41/84 *Pinna* [1986] ECR 1, 24 and Case 33/88 *Allué* [1989] ECR 1591, 12.

[267] Case C–175 *Biehl* [1990] ECR I–1779, 14; Case C–237/94 *O'Flynn* [1996] ECR I–2617, 18 and Case C–124/99 *Borawitz* [2000] ECR I–7293, 30–1.

[268] See, eg: Case C–224/97 *Ciola* [1999] ECR I–2517 at 14; Case C–350/96 *Clean Car* [1998] ECR I–2521 at 29; Case C–326/90 *Commission v Belgium* [1992] ECR I–5517; Case C–175/88 *Biehl* [1990] ECR 1779 and Case 41/84 *Pinna* [1986] ECR 1. Residence requirements do not in all cases meet this requirement. See, eg: Case C–18/95 *Terhoeve* [1999] ECR I–345.

[269] In the context of the free movement of services, it is often far from easy to establish whether a national rule is discriminatory or non-discriminatory. The case law does not provide for crystal-clear criteria on this point. In some cases the Court has indeed held that national rules or measures which do not formally lay down different rules for providers of services established 'at home' and providers based 'abroad' must be regarded as indistinctly applicable (see, eg: Case C–204/90 *Bachmann* [1990] ECR I–249), whilst in other cases it has held that discriminatory rules include those which indirectly give rise to unequal treatment of providers based in other Member States (Case C–484/93 *Svensson and Gustavsson* [1995] ECR I–3955). On this point see also the Opinion of Adv Gen Tesauro in Case C–120/95 *Decker* and Case C–158/96 *Kohll* [1998] ECR I–1831, 44–50.

and has consistently ruled that indirect discriminatory rules may be justified 'by objective considerations independent of the nationality' and if they are necessary for, and proportionate to, the legitimate aim pursued by the national law.[270]

In determining whether or not a given national provision can be justified the Court generally establishes first whether the provision pursues an objective and legitimate aim; it then considers whether the requirement is actually necessary for, and proportionate to, the aim in question.[271] Two examples may illustrate the contours of the indirect discrimination test.

The first is *O'Flynn* (1989).[272] The case concerned an Irish national working in the United Kingdom who had taken responsibility for the funeral of his son in Ireland. Mr O'Flynn applied in the United Kingdom for a funeral payment which was intended to cover the costs of the funeral, but his application was denied on the ground that the burial had not taken place in the United Kingdom. The Court considered the funeral payment to be a social advantage in the sense of Article 7(2) of Regulation No 1612/68 and held that the group of persons who, on the death of a family member, have to arrange a funeral in another Member State will mainly consist of non-nationals. A national provision which makes the payment of funeral expenses subject to the condition that the funeral takes place in the United Kingdom, constitutes in principle indirect discrimination.[273] It was argued that the requirement of having the funeral in the United Kingdom was aimed at avoiding unacceptable increases in costs and the Court implicitly accepted this as a legitimate objective. However, the Court did not accept that the requirement in question was really necessary for this purpose. Expenditure could just as well be kept under control if payment for the funeral abroad were limited to a sum fixed by reference to the costs of funerals in the United Kingdom. The requirement could thus not be regarded as proportional to the valid aim of controlling expenditure.[274]

A second example concerns *Vlassopoulou* (1993).[275] In this case the Court was asked to determine whether the refusal of German authorities to admit to the bar a Greek national who had obtained a Greek law degree and who had

---

[270] Case C–111/91 *Commission v Luxembourg* [1993] ECR I–817, 12; Case C–332/91 *Allué* [1993] ECR I–4309, 15 and Case C–237/94 *O'Flynn* [1996] ECR I–2617, 18.

[271] In some cases the Court follows another approach. Consider *Schumacker* in which the Court was asked whether a national rule which reserved certain tax advantages for workers residing in the territory of the State concerned, was compatible with Art 39 EC. The Court accepted that such a residence requirement can work to the detriment of nationals of other Member States, but it held that discrimination can only be present when different rules are applied to comparable situations or when the same rule is applied to different situations. As regards direct taxation, however, according to the Court the situations of residents and non-residents generally are not comparable. Case C–279/93 *Schumacker* [1995] ECR I–225. In such cases there is in principle no discrimination and no need to consider possibilities for justification.

[272] Case C–237/94 *O'Flynn* [1996] ECR I–2617.

[273] *Ibid*, 21–2.

[274] *Ibid*, 28–9.

[275] Case 340/89 *Vlassopoulou* [1993] ECR 2357.

practised German law for several years on the ground that she had not passed the relevant German exams, was compatible with Article 43 EC. The requirement of passing German exams was likely to affect non-Germans more than Germans and was thus in principle indirectly discriminatory in nature. The right to lay down conditions for admission to the bar may be a justification for such a requirement, but, according to the Court, only when on deciding for an application for the bar a Member State takes the diplomas, certificates or other qualifications obtained by the person concerned into consideration and compare these to qualifications required by national law. If the foreign qualification is found to be equivalent, it must be recognised; if not, the Member State may require the applicant to demonstrate that he has acquired the required skills, knowledge or qualifications.[276]

7.3 Non-Discriminatory Rules Hampering the Free Movement of Persons

The development of the concept of indirect discrimination has significantly contributed to a strengthening of the free movement of persons. Since the early 1990s, however, the Court has appeared willing to go one step further by holding that non-discriminatory rules that hamper the exercise of free movement rights may also be prohibited. The roots of this prohibition are found in the case law of the Court on the free movement of goods. Since *Dassonville* (1974) and *Cassis de Dijon* (1979) the Court has consistently ruled that all national rules which 'directly or indirectly, actually or potentially' hamper intra-Community trade in goods are prohibited, unless they are necessary to satisfy mandatory requirements.[277] The Court has applied this approach first to the freedom to provide services,[278] then to the right of establishment[279] and more recently to

---

[276] *Ibid*, at 16–22. The line of reasoning followed by the Court is similar to the approach the Community legislator has adopted in Dir 89/48 on the mutual recognition of higher-education diplomas. OJ 1989 L 19. On this directive, and the recognition of diplomas in general, see especially: Schneider, *Die Anerkennung von Diplomen in der Europäischen Gemeinschaft* (1995) (with numerous references to other literature).

[277] Case 8/74 *Dassonville* [1974] ECR 837, 5 and Case 120/78 *Rewe-Zentral* (Cassis de Dijon) [1979] ECR 649. On the case law on the free movement of goods see, eg: Voogsgeerd (2000) n 102 above; Maduro, *We the Court—The European Court of Justice & the European Economic Constitution* (1998); Jarvis, *Application of EC law on the Free Movement of Goods by National Courts of the Member States* (1997) and Oliver, *Free Movement of Goods in the European Community* (1996).

[278] Case C–76/90 *Säger* [1991] ECR I–4221 and Case C–384/93 *Alpine Investments* [1995] ECR I–1141.

[279] See, eg: Case 107/83 *Klopp* [1984] ECR 2971 and Case C–175/88 *Biehl* [1990] ECR I–1779. On Art 43 EC and the prohibition of non-discriminatory rules see, eg: Hilson, 'Discrimination in Community Free Movement Law' (1999) *ELRev* 445–62; Marenco, 'The Notion of Restriction on the Freedom of Establishment and the Provision of Services in the Case-Law of the Court' (1992) *YEL* 111–50; Everling, 'Das Niederlassungsrecht in der Europäischen Gemeinschaft' (1990) *DB* 1853–9 and Knobbe-Keuk, 'Niederlassungsfreiheit: Diskriminierungs- or Beschränkungsverbot?— Zur Dogmatik des Art.52 EWG-Vertrag—am Beispiel einiger gesellschaftsrechtlicher Beschränkungen' (1990) *DB* 2573–84.

the free movement of workers.[280] It now seems established case law that the provisions on freedom of movement:

> 'preclude all national provisions . . . which, although applicable without discrimination on grounds of nationality, are nevertheless liable to hinder or make less attractive the exercise of the fundamental freedoms guaranteed by the EEC Treaty by Community citizens.'[281]

As the Court ruled in *Gebhard* (1995), as long as no harmonisation measures have been adopted, nationality-neutral rules or measures which may hamper the exercise of fundamental freedoms guaranteed by the Treaty can only be justified when they are (*i*) applied in a non-discriminatory manner, (*ii*) justified by imperative requirements in the general interest and (*iii*) when they are suitable and necessary for attaining this imperative requirement.[282] The 'justification test' to be applied in the case of non-discriminatory rules is, at least on the face of it, the same as in the case of indirect discrimination on grounds of nationality. The main significance of the case law on non-discriminatory measures is that the justification test is to be applied in a greater number of cases.[283]

In the context of the free movement of goods, the result of the prohibition of non-discriminatory rules has been that virtually any national rule that regulates the marketing of goods had become susceptible to judicial review. The resulting workload on the judiciary has compelled the Court to limit the definition of the notion of measures having equivalent effect in order to exclude certain national

---

[280] Case C–415/93 *Bosman* [1995] ECR I–4291 and Case C–18/95 *Terhoeve* [1999] ECR I–345.

[281] Case C–19/92 *Kraus* [1993] ECR I–1663, 32 and Case C–55/94 *Gebhard* [1995] ECR I–4165, 37. See also: Simm, *Der Gerichtshof der Europäischen Gemeinschaften im föderalem Kompetenzkonflikt—Kontinuität und Neubesinnung in der Rechtsprechung vor und nach 'Maastricht'* (1998) 156–201; Bernard, 'Discrimination and Free Movement in EC Law' (1996) *ICLQ* 82–108; Behrens, 'Die Konvergenz der wirtschaftlichen Freiheiten im europäischen Gemeinschaftsrecht' (1990) *EuR* 145 *et seq* and the Opinion of Adv Gen Lenz in Case C–415/93 *Bosman* [1995] ECR I–4921, 4984–5010. In terms of terminology, the case law on the four common market freedoms shows a clear convergence as to the scope of the prohibitions. In the application of a particular test, however, differences still exist. In particular, a distinction still needs to be made between cases involving cross-border border movement of products and movement of persons. See, eg: Barnard, 'Fitting the Remaining Pieces into the Goods and Persons Jigsaw?' (2001) *ELRev* 35–59; Voogsgseerd (2000) n 102 above, ch 8; Martin, 'Discriminations, Entraves et Raisons impérieur' (1998) *CDE* 561 *et seq*, at p614 *et seq* and Behrens (1992) above.

[282] Case C–55/94 *Gebhard* [1995] ECR I–4165, 37. See also Case C–19/92 *Kraus* [1993] ECR I–1663, 32 and Case C–212/89 *Centros* [1999] ECR I–1459, 34.

[283] The new approach may, however, in some cases also be a step back. In *Bosman* the Court was asked to rule upon the validity of the so-called nationality clauses according to which only a limited number of foreign players could be fielded in matches between club teams. The rules implied direct discrimination on grounds of nationality and, following settled case law, this would have implied that the rules could only be justified under the public policy proviso. The Court, however, held that the rules constituted an obstacle to the free movement of workers and subsequently considered whether the rules could possibly be justified. The Court concluded that the nationality rules could not be justified, but the application of the new approach did enable the Court to uphold nationality criteria applied in the context of matches between national football teams. Case C–415/93 *Bosman* [1995] ECR I–4291 at 121–37.

rules concerning selling arrangements.[284] There are reasons to believe, however, that the implications of the prohibition of non-discriminatory measures for the free movement of persons will not be as far-reaching.[285] The cases in which the prohibition of non-discriminatory rules has so far been applied often concerned rules which seemed to affect non-nationals more than nationals and which could therefore have been decided under the indirect discrimination test.[286] For instance, in *Vlassopolou*, discussed above, the Court spoke in terms of a prohibition of non-discriminatory rules but the rules in question concerning admission to the German Bar obviously affected non-nationals more than nationals.[287]

The cases that have been decided so far by the Court suggest that the added value of the prohibition of non-discriminatory rules for the free movement of persons primarily concerns the possibility of challenging rules imposed by the State of origin which hamper the right to work in other Member States. Consider *Terhoeve* (1999). The case concerned a Dutch national who, during a given year, had been working in the United Kingdom and the Netherlands. The social security contributions Mr Terhoeve had to pay in the Netherlands were greater than if had worked there throughout the year. Mr Terhoeve claimed that the Dutch legislation constituted indirect discrimination on grounds of nationality since it made a distinction on the basis of residence. This argument could not succeed. The residence requirement mainly affected nationals rather than non-nationals. The Court ruled, however, that national provisions which preclude or deter Community citizens from moving to or taking up employment in other Member States may be caught by Article 39 EC.[288] The more recent judgment in *Elsen* (2000) demonstrates that the Member States of origin can also be prohibited from applying rules that impinge on non-economic free movement rights. The case concerned a German national who was living with her husband and son in France. Ms Elsen, who had worked in Germany but never in France, requested the German social security institutions to take into consideration periods she had spent raising her son as insurance periods for the purposes of her old-age pension. The German institutions refused on the ground that under the relevant German rules they could only do so if the child rearing had taken place in Germany. The Court ruled that the German rules were disadvantageous

---

[284] Joined Cases C–267 and C–268/91 *Keck* [1993] ECR I–6097. See also: Poiares Maduro (1998) n 277 above and Weatherill, 'After *Keck*: Some Thoughts on How to Clarify the Clarification' (1995) *CMLRev* 991 *et seq*.

[285] '*Keck*' has so far not been extended to the other freedoms. On the question whether *Keck* can be transposed to the other freedoms see Voogsgeerd (2000) n 102 above, 428–34.

[286] Cp the Opinion of Adv Gen Fennelly in Case C–190/98 *Graf* [2000] ECR I–493, 21.

[287] Cp Case C–204/90 *Bachmann* [1992] ECR I–249.

[288] Case C–18/95 *Terhoeve* [1999] ECR I–345, 39. See also: USZ (1999) nr.67 (with annotation van der Mei). See also: *Bosman* (1995) (where the Court held that the transfer rules in professional football may be caught by Art 39 EC since this provision not only intends to ensure equality of treatment in other Member States but also prohibits the Member State of origin from hindering the right to work in other Member States (Case C–415/93 *Bosman* [1995] ECR I–4291, 97) and Weatherill, 'Annotation *Bosman*' (1995) *CMLRev* 991 *et seq*) and Case C–303/98 *Sehrer* [2000] ECR I–4585.)

to Community citizens who wished to exercise their non-economic free movement rights and that Article 18 EC required the periods in question to be taken into consideration.[289]

7.4 Reverse Discrimination

Throughout its case law the Court has interpreted Community provisions on the free movement of persons broadly. In one[290] significant respect, however, the Court has shown considerable restraint. Treaty provisions such as Articles 18 and 39 EC speak of freedom of movement (with)in the territory of the Member States, and on the face of it, the Articles thus seem to imply that Community citizens can rely on these provisions in all Member States including their own. Yet, from the early years the Court has interpreted the Treaty provisions so as to cover only rights to move to, to be economically active in and to be treated equally in *other* Member States. Community citizens who have never exercised their free movement rights fall outside the scope of Community provisions on the free movement of persons. They and their family members cannot benefit from any of the rights discussed in this chapter. Consider *Morson* (1982). The case concerned two Surinamese nationals who wished to reside in the Netherlands with their children who were already working and living there. Under Dutch law Mrs Morson and Mrs Jhanjan did not enjoy the right to reside in the Netherlands, but they claimed that they had as 'dependent family members in the ascending line' such a right under Article 10 of Regulation

---

[289] Case C–135/99 *Elsen* [2000] ECR I–10409, 34–6. The judgment in *Graf* (2000) demonstrates that there are limits to the prohibition for the Member State of origin to apply rules which may hamper the right to move to other Member States. The case involved a German national who voluntarily terminated his employment in Austria in order to take up a new job in Germany. Mr Graf claimed that he was, under Austrian law, entitled to a compensation from his former employer, but the latter refused to pay the compensation on the ground that the law in question provides that no compensation has to paid where the worker gives notice, leaves prematurely or is responsible for premature dismissal. Graf claimed that the law impeded the free movement of workers and was inconsistent with Art 39 EC. The Court of Justice did not agree. The Court confirmed that non-discriminatory national rules which preclude or deter a worker from moving to other Member States may be covered and prohibited by Art 39 EC, but in order to constitute an obstacle to freedom of movement such rules must affect access of workers to the labour market in other Member States. The Court held that this was not the case with the Austrian law in question because the compensation payment was not dependent on a decision of a worker whether or not to stay with the employer, but rather on the 'future and hypothetical event' that the labour contract is terminated by their employer without such termination being at the initiative or attributable to the worker. Such an event, the Court concluded, is 'too uncertain and indirect a possibility for legislation to be capable of being regarded as liable to hinder the free movement of workers where it does not attach to termination of a contract of employment by the worker himself the same consequence as it attaches to termination which was not at his initiative or is not attributable to him'. Case C–190/98 *Graf* [2000] ECR I–493, 23–5.

[290] To be sure, in some cases the Court also shows restraint by holding that a link between a certain case and Community law is too indirect or uncertain for Community law to apply. See, eg: Case C–190/98 *Graf* [2000] ECR I–493 (see previous footnote); Case C–299/95 *Kremzow* [1997] ECR I–2629 and Case C–379/92 *Peralta* 1994] ECR I–345.

No 1612/68. The Court rejected their claim. The provisions on freedom of movement could not be relied upon because the children were Dutch nationals who had never worked in another Member State. In the view of the Court there was no factor linking the case to situations where Community law applies.[291]

This is not to say that Community citizens can never invoke the free movement provisions *vis-à-vis* their own Member State. When a so-called inter-State element is present they may do so. In particular, such an element is present when Community citizens have been employed or have resided in another Member State and subsequently return to their own Member State. In *Singh* (1992), for instance, the Court held that the Indian spouse of a UK national, who had worked in Germany and subsequently returned to the United Kingdom, could rely on Community law in order to claim the right to enter and reside in the United Kingdom. In *Scholz* (1994), a case brought against an Italian government body, it was accepted that a former German national who had moved to Italy and, through marriage, had acquired Italian and lost German nationality, could rely on Article 39 EC.[292]

Morson and Jhanjan is an example of a case leading to so-called reverse discrimination. This occurs when Member States treat (family members of) their own nationals less favourably than (family members of) nationals of other Member States.[293] At first glance, reverse discrimination seems at odds with the

---

[291] Community law on the free movement of persons does not apply to such 'purely internal situations' in which activities 'are confined in all respects within a single Member State'. See, eg: Case C–41/90 *Höfner* [1991] ECR I–1979, 37 and Case C–332/90 *Steen* [1992] ECR I–341, 9.

[292] Case C–419/92 *Scholz* [1994] ECR I–505. Until recently, it seemed that *private* residence in another Member State did not suffice to establish an inter-State element for the purposes of *economic* provisions for the free movement of workers and the right of establishment. Consider *Werner* (1993). This case concerned a German national who resided in the Netherlands and worked as a self-employed dentist in Germany where he earned most of his income. The Court denied Mr Werner the right to rely on Art 43 EC in order to challenge a German law which in Werner's unlawfully discriminated against non-residents because the case was, in brief, purely internal. Case C–112/91 *Werner* [1993] I–429. It may be assumed, however, that *Werner* no longer stands. In *Elsen* (2000) the Court accepted that a (former) German frontier worker living in France could invoke Arts 18, 39 and 42 EC in order to challenge a German social security rule. See Case C–135/99 *Elsen* [2000] ECR I–10409, 34–6.

[293] In the literature the notion of reverse discrimination (in the context of the free movement of persons, services and goods) has been discussed extensively. See, eg: Vooggsgeerd (2000) n 102 above; Balthasar, 'Inländerdiskriminierung in der EU nach dem EWG-Vertrag und aus österreicher Sicht' (1998) *ZföR* 143–216; Münnich, 'Article 7 EWGV und Inländerdiskriminierung' (1992) *ZfRV* 92–100; Jesserun d'Oliveira, 'Is Reverse Discrimination still Permissible under the Single European Act' in *Centre of Foreign Law and Private International Law—University of Amsterdam, Forty Years On: The Evolution of Postwar Private International Law in Europe* (1990) 71–86; van Ooik, 'Omgekeerde Discriminatie van EEG-Onderdanen' (1990) *MR* 83–6; Greenwood, 'Limits on the Free Movement of Persons in EEC Law' (1987/1988) *YEL* 185–210; Pickup, 'Reverse Discrimination and Freedom of Movement for Workers' (1986) *CMLRev* 135–56; Schlachter, *Discrimination à Rebours—Die Inländerdiskriminierung nach der Rechtsprechung des EuGH und des französichen Conseil d'Etat* (1984); Weiss, 'Inländerdiskriminierung zwischen Gemeinschaftsrecht und nationalem Verfassungsrecht' (1983) *NJW* 2721–6; Kon, 'Aspects of Reverse Discrimination in Community Law' (1981) *ELRev* 75–101; Druesne, 'Remarques sur le Champ d'Application personnel du Droit communautaire: des 'Discriminations à Rebours' Peuvent-elles Tenir en Echec la Liberté de Circulation des Personnes' (1979) *RTDE* 429–39 and Mortelmans, 'Omgekeerde Discriminatie en het Gemeenschapsrecht' (1979) *SEW* 654–74.

prohibition of discrimination on grounds of nationality. *Singh* and *Scholz* demonstrate, however, that the States' own nationals are not discriminated against on grounds of their nationality, but rather on the ground that they have never exercised their free movement rights. In situations where reverse discrimination occurs, there is no differential treatment of nationals and non-nationals but of 'free movers' and 'non-movers.' In *Uecker* (1997) the Court held that such reverse discrimination does not run counter to Article 17 which has established a Union citizenship. That provision, the Court held, 'is not intended to extend the scope *ratione materiae* of the Treaty also to internal situations which have no link with Community law.'[294]

8 THE UNITED STATES

Having set out the main rules and principles governing the free movement of persons within the European Community, the discussion now proceeds with a description and initial analysis of American constitutional law of the so-called right to travel, as the notion of free movement of persons is generally referred to in the United States. After a brief history, this section describes what the right to travel entails and how the American Supreme Court reviews State rules that hamper the exercise of the right to travel or discriminate against those who have exercised this right.

8.1 Right to Travel: A Brief History

Nowhere does the United States Constitution mention the right to travel, a right to freedom of movement or any comparable notion. The omission of a reference to the right to travel has never been seen as a denial of the right. On the contrary, the framers of the Constitution probably took the right to travel so much for

---

[294] Joined Cases C–64/96 and C–65/96 *Uecker and Jacquet* [1997] ECR I–3171, 23. In cases which have no link with Community law, national courts remain free to review national rules under national constitutions. Case C–132/93 *Steen* [1994] ECR I–2715. Johnson and O'Keeffe, 'From Discrimination to Obstacles to Free Movement: Recent Developments Concerning the Free Movement of Workers' (1994) *CMLRev* 1313–46, 1338.

The Community obligation to observe fundamental human rights (see n 237 above) does not exist in 'purely internal cases'. Consider *Kremzow* (1997). The case concerned an Austrian national who had been convicted of murder. In 1993 the European Court of Human Rights, however, held that criminal proceedings against Mr Kremzow had been in breach of Art 6 of the European Convention. Mr Kremzow started an action for damages against the Austrian State. In doing so he claimed, inter alia, that the prison sentence prevented him from exercising his free movement rights under Community law and that Austria was liable in damages under Community law. The Court of Justice, however, held that it had no jurisdiction. The situation of Mr Kremzow was 'not connected in any way with any of the situations contemplated' by the EC Treaty. The deprivation of liberty actually prevented Mr Kremzow from moving to other Member States but was, according to the Court, not sufficiently closely connected with the right to freedom of movement as to bring the situation within the realm of Community law. Case C–299/95 *Kremzow* [1997] ECR I–2629.

granted that they considered any reference to the right superfluous.[295] Ever since the nation's inception, no one has ever questioned the constitutional status of the right to travel. The right simply exists and the absence of an explicit reference to it may, if anything, symbolise how deeply the notion of freedom of movement is rooted in American thinking.

Throughout constitutional history, the Supreme Court and several Justices have stressed the fundamental importance attached to the right to travel.[296] In 1849, for instance, Chief Justice Taney wrote in the *Passenger Cases*:

'For all the great purposes for which the Federal government was formed, we are one people with one common country. We are all citizens of the United States; and as members of the same community, must have the right to pass and repass every part of it without interruption, as freely as in our own States.'[297]

Almost one hundred years later, Justice Jackson held in *Edwards v. California* (1941) that:

'It is a privilege of citizenship of the United States protected from State abridgement, to enter any State of the Union either for temporary sojourn or for the establishment of permanent residence therein . . . If national citizenship means less than this it means nothing.'[298]

Later, in *Shapiro v. Thompson* (1969), Justice Brennan stated:

'The nature of our Federal Union and our constitutional concepts of personal liberty unite to require that all citizens be free to travel throughout the length and breadth of our land uninhibited by statutes, rules, or regulations which unreasonably burden or restrict this movement.'[299]

---

[295] Chafee, 'Three Human Rights in the Constitution of 1787 (1956) at 185; Rosberg, Free Movement of Persons in the United States' in Sandalow and Stein, *Courts and Free Markets—Perspectives from the United States and Europe* (1982) 275–362, at 281. Article IV of the Arts of Confederation—the predecessor of the Constitution—provided that 'to secure and perpetuate mutual friendship and intercourse among the people of the different States in this Union, the free inhabitants of each of these States . . . shall have free ingress and egress to and from any other State . . .'. The framers of the Constitution, however, dropped the phrase 'free ingress and regress'. The Constitution of 1787 converted the confederation into a federation. The right to travel was so elementary that it 'was conceived from the beginning to be a necessary concomitant of the stronger Union the Constitution created'. *United States v Guest*, 383 U.S. 745 (1966) at 757–8.

[296] Justices of the Supreme Court and scholars have debated where the right to travel should be located in the Constitution. The right has been read into various constitutional provisions such as the Due Process Clause of the Fifth Amendment, the Commerce Clause, the Privileges and Immunities Clause of Article IV and the Privileges or Immunities Clause of the Fourteenth amendment. Note, 'The Right to Travel—Quest for A Constitutional Source' (1974) *RutgCLJ* 122–43. In order to prove that the right exists there is, however, no need to ascribe the right to travel to a particular constitutional provision. *Shapiro v Thompson*, 394 U.S. 618 (1969); *Soto-Lopez*, 476 U.S. 898 (1986) at 902 and *Saenz v Roe*, 119 SCt 1518 (1999). *Saenz* strongly suggests, however, that the Court has chosen the Privileges or Immunities Clause of the Fourteenth amendment as the constitutional base of the right to travel.

[297] *Smith v Turner* (the Passenger Cases) 48 U.S. 283 (1849) at 492 (Taney C J, dissenting).

[298] *Edwards v California*, 314 U.S. 160 (1941) at 183 (Jackson, concurring).

[299] *Shapiro v Thompson*, 394 U.S. 618 (1969) at 629.

These glowing descriptions demonstrate that the right to travel has a 'national' as well as a personal value. This right is an important instrument of national unity that strengthens the notion of United States citizens as one people. It has played an important role in the transformation of the several States into a single Nation[300] and it now prevents 'the Balkanization of the Nation.'[301] At the same time, the right to travel is a highly valued personal right[302] that enables individuals to 'explore new horizons' and to pursue their interests in the State of their choice. The right is incidental to United States citizenship and valued as a personal liberty 'as close to the heart of the individual as the choice of what he eats, or wears, or reads.'[303]

Unlike the right to freedom of movement within the European Community, the American right to travel has never been perceived as functional or subordinate to the process of economic integration. The Constitution does aim at integration of the economies of the various States and, obviously, the right to travel serves this process by enabling persons to do business or work in other States. Economic integration, however, is only of secondary importance. The Constitution provides, above all, the legal framework for a political Union. The personal right to move freely from State to State is a product of this political Union[304] and occupies within the constitutional system 'a more protected position . . . than does the movement of cattle, fruit, steel and coal across state lines.'[305]

8.2 Beneficiaries and their Free Movement Rights

The fundamental importance attached to the right to travel is reflected in the personal scope of the right. This scope is, in principle, unlimited. All persons present within the United States enjoy the right to cross inter-state boundaries and all persons entitled to reside in the United States can choose the State in which they wish to live. By comparison with the freedom of movement within the European Community, two differences exist. First, not only United States

---

[300] *Attorney General of New York v Soto-Lopez.* 476 U.S. 898 (1986) at 902.

[301] *New York v O'Neill*, 359 U.S. 1 (1959) at 7–8.

[302] Chafee (1956) n 295 above, at 188.

[303] *Kent v Dulles*, 357 U.S. 116 (1958) at 126.

[304] Varat, 'Economic Integration and Interregional Migration in the United States Federal System' in: Tushnet (ed), *Comparative Constitutional Federalism—Europe and America* (1990) 21–66, at 31–4.

[305] *Edwards v California*, 314 U.S. 160 (1941) at 177. Illustrative of the predominantly political nature of the right to travel is the Supreme Court's decision in *Truax v Raich*. With respect to State restrictions on the employment of aliens, who as we will see also enjoy the freedom to move *within* the United States, the Court held: 'The assertion of an authority to deny to aliens the opportunity of earning a livelihood when lawfully admitted to the State would be tantamount to the assertion of the right to deny them entrance and abode, for in ordinary cases they cannot live where they cannot work'. *Truax v Raich*, 239 U.S. 33 (1915).

citizens but also foreigners enjoy the right to move and reside freely within the United States. With respect to nationals of other States, immigration powers are entrusted to the Federal authorities.[306] The latter hold the exclusive power[307] to determine which foreigners shall be admitted and for how long they are entitled to remain. States, in principle, hold no power to refuse foreigners entry to or presence on their territory. As the Supreme Court found in *Truax v. Raich* (1915), foreigners are 'admitted with the privilege of entering and abiding in the United States, and hence of entering and abiding in any state in the Union'.[308] Second, indigents enjoy the right to reside freely within the United States. As will be demonstrated in chapter 3 of this book, the difference between the European Community, where indigents do not enjoy this right, and the United States is explained by the fact that in the United States poverty is perceived as a national problem for which not only the States but also the Federal authorities hold a responsibility. States cannot isolate themselves from this shared problem[309] by closing their borders. The 'purpose of deterring the in-migration of indigents . . . is constitutionally impermissible.'[310]

At its core, the right to travel inter-State[311] consists of three rights: the right to leave a State, the right to enter another and the right to establish residence in any State.[312] At the time the Constitution was adopted, States did not attempt to hinder or restrict the exercise of these rights. Legal barriers to cross-border movement hardly existed. Over the years, however, States have, for various reasons, imposed limits on inter-state movement. The Supreme Court has always strongly resisted any attempt to hinder or restrict the exercise of the right to

---

[306] The Constitution does not explicitly confer upon Congress the power to regulate immigration. Yet, this power may be read into various provisions such as the federal power over foreign affairs (*United States v Curtiss-Wright Export Corp.*, 299 U.S. 304 (1936) at 318), the power to make a uniform rule on naturalization (Art I § 8, cl.4) or the power to regulate foreign commerce (Art I § 8, cl.3). See also: Note, 'State Burdens on Aliens: A New Preemption Analysis' (1980) *YaleLJ* 940–61, at 944–5.

[307] *Truax v Raich*, 239 U.S. 33 (1915) at 42.

[308] *Ibid*, at 52. In light of the classification of the right to travel as 'an incident of national citizenship' it is debatable whether the right to travel of foreigners is protected by the Constitution. See, eg: *Graham v Richardson*, 403 U.S. 365 (1971) at 375. There is no doubt, however, that the right is at least implicit in the federal immigration scheme. Rosberg (1982) n 295 above, at 294–5.

[309] *Edwards v California*, 314 U.S. 160 (1941) at 173. See also: ch 3, s 8.3.

[310] *Shapiro v Thompson*, 394 U.S. 618 (1969) at 630.

[311] The terms 'right to travel' and 'right to inter-state travel' will be used interchangeably in this ch. It is to be noted, however, that the notion 'right to travel' also covers the right to travel abroad and the rights to move and reside freely within the separate States. The rights to *foreign* travel and *intra*-state travel will not be discussed any further in this ch. On the right to travel abroad see Farber, National Security, 'The Right to Travel, and the Court' (1981) *SCRev* 263–90 and Laursen, 'Constitutional Protection of Foreign Travel' (1981) *ColLRev* 902–31. See also: *Kent v Dulles*, 357 U.S. 116 (1958); *Aptheker v Secretary of State*, 378 U.S. 500 (1964) and *Zemel v Rusk*, 381 U.S. 1 (1965). On the right to travel intra-state see Porter, 'Comment: A Constitutional Analysis of the Right to Travel Intra-State' (1992) *NorthwULRev* 820–57.

[312] The right to travel includes, as a right of personal liberty, also the right not to move at all. TenBroek, *The Constitution and the Right to Free Movement* (1955) 3–6.

travel. In brief, any[313] State[314] measure that hampers cross-border movement or the establishment of residence is unconstitutional unless shown to be necessary for the promotion of an overriding or compelling State interest.[315] The number of cases in which a State can demonstrate such a compelling State interest is limited. A State cannot close its borders in order to protect the employment opportunities of its residents, to limit the number of users of its public roads, to 'keep aliens out' or, as said, earlier on, to prevent indigents from moving to the State for the sole purpose of obtaining welfare benefits. Probably the only circumstances in which States are permitted to stop cross-border movement concern suspects or convicts of a crime. Such persons may be detained[316] and simply cannot 'claim freedom to migrate.'[317] An exception to freedom of movement similar to the public policy proviso under European Community law does not exist under American constitutional law.[318] The right to establish residency is granted unconditionally. The motive for establishing residence in a State is

[313] Even the smallest burdens on the rights are prohibited. Illustrative is the nineteenth century decision in *Crandall v Nevada*. The Court invalidated a State tax of 1 dollar on every person leaving the State. Obviously, the amount of the tax was too small to prevent anyone from actually leaving the State, but the Court reasoned that if 'the State can tax a ... passenger one dollar, it can tax him thousand dollars. If one State can do this, so can every other State. And thus one or more States . . . may totally prevent or seriously burden all transportation of passengers from part of the country to another'. *Crandall v Nevada*, 73 U.S. 35 (1867) at 39. *Crandall* does not necessarily imply that States can never charge inter-state travellers. A burden on the exercise of the right to travel must be present. In *Evansville*, for instance, the Court upheld a charge by a State of 1 dollar per airline passenger to help defray the costs of airport construction and maintenance. The Court denied that the charge burdened the right to travel. The facilities which were provided and paid from charges facilitated rather than hindered the right to travel. *Evansville-Vanderburgh Airport Authority District v Delta Airlines*, 405 U.S. 707 (1972).

[314] The Federal government and private persons are equally prohibited to hinder or restrict the exercise of the right to travel. In *United States v Guest*, which concerned the prosecution of persons who had attacked African-Americans and civil rights workers in order to deprive them of a number of constitutional rights including the right of inter-state travel, the Court held: 'the constitutional right to travel is a right secured against interference from any source whatever, whether governmental or private'. *United States v Guest*, 383 U.S. 745 (1966) at 759 (n 17). The Supreme Court has never been asked whether the Federal government would be entitled to impose limits upon the right to inter-state travel. In the doctrine it is generally assumed, however, that the Federal Government (Congress) does not hold such a power. The right to travel is 'too fundamental' to be limited by any government. Varat (1990) n 305 above, at 46. See also: Rosberg (1982) n 295 above, at 302–3.

[315] Thomson, 'The Right to Travel—Its Protection and Application Under the Constitution' (1971–1972) *UMKCLRev* 66–96, at 95.

[316] *Jones v Helms*, 452 U.S. 412 (1981) at 419.

[317] *Edwards v California*, 314 U.S. 160 (1941) at 184 (Jackson, concurring). States are even under an obligation to send back fugitives from justice to the State where they are charged with a crime. Art IV, S 2 of the Constitution. See also: *Puerto Rico v Branstad*, 483 U.S. 219 (1987).

[318] States do not have the power to refuse entry to or deport persons whom it considers to be a threat to the public order or who are considered to be *persona non grata*. Like poverty, criminality is a national problem from which States cannot isolate themselves by closing their borders. Rosberg (1982) n 295 above, at 291. States may restrict freedom of movement by using their powers under criminal procedural law, but they may not use their 'immigration powers' in order to combat crime. As regards the extent to which states can close their borders for the purposes of protecting public health, the situation is less clear. States still seem to have the possibility of excluding persons suffering from contagious diseases albeit only in very exceptional situations. Rosberg (1982) n 295 above, at 291–4.

irrelevant[319] and individuals do not, as in the European Community, have to prove that they have found employment or possess sufficient financial means to provide for themselves and their family.

8.3 Concept of State Citizenship

The right to take up residence in the State of one's choice, has one important consequence as far as United States citizens are concerned. The Citizenship Clause of the Fourteenth Amendment states that 'all persons born or naturalised in the United States, and subject to the jurisdiction thereof, are citizens of the State wherein they reside.' The right of United States citizens to choose the State in which they wish to live implies the right to choose which State they wish to be a citizen of. Residence and State citizenship coincide.[320] From the moment United States citizens establish residence in a State they automatically become citizens of that State. States do not have the power to determine who its citizens are; they not only lack immigration powers but also 'naturalisation' powers. The Supreme Court, however, has never indicated what is entailed in establishing residence in, and thus acquiring citizenship of, a State. Generally, residence requires physical presence in a State *plus* the intention to remain there for a certain period of time. The Court has admitted though that 'residence' may have different meanings in different contexts.[321] An intention to make a State a permanent home is not necessary, but on occasions the Court has, quite confusingly, also required the absence of a present intention to leave the State. In other cases, State citizenship is to be equated with domicile which is the State with which persons are most closely connected. Persons can have several residences but only one domicile. The difference between residence and domicile is, however, far from clear and in practice often difficult to determine.[322]

8.4 Right to Equal Treatment: Judicial Review under the Equal Protection Clause

The 'virtually unqualified'[323] rights to move and reside freely across inter-State boundaries would have little practical significance if the beneficiaries did not

---

[319] A person can freely choose to live in another State. It 'is immaterial what motives led the person to go there. It makes no difference whether these motives were good or bad or, more specifically, whether the move to the new location was for the purposes of health, to accept a job, to avoid taxation, to secure a divorce, to bring suit in the federal courts or even to facilitate a life of sin or crime'. *Martinez v Bynum*, 461 U.S. 321 (1982) n 10 at 343 (Marshall J, dissenting).

[320] It is 'a privilege of citizenship of the United States . . . to enter any state of the Union . . . for gaining resultant citizenship thereof . . . State citizenship is ephemeral. It results only from residence and is gained or lost therewith'. *Edwards v California*, 314 U.S. 160 (1941) at 183.

[321] *Martinez v Bynum*, 461 U.S. 321 (1982) at 330.

[322] On the concepts of residence and domicile see Reese and Green, 'That Elusive Word, "Residence"' (1953) *VdbiltLRev* 561 *et seq*.

[323] *Califano v Torres*, 435 U.S. 1 (1978) at 4 (n 6).

enjoy constitutional protection on arrival in another State. If the States were free to treat persons coming from other States any way they liked, they could, in theory, deny those persons so many rights that not one of them would consider crossing inter-State borders. Several constitutional provisions protect beneficiaries of the right to travel against discriminatory treatment in, and by, other States. The most relevant are the Equal Protection Clause of the Fourteenth Amendment, the Privileges and Immunities Clause of Article IV § 2 of the Constitution and the Commerce Clause of Article I § 8. The first of the three clauses offers persons who have established residence in another State (residents), people who merely visit other States (non-residents or visitors) and aliens (or foreigners) protection against discriminatory treatment. The latter two clauses are designed to protect non-residents from discriminatory treatment. Before the degree of equal protection offered by the clauses to the beneficiaries of the right to travel is explored, some introductory remarks are made about the Equal Protection Clause. Discrimination against the beneficiaries of the right to travel is only one form of discrimination prohibited by the Clause and the main principles governing the equal protection of the laws have been developed in areas other than those related to the right to travel.

The Equal Protection Clause states that no State shall 'deny to any person within its jurisdiction the equal protection of the laws.'[324] Although originally merely intended to combat racial discrimination, the Clause nowadays applies to any State[325] measure which distributes benefits unequally to different classes of persons.[326] The Clause demands that persons similarly situated must be treated similarly unless there is serious justification or 'need' for dissimilar treatment. Equal protection analysis usually[327] centres around the question whether

---

[324] The literature on the Equal Protection Clause is extensive. See, eg: Klarman, 'An Interpretive History of the Modern Equal Protection' (1991) *MichLRev* 213–316; Perry, 'Modern Equal Protection: A Conceptualization and Appraisal' (1979) *ColLRev* 1023–84; Karst, 'The Supreme Court 1976 Term—Foreword: Equal Citizenship under the Fourteenth Amendment (1977)' (1977) *HarvLRev* 1 *et seq*; Gunther, 'The Supreme Court 1971 Term—Foreword: In Search of Evolving Doctrine on a Changing Court: A Model for a Newer Equal Protection' (1972) *HarvLRev* 1–48 and Tusman and ten Broek, T'he Equal Protection of the Laws' (1949) *CalLRev* 341–81. See also the various handbooks on Constitutional Law such as Rotunda and Nowak, *Treatise on Constitutional Law* (1992) ch 18; Tribe, *American Constitutional Law* (1988) ch 16; Stone *et al*, *Constitutional Law* (1986) ch 5 and Gunther, *Constitutional Law* (1985) ch 9.

[325] The Clause does not apply to the Federal government. However, the Due Process Clause of the Fifth Amendment—'No person shall be deprived of life, liberty, or property without due process of law'—prohibits the Federal Government from denying any persons equal protection of the laws. *Bolling v Sharpe*, 347 U.S. 497 (1954).

[326] 'When a State distributes benefits unequally, the distinction it makes are subject to scrutiny under the Equal Protection Clause of the Fourteenth Amendment'. *Zobel v Williams*, 457 U.S. 55 (1982) at 60.

[327] Strictly speaking, the justification question must be preceded by the question whether or not persons are similarly situated. Persons do not have to be similar or similarly situated in all respects. Similarity must be determined with respect to the purpose of the law. Tusman and tenBroek (1949) n 324 above, at 346. In most cases, however, courts do not explicitly establish the similarity of cases. Usually, and certainly in cases concerning discrimination against the beneficiaries of the right to travel, courts turn directly to the question whether a differential treatment of presumably similar cases can be justified.

the unequal treatment of equal cases can be justified. Courts apply a 'means-end analysis.' They first establish the purpose a State seeks to achieve and, assuming this purpose is legitimate, they then explore how closely the classification applied or the distinction made is related to this purpose.[328] How close this link between means and end must be, and more in general, whether a classification can be justified largely depends on the standard of review to be applied. The Supreme Court has formally adopted three standards of review. Each of these requires a different degree of correlation between means and end, and each reflects a different role of the judiciary *vis à vis* the State legislatures.[329] The selection of one of the standards of review is often decisive for the ultimate decision in a given case.

The first standard involves the 'rational relation test.' A classification will be upheld when it is 'rationally related to furthering a legitimate government interest'[330] or when 'it is conceivable that the classification bears a rational relationship to an end of government that is not prohibited by the Constitution.'[331] In applying this test court show considerable deference toward State legislatures.[332] Laws are presumed to be lawful, classifications will only be invalidated when they are patently arbitrary. For persons challenging a classification it is almost impossible to prove unconstitutionality. Rational relation must be applied to all State classifications and is an expression of the broader principle that States, whenever they act or classify, must obey the minimum requirement of non-arbitrariness.[333]

For a long period of time rational relation was the only test the Court applied. From the 1950s, however, the Supreme Court has heightened the level of scrutiny of certain classifications. Most important, the Court has developed

---

[328] In determining how 'closely' a classification is related to the State purpose, courts do not require a classification to be perfect, ie, when a classification treats all similarly situated persons alike and all persons not similarly situated unalike. A 'classification having some reasonable basis does not offend equal protection merely because it is not made with mathematical nicety or because in practice it results in some inequality'. *Lindsey v Natural Carbonic Gas Co*, 220 U.S. 61 (1911). Perfect classifications hardly exist; classifications are usually over inclusive and/or under inclusive. Classifications are over-inclusive when they do not only burden or benefit similarly situated persons but also persons not so situated. They are under-inclusive when they burden or benefit only part of the similarly situated persons. For a further explanation of these terms see Rotunda and Nowak (1992) n 324 above, at 9–12.

[329] In reviewing a certain classification the strength or the importance of the legislative purpose is also to be weighed. Burnham, *Introduction to the Law and Legal System of the United States* (1995) 339 *et seq*.

[330] *Massachusetts Board of Retirement v Murgia*, 427 U.S. 307 (1976).

[331] Rotunda and Nowak (1992) n 324 above, at 14.

[332] The reason for this deference is that 'the Constitution presumes that . . . even improvident decisions will eventually be rectified by the political process and that judicial intervention is generally unwarranted no matter how unwisely we may think a political branch has acted'. *Vance v Bradley*, 440 U.S. 93 (1978).

[333] As lax as the rational relation test may, it must be noted that the legislative purpose must be legitimate. See, eg: *Metropolitan Life Insurance Co. v Ward*, 470 U.S. 869 (1985) where the Supreme Court held that States may not enact laws which are solely aimed at protecting local businesses from out-of-state competition.

the so-called 'compelling State interest test.' This test is in fact the opposite of the rational relation test. Courts do not presume the constitutionality but rather the unconstitutionality of a classification. 'Strict scrutiny' is applied. Courts do not explore whether there is 'some permissible State purpose' but require States to show that the classification serves a 'compelling' or 'overriding' end. In addition, courts require that the classification is 'precisely tailored to serve'[334] or 'necessary to promote'[335] that compelling State interest. The State must demonstrate that there are no less 'drastic means'[336] available to accomplish the State purpose. The burden of proof is on the State under challenge. A State may have to submit statistical data, studies, etc. in order to defeat a challenge, but this is usually an insurmountable task. As a rule, strict scrutiny leads to the invalidation of a classification.

The compelling State interest test is applied in only two situations. The first concerns 'suspect classifications' such as race, ethnic origin and nationality. In applying strict scrutiny courts offer members of a 'suspect class' extra judicial protection. It concerns persons belonging to a 'discrete and insular' minority who are incapable of protecting interests through the usual political process and who are often subject to pervasive discriminatory treatment.[337] Suspect classifications are those which are thought to be irrelevant in a democratic society. The focus of the inquiry is on the nature of the classification, not on the nature of the benefits or rights denied by the classification. Thus, whenever a State uses a suspect classification strict scrutiny is applied regardless of the benefit denied or the burden imposed by this classification.[338] Strict scrutiny has further been applied to classifications which affect a fundamental interest or the exercise of a 'fundamental right' such as the rights to freedom of speech, to a fair trial, to marriage and family life, to vote, access to justice and, as shown later on, the right to travel. Here, the focus is not so much on the classification itself, but rather on its effect, ie, on the right the classifications impinge upon.[339] The Court has limited the category of fundamental rights for the purposes of equal protection analysis to rights that are explicitly or implicitly guaranteed by the Constitution.[340]

The third standard of review, the so-called 'intermediate test,' is as the 'name' already suggests, to be situated anywhere between rational relation and strict scrutiny review. The test implies that any classification which does not have a

---

[334]   *Plyler v Doe*, 457 U.S. 202 (1982) at 217.

[335]   *Shapiro v Thompson*, 394 U.S. 618 (1969) at 634.

[336]   *Dunn v Blumstein*, 405 U.S. 330 (1972) at 343.

[337]   The classic statement is the one of Justice Stone in footnote four in *United States v Carolene Products Co.*, 304 U.S. 144 (1938): 'Prejudice against discrete and insular minorities may be a special condition, which tends seriously to curtail the operation of those political processes ordinarily to be relied upon to protect minorities, and may call for a more searching judicial scrutiny'.

[338]   Wildenthal, 'State Parochialism, the Right to Travel, and the Privileges and Immunities Clause of Article IV' (1989) *StanfLRev* 1557–95, at 1572.

[339]   Perry (1979) n 324 above at 1077.

[340]   *San Antonio Indep. School Dist. v Rodriguez*, 411 U.S. 1 (1973) at 33–4.

'substantial' relationship to an 'important' public interest violates the Equal Protection Clause.[341] The intermediate test is more flexible than the other two. In applying the intermediate test courts presume a classification to be unconstitutional, but they leave more room for States to defeat a challenge. The outcome of the intermediate standard of review is less predictable and the test leaves much more room for a balancing of the constitutional value of equality of treatment against the State interests classifications serve.

The test emerged against the background of the equal protection model as it existed in the late 1960s, early 1970s. Only two 'equal protection tests' existed at the time: rational relation and strict scrutiny. This 'two-tiered' model was very rigid. Virtually all classifications could pass the first test, almost none the second. This 'all or nothing' model was severely criticised. It was not only argued that in reality the Court had not applied this two-tiered model strictly[342] but also that it should not do so. From classifications such as gender it was thought that the need for strict scrutiny was not as great as race, but that more careful review than mere rationality was appropriate. Similarly, with respect to important interests such as welfare and education, it was claimed that, if they did not qualify for strict scrutiny, they would merit at least a more meaningful form of judicial review than the 'mere rationality test.'[343] The most prominent critic within the Supreme Court, Justice Marshall, argued that the Court should adopt an approach in which due regard should be given to 'the character of the classification in question, the relative importance to individuals . . . of the governmental benefits that they do not receive, and the asserted state interests in support of the classification.'[344] The Court has never adopted such a 'sliding scale,' but the formal adoption of the intermediate test in a number of cases suggests that the criticism of people like Marshall has had at least some effect.[345]

---

[341] *Mills v Babluetzel*, 456 U.S. 91 (1982) at 99.

[342] In *Rodriguez* Marshall J wrote: 'The Court apparently seeks to establish . . . that equal protection cases fall into one of two neat categories which dictate the appropriate standard of review—strict scrutiny and rational relation. But this Court's decisions in the field of equal protection defy such an easy categorization. A principled reading of what this Court has done reveals that it has applied a spectrum of standards in reviewing discrimination allegedly violative of the Equal Protection Clause. This spectrum clearly comprehends variations in the degree of care with which the Court will scrutinize particular classifications, depending I believe, on the constitutional and societal importance of the interest adversely affected and the recognized invidiousness of the basis upon which the particular classification is drawn'. *San Antonio Indep School Dist. v Rodriguez*, 411 U.S. 1 (1973) at 98–9 (Marshall J, dissenting). See also: *Dandridge v Williams*, 397 U.S. 471 (1970) at 520–1 (Marshall J, dissenting).

[343] *Dandridge v Williams*, 397 U.S. 471 (1970) at 520–1 (Marshall, J, dissenting).

[344] *Ibid*, at 520–1 (Marshall J, dissenting) and *Martinez v Bynum*, 461 U.S. 321 (1982) at 345 (Marshall J, dissenting).

[345] In addition, the Court has not always applied the rational relation and strict scrutiny tests in the way described above. In some cases the Court has applied the rational relation test with some 'more bite'. See, eg: *Romer v Evans* (1996) in which the Supreme Court struck down an amendment to the Colorado Constitution that would have prohibited public action aimed at protecting homosexuals from discriminatory treatment under the rational relation test. *Romer v Evans*, 116 SCt 1620 (1996). On this decision see, eg: Jackson, 'Persons of Equal Worth: Romer v Evans and the Politics of Equal Protection' (1997) *UCLALRev* 453–501. Further, the decision in *Adarand Constructors,*

The importance of the intermediate level of scrutiny is still rather limited though. So far, the Court has only applied this standard to 'quasi-suspect' classifications of gender and illegitimacy.[346]

Notwithstanding the rise of the intermediate test, rational relation and strict scrutiny are up until today the most important standards of review. In practice, rational relation is applied in cases concerning 'economics and welfare,' strict scrutiny only when a fundamental right is impeded or a suspect classification is applied. The discussion below will explore how this general equal protection model must be applied to discriminations against individuals who have exercised the right to travel. In principle, the discussion is limited to the question which of the available equal protection tests must be applied. The question whether or not State discriminations can actually be justified will not be addressed here but only in the chapters on minimum subsistence benefits, health care and education. It may be recalled, however, that the choice for a certain test will often be decisive for the ultimate decision: the compelling State interest test generally results in the unconstitutionality of a classification, whilst most classifications can be upheld under the rational relation test. The intermediate test presumes but does not always lead to the unconstitutionality of a classification.

8.5 Residents

As a rule, United States citizens who have established residence in another State will not need a constitutional right to be treated equally with the citizens of that State. According to the first sentence of the Fourteenth Amendment, they are State citizens themselves and, in this capacity, they will usually be entitled to the full panoply of rights and benefits the State accords to its citizens.[347] States, however, do not always treat residents as citizens from the moment they arrive in the State. The enjoyment of many rights or benefits such as welfare, voting and admission to the bar is often made conditional upon the fulfilment of durational residence requirements. These imply that persons must have resided in

Inc v Pena (1995) suggests that the Court may be willing to apply the strict scrutiny test more flexibly. In *Adarand* (515 U.S. 200 (1995)) the Court applied strict scrutiny to a federal programme that encouraged State and local governments to award construction contracts to minority firms, even if non-minority firms had submitted lower bids. The Court dispelled the notion that strict scrutiny is 'strict in theory, but fatal in fact' and this may portend some sort of 'kinder and gentler strict scrutiny'. Rutten, 'Elasticity in Constitutional Review: *Adarand Constructors, Inc. v Pena* and Continuing Uncertainty in the Supreme Court's Equal Protection Jurisprudence' (1997) *SouthCalLRev* 591–642.

[346] Rotunda and Nowak (1992) n 324 above, at 17. See, eg: *Reed v Reed*, 404 U.S. 71 (1971); *Craig v Boden*, 428 U.S. 190 (1976); *Orr v Orr* 440 U.S. 268 (1979) and *Mississipi University for Women v Hogan*, 458 U.S. 718 (1982). On gender discrimination see also: Loenen, *Verschil in Gelijkheid—De Conceptualisering van het Juridische Gelijkheidsbeginsel met Betrekking tot Mannen en Vrouwen in Nederland en de Verenigde Staten* (1992).

[347] 'A citizen of the United States has a perfect constitutional right to go to and reside in any State he chooses, and to claim citizenship therein, and an equality of rights with every other citizen'. *Slaughter-House Cases*, 16 Wall 36 (1873) at 80.

the State for a minimum period of time before they become eligible for certain rights or benefits. The requirements introduce a waiting-period during which 'new,' recently arrived, residents are either denied benefits/rights or have to fulfil conditions of eligibility which 'old,' long-term, residents do not have to meet. Until the expiration of the waiting-period, new citizens are still treated as 'non-citizens,' as outsiders. Waiting-period requirements are discriminatory in nature and at odds with the Fourteenth Amendment's definition of State citizenship. Yet, discrimination against newcomers is not unconstitutional for these reasons alone. Waiting-period requirements may serve legitimate and important State interests.[348]

8.5.1 *Shapiro v Thompson*

Up until the late 1960s, durational residence requirements did not raise serious constitutional objections. Courts merely employed minimal scrutiny and upheld the requirements as being rationally related to the State interests they claimed to serve. In 1969, however, the Supreme Court abandoned much of its traditional deference *vis à vis* durational residence requirements. In *Shapiro v Thompson*[349] the Court invalidated one-year waiting-periods for welfare benefits under the compelling State interest test. The Court held that no longer rational relation but strict scrutiny was to be applied, because in

> 'moving from State to State . . . appellees were exercising a constitutional right, and any classification which serves to penalize the exercise of that right, unless shown to be necessary to promote a compelling governmental interest, is unconstitutional.'[350]

The fundamental right that triggered the compelling State interest test was the right to travel, not a 'right to welfare.' Since any durational residence requirement leads to the denial of a right or benefit for a certain period of time, it seemed that any durational residence requirement would, as a penalty on the right to travel, be subject to strict scrutiny and thus probably be unconstitutional. However, in 'footnote 21' the Court carefully avoided such a far-reaching conclusion:

> 'We imply no view on the validity of waiting period or residence requirements determining eligibility to vote, eligibility for tuition free education, to obtain a license to practice a profession, to hunt or fish, and so forth. Such requirements may promote

---

[348] For instance, durational residence requirements for the right to vote in State elections are said to serve the 'purity of the ballot box'. They are aimed at preventing non-residents from temporarily invading the State, falsely swearing that they are residents eligible to vote and voting for a candidate in the elections who could win by fraud. *Dunn v Blumstein*, 405 U.S. 330 (1972) at 345. In the field of welfare, waiting-periods are intended to discourage indigents from coming to the State in order to collect higher welfare benefits. In the absence of waiting-periods, States would, as they have always claimed, be subjected to substantial additional financial burdens.

[349] *Shapiro v Thompson*, 394 U.S. 618 (1969). See for a detailed analysis of the decision ch 3, s 8.4.

[350] *Shapiro v Thompson*, 394 U.S. 618 (1969) at 634.

compelling state interests on the one hand, or, on the other, may not be penalties upon the exercise of the constitutional right of interstate travel.'[351]

Shapiro, and in particular footnote 21, puzzled many scholars.[352] All durational residence requirements penalise the right to travel in that they all have negative consequences for persons who have recently moved to another State. Yet, the Court listed several requirements that did not constitute 'penalties' on the right to travel which trigger strict scrutiny. What then was to be understood by the term 'penalty' on the exercise of the right to travel? In particular, what durational residence requirements did not constitute 'penalties' for the purposes of equal protection analysis?

One possible explanation could have been that *Shapiro*'s penalty concept had to be read as an obstacle to the right to travel in the sense that only discrimination against newcomers which actually prevents or deters individuals from moving to other States would be covered by the concept.[353] The Court, however, has rejected this 'burden-explanation.' In *Dunn v Blumstein*[354] (1972) the Court held that the argument that durational residence requirements for the right to vote and to stand as a candidate in local elections would not constitute a penalty on the exercise of the right to travel because such requirements would not abridge that right in any constitutionally relevant sense, was a 'fundamental misunderstanding of the law.' Neither *Shapiro* nor any other 'right-to-travel case' relied on the presence of an actual deterrence; the unconstitutionality of durational residence requirements derived from the fact that they deny persons certain benefits or rights on the ground that they have exercised the fundamen-

---

[351] *Shapiro v Thompson*, n 21.

[352] For comments on *Shapiro* see, eg: Note, '*Shapiro v Thompson*: Travel, Welfare and the Constitution' (1969) *NYULRev* 989–1013; Schechner, 'Constitutional Law—Equal Protection— *Shapiro v Thompson*, 394 U.S. 618 (1969)' (1969) *SuffULRev* 572–85; Hammerstrom, 'Constitutional Law—Equal Protection—Residency Requirements' (1970) *CaseWLRev* (pp unknown); Anderson and Lutes, 'The Demise of the Durational Residence Requirement' (1972) *SouthwLJ* 538–68; Note, *The Right to Travel—Quest for a Constitutional Source* (1974) 122–43; Note, 'Durational Residence Requirements From Shapiro *Through* Sosna: The Right to Travel Takes a New Turn' (1975) *NYULRev* 622–80 and McCoy, 'Recent Equal Protection Decisions— Fundamental Right to Travel or 'Newcomers' as a Suspect Class' (1975) *VdbiltLRev* 987–1023. Even Justices of the Supreme Court were confused. In *Shapiro* the dissenting Warren C J warned that 'the Court's decision reveals only the top of the iceberg. Lurking beneath are the multitude of situations in which States have imposed residence requirements including eligibility to vote, to engage in certain professions or occupations or to attend a state-supported university. Although the Court takes pains to avoid acknowledging the ramifications of its decision, its implications cannot be ignored.' *Shapiro v Thompson*, 394 U.S. 618 (1969) at 655 (Warren C J, dissenting).

[353] To be sure, it was beyond doubt that the Court had not intended to say that non-discriminatory State measures which burden the exercise of the right to travel were or might also be prohibited. Such a reading, which would resemble the case law of the Court of Justice on the prohibition of non-discriminatory obstacles to freedom of movement (s 7.4), would clearly reach too far. Rosberg (1982) n 295 above at 306–9 and McCoy (1975) n 352 above, 1025. In *Shapiro* the Court had indicated that the 'problem' created by durational residence requirements was essentially a problem of equal protection. *Shapiro v Thompson*, 394 U.S. 618 (1969) at 627.

[354] *Dunn v Blumstein*, 405 U.S. 330 (1972).

tal right to travel.[355] Thus, the Court's main concern with waiting-period requirements was not that they hinder or burden the exercise of the right to travel, but rather that such requirements constitute, by their very nature, a discrimination against 'newcomers.'[356] The requirements divide the group of State citizens in two categories: 'new' citizens and 'long-term' citizens. Up until the expiration of the waiting-period, the former are still treated as non-citizens, as outsiders. Waiting-periods requirements conflict with the Citizenship Clause of the Fourteenth Amendment and that Clause does not 'provide for, and does not allow, degrees of citizenship based on length of residence'.[357]

Yet, all waiting-periods create, by definition, different classes of State citizens based on the length of residence. This equal-citizenship-interpretation of *Shapiro* would seem to imply, that all durational residence requirements were subject to strict scrutiny and thus, probably, unconstitutional. The Court however wished to leave room for some waiting-periods. It sought the solution for *Shapiro*'s footnote 21 in the importance or the nature of the rights or benefits denied by durational residence requirements. Two years after *Dunn*, in *Memorial Hospital v Maricopa County*[358] (1974), the Court was asked to rule upon the constitutionality of a one-year residence requirement for free non-emergency medical care for indigents. The Court classed the waiting-periods as a 'penalty.' Whatever

> 'the ultimate parameters of the Shapiro penalty analysis (. . .), it is at least clear that medical care is as much 'a basic necessity of life' to an indigent as welfare assistance' . . . And, governmental privileges or benefits necessary to basic sustenance have often been viewed as being of greater constitutional significance than less essential forms of governmental entitlements.'[359]

The right to interstate travel, the Court said, 'must be seen as insuring new residents the same vital government benefits and privileges in the States to which

---

[355] In subsequent case law the Court has confirmed that *Shapiro*'s penalty concept is not to be read as a burden on the right to travel. Ten years after *Dunn*, in *Zobel v Williams* (1982), it held that 'the right to travel, when applied to residence requirements, protects new residents of a state from being disadvantaged because of their recent migration or from otherwise being treated differently from longer term residents'. *Zobel v Williams*, 457 U.S. 55 (1982) n 6. On *Zobel* see also: Kalen, 'Durational Residency Requirements and the Equal Protection Clause: *Zobel v Williams*' (1983) *JUrbContL* 329–59 and Cohen, 'Equal Treatment for Newcomers: The Core Meaning of National and State Citizenship' (1984) *ConstComm* 9–19. See also: *Attorney General of New York v Soto-Lopez*, 476 U.S. 898 (1986) where the Court held that the right to travel 'protects residents of a State from being disadvantaged, or from being treated differently, simply because of the timing of their migration, from other similarly situated residents' (at 904) and *Memorial Hospital v Maricopa County*, 415 U.S. 250 (1974) in which the Court stated that *Shapiro* did 'not rest upon a finding that denial of welfare actually deterred travel' (at 258–9).

[356] McCoy (1975) n 352 above, at 1010.

[357] *Zobel v Williams*, 457 U.S. 55 (1982) at 69 (Brennan J, concurring). Rosberg (1982) n 295 above, at 309 and 311; Garth (1986) n 7 above, at 109; Cohen (1984) n 355 above, at 17 and Brennan J in *Zobel v Williams*, 457 U.S. 55 (1982) at 69–70 (Brennan J, concurring).

[358] *Memorial Hospital v Maricopa County*, 415 U.S. 250 (1974). See further on *Memorial Hospital* ch 5, s 5.2.

[359] *Ibid*, at 259.

they migrate as are enjoyed by other residents.'[360] In a footnote the Court suggested that tuition waiting-period requirements did not constitute 'penalties' on the right to travel because these would not involve the 'immediate and pressing need for preservation of life and health.'[361] *Maricopa County* thus implied that only durational residence requirements which lead to the denial of a 'basic necessity of life' or 'vital governmental benefit' would constitute a 'penalty' on the exercise of the right to travel.[362]

8.5.2 Saenz v Roe

Maricopa County, however, did not end the debates on, and the controversy surrounding, *Shapiro*'s penalty on the right to travel analysis. The Supreme Court had never explained why the meaning of the term 'penalty' would have to depend on the 'importance' of the right/benefit withheld[363] and it had failed to give sufficiently clear criteria for determining the significance of the right or benefit.[364] Moreover, the Court itself did not apply penalty-analysis consist-

---

[360] *Memorial Hospital v Maricopa County*, at 261.

[361] *Ibid*, at 260 (n 15).

[362] In later rulings the Court confirmed *Maricopa*'s 'solution' for *Shapiro* (see, eg: *Zobel v Williams*, 457 U.S. 55 (1982) at 64 (n 11) and *Attorney General of New York v Eduardo Soto-Lopez*, 476 U.S. 898 (1986) at 907–9)), even though the Court relaxed *Maricopa* somewhat. Poppe, 'Defining the Scope of the Equal Protection Clause with Respect to Welfare Waiting Periods' (1994) ChicLRev 291–323, at 298. In *Soto-Lopez* the Court held that a provision of the New York Constitution which granted a civil service employment preference only to those veterans who were residents of New York on the moment they entered the military service, 'penalized' the right to travel. The Court found that even though the civil employment preference 'may not rise to the same level of importance as the necessities of life and the right to vote, it is unquestionably substantial'. *Attorney General of New York v Eduardo Soto-Lopez*, 476 U.S. 898 (1986) at 908. A 'penalty' on the right to travel did not have to deprive new residents of 'basic necessities of life' in order to constitute a 'penalty'. The deprivation of a 'very important' or 'significant' right or benefit would suffice.

[363] Indeed, the Court has never given a theoretically sound explanation as to why the importance of the right/benefits would have to be decisive. The Court had held that penalty-analysis falls under the fundamental rights branch of the equal protection model and the Court had chosen the right to travel as the fundamental right which may trigger the compelling State interest test. It was not understandable, however, why the presence of a penalty on the right to travel depended not on the degree to which travel is actually deterred but rather on the importance or nature of the right/benefit denied during the waiting-period. Furthermore, the true problem of waiting-periods is that they imply, by their very nature, discrimination against newcomers. The problem lies in the requirements themselves and one could therefore have concluded that in *Shapiro* the Court intuitively established newcomers as a suspect class for equal protection purposes. McCoy (1975) n 352 above, at 1010. Suspect classifications are, however, as noted in s 8.4, subject to strict scrutiny regardless of the benefit or right denied. In *Maricopa* and *Soto-Lopez*, however, the Court did make the application of strict scrutiny dependent upon the right/benefit denied and the judgments thus made clear that waiting-periods requirements were not treated as suspect classifications. In sum, penalty-analysis fitted poorly into the classic equal protection model. It seemed to fall somewhere in between the fundamental rights branch and the suspect classification branch of this model.

[364] The Court seemed to determine the meant significance on an ad hoc basis. It was virtually impossible to distil any criteria from the case law. The Court had held that welfare, medical care and civil employment were 'vital benefits', but it had also refused to class the right to file for a divorce (*Sosna v Iowa*, 419 U.S. 393 (1975)) and education as 'vital'. Why was civil employment any more 'vital' than the right to file for a divorce or education? Why were waiting-periods for civil employment subject to strict scrutiny and tuition waiting-periods merely to rational relation?

ently.[365] In brief, the Court was accused of not having given sufficient guidance as to when a particular standard of review was to be applied. 'Penalty-on-the-right-to-travel-analysis' was classed as a 'failure' and the Court was called upon to develop an alternative framework for reviewing waiting-period require-ments. The suggested alternatives all had in common that the Court should abandon the classic equal protection model and rely much more on an inter-mediate level of scrutiny which would enable courts to weigh the States' inter-ests in discriminating against newcomers against the principle of equality of treatment.[366]

Quite recently, the Court has indeed moved away from *Shapiro*'s penalty analysis in *Saenz v Roe* (1999). As in *Shapiro* the Court was asked to rule upon the constitutionality of one-year residence requirements for welfare benefits. The debates about the appropriate standard of review to be applied to waiting periods requirements (for welfare benefits)[367] persuaded the Court to focus on the source of the constitutional right to travel. The Court distinguished three different components of the right to travel: the right to leave and enter States, the right to equal treatment in States which beneficiaries visit and, for those who elect to become permanent residents of a State, a right to be treated like other

---

[365] Consider *Sosna v Iowa*, 419 U.S. 393 (1975). The Court was asked to rule upon the constitu-tionality of a one-year residency requirement for the right to file for a divorce. In selecting the stan-dard of review it would, in the light of *Maricopa County*, have been most logical if the Court had asked itself whether the right to divorce constituted a 'basic necessity of life'. The Court, however, did not apply penalty-analysis at all. It did not even indicate which equal protection test it applied. The Court merely asked itself whether Iowa's waiting-period requirement may 'reasonably be justified'. The Court, in employing what dissenting Justice Marshall called an 'ad hoc balancing test', answered the question in the affirmative: 'a State such as Iowa may quite reasonably decide that it does not wish to become a divorce mill for unhappy spouses'. *Sosna v Iowa*, 419 U.S. 393 (1975) at 407. Even though it is difficult to establish the Court's real motives, it seemed that the Court simply did not want to apply penalty-analysis because this would inescapably have lead to the conclusion that the waiting-period for the right to divorce would constitute a 'penalty'. The right to marriage has been recognised as a fundamental right and it may therefore have been somewhat 'awkward' to argue that the right to dissolve a marriage would not be significant enough for the waiting-period to be classed as a penalty. In *Sosna* the Court argued that the durational residence requirement at issue in *Sosna* merely delayed her access to courts. Unlike the requirements chal-lenged in *Shapiro* and *Memorial Hospital*, the *Sosna*-requirement did not prevent applicants from obtaining the benefit they claimed. This 'mere delay' argument was not convincing. *Sosna v Iowa*, 419 U.S. 393 (1975) at 421–2 (Marshall J, dissenting) and Note (1975) n 352 above, at 664–5. *Sosna* suggested that the Court preserved for itself the opportunity not to apply penalty analysis where this analysis does not enable a presumably desired conclusion to be reached.

[366] This result could for example have been reached by applying a balancing act similar to the one applied by the Court in *Sosna* (see previous footnote), by treating some waiting-periods require-ments as 'quasi suspect' classifications (see in particular Poppe (1994) n 362 above, at 303–14), by reviewing discriminations against new citizens under the Privileges and Immunities Clause of Art IV § 2 of the Constitution (*Zobel v Williams*, 457 U.S. 55 (1982) at 73–81 (O'Connor J, concurring), the Commerce Clause, the Citizenship Clause of the Fourteenth Amendment (Cohen, 'Discrimination Against New State Citizens: An Update' (1994) *ConstComm* 73 *et seq*) or the Privileges or Immunities of the Fourteenth Amendment. See also: Zubler, 'The Right to Migrate and Welfare Reform: Time for *Shapiro v Thompson* to Take a Hike' (1997) *ValpULRev* 893–950; Poppe (1994) n 362 above, at 293–303; Katz, 'More Equal Than Others, The Burger Court and the Newly Arrived State Resident' (1989) *NewMexLRev* 329–76 and Wildenthal (1989) n 338 above.

[367] See also: ch 3, s 8.4.

citizens of that State.[368] At issue in *Saenz* was this third aspect of the right to travel, which involved 'the right of the newly arrived citizen to the same privileges and immunities enjoyed by other citizens of the same State.'[369] The Court held that that right is protected not only by the new arrivals' status as a State citizen, but also by their status as citizens of the United States. The Court quoted the Privileges or Immunities Clause of the Fourteenth Amendment which provides that 'No State shall make or enforce any law which shall abridge the privileges and immunities of citizens of the United States.' The Court explained that despite fundamentally different views on the meaning of the Clause,[370] it has always been common ground that this Clause protects the third component of the right to travel:

> 'The States have not now, if they ever had, any power to restrict their citizenship to any classes or persons. A citizen of the United States has a perfect constitutional right to go to and reside in any State he chooses, and to claim citizenship therein, and an equality of rights with every other citizen; and the whole power of the nation is pledged to sustain him in that right. He is not bound to cringe any superior, or to pray for any act of grace, as a means of enjoying all the rights and privileges enjoyed by other citizens.'[371]

The Court further stated that newly arrived citizens 'have two political capacities, one state and one federal' and this added special force to the claim that such citizens have the same rights as others who share their citizenship. Neither mere rationality nor some intermediate standard of review should be used to judge the constitutionality of a State rule that discriminates against some of its citizens because they have been domiciled in the State for less than a year. The appropriate standard 'may be more categorical than that articulated in *Shapiro* . . . , but it surely is no less strict.'

In *Saenz* the Court thus did depart from the controversial penalty on the right to travel analysis it had developed in *Shapiro*. Discrimination against new, recently arrived, residents must be reviewed under the Privileges or Immunities Clause rather than the Equal Protection Clause of the Fourteenth Amendment. The new legal framework for reviewing waiting-period requirements does more

---

[368] *Saenz v Roe*, 119 S.Ct.1518 (1999). On *Saenz* see, eg: Lashbrook, 'Back from a Long Vacation: The Privileges and Immunities Clause of the Fourteenth Amendment' (2001) *CapULRev* 481–512; Douglas, 'A Return to First Principles? *Saenz v Roe* and the Privileges and Immunities Clause' (2000) *UtahLRev* 305–58; Nelson, 'Unanswered Questions: The Implications of *Saenz v Roe* for Durational Residence Requirements' (2000) *KansLRev* 193–221; Nixon, '"Rational Basis with a Bite": A Retreat from the Constitutional Right to Travel' in *Law and Equality* (2000) 209–42 and Wolff, 'Right Road, Wrong Vehicle?: Rethinking Thirty Years of Right to Travel Doctrine: *Saenz v Roe*, 119 S.Ct.1518' 307–35.

[369] *Ibid.*

[370] Cp the majority opinion and the various dissenting opinions in the *Slaughter House cases* 83 U.S. (16 Wall.) 36 (1873). See also: Stone *et al* (1986) n 324 above, at 698–707.

[371] *Saenz v Roe*, 119 S.Ct.1518 (1999) (quoting the dissenting opinion of Bradley J in the *Slaughter House Cases*, 16 Wall.36 (1873).

justice to the true concerns of the Court regarding such requirements than penalty on the right to travel analysis. The requirements are not constitutionally controversial because they affect the right to travel, but rather because they divide the group of State citizens in two categories: 'new' citizens and 'long-term' citizens. It is a privilege of United States citizenship of which State one wishes to become a citizen; the right to travel is merely the means for choosing State citizenship. *Saenz*, however, does raise many questions as to how the validity of durational residence requirements must be determined under the Privileges or Immunities Clause. The Court invalidated welfare waiting-period requirements, but, as shown later on in this book,[372] it also indicated that not all waiting-periods are unconstitutional. The Court did not provide much guidance as to how these conclusions must be reached under the Privileges or Immunities Clause. In fact, the Court did not say much more than that the appropriate standard 'may be more categorical' than the one articulated in *Shapiro*, but 'it surely is no less strict.' Until *Saenz* the Court had interpreted the Privileges and Immunities Clause in one decision only (the so-called *Slaughter House cases* (1873)),[373] and in this decision it had held that the privileges and immunities guaranteed by the Fourteenth Amendment were limited to those 'belonging to a citizen of the United States as such.'[374] The Clause was not intended 'as a protection to the citizen of a State against the legislative power of his own State.'[375] *Saenz* 'breathes new life into the previously dormant Privileges or Immunities Clause,'[376] but the decision does not reveal which principles must be applied when reviewing durational residence requirements in areas other than welfare.

8.6 Non-Residents

States make the enjoyment of many rights and benefits (eg welfare, admission to the bar, free public education, voting, public employment, etc.) conditional upon residence in, and thus citizenship of, the State. Unlike durational residence requirements, simple residence requirements do not make a distinction between classes of State citizens or residents. They distinguish residents and non-residents. Residence requirements do not conflict with the Fourteenth Amendment's demand for equal State citizenship. Therefore, non-residents' right to equal treatment is not as strongly protected as the equivalent right of

---

[372] See especially: ch 5, s 5.2.
[373] To be sure, in *Colgate v Harvey*, 296 U.S. 404 (1935) the Court did invoke the Clause in order to invalidate a State income tax levied against in-State residents, but this decision was overruled five years later in *Madden v Kentucky*, 309 U.S. 83 (1940).
[374] *Slaughter House Cases*, 83 U.S. (16 Wall.) 36 (1873) at 75.
[375] *Ibid*, at 74.
[376] *Saenz v Roe*, 119 SCt 1518 (1999) (Rehnquist C J, dissenting).

'new' residents/citizens. Residence requirements are merely subject to the rational relation test under the Equal Protection Clause,[377] and *Saenz v Roe* indicates that the Privileges or Immunities Clause only objects to discrimination against residents, and not to non-resident discrimination.

8.6.1 Privileges and Immunities Clause

However, United States citizens who visit other States are not 'true outsiders' or 'strangers' who can be denied rights or benefits merely on the ground that they are not State citizens. They visit other States in their capacity as citizen of the United States and they enjoy in this capacity the specific protection offered by the Privileges and Immunities Clause of Article IV § 2 of the Constitution. The Clause reads: 'The Citizens of each State shall be entitled to all Privileges and Immunities of Citizens in the several States.'[378] The Clause is an equality provision which offers non-residents a right to equal treatment with respect to the privileges and immunities States grant to their own citizens.[379] The purpose of the Clause is, as the Court held in *Paul v Virginia* (1869):

---

[377] *Shapiro*'s penalty-analysis was of no relevance. In *Maricopa County* the Court said 'the right to travel was involved in only a limited sense in Shapiro. The Court there was only concerned with the right to migrate, resettle, find a new job, and start a new life'. *Memorial Hospital v Maricopa County*, 415 U.S. 250 (1974) at 255. In *Martinez v Bynum* (1982) the Court further explained that a bona fide residence requirement 'does not burden or penalize the right of inter-state travel . . . for any person is free to move to a State and to establish residence there. A bona fide residence requirement simply requires that the person does establish residence before demanding the services that are restricted to residents'. *Martinez v Bynum*, 461 U.S. 321 (1982) at 328–9. In *Martinez* the Court added that a residence requirement neither implicates a 'suspect classification'. *Martinez v Bynum*, 461 U.S. 321 (1982) at 328 (n 7). In terms of citizenship, then, the Court prohibited in *Shapiro* only discrimination against 'new' State citizens, not discriminations against citizens of other States.

[378] On the Privileges and Immunities Clause of Art IV § 2 see, eg: Wildenthal (1989) n 338 above, at 1560–4; Gergen, 'The Selfish State and the Market' (1988) *TexLRev* 1099–153; Bogen, 'Privileges and Immunities Clause of Art IV' (1987) *CaseWLRev* 794–861; Gonzalez, 'The Interstate Privileges and Immunities: Fundamental Rights or Federalism' (1986) *CapULRev* 493–513; Zwicker, 'Equal Protection III: Non-Resident Discrimination'. (1986) *ASAL* 469–94; Varat, '"State Citizenship" and Interstate Equality' (1982) *ChicLRev* 487 *et seq*; Simson, 'Discrimination Against Nonresidents and the Privileges and Immunities Clause of Article IV' (1979) *UPennLRev* 379–401 and Antieau, 'Pauls's Perverted Privileges or the True Meaning of the Privileges and Immunities Clause of Article IV' (1967) *W&MLRev* 1–38.

[379] Taken literally, the Clause could be read so as to guarantee all United States citizens a set of substantive rights which they can enjoy in every State of the Union. Bogen (1987) n 378 above, at 842. The Supreme Court has rejected such a reading of the Clause. *Baldwin v Fish*, 436 U.S. 371 (1978) at 382. The Privileges *and* Immunities Clause of Article IV § 2 is an equality provision, it does not create privileges and immunities. Laycock, 'Equal Citizens of Equal and Territorial States: The Constitutional Foundations of Choice of Law' (1992) *ColLRev* 249–337, at 262. A set of universal substantive rights is guaranteed, however, by the Privileges *or* Immunities Clause of the Fourteenth Amendment. This Clause concerns incidents of *national* citizenship and includes eg, the right to petition Congress, to enter public lands, to vote for national offices, and, as described in the previous sub-section, a right for new residents to claim benefits under the same conditions as long-term residents.

'to place the citizens of each State upon the same footing with citizens of other States, so far as the advantages resulting from citizenship in those States are concerned. It relieves them from the disabilities of alienage in other States; it inhibits discriminating legislation against them by other States; . . . and it secures them in other States the equal protection of the laws. It has been justly said that no provision in the Constitution has tended so strongly to constitute the citizens of the United States one people as this. Indeed, without some provision of the kind removing from the citizens of each State the disabilities of alienage in the other States, and giving them equality of privilege with citizens of other States, the Republic would have constituted little more than a league of States; it would not have constituted the Union which now exists.'[380]

The Privileges and Immunities Clause is thus not only an individual rights provision which insures 'a citizen of State A who ventures into State B the same privileges which the citizens of State B enjoy'[381] but also a 'national unity' provision which 'intends to fuse into one nation a collection of independent sovereign states.'[382] The Privileges and Immunities Clause 'builds a bridge between personal rights and federalism'[383] and it 'facilitates federalism by preventing parochialism in the treatment by a state of citizens of other States.'[384]

Even though the Clause is drafted in absolute, uncompromising terms, it does not prohibit all conceivable forms of discrimination against non-residents. Non-residents do not have to be treated as if they were residents of the State they visit. A State, as the Court held in *Baldwin v Fish* (1978), does not have to:

'apply all its laws or all its services equally to anyone. Some distinctions between residents and nonresidents merely reflect the fact that this is a Nation composed of individual States, and are permitted; other distinctions are prohibited because they hinder the formation, the purpose, or the development of a single Union of those States'.[385]

The Supreme Court has developed a number of principles on how permissible differences in treatment should be distinguished from impermissible discrimination

---

[380] *Paul v Virginia*, 75 U.S. (8 Wall.) 168 (1869) at 180–1 as quoted in *Baldwin v Fish*, 436 U.S. 371 (1978) at 380–1. See also the Slaughterhouse Cases where the Court held that the sole purpose of the Clause 'was to declare to the several states, that whatever those rights, as you grant or establish them to your own citizens, or as you may limit or qualify, or impose restrictions on their exercise, the same, neither more or less, shall be the measure of the rights of citizens of other states within your jurisdiction'. *Slaughtherhouse Cases*, 83 U.S. (16 Wall) 36 (1873) at 77.
[381] *Toomer v Witsell*, 334 U.S. 385 (1948) at 395.
[382] *Ibid.*
[383] Tribe (1988) n 324 above, at 528.
[384] Gonzalez (1986) n 378 above, at 497.
[385] *Baldwin v Fish*, 436 U.S. 371 (1978) at 383.

against non-residents.[386] Usually, the Court follows a two-step inquiry. The first step involves asking the question whether the rights or benefits involved constitute one of the privileges and immunities protected by the Clause. The Court has limited the scope of the Clause to privileges and benefits which are in their nature 'fundamental' or which are 'basic and essential activities, interference with which would frustrate the purposes of the formation of the Union.'[387] The Court has never given a general definition of the term 'privileges and immunities.' It has even explicitly refused to do so.[388] Instead the Court has determined on a case-by-case basis whether certain privileges or activities are protected. So far it has classed as 'fundamental', eg, the right to do business,[389] the right to practice law[390] and the right to secure abortions.[391] Recreational activities such as, eg, elk-hunting[392] are not fundamental for the purposes of the Privileges and Immunities Clause. Whenever a right or activity is not considered to be 'fundamental,' the Court's inquiry under the Privileges and Immunities Clause ends. The residence requirement is then subject to the rational relation test of the Equal Protection Clause only and thus has a good chance of being upheld. In case a fundamental right or benefit is present, the Court proceeds to the second step of the inquiry under the Privileges and Immunities Clause. The Court asks (*i*) whether there is a substan-

---

[386] In determining which discrimination against citizens of other States is valid and which is not, the Court has relied on various other principles or exceptions. In a number of commercial cases the Court accepted a so-called 'proprietary exception' to the Privileges and Immunities Clause according to which the Clause would not apply to State decisions regarding the use and distribution of 'State property' (such eg, natural resources) and which thus entitled States to preserve the benefits of this 'property' for their own citizens. See, eg: *McCready v Virginia*, 94 U.S. 391 (1877); *Toomer v Witsell*, 334 U.S. 385 (1948) and *Hicklin v Orbeck*, 437 U.S. 518 (1978). In theory, the exception could be relevant for the purposes of the subject of this study in the sense that one could argue that public benefits constitute the 'common property' of the citizens of a State. Such collectively created and financed services would then fall outside the scope of the Clause and States would be free to exclude non-citizens from them. However, the Court has never applied the exception in welfare, health care and education cases and, although the Court has not wholly abandoned the exception (*Baldwin v Fish*, 436 U.S. 371 (1978) at 386), the current relevance of the exception seems minimal. See in particular Varat (1981) n 378 above, at 494–8 and 505–8. See also: Wells and Hellerstein, 'The Governmental-Proprietary Distinction in Constitutional Law' (1980) VirgLRev 1073 *et seq.*

In cases decided under the Privileges and Immunities Clause (and the Commerce Clause) the Court has also applied a 'market participant exception'. The basic notion is that a State may use its resources to provide benefits to its own citizens and that it does not have to share those resources with citizens from other States. See, eg: *Reeves, Inc. v Stake*, 447 U.S. 429 (1980) and *White v Massachusetts Council of Construction Employers, Inc.*, 460 U.S. 204 (1982). On this market participation exception see also: Varat (1981) n 378 above and Levmore, 'Interstate Exploitation and Judicial Intervention' (1983) VirgLRev 563–630.

[387] *Baldwin v Fish*, 436 U.S. 371 (1978) at 383.

[388] 'We do not decide to the full range of activities that are sufficient basic to the livelihood of the Nation that States may not interfere with a nonresident's participation therein without similarly interfering with a resident's participation.' *Baldwin v Fish*, 436 U.S. 371 (1978) at 388.

[389] See, eg: *Toomer v Witsell*, 334 U.S. 385 (1948) and *Hicklin v Orbeck*, 437 U.S. 518 (1978).

[390] *Supreme Court of New Hampshire v Piper*, 470 U.S. 274 (1985) at 281.

[391] *Doe v Bolton*, 410 U.S. 179 (1973).

[392] *Baldwin v Fish*, 436 U.S. 371 (19878) at 388.

tial reason for the difference in treatment, (*ii*) whether the discrimination bears a substantial relationship to the State's objective and (*iii*) whether less restrictive means are available.[393] The 'substantial reason test' must be located anywhere between the rational relation and the compelling state interest test of the Equal Protection Clause. The level of scrutiny comes close to the level exercised under the intermediate test of the Equal Protection Clause.

The Court's interpretation of the Privileges and Immunities Clause, and in particular the 'fundamentality' requirement, has been severely criticised in legal doctrine. The Court has never adequately explained why the scope of the Clause should be limited to 'fundamental' rights and benefits[394] and, as said, it has not defined the term 'fundamental.'[395] It has given some guidance by speaking of 'basic and essential activities, interference with which would frustrate the purposes of the formation of the Union,'[396] but the Court has never indicated how or where the borderline between fundamental and non-fundamental privileges

---

[393] *Supreme Court of New Hampshire v Kathryn Piper*, 470 U.S. 274 (1985) at 284 and *Barnard v Thorstenn*, 489 U.S. 546 (1989) at 552–3.

[394] The argument that discrimination in the grant of 'non-fundamental' privileges and immunities does not 'bear upon the vitality of the Nation' or does not realistically threaten the social, economic and political unification, is not persuasive. Cp Varat (1981) n 378 above, at 511. In the case of non-fundamental rights or benefits, discriminations against non-residents may be even more hostile or serious than in the case of fundamental rights. Do non-residents feel less an 'outsider' when they are denied access to public parks or libraries than when they are refused admission to the bar? Any discrimination on the ground of non-residence simply implicates a 'disability of alienage', conflicts with the notion of United States citizens as one people and potentially threatens national unity and cohesion. Arguably, any such discrimination is at odds with the object of the Privileges and Immunities Clause.

[395] The history of the Clause does not explain either why the Clause should be limited to 'fundamental' privileges and immunities. The framers did not in any way indicate that the scope of the Clause should or would be limited to certain privileges and immunities. They saw the Clause as an equality provision intended to facilitate 'an effective federal system by prohibiting states from asserting parochial interests to the detriment of an effective federal system'. Gonzalez (1986) n 378 above, at 498–9. On the framers' purpose in drafting the Clause see also: Bogen (1987) n 378 above, at 843–5. The fundamentality requirement finds its roots in *Corfield v Coryell* (1823) where Washington J said: 'What are the privileges and immunities of citizens in the several States? We feel no hesitation in confining these expressions to those privileges and immunities 'which are, in their nature, fundamental; which belong, of right, to the citizens of free governments; and which have, at all times, been enjoyed by the citizens of the several states which compose the Union'. Washington J mentioned inter alia the right to travel, the right to property, the right to claim the benefit of the 'writ of habeas corpus'. *Corfield v Coryell* as quoted in *Baldwin v Fish*, 436 U.S. 371 (1978) at 395 (Brennan J, dissenting). Washington J, however, did not read the Privileges and Immunities Clause as an equality provision, but rather as a Clause which guaranteed a number of uniform substantive 'fundamental rights' or 'natural rights' to all United States citizens which should be respected by all States regardless of the rights or benefits which a State grants to its own citizens. The language of the Clause leaves room for such an interpretation. Since *Corfield*, however, the Court has, in numerous cases, indicated that it does not consider that the Clause guarantees a number of 'substantive rights'. Since 1867, this role is fulfilled by the Privileges *or* Immunities Clause of the Fourteenth Amendment. Like the framers, the Supreme Court sees the Privileges and Immunities Clause of Article IV § 2 as an anti-discrimination clause and it is therefore not easy to understand why the Court still adheres to *Corfield*'s fundamentality requirement.

[396] *Baldwin v Fish*, 436 U.S. 371 (1978) at 387.

and immunities must be drawn.[397] Therefore, arguments have increasingly been made that the 'fundamentality' requirement should no longer be applied.[398]

8.6.2 Dormant Commerce Clause

In addition to the equality of treatment guaranteed by the Equal Protection Clause and the Privileges and Immunities Clause, individuals are protected against discriminatory treatment in other States by the Commerce Clause.[399] This Clause provides that Congress has the power 'to regulate commerce . . . among the several States . . .'. From the beginning,[400] it has been recognised that the Clause not only entails an affirmative grant of congressional power, but also acts as a 'self-executing limitation on the power of the States.'[401] As the provisions of the EC Treaty on the free movement of goods, persons and services, the so-called 'dormant' Commerce Clause may be regarded as a 'negative integration provision' which acts as a constitutional check on State legislation even if no 'positive' legislative measures have been taken by the political institutions at

---

[397] One thing is clear though, and that is that under the Privileges and Immunities Clause the term 'fundamental' must be defined other than under the Equal Protection Clause. Otherwise, the Privileges and Immunities would be superfluous and empty. Varat (1981) n 378 above at 515 and Tribe (1988) n 324 above, at 535.

[398] See, eg: Brennan's J dissenting opinion in *Baldwin v Fish*, 436 U.S. 371 (1978) at 402 (Brennan, J, dissenting, joined by Marshall and White). See also: eg, Gonzalez (1986) n 378 above, at 510–13; Varat (1981) n 382 above, at 509–16 and Simson (1979) n 378 above, at 383–6. The Justices and scholars who have expressed this view, thus contend that all residence requirements must be scrutinised under the substantial relation test. The 'non-importance' of the benefit/right may, if at all, be one element to be considered in balancing non-residents' right to equal treatment against the States' interests in preserving these right/benefits to their own residents, but it is simply not clear why this 'non-importance' should be given so much weight as to escape scrutiny under the Privileges and Immunities Clause.

[399] The commerce clause is primarily concerned with cross-border commerce, whilst the Privileges and Immunities Clause more generally protects United States citizens in other States against unequal treatment on the ground that they lack citizenship of the State concerned. The material scope of the two clauses may overlap The Privileges and Immunities Clause has for instance been applied in a number of commercial cases (see, eg: *Toomer v Witsell* 334 U.S. 385 (1948)), whilst the Court has given a very wide interpretation to the scope of the Commerce Clause so as to include issues which are not typically trade related (see, eg: *Edwards v California*, 314 U.S. 160 (1941)— transportation of 'indigents'). On the relationship between both clauses see also: Varat (1981) n 378 above, at 499–501. The personal scope of the Commerce Clause is broader than that of the Privileges and Immunities Clause. Unlike the former, the latter does not apply to corporations (*Paul v Virginia*, 75 U.S. (8Wall.) 168 (1869) at 177–82) and aliens (*Blake v McClung*, 172 U.S. 239 (1889) at 247.

[400] Loffredo, 'If You Ain't Got The Do, Re, Mi: The Commerce Clause and State Residence Restrictions on Welfare' (1993) *YaleLPRev* 147–202, at 173 (n 166) stating that the drafters of the Constitution had already recognised this 'negative' side of the Commerce Clause.

[401] *South-Central Timber Dev v Wunnicke*, 467 U.S. 82 (1984) at 87. See also: Redish and Nugent, 'The Dormant Commerce Clause and the Constitutional Balance of Federalism' (1987) *DukeLJ* 569 *et seq*; Kommers and Waelbroeck, 'Legal Integration and the Free Movement of Goods: The American and the European Experience' in Cappelletti *et al*, *Integration Through Law—Europe and the American Federal Experience* (1986) 165–227; Blasi, 'Constitutional Limitations on the Power of States to Regulate the Movement of Goods in Interstate Commerce' in Sandalow and Stein (eds), *Courts and Free Markets: Perspectives from the United States and Europe* (1982) 174–221 and Tushnet, 'Rethinking the Dormant Commerce Clause' (1979) *WisLRev* 125–65.

federal level. The main principle on which the dormant Commerce Clause is based is that 'one State in its dealings with another may not place itself in a position of economic isolation . . . by establishing an economic barrier against competition with the products of another or the labor of its residents.'[402] The 'negative' or dormant Commerce Clause primarily protects companies and individuals when doing business in other States, but the Supreme Court has construed the term 'commerce' quite broadly.

Since the 1930s, the Court has followed a 'two-tiered' approach in reviewing State legislation under the dormant Commerce Clause.[403] As regards statutes or rules that directly or overtly discriminate against 'economic actors' established in other States, the Court applies the 'strictest scrutiny.'[404] Protectionist statutes and rules are in principle unconstitutional. In theory, States can escape unconstitutionality when they can demonstrate that a particular regulation is narrowly tailored to achieve a legitimate and non-protectionist interest, but the case law indicates that this is virtually impossible.[405] As regards such discriminatory measures, a virtual *per se* rule of invalidity is applied. State rules which are non-protectionist and non-discriminatory in aim and effect, and which only have minimal impact on interstate trade, are subject to a more flexible test. In *Pike v Bruce* (1970) the Court defined the basic contours of the test to be applied:

> 'Where the statute regulates evenhandedly to effectuate a legitimate local public interest, and its effects on interstate commerce are only incidental, it will be upheld unless the burden imposed on such commerce is clearly excessive in relation to the putative local benefits . . . If a legitimate local purpose is found, then the question becomes one of degree. And the extent of the burden that will be tolerated will of course depend on the nature of the local interest involved, and on whether it could be promoted as well as with a lesser impact on interstate activities.'[406]

The '*Pike*-test' is thus a balancing test in which the Federal interest of promoting economic integration is weighed against non-protectionist State interests.[407] As is inherent in such a balancing test, the judicial outcomes in individual cases are often hard to predict.[408]

---

[402] *Philadelphia v New Jersey*, 437 U.S. 617 (1978) at 624.

[403] *Brown-Forman Distillers v New York State Liqor Auth*, 476 U.S. 573 (1986) at 578–9.

[404] *Sporhase v Nebraska ex rel Douglas*, 458 U.S. 941 (1982) at 958.

[405] So far only one State rule has been upheld under the strict scrutiny of the Commerce Clause. *Maine v Taylor*, 477 U.S. 131 (1986) in which the Court accepted that Maine could apply a statute which prohibited the importation of parasitic baitfish which posed a unique threat to the environment of Maine. The State was able to convince the Court that there were no less discriminatory means sufficient to protect the environment.

[406] *Pike v Bruce*, 397 U.S. 137 (1970) at 142.

[407] The test resembles the 'rule of reason test' applied by the European Court of Justice, but it must be noted that the Supreme Court is often less strict than its European counterpart. Many laws or regulations which would probably not have been able to pass the tests under Arts 28 and/or 49 of the EC Treaty, have been upheld under the American Commerce Clause. Kommers and Waelbroeck (1986) n 401 above, at 224.

[408] In a number of cases decided under the Commerce Clause the Court has applied a 'proprietary exception' and a 'market participant exception' comparable to the ones applied under the Privileges and Immunities Clause. See also: n 386 above.

8.7 Aliens

A third category of 'out-of-staters' that, upon arrival in a State, is often faced with discriminatory treatment consists of aliens (or foreigners). As United States citizens, aliens may be discriminated against on the ground that they do not reside or have not resided long enough in the State concerned. This form of discrimination is not to be discussed here. Constitutional law on residence and durational residence requirements, as described in the previous sub-sections, applies in principle equally to aliens.[409] The focus is here rather on discrimination based on alienage, ie, the status of not being a United States citizen.[410] It concerns discrimination that disadvantages aliens on the ground that they lack United States citizenship.[411]

8.7.1 Equal Protection Analysis

As the Supreme Court ruled as far back as in 1886, aliens enjoy equal protection of the laws.[412] Yet, constitutional law on alienage classification began in fact

---

[409] This conclusion is not entirely obvious. Aliens do not fall under the personal scope of the Privileges and Immunities Clause (Varat (1981) n 378 above at 525 and Simson (1979) n 378 above, at 380) and it is not entirely certain whether aliens enjoy the constitutional right to travel (*Graham v Richardson*, 403 U.S. 365 (1971) at 375). It is debatable whether aliens challenging 'nationality neutral' (durational) residence requirements can benefit from '*Shapiro*', the Privileges or Immunities Clause of the Fourteenth Amendment and/or the Privileges and Immunities Clause of Article IV § 2. Aliens, however, do enjoy the protection of the Equal Protection Clause. The mere fact that they would not have the same opportunity as United States citizens to challenge 'nationality-neutral' (durational) residence requirements, constitutes a discrimination based on alienage, which is subject to the compelling State interest test under the Equal Protection Clause. Varat (1981) n 378 above, at 527.

[410] A distinction must be made between discriminations based on alienage and discriminations based on nationality. The former term covers discrimination against of aliens on the ground that they do not possess United States citizenship. It is of no relevance which specific nationality an alien possesses. The term discrimination based on alienage resembles the term discrimination based on nationality as used within the context of the EC Treaty. The notion of discrimination based on nationality (or national origin) applies under United States law to discrimination based on the specific nationality an alien may have. It concerns discriminatory treatment of eg, a Dutch or Japanese person on the ground that they are Dutch or Japanese, not on the ground that they lack United States citizenship. Discrimination based on nationality comes close to discrimination based on race. Therefore, nationality is a suspect classification for equal protection purposes; the criterion can only withstand strict scrutiny in the most exceptional circumstances. See, eg: *Korematsu v United States*, 323 U.S. 214 (1944) and *Hirabayashi v United States*, 320 U.S. 81 (1943).

[411] On constitutional law on State discrimination against foreigners see, eg: Rubio Marín, *Stranger in Your Own Home—The Incorporation of Resident Aliens into the Political Community: Theory and Constitutional Practice in Germany and the United States* (1997); Rotunda and Nowak (1992) n 324 above, § 18.11—§ 18.13; X, 'Developments in Law—Immigration Policy and the Rights of Aliens' (1983) *HarvLRev* 1286–465; Note, *State Burdens* (1980) n 306 above, at 940–61; Levi, 'The Equal Treatment of Aliens: Preemption or Equal Protection? (1979) *StanfLRev* 1069–91; Hull, *Without Justice for All—The Constitutional Rights of Aliens* (1980) and Note, 'A Dual Standard for State Discrimination Against Aliens' (1979) *HarvLRev* 1516 *et seq*.

[412] *Yick Wo v Hopkins*, 118 U.S. 365 (1886). Aliens have a 'right to enter and abide in any State of the Union . . . on an equality of legal privileges with all citizens under non-discriminatory laws'. *Takahashi v Fish*, 334 U.S. 410 (1948) at 420.

only in 1971 with the decision in *Graham v Richardson*.[413] Between 1886 and 1971 aliens' right to equal treatment did not have significant substance. Like durational residence requirements, alienage classifications were merely scrutinised under the rational relation test and generally upheld. The Court accepted a so-called 'public interest doctrine' which implied, in short, that States had an interest in favouring citizens above aliens in the grant of rights and governmental benefits for as long as this interest entailed 'something' more than a mere hostility toward aliens.[414] Aliens were viewed and treated as 'guests' invited to advance the welfare of United States-citizens. In *Graham*, however, the Court considerably strengthened aliens' right to equal treatment. Aliens, the Court held, constitute a prime example of a 'discrete and insular minority' for whom 'heightened judicial solicitude' under the Equal Protection Clause is appropriate.[415] The Court invalidated State statutes that denied welfare benefits to permanent resident aliens under the compelling State interest test. Strict scrutiny was to be applied not because alienage classifications in question impinged on the fundamental right to travel, but rather because they were said to be 'inherently suspect.'[416]

With *Graham*, however, also began the confusion. If alienage were actually a suspect classification, then all discrimination based on alienage would, regardless of the right or benefit denied, have to be strictly scrutinised and, thus, would probably have to be invalidated. It seemed unlikely, however, that the Court had intended to say that all aliens should be treated equally with United States citizens in all respects. Discrimination against aliens may serve legitimate and important interests. The Court has recognised this and created a number of exceptions to *Graham*. First, the Court has accepted a so-called 'political community exception.' States are entitled to preserve the 'basic conception of a political community' by limiting to United States citizens voting rights and eligibility for office which 'participate directly in the formulation, execution, or review of broad public policy.'[417] Political alienage classification does not have to be treated as suspect[418] and is, under the Equal Protection Clause, merely subject to rational relation review. Secondly, the Court has held

---

[413] *Graham v Richardson*, 403 U.S. 365 (1971).

[414] Rotunda and Nowak (1992) n 324 above, at 221.

[415] *Graham v Richardson*, 403 U.S. 365 (1971) at 372.

[416] *Ibid*, at 376.

[417] *Sugarmann v Dougall*, 413 U.S. 634 (1973) at 647. See also: *Foley v Connelie*, 435 U.S. 291 (1978); *Ambach v Norwick*, 441 U.S. 68 (1979) and *Cabell v Chavez-Salido*, 454 U.S. 432 (1982). See also: Rotunda and Nowak (1992) n 324 above, at 226–32; X, 'Developments in Law—Immigration Policy and the Right of Aliens' (1983) n 411 above, at 1405–6 and Hull, 'Resident Aliens and the Equal Protection Clause: The Burger Court's Retreat From *Graham v Richardson*' (1980) *BrookLRev* 1–42.

[418] The Court could have held that the 'preservation of the political community' constitutes a compelling State interest and that political alienage classifications could withstand strict scrutiny. Yet, this would have required a loosening of the strict scrutiny standard and the Court may have been reluctant to do so because of the implications for the application of the test in other, and in particular, racial cases. Levi (1979) n 411 above, at 1089.

that undocumented aliens, because of their illegal presence, do not have to be treated as a suspect class.[419] In principle, undocumented aliens enjoy only minimal protection from the rational relation test.[420] Thirdly, the Court has refused to treat alienage classifications applied by the Federal authorities as 'suspect.' In *Matthews v Diaz*[421] (1976), the most important decision concerning Federal discrimination against foreigners, the Court stated that it is 'the business of the political branches of the Federal Government, rather than of either the States or the Federal judiciary, to regulate the conditions of entry and residence of aliens.' Immigration decisions 'may implicate ... relations with foreign powers' which must be made 'in the light of changing political and economic circumstances.' The Supreme Court considers itself an inappropriate forum for making such decisions and it has therefore only applied the most minimum level of scrutiny to Federal alienage classifications.[422] The Federal authorities are largely free to determine the conditions under which foreigners are admitted.

The Court's application of the Equal Protection Clause in alienage cases has been severely criticised.[423] The Court has applied different standards of review but has failed to give sufficient guidance as to when a particular test must be applied. The case law leaves one with the impression that the Court simply creates a new exception whenever it wishes to uphold discrimination against aliens thereby leaving it largely uncertain whether in future cases more alienage classifications will be exempt. The most notable omission is that the Court has never explicitly decided whether or not the biggest group of aliens, i.e., the nonimmigrants which include temporary foreign workers, tourists, businessmen, etc., must be treated as a suspect class.[424] If the group of non-immigrants, as the Court seems to have suggested,[425] is not covered by *Graham*, one would have to conclude that alienage constitutes a suspect classification only by exception.

---

[419] *Plyler v Doe*, 457 U.S. 202 (1982) at 223.

[420] In exceptional circumstances, however, this may be different. In *Plyler v Doe* (1982) the Court applied the intermediate test to a Texas Statute which denied undocumented school-age children the access to free public education offered to other children. The Court, however, did not wish to limit itself to rational relation because the case involved, on the one hand, 'innocent' children who could 'affect neither their parents' conduct nor their own status' and, on the other hand, the case concerned education which was not just 'some' governmental benefit. *Plyler v Doe*, 457 U.S. 202 (1982) at 218–24.

[421] *Matthews v Diaz*, 426 U.S. 67 (1976). See also: *Hampton v Mow Sun Wong*, 426 U.S. 88 (1976).

[422] Federal discrimination against foreigners is not to be reviewed under the Equal Protection Clause of the Fourteenth Amendment but under the equal protection component of the Due Process Clause of the Fifth Amendment. The differential attitude of the Supreme Court towards Federal immigration authorities is not free from criticism. Guendelsberger, 'Equal Protection and Resident Alien Access to Public Benefits in France and the United States' (1993) *TulLRev* 699–730.

[423] See, eg: Rotunda and Nowak (1992) n 324 above, at 217–20; Note (1980) n 411 above; Levi (1979) n 411 above and Note (1979) n 411 above.

[424] Rosberg (1983) n 295 above, at 401.

[425] *Elkins v Moreno*, 435 U.S. 647 (1978).

Such a conclusion is at odds with *Graham* and implies an erosion of the equal protection of aliens.[426]

8.7.2 Pre-emption Analysis

The 'failure' of equal protection analysis has prompted a number of commentators to advocate another legal technique for evaluating alienage classifications: pre-emption analysis. Under the pre-emption doctrine State discrimination against aliens is judged on its compatibility with the conditions of admission set by Federal immigration authorities. The starting-point is that immigration and alien policy falls within under the exclusive power of the Federal government. It is up to the Federal immigration authorities to decide which, and the conditions under which, aliens are admitted to the United States. States do not hold such powers. They are bound by the immigration conditions set by the Federal authorities. It 'is not for the States to alter the terms of immigration with new burdens'.[427] State statutes which impose additional discriminatory burdens on aliens conflict with the exclusive federal power to regulate immigration and are, accordingly, invalid. In a number of alienage cases the Court has indeed applied pre-emption analysis. In *Takahashi v Fish*[428] (1948), for example, the Court invalidated a California Statute which denied fishing licences to resident aliens by engaging in pre-emption analysis. The Court held that resident aliens have been lawfully admitted to the United States and entitled to 'enter and abide in any State in the Union on an equality of legal privileges with all citizens under non-discriminatory laws.'[429] The challenged statute was said to conflict with the exclusive power of the Federal government to regulate immigration and was thus not permissible. Similarly, in *Graham v Richardson* (1971) the Court invalidated the welfare statutes in question (also) on the basis of what it called 'federal-state relations.' Congress, the Court reasoned, had declared that 'resident aliens who become public charges . . . are not subject to deportation, and that as long as they are here they are entitled to the full and equal benefit of all state laws for the security of persons and property.'[430] The State statutes at issue thus encroached upon exclusive Federal immigration power and were, consequently, invalid.[431]

---

[426] Furthermore, in cases in which strict scrutiny does not have to be applied, the Court would have given States too much discretion in discriminating against aliens. The 'political community exception' would allow States to exclude aliens from governmental positions which are only tenuously related to the formulation or execution of high level policy. Hull (1980) n 411 above, at 40. For similar criticism as regards Federal alienage classifications see Guendelsberger (1993) n 422 above.

[427] Levi (1979) n 411 above, at 1070.

[428] *Takahashi v Fish*, 334 U.S. 410 (1948).

[429] *Ibid*, at 420.

[430] *Graham v Richardson*, 403 U.S. 365 (1971) at 378.

[431] *Ibid*, at 378.

8.7.3 *Pre-emption and/or Equal Protection Analysis?*

Advocates of pre-emption analysis claim that this technique recognises, much more than equal protection analysis, that immigration and alien policy are exclusively federal affairs.[432] Furthermore, 'pre-emption' would far better explain the results in alienage cases. For instance, the Federal authorities allow permanent resident aliens to establish domicile and this would thus imply that such aliens are admitted as full members of America's 'social-economic society.' Admission for permanent residence, however, does not imply the grant of United States citizenship and the immigration authorities would thus implicitly allow States to deny immigrant aliens the right to vote and to exclude them from political offices.[433] The Court would, in cases in which it formally applied equal protection analysis, in fact, have followed 'an unarticulated theory of pre-empting.'[434]

Nonetheless, the argument for an increased use of the pre-emption technique does not, and cannot, mean that equal protection analysis should be abandoned altogether. More than once, the Court has held that the Federal authorities do not hold the power to authorise States to violate the Equal Protection Clause.[435] Pre-emption analysis is only useful when the Federal authorities indicate that aliens have to be treated equally. In cases in which the Federal authorities do not prescribe equality of treatment, one necessarily has to engage in equal protection analysis. Furthermore, pre-emption analysis does not in all cases enable courts to determine the (un)constitutionality of alienage classifications. The Federal government does not always indicate in detail which right/benefits aliens can(not) enjoy. This particularly holds true for the heterogeneous group of the non-immigrants. It is, as the Court seems to have admitted,[436] simply not always possible to 'read into' Federal policy that a State must treat such aliens equally. Lastly, it would seem that the problem with the Court's application of the Equal Protection Clause does not so much lie in the Clause itself but rather in the fact that the Court has adhered to the classic two-tiered equal protection model. In *Graham* the Court wished to strengthen the legal status of aliens and the only opportunity the Court had, under the classic equal protection model, was to treat alienage as a suspect classification.[437] The strictness of the compelling State interest test, however, has forced the Court to exempt an increasing number of alienage classifications from suspect treatment. The uncertainty

---

[432] Note (1980) n 411 above, at 944. See also: Perry (1979) n 324 above, at 1060–5 and Levi (1979) n 411 above, at 1069.

[433] Levi (1979) n 411 above, at 1070.

[434] *Ibid.*

[435] *Shapiro v Thompson*, 394 U.S. 618 (1969) at 641 and *Graham v Richardson*, 403 U.S. 365 (1971) at 382.

[436] *Toll v Moreno*, 458 U.S. 1 (1982) at 12.

[437] Nowak, 'Realizing the Standards of Review under the Equal Protection Guarantee—Prohibited, Neutral and Permissive Classifications' (1974) *GeorgeLJ* 1071 *et seq*, at 1099.

regarding the test to be applied and the erosion of aliens' right to equal treatment are the almost inevitable result of the classic equal protection model. Yet, this is not to say equal protection analysis cannot provide an adequate technique for reviewing alienage classifications. Legal certainty and an adequate protection of aliens' right to equal treatment could be achieved if the Court would subject alienage classification to an intermediate level of scrutiny. This test allows courts to give due regard to both aliens' right to equal treatment and the States' interest in discriminating against aliens. Indeed, all the Court's decisions in alienage cases would appear to be quite consistent if the Court had applied the intermediary test.[438]

Pre-emption and equal protection analysis are not mutually exclusive. Rather, they are complementary legal methods for reviewing alienage classifications. Immigration and alien policy are predominantly Federal affairs and States should simply not be entitled to thwart these policies. Pre-emption is the starting-point. Whenever Federal policy demands or prescribes equality of treatment, States must act accordingly. In all other cases, one necessarily has to resort to equal protection analysis. Preferably, the Court should apply the intermediate level of scrutiny. For as long as the Court adheres to the classic two-tiered equal protection model, legal uncertainty as to the true principles underlying the Court's jurisprudence is likely to remain.[439]

8.7.4 Categories of Aliens

As chaotic and confusing as the Court's jurisprudence on discrimination against aliens may be, it is possible to bring some structure to constitutional rules applicable to State discrimination against aliens. The outcomes of the several alienage decisions reveal that aliens enjoy an ascending scale of rights as their contribution to society increases. In determining the validity of alienage classifications the Court appears to make a distinction between, at least, three categories of aliens.

The first category consists of aliens who have been lawfully admitted by the Federal authorities for permanent residence. Such immigrants or permanent residents are, of all aliens, the most like United States citizens. They have made the United States their permanent home, are fully taxable and integrated in social

---

[438] Rotunda and Nowak (1992) n 32 above, at 217.

[439] One could even argue that there is formally no need at all for pre-emption analysis. The Equal Protection Clause does allow courts to give due regard to the Federal interest in immigration and alien policy. One could simply argue that whenever Federal authorities prescribe that aliens have to be treated equally, States no longer have an interest which may justify a discrimination against aliens. Such discrimination might not, even under the rational relation test, withstand judicial scrutiny. Basically, however, such a view implies an incorporation of the pre-emption doctrine in equal protection analysis. For the purposes of clarity it is therefore preferable to speak of equal protection and pre-emption analysis as complementary legal techniques for evaluating alienage classifications.

and economic life and they may even be called into the armed forces. The only difference between them and United States citizens is that they do not possess United States citizenship.[440] The right to equal treatment is strongly protected. Under the Equal Protection Clause, permanent resident aliens enjoy the protection of the compelling State interest test except in cases concerning voting rights and public employment.

The second class consists of non-immigrant aliens. The category of non-immigrants is highly heterogenous and includes, for instance, aliens who merely visit the United States as well as aliens who have lived there for years without ever acquiring permanent resident status or United States citizenship. The principles governing the equal treatment of non-immigrants are not as clear as in the case of permanent resident aliens. *Toll v Moreno*[441] (1982) demonstrates that State alienage requirements must be held invalid if the Federal immigration authorities have explicitly or implicitly indicated that non-immigrant aliens should be treated equally.[442] In most other cases involving non-immigrants pre-emption analysis will not be of much help. One has to resort to equal protection analysis. The Court has never indicated which standard of review must be applied to State discrimination against non-immigrants,[443] but, as argued earlier on, the Court should preferably apply the intermediate level of scrutiny.

Undocumented or illegal aliens constitute the third category of aliens. These are aliens who have entered the United States contrary to Federal law and aliens who have decided to stay after the expiration of the temporary period for which they were initially allowed to stay. In spite of their illegal presence in the United States, undocumented aliens are entitled to equal protection from the law.[444] In *Plyler v Doe*[445] (1982) the Court held, as noted earlier on, that their illegal presence prevents them from being treated as a suspect class.[446] State discrimination against undocumented aliens is, in principle, only scrutinised under the rational

---

[440] Once aliens are admitted to permanent residence, they are 'virtually full-fledged members of the American community, sharing the burdens of membership as well as the benefits'. Rosberg, 'The Protection of Aliens from Discriminatory Treatment by the National Government' (1977) *SC Rev* 275–339, at 337.

[441] *Toll v Moreno*, 458 U.S. 1 (1982).

[442] *Ibid*, at 12–13.

[443] Rosberg (1983) n 295 above, at 401.

[444] The 'protection of the Fourteenth Amendment extends to anyone, citizen or stranger, who *is* subject to the laws of a State . . . That a person's initial entry into a State, was unlawful, . . . cannot negate the simple fact of his presence within the State's territorial perimeter. Given such presence, . . . he is entitled to the equal protection of the laws that a State may choose to establish'. *Plyler v Doe*, 457 U.S. 202 (1982) at 215.

[445] *Plyler v Doe*, 457 U.S. 202 (1982). On *Plyler* and the equal treatment of undocumented aliens see Rosberg (1982) n 295 above; Perry, 'Equal Protection, Judicial Activism, and the Intellectual Agenda of Constitutional Theory: Reflections on, and Beyond, Plyler v Doe' (1983) *UPittLRev* 329 *et seq* and X, *Developments in Law* (1983) n 411 above, at 1400–33.

[446] *Plyler v Doe*, 457 U.S. 202 (1982) at 223.

relation test[447] with the result that States can deny illegal aliens virtually all benefits accorded to citizens and lawfully admitted aliens.[448]

9 CONCLUSIONS

As noted in Section 1, most questions concerning cross-border access to welfare state services within the European Community and the United States must be answered on the basis of the general rules and principles governing the free movement of persons. The discussion in the previous sections has demonstrated that there are significant differences between the rules governing this freedom of movement. Critics might even say that there are too many differences in order to make useful a comparative analysis of the degree to which European Community law and American constitutional law entitle individuals to gain access to public benefits systems in other States. Differences are decreasing however. In particular, European Community law on the free movement of persons has proven to be quite dynamic. Over the years, Community law has transformed the initial economically determined freedom of movement into a general freedom of movement which increasingly resembles the American right to travel. Freedom of movement is now a right which nationals of Member States enjoy merely in their capacity as citizens of the Union and upon arrival in another State, Union citizens enjoy a right to equal treatment which reaches almost as far as the right to equal treatment enjoyed by the beneficiaries of the American right to travel. Both European and American law entitle citizens who have moved to other States to gain (equal) access to social and public benefits and, at least on the face of it, the non-discrimination tests applied by the European Court of Justice and the American Supreme Court show clear similarities. For instance, both courts are very strict as regards State rules or measures which directly discriminate against citizens of other States. To nationality requirements the European Court applies a virtual per se rule of prohibition, whilst the American Supreme Court subjects waiting-period requirements to the virtually insurmountable compelling State interest test. Further, the substantial relation test applied under the American Privileges and Immunities Clause, the Commerce Clause as well as the intermediate test adopted under the Equal Protection Clause resemble the test which the Court of Justice applies when reviewing national rules which indirectly discriminate against non-nationals or which merely hamper freedom of movement.

---

[447] To be sure, States have to guarantee undocumented aliens the same equal protection as regards fundamental rights as they have to afford United States citizens and lawfully admitted aliens. X, *Developments in Law* (1983) n 411 above, at 1445–6. Fundamental rights trigger the compelling State interest test on their own and all classifications which impede these rights are subject to strict scrutiny regardless of the status of person whose rights are impeded.

[448] In *Plyler* the Court held that 'persuasive arguments support the view that a State may withhold its beneficence from those whose very presence within the United States is the product of their own unlawful conduct'. *Plyler v Doe*, 457 U.S. 202 (1982) at 219.

Bearing in mind the existing differences as well as the increasing similarities between American constitutional and European Community law, the discussion now proceeds with an examination of the law governing cross-border access to specific public benefits which have been selected for the purposes of this book.

3

Minimum Subsistence Benefits

From the European (Economic) Community's inception, its Member States have objected to a free movement of persons which would enable individuals in need of social assistance benefits to move to and to establish residence in other Member States. Those Member States now located in the geographical heart of the Community especially have always feared that the comparatively high level of their benefits would attract nationals from the 'southern' and 'poorer' Member States. A large influx of Community citizens moving for the sole purpose of collecting higher benefits, so the argument runs, could affect the financing of social assistance schemes.

Initially, the objections to 'social tourism' remained largely hidden. The original EEC Treaty merely prescribed freedom of movement for employed and self-employed persons and it was presumed of such persons that they would provide for themselves and their family members with income earned from work. When from the early 1970s, however, the Court of Justice started to interpret Community provisions on the free movement of workers broadly, and in particular when the first plans for the realisation of a general right of residence for all Community citizens were launched, Member States were quick to express their concerns and objections. The conflict between the goal of realising a free movement of persons, on the one hand, and the need to protect social assistance schemes, on the other hand,[1] came to the surface.

This chapter explores how Community law has sought to settle this conflict by examining the degree to which it gives individuals in need of social assistance(-like) benefits the right to move to other Member States and to claim such benefits there. Section 2 puts the subject in its proper context by (*i*) describing the main characteristics of the Member States' social assistance schemes, (*ii*) the ways in which Member States have traditionally regulated the access of 'needy' foreigners to their territory and benefit schemes and (*iii*) the case law of the Court of Justice on the application of the Community's rules on the coordination of social security schemes to social assistance(-like) benefits. The subsequent four sections deal with the free movement and social assistance rights of

---

[1] On the conflict between the 'free movement interest' and the 'public benefit interest' see further ch 1 s 2.

economic residents (section 3), non-economic residents (section 4), non-residents (section 5) and third country nationals (section 6).[2] After a brief summary and evaluation (section 7), the discussion proceeds in Section 8 with an analysis of the law governing cross-border access to social assistance schemes within the United States. As described in the previous chapter, the American Constitution guarantees a right to travel, which, in principle, entitles all persons present, or established, in the United States to move freely among the States. Like the Member States of the European Community, however, the American States have always resisted a freedom of movement for persons in need of social assistance or welfare benefits. Many States have feared that the comparatively high level of their benefits would have a magnetic effect on 'indigents' from other States and they have claimed the power to put up legal barriers in order to avoid 'free-riding indigents' affecting the financial stability of their benefit schemes. Section 9 explores whether, and if so, to what extent, American States are entitled to impose such legal restrictions and how American constitutional law has settled the conflict between the 'free movement interest' and the 'social assistance interest.' In the final section the findings of this chapter will be evaluated. Can, or should, Community law on the free movement of persons and cross-border access to social assistance be adjusted or improved, and what lessons can possibly be learned from the United States?

At the outset, some comments need to be made about terminology. Above, reference has been made to social assistance-like benefits and the title of this chapter refers to minimum subsistence benefits. There are two reasons for this. First, the discussion of European Community law will not only include the traditional social assistance schemes, but also the so-called 'mixed,' 'hybrid' or 'special non-contributory' benefit schemes. The main features of these benefit schemes will be described in the next section, but these benefits, like social assistance benefits, are funded out of tax revenues and aimed at giving recipients a minimum means of subsistence. Secondly, the term 'social assistance benefits' is rarely used in the United States. Publicly funded benefits that aim to offer the 'poor' a minimum of financial means are usually referred to as 'welfare benefits.' The 'European' sections of this chapter speak of social assistance and mixed benefits and the term welfare benefits will be used in the 'American' section. All benefits to be dealt with, however, are funded out of the public purse, aimed at offering beneficiaries minimum means of subsistence and they may therefore all be referred to as minimum subsistence benefits.[3]

---

[2] For a brief description of the four categories and the main principles governing their legal status under Community law, see ch 2, ss 2–5.

[3] The term is derived from Vonk, 'De Coördinatie van Bestaansminimumuitkeringen in de Europese Gemeenschap' (1991) at 40–1.

2 MINIMUM SUBSISTENCE BENEFITS AND THE EUROPEAN COMMUNITY

2.1 Minimum Subsistence Benefit Schemes of the Member States

In each of the Member States governments hold a certain responsibility for the financial well being of the population. Persons who, due to unemployment, sickness, old age or disability are no longer able to generate an income from work, should be assured of maintaining (the main) part of their income and every member of society should possess the minimum means for subsistence.[4] In furtherance of this responsibility, Member States' governments have established numerous social benefit schemes.[5] Traditionally, a distinction has been made between social security (or insurance) benefit schemes and social assistance schemes.[6]

Social security schemes are State created systems which oblige or enable specific categories of persons such as workers to insure themselves against loss of income resulting from unemployment, sickness, invalidity or old age. Social security schemes place the beneficiaries in a legally defined position that is largely determined by their personal 'insurance record.' The payment of social charges by workers and their employers (to a social insurance fund) entitles workers to benefits when the insured risk occurs. The level of benefits is fixed and generally does not depend on other possible sources of income. The benefits are granted as of right and in principle funded out of the collectively paid contributions.

Social assistance schemes are different in nature.[7] The schemes offer minimum financial means to all members of society who are not able to provide for themselves and their dependent family members. Social assistance is subsidiary in nature. Benefits are only granted to persons who have no other financial

---

[4] De Kam *et al*, Leer van de Social Zekerheid (1989) at 18–20.

[5] For an overview of the benefit schemes in the Member States see eg Einerhand, 'Sociale Zekerheid: Een Europese Vergelijking', (1997) 5–20 in: *TvA* (1997) 5–20; Pieters (ed), *Social Security Law in Fifteen Member States of the European Union* (1997); Einerhand, 'Sociale Zekerheid: Stelsels en Regelingen' in Enkele Europese Landen (1995) and Pieters/Schell, *Inleiding to het Sociale Zekerheidsrecht van de Landen van de Europese Gemeenschap* (1990).

[6] Two other types of benefits can be identified. The first consists of benefits for 'common risks' which are given regardless of the payment of any contributions. Examples of these 'universal' benefits are child benefits paid to families irrespective of financial means. The second 'other' type concerns social compensation benefits for victims of certain misfortunes for which the State accepts responsibility. These include eg vaccination damage payments. See White, EC Social Security Law (1999) at 6.

[7] On the traditional distinction between social assistance and security see eg Forde, 'Social Assistance and the EEC's Regulations', in: *LIEI* (1978) 9–28 and Perrin, Les Prestations non contributive et la Sécurité sociale, in: *DS* (1961) 179–88. The organisation of social assistance schemes differs considerably. For an overview of social assistance schemes in various European countries see eg Einerhand, 'Bijstand een Internationale Vergelijking,' in: *SMA* (1997) 207–20; Eardley *et al*, *Social Assistance in OECD Countries: Synthesis Report* (1996) and *Council of Europe, Social Assistance Benefits in Cash and in Kind in the Council of Europe Member States and Finland* (1982).

means be it income from work or social security benefits. Social assistance is the last stage of governmental help which, in most Member States, serves as a financial safety net for those in financial need. The schemes take beneficiaries' financial need rather than their insurance record as the starting-point. Usually, the grant of social assistance benefits is preceded by a means test. Social assistance schemes are non-contributory benefit schemes. They are paid out of tax revenues; payment of taxes is not a prerequisite for individual enjoyment of social assistance benefits. Under the poor relief systems, out of which social assistance systems have grown,[8] grant as well as the level of social assistance benefits were dependent upon the discretionary power of the competent administrative body. Benefits were accorded as a privilege; they were seen as a form of governmental charity.

Over the years, the traditional distinction between social security and social assistance has become blurred.[9] Today, social assistance benefits are also granted as of right, whilst social security schemes often contain features which traditionally characterised social assistance. Insurance-based schemes may contain a means test,[10] they are often also financed by the State and benefits may be granted irrespectively of the actual payment of social charges.[11] Often, it is quite difficult, if possible at all, to label benefit systems as either social insurance or social assistance. Many benefit schemes aim to provide specific categories such as the disabled or the elderly with minimum means of subsistence. Such categorical benefit schemes, which may be granted as a substitute for classic social assistance or as a supplement to insufficient social security benefits, resemble social assistance in that they are financed out of the public budget, not dependent on the payment of taxes, subsidiary to social security benefits and preceded by a, often limited, means test. However, such minimum subsistence benefit systems are also insurance-like because they are only made available for specific categories of persons and often administered by social security funds.

A typical example concerns the Netherlands Law on the Provision of Income for Unemployed Workers who are Elderly or Suffering from Partial Incapacity to Work (the so-called IOAW). The law is intended to provide elderly persons

---

[8] On the origin of social assistance schemes see eg Vonk (1991) n 3 above, at 30–5; Hepple, 'Welfare Legislation and Wage Labour', in: Hepple (ed), *The Making of Labour Law in Europe— A Comparative Study of Nine Countries up to 1945* (1986) 115–53; Schulte/Trenk Hinterberger, 'Sozialhilfe, eine Einführung' (1986) 37–46 (Germany) and van der Valk, *Van Pauperszorg tot Bestaanszekerheid—Een Onderzoek naar de Ontwikkeling van Armenzorg in Nederland tegen de Achtergrond van de Overgang naar de Algemene Bijstandswet 1912–1965* (1986) (the Netherlands).

[9] van der Mei, 'De Rechtmatigheid van Woonplaatsvereisten voor Bestaansminimumuitkeringen onder het EG-Recht,' in *SMA* (1999) 451–9; van der Mei, 'Het Vrij Verkeer van Personen binnen de Europese Gemeenschap en de (Niet-)Exporteerbaarheid van "Gemengde" Bestaansminimumuit-keringen', in *USZ* (1997) 895–902 and Laske, 'The Impact of the Single European Market on Social Protection for Migrant Workers', in *CMLRev* (1993) 515–40, at 528.

[10] Schell/Pieters, 'De Middelentoets in Rechtsvergelijkend Perspectief', (1989) at 174.

[11] On this development see in particular the opinion of Adv Gen Mayras in Case 1/72 *Frilli* [1972] ECR 457 at 468–75.

who have lost employment with minimum means of subsistence without sub-jecting beneficiaries to the means test of the general social assistance scheme. IOAW benefits are funded out of the public purse and they are provided and administered by the same bodies that are responsible for social assistance benefits. However, the means test under the IOAW is limited (test of partners' income, no test concerning property) and the benefits are only granted to specific categories of unemployed persons. Benefits such as the ones offered under the IOAW contain a mixture of social security and social assistance features. They are recognised as a separate category of social benefits that can be situated anywhere between social security and social assistance. They may be referred to as 'mixed,' 'hybrid' or 'special non-contributory' benefit schemes.[12]

2.2 Conditions of Access

The minimum subsistence benefit schemes of the Member States have tradi-tionally been based on the principle of territoriality. Residence on the national territory is a condition for acquiring the right to social assistance and mixed benefits as well as for payment of such benefits. On the basis of national law, minimum subsistence benefits are not exportable.

The territorial limitation of benefit schemes, and social assistance systems in particular, has been defended on various grounds. A first, rather concrete, one is that application of a proper means test to persons living outside the territory of the State would raise technical and administrative difficulties.[13] A second rea-son ground is that the level of benefits is calculated on the basis of the cost of liv-ing in the national territory. Non-residents would otherwise be entitled to benefits that are either 'too high' or 'too low.'[14] A third, more theoretical,

---

[12] See eg van der Mei (1999) n 9 above, at 452 and Vonk (1990) n 3 above, at 37–8. The assimila-tion of social insurance and social assistance is in particular a characteristic of the benefit schemes in the original Member States. In these States two guaranteed minimum income benefit schemes can, roughly speaking, be distinguished: general social assistance schemes which grant subsistence benefits to all members of society irrespective of the cause of their need and mixed benefit schemes which apply to specific categories of persons. Both types of benefits are granted as of right and are generally paid out of the public budget. In southern Member States the picture is often different. 'The general schemes in existence in these States resemble the traditional poor relief systems. A basic right for all 'members of society' to minimum means of subsistence does not exist. See eg Adler, 'The "Habitual Residence Test" in the UK', in: Eichenhofer (ed), *Social Security of Migrants in the European Union of Tomorrow* (1997) 53–9, at 57. Next to these charitable systems several regula-tions for specific and small groups of persons like the blind, disabled, victims of earthquakes, etc. exist. Vonk (1990) n 3 above, at 34. For brief descriptions of these schemes see the relevant chapters in Schell/Pieters (1990) n 10 above and Council of Europe (1982) n 7 above.

[13] See eg the observations of the European Commission in Case 24/74 *Biason* [1974] ECR 999 at 1004.

[14] Schulte, 'Pflegeleistungen zwischen Sozialer Sicherheit und Sozialer Hilfe—Aspekte der Europarechtlichen Abgrenzung', in Sieveking (Hrsg.) *Soziale Sicherung bei Pflegebedürftigkeit in der Europäischen Union* (1998) 143–59, at 154.

ground is that the welfare responsibility of governments only applies to residents and not to non-residents. Only residents are part of the solidarity of shared welfare. The most important argument for the principle of territoriality, however, has always been, and still is, financial in nature. If States were obliged to grant social assistance and mixed benefits to residents and non-residents alike, the financing of these schemes would be affected. Since minimum subsistence benefits are funded out of revenue from taxes paid mainly by residents, States have limited eligibility for benefits to residents.

The above is not to say that States merely regulate access to their social assistance schemes through residence requirements. The picture is more complicated. First, some States have simply denied non-nationals benefits altogether. Secondly, States, and in particular the ones with comparatively high benefit levels, have always recognised that social assistance systems could have a magnetic effect on nationals of other States. Traditionally, immigration policy has been used in order to safeguard the funding of social assistance schemes. Whether or not non-nationals are able to provide for themselves and their family members is one of the most important factors States have considered when deciding on admission for residence. Generally, non-nationals in need of social assistance have been refused admission. Under the guest worker system, as it existed in the 1950s and 1960s, non-nationals were required to contribute to the funding of social assistance schemes by paying taxes, but once they became in need of social assistance they would lose their right to residence. From the perspective of social assistance schemes, guest workers were supposed to be contributors to the welfare state and social assistance schemes; they were not supposed to become a burden on these schemes. Today, being in need of social assistance is usually still a ground for refusing non-nationals residence, but the right to reside is no longer automatically lost the moment a foreigner becomes in need of social benefits. After a minimum period of employment or residence[15] non-nationals may become eligible for social assistance benefits. Up until the expiration of the minimum period of residence or employment, however, being in need of social assistance may still lead to the loss of the right to reside.[16]

[15] Most Member States apply a period of around five years. Vonk (1990) n 3 above, at 194. See for instance the European Convention on Social and Medical Assistance. Art 1 of this Convention provides that the State parties to the Convention shall ensure that nationals of other State parties who are legally residing in their territory are treated equally as regards social (and medical) assistance. Art 6 further states that States shall not repatriate nationals of other contracting parties solely on the ground that they are in need of assistance. The latter article seems to eliminate the power to end the residence of non-nationals in need of social assistance, but Art 7 makes some significant exceptions to this rule. Such persons may be repatriated if they have not resided in the State territory for a period of five years (or ten years for persons who were older than 55 years on the moment of entering the State), are in a fit state of health to be transported and have no close ties to the State of residence. The Convention does not seem to confer upon individuals strong legally enforceable rights. It only imposes on the contracting party State the duty to show restraint in repatriating non-nationals. See further Vonk (1991) n 3 above, at 204–14.

[16] See in general Vonk (1990) n 3 above, at 195–201. For the Netherlands see Swart, *De Toelating and Uitzetting van Vreemdelingen* (1978) at 241–52 and as regards Germany Schuler, *Das Internationale Sozialrecht der Bundesrepublik Deutschland* (1988) at 775–9.

Being in need of minimum subsistence benefits may thus affect the residence status of non-nationals. The reverse also holds true. The residence status of non-nationals is relevant for entitlement to minimum subsistence benefits. First, the right to claim benefits has been made conditional upon lawful residence in the State territory. As a rule, non-nationals who are illegally residing in the national territory have been excluded. Non-nationals can only obtain benefits upon presentation of a valid residence permit or residence entitlement. Secondly, the right to receive minimum subsistence benefits has often been made conditional upon fulfilment of minimum periods of residence. Generally, such durational residence requirements apply to non-nationals only.[17] Nationals only have to fulfil the 'simple' residence requirement.[18]

The practical result of national immigration laws and rules governing minimum subsistence benefits is that many persons in need of such benefits cannot move to other (Member) States. Because they are not entitled to export their benefits, beneficiaries will often be unable to demonstrate that they can provide for themselves in the State where they wish to live. The combined application of immigration laws and the territoriality principle enshrined in the laws and regulations governing minimum subsistence benefits prevents the 'needy' from moving to other States.

2.3 Application of Regulation No 1408/71 to Minimum Subsistence Benefits

For the purposes of this chapter it is important to establish whether minimum subsistence benefits are covered by social security Regulations No 1408/71 and No 574/72.[19] Application of these regulations may have legal effects that do not necessarily follow from the general provisions on freedom of movement and nondiscrimination such as the exportability of benefits and the application of aggregation rules.[20]

---

[17] Compare von Maydell, 'Treatment of Third-Country Nationals in the Member States of the European Union and the European Economic Area in Terms of Social Law—General report', in *Commission of the European Communities/Departemento de Relações Internaçiônais e Convençoes de Segurança Social, Social Security in Europe—Equality between Nationals and Non-Nationals* (1995) 139–54, at 148–51.

[18] There are more situations in which non-nationals are, or have been, treated less favorably than nationals of the host State. Even if non-nationals have resided in the host State for the required minimum period they may be confronted with other conditions that can only or more easily be met by nationals. For instance, mixed benefits that are granted as a supplement to another social security benefit are often only awarded as a supplement to other social security benefits provided by the host State. Often migrants only receive social security benefits from the State of their origin and are thus in a less favorable position than persons who have never lived or worked in another Member State. Furthermore, in applying the means test Member States often leave certain income sources or assets out of consideration. In many cases, however, this exclusion only applies to income or assets in the host State.

[19] For a brief introduction to the regulations see ch 2 s 6.

[20] Lyon-Caen, Social Security and the Principle of Equal Treatment in the EC Treaty and Reg No 1408/71, in *Commission of the European Communities/Departemento de Relações Internaçionais e Convenções de Segurança Social* (1995) 45–73, at 52.

According to Article 4(1), Regulation No 1408/71 applies to sickness and maternity benefits, invalidity benefits, old age benefits, survivors' benefits, benefits in respect of accidents at work and occupational diseases, death grants, unemployment benefits and family benefits. The list of Article 4(1) is exhaustive.[21] Article 4(4) specifically excludes 'social and medical assistance, benefit schemes for victims of war or its consequences' from the scope of application.[22] The classic social assistance benefits are thus not covered.

Difficult questions have arisen as regards the application of the regulations to mixed benefit schemes. From the early 1970s, the Court of Justice has in various cases been asked to determine whether or not such benefits are covered by Regulation No 1408/71.[23] The text of Regulation No 1408/71 did not give the Court much to go by. That mixed benefits are non-contributory could be no reason for excluding these benefits from the scope of application. Article 4(2) provides that Regulation No 1408/71 applies to all general and special social security schemes, whether contributory or non-contributory.[24] Further, Article 5 of the regulation, which provides that every Member State has to notify the President of the Council of the legislation that comes under the scope of the Regulation, did not seem to be of much help. Such notifications do not define the scope of the Regulation. Benefit schemes that have been notified are covered

[21] See eg Case C–66/92 *Acciardi* [1993] ECR I–4567 and Case 122/84 *Scrivner* [1985] ECR 1029 at 19.

[22] The reasons behind the exclusion of social assistance are not entirely clear. It has been suggested that the exclusion relates to the fact that at the time the original Reg No 3/58 was adopted, most Member States were bound by the European Convention on Social and Medical Assistance (1953). See Bender, 'Die Sozialhilfe im System Ausländerrechts, in Demokratie und Recht' (1974) 36–42, at 37. Also, it might be that there was no rational motive for excluding social assistance and that the drafters of Reg No 3/58 simply continued to apply the principles of the European Interim Agreements of the Council of Europe that did not apply to social asisstance benefits. Vonk (1991) n 3 above, at 249–50 and Schulte, 'Pensions and Social Security', in Carlier/Verwilghen, *Thirty Years of Free Movement of Workers in Europe* (2000) 143–58, at 145.

[23] See Case 1/72 *Frilli* [1972] ECR 457; Case 187/73 *Callemeyn* [1974] ECR 553; Case 24/74 *Biason* [1974] ECR 999; Case 39/74 *Costa* [1974] ECR 1251; Case 7/75 *Mr and Mrs F* [1975] ECR 679; Case 39/76 *Mouthaan* [1975] ECR 1901; Case 63/76 *Inzirillo* [1976] ECR 2057; Case 139/82 *Piscitello* [1983] ECR 1471; Case 261/83 *Castelli* [1984] ECR 3199; Case 249/83 *Hoeckx* [1985] ECR 982; Case 122/84 *Scrivner* [1985] ECR 1029; Joined Cases 379–381/85 and 93/86 *Giletti and others* [1987] ECR 955; Case 147/87 *Zaoui* [1987] ECR 551; Case 236/88 *Commission v France* [1990] ECR I–3163; Case 356/89 *Newton* [1991] ECR I–3017; Case C–66/92 *Acciardi* [1993] I–4567 and Case C–78/91 *Hughes* [1992] ECR I–4839.

For descriptions of the case law see van der Mei (1999) n 9 above; van der Mei (1997) n 9 above; Schulte (1998) n 14 above; Verschueren, 'Libre Circulation des Personnes et Protection Sociale Minimale', in *RMUE* (1996) at 83–105; Verschueren, Les Prestation spéciales à Caractère non contributif et le Règlement Communautaire, in *DS* (1995) 921–30; Pennings, 'Bijstandsuitkeringen' en het Recht op Vrij Verkeer van Werknemers, in: MR (1992) p 146–55; Vonk (1990) n 3 above, at 318–36 and Watson, 'Minimum Income Benefits: Social Security or Social Assistance', in *ELRev* (1985) 335–43.

[24] Taking the financing method as a distinguishing criterion would be rather 'artificial' since many benefit schemes are financed from different sources. They are often both contributory and non-contributory in nature. See Advocate General Roemer in his Opinion in Case 28/68 *Torrekens* [1969] ECR 125 at 140.

by the Regulation, but the fact that certain schemes are not notified does not necessarily mean that they fall outside the field of application of the Regulation.[25] Finally, it was clear that the national classification of benefits as social assistance or social security could not be a relevant factor. If it were, Member States could unilaterally exclude certain benefits from the regulation.[26]

In the absence of concrete guidance provided by the Regulation, it was wholly up to the Court to determine whether and, if so, under which conditions mixed benefits are covered by the regulation. The first case in which the Court was asked to address the issue was *Frilli* (1972). The case concerned an Italian national who lived in Belgium and who, by virtue of previous employment, received a retirement pension there. This pension, however, did not suffice for meeting the basic costs of living. Mrs Frilli therefore applied for payment of a guaranteed income for old people. Her request was rejected on grounds of her nationality. In order to establish whether Mrs Frilli could claim equality of treatment under Regulation No 3/58, the predecessor of Regulation No 1408/71, the Court had to determine whether the benefit in question fell within the scope of the regulation. The Court observed that:

> 'Although it may seem desirable, from the point of view of applying the regulation, to establish a clear distinction between legislative schemes which come within social security and those which come within assistance, it is possible that certain laws, because of the classes of persons to which they apply, their objectives, and the detailed rules for their application, may simultaneously contain elements belonging to both categories mentioned and thus defy any general classification.'[27]

The Belgian guaranteed income for older people had certain affinities with social assistance, in particular where it prescribed need as an essential criterion for its application. The Court stated, however, that the benefit nevertheless approximated social security because it did not prescribe consideration of each individual case, which is a characteristic of social assistance, and it conferred on recipients a legally defined position giving them the right to a benefit which is analogous to old age pensions. Such legislation, the Court held, 'in fact fulfils a double function.' It 'consists on the one hand in guaranteeing a subsistence level to persons wholly outside the social security system, and on the other hand in providing an income supplement for persons in receipt of inadequate social security benefits."[28] The Court concluded that as regards workers who have completed periods of employment in a Member State, reside in that State and who are entitled to a pension there, legislative provisions giving elderly residents a legally protected right to a minimum pension fall within the scope of Regulation No 3/58.[29]

---

[25] Case 35/77 *Beerens* [1977] ECR 2249, 9 and Case C–85/99 *Offermans* [2001] ECR I–0000, 26.

[26] See eg Case 79/76 *Fossi* [1977] ECR 667.

[27] Case 1/72 *Frilli* [1972] ECR 457, 13. See also Case 39/74 *Costa* [1974] ECR 1251, 6 and Case C–356/89 *Newton* [1991] ECR I–3017, 12.

[28] *Ibid*, at 15.

[29] *Ibid*, at 18.

In later cases the Court has followed a similar approach. After having established that the benefit schemes under consideration fulfilled a double function, the Court assessed these benefits on the basis of their purpose and specific features.[30] Even though the Court has not always been consistent, one may conclude from the case law that a social benefit had to meet the following conditions in order to come within the ambit of the Regulation:

(i) the legislation under which the benefit is granted must place claimants in a legally defined position as a result of which they have an absolute right to benefit;[31]
(ii) the benefit must cover one of the risks enumerated in Article 4(1)[32] and
(iii) recipient must have been subject to the social security system of the State under whose legislation the benefit is made available.[33]

When a benefit satisfied these criteria, the Court classified it as a social security benefit falling within the ambit of Regulation No 1408/71. In *Acciardi* (1993), for instance, the Court concluded that the Netherlands IOAW, mentioned in section 2.1, fell within the scope of the Regulation. The benefit in question was partly dependent on the income of the applicant and/or the spouse, but this did

---

[30] The distinction between benefits that are excluded from the field of application of Reg No 1408/71 and benefits that come within it 'rests entirely on the factors relating to each benefit, in particular its purpose and the conditions for its grant'. Case 9/78 *Gillard* [1978] ECR 1661, 12 and Case 139/82 *Piscitello* [1983] ECR 1471, 10.

[31] 31 Case 1/72 *Frilli* [1972] ECR 457, 18 and Case 139/82 *Piscitello* [1983] ECR 1471, 11.

[32] 32 Case 249/83 *Hoeckx* [1985] ECR 982, 12 and Case 122/84 *Scrivner* [1985] ECR 1029, 19. The fact that a mixed benefit constitutes the sole source of income of recipients does not prevent application of Reg No 1408/71. When a benefit may be paid as a supplement to another social security benefit, it in principle falls within the scope of the regulation. Case 139/82 *Piscitello* [1983] ECR 1471, 13.

[33] 33 Case C–356/89 *Newton* [1991] ECR I–3017, 19. Newton was a British national who was working as a self-employed person in France, when became the victim of a car accident as a result of which he became paralysed. He returned to the United Kingdom where he applied for, and was awarded, a so-called mobility allowance. This was a minimum income benefit granted to persons who, due to physical disability, were unable to walk. The national law required *inter alia* that the beneficiaries were 'ordinarily present' on the territory of the United Kingdom. Thus, when Newton decided to move back to France the competent administrative authorities withdrew the mobility allowance. In order to be able to export his allowance on the basis of Art 10 of Reg No 1408/71 (see further s 5.2), it had to be established that the mobility allowance was covered by Regulation No 1408/71. Mr Newton had never worked in the United Kingdom and had never been subject to the social security system of the United Kingdom. In the proceedings before the Court, the Commission therefore argued that Mr Newton could not export his allowance because if he could, there would be a danger that persons who have never worked and lived in a certain State could nonetheless claim certain mixed benefit schemes. Unlike Adv Gen Darmon, the Court accepted the Commission's argument. In the Court's view, the benefits could not be regarded as being covered by Reg No 1408/71 in the case of persons who have only been subject to the legislation of States other than the one whose legislation is invoked. *Ibid*, at 15–16. The Court recognised the financial concerns of the Member States. Any other conclusion would affect the stability of the system instituted by the national legislation. The co-ordination system set up by the two social security regulations is aimed at promoting free movement of persons, but the provisions of the regulations cannot be interpreted in such a way as to upset national systems. *Ibid*, at 17–19.

not imply that it was to be classed as a social assistance benefit. In the Court's view, the IOAW provided a legally defined criterion which gave entitlement to the benefit without the competent authority being able to take other personal circumstances into consideration. The grant of the IOAW benefit did not depend on an individual assessment of the claimant's personal needs and since the benefit was directly related to the risk of unemployment, it was classified as an unemployment benefit for the purposes of the Regulation.[34]

In 1992 the case law of the Court has largely been codified. Regulation No 1247/92[35] has inserted a new Article 4(2a) in Regulation No 1408/71 which states that the regulation applies to:

> 'Special non-contributory benefits which are provided under legislation or schemes other than those referred to in paragraph 1 or excluded by virtue of paragraph 4, where such benefits are intended: (a) either to provide supplementary, substitute or ancillary cover against the risks covered by the branches of social security referred to in paragraph 1(a) to (h), or (b) solely for the protection of the disabled.'

The first two of the above-mentioned conditions have been codified. The third is no longer applicable.[36] In sum, mixed benefits fall within the scope of Regulation No 1408/71,[37] but the classic social assistance benefits are still excluded by virtue of Article 4(4).

3 ECONOMIC RESIDENTS

Having put the subject of this chapter in its proper context, the discussion can now proceed with an analysis of the Community rules and principles governing cross-border access to minimum subsistence benefit schemes. For the purposes of this book four categories have been identified: economic residents, non-economic residents, non-residents and third country nationals.[38] This section discusses the category of economic residents, and Community workers and their family members in particular.[39]

---

[34] Case C–66/92 *Acciardi* [1993] ECR I–4567, 15–19.

[35] OJ 1992 No L 136. On the background of this Reg see s 5 of this chapter and Opinion of Adv Gen Jacobs in Case C–132/96 *Stinco* [1998] ECR I–5225, 22–3.

[36] See Case C–20/96 *Snares* [1997] ECR I–6057, 48 and Verschueren (1996) n 23 above, at 99.

[37] Lyon-Caen (1995) n 20 above, at 54.

[38] See ch 2 s 2–5.

[39] The category of economic residents also covers the self-employed beneficiaries of the right of establishment and their family members. The rights of beneficiaries of Art 43 EC concerning movement to, and eligibility for minimum subsistence benefits, in other Member States will not be discussed separately. The basic assumption is that the self-employed and their family members enjoy the same rights as workers and their family members do. See further ch 2 s 2.4.

3.1 Community Workers

When the Community institutions realised the free movement of workers during the 1960s, they had not considered granting workers a right to claim minimum subsistence benefits in the State of employment. In their view, workers were supposed to provide for themselves with the income earned from full-time employment. National rules governing minimum wages would guarantee that workers did not fall below the minimum subsistence level in the host State and in case they were unable to work due to illness, incapacity or retirement, the Community's social security rules would entitle workers to a wage-replacing social security benefit. Rights concerning minimum subsistence benefits were not provided for. Regulation No 1612/68 does not contain any provision specifically dealing with social assistance and other minimum subsistence benefits and, as noted, Article 4(4) of the Regulation No 1408/71 explicitly excludes social assistance from the scope of this regulation.

From the early 1970s, however, the Court of Justice has broadly interpreted the provisions on the free movement of workers. The Court has extended the scope of the right to equal treatment and it has recognised that Article 39 EC can also be relied upon by work-seekers, part-time workers and other 'flexible' workers whose income may fall below the minimum subsistence level. Are such 'needy' Community citizens entitled to claim social assistance or mixed benefits in the Member State where they work?

3.1.1 Right to Reside

Before considering whether Community citizens have the right to claim minimum subsistence benefits in the State of employment, it is necessary to determine whether being in need of such benefits affects their right to establish residence in that State.[40] Can Community citizens who have found and taken up

---

[40]   The right to enter the territory of another Member State is not affected by being in need of minimum subsistence benefits. This right is only subject to the public policy proviso and it is settled case law that Member States cannot rely on this proviso for economic ends. See further ch 2 s 7.2.

In Case 36/85 *Bonincontro* the Court was asked whether being in need of social assistance benefits could possibly be regarded as a threat to public policy and thus be a reason to refuse residence or to expel a national of another Member State on the basis of Art 39(3) EC. See OJ 1985 C 59. The case, however, was withdrawn. Most probably, the Court would have answered the question in the negative. See Verschueren, *Internationale Arbeidsmigratie* (1990) at 393, n 86 and Hailbronner, Aufenthaltbeschränkungen gegenüber EG-Angehörigen und neuere Entwicklungen im EG-Aufenthaltsrecht, in *ZAR* (1985) 108–16, at 112–13. On this point see further Schulz, *Freizügigkeit für Unionsbürger* (1997) at 305–7.

Further, the right to stay of Community citizens who wish to seek work in other Member States cannot be refused or ended on the ground that beneficiaries are not able to provide for themselves. In 1968 the Member States included in the minutes of the meeting at which Reg No 1612 was adopted a declaration which stipulated that in case Community citizens should 'be taken charge of by national assistance (social welfare)' in the State where they seek work, they could 'be invited to leave the territory of this . . . State'. See ch 2 s 2.2.1. In *Antonissen* (1991), however, the

employment but whose remuneration falls below the minimum subsistence level acquire the status of worker and the right to reside in the State of employment?

The issue arose in *Levin* (1982).[41] The case concerned a British national who wished to reside with her South African husband in the Netherlands. The application for a residence permit was rejected on the ground that Mrs Levin was not engaged in gainful occupation in the Netherlands. She appealed the decision. During the course of the proceedings she accepted a 20 hour-a-week job as a cleaning lady. The income she derived from this job fell below the minimum subsistence level. Mrs Levin claimed that this could be no reason to withhold the requested residence card because she and her husband had property and income enough to support themselves. Before the Court of Justice, the Dutch government argued that persons such as Mrs Levin who only work for a limited number of hours, who earn less than the host State's minimum subsistence level and who move to other States lacking the primary intent of working, cannot claim to be Community workers and acquire the right to reside.

The Court rejected the Dutch arguments. The concept of Community worker should not be determined by reference to national rules on minimum working hours, wages or subsistence levels. Rather, the concept should be clarified within the Community legal order.[42] The Court held that part-time work could be an effective means to improve a person's living conditions. The concept of worker may therefore also apply to 'persons who pursue or wish to pursue an activity as an employed person on a part-time basis only and who, by virtue of that fact obtain or would obtain only remuneration lower than the minimum wage guaranteed in the sector under consideration.'[43] The income can be supplemented by private resources or by the earnings of an accompanying family member.[44] The purpose of the movement to another Member State was considered to be immaterial.[45]

From a social assistance perspective, *Levin* was not yet so controversial. Apparently, the Levins had sufficient financial means; they did not ask for, and were not likely to become in need of, social assistance. However, the judgment

---

Court held that the declaration had no legal significance. Case C–292/89 *Antonissen* [1991] ECR I–745, 18. Hence, the declaration does not entitle the host States to end the stay of work-seekers on the ground that they are in need of minimum subsistence benefits. There also does not seem to be any sound reason for limiting the right to stay of work-seekers on the ground that they lack sufficient financial means. Work-seekers can be denied minimum subsistence benefits in the State where they seek work on the ground that they do not satisfy the requirement of being a 'habitual resident' of the State in question. See s 5.2.5.

[41] Case 53/81 *Levin* [1982] ECR 1035.

[42] *Ibid*, at 11.

[43] *Ibid*, at 16.

[44] *Ibid*.

[45] The immigration rights of Art 39 EC are granted in order to facilitate the right to work in other Member States. Following some suggestions that had been made in the literature (eg Hartley, *EEC Immigration Law* (1978) at 4–5), Adv Gen Slynn concluded that the rights to enter and reside in another Member States are conditional on it being shown that the work in another Member State is the genuine and substantial purpose of Community citizens exercising these rights. The Court, however, rejected this view. Case 53/81 *Levin* [1982] ECR 1035, 22.

did raise the question whether the right to reside of a Community worker could also be obtained by part-time workers who have no other sources of income and who are in need of social assistance benefits. The question was put to the Court in *Kempf* (1985).[46] The case involved a German music teacher who for twelve hours a week taught guitar lessons in the Netherlands. His application for a residence card was rejected on the ground that he had obtained a supplementary social assistance-like benefit. Was the refusal to grant him the residence card compatible with Article 39 EC? The Court concluded that the fact that social assistance benefits are enjoyed can be no reason for denying the status of Community worker because it 'is irrelevant whether . . . supplementary means of subsistence are derived from property or from the employment of a member of his family . . . or whether . . . they are obtained from financial assistance drawn from . . . public funds' of the host State.[47]

3.1.2 Right to Claim Minimum Subsistence Benefits

Thus, being in need of social assistance or other minimum subsistence benefits does not affect the right to establish residence as a Community worker in the State of employment. Neither in *Levin* nor in *Kempf*, however, did the Court go into the question whether workers who have established residence in the State of employment[48] can also claim minimum subsistence benefits there.

A few months before the judgment in *Kempf*, however, the Court had addressed the issue in *Hoeckx* (1985).[49] Mrs Hoeckx was a Dutch national who had claimed a minimum subsistence allowance in Belgium. The allowance, the so-called *minimex*, was refused because Mrs Hoeckx had not lived in Belgium for five years prior to her application. The first question the Court of Justice had to answer was whether the *minimex* fell within the scope of Regulation No 1408/71. An affirmative answer would have implied that Mrs Hoeckx could have invoked Article 3 of the Regulation in order to challenge the durational residence requirement. The Court held, however, that the benefit was not covered by the Regulation. The law governing the *minimex* did confer upon recipients of the allowance a legally defined position, but the benefit was in the view of the Court not linked to one of the risks mentioned in Article 4(1) of the Regulation.[50] In other words, the *minimex* was regarded as a general social assistance benefit, which by virtue of Article 4(4) was excluded from Regulation No 1408/71.[51] This

[46] Case 139/85 *Kempf* [1986] ECR 1741.

[47] *Ibid*, at 14.

[48] On the question whether workers who have decided not to establish residence in the State of employment can claim minimum subsistence benefits there, see s 5.

[49] Case 249/83 *Hoeckx* [1985] ECR 982.

[50] *Ibid*, at 13–15.

[51] Only mixed minimum subsistence benefits that are linked to one of the risks referred to in Art 4(1) can fall under Reg No 1408/71. See eg Case 1/72 *Frilli* [1972] ECR 457 (guaranteed income for old people) and Case 187/73 *Callemeyn* [1974] ECR 553 (benefits for disabled persons).

conclusion, however, did not mean that Mrs Hoeckx lost her case. The Court held that she could invoke Article 7(2) of Regulation No 1612/68, which provides for a right to equal treatment as regards 'social advantages.' The Court reiterated that social advantages are all those advantages or benefits 'which, whether or not linked to a contract of employment, are generally granted to national workers primarily because of their objective status of workers or by virtue of the mere fact of their residence on the national territory.' The Court concluded that benefits guaranteeing a minimum means of subsistence 'in a general manner' constitute social advantages for the purposes of Article 7(2) of Regulation No 1612/68.[52]

Thus, Community workers who wish to claim access to general social assistance schemes may rely on Article 7(2) of Regulation No 1612/68 and, as regards mixed benefits, they can alongside this provision,[53] invoke Article 3 of Regulation No 1408/71. The mere fact, however, that 'needy' Community workers are entitled to invoke these provisions does not automatically imply that they can actually receive minimum subsistence benefits. Article 7(2) and Article 3 provide for a right to equal treatment, which implies that Community workers must in principle meet the same eligibility requirements as the nationals of the host State. Thus, in order to receive a benefit Community workers must be available for work, lack other sources of income, etc. As a rule, such eligibility criteria do not violate the nondiscrimination principle. The same does not hold true for national rules that make enjoyment of benefits conditional upon a minimum period of residence in the State of employment. Read together, *Kempf* and *Hoeckx* would seem to have increased the magnetic effect of the benefit schemes of the 'richer' Member States and it had been argued that Member States should be entitled to apply durational residence requirements in order to protect themselves against 'social tourism.'[54] The Court, however, has not accepted the validity of such requirements. As noted, in *Hoeckx* the Court had to answer whether a five-year residence requirement for the Belgian *minimex*, which only applied to non-nationals, was compatible with Article 7(2) of Regulation No 1612/68. The Court concluded that such a requirement implies 'an additional condition imposed on workers who are nationals of a Member State' which constitutes a direct discrimination on the basis of the nationality

---

[52] Case 249/83 *Hoeckx* [1985] ECR 982, 20–2. For a similar conclusion see Case 122/84 *Scrivner* [1985] ECR 1029, 26. See further also the judgment in *Reina* where the Court held that the concept of 'social advantages' covers 'not only benefits granted as of right' but also rights offered 'on a discretionary basis'. Case 65/81 *Reina* [1982] ECR 33, 17.

[53] The social security benefits covered by the Regulation can in principle also be classed as 'social advantages' for the purposes of Art 7(2) of Reg No 1612/68. See further ch 2 s 6 (n 219).

[54] Compare eg Steiner, 'The Right to Welfare: Equality and Equity under Community Law', in: *ELRev* (1987) 477 *et seq.*, at 41 and Hailbronner, 'Die neuere Rechtsprechung zum EG-Freizügigkeitsrecht', in: ZAR (1988) 3–13, at 6.

of the workers.[55] Member States thus are not entitled to make eligibility for minimum subsistence benefits conditional upon the fulfilment of durational residence or employment requirements.[56]

3.1.3 Effective and Genuine Work

Community workers who earn less than the minimum subsistence level in the State of employment are entitled to establish residence there and, from the moment they actually do so, they are entitled to supplement their income with minimum subsistence benefits under the same conditions as the nationals of the host State. This does not imply, however, that the Court has disregarded Member States' concerns regarding 'social tourism.' On the contrary, due regard has been given to these concerns. The Court has not done so by accepting the legality of durational residence requirements for entitlement to minimum subsistence benefits, by entitling Member States to refuse needy workers

---

[55] Case 249/83 *Hoeckx* [1985] ECR 982, 23–4. In response to the judgment in *Hoeckx*, the Belgian legislator decided to delete the nationality requirement and to impose the rule that all persons regardless of their nationality had to meet the five-year residency requirement. See Van den Bogaert, The Consequences of the Gaygusuz Judgement for Belgian Social Security, in: Van den Bogaert (ed), *Social Security, Non-Discrimination and Property* (1997) 123–48, at 41. In the view of the European Commission, however, the Belgian rules were still contrary to Art 7(2) and the Commission subsequently started an infringement procedure (Art 169 (now 226) of the Treaty). In *Commission v Belgium* (1992) the Court concluded that the waiting-period requirement worked to the disadvantage of nationals from other Member States. The requirement constituted an indirect discrimination on grounds of nationality and it was held to be at odds with both Art 7(2) of Reg No 1612/68 and Art 3 of Reg No 1408/71. Case C–326/90 *Commission v Belgium* [1992] ECR I–5517, 2–3.

[56] This is not to say that the length of residence in the State is in all circumstances an irrelevant factor. See further s 5.2.5.

Art 10a of Reg No 1408/71 provides for an extended right to equal treatment as regards mixed benefits. Art 10a(1) provides that mixed benefits falling within the ambit of Art 4(2a) shall be granted exclusively in the territory of the Member State in which beneficiaries reside, provided such benefits have been listed in the newly created Annex IIa. In other words, residence requirements for entitlement mixed benefits can be validly applied. See further s 5. In addition, however, Art 10a contains a number of provisions that partly compensate for the Member States' right to deny non-residents mixed benefits. In order to secure that beneficiaries will actually be able to receive mixed benefits in the State of residence, Art 10a(2) states that the institution which is to grant mixed benefits shall, where necessary, regard periods of employment, residence or insurance completed in other Member States as though they had been fulfilled in its own territory. Art 10a(3) further provides that a Member State whose legislation makes the grant of a supplementary benefit subject to the prior award of a particular social security benefit under its own legislation, is to treat a corresponding benefit awarded under the legislation of another Member State, as if it were awarded under its own legislation. The supplementary benefit is then added to that foreign corresponding benefit. See COM(85) 396 final. Finally, Art 10a(4) provides that where the legislation of a Member State makes entitlement to a mixed benefit for disability or invalidity subject to the condition that the disability or invalidity should be diagnosed for the first time in the territory of that Member State, this condition shall be deemed to be fulfilled where such diagnosis is made for the first time in the territory of another Member State. See further Art 2a of Reg No 574/72 (as inserted by Reg No 1945/93—OJ 1993 L 181) and Decs No 151 and No 152 of the Administrative Commission on the implementation of Art 10a (OJ 1994 L 244).

residence on public policy grounds[57] or by allowing the States to deny benefits to workers whose primary intent for moving is to obtain comparatively high benefits.[58] Rather, the Court has given regard to the host States' interests in its interpretation of the concept of Community worker. As noted in Section 3.1.1, in *Levin* and *Kempf* the Court was willing to give quite a broad interpretation to the concept by accepting that part-time workers who might be in need of minimum subsistence benefits can also obtain the status of Community worker. However, not all part-time workers can do so. In *Levin* the Court held that a minimum amount of work must be performed. The work must be 'effective and genuine.' Activities that are on such a small scale that they have to be regarded as purely 'marginal and ancillary' do not suffice.[59] The Court has never indicated how many hours must be worked, but from the case law the conclusion could be drawn that a Community citizen must work approximately half of the number of normal working hours in a given sector in order to obtain the status of worker and the connected right to equal treatment as regards minimum subsistence benefits.[60] One cannot be certain of the Court's true motives,[61] but by introducing the criterion of 'effective and genuine work' the Court did create a threshold for Community citizens who, through the pursuit of economic activities during a small number of hours, would try to obtain the status of Community worker, the right to reside and the right to claim social advantages under Article 7(2) of Regulation No 1612/68.

3.1.4 Loss of Effective and Genuine Work

So far the Court has never indicated whether Member States must also grant minimum subsistence benefits to nationals of other Member States who have acquired the status of Community worker but who later lose their effective and genuine employment. If unemployed workers could indeed claim such

---

[57] See n 40 above.

[58] Case 53/81 *Levin* [1982] ECR 1035 at 21.

[59] *Ibid*, at 17.

[60] See Jørgensen, *Union Citizens—Free Movement and Non-Discrimination* (1996) at 31 and ch 2 s 2.2.4.

[61] It would seem, however, that the Court has indeed deliberately chosen to give regard to the Member States' welfare state interests through the interpretation of the notion of worker. The concept of worker may not be defined by reference to national law (Case 53/81 *Levin* [1982] ECR 1035, 11), but the three requirements of work, remuneration and subordination which the Court has laid down (Case 66/85 *Lawrie Blum* [1986] ECR I–2121, 17—see ch 2 s 2.2.4) do indicate that the Court itself has been inspired by national definitions of the concept of worker. The requirement that the work must also be 'effective and genuine', at least to the knowledge of the present author, cannot be found in the labour laws of any of the Member States. The work performed by Community citizens whose jobs are according to the Court to be considered as 'marginal and ancillary' may often very well be classed as economic activities and indeed part-time workers are, as a rule, seen and treated as workers under national labour laws. The new and unique requirement that work must be 'effective and genuine' for the purposes of Art 39 EC has been introduced by the Court itself and it is hard to find any other explanation than that this was done in defence of the welfare state interests of the Member States.

benefits,[62] the status of Community worker could possibly be open to abuse. Community citizens who wish to obtain social assistance benefits in another Member State could take up employment there, then give up their job and subsequently, as Community workers, claim the desired benefits under Article 7(2).

From existing case law, it does not become entirely clear whether and, if so, under which conditions, unemployed workers can obtain, or retain, minimum subsistence benefits. In *Martínez Sala* (1998) the Court held that once 'the employment relationship has ended, the person concerned as a rule loses his status of worker,' and this would seem to imply that the right to invoke Article 7(2) of Regulation No 1612/68 ceases to exist.[63] However, the Court, rather cryptically, added that the status of worker 'may produce effects after the relationship has ended.'[64] The Court has never fully explained what these effects entail, but the afore cited phrase could best be interpreted to mean that unemployed workers retain the right to invoke Article 7(2) as long as they still hold the right to reside in the host State as guaranteed by Article 39 EC.[65] Article 7(1) of Directive No 68/360 indicates that voluntary unemployment leads to the loss of the right to reside and, arguably, the right to equal treatment as regards social advantages.[66] The danger of abuse of the status of worker thus seems minimal.

---

[62] Unemployed workers may become entitled to unemployment benefit, but this is not necessarily the case. Workers may have worked long enough to become eligible for unemployment benefits or they may, after temporary enjoyment of such benefits, become in need of minimum subsistence benefits.

[63] To be sure, this may be different for workers who acquire the so-called right to remain. See Art 7 of Reg No 1251/70 and ch 2 s 2.2.4.

[64] Case C–85/96 *Martínez Sala* [1998] ECR I–2691, 32.

[65] See ch 2 s 2.2.

[66] See Art 7 of Dir No 68/360 and ch 2 s 2.2. To be sure, this does not necessarily imply that the voluntarily unemployed can never claim minimum subsistence benefits. They may be able to do so in their capacity as 'non-economic resident'. See further s 4.

The legal situation may be different for those who voluntarily give up their job in order to commence studying. Such student-workers can retain the status of worker, and thus invoke Art 7(2) of Reg No 1612/68, provided there is 'some continuity between the previous occupational activity and the course of the study; there must be a relationship between the purpose of the study and the previous occupational activity'. Case 39/86 *Lair* [1988] ECR 3161, 37. See further s 5 s 3.2.3.

Grzelczyk (2001) suggests that such relationship is not required in all cases. The case concerned a French student who was studying sports at the University of Louvain, Belgium. During the first three years of his studies Mr Grzelczyk was able to provide for himself by the income earned from various small jobs. In the fourth and final year, however, he was no longer able to combine his studies and employment. Since his parents were not able to maintain him, Mr Grzelczyk applied for a social assistance benefit in Belgium. His application was rejected on the ground that social assistance benefits could only be awarded to Belgian nationals and Community citizens falling within the ambit of Regulation No 1612/68. The national court which has to decide the case asked the Court of Justice, *inter alia*, whether denying Mr Grzelczyk the requested benefit is compatible with Arts 12 and 18 EC. The Belgian court had not included the provisions on the free movement of workers in its preliminary questions because it assumed that Mr Grzelczyk did not fulfil the criteria for treatment as a worker. Advocate General Alber, however, and probably also the Court, however, had doubts about that assumption. In his Opinion Adv Gen Alber did consider whether Mr Grzelczyk could possibly still be classed as a worker in the sense of Art 39 EC. In principle, loss of employment leads to the loss of the status of worker (compare Case C–85/96 *Martínez Sala* [1998] ECR I–2691, 32) but, under reference to *Lair* and *Brown*, the Adv Gen stated that the status of worker and the

Involuntary unemployment does not lead to the loss of the right to reside. This right continues for as long as the period for which the residence card was issued has not expired.[67] Arguably, during this period the involuntary unemployed retain the right to claim equal treatment as regards minimum subsistence benefits under Article 7(2) of Regulation No 1612/68.[68]

3.2 Family Members

The drafters of Regulation No 1612/68 had recognised that a free movement of workers, which is practical and relevant, could not be realised without giving workers the right to be joined by their family members. Article 10 of the regulation entitles the workers' spouse, (grand)children who are under the age of 21 years or dependent and the dependent (grand)parents to install themselves with the worker in the host State.[69] The question whether these family members could possibly claim minimum subsistence benefits in the host State did not seem to arise. Workers were supposed to be full-time workers who would provide for themselves and their families. Family members were assumed to be dependent on the worker, not on the host State. Yet, over the years the Court has strengthened the legal status of family members of Community workers. In doing so, the Court has been inspired by the preamble of Regulation No 1612/68 according to which the free movement of workers requires the abolition of all obstacles to the integration of the worker's family into the host State's society.

---

right to invoke Art 7(2) of Reg No 1612/68 can be retained when a worker gives up employment in order to commence study which is substantially related to the nature of the work that he was last engaged in. From the information given by the national court it did not become clear whether Mr Grzelczyk satisfied the requirement of a link between his work and his studies. Adv Gen Alber, however, did not deem this to be decisive. *Lair* and *Brown* concerned Community citizens who had first worked and subsequently embarked on a study. In such cases a link between the work and the studies needs to be established in order to avoid 'real students' claiming student grants. In the Adv Gens view, the case of Mr Grzelczyk was different because he had been working and studying at the same time. In such cases, Alber did not consider it necessary to insist on a link between studies and work. Opinion of Adv Gen Alber in Case C–184/99 *Grzelczyk* [2001] ECR I–6193, 98–101. In its judgment the Court seemed to approve the Adv Gens reasoning and conclusions. Because the national court had limited its question to Arts 12 and 18 EC, the Court did not deem it necessary to go into the question whether Grzelczyk could retain worker status. The Court expressly added, however, that it was for the national court to determine, in the light, in particular, of the Opinion of the Adv Gen whether or not the facts and circumstances of the case are such as to permit Mr Grzelczyk to be regarded as a worker for the purposes of Community law. Case C–184/99 *Grzelczyk* [2001] ECR I–6193, 18.

[67] See ch 2 s 2.2.4.

[68] Even if one were to assume that such involuntarily unemployed persons are no longer to be regarded as Community workers, they would still be entitled to equality of treatment as regards minimum subsistence benefits. Such unemployed persons would still be 'nationals of the Member States legally residing in another Member State' who are, as follows from the judgment in *Martínez Sala* and *Grezlczyk* entitled to claim access to minimum subsistence benefit schemes under Art 12 EC. See further ch 2 s 3 and s 4 of this chapter.

[69] For further details see ch 2 s 2.3.

Does this imply that family members who are in need of minimum subsistence benefits have the right to claim such benefits in that State?

3.2.1 *Right to Reside*

As in the case of Community workers themselves, it is first to be established whether being in need of minimum subsistence benefits possibly affects the right of family members to reside in the host State. As regards the spouse and (grand)children below the age of 21 years no problems arise. Article 10 of Regulation No 1612/68 makes the right to reside in the host State only condi-tional upon the availability of adequate housing.[70] As regards (grand)children of 21 years or older and (grand)parents, the situation is less clear. Article 10 does not contain a financial means requirement comparable to those contained in the three 1990 residence directives applying to non-economic residents,[71] but the provision does require that the family members concerned are dependent on the worker. What does this imply? Do family members who have been working in the State of origin but are still living with the worker not have the right to join the worker into the State of employment? Do children who have already left their parents' house and obtained social assistance(-like) benefits in the State of origin, have the right to join the worker? Do children who as a minor have acquired the right to reside, lose this right when they apply after their 21st birth-day for social assistance(-like) benefits? More in general, can the requirement of being dependent on the worker be met by family members who are dependent on minimum subsistence benefits?

In order to answer such questions the *Lebon* case (1987)[72] must be considered. Ms Lebon was a 24 year old French woman who had lived almost her entire life in Belgium and who claimed equality of treatment as regards eligibility for social assistance benefits, the so-called *minimex*, as a family member of a Community worker.[73] Her claim was refused and Ms Lebon subsequently appealed that decision. At first glance, Ms Lebon seemed to have a strong case. In earlier judgments the Court had already concluded that minimum subsistence benefits constitute 'social advantages' for the purposes of Article 7(2) of Regulation No 1612/68[74] and that family members may also rely on this provi-sion.[75] For instance, in *Castelli* (1984) the Court had had no difficulty in con-

---

[70] See Art 10(3) of Reg No 1612/68.

[71] See ch 2 ss 3.1 and 3.2.

[72] Case 316/85 *Lebon* [1987] ECR 2811.

[73] Ms Lebon's parents had exercised their right to remain in accordance with Art 39(3)d EC and Reg No 1251/70. The legal status of the beneficiaries of this right to remain in the host State is iden-tical to that of Community workers and their family members and for the purposes of this study these beneficiaries are treated as though they were still holding the status of Community worker or family member of Community worker. See further ch 2 ss 2.2. and 2.3.

[74] Case 249/83 *Hoeckx* [1985] ECR 982, 20–2.

[75] See eg Case 261/83 *Castelli* [1984] ECR 3199, 9–10 and Case 94/84 *Deak* [1985] ECR 1873, 26.

cluding that the mother of an Italian worker in Belgium could rely on Article 7(2) in order to claim a non-contributory income benefit that was intended to provide old people with minimum means for subsistence.[76] In the proceedings before the Court in *Lebon*, however, the Dutch government had argued that family members of workers who have reached the age of majority and who are not dependent on the worker do not have the right to reside in the State of employment under Article 10 of Regulation No 1612/68. For this reason they would neither be entitled to claim benefits under Article 7(2). The Court did not agree. If this line of reasoning were accepted, family members in need of social assistance could lose their status of family member and even their right to reside. In practice it would be impossible for such family members to claim social assistance benefits and this would seriously undermine the right to equal treatment granted to Community workers. The status of dependent family members must be considered independently of the claim for or the grant of benefits such as the *minimex*.[77] That status, the Court stated, is held by family members who are factually supported by the worker.[78]

3.2.2 Right to Claim Minimum Subsistence Benefits

That being in need of minimum subsistence benefits cannot affect the right to reside does not necessarily imply that family members can also claim such benefits in the host State. The above-mentioned argument of the Netherlands government in *Lebon* was financially motivated. If all family members who have acquired the right to reside in the State of employment could rely on Article 7(2) of Regulation No 1612/68, the pressure on the budget out of which minimum subsistence benefits are funded would increase. The German government had even warned of situations in which workers, by temporarily giving financial support, would enable family members to obtain the right to reside in the host State and to claim upon arrival social assistance under Article 7(2). The status of family member could possibly be open to abuse if family members could rely on both Article 10 and Article 7(2) of the Regulation. The Court appeared sensitive to these concerns. In *Lebon* the Court confirmed that family members may rely on Article 7(2), but it now specified earlier judgments such as *Castelli* in ruling that family members can only indirectly benefit from this provision. Benefits

---

[76] Case 261/83 *Castelli* [1984] ECR 3199, 9–10.

[77] Case 316/85 *Lebon* [1987] ECR 2811, 20.

[78] The Court rejected the view that family members can only be regarded as dependants in cases where national law confers upon family members a right to maintenance on the part of the worker. If that were the case 'the composition of the family would depend on national legislation, which varies from one State to another', and that 'would lead to the application of Community law in a manner that is not uniform'. The status of dependent family member of a worker is the result of a factual situation and applies to family members who are supported by the worker without there being a need to determine the reasons for recourse to the worker's support or to raise the question whether the person concerned is able to support himself by taking up employment. Case 316/85 *Lebon* [1987] ECR 2811, 21–2.

only qualify as 'social advantages' if, and in as far as, they may be regarded as social advantages for the worker himself. This implied, according to the Court, that family members such as Ms Lebon who are 21 years or older and who are no longer dependent on the Community worker, cannot claim equal treatment as regards social assistance benefits under Article 7(2). As regards such family members, the benefits do not constitute a social advantage in the sense of Article 7(2) for the worker.[79]

Lebon implied a compromise. On the one hand, the Court promoted freedom of movement by holding that dependence on minimum subsistence benefits cannot in itself affect the right of family members to reside in the host State. On the other hand, the Court had regard to the financial interests of the host States by stipulating that reliance on Article 7(2) is preserved for family members who are dependent on, ie, actually supported by,[80] the worker. As a result, family members do not seem to have a right to claim minimum subsistence benefits in their own right. Independent family members have no right to equal treatment under Article 7(2). Dependent family members can rely on this provision, but as members of the workers' family they will often be unable to claim benefits in their own right under national law. What the Court implicitly seems to have said is that family members can reside in the State of employment, but that they either have to provide for themselves or have to be taken care of by the workers.[81]

Lebon, and the exclusion of independent family members from Article 7(2) in particular, was problematic however. Safeguarding the financial stability of minimum subsistence benefit schemes is a legitimate interest that deserves protection under Community law, but the requirement of being dependent on the

---

[79] 79 Case 316/85 *Lebon* [1987] ECR 2811, 13. See also Case C–185/96 *Commission v Greece* [1998] ECR I–1095, 21.

[80] The Court did not clarify what the workers' support should consist of. It would seem, however, that this support has to be valuable in financial terms. Otherwise, and if for instance 'moral support' would suffice, the requirement of dependence in terms of Art 7(2) would have little practical significance. Compare also *Bernini* where the Court held that benefits can only be regarded as social advantages for workers when they continue to support the family member. Case C–3/90 *Bernini* [1992] ECR I–1071, 25.

[81] Until recently, the possibility for dependent family members of relying on Art 7(2) of Reg No 1612/68 was particularly relevant as regards social security benefits. In *Kermaschek* the Court had ruled that family members enjoy only derived rights (ie rights which are under national law specifically offered to, or for, family members such as family allowances and co-insurance for health care) under Reg No 1408/71 to the exclusion of 'personal rights' (ie rights which are granted to beneficiaries in their capacity as workers, residents or nationals). The latter were under the regime of Reg No 1408/71 preserved for the employed and self-employed persons. Case 40/76 *Kermaschek* [1976] ECR 1669, 7. In *Schmid* (1993), for instance, the Court held that a German national could not rely on Art 3 in Belgium in order to claim a disability benefit on behalf of his dependent daughter because the benefit did not constitute a derived right. The Court ruled, however, that Art 7(2) could be relied upon. Case C–310/91 *Schmid* [1993] ECR I–3011, 12–14. More recently, however, the *Kermaschek*-rule has been limited in *Cabanis-Issarte* (Case C–87/94 [1996] ECR I–2097—see ch 2 s 6). The judgment suggests that independent family members can now claim equal treatment as regards mixed minimum subsistence benefits with the exception of those which are linked to the risk of unemployment, industrial accident and occupational diseases. Compare Peers, 'Equality, Free Movement and Social Security', in *ELRev* (1997) 342–51, 347.

worker seems unnecessarily strict. Why would a child who was born in the host State and has separated from the parent-worker, be denied the right to claim social assistance benefits under the same conditions as nationals of the host State? Why should family members who have lived in the host State for a long period of time and who have socially and culturally integrated in the host State, have to remain dependent on the worker? Denial of the right to rely on this provision is hard to compare with the objectives of promoting freedom of movement and the integration of the workers' family in the host State. From the perspective of avoiding abuse, the requirement is overly inclusive.

The judgments in *Martínez Sala* (1998) and *Grzelczyk* (2001) suggest that the Court[82] has recognised the point and that it has moved away from *Lebon*. The cases will be discussed in further detail in the next section. However, it may already be pointed out that the Court ruled in *Martínez Sala* that nationals of the Member States who are lawfully residing in the territory of another Member State can invoke Article 12(1) EC in order to claim equal treatment as regards all rights and benefits falling within the scope of Regulation No 1408/71 and Article 7(2) of Regulation No 1612/68.[83] In *Grzelczyk* the Court concluded that Community students can, under certain conditions claim equality of treatment as regards social assistance.[84] No certainty exists, but *Martínez Sala* and *Grzelczyk* do not seem to leave room for any conclusion other than that independent family members who hold the nationality of a Member State[85] and who have installed themselves with the worker in the State of employment, are entitled to rely on Article 12(1) EC in order to claim access to minimum subsistence benefits under the same conditions as the nationals of the host State.

That dependent family members enjoy the right to equal treatment as regards all minimum subsistence benefits does not yet imply that they will actually be able to receive minimum subsistence benefits. In principle, family members must

---

[82] The Commission has already taken the initiative to repair *Lebon* by proposing to confer upon all family members an independent right to equal treatment as regards social advantages. The proposed new Art 10(3) of Reg No 1612/68 reads: 'Members of the family entitled to live in a Member State under the terms of paragraphs 1 and 2 shall be entitled to all financial, tax, social, cultural or other advantages available to nationals'. COM(1998) 394 def.

[83] Case C–85/96 *Martínez Sala* [1998] ECR I–2691, 57 and 60–1.

[84] Case C–184/99 *Grzelczyk* [2001] ECR I–6193, 46.

[85] It is less certain whether independent family members who lack the nationality of one of the Member States can rely on Art 12(1) EC. Compare More, The Principle of Equal Treatment: From Market Unifier to Fundamental Right?, in: Craig/de Búrca (eds), *The Evolution of EU Law* (1999) 517–51, at 540. It is submitted, however, that family members who have been admitted for residence by virtue of Art 10(1) of Reg No 1612/68 can rely on Art 12(1) EC. In *Martínez Sala* and *Grzelczyk* the Court only spoke of Union citizens lawfully residing in the territory of another Member State, but it seems indisputable that third country family members who have made use of the right to reside guaranteed by Art 10(1) fall within the personal scope of Community law and, thus, Art 12(1) EC. It still seems doubtful, however, whether family members who have been admitted in the State of the workers' employment by virtue of Art 10(2) of Reg No 1612/68 can claim equal treatment under Art 12(1) EC in their own right.

meet the same conditions as nationals of the host State[86] in order to become entitled to obtain minimum subsistence benefits. As in the case of Community workers, however, the right of family members to claim such benefits cannot be made conditional upon a minimum period of residence in the State. In *Mr and Mrs F.* (1975) the Court was asked to determine whether the right to a benefit for disabled children could be preserved for nationals of the host State and non-nationals who have resided in the territory of that State for a minimum period of fifteen years. The Court answered the question within the terms of Regulation No 1408/71. It concluded, in rather general terms, that as regards such invalidity benefits neither the worker himself nor the members of his family may, as compared with the host State's nationals, be placed in a less

---

[86] As regards family members, the question has arisen whether they must be treated equally as the host State nationals or as the family members of the latter. Consider *Taghavi* (1992). The case concerned the Iranian wife of an Italian worker in Belgium who had applied for an invalidity allowance. The benefit was a mixed benefit that was awarded only to Belgian nationals residing in Belgium. On this ground, the application of Mrs Taghavi was rejected and she subsequently appealed the decision. The Belgian court asked the Court to determine whether the refusal to grant the allowance was compatible with Art 3 of Reg No 1408/71. The Court concluded that Mrs Taghavi could not rely on this non-discrimination provision because the allowance could not be classed as a derived right. Case C–243/91 *Taghavi* [1992] ECR I–4401, 8–9. The European Commission had argued, however, that persons as Mrs Taghavi could claim the benefits on the basis of Art 7(2) of Reg No 1612/68. Invalidity benefits such as the one Mrs Taghavi can in principle be regarded as 'social advantages' and Mrs Taghavi was dependent on her husband. The problem, however, was that the family members of Belgian nationals were under the Belgian law in question neither entitled to claim the invalidity benefits. The Court thus had to determine whether the third country family members should be treated equally with the nationals of the host State or with the third country family members of such nationals. In case it would accept that Mrs Taghavi would have to be treated equally with Belgian nationals, a reverse discrimination would occur. If the Court would deny persons as Mrs Taghavi the right to invoke Art 7(2) in such cases, it would accept a rule which may induce workers not to remain in the host State and which thus hampers the free movement of workers. Compare the Opinion of Advocate General van Gerven in Case C–243/91 *Taghavi* [1992] ECR I–4401, 4414. In *Taghavi* the Court chose for the former solution. Since the family members of Belgian nationals could not claim the allowance in question, there was no 'social advantage' for nationals workers and Art 7(2) could therefore not apply. Case C–243/91 *Taghavi* [1992] ECR I–4401, 11. On *Taghavi* see Verschueren, 'Het Arrest Taghavi en de Tegemoetkoming aan niet-EG-familieleden van EG-werknemers', in *MR* (1993) 74–5.

One year later, however, the Court seems to have come back from *Taghavi* in *Schmid*. The case concerned the refusal by Belgian authorities to grant a disability benefit to the daughter of a German national on the ground that she had never worked in Belgium and did not possess Belgian nationality. Under the Belgian law, also the non-Belgian family members of Belgian nationals could not claim the benefits in question. Ignoring *Taghavi*, the Court concluded in *Schmid* that any provision which makes entitlement to a social advantage conditional upon nationality is compatible with Art 7(2), even if it also applies to family members of national workers. Since such a criterion would be more easily fulfilled by the family members of national workers than by family members of workers from other Member States, the Court concluded that the refusal to grant the disability benefit was incompatible with Art 7(2). Case C–310/91 *Schmid* [1993] ECR I–3011, 24–5.

The two judgments, which were delivered by different chambers of the Court, are at odds with each other and could certainly need more clarification from the (full) Court. Compare Pennings, Introduction to European Social Security Law (1998) at 106–7. Until the Court does so, it may be assumed that *Schmid* has 'overruled' *Taghavi* and that the Court has sacrificed the objections against reverse discrimination for the goal of promoting a genuine free movement of workers. Compare the Opinion of Adv Gen van Gerven in case C–243/91 *Taghavi* [1992] ECR I–4401, 15–16 and Martin/Guild, *Free Movement of Persons* (1996) 139–40.

favourable position simply because they do not posses the nationality of the State.[87] Thus, family members have equal access to benefit schemes from the moment they establish residence in the host State.[88]

[87] Case 7/75 *Mr and Mrs F* [1975] ECR 679, 17. The judgment in *Mr and Mrs F* still leaves room for the conclusion that durational residence requirements for eligibility for minimum subsistence benefits which apply to nationals and non-nationals alike could survive judicial scrutiny, but by analogy with the judgment in *Commission v Belgium* (1992), discussed above in s 3.1.3, one may assume that such requirements are also invalid.

[88] The rights discussed in this section are conditional upon the status of family member of a Community worker. In principle, loss of the status of family member leads to the loss of the right to reside and the right to claim minimum subsistence benefits. Two situations may be distinguished.

First, the family relationship itself may end. In practice, this will most often occur as a result of divorce. Where the marriage is dissolved by the competent authorities (see Case 267/83 *Diatta* [1985] ECR 567, 20), the former spouse of the worker will have to place him- or herself in another category in order to retain residence and possibly claim minimum subsistence benefits. For spouses who hold the nationality of a Member State, this implies that they will have to obtain residence as an employed person (Art 39 EC), a self-employed person (Art 43 EC) or as a 'non-economic resident' (1990 residence directives). For spouses who merely hold the nationality of a third State, a divorce may have harsher implications. They have no right to claim residence in their own right. The Commission has recognised this and proposed to offer third country divorcees basically the same rights as Community citizens. Family members of workers who fall within the scope of Art 10(1) of Reg No 1612/68 but lack the nationality of a Member State, are proposed to be given the right to retain the right of residence if the marriage is dissolved on condition that they have lived in that country for a period of three consecutive years. In the proposed new Art 11 it is further stated that such family members retain the right to work when they have lived in the host State for a period of at least five consecutive years. See COM(1998) 394(01).

The wording of the proposed provisions suggests that third country nationals whose marriage has been dissolved after more than three but less than five years of residence have no, or even loose the, right to work as an (self-)employed person. This, however, is not the case. In its proposal for amending Dir No 68/360 the Commission has included a new Art 4a which provides that in the event of dissolution of the marriage, Member States shall recognise the right of residence of family members who do not hold the nationality of one of the Member States, but who have lived in a Member States for three years and who are still pursuing economic activities on presentation of a contract or certificate of employment or a declaration of self-employment. See the proposed Art 4a(3) of Dir No 68/360 (COM(1998) 394((02). Third country nationals who are not economically active must provide evidence that they have sufficient financial resources for themselves and their dependants and that they have health insurance cover. The provisions of Dir No 90/364 apply *mutatis mutandis*. See the proposed Art 4a(2) of Dir No 68/360 (COM(1998) 394((02). See also Sewandono, 'Het Commissievoorstel tot Wijziging van Verordening (EEG) nr.1612/68: Meer Bescherming van Familie- en Gezinsleven en Meer Gelijke Behandeling', in *SEW* (1999) 284–90.

Secondly, family members may lose their privileged status when the working parent, spouse or child gives up their status of Community worker. Family members of workers who return to the State of origin are supposed to join the worker. Where they wish to remain in the host State, family members will have to obtain a new residence right as a (self-)employed person or as a 'non-economic resident'. The above-mentioned Commission proposal does not seem to cover cases where the worker returns to the State of origin. Third country nationals will have to join the returning worker. In some cases, however, family members are entitled to stay. *Echternach* (1989), for instance, indicates that family members of workers who have returned to the State of origin can retain the status of family member in the host State for the period they need to finalise their education in cases where it is not possible to complete the studies in the State of origin. Joined Cases 389 and 390/87 *Echternach* [1989] ECR 723. See further ch 5 s 3.3.3. Further, in *Fahmi* the Court has rejected the view advocated by Adv Gen Alber that the right to claim equal treatment as a Community worker or a family member of a worker under Art 7(2) of Reg No 1612/68 can be retained in case the worker has returned home but receives a pension from, and which is taxable in, the (former) host State. Case C–33/99 *Fahmi* [2001] ECR I–2415, 47.

3.3 Conclusions

On the basis of the foregoing, one must conclude that Community law on cross-border access to minimum subsistence benefits has undergone significant changes since the 1950s and 1960s. In the view of the drafters of Article 39 EC and Regulation No 1612/68, Community citizens who were in need of social assistance(-like) benefits would not have a right to reside in other States and they would not enjoy equality of treatment as regards such benefits. Today, however, 'needy' Community workers and their dependent family members have the right to reside in the State of employment and, from the moment they establish residence in the State of employment, they are entitled to receive minimum subsistence benefits under the same conditions as the nationals of that State. Family members who are not dependent on the worker cannot claim a right to establish residence in the State where the worker is employed, but *Martínez Sala* suggests that when, and for as long as, they do lawfully reside there, they are entitled to claim equal access to minimum subsistence benefit schemes.

The Court has thus interpreted the Community provisions on the free movement of workers as to embody a certain degree of financial solidarity between nationals of the host States and nationals of other Member States. This solidarity, however, is limited. The Court of Justice, which has largely been responsible for the progress that has been made, has not sacrificed the 'social assistance interest' for the purpose of promoting freedom of movement. Workers' right to reside and right to claim minimum subsistence benefits in the State of employment are conditional upon the pursuit of 'effective and genuine' work. This requirement constitutes a barrier to Community citizens and their family members who consider moving to other Member States for the sole purpose of collecting benefits. For the host States, the requirement serves as a safeguard against 'social tourism."

4 NON-ECONOMIC RESIDENTS

4.1 Introduction

From the early 1970s, Community institutions have worked on a general right of residence which would no longer be linked to, or conditional on, the pursuit of economic activities, but be granted as an independent right that nationals of the Member States would enjoy in their capacity as European citizen.[89] From the beginning, it was undisputed that this anticipated right should not affect the funding of Member States' minimum subsistence benefit schemes. At all

---

[89] See ch 2 s 4.1.

costs, social tourism was to be avoided.[90] Thus, when in 1979 the European Commission sent its first proposal for a directive on a general right of residence to the Council,[91] it included a provision which allowed Member States to require from nationals of other Member States 'to provide proof of sufficient resources for their own needs and the dependent members of their family."[92] The inclusion of this financial means requirement did not allay the concerns and objections of the Member States. The Council negotiations[93] proved difficult. It was only following the judgment of the Court in *Gravier* (1985),[94] in which the Court laid down the legal foundations for a free movement of students, and the subsequent replacement of the original 1979 proposal by three new Commission proposals, that Member States could reach agreement on Directives No 93/96 (*ex* Directive No 90/366),[95] No 90/365 and No 90/364, which offered a right of residence to students, pensioners and 'other' Community citizens respectively.[96]

4.2 Right to Reside and Right to Claim Minimum Subsistence Benefits

4.2.1 Directives Nos 93/96, 90/365 and 90/364

The preambles to the three directives stress that beneficiaries must not become an 'unreasonable burden' on the public finances of the host Member State. This financial safeguard for the Member States is set out in Article 1 of each of the directives. Pensioners shall be granted the right of residence when they receive invalidity, early retirement or other pensions or old age benefits which are of an amount sufficient to avoid becoming a burden on the social security system of

---

[90] Compare Fries/Shaw, Citizenship of the Union: First Steps in the European Court of Justice, in *EPL* (1998) 533–59, at 536.

[91] OJ 1979 C 204; COM(79) 215 final.

[92] Art 4(2) of the 1979 draft directive. The Commission observed that the financial means requirements would discourage 'population movements being undertaken with the sole aim of obtaining the most favourable social benefits'. COM(80) 358 final at 3. The draft directive did not define what was to be understood by 'sufficient means'. It merely provided that 'Member States may not require the resources to be greater than the minimum subsistence level defined under their own law' which basically implied that the resources should at least be as great as to avoid that beneficiaries and their family members becoming a charge on the public purse of the host State.

[93] The Member States had considerable difficulty in agreeing on which family members would be given the right to join the principal beneficiary and whether students would have to demonstrate that they possess enough financial means. See further ch 2 s 4.1. On the Council negotiations on the 1979 draft directive see O'Leary, *The Evolving Concept of Community Citizenship—From the Free Movement of Persons to Union Citizenship* (1996) at 109–18; Bolly, 'Droit d'entrée et de Sejour des Ressortissant communautaire: Développements récents', in *ActduDr* (1990) 735–48; Taschner, 'Free Movement of Students, Retired Persons and other European Citizens—A Difficult Legislative Process', in Schermers *et al* (eds), *Free Movement of Persons in Europe* (1993) 427–36 and van Nuffel, 'Een Bijna Algemeen Verblijfsrecht in de Europese Gemeenschap—Commentaar op de Verblijfsrecht-Richtlijnen van 28 juni 1990', in *SEW* (1990) 887–903.

[94] Case 293/83 *Gravier* [1985] ECR 593. See further ch 4 s 4.

[95] 95 See ch 5 n 176.

[96] See further ch 2 s 4.1.

the host State. The residual class of 'other Community citizens' must have sufficient means to provide for themselves and their family members.[97] The pensions and resources of the two categories are deemed sufficient where they are higher than the level of resources below which Member States may grant social assistance benefits to its own nationals.[98] The financial means requirement to be met by students is less strict. Students only have to assure the relevant national authorities that they have enough resources in order to avoid becoming a 'public burden.' Directive No 93/96 does not require resources of any specific amount, nor that they be evidenced by specific documents.[99]

The drafters of the 1990 residence directives had not intended to confer upon beneficiaries[100] a right to equal treatment as regards social assistance or other minimum subsistence benefits. First, in *Lair* (1988) and *Brown* (1988) the Court had concluded that maintenance grants for students did not come within the scope of Article 12(1) EC because such grants would be matters of educational policy, which as such had not been brought within the ambit of the Treaty, and social policy, which falls within the competence of the Member States,[101] and this did not seem to leave room for any conclusion other than that Community

---

[97] Next to the financial means requirement, beneficiaries must satisfy the requirement of being insured for all medical risks in the host State. See further ch 4 s 3.3.3.

[98] Where this requirement cannot be applied in a Member State, the resources are deemed sufficient if they are higher than the level of the minimum social security pension paid by the host Member State. See Art 1(1), third paragraph of Dir No 90/364 and No 90/365.

In the view of the European Commission, Dir Nos 90/364 and 90/365 are not correctly transposed by national measures which arbitrarily limit the types of resources that can be taken into account or which impose excessive demands with regard to the types of supporting documentation accepted. European Commission, Report to the Parliament and the Council on the Implementation of Dir 90/364, 90/365 and 93/96 (1998) at 10.

The directive for pensioners requires that the pension or the benefit that is received must be 'sufficient'. This could imply that Community citizens who receive pensions which are relatively low and fall below the minimum subsistence level in other Member States, cannot rely on Dir No 90/365. Such pensioners, however, may possess other financial resources which together with the pension would be 'sufficient'. In such cases pensioners may rely on Dir 90/364. See Martin/Guild (1996) n 86 above, at 220.

[99] Case C–184/99 *Grzelczyk* [2001] ECR I–6193, 40. In merely requiring a declaration, Dir No 93/96 differs from Dir Nos 90/365 and 90/364. That difference is explained by the special characteristics of student residence in comparison with that of pensioners and 'other' Community citizens. *Ibid*, at 41. More concretely, the difference may be explained by the fact that the students' right to reside is limited to the duration of the studies, whilst the right of the other two categories is not (Case C–424/98 *Commission v Italy* [2000] ECR I–4001, 40 and 45) or, possibly, by the fact that the Community legislator wished to avoid introducing an additional requirement for the residence rights of students (Opinion of Adv Gen Alber in Case C–184/99 *Grzelczyk* [2001] ECR I–6193, 86). See further ch 5 s 4.4.

[100] The right to reside is also granted to the spouse and the dependent (grand)children and (grand)parents of pensioners and 'other Community citizens'. In *Commission v Italy* (2000) the Court held that in applying the financial means requirements Member States have a certain discretion and that they therefore do not have to apply identical criteria in relation to the family members of beneficiaries of Dir No 90/364 and Dir No 90/365. Case C–424/98 *Commission v Italy* [2000] ECR I–4001, 26. Students are only entitled to bring their spouse and their dependent children. Art 1 Dir No 93/96.

[101] 101 Case 39/86 *Lair* [1988] ECR I–3161, 14–151 and Case 197/87 *Brown* [1988] ECR I–3205, 25.

citizens could neither rely on Article 12(1) EC in order to claim social assistance or other minimum subsistence allowances. Second, in the drafters' view being in need of such benefits would lead to the loss of the right to reside. Each of the three directives states that the right of residence only exists for as long as beneficiaries of that right fulfil the financial means requirement.[102]

The rulings in *Martínez Sala* (1998) *and Grzelczyk* (2001), however, demonstrate that being in need does not necessarily end lawful residence status and that economically inactive Community citizens may have a right to minimum subsistence benefits in the host State.

4.2.2 Martínez Sala

Martínez Sala concerned a Spanish national who had lived in Germany since 1968. Between 1976 and 1989, Ms María Martínez Sala had had various jobs, but since 1989 she was wholly dependent on social assistance benefit (*Sozialhilfe*). Ms Martínez Sala could not be expelled. Both Germany and Spain are parties to the 1953 Convention on Social and Medical Assistance, which provides that nationals of the contracting parties shall not be repatriated on the sole ground that they are in need of assistance. In 1993 Martínez Sala applied for a child-raising allowance for her new born child. Her application was denied on the ground that she did not possess a valid residence permit. Ms Martínez Sala only possessed a document certifying that she had applied for a residence permit.

Was Germany entitled to make the right to social security benefits subject to the presentation of a residence permit? In case Ms Martínez Sala could still be regarded as a worker, the question was to be answered in the negative. The duty to present a residence permit constitutes a discrimination on grounds of nationality because no comparable duty is imposed on nationals of the host State[103] and from previous case law it followed that the German child-raising allowance falls within the scope of both Regulation No 1408/71[104] and Article 7(2) of Regulation No 1612/68.[105] The referring German court, however, had not submitted enough information to the Court of Justice in order to determine whether Ms Martínez Sala could be regarded as a worker for the purposes of

---

[102] Art 3 of Dir No 90/364 and No 90/365 and Art 4 of No 93/96. Further, at the time such benefits did not seem to come within the scope of Community law.

[103] In *Royer* the Court had already held that for the purposes of the right of residence, a residence permit can only have declaratory and probative force. Case 48/75 *Royer* [1976] ECR 497. In *Martínez Sala* the Court concluded that the same must apply for the purposes of the grant of social security benefits. Case C–85/96 *Martínez Sala* [1998] ECR I–2691, 53–4.

[104] In an earlier judgment the Court had already concluded that the child-raising allowance which Ms Martínez had applied for, falls within the scope of Reg No 1408/71. Joined Cases C–245/94 and C–312/94 *Hoever* [1996] ECR I–4895. The German Government had argued that the Court should reconsider that judgment, but the Court saw no reasons for doing so. Case C–85/96 *Martínez Sala* [1998] ECR I–2691, 24.

[105] Case C–85/96 *Martínez Sala* [1998] ECR I–2691, 26.

either one of the two Regulations. The question therefore arose whether Ms Martínez Sala could invoke Article 12(1) EC in order to challenge the German rules. The German Government had argued that she could not do so because the benefit in question would fall outside the material scope of Article 12(1) EC and Ms Martínez Sala herself would not fall within the personal scope of the Treaty.

The Court could not agree. As regards the material scope of Article 12 EC, the Court held that the child-raising allowance in question fell within the scope of both Regulation No 1408/71 and Article 7(2) of Regulation No 1612/68. This implied, according to the Court, that the allowance 'indisputably' fell within the scope of Community law, and thus Article 12(1) EC.[106] As to the personal scope of Article 12, the European Commission had argued that, in case Ms Martínez Sala could indeed not be regarded as a worker, she would have a right to reside under Article 18(1) EC and thus fall within the scope of the Treaty. The Court did not address the possible importance of Article 18(1) EC. In the view of the Court, it was not necessary to examine whether a person like Ms Martínez Sala can rely on Article 18 EC in order to obtain recognition of a new right to reside in the territory of the host State Germany since she had already been authorised to reside there. As a national of a Member State who is lawfully residing in the territory of another Member State, Ms Martínez Sala came, according to the Court, within the personal scope of the Treaty provisions on European Citizenship. Article 17(2) attaches to the status of citizen of the Union the rights and duties laid down by the Treaty, including the right laid down in Article 12 not to suffer discrimination on grounds of nationality within the material scope of the Treaty. Consequently, citizens of the Union who are lawfully residing in the territory of another Member State can rely on Article 12 of the Treaty in 'all situations which fall within the scope *ratione materiae* of Community law.'[107]

Like the child-raising allowances Ms Martínez Sala had applied for, minimum subsistence benefits are covered by Regulation No 1408/71 and/or Article 7(2) of Regulation No 1612/68. Therefore, the judgment[108] could already have been interpreted as to imply that non-economic residents who are lawfully residing in the territory of another Member State are entitled to claim minimum subsistence benefits under the same conditions as nationals of the host State. One could not be certain, however. First, one had to be careful not to read too much into the *Martínez Sala* judgment which concerned quite unique facts, was not extensively reasoned and which had been critically commented upon in the

---

[106] *Ibid*, at 57.

[107] *Ibid*, at 60–5.

[108] For comments on *Martínez Sala* see eg Schrauwen, 'Sink or Swim Together? Developments in European Citizenship', in *Ford ILJ* (2000) 778–94; Tomuschat, 'Annotation *Martínez Sala*', in *CMLRev* (2000) 449–57; Becker, 'Freizügigkeit in der EU—Auf dem Weg vom Begleitrecht zur Bürgerfreiheit', in *EuR* (1999) 522–33 and O'Leary, 'Putting Flesh on the Bones of European Union Citizenship', in *ELRev* (1999) 68–79.

doctrine.[109] Secondly, the judgment did not clarify the concept of lawful residence. The judgment did indicate that lawful residence may derive from international or national law,[110] but it left unanswered the question whether economically inactive Community citizens who are not able to provide for themselves can derive lawful residence status from Community law, and Article 18(1) EC in particular. The question was of the utmost significance. If, as the German government had argued in *Martínez Sala*, the right would not be based on Article 18(1), it would have to regarded as a right accorded by Member States in accordance with the provision of Directive No 90/364. In the German view, the reference in Article 18(1) to the 'limitations and conditions laid down in this Treaty and by the measures adopted to give it effect' would have to be read as to relate to the existence of the right itself. Community citizens who do not, or no longer, meet the financial means requirement would have no right of residence under Community law and fall outside the personal scope of Community law and, thus, Article 12(1) EC.[111] However, if, as the European Commission had argued, Article 18(1) EC would constitute the source of the general right of residence, the 'limitations and conditions' would have to be interpreted as to relate to the exercise of the right to reside. This would imply that Community citizens who are living in a Member States other than the one of which they hold the nationality would have to be regarded as lawful residents, and be entitled to equal treatment under Article 12(1), when and for as long as the host State does not make use of its power to refuse residence to, or to end lawful residence status of, 'needy' nationals of other Member States. In *Martínez Sala* the Court saw no need to examine whether economically inactive Community citizens who are in need of social assistance benefits can possibly rely on Article 18 EC in order to claim a right of residence.[112] In *Grzelczyk*, however, the Court did address the issue.

4.2.3 Grzelczyk

Grzelczyk involved a French student who was studying sports at the University of Louvain, Belgium. During the first three years of his studies Mr Grzelczyk

---

[109] See in particular Tomuschat (2000) n 108 above.

[110] Fries/Shaw (1998) n 90 above, at 558.

[111] Opinion of Adv Gen La Pergola in Case C–85/96 *Martínez Sala* [1998] ECR I–2691, 15.

[112] In previous cases the Court had also never expressly gone into the question whether the general right of residence is now based on Art 18(1) EC. In cases such as *Skanavi* (1996) and *Stöber and Pereira* (1997) the question did arise, but the Court did not have to consider the provision because the cases under consideration could be decided on the basis of Art 43 EC. Case C–193/94 *Skanavi* [1996] ECR I–929 and Joined Cases C–4/95 and C–5/95 *Stöber and Pereira* [1997] ECR I–511. Furthermore, in *Wijsenbeek* (1999), in which the Court was asked whether a duty to present a passport on entry into a Member State is compatible with Art 18 EC, the Court did not address the issue. Even if under Art 17 or Art 18 EC 'nationals of the Member States did have an unconditional right to move freely within the territory of the Member States', Member States still have the right to impose on all persons wishing to enter their territory the duty to establish that they are nationals of the Member States. Case C–378/97 *Wijsenbeek* [1999] ECR I–6207, 42–3.

defrayed his own costs of maintenance, accommodation and studies by taking on various minor jobs and by obtaining credit facilities. In the fourth and final year, however, he was no longer able to combine his studies with employment. Since his parents were unable to bear the costs of his maintenance, Mr Grzelczyk applied for a minimum subsistence allowance (*minimex*). Initially, the competent authority awarded Mr Grzelczyk the *minimex*, but it later withdrew the allowance on grounds of his nationality. According to Belgian legislation, persons not possessing Belgian nationality were only eligible for a minimum subsistence allowance when they came within the scope of EC Regulation No 1612/68 on the free movement of workers. Mr Grzelczyk, so the Belgian authorities argued, was not a worker but a student. Mr Grzelczyk challenged the decision to withdraw the *minimex* from him before a Belgian court, which stayed the proceedings to ask the Court of Justice whether the refusal to grant Mr Grzelczyk the allowance was compatible with Articles 12(1) and 18(1) EC.[113]

In answering the question the Court commenced by stating that a student of Belgian nationality who found himself in exactly the same circumstances as Mr Grzelczyk would have been entitled to receive a social assistance benefit. Mr Grzelczyk was discriminated against on grounds of his nationality. Since Article 12(1) EC prohibits discrimination on grounds of nationality only within the scope of application of the Treaty, the core question to be answered was whether Mr Grzelczyk's situation was covered by Community law. Article 12 EC, so the Court held, must be interpreted in conjunction with the Treaty provisions on European Union citizenship which is 'destined to be the fundamental status of nationals of the Member States, enabling those who find themselves in the same situation to enjoy the same treatment in law irrespective of nationality".[114] Confirming *Martinez Sala*, the Court held that Community citizens lawfully residing in the territory to another Member State can rely on Article 12 EC in all situations which fall within the scope *ratione materiae* of Community. Those situations, the Court stated, include 'those involving the exercise of fundamental freedoms guaranteed by the Treaty and those involving the exercise of the right to move and reside freely in another Member States, as conferred by Article [18] of the Treaty'.[115] Article 12(1) must be read in conjunction with Article 18(1) EC which provides for rights to move and reside freely within the Community, subject to conditions and limitations laid down in the Treaty and secondary legislation. The Court held that the 1990 residence directives do not prevent Member States from taking the view that a student who has recourse to social assistance no longer fulfils the conditions for the right to reside or from taking measures, within the limits imposed by Community law, either to with-

---

[113] Probably, however, Mr Grzelczyk could still be classified, and claim social assistance, as a Community worker. See n 66 above.

[114] Case C–184/99 *Grzelczyk* [2001] ECR I–6193, 30–1.

[115] *Ibid*, at 33.

draw the residence permit or not to renew it.[116] According to the Court, however, in no case may such measures become the automatic consequence of a
student having recourse to social assistance. Article 4 of Directive No 93/96 does
provide that the right of residence is to exist for as long as beneficiaries fulfil the
conditions for acquiring that right among which the financial means requirements, but the sixth recital of the preamble to the directive envisages that
beneficiaries must not become an unreasonable burden on the public finances of
the host State. The Court concluded that Directive No 93/96, like Directives No
90/364 and No 90/365, 'thus accepts a certain degree of solidarity between
nationals of the host Member State and nationals of other Member States, particularly if the difficulties which a beneficiary of the right of residence encounters are temporary".[117]

In conclusion, the Court held that Articles 12(1) and 17(1) EC preclude application of national rules which make entitlement of nationals of other Member
States to non-contributory social benefits such as the *minimex* conditional upon
their falling within the scope of Regulation No 1612/68 where no such condition
is imposed on nationals of the host State.[118]

4.2.4 Conclusions

Grzelczyk confirms that all Community citizens who are lawfully residing in the
territory of another Member State can rely on Article 12(1) EC in order to claim
social assistance, and as one may safely assume, mixed benefits in other Member
States under the same conditions as nationals of the host State. Further, the
judgment shows that the economically inactive Community citizens who are
not able to provide for themselves can claim lawful residence on the basis
of Community law. Article 12(1) EC, so the Court held, guarantees a right to
equal treatment to all Community citizens who have exercised the fundamental

---

[116] *Ibid*, at 42.

[117] *Ibid*, at 44. The Court added that a student's 'financial position may change with the passage
of time for reasons beyond his control' and that the 'truthfulness of a student's declaration' concerning his resources 'is therefore to be assessed only at the time that it is made'. *Ibid*, at 45.

[118] *Ibid*, at 46. The Belgian Government had feared that, if the Court were to find that persons as
Mr Grzelczyk may indeed receive the *minimex*, that 'systems of social allowances for students' will
be upset and it therefore asked the Court in such an event to limit the effects of the judgment in time.
The Court refused to do so. It held that it is settled case law that financial consequences which might
ensue for a Member State from a preliminary ruling do not in themselves justify limiting the tem-
poral effect of the ruling. The Court has only been willing to do so where there was a risk that serious economic repercussions owing in particular to the large number of legal relationships entered
into in good faith on the basis of rules considered to be validly in force and where it appeared that
both individuals and national authorities had been led into adopting practices which did not comply with Community law by reason of objective, significant uncertainty regarding the implications
of Community provisions, to which the conduct of other Member States or the Commission may
even have contributed. In the Court's view, however, the Belgian Government had not produced any
evidence to show that any objective and significant uncertainty regarding the implications of the
Treaty provisions on Union citizenship had led its authorities to adopt practices which did not comply with those provisions. *Ibid*, at 48–55.

freedoms guaranteed by the Treaty or the right to move and reside freely in another Member State, 'as conferred by Article 18 EC'.[119] The general non-economic right of residence is indeed based on Article 18(1) EC and it thus indeed seems, as the Commission had argued, that the 'conditions and limitations' mentioned in Article 18(1) EC relate to the exercise rather than the existence of the right to reside. Consequently, Member States that do not make use of their power to take measures ending lawful residence status of economically inactive nationals of other Member States must award these Community citizens minimum subsistence benefits under the same conditions as their own nationals. Put differently, Union citizens who are actually residing in the territory of another Member State are, as lawful residents, entitled to be treated

---

[119] Arguably, this conclusion could already have been read into the Court's ruling in *Elsen* (2000). The case involved a German national who was living with her husband and son in France. Mrs Elsen, who had worked in Germany but never in France, requested the German social security institutions to take into consideration the periods she had spent rearing her son as insurance periods for the purposes of her old-age pension. The German institutions refused on the ground that the applicable German rules only allowed them to do so when the child rearing has taken place in Germany. The Court concluded that the German rules were disadvantageous to Community citizens who wish to exercise their non-economic free movement rights and that, by not taking into account the periods devoted to child-rearing completed in France, the German social security institution had acted contrary to Art 18 EC. Case C–135/99 *Elsen* [2000] ECR I–10409, 34–6. *Elsen* indicated that Art 18 has legal force and strongly suggested that the right to reside has acquired 'constitutional status'. After all, how does explain that Mrs Elsen could claim rights under Art 18(1) if her right to reside in France was not based on this provision?

The conclusion that the right to reside is now protected by the Treaty is also the most, if not the only, logical interpretation of the provision. In the words of Adv Gen La Pergola: 'Now that Art 8a (now 18: APvdm) of the Treaty has entered into force, the right of residence can no longer be considered to have been created by the directive . . . That legislation was adopted by the Council to cover situations in which citizens did not enjoy a right of residence under other provisions of Community law. Now, however, we have Art 8a of the Treaty. The right to move and reside freely throughout the whole Union is enshrined in an act of primary law and does not exist or cease to exist depending on whether or not it has been made subject to limitations under other provisions of Community law, including secondary legislation. The limitations provided for in Art 8a itself concern the actual exercise but not the existence of the right'. Opinion of Adv Gen La Pergola in Case C–85/96 *Martínez Sala* [1998] ECR I–2691, 18.

See further also the Opinion of Adv Gen Cosmas in Case C–378/98 *Wijsenbeek* [1999] ECR I–6207, 79–87, the Opinion of Adv Gen Alber in Case C–184/99 *Grzelczyk* [2001] ECR I–6193, 120 and Opinion of Adv Gen Geelhoed in Case C–413/99 *Baumbast,* pending, at 48–63.

On this point and the direct effect of Art 18(1) EC see further eg Martin/Guild (1996) n 86 above, at 97; O'Leary (1996) n 93 above, at 141–2; Koenig/Pechstein, *Die Europäische Union* (1995) at 178; Wouters, 'European Citizenship and the Case-law of the Court of Justice of the European Communities on the Free Movement of Persons', in Marias (ed), *European Citizenship* (1994) 25 *et seq*, at 49 and Douglas-Scott/Kimbell, 'The Adams Exclusion Order Case: New Enforceable Civil Rights in the post-Maastricht European Union?', in: *PubLaw* (1995) 516–25, at 520–1 and Report of the High Level Panel on the Free Movement of Persons (1998) at 17.

Finally, textual support for the above conclusion can also be found in Art 18(2) EC, which empowers the Council to adopt measures with a view to *facilitating* the *exercise* of the free movement rights referred to in the Art's first paragraph. If the drafters of the Treaty had actually intended to say that freedom of movement is not a Treaty based right, then they should have empowered the Council to *extend* free movement rights.

equally as regards minimum subsistence benefits until the moment the host State executes measures to end their lawful residence status.[120]

The most remarkable aspect of *Grzelczyk* is that the Court has imposed limitations on Member States' powers to end lawful residence status of 'needy' nationals of other Member States. Having recourse to social assistance is not a sufficient reason for withdrawing residence permits or refusing to offer new permits. In order to take measures, Member States must demonstrate that nationals of other States have or will become an 'unreasonable' burden on the social assistance scheme. Contrary to the intentions of those who drafted and adopted Directives No 93/96, No 90/365 and No 90/364, the Court reads into these directives 'a certain degree of financial solidarity between nationals of a host Member State and nationals of other Member States".

The Court is likely to be criticised on this point. In comments on *Martínez Sala* the Court had already been accused of having gone too far and of not giving sufficient regard to the Member States' interests. Article(s) 12 (and 18) EC, so it was argued, should not be interpreted as to impose on Member States the obligation to grant benefits that have not been anticipated for and that 'have not been earned by the claimant on account of his or her participation in the collective work process of a given society'.[121] *Grzelczyk*, however, suggests that the

---

[120] This conclusion raises a series of new questions. What should the measures taken by the Member States consist of? From which moment on does lawful residence become unlawful residence? O'Leary has argued that Community citizens must be regarded as lawful residents until they are subject to formal proceedings to effect deportation. O'Leary, 'The Principle of Equal Treatment on Grounds of Nationality in Art 6 EC—A Lucrative Source for Member State Nationals?' in O'Leary/Tiilikainen (eds) *Citizenship and Nationality Status in the New Europe* (1998) 105–36, at 134. Yet, what does this imply? Are Community citizens unlawful residents from the moment they are informed by the immigration authorities that they have to leave the host State's territory? In the light of Art 1 of Protocol 7 to the European Convention on Human Rights (procedural safeguards as regards the expulsion of aliens) and by analogy with Arts 8 and 9 of Directive No 64/221 (on the co-ordination of special measures concerning the free movement rights which are justified on grounds of public policy, public security or public health—OJ 1963/1964 (Spec. English Edn) 117—see further ch 2 s 7.1), it would seem that Community citizens have a right to appeal expulsion decisions. By analogy with the case law on Dir No 64/221, it could be argued that such Community citizens retain the status of lawful resident, and thus the right to equal treatment as regards minimum subsistence benefits, until they have been able to complete the formalities to avail themselves of that remedy and the competent authority has reached a decision. Compare Case 48/75 *Royer* [1976] ECR 497 and Case C–175/94 *Gallagher* [1996] ECR I–4253. If Community citizens who are challenging decisions of immigration authorities are indeed to be regarded as lawful residents until the moment a decision on appeal has been made, can the institutions responsible for payment of social assistance benefits require the presentation of a document stating that they have actually started the procedure or are they obliged to grant benefits to those who can prove to be actual residents until they have received the decision of the appeal body? Does a negative decision on appeal end lawful residence or does such a decision merely imply an authorisation for the immigration authorities to end lawful residence? In answering such questions, is any distinction to be made between Community citizens who apply for a residence card for the first time and Community citizens who have acquired such a card but later cease to meet the financial means requirement? Can Community citizens who know in advance that they are unable to meet the financial means requirement in another Member State but nonetheless move there, claim lawful residence status and social assistance benefits for the duration of the appeal procedure?

[121] Tomuschat (2000) n 108 above, at 455.

Court has dismissed such critiques altogether and it is submitted that it was right in doing so. The crux of the problem and the critique concerns the possible burden on social welfare systems. It seems quite unlikely, however, that the funding social assistance schemes will be seriously affected as a result of *Martínez Sala* and *Grzelczyk*. Firstly, and most important, the Court remained wholly silent on the financial means requirement contained in Article 1 of the three 1990 residence directives. Economically inactive Community citizens who wish to install themselves in another Member States can still be required to present proof that they will not become a burden on the host State's social assistance schemes. *Grzelczyk* does not imply recognition of a general, unconditional right to freedom of movement. The ruling merely implies that Union citizens who have initially convinced the host State's authorities that they are able to provide for themselves but who, contrary to initial expectations, become temporarily in financial need do not automatically lose their right to reside. Secondly, *Grzelczyk* does not necessarily imply that Community students can actually claim social assistance in the host State. The ruling merely implies that Community students can claim social assistance benefits where, and under the same conditions as, national students have right to such benefits. National social assistance laws, however, may contain eligibility criteria which students often are not able to meet such as the requirements that social assistance must seek or be available for full-time employment and in many cases persons pursuing studies are categorically excluded from social assistance entitlement. Further, as will be argued in Section 5, Article 12(1) EC does not object to national rules which make entitlement to social assistance and other minimum subsistence benefits subject to requirements of 'habitual residence' or 'domicile' on the national territory. As a rule, pensioners and 'other' Community citizens meet such requirements, but the same does not hold true for Community students. As a rule, Community students must be regarded as having their habitual residence in the State where they lived prior to their studies.[122]

5 NON-RESIDENTS

5.1 Introduction

Member States' laws and rules on minimum subsistence benefits are all based on the principle of territoriality.[123] Benefits have traditionally been preserved for residents; non-residents have been excluded. At first glance, the legality of residence requirements seems beyond doubt. If Member States were obliged to grant minimum subsistence benefits to residents and non-residents under the same

---

[122] See van der Mei, 'Freedom of Movement and Financial Aid for Students: Some Reflections on *Grzelczyk* and *Fahmi Esmoris-Cerdeiro Pinedo Amoris*', in *EJSS* (2001).

[123] See s 2.2.

conditions, the funding of their benefit schemes would be jeopardised.[124] The validity of residence requirements, however, is not entirely obvious as regards some categories of non-residents who have certain 'economic ties' with the State concerned because they work and/or pay taxes there or have done so in the past. Why would frontier workers be denied a right to claim minimum subsistence benefits in the State where they are employed and (may) pay taxes? Why would Community citizens who have lived and worked their entire life in a given Member State have to lose entitlement to minimum subsistence benefits the moment they decide to live in another Member State? Recipients of such benefits may be discouraged from working or moving elsewhere if they cannot export their benefit. Due to the financial means requirements contained in the 1990 residence directives, it might for some of them even be impossible to take up residence in other Member States. Case law demonstrates that the validity of residence requirements for minimum subsistence benefits has indeed been quite controversial. A distinction must be made between mixed, hybrid or special non-contributory benefits, on the one hand, and classic social assistance benefits, on the other hand.

5.2 Mixed Benefits

5.2.1 Application of Article 10 of Regulation No 1408/71

Questions concerning the validity of residence requirements have played a central role in the Court's case law on the application of Regulation No 1408/71 to mixed benefits.[125] Article 10 of this regulation allows for the exportability of benefits. It reads:

'Save as otherwise provided in this regulation, invalidity, old-age or survivors' cash benefits, pensions for accidents at work or occupational diseases and death grants acquired under the legislation of one or more Member States shall not be subject to any reduction, modification, suspension, withdrawal or confiscation by reason of the fact that the recipient resides in the territory of a Member State other than that in which the institution responsible for payment is situated'.[126]

---

[124] van der Mei (1999) n 9 above, at 451.

[125] See s 2.3 above.

[126] The aim of Art 10 is 'to promote freedom of movement for workers and members of members of their family by protecting them against any adverse consequences which might arise as a result of the transfer of their residence from one Member State to another. The provision therefore seeks to ensure that such persons retain their rights to benefits, pensions and allowances to which they are entitled under the legislation of one or more Member States if they reside in the territory of a Member State other than that in which the institution responsible for payment is situated'. Case 139/82 *Piscitello* [1983] ECR 1427, 15. See also Joined cases 379–381/85 and 93/86 *Giletti and others* [1987] ECR 955, 14.

Under national law residence requirements may have different purposes. They can be applied as a condition for insurance cover, as a condition for entitlement to benefits or as a condition for payment of benefits. See eg *Keunen, Schets van het Europees Socialezekerheidsrecht—Europese*

Article 10 may be regarded as the general export provision of the Regulation No 1408/71. For sickness and maternity benefits, unemployment benefits and family benefits specific export provisions exist. Upon reading of Article 10, one might be tempted to conclude that once it is decided that a benefit is covered by the Regulation, it is also exportable. Case law demonstrates, however, that this conclusion is not as obvious as it may seem.

5.2.1.1 *Biason*

Consider *Biason* (1971). The case concerned an Italian woman who received a supplementary allowance in France in addition to an invalidity pension. This tax-funded allowance, which was only granted to persons in receipt of invalidity pensions, was withdrawn the moment Mrs Biason moved to Italy. She claimed that the withdrawal was inconsistent with Article 10 of Regulation No 3/58, the predecessor of the current Article 10 of Regulation No 1408/71. In the proceedings before the Court of Justice, the European Commission strongly argued against the exportability of mixed benefits. Article 10 would only apply to insurance-like benefits. Such benefits may be regarded as 'deferred income' and 'must of necessity be exportable. Mixed benefits, however, are usually financed out of the public budget and they are generally regarded as an expression of the welfare solidarity between the residents of a State. Persons who wish to export such mixed benefits are no longer residents and thus no longer part of the shared welfare solidarity.[127]

The Court first had to determine whether the supplementary allowance Mrs Biason received, fell within the scope of Regulation No 3/58. The Court held that the French legislation conferred upon recipients a legally defined position and that the allowance was linked to the risk of invalidity mentioned in Article 4(1)(b) of Regulation No 1408/71. So far as Mrs Biason was concerned, the allowance was therefore a social security benefit within the meaning of the Regulation.[128] In the view of the Court, the allowance was also exportable. Article 10(2) of Regulation No 3/58 entitled Member States to exclude certain non-contributory benefits from the export provision in Article 10(1) by including benefits in an annex to the Regulation for 'benefits not payable abroad'. The

---

Coördinatieregels inzake Sociale Zekerheid (2001) 75–9 and Sakslin, 'The Concept of Residence and Social Security: Reflections on Finnish, Swedish and Community Legislation', in *EJML* (2000) 157–83, at 161. Within the context of Reg No 1408/71, residence requirements applied as a condition for insurance cover are waived by the rules determining the applicable legislation contained in Arts 13 *et seq*. Art 10 of the regulation prevents application of residence criteria that are used as conditions for entitlement to or payment of benefits. The Court makes no distinction between the latter two types of requirements. Art 10 entitles non-residents to acquire rights to benefits and to payment of already acquired rights. See eg Case 51/73 *Smieja* [1973] ECR 1213; Case 276/81 *Camera* [1982] ECR 2213; Case 284/84 *Spruyt* [1986] ECR 685 and Joined Cases 379–381/85 and 93/86 *Giletti* [1987] ECR 955.

[127] See the observations of the Commission in Case 24/74 *Biason* [1974] ECR 999, 1004. Furthermore, the Commission claimed that the assessment of financial resources in the context of the means test would be largely impossible when such benefits are exported to other States.

[128] Case 24/74 *Biason* [1974] ECR 999, 15–16.

French supplementary allowance was not set out in the annex and the Court therefore simply concluded that a person such as Mrs Biason could continue to receive the benefit while staying in another Member State.[129]

5.2.1.2   *Piscitello*

The line of reasoning followed by the Court in *Biason* was rather formal. Basically, the Court reasoned that if France had wished to limit the export of the benefit in question, it should have included it in the annex. As France had not done so, Mrs Biason could 'simply' export her benefit. The possibility of excluding certain benefits from the export provision was abolished, however, when Regulation No 1408/71 was adopted. At first glance, this would seem to have increased the possibility of exporting mixed benefits. France, however, held to the view that mixed benefits could not be exported. The European Commission, acting in response to a number of complaints it had received from recipients of French supplementary benefits whose benefits were stopped on the moment they moved to another Member State, commenced in 1980 an infringement procedure under Article 226 (formerly 169) E(E)C. France subsequently submitted to the Council a communication in which it referred to the specific problems regarding the exportability of non-contributory minimum subsistence benefits. France proposed to bring these mixed benefit schemes under Regulation No 1612/68 and to insert into this regulation a special provision which would limit the export of such benefits. In response, the Commission postponed the infringement procedure without, however, directly sending a legislative proposal to the Council. The Commission only did so following the Court's decision in *Piscitello* (1983).[130]

Mrs Piscitello was an Italian national who was living and receiving a social aid pension in Italy. The benefit was granted to all persons of 65 years and older whose income fell below the minimum income fixed by law. The benefit was Mrs Piscitello's only source of income. When she transferred her residence to Belgium, the Italian authorities withdrew the pension on the ground that she was no longer resident in Italy. Mrs Piscitello challenged the withdrawal in an Italian court which initiated a procedure under Article 177 (now 234) E(E)C in order ask the Court of Justice whether the benefit at issue was covered by the Regulation and, if so, whether it could be exported. The Italian and British governments had argued that the conclusions drawn in *Biason* could not be extended to the case of Mrs Piscitello. *Biason* concerned the exportability of an allowance that was granted as a supplement to another social security benefit. Mrs Piscitello's benefit, however, constituted her only source of income. It was a benefit financed solely out of public funds that served for Mrs Piscitello, in fact, as a social assistance benefit. No Community machinery existed for assessing the income that might be received in other Member States or for sharing the

---

[129] *Ibid*, at 17–22.
[130] Case 139/82 *Piscitello* [1983] ECR 1427.

costs involved amongst the Member States. The exportability of benefits, so the two governments argued, would cause disruption to the national systems.[131]

The Court was not persuaded by these arguments. It had no difficulty in concluding that the benefit scheme fell within the Regulation[132] and that Mrs Piscitello's benefit was amongst the benefits referred to by Article 10. Since Regulation No 1408/71 did not contain specific provisions applying to such a pension, the Court ruled 'that the waiver of residence clauses provided for in Article 10(1) of that regulation applies to the benefit in question'.[133]

5.2.1.3 *Commission v France*

Piscitello implied that all benefits covered by the Regulation were, in principle, also exportable. On the one hand, this seemed to have far-reaching consequences. The conclusion that minimum subsistence benefits that are not granted as a supplement to other social security benefits can be exported, implied that also persons who have never paid social security premiums or contributions could export benefits. More generally, *Piscitello* raised the fundamental issue whether Member States had been forced to extend their welfare responsibility to certain categories of non-residents. On the other hand, however, the implications of *Piscitello* did not have to be so problematic. Article 10 contains the phrase 'Save as otherwise provided in this regulation' and the Court had expressly stated that mixed benefits are only exportable because the Regulation did not contain any specific provision for such benefits. The Court had thus left open the possibility for the Community legislator to amend the Regulation and to include in it specific provisions which would entitle Member States to limit the export of mixed minimum subsistence benefits.

Two years after the judgment in *Piscitello* the Commission responded to the Court's implicit call by submitting a proposal to the Council to amend Regulation No 1408/71.[134] In brief, the proposal suggested that mixed benefits would be brought under the material scope of Regulation No 1408/71 and that a new Article 10a would be introduced which would entitle the Member States to limit the right to receive mixed benefits to Community citizens residing within their territory. The Council did not directly adopt the Commission's proposal. Faced with a lack of progress in the Council negotiations, the Commission decided in 1988 to carry on the infringement procedure against France. This Member State still held the view that mixed benefits should not be exportable; it even refused to implement the ruling in *Piscitello*.[135] In the proceedings before the Court, the French government referred to the Commission's proposal suggesting that it could be relieved from the obligation to allow

[131] *Ibid*, at 1434.
[132] *Ibid*, at 8–13.
[133] *Ibid*, at 16.
[134] COM(85) 396 final.
[135] It has been suggested that France did so in order to constraint the other Member States to adopt the Commission's proposal. Lyon-Caen (1995) n 20 above, at 52 (n 20).

beneficiaries to export the benefits at issue. In *Commission v France* (1990), however, the Court stated that 'the fact that a proposal which could terminate an infringement is submitted to the Council cannot relieve the member State responsible for that infringement of its obligation to comply with the provisions of Community law in force'.[136] It was not for the Court to anticipate any amendments that might be made by the Community legislature.[137] The French government had further argued that Member States fix the level of mixed benefits on the basis of a specific economic and social environment. The level of the French benefit was designed to guarantee a minimum means of subsistence at the level fixed in France. In the French view, the possibility of exporting such benefits would carry the risk of social regression as a result of the differences in national laws and the disparity in standards of living. The Court did not accept the argument. The fact that a mixed benefit 'is linked to a specified economic and social environment cannot, under Community law as it now stands, constitute a ground for' excluding the application of Article 10 to mixed benefits.[138]

5.2.2 Regulation No 1247/92: The Insertion of Article 10a and Annex IIa

The Court thus put pressure on the Council to take legislative action to co-ordinate mixed benefit schemes. Two years after *Commission v France*, the Council did indeed do so by adopting Regulation No 1247/92,[139] which inserted a specific co-ordination mechanism for mixed benefits into Regulation No 1408/71.

As stated in Section 2.3, a new Article 4(2a) was included which has brought within the scope of Regulation No 1408/71 'special non-contributory benefits which are provided under legislation or schemes other than those referred to in paragraph 1 or excluded by virtue of paragraph 4' that are intended either 'to provide supplementary, substitute or ancillary cover against the risks covered by the branches of social security referred to in paragraph 1(a) to (h)' or 'solely as specific protection for the disabled'. As follows from the preamble to Regulation No 1247/92, the benefits in question are regarded as social security benefits.

In addition, a new Article 10a was inserted which, in its first paragraph, provides that by way of derogation of Article 10, the mixed benefits falling within the ambit of Article 4(2a) shall be granted exclusively in the territory of the Member State in which beneficiaries reside. The main justification for this rule

---

[136] Case C–236/88 *Commission v France* [1990] ECR I–3163, 19.

[137] Opinion of Adv Gen van Gerven in Case C–236/88 *Commission v France* [1990] ECR I–3162, 3175.

[138] Case C–236/88 *Commission v France* [1990] ECR I–3163, 13. The French government had further claimed that the export of mixed benefits would raise serious problems of management, co-ordination and substance that can only be resolved by Community legislation. The Court responded that such practical difficulties must not prejudice the rights which individuals derive from Community law. *Ibid*, at 17.

[139] OJ 1992 No L 136. The regulation was adopted on 1 May 1992 and came into force on 1 June 1992.

is that mixed benefits are intended to provide recipients with financial means at minimum subsistence level. This level must be determined by the cost of living and the social and economic environment in the State of residence.[140] The benefits are granted by, and at the expense of, the institution of this State in accordance with the legislation applicable there. Member States are entitled to deny non-residents benefits provided such benefits have been listed in the newly created Annex IIa.[141] Mixed benefits that have not been listed in the annex do not fall under Article 10a(1),[142] with the result that they, in principle, can be exported on the basis of the general provision of Article 10.

By adopting Regulation No 1247/92 the Community legislator thus introduced a mechanism for mixed benefits comparable to the one that existed under the original Regulation No 3/58.[143] Member States may apply residence requirements for entitlement to or payment of mixed benefits, provided these have been listed in Annex IIa. As regards benefits that have not been listed, residence requirements cannot be applied.

In addition, Article 10a contains a number of provisions that partly compensate for the Member States' right to limit the export of mixed minimum subsistence benefits. In order to secure that beneficiaries will actually be able to receive mixed benefits in the State of residence, Article 10a(2) states that the institution which is to grant mixed benefits shall, where necessary, regard periods of employment, residence or insurance completed in other Member States as though they had been fulfilled in its own territory. Article 10a(3) further provides that a Member State whose legislation makes the grant of a supplementary benefit subject to the prior award of a particular social security benefit under its own legislation, is to treat a corresponding benefit awarded under the legislation of another Member State, as if it were awarded under its own legislation. The supplementary benefit is then added to that foreign corresponding benefit.[144]

---

[140] Verschueren (1996) n 23 above, at 100.

[141] The inclusion of mixed benefits in Annex IIa requires a unanimous decision of the Council. Keunen (2001) n 126 above, at 62. Annex IIa now contains more than fifty types of national benefits that usually concern financial support benefit for handicapped persons, retired persons or family benefits. Verschueren (1996) n 23 above, at 97 and Opinion of Adv Gen Jacobs in Case C–43/99 *Leclere* [2001] ECR I–4265, 74.

[142] Art 10a cannot result in the withdrawal of rights obtained prior to the entry into force of Reg No 1247/92. See Art 2 of Reg No 1247/92.

[143] Art 10a has the function of determining the applicable legislation. It is a specific conflict rule that deviates from, and takes precedence over, the general conflict rules laid down in Arts 13 *et seq.* of the Regulation. Compare Sakslin (2000) n 126 above, at 173.

[144] See COM(85) 396 final. Finally, Art 10*a*(4) provides that where the legislation of a Member State makes entitlement to a mixed benefit for disability or invalidity subject to the condition that the disability or invalidity should be diagnosed for the first time in the territory of that Member State, this condition shall be deemed to be fulfilled where such diagnosis is made for the first time in the territory of another Member State. See further Art 2a of Reg No 574/72 (as inserted by Reg No 1945/93—OJ 1993 L 181) and Decisions Nos 151 and 152 of the Administrative Commission on the implementation of Art 10a (OJ 1994 L 244).

5.2.3 *Snares: The Validity of Article 10a*

Since the coming into force of Regulation No 1247/92, the debates and controversies regarding the portability of mixed benefits seemed to have come to an end. In the beginning of 1996, however, the discussions seemed to start all over again when the *Snares* case was put to the Court. Mr Snares was a British national who had been working and been subject to the British social security system for more than 25 years. In April 1993 he became the victim of a serious accident. Mr Snares applied for and was awarded a disability living allowance. This allowance was non-contributory, linked to incapacity for work, not subject to a means test and granted, *inter alia*, to persons whose walking ability was impaired. On 1 November 1993 Mr Snares informed the competent institution that he wished to establish himself permanently in Tenerife, Spain, so that his family members who lived there, could take care of him. The relevant institution informed Mr Snares that from the date of his departure to Spain he could no longer receive the mobility allowance since the British legislation provides that the benefits can only be granted to persons who are 'ordinarily resident' in Great Britain. Mr Snares challenged the decision and the national court referred the case to the Court of Justice for a preliminary ruling.

The main[145] question the Court had to answer was whether Regulation No 1247/92 was valid in the light of Articles 51 (now 42) and 235 (now 308) of the Treaty in so far as that regulation makes the right to receive mixed benefits subject to residence clauses. In other words, was the Community legislator empowered to adopt a rule authorising the States to restrict the exportability of mixed benefits? The Court recalled some of its previous case law and stated that on numerous occasions it had pointed out that the principle of the exportability of social security benefits applies so long as no derogating provisions have been adopted by the Community legislator. The Court further reiterated the ruling in *Lenoir* (1988)[146] in which it had held that the grant of benefits closely linked with the social environment may be made subject to a condition of residence in the competent State. The fact that a person such as Mr Snares did not satisfy the conditions applied by his new State of residence to the award of an invalidity benefit could not invalidate Article 10a of Regulation No 1408/71. The system introduced by Regulation No 1247/92 contains rules whose very purpose is to protect the interests of migrant workers. The Court referred in this regard to the second, third and fourth paragraphs of Article 10a that strengthen the right to equal treatment in the State of residence as regards mixed benefits.[147]

---

[145] The first question to be answered was whether the position of persons like Mr Snares, who, after the entry into force of Reg No 1247/92, satisfy the conditions for the award of mixed benefits, is governed exclusively by the co-ordination rules established by Art 10a. The Court answered the question in the affirmative. Mr Snares did fall within in the personal scope of the Regulation, the allowance was covered by Art 4(2a) and the disability allowance was mentioned in Annex IIa of the Regulation. Case C–20/96 *Snares* [1997] ECR I–6057 at 30–9.

[146] Case 313/86 *Lenoir* [1988] ECR 5391 at 16.

[147] Case C–20/96 *Snares* [1997] ECR I–6057, 51.

The conclusion drawn in *Snares* logically followed from the case law that the Court has developed under Regulation No 1408/71 since the early 1970s. In various cases the Court had accepted the exportability of mixed benefits on the basis of Article 10 of the regulation, but it had always indicated that the Community legislator was empowered to amend the regulation on this point. By adopting Regulation No 1247/92 the legislator responded to this implicit call and in *Snares* the Court therefore did not have much difficulty in concluding that the legislator was indeed entitled to authorise the Member States to limit the exportability of mixed benefits.[148]

5.2.4 Jauch *and* Leclere: *Scope of Article 10a and Legal Effect of the Inclusion of Benefits in Annex IIa*

Member States are thus entitled to make enjoyment of special non-contributory benefits conditional upon residence on the national territory provided such benefits have been listed in Annex IIa of Regulation No 1408/71.[149] In *Jauch* (2001) and *Leclere* (2001) the Court was asked to clarify the scope of Article 10a and the legal effect of the inclusion of benefits in Annex IIa.

Jauch concerned a German national residing in Germany who had previously worked in Austria. In the latter State, he requested payment of a care allowance which was intended to provide care and assistance, in the form of a flat-rate payment, to persons reliant on care in order to improve their opportunity of leading a life which is autonomous and meets their needs. The competent authorities rejected Mr Jauch's claim on the ground that he did not meet the requirement of being habitually resident in Austria. That requirement, so it was argued, could validly be applied because the care allowance was expressly listed in Annex IIa to Regulation No 1408/71. The national court that was to decide in the case, however, had doubts as to whether the care allowance could be regarded as a special non-contributory benefit within the meaning of Article 10a. In *Molenaar* (1998) the Court had held that the German equivalent of the Austrian care allowance, the so-called *Pflegegeld*, was to be classified as a sickness benefit in cash for the purposes of Article 19(1)(b), which prohibits application of residence requirements for entitlement to such benefits.[150] The Austrian court decided to refer the case for preliminary ruling essentially asking the Court of Justice whether in the case before it had to apply either Article 10a or Article 19.

---

[148] The validity of Art 10a has been confirmed by the Court in Case C–297/96 *Partridge* [1998] ECR I–3467, Case C–90/97 *Swaddling* [1999] ECR I–1075; Case C–215/99 *Jauch* [2001] ECR I–1901, 21 and Case C–43/99 *Leclere* [2001] ECR I–4265, 32.

[149] Remarkably, in the Commission's 1998 proposal (COM (1998) 779 final) for a simplification of the social security co-ordination rules one no longer finds a specific regime for mixed benefits. This would seem to suggest that the Commission has proposed re-introducing the exportability of mixed benefits again. Compare Pennings, Het Einde van de Exporteerbaarheid van Wajong-Uitkeringen?, in *MR* (2000) 71–4, at 73.

[150] Case C–160/96 *Molenaar* [1998] ECR I–843, 25. On *Molenaar* see ch 4 n 43.

In the proceedings before the Court the Austrian government argued that the mere fact that a benefit has been included in the list of Annex IIa sufficed for it to be classed as a special non-contributory benefit. In support of this argument, the Austrian government referred to *Snares* in which the Court had held that the mere fact that the British legislation on disability living allowances was referred to in Annex IIa was to be accepted as establishing that benefits granted under that legislation were special non-contributory benefits.[151] The argument was doomed to, and indeed did, fail. If it had been accepted, Member States could, free from any judicial supervision, decide which benefits they wish to include in Annex IIa. Obviously, this is not what the Court had intended to say.[152] In *Jauch* the Court held that provisions derogating from Article 10's principle of exportability, such as Article 10a, must be interpreted strictly and this meant, according to the Court, that Article 10a and Annex IIa can apply only to benefits covered by Article 4(2a) of Regulation No 1408/71.[153]

Subsequently, the Court examined whether the Austrian care allowance could be classified as a special non-contributory benefit. In the Court's view, the allowance could not be regarded as non-contributory. In brief, the Austrian care allowances were funded out of the public purse, but the public means needed to pay for the allowances were generated through an increase in sickness insurance contributions.[154] The care allowances could also not be classified as 'special'. In the Court's view, the Austrian allowances were essentially of the same character as the German *Pflegegeld*. They were granted objectively on the basis of a legally defined situation in order to improve the state of health and quality of life of persons reliant on care. Thus, the allowances did not come under Article 4(2a) of Regulation No 1408/71; they were to be classified as a 'sickness benefit in cash', which, by virtue of Article 19(1)(b), must be provided irrespective of the Member State in which a beneficiary is resident.[155]

Leclere involved a former Belgium frontier worker who had worked in Luxembourg and who lived with his wife in Belgium. After the birth of their child, Mr and Mrs Leclere applied in Luxembourg for various allowances among which a maternity allowance. According to the relevant Luxembourg rules, such allowances could be granted to every pregnant woman and every woman who has given birth provided she was officially resident in Luxembourg. Since Mrs Leclere did not meet the latter requirement, the allowance was denied. The maternity allowance was listed in Annex IIa to Regulation No 1408/71, but this could not save the Luxembourg residence requirement. The Court held that it follows from the actual wording of Article 4(2a) of the regulation that the only benefits to which that provision can be taken to refer are

---

[151] Case C–20/96 *Snares* [1997] ECR I–1075 at 30. Compare also Case C–297/96 *Partridge* [1998] ECR I–3467 at 31 and Case C–90/97 *Swaddling* [1999] ECR I–1075 at 24.
[152] Compare Keunen, Annotation *Jauch*, in: RSV (2001) 671–4, at 671.
[153] Case C–215/99 *Jauch* [2001] ECR I–1901, 20–2.
[154] *Ibid*, at 33.
[155] *Ibid*, at 36.

those not covered by general legislation relative to the schemes referred to in Article 4(1).[156] Since the maternity allowances in question were paid to every pregnant woman and to every woman who has given birth, it could not be regarded, in relation to the benefits referred to in Article 4(1) of Regulation No 1408/71, as being in the nature of a special allowance. The allowances, so the Court seemed to say, were to be regarded as maternity allowances for the purposes of the export provision of Article 19(1)(b) of the regulation. Since the maternity allowances were not covered by Article 10a, the Court held that Annex IIa to the regulation was invalid in so far as it covers the Luxembourg maternity allowance.[157]

Jauch and *Leclere* demonstrate that Article 10a and Annex IIa only apply to benefits that can actually be regarded as special and non-contributory benefits in the sense of Article 4(2a) of Regulation No 1408/71. The Court supervises whether benefits listed in Annex IIa meet the requirements mentioned in Article 4(2a) and, in case they do not, references in the annex will be declared invalid.

'Special non-contributory benefits' constitute a separate category of benefits, which must be distinguished from, on the one hand, social assistance benefits that by virtue of Article 4(4) are excluded from Regulation No 1408/71 and its export provisions and, on the other hand, the social security benefits falling under Article 4(1) of the regulation, which can be exported on the basis of Article 10 or one of the specific export provisions of Regulation No 1408/71.

The demarcation *vis-à-vis* social assistance does not give rise to many interpretation problems. In order to determine whether a given benefit is covered by the Regulation No 1408/71 or excluded by virtue of Article 4(4), two criteria must be applied. First, from the preamble to Regulation No 1408/71 it follows that special non-contributory benefits constitute social security benefits, which implies that they fall within the scope of Regulation No 1408/71 only when they are granted as a legally defined right. This requirement excludes from the scope of the regulation social assistance and other minimum subsistence benefit schemes of a charitable nature under which the competent institutions enjoy great discretion as regards both grant and level of the benefits. Secondly, in order to fall under Regulation No 1408/71 benefits must be classifiable as social security benefit covered by the regulation, which implies that they must relate to, or be granted to cover, one of the risks mentioned in Article 4(1).

The demarcation line between special non-contributory benefits and the social security benefits covered by Article 4(1) is more difficult to draw. On this point, *Jauch* and *Leclere* are not wholly clear. The benefits in question were regarded as sickness benefits and maternity benefits respectively, which could be exported on the basis of Article 19(1)(b) of Regulation No 1408/71. The Court did not, however, truly explain why the benefits in question could not be regarded as special non-contributory within the meaning of Article 4(2a). In

---

[156] Case C–43/99 *Leclere* [2001] ECR I–4265, 35.
[157] *Ibid*, at 36–8.

Jauch the Court did not say much than that the care allowance was essentially intended to supplement sickness insurance benefits in order to improve the state of health and quality of life of beneficiaries, whilst in *Leclere* the Court simply seems to have regarded the allowances at issue as classic maternity benefits. In the light of the preamble to Regulation No 1247/92, in which it is indicated that the regulation sought to take account of the case law of the Court on the application of Regulation No 1408/71 to mixed or hybrid benefits, it would seem, however, that the distinguishing feature of the benefits covered by Article 4(2a) is that they are intended to grant beneficiaries a minimum of financial means sufficient to meet the basic costs of subsistence. In other words, it would seem that financial need, as the case law which led to Regulation No 1247/92 would seem to require, serves as the criterion separating the special non-contributory benefits of Article 4(2a) from the benefits falling within the ambit of Article 4(1).[158]

In sum, the term 'special' in Article 4(2a) seems to have a twofold meaning and purpose. In relation to Article 4(4) of the regulation, the term distinguishes mixed benefits from the classic social assistance benefits guaranteeing minimum means of subsistence 'in a general manner'. The term 'special' would seem to refer to the personal scope of benefit schemes so as to include schemes applicable to 'special groups' such as the elderly or the disabled to the exclusion of schemes applicable to the entire resident population. In relation to Article 4(1), the term 'special' seems to refer to the objective of benefit schemes. Article 4(1) covers benefit schemes, be they contributory or non-contributory, that intend to give protection against the financial implications of sickness, maternity, unemployment, old age, etc. Such benefits can be exported on the basis of Article 10 or one of the specific export provisions of the regulation. Article 4(2a) applies to publicly funded benefits which are intended to guarantee beneficiaries minimum means of subsistence. Such benefits are linked to the particular social and economic context in the Member State where beneficiaries live[159] and, provided they are listed in Annex IIa, they cannot be exported.

5.2.5 Residence

From all the foregoing it follows that Member States must grant minimum subsistence benefits to nationals of other Member States who are lawfully residing within their borders under the same conditions as their own nationals, but that they are under no obligation to award such benefits to those living outside their borders. Lawful residence serves as the criterion determining the Member State

---

[158] Compare the Opinion of Adv Gen Jacobs in Case C–43/99 *Leclere* [2001] ECR I–4265, 75.

[159] Compare Resolution of the Administrative Commission of 29 June 2000 concerning criteria for the inclusion of benefits as 'special non-contributory benefits' in Annex II, s III or in Annex IIa of Reg (EEC) No 1408/71 (OJ 2001 C 44).

in which Community citizen can, when necessary, apply for and, when substantive eligibility criteria are met, receive minimum subsistence benefits.

It is thus of the utmost importance to establish what the notion lawful residence precisely entails. The concept comprises two elements. The first concerns the legality of residence and has already been addressed. The second element involves the notion of residence itself. What does it take to establish residence in another Member State?

Community law does not provide a crystal clear answer. Regulation No 1408/71 defines 'residence' as 'habitual residence' which must be distinguished from 'stay' which means 'temporary residence'.[160] In the recent *Swaddling* case (1999) the Court held in relation to Article 10a that residence implies the place or State where a person 'habitually resides' or where the 'habitual centre of their interests is found'.[161] Vague as these descriptions may be, they do reveal that residence entails more than just the place or State where an individual effectively lives. Individuals may very well live in more than one place or State, but they can claim social assistance or mixed benefits in one State only. For the purposes of minimum subsistence benefits, the term residence cannot have the meaning commonly given to it. As regards persons who live in or have ties with more than one State, a choice has to be made. 'Habitual residence' may be equated with 'domicile'. The concept is equally elusive and whilst it often coincides with residence, it does not have an identical meaning. Domicile can be defined as the place where a person has his principal establishment which serves to link a given act or fact to a specific legal order,[162] or the place or State with which a person is most closely connected.[163]

Application of the notion of 'habitual residence' is often far from easy. Consider *Swaddling* (1999). The case concerned the social security legislation of the United Kingdom under which eligibility for income support benefits was made conditional upon 'habitual residence' in the country. The requirement was introduced in order to tackle social security abuses by Community citizens[164] and to exclude in particular work-seekers from such benefit schemes. Under the United Kingdom legislation, 'habitual residence' implies that a claimant has a 'settled purpose of establishing residence' in the country and has resided there for 'an appreciable period'. This definition of 'habitual residence' was applied to a Mr Swaddling, a British national who, after having worked in France, returned to the United Kingdom in January 1995. Mr Swaddling was

---

[160] See Art 1(h) and (i) of Reg No 1408/71.

[161] Case C–90/97 *Swaddling* [1999] ECR I–1075, 29–30.

[162] See Garot, 'A New Basis for European Citizenship: Residence?', in La Torre (ed), *European Citizenship: An Institutional Challenge* (1998) 229–48, at 236–9. Compare further Corson, 'Reform of Domicile Law for Application of Transients, Temporary Residents and Multi-Based Persons', in *ColJLSP* (1981) 327–64.

[163] Reese/Green, 'That Elusive Word, "Residence"', in *VdbiltLRev* (1953) 561–80, at 562. To be sure, under national law one may often find wholly different definitions of the two terms. The descriptions given above only have significance for this chapter.

[164] O'Leary (1998) n 120 above, at 134.

granted the income benefit but only from the beginning of March. For January and February the benefit was denied because during these months Mr Swaddling had not yet resided in the United Kingdom for an 'appreciable period'. The benefit Mr Swaddling had applied for was listed as a mixed benefit in Annex IIa to Regulation No 1408/71 and was thus covered by Article 10a. This implied that the United Kingdom was entitled to preserve eligibility to the benefits for residents. Yet, was Mr Swaddling to be regarded as a resident? The Court held that the phrase 'the Member State in which they reside' in Article 10a of the regulation refers to the State in which the persons concerned 'habitually reside' or where the 'habitual centre of their interests is found'. In this context, account should be taken in particular of the person's family situation, the reasons which have led him to move, the length and continuity of his residence, the fact that a person is in 'stable employment' and his 'intention as it appears from all the circumstances'.[165] The Court held that the length of a person's residence could not be regarded as an 'intrinsic element' of the concept of residence. The mere fact that a person like Mr Swaddling had not resided in the country for 'an appreciable period' could in itself be no reason for classing him as a non-resident and denying him the claimed benefit.

The concept of habitual residence, as *Swaddling* demonstrates, does not have a fixed meaning. It is a concept which Member States and their courts have to apply on a case-by-case basis in accordance with a number of qualitative (eg, family situation, place of stable employment etc.) and quantitative (eg, duration of envisaged or actual residence) factors which in themselves are never decisive and which, depending on the facts of a given case, may have to be given different weight. Outcomes of individual cases are hard to predict and it is quite difficult to draw more general conclusions from the case law. *Swaddling* would seem to imply that work-seekers are not to be regarded as habitual residents of the host State for the purposes of social assistance laws. Until the moment they find employment, work-seekers indeed seem to have the closest ties with the State that they moved from.[166] Yet, does this imply that Community citizens who have worked and live in another Member State and who, after having become unemployed, seek a new job in the host State can be classed as residents for minimum subsistence laws? Further, in cases such as *Reibold* (1990)[167] and

---

[165] Case C–90/97 *Swaddling* [1999] ECR I–1075, 30.

[166] In *Lebon* (1987) the Court held that only workers can claim equal treatment as regards social advantages under Art 7(2) of Reg No 1612/68. Case 316/85 *Lebon* [1987] ECR 2811, 26. Recently, the Court seems to have partly come back from *Lebon* in *Martínez Sala* (1998) where it concluded that 'persons genuinely seeking work must . . . be classed as a worker'. Case C–85/96 *Martínez Sala* [1998] ECR I–2691, 32. Work-seekers now seem entitled to invoke Art 7(2) (compare O'Leary (1999) n 108 above, at 76), but that conclusion merely implies that work-seekers can no longer be denied equal treatment as regards 'social advantages' on grounds of their nationality (van der Steen, 'De Europese Burger Krijgt Handen en Voeten', in *NTER* (1998) 163–6, at 165). *Martínez Sala* does not prohibit Member States from denying work seekers minimum subsistence benefits on the ground that they lack residence status.

[167] Case C–216/89 *Reibold* [1990] ECR I–4163.

Knoch (1992)[168] the Court suggested that teachers or professors who participate in exchange programmes are not to be regarded as residents of the host State for the purposes of unemployment benefits. Without establishing a general rule, the Court seemed to have indicated that such providers of education are still to be seen, and treated, as residents of the home State because the length of employment is normally limited at the outset and the work performed is often interrupted by long holiday periods which may be spent in the State of origin. Similar arguments could be made as regards Community students. Students often spend most of their time in the host State, but given the limited duration of their studies and the fact that many students spend holidays 'at home', the State of origin would seem their 'habitual residence'.

The determination of a Community citizen's 'habitual residence' entails an assessment of facts that may vary from case to case. For this reason, it is quite understandable that the Court has refrained from giving a detailed general definition and chosen merely to enumerate a number of factors which Member States and national courts have to apply in individual cases. The result, however, is that Member States enjoy a wide margin of discretion in interpreting the notion of 'habitual residence'. In practice, the notion may be given quite different meanings and the danger exists that Community citizens might be denied minimum subsistence because of overly restrictive and 'self-serving' interpretations of the notion of 'domicile'. In 'the spirit of juridical justice',[169] it would be desirable if the Court, when given the opportunity, were to provide further clarification and guidance.

5.3 Social Assistance Benefits

Regulation No 1408/71 does not apply to classic social assistance schemes. Therefore, the question whether or not Member States can make entitlement to such benefits conditional upon residence in the national territory must be answered on the basis of the general provisions governing free movement of persons.

From the rulings in *Martínez Sala* and *Grzelczyk* it follows that Community citizens who have decided to move to another Member State fall within the scope of Community law and that they enjoy under Article 12(1) EC a right to equal treatment as regards virtually all social benefits including social assistance allowances. It can safely be assumed, however, that the rulings cannot be interpreted as to confer upon Community travellers a right to social assistance in the State they visit. Article 12(1) EC precludes nationality criteria but does not prohibit residence requirements for entitlement to social assistance.

---

[168] Case C–102/91 *Knoch* [1992] ECR I–4341.
[169] Garot (1998) n 162 above, at 239.

The question could be raised, however, whether frontier workers and other workers who have decided not to establish residence in the State of employment can claim social assistance in that State. Does employment in the State's territory suffice for entitlement to such assistance? Regulation No 1612/68 does not contain an export provision comparable to Article 10 of the social security regulation.[170] The case law of the Court on Regulation No 1612/68, however, raises the question whether residence requirements for social assistance are compatible with Article 7(2) of this regulation. As the Court ruled in *Hoeckx* (1985)[171], social assistance benefits must be regarded as 'social advantages' and this implies that Community workers and their dependent family members enjoy equality of treatment as regards such benefits. Yet, can they be required to establish, or keep, their residence in the State of employment?

A first case to be discussed in this context is *Meints* (1998).[172] The case concerned a German frontier worker who was working on a farm in the Netherlands and residing in Germany. Following set-aside measures taken by his employer, Mr Meints lost his job. He applied for a benefit which was made available to workers whose contract of employment has been terminated as a result of the setting aside of land by their former employer. Under the Netherlands legislation enjoyment of this special benefit was conditional upon the receipt of 'normal' unemployment benefits. Since Mr Meints was wholly unemployed and not residing in the Netherlands, he could not claim the latter benefits in the Netherlands,[173] and his application for the special benefit was therefore denied. Appealing that decision, Mr Meints claimed, *inter alia*, that the residence requirement was contrary to Article 7(2) of Regulation No 1612/68. The French and the Netherlands governments argued that residence requirements for benefits which can be classified as social advantages were valid because Article 7(2) would not provide for the possibility of exporting such advantages. The Court rejected this argument by referring to the fourth recital of the preamble to of Regulation No 1612/68 which states that the right of free movement must be enjoyed 'without discrimination by permanent, seasonal and frontier workers'. Frontier workers thus can invoke Article 7(2).[174] The Court further held that the residence requirement in question could be more easily met by nationals than by nationals of other Member States. The requirement constituted an indirect discrimination by reason of nationality.

Hoeckx and *Meints*, however, did not necessarily imply that residence requirements for social assistance benefits are indeed prohibited by Article 7(2) of Regulation No 1612/68. It is settled case law that the concept of social advantages

---

[170] Altmaier, 'Europäisches koordinierendes Sozialrecht—Ende des Territorialitätsprinzip?', in Eichenhofer/Zuleeg (Hrsg.), *Die Rechtsprechung des Europäischen Gerichtshof zum Arbeits- und Sozialrecht im Streit* (1995) 71–91, at 81.

[171] Case 249/83 *Hoeckx* [1985] ECR 982, 20–2.

[172] Case C–57/96 *Meints* [1997] ECR I–6689.

[173] See Art 71(1)(a)(ii) of Reg No 1408/71.

[174] Case C–57/96 *Meints* [1998] ECR I–6689, 50–1.

covers all advantages which are granted to 'national workers because of their objective status as workers' or by 'virtue of the mere fact of their residence on the national territory'. *Meints* concerned benefits which beneficiaries enjoyed in their capacity as (former) workers and the judgment could therefore still be read so as to imply that residence requirements for benefits which are offered by virtue of residence, such as social assistance, do not violate Article 7(2).[175] This interpretation of *Meints*, however, is hard to compare with the ruling in *Meeusen* (1999).[176] The case, which will be discussed in further detail in chapter 5, concerned a Belgian child of a Belgian frontier worker who was working in the Netherlands. Ms Meeusen, who was residing in Belgium, claimed student financial aid in the Netherlands for her studies in Antwerp. The Netherlands government argued that a person such as Ms Meeusen could not rely on Article 7(2) because this provision is intended to promote the integration of the worker and his family in the host State. Frontier workers, however, have chosen not to establish residence in, and to become a member of the society of, the State of employment. The Court, however, reasoned that such an interpretation disregarded the wording of Regulation No 1612/68. Under reference to *Meints*, the Court stated that frontier workers may enjoy rights under Article 7(2) and it concluded that:

> 'In a situation where national legislation . . . does not impose any residence require-
> ment on the children of national workers for financing of their studies, such a require-
> ment must be regarded as discriminatory if it is imposed on the children of workers
> who are nationals of other Member States.'[177]

As with student grants, social assistance benefits can be regarded as benefits that are not granted to beneficiaries in their capacity as worker, but rather because of their residence in the national territory. A combined reading of *Hoeckx*, *Meints* and *Meeusen* would thus seem to lead to the conclusion that frontier workers, other workers not residing in the State of employment and their dependent family members can rely on Article 7(2) of Regulation No 1612/68 in order to claim social assistance benefits under the same conditions as nationals of the host State.

The practical significance of this conclusion, however, seems minimal. It would indeed imply that national rules that deny non-nationals social assistance benefits on the ground that they do not possess the nationality of the State in question. Yet, the mere fact that frontier workers can rely on Article 7(2) does not necessarily imply that residence requirements which are applied to nationals and non-nationals alike violate this provision. In fact, one may safely assume that Article 7(2) does not prohibit application of such residence requirements. First, so far the Court has never applied the indirect discrimination test of Article 7(2) to residence requirements for benefits such as social assistance that

---

[175] Compare the Opinion of Adv Gen Alber in Case C–255/99 *Humer*, pending, at 86 and Sewandono, *Werknemersverkeer en Gezinsleven* (1998) at 225–6.
[176] Case C–337/97 *Meeusen* [1999] ECR I–3289.
[177] *Ibid*, at 23.

are granted to national workers by virtue of residence on the national territory. There is no certainty that, in relation to frontier workers and their dependent family members, social assistance can be regarded as a 'social advantage'. The Court has never held that Article 7(2) obliges Member States to treat non-resident workers equally as resident workers with respect to benefits that are awarded by virtue of residence. Second, in case non-residents can benefit from the indirect discrimination test as regards residence-based social benefits, residence requirements for social assistance can most probably be justified. Such requirements mainly affect non-nationals but they can be saved when necessary for, and proportional to, the protection of a legitimate public interest.[178] Residence requirements for social assistance benefits may be regarded as a prerequisite for safeguarding the funding and organisation of social assistance schemes. Any other conclusion is hard to compare with the Court's conclusions in *Snares* that benefits that are linked with the social environment can be made subject to the condition of residence in the competent State.

5.4 Conclusions

Member States' minimum subsistence benefit schemes are territorial systems based on a form of 'membership' which has always been, and still is, primarily defined in terms of residence on the State territory. Regulation No 1408/71 and Regulation No 1612/68 do require that non-nationals lawfully residing on national territory can obtain such benefits under the same conditions as the States' own nationals, but they do not demand from States' to extend their 'welfare responsibility' to persons living outside their borders. Residence requirements for mixed benefits and social assistance benefits do not violate the provisions of the two regulations. Community citizens can claim minimum subsistence benefits in one Member State only. The criterion of 'lawful' residence determines which Member State is responsible for persons in need of such benefits.

6 THIRD COUNTRY NATIONALS

The Community provisions on the free movement of persons and the co-ordination of social security schemes apply in principle only to Community citizens.[179] Third country nationals can only claim minimum subsistence benefits under these provisions when they can be classed as a family member of a Community citizen who has established residence in another Member State. The exclusion from the free movement and social security regime does not imply, however, that Community law has nothing to offer 'needy' nationals of

---

[178] Case C–237/94 *O'Flynn* [1996] ECR I–2617, 17 and 20.

third countries. Third country nationals enjoy social rights under various agreements which the Community and its Member States have concluded with third States. This section explores whether, and if so, the conditions under which, third country nationals can claim minimum subsistence benefits under the Agreement on the European Economic Area (EEA), the E(E)C-Turkey Association Agreement and the agreements which have been concluded with the Maghreb countries Morocco, Algeria and Tunisia.[180]

6.1 EEA Nationals

The EEA Agreement aims to promote a continuous and balanced strengthening of trade and economic relations between the European Community and its Member States, on the one hand, and Norway, Iceland and Liechtenstein, on the other hand.[181] In order to achieve these objectives, the Agreement has extended the scope of the common market freedoms to the nationals and the territories of the three countries concerned. Article 28 of the Agreement applies to the free movement of workers and is phrased similarly to Article 39 of the EC Treaty. The secondary legislation adopted under Article 40 of the Treaty, including Regulation No 1612/68, has been integrated into the EEA Agreement. Further, Article 29 EEA largely reproduces Article 42 EC and Regulations No 1408/71 and No 574/72 have been made applicable to EEA nationals.[182] In as far as the free movement of workers is concerned, the legal status of the nationals of the three States and their family members under the EEA Agreement is in principle

---

[179] See ch 2 ss 5 and 6. The Commission, however, has proposed to bring third country nationals within the ambit of the Reg No 1408/71 (COM(97) 561 final and COM(1998) 779 final) and it has submitted to the Council a Proposal for A Directive concerning the Status of Third-Country Nationals who are Long-Term Residents (COM(2001)127 final), which includes the right to reside in other Member States..

[180] For brief descriptions of these agreements and the relevant free movement and/or equal treatment provisions, see ch 2 s 5. This section does not discuss the possible implications for minimum subsistence benefits of the judgment of the European Court of Human Rights in *Gaygusuz*. Judgement of 16 September 1996, Case No 39/1995/545/631. In this case Austria was condemned for rejecting the application of a Turkish national for emergency assistance for unemployed persons on the ground of his nationality. In brief, the Strasbourg court concluded that the Austrian rejection was in breach of Art 14 of the European Convention (non-discrimination principle) read in conjunction with Art 1 of the first Protocol to the Convention (the right to property). Fundamental rights such as those contained in the European Convention are, as general principles of law, also protected by Community law (see ch 2 n 237), but so far there are no indications that *Gaygusuz* has any implications for Community rules governing freedom of movement and entitlement to non-contributory benefits such as minimum subsistence benefits. On *Gaygusuz* see Verschueren, 'EC Social Security Coordination Excluding Third Country Nationals: Still in Line with Fundamental Rights after the *Gaygusuz* Judgment?', in *CMLRev* (1997) 991–1017 and the various contributions in Van den Bogaert (ed), *Social Security, Non-Discrimination and Property* (1997).

[181] Art 1 EEA.

[182] OJ 1994 L 1. See further Sakslin, 'The Agreements on the European Economic Area', in Jorens/Schulte (eds), *European Social Security Law and Third Country Nationals* (1998) 399–417.

identical to the status of the category of the economic residents discussed in section 3. Thus, when the work they perform in another EEA State is classed as 'effective and genuine', EEA workers and their dependent family members are eligible for minimum subsistence benefits under the same conditions as the nationals of the host State from the moment they take up residence in that State. It is not certain whether the same conclusion can be drawn as regards economically inactive EEA nationals[183] who have established residence in another State. The three residence directives of 1990 for students, pensioners and 'other' Community citizens have been extended to EEA nationals and Article 4(1) EEA contains a non-discrimination clause phrased similarly to Article 12(1) EC. It could be argued that 'needy' EEA nationals who are lawfully residing in another EEA State can invoke Article 4(1) EEA in order to claim equal access to minimum subsistence benefits in the host State. Uncertainty exists, however, because the EEA agreement does not provide for an equivalent of European Union citizenship. The reasoning followed by the Court in *Martínez Sala*, and the conclusions drawn in Section 4, cannot be automatically transposed to EEA nationals.

6.2 Maghreb Nationals

Neither the 1978 Maghreb agreements nor the more recent Euro-Mediterranean agreements that the Community and its Member States have concluded with Tunisia and Morocco confer upon Maghreb nationals a right to freedom of movement. However, the various agreements do contain a number of provisions on social security.[184] The first paragraph of Article 65 of the Euro-Mediterranean agreement with Morocco, which replaced Article 41(1) of the original co-operation agreement, offers Moroccan nationals who are residing in one of the EC Member States a right to equal treatment in the field of social security. The subsequent three paragraphs grant Moroccan nationals a right to aggregation of insurance, employment or residence periods for various social security benefits, a right to family allowances for family members residing within the Community and a right to transfer old-age pensions to Morocco. Article 42 states that the Co-operation Council shall adopt measures implementing the principles set out in Article 41. Virtually identical provisions are found in Articles 39 and 40 of the Agreement with Algeria and Articles 65 and 67 of the Euro-mediterranean agreement with Tunisia.

What do the above provisions entail for Maghreb nationals who wish to obtain social security benefits, and minimum subsistence benefits in particular, in the Member State in whose territory they reside? For quite some time it seemed that Maghreb nationals could not enjoy any rights under the social

---

[183] The same holds true for the independent family members of EEA workers.
[184] For a brief overview see ch 2 s 5.3 and s 6.

security provisions. The Co-operation Councils established by the respective agreements have not taken any implementing measures.[185] The social security provisions seemed nothing but 'dormant provisions' lacking legal and practical significance. Since the early 1990s, however, the Court of Justice has breathed life into these provisions in cases such as *Kziber*[186] (1991), *Yousfi*[187] (1994) and *Krid*[188] (1995).

Kziber concerned a Moroccan national who lived in Belgium with her Moroccan parents and who, for reasons of her nationality, had been refused an unemployment benefit for young workers who have just completed their studies. In order to determine whether the refusal was compatible with Article 41(1) of the Morocco co-operation agreement, the Court first had to determine whether this provision has direct effect. The Court ruled that this Article can indeed be directly relied upon. Article 41(1) lays down a clear, precise and unconditional prohibition of discrimination on grounds of nationality; the direct applicability of this provision cannot be made conditional for the sole reason that Article 42 envisages implementing measures to be adopted by the Co-operation Council.[189]

The second question the Court had to answer in *Kziber* concerned the precise meaning of the term 'social security'. The Court held that this term 'must be understood by means of analogy with the identical concept in Regulation No 1408/71'. Since Article 4(1) of this Regulation includes unemployment benefits in the scope of the Regulation, the Court held that the benefits Ms. Kziber had applied for were also covered by Article 41(1) of the Morocco agreement.[190] In *Yousfi* (1994) the Court was confronted with the question whether mixed minimum subsistence benefits are also covered by Article 41(1). The case concerned the Moroccan son of a Moroccan worker living Belgium who after an accident at work applied for a disability allowance. This mixed benefit was denied on the

[185] Recently, however, proposals for social security measures have been made in the context of the Euro-Mediterranenan agreements with Morocco (http://europa.eu.int/eur-lex) and Tunisia (COM(2000) 216 def).

[186] Case C–18/90 *Kziber* [1991] ECR I–199. On this judgment see eg Vonk, 'Het HvJEG-arrest in de zaak Kziber—Een Levenskus voor de Slapende Paragrafen in de EG Samenwerkings-overeenkomsten', in *MR* (1991) 149–51.

[187] Case C–103/93 *Yousfi* [1994] ECR I–1353.

[188] Case C–103/94 *Krid* [1995] ECR I–719.

[189] *Ibid*, at 16–23. The Court confirmed this conclusion in Case C–58/93 *Yousfi* [1994] ECR I–1353, 19. The identically phrased provision contained in Art 39 of the Algeria agreement is, as the Court held in *Krid* (Case C–103/94 [1995] ECR I–719, 23–4) also directly applicable. One may safely assume that the same holds true for provision in the Euro-Mediterranean Agreements with Morocco and Tunisia.

[190] Case C–18/90 *Kziber* [1991] ECR I–199, 25–6. In the proceedings before the Court it had been argued that unemployment benefits would not be covered by Art 41(1) because Art 41(2) (aggregation rule) does not apply to unemployment benefits and no unemployment insurance scheme exists in Morocco. The Court, however, reasoned that the fact that Art 41(2) does not mention unemployment benefits is merely relevant for the application of the aggregation rule; it cannot warrant the conclusion that such benefits are excluded from the term 'social security' in Art 41(1) of the Agreement. Case C–18/90 *Kziber* [1991] ECR I–199, 26.

ground of Yousfi's nationality. Disability allowances were initially not mentioned in Article 4(1) of Regulation No 1408/71, but, as described earlier in this chapter, the Court had already concluded that benefits can be regarded as being covered by the Regulation when the legislation under which they are granted places claimants in a legally defined position as a result of which they have an absolute right to benefit and the benefits cover one of the risks enumerated in Article 4(1).[191] The disability allowance Mr Yousfi had applied for met these conditions and, following the rule established in *Kziber*, the Court therefore concluded that such benefits therefore fell within the scope of Article 41(1) of the Morocco agreement.[192] In *Krid* the Court concluded that a widow of an Algerian worker in Belgium could be denied a supplementary allowance which was, *inter alia*, granted to recipients of old-age pensions or invalidity benefits who lack sufficient means of subsistence on grounds of her nationality. The allowance was a mixed benefit in the sense of Article 4(2)a of Regulation No 1408/71, as inserted by Regulation No 1247/92. The latter regulation had already came into force at the time Ms. Krid applied for the allowance. Therefore, the Court did not have much difficulty in concluding that the allowance was also to be considered as a social security benefit for the purposes of Article 39(1) of the agreement with Algeria.[193]

The non-discrimination provisions enshrined in the social security provisions of the co-operation agreements may thus be directly relied upon in court and the material scope of these provisions coincides with the scope of Article 3 of Regulation No 1408/71. This did not imply, however, that the applicants in the three cases could indeed invoke the provisions. The social security provisions apply to workers of Moroccan, Algerian or Tunisian nationality and family members living with them. In *Yousfi* the Court held that the term 'workers' encompasses 'both active workers and those who have left the labour market after reaching the age required for receipt of an old-age pension or after becoming victims of the materialisation of one of the risks creating entitlement to allowances falling under other branches of social security'.[194] Mr Yousfi, who had become incapable of working after an accident at work, could be classed as a worker for the purposes of Article 41(1).[195] The claimants in *Kziber* and *Krid*, however, were not workers but family members of workers. In both cases it was argued by governments represented in the proceedings before the Court that, by analogy with the '*Kermaschek*-rule' adopted by the Court under Regulation No 1408/71, the applicants could only enjoy derived rights as family members. The unemployment benefits for young workers in *Kziber* and the supplementary allowance for old people in *Krid* would have to be classified as 'personal rights'

---

[191] See s 2.3 above.
[192] Case C–103/93 *Yousfi* [1994] ECR I–1353, 28.
[193] Case C–103/94 *Krid* [1995] ECR I–719, 37.
[194] Case C–58/93 *Yousfi* [1994] ECR I–1319, 21.
[195] *Ibid*, at 23.

which could be denied to applicants. In his Opinion in *Kziber* Advocate General van Gerven agreed with this line of reasoning. In his view it could not be accepted that family members of Moroccan workers could possibly enjoy more extensive rights than family members of Community workers residing in other Member States.[196] The Court, however, took another view. In *Kziber* it simply held that family members of Moroccan workers who fulfil the requirements for entitlement to (unemployment) benefits may not be refused such benefits on the ground of their nationality.[197] In *Krid* the Court reached a similar conclusion and, after referring to the text of Article 39(1) of the Algeria agreement, it stated that the personal scope of this provision is not the same as the scope of Regulation No 1408/71. Therefore, the *Kermaschek* case law 'distinguishing between derived rights and the personal rights of members of the migrant workers' families . . . cannot be applied in the context of the Agreement'.[198]

Workers who hold the nationality of one of the three Maghreb countries and members of the family who are living with them,[199] thus enjoy a right to claim minimum subsistence benefits which are covered by Regulation No 1408/71 under the same conditions as the nationals of the host State.[200] This is not to say that nationals of the Maghreb countries are in an equally privileged position with Community citizens.[201] First, Maghreb nationals do not seem to enjoy

[196] Opinion of Adv Gen van Gerven in Case C–18/90 *Kziber* [1991] ECR I–199, 18.

[197] Case C–18/90 *Kziber* [1991] ECR I–199, 28.

[198] Case C–103/94 *Krid* [1995] ECR I–719, 39. See also Case C–126/95 *Hallouzi-Choho* [1996] ECR I–4807, 30 and Case C–113/97 *Babahenini* [1998] ECR I–183, 24. In *Kziber* and *Krid* the Court thus accepted that family members of Maghreb workers may indeed enjoy more extensive rights than family members of workers holding the nationality of a Member State. This could already be seen as a sign that the Court was 'preparing' itself for the conclusion in *Cabanis-Issarte* (1996—see ch 2 s 6) that the distinction between derived rights and personal rights should no longer or at least be less relevant for the legal status of family members of European workers under Regulation No 1408/71. Compare Jorens, *De Rechtspositie van Niet-EU-Onderdanen in het Europees Socialezekerheidsrecht* (1996) at 326–7.

[199] Art 41(1) of the Morocco agreement and the equivalent provisions of other Maghreb agreements do not define the term 'family members living with them'. The Court has held, however, that the term not only covers spouses and children but also relatives in the ascending line who are living with the worker in the host State. Case C–179/98 *Mesbah* [1999] ECR I–7955, 43–8. Family members who have installed themselves with the worker in the host State after the latter has acquired the nationality of the host State, however, are not entitled to benefit from Art 41(1). This conclusion does not differ where the worker still possesses a Maghreb nationality. *Ibid.*, at 41.

[200] So far the Court has not explicitly determined whether the prohibition enshrined in the non-discrimination provisions also covers indirect discrimination by reason of nationality. *Kziber* and subsequent cases suggest, however, that the Court draws inspiration from the Community provisions on freedom of movement, and equality of treatment in particular, while interpreting the Maghreb provisions. It could thus be argued that durational residence or employment requirements for mixed benefits are also at odds with provisions in the Maghreb agreements.

[201] In one respect, however, Maghreb nationals are in a more privileged position than Community citizens. It is settled case law that Reg No 1408/71 replaces social security conventions previously concluded by the Member States, even where these conventions are more favourable for beneficiaries than Reg No 1408/71. See ch 2 n 208. The Maghreb agreements, however, cannot affect rights enjoyed under agreements Member States have concluded with Maghreb countries. See eg Art 68 of the Euro-Mediterranean Agreement with Morocco and Jorens, Non-European Union

equality of treatment as regards the classic social assistance benefits. Such benefits are excluded from Regulation No 1408/71 and, thus, the social security provisions of the Maghreb agreements. The latter agreements do not contain clauses comparable to those contained in Article 7(2) of Regulation No 1612/68[202] or Article 12 of the EC Treaty, into which a right to equal treatment as regards social assistance benefits could possibly have been read. Secondly, the agreements do not confer upon Maghreb nationals a right to reside in the State of employment.[203] Being in need of minimum subsistence benefits can be a reason for refusing Maghreb nationals a work and residence permit or withdrawing such permits.[204]

6.3 Turkish Nationals

Article 12 of the 1963 Association Agreement between the European Community and Turkey provides that the Contracting Parties agree to be guided by Articles 39 (formerly 48) *et seq.* of the EC Treaty for the purpose of progressively realising a free movement of workers between them. So far, however, the EC-Turkey Association Council has not yet adopted all necessary measures. Up until today, it is for the Member States to decide whether Turkish nationals are admitted to their labour market and territory.[205]

Once admitted to a national labour market, however, Turkish workers enjoy various rights. Decision No 1/80 of the Association Council grants Turkish workers (Article 6) and their family members (Article 7) employment rights which enable them to gradually integrate in the labour market of the host State and which encompass rights of residence.[206] In addition, Turkish nationals enjoy rights in the field of social security. In furtherance of Article 39 of the Additional Protocol of 1970, in 1980 the Association Council adopted Decision No 3/80 on the application of social security schemes to the benefit of Turkish workers moving between the Member States of the Community. By analogy

---

Nationals and the Co-ordination of European Social SecurityLaw: The International Agreements Concluded by the European Union with Third Countries and Conflict Rules in European Social Security Law, in Jorens/Schulte (eds), *European Social Security Law and Third Country Nationals* (1998) 1–110, at 12–13.

[202] Compare the Opinion of Adv Gen van Gerven in Case C–18/90 *Kziber* [1991] ECR I–199, 19.

[203] See eg Case C–416/96 *El-Yassini* (1999) ECR I–1209. See further ch 2 n 204.

[204] The situation might be different where a Member State has voluntarily granted a Maghreb national a work permit the duration of which exceeds the accompanying residence permit. In such a situation a Maghreb national can claim a right to reside until the expiration of the period for which the work permit is granted (Case C–416/96 *El-Yassini* (1999) ECR I–1209, 64–66) and, during this period, probably also a right to claim equality of treatment as regards mixed benefits.

[205] Ch 2 s 5.3.

[206] See eg Case C–171/95 *Tetik* [1997] ECR I–329, 24; Case C–237/91 *Kus* [1992] ECR I–6781, 27–36 and Case C–355/93 *Eroglu* [1994] ECR I–5113, 20 and 23.

with the provisions of Regulation No 1408/71, Decision No 3/80 aims to avoid Turkish workers losing certain social security rights when they decide to move to another Member State.[207] The Decision provides for a right to equal treatment in social security matters (Article 3), a right to export certain benefits (Article 6) and it extends the application of most rules determining the applicable legislation contained in Articles 13 *et seq.* of Regulation No 1408/71 to Turkish workers (Article 9). For the most part, the provisions of Decision No 3/80 refer to provisions of Regulation No 1408/71 and, less frequently, to Regulation No 574/72.

Until recently, however, Decision No 3/80 did not have any practical significance for Turkish workers who wished to claim minimum subsistence benefits or other social security rights in the host State. In order to be implemented, decisions of the Association Council require a unanimous decision of the Council on the part of the Community. In 1983 the European Commission had submitted a proposal for such a decision to the Council, but this proposal has not been adopted.[208] Two quite recent judgments of the Court demonstrate, however, that Decision No 3/80 does have legal effect.

The first was the one in the *Taflan-Met* (1996) case.[209] Mrs Taflan-Met and two other Turkish widows had applied for widows pensions in the Netherlands where their former husbands had worked. The Dutch social security system is based on risk which implies that insured persons or their survivors are only entitled to receive benefits when the insured risk materialises at a time when the insured is covered by the Netherlands legislation. The husbands of the three widows, however, had died in Turkey and the pensions were therefore denied. The Court of Justice was asked to determine whether the refusal to grant the pensions was compatible with a number of provisions of Decision No 3/80. It ruled that the binding effect of the decision of the Association Council could not depend on any implementing measures. In the absence of a provision on the date of the coming into force of the Decision, the Court held that Decision No 3/80 was supposed to have come into force on the day the decision was adopted, ie 19 September 1980.[210] This conclusion, however, did not help the Turkish widows very much. The Court concluded that the specific provisions they had relied upon were not directly effective. In reaching this conclusion the Court drew a comparison with Regulation No 1408/71 and the implementing Regulation

---

[207] For more extensive descriptions of the Decision see eg Centel, 'The Social Security of the Turkish Workers in Europe within the Framework of the Association Agreement', in: Jorens/Schulte (eds) *European Social Security Law and Third Country Nationals* (1998) 281–97 and Hänlein, 'Problems Concerning Decision No 3/80 of the Council of Association—A Point of View from a EU Perspective', in Jorens/Schulte (eds) *European Social Security Law and Third Country Nationals* (1998) 299–322.

[208] The reason for this is that Greece, which became a Member State a few weeks after the adoption of Dec No 3/80, was not willing to agree to any decision in favour of Turkey. See Hänlein (1998) n 207 above, at 305.

[209] Case C–277/94 *Taflan-Met* [1996] ECR I–4085.

[210] *Ibid*, at 21.

No 574/72. The Court held that the main principles set out in the former Regulation could only have been given practical effect because of the procedures and formalities contained in the latter Regulation. The coming into force of Regulation No 574/72 was thus a prerequisite for the enforcement of the rights enshrined in Regulation No 1408/71. The Commission's proposal of 1983 does contain implementing measures comparable to ones contained in Regulation No 574/72, but for as long as this proposal has not been adopted, the provisions of Decision No 3/80 could not, according to the Court, be enforced in court.[211]

After *Taflan-Met* Decision No 3/80 seemed a 'walking corpse': the decision had come into force but in the absence of any implementing measure its provisions could not be applied.[212] The reasoning[213] and the conclusion of the Court in *Taflan-Met*, however, was not persuasive. As regards certain rights that require the co-operation of social security institutions, such as rights concerning the aggregation of insurance periods, implementing measures may be necessary for their enforceability. This does not seem to be the case, however, for other rights guaranteed by Decision No 3/80 such as, in particular, the right to equal treatment. Article 3 contains a non-discrimination provision which is phrased in similar terms to Article 3 of Regulation No 1408/71. Why would Turkish nationals be denied the right to invoke this non-discrimination provision in court? The Court addressed this question in *Sürül* (1999).[214]

The case concerned a Turkish woman who had been authorised to reside in Germany with her Turkish husband who was studying and working there. After the birth of their child, Mrs Sürül was given family allowances as well as a supplementary allowance for persons with a low income. The competent social security institution, however, terminated payment of the family allowances on the ground that Mrs Sürül could no longer produce a residence entitlement or permit. Mrs Sürül, who only possessed an 'accessory residence authorisation', challenged that decision in court. The German court referred the case to the Court of Justice asking whether the refusal to grant family allowances was compatible with Article 3 of the Decision. The Court held that the reasoning followed in *Taflan-Met* merely applied to provisions of Decision No 3/80 which actually require additional measures for their application in

---

[211] *Ibid*, at 31–7. On *Taflan-Met* see eg Bulterman, Annotation *Taflan-Met*, in *CMLRev* (1997) 1497–507; Peers, 'Equality, Free Movement and Social Security', in *ELRev* (1997) 342 *et seq.*; Verschueren, 'Na het Arrest Taflan-Met: Is er Leven na de Dood?—Besluit 3/80 (Sociale Zekerheid) van de Associatieraad EEG-Turkije Bestudeerd', in: *MR* (1997) 29–34, at 30 and Zuleeg, 'Das Urteil Taflan-Met des Europäischen Gerichtshofs', in *ZIAS* (1997) 170 *et seq.*

[212] Verschueren (1997) n 211 above, at 33.

[213] Hänlein has criticised the Court's reasoning on the ground that Dec No 3/80 itself refers to the most relevant implementing provisions of Reg No 574/72. Hänlein, 'Fehlende unmittelbare Wirkung der Bestimmungen des Assoziationsratsbeschlusses EWG-Türkei über `Invalidität' und Renten bei "Alter und Tot"', in *EASr* (1997) 21–3.

[214] Case C–262/96 *Sürül* [1999] ECR I–2685. On this judgment see eg Peers, 'Social Security Equality for Turkish Nationals', in *ELRev* (1999) 627–37; Pennings, 'Het Arrest Sürül: Een Arrest dat Knaagt aan de Koppelingswet', in *SMA* (1999) 442–50 and Verschueren, 'The Sürül Judgment: Equal Treatment for Turkish Workers in Matters of Social Security', in *EJML* (1999) 371 *et seq.*

practice. The application of the non-discrimination principle embodied in Article 3(1) of the Decision, however, does not raise problems of a technical nature as is the case with the rules concerning aggregation of insurance periods or the rules for determining the applicable legislation.[215] The Court held that Article 3 of Decision No 3/80 is a precise and unconditional provision, which does not require any additional measures in order to be directly relied upon in national courts.[216] As to Mrs Sürül's substantive claim, the Court held that if she could be classed as a worker or a family member of a worker for the purposes of Decision No 3/80, as a Turkish national who has been authorised to reside, and actually resides, in the host Member State she could not be denied social security benefits such as family allowances on the ground that she only held a conditional residence authorisation. A national rule which makes eligibility for social security benefits subject to the possession of a residence permit covers, by its very nature, only non-nationals and is thus caught by the non-discrimination provision of Article 3(1) of Decision No 3/80.[217]

It follows that Article 3(1) of Decision No 3/80 produces direct effect. Although the Court did not set out a general rule for interpreting the scope of the Decision, it would seem that, since the date of the *Sürül* judgment,[218] Turkish nationals who are lawfully residing in the territory of a Member State and as workers or family members of workers covered by Decision No 3/80, are entitled to claim equal access to all benefit schemes falling within the scope of Regulation No 1408/71 including mixed benefit schemes. *Sürül*, however, leaves a number of questions unanswered. For instance, are Turkish nationals entitled to equality of treatment as regards the classic social assistance benefits? Such benefits are not covered by Regulation No 1408/71 and Decision No 3/80. Article 9 of the 1963 Association Agreement, however, contains a general non-discrimination clause which prohibits discrimination on grounds of nationality 'in accordance with the principle laid own in Article 7 of the EEC Treaty' (now Article 12 EC). Even though no 'Turkish equivalent' of Article 7(2) of Regulation No 1612/68 exists, the possibility cannot be excluded that the afore mentioned Article 9 might cover 'social advantages'.[219] Further, does the being in need, or enjoyment, of minimum subsistence benefits affect the right of Turkish nationals to reside in the host State? The Court has never answered this question, but on the basis of existing case law one could conclude that Member States are entitled to deny 'needy' Turkish nationals the right to establish residence in their territory, but that those who have been admitted are entitled to retain their residence right when, and for as long as, they continue to satisfy the conditions laid down in Articles 6 or 7 of

---

[215] Case C–262/96 *Sürül* [1999] ECR I–2685, 54–7.

[216] *Ibid*, at 74.

[217] *Ibid*, at 101–5.

[218] The Court time-limited the effect of its judgment. In principle, Art 3(1) of Dec No 3/80 can only be relied upon in support of claims relating to benefits in respect of periods prior to the date of the judgment (ie 4 May 1999). Case C–262/96 *Sürül* [1999] ECR I–2685, 106–13.

[219] See Peers (1999) n 214 above, at 635.

Decision No 1/80. These provisions directly confer precise and unconditional rights upon Turkish nationals that cannot be made conditional upon additional requirements imposed by the host State.[220]

7 CONCLUSIONS

In section 1 the goal was set to establish the degree to which Community law entitles individuals who are not able to provide for themselves to move to, and to obtain minimum subsistence benefits in, other Member States. This chapter has demonstrated that the legal status of the 'needy' has been strengthened in the last three decades. At the end of the 1960s it was still wholly up to the Member States to decide whether 'needy' nationals of other States would be admitted for residence in their territory and, if so, whether they would be offered minimum subsistence benefits. Today, the legal status of 'needy' nationals of third countries is fragmented and in many respects still not very well developed, but nationals of Member States have acquired a right to equal to treatment as regards eligibility for minimum subsistence benefits when, and for as long as, they are lawfully domiciled in another Member State. Both the Community provisions on free movement of workers and the 1990 residence directives accept a certain degree of solidarity between Community citizens of the various Member States. This solidarity, however, is still limited. The Court of Justice, which has largely been responsible for all the progress that has been made, has not ignored the financial interests of Member States. It has accepted the validity of rules which limit entitlement to minimum subsistence benefits to Community citizens residing (or domiciled) within their borders and, in brief, it has allowed Member States to deny residence/domicile in their territory to nationals of other Member States who do not perform 'effective and genuine' work and who are unable to provide for themselves and their families.

The fact that the Court has had regard to the financial concerns of the Member States may be understandable, but, as it stands today, Community law in the field under examination is not free from criticism. Article 18(1) EC confers upon all citizens of the European Union the fundamental non-economic right to establish residence in any Member State. For many Union citizens who are in need of minimum subsistence benefits, however, this right lacks practical relevance. Union citizenship is a political rather than an economic concept that only has limited meaning for as long as some citizens are denied freedom of movement because of their economic status.[221] The question arises whether, and if so, how, the legal status of 'needy' Union citizens could possibly be improved. Is it possible to realise, or to move closer to, a general right of residence without undermining the funding of minimum subsistence benefit schemes?

---

[220] Compare Case C–36/96 *Günaydin* [1997] ECR I–5143, 39 and 40.
[221] Compare O'Leary (1996) n 93 above, at 99.

Before attempting to answer the question, it is useful to first take a look at American constitutional law. As noted in the introductory section, the United States Constitution guarantees a right to travel which includes both a right to cross the inter-State boundaries and a right to reside freely in any of the States. Does this right also apply to those who are in need of welfare benefits, and if so, does it also include a right to claim such benefits in other States? How has American Constitutional law settled the conflict between the 'free movement interest' and the 'welfare interest'? What lessons are there to be learned for the European Community?

8 THE UNITED STATES

8.1 The American Welfare System: A Brief Introduction

American constitutional law on cross-border access to welfare must be placed against the background of the history and the structure of the American welfare system. The roots of the system can be traced back to the Elizabethan Poor Laws adopted in the early 1600s in England.[222] Like the Poor Law system, the original American welfare system was essentially local in character. Not the Federal government, but State and local governments bore the responsibility for handling the problem of poverty. In fact, 'the' welfare system consisted of a large number of separate and independent welfare systems. These were not social systems in the sense that they reflected a solidarity of the 'rich' with the 'poor'. The poor were regarded as a 'moral pestilence'; welfare was merely offered in order to protect the elite from beggary, crime and other problems the poor were associated with.

The Great Depression of the 1930s demonstrated the inadequacies of the local structure of the welfare system. Tax revenues decreased whilst the number of people in need of public assistance increased. About four million people, most of them indigents,[223] 'tried to seek their luck' in other States. This enormous flow of indigents across the inter-state borders constituted visible proof for the view that poverty was no longer a problem which State and local governments could solve individually. It had become a national problem that called for a national solution. Furthermore, it was recognised that the poor could no longer be regarded as a 'moral pestilence'; they were rather seen as victims of the economic recession who lacked financial means due to circumstances beyond their

---

[222] On the English origins of the American welfare system see, eg: Camissa, *From Rhetoric to Reform?—Welfare Policy in American Politics* (1998) ch 2; Trattner, *From Poor Law to Welfare State: History of Social Welfare Law in America* (1989); tenBroek, 'California's Dual System of Family Law: Its Origin, Development and Present Status' (1964) *StanfLRev* 257 et seq; Mandelker, 'The Settlement Requirement in General Assistance' (1955) *WashULQ* 355–77 and Riesenfeld, 'The Formative Era of American Public Assistance Law' (1955) *CalLRev* 175 et seq.

[223] Adams, 'State Control of Interstate Migration of Indigents' (1942) *MichLRev* 711–33, at 713.

control. Federal participation was required to guarantee that every person had an income sufficient for at least the essential needs of life. These new perceptions on poverty and welfare were expressed in the New Deal politics and ultimately resulted in the Social Security Act of 1935.[224] The Act's title on Public Assistance introduced welfare programmes for four categories of indigents: the aged, the blind, the disabled and dependent children. Indigents not falling within one of these 'categorical' assistance programmes were left to the traditional general welfare programmes, which remained wholly within the responsibility of the States. The Social Security Act did not federalise welfare in the sense that the programmes were organised, administered and financed by Federal authorities. The States remained the central governmental entities in the field. The Act also did not oblige States to develop or to improve welfare programmes. Its purpose was to encourage the States to provide new and enhanced welfare programmes by making available federal financial aid for States participating in the programme. Federal funding, which itself was financed by a tax introduced by the Social Security Act and made available in the form of matching grants, i.e., subsidies that are contingent upon the amount States have decided to spend on welfare, was made subject to detailed requirements. In brief, the Federal authorities determined which categories of people were to be eligible for public assistance; the States set the level of the benefits.[225] The programmes were 'major experiments in 'cooperative federalism', . . . combining state and federal participation to solve the problems of the depression'.[226]

The complex system of co-operative federalism introduced by the Social Security Act was partially simplified in 1973 by the Supplemental Security Income Program (SSI) adopted by Congress. SSI federalised three of the four categorical programmes; the most important, Aid for Families with Dependent Children (AFDC), was excluded. The administration and funding of the three programmes were brought under the sole responsibility of the Federal authorities. The SSI programme introduced a nationwide uniform benefit level for the aged, blind and disabled.[227] States no longer played a role in the provision, administration and financing of these three programmes. Further, in response to the growing concerns about the (federal) financing of the welfare system, the welfare system was significantly altered in 1996 by the Personal Responsibility and Work Opportunity Act (PRWORA). The Act has replaced the AFDC programme by the Temporary Assistance for Needy Families (TANF) which has eliminated the federal entitlement to welfare benefits, replaced the original

---

[224] Social Security Act, 49 Stat. 620 (1935). The power to adopt the Act derived from Art I s 8 of the Constitution that grants Congress the power to provide for the 'general Welfare' of the United States. For a discussion of the structure and administrative operation of the social security system see, eg: Wedemeyer and Moore, 'The American Welfare System' in tenBroek, *The Law of the Poor* (1966) 2–33 and LaFrance, *Welfare Law: Structure and Entitlement* (1979).

[225] *Dandridge v Williams*, 397 U.S. 471 (1970).

[226] *Shapiro v Thompson*, 394 U.S. 618 (1969) at 645 (Warren J, dissenting).

[227] LaFrance (1979) n 224 above, at 22.

matching grants for the States by block grants ie, lump sum payments, and limited the receipt of benefits to a maximum duration of two years. TANF implies a decentralisation of the welfare system. Much more then under the AFDC programme, States are free to determine whether, and if so, under which conditions benefits are made available.[228]

The current American welfare system provides for three different types of welfare programmes. The first, SSI, is administered and financed by the Federal authorities. It guarantees the aged, the blind and the disabled a universal annual income. The second type, TANF (the former AFDC), is partly financed by the Federal government but falls under the responsibility of the States. The third concerns the general assistance programmes (or 'Home Relief'). These programmes serve as a safety net for all those indigents who are not eligible for benefits under one of the other programmes. They are purely local in character; the Federal authorities do not administer or fund these programmes. This section examines constitutional law with regard to cross-border access to TANF- (and AFDC-)benefits as well as general social welfare benefits.[229] The SSI-benefits are not included in the discussion as the conflict between the 'free movement interest' and the 'public facilities interest' does not arise under this federal programme.

9.2 Conditions of Access

The States' policies regarding cross-border access to their welfare programmes have always been aimed at preserving benefits for the States' own citizens.[230] Non-residents have been denied welfare; residence in the State is a prerequisite for eligibility for welfare benefits. In addition, States have always attempted to prevent or discourage indigents from other States establishing residence in their territory.[231] Initially, States did so in order to protect public order. By using their police or 'immigration' power States prohibited indigents from establishing residence in the State and indigents who were 'found' within State borders could be

---

[228] Camissa (1998) n 222 above, at 117–22.

[229] The level of welfare benefits is by comparison with many of the European systems relatively low. For instance, the average AFDC benefit for a family with three children in 1988 was $ 501. This amounted to 63% of the poverty line. For further figures see Peterson and Rom, *Welfare Magnets* (1990). The variation between benefit levels in the different States has historically been wide. Taking into consideration the differences in living costs, the benefit level in the most generous States was approximately five times as high as in the least generous States. *Centre on Social Policy and Law, Living at the Bottom: An Analysis of AFDC Benefit Levels* (1993) at 25 and Peterson and Rom (1991) at 6–10 above. In addition to the social welfare benefits, indigents may enjoy a number of 'in-kind' benefits such as medical care (see also: ch 4, s 5.1), public housing and food stamps. See also: LaFrance (1978) n 224 above, at 155–93.

[230] Cp Loffredo, 'If You Ain't Got the Do, Re, Mi' The Commerce Clause and State Residence Restrictions on Welfare' (1993) *YaleLPR* 147–202, at 154.

[231] See also: Trattner (1984) n 222 above.

sent back to the State they came from.[232] The main motive for 'keeping indigents out', however, has always been financial in nature. States, and in particular the more generous ones, have always feared that their welfare systems would attract indigents moving to the State for the sole purpose of collecting benefits. A large influx of indigents could affect the States' ability to maintain their benefit schemes. States have therefore always, and in particular when their economies experienced a downturn[233], attempted to decrease the magnetic effect of welfare systems. The typical legal instrument used for this purpose is the durational residence requirement. By denying indigents welfare during an initial period of time, States have aimed to discourage indigents or persons likely to become public charges, from coming to the State. The last legal instrument by means of which States have tried to protect their welfare systems is the alienage classification. By denying aliens welfare or by making their eligibility for welfare subject to a long period of residence within the (United) State(s), States attempted to reduce the pressure on their welfare budgets. Often, States claimed to have a 'special public interest' in favouring United States citizens in granting welfare. Aliens were not perceived as 'equal members of society' but rather as guests who might be granted the privilege of welfare benefits but who had no right to such assistance.

The next sub-sections explore the degree to which indigents are entitled to move to and to collect welfare benefits in other States by discussing the constitutionality of the four legal instruments by means of which States have traditionally attempted to regulate cross-border access to welfare programmes by using four legal instruments: the police or immigration power, the durational residence requirement, the residence requirement and the requirement of United States citizenship.

8.3 Edwards: Recognition of a Freedom of Movement for Persons in Need of Welfare Benefits

The power of States to deny indigents entrance and residence is at odds with the constitutional right to travel.[234] This right is as old as the Constitution itself, but up until the middle of the twentieth century constitutional law did not object to the use of the police or 'immigration power'. Indigents did not enjoy the right to

---

[232] Mandelker, 'Exclusion and Removal Legislation' (1956) *WisLRev* 57 *et seq*, at 57. It is hard to discover the extent to which States actually used this power. A comprehensive and effective border control system has never existed but during the Depression of the 1930s some States appear to have installed border patrols to bar the entry of the poor. It is not unlikely that many States have made use of their police power by removing indigents from their territory and sending them back to their home States. Rosberg, 'Free Movement of Persons in the United States' in Sandalow and Stein (eds), Courts and Free Markets—Perspectives from the United States and Europe (1982) 273–384, at 288–9.

[233] Davis, 'The Evolving Right to Travel: *Saenz v Roe*' (1999) *Publius* 95–110, at 100.

[234] See ch 2, s 8.1 and 8.2.

travel.[235] Illustrative is the Supreme Court decision in *Mayor of the City of New York v. Miln* (1837).[236] The case involved a New York statute that required the master of any ship to report to the mayor on the names and origins of the passengers. A person who was deemed 'liable to become chargeable on the City' could be removed 'to the place of his last settlement'. The Supreme Court sustained the statute. The Court spoke of the 'danger' of a State's citizens being subjected to a heavy charge in the maintenance of indigents and stated that it is 'as competent and as necessary for a State to provide precautionary measures against the moral pestilence of paupers, vagabonds, and possibly convicts'. The Court even held it the duty of the State to protect its citizens from this 'evil'.[237] The power to exclude indigents, which 'undeniably existed at the formation of the Constitution', was not taken away from the States.

In 1941, six years after the coming into force of the Social Security Act, the Court moved away from *Miln* in *Edwards v. California*.[238] The case concerned a California statute which made it a misdemeanour to bring or assist 'in bringing into the state any indigent person who is not a resident of the State knowing him to be an indigent person'. A California resident brought an unemployed relative to California to help him to have a new start in life and was sentenced to six months' imprisonment for doing so. Before the Supreme Court, the State of California attempted to justify the statute by referring to the huge influx of migrants into California which had resulted in problems of health, morals, and especially finance, the proportions of which were staggering. The Supreme Court recognised the seriousness of California's concern, but, nonetheless, it held the statute to be unconstitutional. The Court stated that:

'None is more certain than the prohibition against attempts on the part of any single state to isolate itself from difficulties common to all of them by restraining the transportation of persons and property across its borders. It is frequently the case that a State might gain a momentary respite from the pressure of events by the simple expedient of shutting its gates to the outside world. But in the words of Mr Justice Cardozo: "The Constitution was framed under the dominion of a political philosophy

---

[235] In support of this view reference was often made to Art IV of the Arts of Confederation which stated that 'the free inhabitants of each of these States, *paupers, vagabonds and fugitives from justice excepted*, shall be entitled to all privileges and immunities of free citizens in the several States; and the people of each State shall have free ingress and egress to and from any State . . .' (*ital:* APvdM). When the clause was incorporated in Art IV of the Constitution the explicit exclusion of paupers and vagabonds was, like the terms 'free ingress and egress' (ch 2, s 8.1), dropped. Art IV, however, was considered to be based on the same principles of the fourth Art of the Arts of Confederation. It was therefore generally assumed that paupers or indigents were not entitled to the privileges and immunities of citizenship, including the right to travel. Rosberg (1982) n 232 above, at 288.

[236] *Mayor of the City of New York v Miln*, 36 U.S. 102 (1837).

[237] *Ibid* 36 U.S. 102 (1837) at 142–3. See, also: *Smith v Turner (The Passenger Cases)*, 48 U.S. 283 (1849); *Railroad Co. v Husen*, 95 U.S. 465 (1877) (a State may use its police power 'to exclude from its limits convicts, paupers, idiots, and lunatics, and persons likely to become a public charge . . .') and *Plumley v Massachusetts*, 155 U.S. 461 (1894).

[238] *Edwards v California*, 314 U.S. 160 (1941).

less parochial in range. It was framed upon the theory that the peoples of the several States must sink or swim together, and in the long run prosperity and salvation are in union and not division'".[239]

The Court explained that:

'Recent years, and in particular the past decade, have been marked by a growing recognition that in an industrial society the task of providing assistance to the needy has ceased to be local in character. The duty to share the burden, if not wholly to assume it, has been recognized not only by State governments, but by the Federal government as well. The changed attitude is reflected in the Social Security laws under which the Federal and State governments cooperate for the care of the aged, the blind and dependent children'[240].

Before the Court reached a conclusion it explicitly considered the contention that the limitation of this State power would be subject to an exception for 'paupers'. The Court admitted that support for this contention could be found in earlier decisions of the Court such as *New York v Miln*. Yet, the Court found itself no longer bound by those observations:

'New York v. Miln was decided in 1837. Whatever may have been the notion then prevailing, we do not think that it will now be seriously contended that because a person is without employment and without funds he constitutes a 'moral pestilence'. Poverty and immorality are not synonymous'.[241]

The Court concluded that States no longer held the power to interfere with the cross-border movement of persons, including indigents. Implicitly, then, the Court recognised that indigents enjoyed the rights to travel including both the right to cross the inter-state boundaries and the right to choose the State of residence.

Edwards could be regarded as a response of the Supreme Court to the transformation of the welfare system. The Social Security Act of 1935 had established a single welfare union in which not only the States but also the Federal government held a responsibility for guaranteeing every individual a 'minimum income' sufficient for at least the 'essential needs of life'. In this newly created welfare union there was, in the view of the Court, no longer room for 'any single State to isolate itself from difficulties common to all' by 'shutting its gates' for indigents.[242] Indigents were no longer seen as 'second-class' citizens. Rather, they were regarded as 'equally deserving' United States citizens who, like other citizens of the Union, should have the right to move to and to pursue

[239] *Ibid*, at 173–4.
[240] *Ibid*, at 175.
[241] *Ibid*, at 177.
[242] *Ibid*, at 173–4.

their interests in the State of their choice.[243] A 'man's mere property status', as the concurring Justice Jackson put it, could no longer, 'be used by a state to test, qualify, or limit his rights as a citizen of the United States'.[244] The right to travel may always have been 'inherent in the nature of the Union',[245] but the right was only granted to indigents after the establishment of the 'welfare Union'.

8.4 Residents

8.4.1 *Post-*Edwards *Debates*

Edwards did not yet guarantee that indigents also enjoyed in practice a greater freedom of movement. Virtually all States made eligibility for welfare benefits conditional upon the fulfilment of durational residence requirements. States had always imposed such requirements and they continued to do so after '1935'.[246] The Social Security Act had not established a uniform welfare benefit level nor had it provided for a system under which States were reimbursed for the costs of the benefits offered to recently arrived indigents. In the States' view, they still needed to protect themselves against 'welfare migration'. The States found support for their view in the Social Security Act itself which explicitly allowed them to impose, within certain limits,[247] waiting-period requirements. The practical

---

[243] 'It is a privilege of citizenship of the United States, protected from State abridgement, to enter any state of the Union, either for temporary sojourn or for the establishment of permanent residence therein and for gaining resultant citizenship thereof. If national citizenship means less than this, it means nothing'. *Edwards v California* 314 U.S. 160 (1941) at 183–4 (Jackson J, concurring). Justice Douglas held that to deny indigents freedom of movement would 'introduce a caste system utterly incompatible with the spirit of our system of government. It would permit those who were stigmatised by a State as indigents, paupers, or vagabonds to be relegated to an inferior class of citizenship. It would prevent a citizen, because he was poor, from seeking new horizons in other States. It might thus withhold from large segments of our people that mobility which is basic to any guarantee of freedom of opportunity. The result would be a substantial dilution of the right of national citizenship, a serious impairment of the principles of equality'. *Edwards v California* 314 U.S. 160 (1941) at 181 (Jackson J, concurring). The majority in *Edwards* did not speak in 'right-to-travel-terms' because it considered the transportation of persons to be 'commerce' and dealt with the case under the Commerce Clause.

[244] *Edwards v California* 314 U.S. 160 (1941) at 183–4 (Jackson J, concurring).

[245] Ch 2, s 8.1.

[246] During the 1940s and 1950s, a number of States concluded compacts with other States in which the parties agreed to waive durational residence requirements for their mutual citizens. See *Shapiro v Thompson*, 394 U.S. 618 (1969) at 635–6 (nn 15 and 16). Some States reduced the duration of the residence period required for welfare eligibility even unilaterally, but only a few abolished waiting-periods entirely. Many States even increased the duration of residence required for eligibility for general assistance programmes. Altmeyer, 'People on the Move: Effect of Residence Requirements for Public Assistance' (1946) *SocSecBull* 4 *et seq*, at 4 and National Travellers Aid Ass'n, *One Manner of Law—A Handbook on Residence Requirements in Public Assistance* (1961).

[247] During the debates on the Social Security Act in Congress in the 1930s, welfare durational residence requirements had been subject of heated discussions. Advocates of lengthy waiting-period requirements had emphasised the 'danger' of a high influx of persons seeking higher welfare benefits, whilst the opponents of such requirements had stressed the unfairness of the requirements to those who were forced by the Depression to seek work in other States. Advocates and opponents

significance of *Edwards'* right to travel was still minimal. Indigents who moved to another State risked a temporary loss of their 'basic income'. In the years after *Edwards*, however, welfare waiting-periods became the subject of heated debates.[248] In the literature it was increasingly argued that the temporary denial of welfare to migrating indigents was at odds not only with *Edwards'* right to travel but also with the basic philosophy of the Social Security Act that every person should have a 'basic income' sufficient for the 'essential needs of life'.[249] Furthermore, the justifications offered by States for waiting-periods were said to have no basis in fact. The administrative costs of enforcing the requirements would exceed the probable costs of granting welfare to 'newcomers'; data were presented which would indicate that indigents would not move to other States for the purpose of obtaining welfare benefits.[250] In the absence of a 'need' for the requirements, waiting-periods would have to be held unconstitutional as unnecessary burdens on the right to travel and/or arbitrary denials of the equal protection of the laws.[251]

8.4.2 *Shapiro v Thompson*

It was not until 1969, however, that the issue of the constitutionality of welfare waiting-period requirements was brought before the Supreme Court. In *Shapiro v Thompson*[252] the Court was asked to rule upon the constitutionality of the statutes of two States and the District of Columbia which all made eligibility for AFDC-benefits conditional upon one year of residence in the State. Each of the applicants met all the requirements for the benefits except this one. The Court opened the decision by defining the constitutional problems raised by the waiting-periods as problems of equal protection:

reached a compromise implying that Federal funding would be made subject to durational residence requirements not exceeding a maximum -one year for AFDC- to be set by Congress. See dissenting opinion of Chief Justice Warren in *Shapiro v Thompson*, 394 U.S. 618 (1969) at 646 and Rosenheim, 'Shapiro v Thompson 'The Beggars are Coming to Town'' (1969) *SCRev* 303–46, at 313.

[248] See, eg: LoGatto, 'Residence Laws—A Step Forward or Backward?' (1961) *CathLaw* 101 *et seq*; Note, 'Residence Requirements in State Public Welfare Statutes-I' (1966) *IowaLRev* 1080–95; Note, 'Residence Requirement for Public Relief: An Arbitrary Prerequisite' (1966) *ColJLSP* 133–43 and Harvith, 'The Constitutionality of Residence Tests for General and Categorical Assistance Programs' in tenBroek, *The Law of the Poor* (1966) 243–317.

[249] The unconstitutionality of welfare waiting-periods was also claimed to be implied in *Edwards*. This conclusion was not only based on the 'sink-or-swim-together-rationale' of the decision but also on a dictum in *Edwards* in which the Court had said that the nature and extent of a State's obligation 'to afford relief to newcomers is not here involved. We do, however, suggest that the theory of the Elizabethan poor laws no longer fits the facts'. *Edwards v California*, 314 U.S. 160 (1941) at 174.

[250] For an overview of research and literature on 'welfare migration' before 1969 see, eg: Peterson and Rom (1991) n 229 above, at 151–2 and Long, 'Poverty States and Receipt of Welfare Among Migrants and Nonmigrants in Large Cities' (1974) *ASRev* 46–56.

[251] See especially: Harvith (1966) n 248 above.

[252] *Shapiro v Thompson*, 394 U.S. 618.

'There is no dispute that the effect of the waiting-period requirement . . . is to create two classes of needy resident families indistinguishable from each other except that one is composed of residents who have resided a year or more, and the second of residents who have resided less than a year. in the jurisdiction. On the basis of this sole difference the first class is granted and the second class is denied welfare aid upon which may depend the ability of the families to obtain the very means to subsist-food, shelter and other necessities of life'.[253]

The main question to be answered by the Court was whether the discrimination against 'new' indigent residents could be justified. The primary justification put forward by the States concerned the preservation of the 'fiscal integrity' of welfare programmes. The States contended that if indigents could be deterred from entering the State by denying them welfare benefits during the first year, state programmes to assist long-term residents would not be impaired by a substantial influx of newcomers. The Court did not doubt that a one-year waiting-period 'was well suited to discourage the influx' of indigents but it held that the purpose of deterring in-migration could not serve as justification for the classification created by the waiting-period requirement. It confirmed the constitutional status of the right to travel and stated that if a law has 'no other purpose . . . than to chill the assertion of constitutional rights by penalizing those who chose to exercise them, then it is patently unconstitutional'.[254]

The States had argued, however, that even if it were forbidden to deter the entry of all indigents, the waiting-period could be justified as an attempt to discourage those indigents from entering the State who might come for the sole purpose of obtaining higher welfare benefits. The Court responded negatively to this 'free-rider argument'. The requirements were 'all-inclusive'. They did not only result in a denial of welfare to persons who came to the States for the sole purpose of collecting higher welfare benefits, but they also withheld benefits from the great majority who came to the State for other purposes. More fundamentally, however, the Court held that

'A State may no more try to fence out those indigents who seek higher welfare benefits than it may try to fence out indigents generally. Implicit in any such distinction is the notion that indigents who enter a State with the hope of securing higher welfare benefits are somehow less deserving than indigents who do not take this consideration into account. But we do not perceive why a mother who is seeking to make a new life for herself and her children should be regarded as less deserving because she considers, among others, the level of a State's public assistance. Surely such a mother is no less deserving than a mother who moves into a particular State in order to take advantage of its better educational opportunities'.[255]

---

[253] *Ibid*, at 627.
[254] *Ibid*, at 631.
[255] *Ibid*, at 631–2.

The States further presented a 'past-contributions-argument' which suggested that welfare waiting-periods could be sustained as an attempt to distinguish between new and old residents on the basis of the contributions made to the community through the payment of taxes. The Court rejected this argument too. A State may legitimately attempt to limit its expenditure but a State may not seek to achieve such a purpose by invidious distinctions between classes of its citizens.[256] Accepting the past-contributions argument would permit States to bar new residents from schools, parks, and libraries or deprive them from police and fire protection. It would even permit States to apportion all benefits and services according to the past contributions of citizens. The Equal Protection Clause, the Court said, prohibits such an apportionment of state services.[257]

In rejecting the free rider and the past-contributions arguments the Court did not (have to) decide which of the equal protection tests[258] was to be applied. Both arguments were held to be constitutionally unacceptable; they simply could not justify the welfare waiting-periods. The States, however, had offered a number of additional justifications that were accepted by the Court as legitimate. The Court held that strict scrutiny was to be applied since 'in moving from State to State . . . appellees were exercising' the fundamental right to travel and 'any classification which serves to penalise the exercise of that right, unless shown to be necessary to promote a compelling State interest, is unconstitutional'.[259] In *Shapiro* the defending States could not demonstrate that the requirements were necessary for a compelling State interest. They had claimed that durational residence requirements could be sustained as objective tests of *bona fide* residence and as a safeguard against the fraudulent receipt of welfare payments. One year of residence would, in other words, ensure that an applicant was actually a resident of the State and not, in fact, a non-resident faking residence for the purpose of obtaining welfare in another State in addition to the benefits received in the State where the indigent actually resides. The Court, however, did not consider a one-year waiting-period a necessary means for determining bona fide residence and avoiding double payments. Less drastic

---

[256] *Ibid,* at 633.

[257] *Ibid.*

[258] On the equal protection clause and the various tests that may have to be applied, see ch 2, s 8.4.

[259] *Shapiro v Thompson*, 394 U.S. 618 (1969) at 634. The fundamental right that triggers strict scrutiny was the right to travel, not a right to welfare. In *Dandridge v Williams* (1970) the Supreme Court concluded that the constitution does not guarantee a right to welfare payments. The administration of welfare, the Court reasoned, raises 'intractable economic, social and even philosophical problems' that are not 'the business of the Court'. *Dandridge v Williams*, 397 U.S. 471 (1970) at 485–7. Under the Equal Protection Clause wealth criteria are merely subject to rational relation review. See also: Bork, 'The Impossibility of Finding Welfare Rights in the Constitution' (1979) *WashULRev* 695 *et seq*; Loffredo, 'Poverty, Democracy and Constitutional Law' (1993) *UPennLRev* 1277 *et seq* and Hershkoff, 'Positive Rights and State Constitutions: The Limits of Federal Rationality Review' (1999) *HarvLRev* 1131–96.

means were thought to be available for determining bona fide residency.[260] The Court concluded the States did not use, and had no need to use, one-year waiting-periods for the purposes suggested. Even under the rational relation test of the Equal Protection Clause the requirements would have been unconstitutional.

Before the Court could reach a final conclusion, it had to deal with what may, at first, have seemed the strongest argument of the defending States. *Shapiro* concerned categorical assistance programmes (AFDC) for which Congress had authorised the States to impose durational residency requirements not exceeding a maximum of one year. The States argued that they had not exceeded this maximum and that they were therefore justified in imposing the requirements. In the view of the States the real issue was not whether, acting on their own, they were permitted to impose (minimal) durational residence requirements, but rather whether Congress could authorise States to impose such requirements.[261] The Court rejected this argument by stating that regardless of the possible approval by Congress, it was the State legislation that infringed the constitutional rights of freedom of travel and equal protection of the laws. In the view of the Court, the constitutional questions were posed by State legislation, not by any federal statute. The Court added, however, that even if it could be argued that *Shapiro* involved the constitutionality of a federal statute, the waiting-periods at issue would be unconstitutional. Congress is prohibited from denying public assistance to otherwise eligible poor persons solely on the ground that they have not been residents of a State for one year prior to their application for welfare. 'Congress', the Court said, 'may not authorise the States to violate the Equal Protection Clause'.[262]

From a welfare perspective,[263] *Shapiro* did not come as a real surprise. Prior to the decision calls had already been made for welfare waiting-periods to be held unconstitutional. By rejecting the free rider and the past-contributions argument and by holding that the requirements must be reviewed under the strict scrutiny test, the Court made it patently clear that there was no longer

---

[260] Before granting welfare, the responsible authorities investigate the applicant's employment, housing and family situation and in the course of the inquiry necessarily learn whether or not the applicant is a resident or not. The hazard of double payments could in the view of the Court simply be prevented by a call or letter from the authorities to the welfare authorities of the State an applicant came from. *Shapiro v Thompson*, 394 U.S. 618 (1969) at 636–7. Nor did the Court accept the argument that a one-year waiting-period could be justified as a means of encouraging 'newcomers' to join the labour market promptly. The Court simply held that this logic would also require a similar waiting-period for long-term residents of the State. *Shapiro v Thompson*, 394 U.S. 618 (1969) at 637–8.

[261] On this argument see in particular Chief Justice Warren, dissenting in *Shapiro*. *Shapiro v Thompson*, 394 U.S. 618 (1969) at 647–8.

[262] *Shapiro v Thompson*, 394 U.S. 618 (1969) at 641.

[263] To be sure, *Shapiro* did cause a stir in the legal doctrine. Most of the confusion and criticism, however, concerned the implications of the Court's conclusion that any classification which serves to penalise the exercise of that right is subject to strict scrutiny, for waiting-period requirements in areas other than welfare. See also: ch 2, s 8.5.

room for welfare waiting-periods. *Shapiro* largely built on the 'sink-or-swim-together' rationale of *Edwards*. States were no longer permitted to shift the burden of the poor to other States. In a single welfare Union, in which the task of 'taking care of the needy' is shared by the States and the Federal authorities, States were not only prohibited from 'isolating' themselves from the poverty problem by shutting the gates to their State territory but also from closing the gates to their welfare systems. *Shapiro* made *Edwards'* right to freedom of movement a practical reality for indigents. In the single welfare Union indigents can, as 'equally deserving' United States citizens, move to the State where they think they can pursue their interests best without being discouraged by a temporary loss of their 'basic income' even if the sole motive for moving to another State is to collect higher welfare benefits there. From the moment indigents establish residence in a State, they can, as 'equally deserving' State citizens, apply for welfare.

Shapiro, however, was also more than the logical follow-up from *Edwards*. It was only in *Shapiro* that the Court was confronted with the 'welfare magnet problem'. Unlike Congress and the dissenting Chief Justice Warren,[264] the majority of the Justices in *Shapiro* did not consider this problem serious enough to uphold the waiting-period requirements. Why? The answer is not to be found in the Federal funding that has been made available under the Social Security Act. Five years after *Shapiro*, the Court held in *Maricopa County v Memorial Hospital* (1973) that whether or not a programme is federally funded is irrelevant to the applicability of *Shapiro*'s penalty-analysis.[265] It is hard to know whether, or to what extent, the welfare magnet problem played a role in the deliberations within the Court,[266] but the conclusions drawn, and the reasoning followed, in *Shapiro* do suggest that the majority did not see a need for the challenged requirements. It does not seem very likely that the Court would have rejected the free-rider and past-contributions arguments in such strong terms if it had expected that the abolition of welfare waiting-periods would incite large numbers of indigents to move to other States. Further, the Court subjected welfare waiting-periods to strict scrutiny under the equal protection test. It explicitly, however, added that even under the traditional equal protection tests a

[264] Warren C J was of the view that 'Congress quite clearly believed that total elimination of durational requirements would be self-defeating because the prospect of a sudden influx of new residents might deter the States from significantly increasing categorical assistance benefits', and that these legislative realities could not be ignored in assessing the validity of the congressional decisions to authorize' durational residence requirements for welfare benefits. Schwartz, *Super Chief—Earl Warren and his Supreme Court—A Judicial Bibliography* (1983) at 726 (quoting from a draft opinion in *Shapiro*).

[265] *Memorial Hospital v Maricopa County*, 415 U.S. 250 (1973) at 261. This conclusion was already implicit in the *Shapiro*-decision. The decision implied that waiting-periods for general purely State-funded assistance programmes were in principle also unconstitutional. Furthermore, *Shapiro* itself only involved categorical welfare programmes, but the Court spoke in general terms of 'welfare' and 'public assistance' and did not in anyway indicate that an exception for general welfare programmes was to be made.

[266] On the discussions within the Court in *Shapiro* see *Schwartz* (1983) n 264 above at 725–32.

classification of welfare applicants according to whether they have lived in the State for one year would seem 'irrational'[267] and unconstitutional. It is hard to understand, however, why waiting-periods are 'irrational' or 'arbitrary', where their invalidation could possibly result in a large influx of indigents and increase in welfare costs. As undesirable and objectionable a limitation of indigents' right to travel and equal protection may be thought to be, waiting-periods do for that reason seem not to be 'without any reasonable basis'. Thus, even though it is hard to prove, *Shapiro* suggested that the Court did not refrain from invalidating durational residence requirements for welfare benefits because it did not expect that welfare-induced migration would occur.

8.4.3 *From* Shapiro *to* Saenz

In *Shapiro* the Supreme Court ordered the States to abolish welfare waiting-period requirements. In subsequent years, the States indeed did so. No claims of welfare migration were made. It seemed that *Shapiro* had definitively settled the earlier controversies regarding the need for, and the validity of, welfare waiting-period requirements. Since the late 1980s,[268] however, the welfare migration issue has returned to the political agenda of many States and the Federal institutions. States such as Wisconsin,[269] Minnesota and California claimed that they were confronted with an increased influx of indigents from other States. In order to protect the financing of their welfare benefit schemes these States decided to re-introduce waiting-periods. In order to avoid conflicts with *Shapiro*, Wisconsin imposed a durational residence requirement of merely sixty days -instead of one year- and exempted persons who were born in the State, had previously lived there for one year, came to Wisconsin to join family members or to accept a job offer, from the denial of welfare benefits during the first sixty days of residence. The purpose was thus to deter only 'free-riding indigents' from coming. Minnesota and California responded to claimed increases in the number of welfare recipients by applying two-tier benefit schedules. In Minnesota newcomers were only granted 60 per cent of the basic welfare benefits during the first six months, whilst in California newcomers were only offered welfare up to the level of the State they came from provided this benefit was lower than the benefit level in California during the first twelve months of residence.[270] The Federal

---

[267] *Shapiro v Thompson*, 394 U.S. 618 (1969) at 638.

[268] For some first comments about the expected impact of *Shapiro* see, eg Chambers, 'Residence Requirements for Welfare Benefits: The Consequences of their Unconstitutionality' (1969) *SW* 29–37.

[269] On Wisconsin's welfare magnet problem see Peterson and Rom (1990) n 229 above, ch 2.

[270] Both the Minnesota and California waiting-periods have been invalidated in court. For Minnesota, see *Mitchell v Steffen*, Minn SupCt, No.C3–92–239, 8/6/93 (as published in the USLWeek of 8 August 1993, 62 LW 2111). For California see *Green v Anderson*, N.93–15306 9th Cir, 29 April 1994 (as published in United States Law Week 61 LW 2475). The courts in question basically followed *Shapiro* and concluded that the challenged statutes penalised the right to travel. The States could not demonstrate a compelling State interest for which the welfare waiting-periods were necessary. The Wisconsin Statute, however, has been upheld by the Supreme Court of that

authorities seemed to support a re-introduction of waiting-periods for AFDC-benefits. Prior to the coming into force in 1996 of the PRWORA, they allowed (ie by not refusing Federal funding) a number of States to experiment with various types of relatively short waiting-periods,[271] and PRWORA itself explicitly allowed the States to apply 'the rules (including benefit amounts) of the programme . . . of another State if the family has moved to the State from the other State and has resided in the State for less than 12 months'.[272]

The introduction of waiting-period requirements fully re-opened the welfare magnet debate in which two separate, but closely intertwined, issues played a role. The first concerned the question whether there was actually a need for the newly introduced requirements. Was the fear of 'welfare migration' justified? Views differed. Several empirical studies on the mobility of welfare recipients were conducted and these reached different and conflicting conclusions. Some scholars[273] claimed to have demonstrated that States like Wisconsin, Minnesota and California were faced with welfare migration and that there was indeed a need to take measures in order to safeguard these States' welfare systems. These scholars did not claim that 'large numbers of poor people rush from one state to another with every modest adjustment in state benefit levels', but they did suggest that 'as people make major decisions about whether they should move or remain where they are, they take into account the level of welfare a state provides and the extent to which that level is increasing'. The poor would do this 'roughly to the same extent that they respond to differences in wage opportunities in other state'.[274] Other scholars, however, questioned the validity of this

State. This Court concluded that a sixty-day waiting-period 'was substantially less onerous' than the one-year period in *Shapiro* and that the Wisconsin waiting-period did not penalise the right to travel. The Court referred to the State's 'legitimate' interests in 'preserving the public fisc' and 'conserving scarce taxpayers' funds'. *Jones v Milwaukee County*, 485 NW2d 21 (as published in USLWeek 61 LW 2027 (1992)). See also: Poppe, 'Defining the Scope of the Equal Protection Clause with Respect to Welfare Waiting-Periods' (1994) *ChicLRev* 291–323, at 300–3. The decision of the Wisconsin Supreme Court was hard to compare with *Shapiro*. The very purpose of the waiting-period was to discourage free-riding indigents from coming and to deny newcomers welfare for the sole purpose of saving money. Cp Loffredo (1993) n 230 above, at 167.

[271] Schram and Krueger, "Welfare Magnets' and Benefit Decline: Symbolic Problems and Substantive Consequences' (1994) *Publius* 61–82, 80–1 (referring in n 72 to a review of the federal waiver process to Wiseman, Welfare Reform in the States) and Bennet and Sullivan, 'Disentitling the Poor: Waivers and Welfare 'Reform'" (1993) *UMJLR* 741–84.

[272] 42 U.S.C.A. § 604(c) (Supp 1997). Since 1996 the number of States which decided to re-introduce durational residence requirements increased to fifteen. Allard, 'Revisiting *Shapiro*: Welfare Magnets and State Residency Requirements in the 1990s' (1998) *Publius* 45–66, at 55. It may be recalled that PRWORA replaced the AFDC programme with the TANF programme. The original matching grants were replaced by block grants, the new States were given much more freedom as to how they wished to organise welfare. PRWORA decentralised the welfare systems and increased the danger of a 'welfare race to the bottom'.

[273] Clark, *Does Welfare Affect Migration?* (1990); Peterson and Rom (1990) n 229 above; Peterson and Rom, 'American Federalism, Welfare Policy, and Residential Choices' (1989) *APSRev* 711–28 and Gramlich and Laren, 'Migration and Income Redistribution Responsibilities' (1984) *JHR* 489–511.

[274] Peterson and Rom (1990) n 229 above, at 83.

'evidence' and argued that there was no or hardly any welfare migration.[275] This group of scholars did not doubt that some States may have been faced with a larger number of 'new' indigents from other States, but they did deny that the poor would move to other States for the sole purpose of obtaining higher welfare benefits. Like others, the poor would primarily move to the places or States where jobs are available. If there was any welfare migration, it would be a secondary factor and it would not take such drastic forms as to force States either to raise taxes or to lower welfare benefit levels. The welfare magnet issue was, in their view, largely symbolic. State policymakers would use the symbol of the welfare magnet in order to defend refusals to raise welfare benefits.[276]

The second issue in the welfare magnet debates was a legal one. It concerned the constitutionality of the waiting-period requirements. At first glance, the durational requirements that were introduced seemed unconstitutional. *Shapiro* did not exclude the possibility that relatively short waiting-period requirements for welfare could be upheld when they are applied as tests of bona fide residence, but the newly introduced waiting-periods did not serve this goal. They seemed aimed at deterring free-riding indigents from the 'poorer' States from coming and protecting the funding of benefit schemes by denying recently arrived State citizens welfare. Both objectives were declared unconstitutional in *Shapiro*. The fact that PRWORA authorises States to apply the said requirements did not seem to alter that conclusion since *Shapiro* indicated that Congress does not have the power to permit the States to violate the Equal Protection Clause.[277] However, advocates of welfare waiting-period requirements increasingly made calls upon the Supreme Court to move away from *Shapiro*. The alleged existence of welfare migration would compel the Court to recognise that States are, in certain circumstances, entitled to discourage indigents from migrating in

---

[275] See, eg Dye, 'The Policy Consequences of Intergovernmental Competition' (1990) *CatoJ* 59–73 and Schram and Krueger (1994) n 271 above, at 74–9 (referring to other inter alia Hanson and Hartman, *Do Welfare Magnets Attract?* (1994) and Walker, *Migration Among Low-Income Households: Helping the Witch Doctors Reach Consensus* (1994)).

[276] Schram and Krueger (1994) n 271 above, at 82. Cp also Allard and Danziger, 'Welfare Magnets: Myth or Reality?' (2000) *JoP* 350–68.

[277] One could of course have tried to 'read' into *Shapiro* a possibility that welfare waiting-periods were nonetheless constitutional. Some such attempts were indeed made. In *Shapiro* the Court accepted as legitimate a number of State interests which could possibly justify waiting-periods provided they could be demonstrated to be necessary for the promotion of a compelling State interest test. In particular, *Shapiro* left room for the suggestion that the requirements could possibly be sustained if they serve as tests of bona fide residency. In *Shapiro* the Court merely held that a *one-year* waiting-period could not be upheld on this ground, but the decision did not exclude the possibility that shorter waiting-periods (of one or two months) might be constitutional where they function as tests of bona fide residence. In the field of voting, the Court had similarly shot down one-year waiting periods (*Dunn v Blumstein*, 405 U.S. 330 (1972), but it had accepted durational residence residence requirements of up to 50 days in as far as they serve as reasonable tests of bona fide residence. *Martson v Lewis*, 410 U.S. 679 (1973) and *Burns v Fortson*, 410 U.S. 686 (1973). See also: LaFrance (1979) n 224 above, at 253; Rosberg (1982) n 232 above, at 312. Furthermore, it had been argued that welfare waiting-periods could possibly be upheld in as far as they are used as a means to encourage indigents to join the labour force as soon as possible. Poppe (1994) n 270 above, at 317–23.

order to protect their welfare programmes, to abandon penalty-on-the-right-to-travel-analysis and to develop an alternative legal framework under which (welfare) waiting-periods must be reviewed.[278]

8.4.4 Saenz v Roe

In the light of post-*Shapiro* developments and debates, it was inevitable that the question of the constitutionality of welfare waiting-period requirements would be brought before the Supreme Court again. This indeed happened in *Saenz v Roe* (1999).[279] The case concerned the previously mentioned California statute which limited the amount of welfare benefits payable to families that had resided in the State for less than twelve months to the amount payable by the State of the family's prior residence. The relevant provisions of the 1992 California statute were challenged by three women who had all recently moved from other States to California to live with relatives in order to escape abusive family circumstances. Since the benefit levels in the States which the women had moved from were lower than the Californian benefits, their benefits were limited to the benefit level in those other States. In support of the durational residence requirements for its welfare benefits, the State of California had advanced only fiscal justifications. In brief, the statute would save some 10.9 million dollars in annual welfare costs. Under the compelling State interest test of the Equal Protection Clause this argument could not stand, but California claimed that the requirements would merely have to satisfy the much more lenient rational relation test. Since the California statute did not wholly deprive recently arrived

---

[278] It had been suggested that the Court should ground the right to travel or migrate in, and review welfare waiting-period requirements under, the citizenship clause of the Fourteenth Amendment which provides that United States citizens are citizens of the State wherein they reside. Cohen, 'Discrimination Against New State Citizens: An Update' (1994) *Constitutional Commentary* 74 *et seq* and Zubler, 'The Right to Migrate and Welfare Reform: Time for *Shapiro v Thompson* to Take a Hike' (1997) *ValpULRev* 893–950. On the face of it, this clause would not seem to leave any room for durational residence requirements. However, it was argued that the Clause does allow the Federal government to authorise the States to treat 'new' State citizens differently than other residents. Under the Citizenship Clause 'any State discrimination against newcomers would be per se unconstitutional unless Congress specifically authorized it'. Zubler (1997) above at 946. Other suggested means for subjecting durational residence requirements to an intermediate level of judicial scrutiny involved an *ad hoc* balancing test, review under the Privileges and Immunities Clause of Art IV § 2 of the Constitution and classing 'new' residents as a semi-suspect class. See also: ch 2, s 8.6.

[279] In 1995 the question on the validity of durational residence requirements had already been brought before the Supreme Court in *Anderson v Green* (USLWeek 7 February 1995 63 LW 3581). The Court, however, did not decide upon the case because it was not 'ripe' (United States Law Week 21 February 1995 63LW 4162–3). The challenged California statute in this case would only take effect upon receipt of a waiver of the Federal government. Initially, such a waiver was granted but later the waiver was vacated. In the absence of a waiver California simply granted welfare to new residents upon arrival in the State under the same conditions as 'old' residents. Since PRWORA took effect in 1996, no specific approval of waiting-periods was required. Wolff, 'Right Road, Wrong Vehicle?: Rethinking Thirty Years of Right to Travel Doctrine: *Saenz v Roe*, 119 S.Ct.1518' (2000) *UDayLRev* 307–35.

residents from welfare payments, it would not constitute a penalty on the right to travel.

In response to debates about the appropriate standard of review to be applied to (welfare) residency requirements, the Court reconsidered in *Saenz* the rules and provisions governing the right to travel. As described earlier on in this book[280], the Court moved away from *Shapiro*'s penalty-on-the-right-travel-analysis: it indicated that State statutes which discriminate against State citizens on the ground that they have not lived long enough in the State must be reviewed under the Privileges *or* Immunities of the Fourteenth Amendment which provides that 'No State shall make or enforce any law which shall abridge the privileges or immunities of citizens of the United States'. This change in the Court's approach towards durational residence requirements, however, did not in any way affect its view on welfare waiting-period requirements. The Court condemned the requirements in terms that were as clear and unequivocal as the ones it had used in *Shapiro*.

First, the fact that the Privileges or Immunities Clause rather than the Equal Protection Clause was to be applied did not imply a relaxation of the level of judicial scrutiny. Neither mere rationality nor some intermediate standard of review should be used in order to judge the validity of rules such as durational residence requirements which discriminate against a State's own citizens. The appropriate standard, the Court held, may be 'more categorical than that articulated in *Shapiro* . . . but it surely is no less strict'[281]. Secondly, even though California had disavowed that its waiting period requirements were introduced to deter indigent residents of other States from coming to California, the Court expressly rejected the 'free rider argument'. The Court recognised that even though it may be:

> 'Reasonable to assume that some persons may be motivated to move for the purpose of obtaining higher benefits, the empirical evidence . . . indicates that the number of such persons is quite small—surely not large enough to justify a burden on those who had no such motive'.

Repeating *Shapiro*, the Court held the purpose of discouraging indigents from moving to be 'unequivocally impermissible'. Thirdly, the Court did not accept the fiscal justification raised up by California. The Court calculated that the State could just as well save the envisaged 10.9 million if it were to decrease the benefits of all welfare recipients by a mere 72 cents per month. The Court explicitly held, however, that its rejection of the fiscal argument did not rest on the weakness of California's claim. Rather, it rests on the fact that the Citizenship Clause of the Fourteenth Amendment, which expressly equates citizenship with residence and does not 'allow for . . . degrees of citizenship based on length of residence'. The length of residence in California and the identity of the prior

---

[280] Ch 2, s 8.5.
[281] *Saenz v Roe*, 119 S.Ct.1518 (1999).

States of residence do not have any relevance to the need of applicants for welfare benefits nor do those factors, according to the Court, bear any relationship to the State's interest in making an equitable allocation of funds to be distributed among needy State citizens. Citing *Shapiro* the Court held that States are not entitled 'to apportion all benefits and services according to the past contributions of its citizens' and it concluded that the 'State's legitimate purpose in saving money provides no justification for its decision to discriminate among equally eligible citizens'.

Fourthly, and lastly, the Court rejected the view that the durational residence requirements under consideration could be upheld on the ground that Congress had given its approval to the requirements when it adopted PRWORA. Because the TANF programme gives States much broader discretion in setting benefit levels and eligibility criteria than AFDC did, it was argued before the Court that the 1997 programme would provide new incentives for welfare recipients to change their residences and incite States to engage in a 'race to the bottom' in setting benefit levels. The Court, however, was not persuaded. It could not see why the disparities among the States' benefit systems would be any greater under TANF than under AFDC; and it held that the savings which could possibly result from the discriminatory Californian statute could just as well be achieved by non-discriminatory means which would have only a minuscule impact on benefit levels. Where in *Shapiro* the Court had concluded that Congress is not empowered to authorise States to violate the Equal Protection Clause, the Court now held in *Saenz* that the same holds true for all Clauses of the Fourteenth Amendment. The protection afforded by the Citizenship Clause implies a limitation on the powers of the National Government as well as the States. In conclusion, the Court held the California statute to be unconstitutional.

In *Saenz v Roe* the Supreme Court may have altered the legal framework for reviewing durational residence requirements, but this does not imply that the Court has also altered its view on the legality of welfare waiting-periods. Such requirements are unconstitutional.[282] In fact, from a welfare perspective, *Saenz* is quite similar to *Shapiro*: under the Privileges or Immunities Clause welfare waiting periods are subject to a standard of review which is at least equally strict as the compelling State interest test of the Equal Protection Clause, both Clauses of the Fourteenth Amendment do not allow Congress to authorise discriminatory State measures in the field of welfare and the Court confirmed that the free-rider and past-contribution arguments are constitutionally unsound. Thus, all United States citizens regardless of their economic status, enjoy the constitutional privilege of acquiring citizenship of the State of their choice and of being

---

[282] To be sure, *Saenz* still leaves room for the conclusion that (relatively short) welfare waiting-period requirements might survive judicial scrutiny when they are applied in order to establish bona fide residence. Cp n 259 above. In *Saenz* it was undisputed that respondents were bona fide residents and the Court therefore saw no need to consider what weight must be given to a citizen's length of residence in cases where State citizenship is questioned.

treated as citizens from the moment they establish residence in that State. The main difference between the two decisions is that *Saenz* is more explicit in the rejection of the financial arguments of the State. In brief, the Court does not see a practical need for durational residence requirements because it does not expect that applicants for welfare benefits will, if at all, move in such great numbers to other States as to seriously affect the funding of the States' welfare systems.

8.5 Non-Residents

In *Edwards*, *Shapiro* and *Saenz* the Court has thus removed from the States two legal instruments by means of which they have traditionally regulated cross-border access to their welfare programmes: the police or 'immigration' power and the durational residence requirement. *Shapiro* indicated, however, that the Court does approve of the use of the third instrument originating from the Elizabethan Poor Laws: the residence requirement. The Court said that the 'residence requirement and the one-year waiting-period are distinct and independent prerequisites' for welfare under any programme.[283] In *Shapiro* the Court granted indigents the right to establish residence in the State of their choice and to claim welfare benefits as 'equally deserving' State citizens. The Court merely prohibited discrimination among State citizens, not discriminations between State citizens and citizens of other States.[284]

Indigents who have not yet established residence in a State are thus not eligible for welfare. Does this also imply, then, that indigents who have moved to another State and have given up residence/citizenship, can no longer claim welfare benefits? In other words, are welfare benefits exportable?[285] The issue came before the Court in *Califano v Torres* (1978),[286] a case that involved a section of the Social Security Act which denied SSI-benefits to persons living in Puerto Rico. The District Court there held that the Constitution requires that a person who moves to Puerto Rico must be given benefits 'superior to those enjoyed by

---

[283] *Shapiro v Thompson*, 394 U.S. 618 (1969) at 636. *Shapiro*'s analysis only applies to the right to migrate and thus only to durational residence requirements. *Memorial Hospital v Maricopa County*, 415 U.S. 250 (1973) at 255. See also: ch 2, 8.5.

[284] Under the Equal Protection Clause residence requirements are only subject to the flexible rational relation test. The Court has never reviewed welfare residence requirements under the Privileges and Immunities Clause. ch 2, s 8.6.1. It can safely be assumed, however, that the Court would uphold the requirements under this Clause. The requirements are subject to the 'substantial relation test' of this Clause—welfare is obviously 'fundamental'—but it seems beyond doubt that welfare residence requirements are 'substantially' related to the legitimate objective of maintaining welfare programmes. In the absence of residence requirements the 'benefits' of the welfare system would 'spill over' to other States and States would not be able to financially maintain their welfare programmes.

[285] Prior to *Shapiro*, some States allowed their former residents to export welfare benefits for the period they could not yet claim welfare in the 'new' State. *Shapiro v Thompson*, 394 U.S. 618 (1969) at 637.

[286] *Califano v Torres*, 435 U.S. 1 (1978).

other residents of Puerto Rico if the newcomer enjoyed those in the State from which he came'.[287] The Supreme Court disagreed by stating that this

> 'Court has never held that the constitutional right to travel embraces any such doctrine, and we decline to do so now. (. . .) Such a doctrine would apply with equal force to any benefits a State might provide for its residents, and would require a State to continue to pay those benefits indefinitely to any person who had once resided there. And the broader implications of such a doctrine in other areas of substantive law would bid fair to destroy the independent power of each State under our Constitution to enact laws uniformly applicable to all of its residents'.[288]

Indigents who move to, and establish residence in, another State are eligible for welfare in the 'new' home State, but can no longer claim welfare in the 'old' home State. Welfare benefits are in principle not exportable. The movement to another State does not lead to a loss of the right to claim welfare, but it may imply a loss of income where the indigent moves to a State where welfare benefits are lower. Migrating indigents do not have a constitutional right to retain a certain minimum income nor can they 'double their income' by moving to another State. The Social Security Act did not demand an invalidation of welfare residence requirements. The Act did not transform welfare system(s) into a unitary system under which the Federal authorities were fully responsible for the provision, financing and administration of welfare. The constitutionality of residence requirements merely reflects the fact that the single welfare Union is based on a federal system of government in which States are still the primary responsible governmental entities.

8.6 Aliens

A third category of individuals that has often been denied welfare is that of aliens. Up until the 1970s, it seemed beyond doubt that States were entitled to exclude aliens from their welfare systems. The Supreme Court recognised that States had a 'special public interest' in favouring United States citizens over foreigners in the distribution of welfare. Illustrative are the following words of Justice Cardozo in *People v Crane* (1915):

> 'To disqualify aliens is discriminatory indeed, but not arbitrary discrimination, for the principle of exclusion is the restriction of the resources of the state to the advancement and profit of the members of the state. Ungenerous and unwise such discrimination may be. It is not for that reason unlawful. . . The state in determining what use shall be made of its own moneys, may legitimately consult the welfare of its own citizens rather than that of aliens. . . . In its war against poverty, the state is not required to dedicate its own resources to citizens and aliens alike.'[289]

[287] *Ibid*, at 4.
[288] *Ibid*, at 4–5.
[289] *People v Crane*, 214 NY 154, 108 NE 427 (1915) at 429–30 (as quoted in *Graham v Richardson*, 403 U.S. 365 (1971) at 373).

Welfare alienage classifications were merely scrutinised under the rational relation test of the Equal Protection Clause and were, thus, generally upheld. Two years after *Shapiro*, however, the Court considerably strengthened the legal status of 'needy' aliens, and in particular resident aliens, in *Graham v Richardson*[290] (1971).

8.6.1 Permanent Residents

In *Graham* the Court was asked to rule upon the constitutionality of an Arizona statute which made eligibility for categorical welfare benefits for aliens dependent upon fifteen years of residence within the United States and a Pennsylvania statute which wholly excluded aliens from general welfare programmes. Both Arizona and Pennsylvania argued that they had a 'public interest' in favouring citizens over aliens in the distribution of welfare benefits. The Court rejected the States' argument. It held that alienage classifications were 'inherently suspect' and therefore subject to strict judicial scrutiny.[291] Citing *Shapiro*, the Court stated that a

> 'State has a valid interest in preserving the fiscal integrity of its programs. It may legitimately attempt to limit its expenditures . . . for public assistance . . . But a State may not accomplish such a purpose by invidious distinctions between classes of its citizens . . . The saving of welfare costs cannot justify an other wise invidious classification'.[292]

The Court concluded that 'a concern for fiscal integrity is no more compelling a justification' for the requirement of United States citizenship than it was for the waiting-period requirement. The justification of limiting welfare expenses was particularly inappropriate and unreasonable when the class that was discriminated against consists of resident aliens. Like citizens, aliens pay taxes and they contribute to the economic growth of a State. There can be no 'special public interest' in tax revenues to which aliens have contributed on an equal basis with residents'.[293] An additional reason why the classifications in question could not be upheld, emerged from what the Court called 'federal-state relations'.[294] *Graham* concerned permanent residents. Such aliens enjoy the rights to reside and to be treated equally in any State[295] and Congress had explicitly declared that when resident aliens become 'public charges for causes arising after their entry, they are entitled to the full and equal benefit of all state laws for the security of persons and property'.[296] The statutes in question conflicted with this Federal policy: an 'alien, becoming indigent and unable to work, will be unable

---

[290] *Graham v Richardson*, 403 U.S. 365 (1971).
[291] Ch 2, s 8.7.
[292] *Graham v Richardson*, 403 U.S. 365 (1971) at 374–5.
[293] *Ibid*, at 376.
[294] *Ibid*, at 377.
[295] *Ibid*, at 378 (citing *Takahashi v Fish*, 334 U.S. 410 (1948) at 420).
[296] *Ibid*, at 378.

to live, where . . . he cannot secure the necessities of life, including food, clothing and shelter'.[297] Finally, the Court rejected Arizona's argument that its fifteen-year residence requirement for aliens would be authorised by Federal law and could thus be upheld. The Court admitted that Congress has broad powers to determine the conditions under which aliens are admitted to the United States, but it held, citing *Shapiro* again, that Congress does not have the power to authorise individual States to violate the Equal Protection Clause.[298] In conclusion, the Court held the challenged statutes unconstitutional.

Graham implied that aliens whose right to reside in the United States is *not* conditional upon their *not* becoming a public charge, can move to and claim welfare in the State of their choice. *Graham* extended the 'sink-or-swim' rationale of *Edwards* and *Shapiro* to aliens. States cannot shift the poverty problem to other States by denying welfare to those aliens who have been allowed by the Federal authorities to stay or remain in the United States even if they become in need of welfare. States have to treat such aliens equally with United States citizens; they are prohibited to 'keep indigent permanent resident aliens out'.

8.6.2 Undocumented Aliens

Graham and its conclusion that aliens constitute a suspect class did not imply that all aliens can claim State welfare benefits under the same conditions as United States citizens. The question whether aliens are likely to become dependent upon social welfare is one of the most important the Federal immigration authorities consider. Without discussing Federal immigration policy in detail, it can be said, albeit somewhat oversimplified, that aliens likely to become a burden on the public purse are, in principle, not admitted and that the right to reside of aliens who are admitted is made conditional upon their not becoming a public charge.[299] With the exception of permanent resident aliens, aliens lose, in principle, their right to reside in the country when they become in need of social welfare after admission. They are subject to deportation. Aliens who are deported do not, needless to say, have a right to claim welfare.

---

[297] *Ibid,* at 379–80.

[298] *Ibid,* at 382. See also: Guendelsberger, 'Equal Protection and Resident Aliens Access to Public Benefits in France and the United States' (1993) *TulLRev* 631–76, at 720–1. s 402 of PRWORA gives States the option to deny TANF benefits to aliens lawfully residing in the United States. Because of *Graham* it would seem, however, that such denials are incompatible with the Equal Protection Clause. Chang, 'Immigrants under the New Welfare Law: A Call for Uniformity, a Call for Justice' (1997) *UCLALRev* 205–80, at 266 and Note, 'Welfare Reform: Treatment of Legal Immigrants' (1997) *HarvLRev* 1191 *et seq.*

[299] The Federal immigration law bars the admission of any alien 'who in the opinion of the consular officer at the time of application for a visa, or in the opinion of the Attorney General at the time of application for admission or adjustment of status' is likely to become a public charge. Immigration and Nationality Act § 212(a)(4), 8 USC § 1182(a)(4) (SupplII 1990). Additionally, an alien who 'within five years after the date of entry . . . has become a public charge from causes not affirmatively shown to have arisen since entry is deportable'. INA § 241 (a)(5), 8USC § 1252 (a)(5).

The only question left, then, is whether States can deny welfare to aliens who have lost their right to reside but who have not (yet) been deported. In other words, do undocumented or illegal aliens have a constitutional right to claim social welfare benefits? At the present state of the law, they probably do not have such a right. In *Plyler v Doe* (1982) the Court held that illegal aliens do enjoy equal protection from the law, but that their illegal presence does prevent them from being considered a suspect class.[300] Undocumented aliens only enjoy the minimal protection of the rational relation test. A denial of social welfare to aliens who have entered or remained in the country illegally does not seem to be wholly invidious or arbitrary[301] and one may thus assume that States are under no constitutional obligation to grant illegal aliens social welfare.[302] The main reason, however, that undeported illegal aliens cannot claim welfare seems to lie in Federal-State relations. In *Plyler*, Chief Justice Burger held that 'a state has no power to prevent unlawful immigration, and no power to deport illegal aliens. . . . If the Federal Government, properly chargeable with deporting illegal aliens, fails to do so, it should bear the burdens of their presence here'.[303] Basically, the legal status of illegal aliens, and their eventual welfare rights, is the responsibility of the Federal government, not the States.[304]

Constitutional law on aliens' access to welfare demonstrates that the United States also constitutes towards 'the outside world' a single welfare Union.

---

[300]   *Plyler v Doe*, 457 U.S. 202 (1982) at 215 and 223.

[301]   Cp Legomsky, 'Immigration, Federalism and the Welfare State' (1995) *UCLALRev* 1453–74, at 1468.

[302]   302 It has been argued, however, that State laws which deny undocumented aliens access to subsistence benefits should be subject to a significant or intermediate level of scrutiny. Clarke, 'State Legislation Denying Subsistence Benefits to Undocumented Aliens: An Equal Protection Approach' (1983) *TexLRev* 859–92.

[303]   *Ibid*, at 242 (Burger, C J, dissenting).

[304]   The issue of the social welfare rights of illegal aliens became the subject of heated debates at the end of 1994 when California voters approved Proposition 187. This Proposition was designed to make illegal aliens ineligible for most social welfare benefits, health care facilities and education. See, eg Schuler, 'Equal Protection and the Undocumented Immigrant: California's Proposition 187' (1996) *Boston CTWLJ* 275–312; Abriel, 'Rethinking Preemption for Purposes of Aliens and Public Benefits' (1995) *UCLALRev* 1597–630; Neuman, 'Aliens as Outlaws: Government Services, Proposition 187, and the Structure of Equal Protection Doctrine' (1995) *UCLALRev* 1425–52 and X, 'Unenforced Boundaries: Illegal Immigration and the Limits of Judicial Federalism' (1995) *HarvLRev*.

It may come as no surprise that it is the State of California in which debates regarding welfare rights of illegal aliens have been so heated. 40% of all illegal aliens present in the United States (have) settle(d) in California. Another 40% have settled in only six other States (Arizona, Florida, Illinois, New Jersey, New York and Texas). The main problem regarding illegal aliens' welfare rights lies in the Federal-State relations and in particular which government should bear the financial responsibility for illegal aliens. In general, the costs of granting illegal aliens welfare, education or other governmental benefits are, roughly speaking, equal to the taxes generated from these aliens. Yet, the costs are for the biggest part borne by the six or seven States which host most illegal aliens, whilst the biggest part of the tax revenues goes to the Federal government. The latter does not seem willing, however, to compensate the States which in practice bear the burden of offering illegal aliens governmental benefits. The Federal government does not reimburse the States for the AFDC-expenditures made on behalf of illegal aliens. X, *Unenforced Boundaries* (1995) at 1656 above and Legomsky (1995) n 301 above, at 1470–3.

A single decision, made by the Federal immigration authorities, determines whether or not an alien is entitled to be eligible for welfare. Aliens who have been allowed by the Federal authorities to stay in the United States when in need of welfare, can move to and are entitled claim welfare in the State of their choice. All other aliens do not have a constitutional right to claim welfare in either one of the States.

8.7 Summary and Conclusions

American constitutional law on cross-border access to social welfare benefit schemes has undergone drastic changes over the years. Prior to the transformation of the welfare system in the 1930s it was virtually impossible for indigents to establish residence and obtain welfare benefits in other States. The States' responsibility for the poverty problem was limited to their territory and the indigents living therein. The 'immigration' of indigents from other States was perceived as a threat to both public order and the States' ability to maintain adequate welfare programmes. The local structure of 'the' welfare system, required indigents to stay where they were and States were permitted to refuse migrating indigents residence in the State and to deny them welfare during the first months or years of residence in the State. The Social Security Act of 1935, however, opened the door for a strengthening of the legal status of indigents. The Act embodied the notion that every person should have a right to an income sufficient for at least the 'essential needs of life' and recognised that poverty and welfare had become matters of common concern which the States and the Federal government had to handle together. The Supreme Court responded by holding that in the newly established welfare union there was no longer room to deny indigents the fundamental right to travel (*Edwards*) and to allow States to deny welfare benefits to new, recently arrived, indigent residents (*Shapiro*, *Saenz*) and permanent resident aliens (*Graham*). In sum, all indigents lawfully residing in the United States now enjoy the freedom to choose in which State they wish to live and claim welfare.

When one compares American constitutional law and European Community law on cross-border access to welfare or minimum subsistence benefit schemes, one must conclude that the conflict between the 'free movement interest', on the one hand, and the 'minimum subsistence interest', on the other hand, has been settled differently. On both sides of the Atlantic, States are entitled to make eligibility for minimum subsistence benefits subject to the requirement of residence in the State territory, but the degree to which individuals in need of such benefits may move freely between States differs. In the European Community, this right is limited to Community (and EEA) workers and their family members. Member States are protected against the feared social tourism by the threshold requirements of 'effective and genuine work' (Article 39 EC—status of Community worker), the possession of sufficient financial means (1990 residence directives) as well as by the power to regulate the immigration of virtually all third country nationals. In the United States, however, all persons entitled to reside in the country can choose in which States they wish to live and to claim welfare benefits on the same basis as residents already living there. The individual States lack powers to protect themselves against a possible influx of 'free-riding' welfare applicants and recipients. In the United States the conflict between the two interests referred to above has basically been settled to the benefit of the 'free movement interest', whilst in the European Community the 'minimum subsistence interest' has so far proven to be of greater weight.

What explains the differences between American constitutional law and European Community law? Why has it been possible to realise a general freedom of movement in the United States, whilst in the European Community it has not? Given the different historical, political and legal backgrounds against which the law governing freedom of movement of persons has developed, it is far from easy, if not impossible, to give a single or definite answer to these questions. Nonetheless, several factors may explain the differences.

The first one concerns the constitutional position of the Supreme Court and the European Court of Justice, and the 'legal tools' the two courts have had at their disposal. From the very beginning it has never been questioned that all Americans enjoy, as citizens of the Union, the right to move and reside freely among the States[305] and since 1868 they enjoy constitutional protection under the Equal Protection Clause, the Privileges or Immunities Clause and/or the Citizenship Clause of the Fourteenth Amendment. The right to travel and the various constitutional Clauses have provided the Supreme Court with tools which it could use to invalidate welfare waiting-period requirements and to conclude that all United States citizens and the permanent resident foreigners have the right to claim equal access to welfare from the moment they establish residence in the State of their choice. Until recently, however, the European Court of Justice did not seem to possess comparable tools that it could use in order to make a contribution to the realisation of a right of residence for all European citizens. It is only since 1993 that the notion of a European citizenship and a general right to freedom of movement for all citizens are enshrined in the Treaty itself and the free movement rights are, according to the wording of Article 18 EC, still conditional upon certain limitations.

A second factor concerns the structure of the American and European 'welfare systems'. The reasoning of the Supreme Court in *Edwards*, *Shapiro* and *Saenz* was largely based on the 'sink-or-swim-together-rationale' reflected in the Social Security Act. Poverty and the problems caused by the 'migrating' poor have since 1935 been perceived as common problems for which not only individual States but also the Federal government hold a responsibility. Federal funding did not constitute the direct basis for the invalidation of welfare waiting-periods but the common welfare responsibility has inspired the Court

---

[305] See also ch 2, s 8.1.

to conclude that States were no longer entitled to shift the responsibility for these common problems by 'closing the gates' to their territory. In the European Community, however, the notion is still predominant that the responsibility for citizens who do not contribute to but rather seem to burden economic development must be borne not by the Community, but by the individual States. It may perhaps not be correct to speak of 'the' American welfare state, but there is no doubt that the United States has evolved much further than the European Community towards a 'welfare Union'.[306]

A third factor which may help to explain the differences in the law governing freedom of movement of the 'poor' concerns the fear for welfare migration or social tourism. In *Shapiro* the Supreme Court did not confirm *Edwards'* right to travel, and it did not confer upon the 'migrating poor' a right to equal treatment as regards welfare benefits, because the Federal funding made available under the Social Security Act safeguarded the financial stability of welfare systems. At least in theory, the welfare magnet problem still existed and it still does so today. As *Saenz* expressly indicates, the Court has recognised a 'genuine' right to freedom of movement for the 'poor' simply because it did not, and does not, expect that welfare recipients would move to other States in such large numbers as to seriously affect welfare benefit schemes. In the European Community, however, the fear of becoming a 'welfare magnet' is still very strong among the Member States. This is reflected in the financial means requirements contained in the 1990 residence directives, Article 18(1) EC, which states that the right to freedom of movement is subject to the conditions and limitations laid down in the Treaty and secondary legislation as well as the requirement of 'effective and genuine work' for obtaining the status of Community worker.

9 TOWARDS A GENERAL RIGHT OF RESIDENCE IN THE EUROPEAN COMMUNITY

9.1 Introduction

Turning back to the European Community, it may be recalled that the legal status of persons in need of minimum subsistence benefits has been significantly strengthened in the course of the last three decades. Four decades ago, Community law had virtually nothing to offer to 'needy' persons who wished to establish residence, and claim minimum subsistence benefits, in other Member States. Today, all nationals of the Member States enjoy, in their capacity as citizens of the European Union, the right to move to and reside in other Member States (Article 18 EC) and to claim equal treatment as regard access to minimum subsistence benefit schemes (Article 12 EC) when, and for as long as, they are lawfully residing in the territory of another Member State.

---

[306] Cp Garth, 'Migrant Workers and Rights of Mobility in the European Community and the United States: A Study of Law, Community and Citizenship in the Welfare State' in Cappelletti *et al*, *Integration Through Law—Europe and the American Federal Experience* (1986) 85–163 at 115.

For many Community citizens who are in need of minimum subsistence benefits, however, the progress that has been made does not have much practical meaning. Article 18(1) EC stipulates that free movement rights are subject to 'limitations and conditions' laid down in the Treaty and secondary legislation. Community citizens who wish to establish residence in another Member State can still be required to demonstrate that they have obtained 'effective and genuine' employment (Article 39 EC—*Levin*) or that they possess sufficient finances to support themselves and their family members (Article 1 of Directive No 90/364). In addition, economically inactive Community citizens can still lose their right to reside when they become an unreasonable burden on the host State's social assistance scheme (Article 3 of Directive No 90/364—*Grzelczyk*). As argued in Section 7, from the perspective of Union Citizenship the financial means requirement for exercising the right to reside is problematic. Union citizenship is a political rather than an economic concept which is deprived of much of its meaning as long as Community law denies the 'fundamental and personal right'[307] to freedom of movement to some of its citizens just because of their economic status.[308]

This final section addresses the question whether and, if so, how, one could move closer to, or possibly even realise, a general right of residence for all Union citizens including all those who are dependent on minimum subsistence benefits. Is it possible to realise a general right of residence which is not subject to a financial means requirement and which, for all beneficiaries, encompasses a right to obtain minimum subsistence benefits in the State in which they have chosen to live? Can this goal be achieved without threatening the financial integrity of the national benefit systems? What lessons can possibly be learned in this regard from the United States? In an attempt to answer such questions, this section considers both legislative and judicial options. The number of issues involved is too large, and the subject is too politically loaded, however, to come up with a single solution which would be acceptable for all (Member States). The observations below merely intend to give impetus to the discussion about how a general right of residence could possibly be realised.[309]

9.2 Freedom of Movement versus the Financial Stability of Social Assistance Schemes

In order to see how a general right of residence could possibly be realised, one should ignore for a moment the historical factors that have influenced the development of the free movement of persons. This allows us to take a step from the specific legal issues involved and to approach the conflict between the desire to

---

[307] COM (97) 230 at 4.1.

[308] Cp O'Leary (1996) n 93 above, at 99.

[309] For the sake of convenience, the discussion in this section is limited to Community citizens who are in need of social assistance benefits. The specific issues that may arise as regards mixed, hybrid or special non-contributory benefits will not be dealt with separately.

realise a general freedom of movement and the need to maintain social assistance schemes, from a more theoretical perspective. Some elements of the economic theories on fiscal federalism may be of help in this regard.[310] The theories, which start from the presumption that a general right to freedom of movement exists, may contribute to a better understanding of the impact which inter-State mobility of persons may have on the organisation and funding of social assistance schemes in multi-tiered governmental entities, such as the United States and the European Community, in which the task of establishing and financing social assistance schemes is carried out at (Member) State level.

9.2.1 Race to the Bottom Hypothesis

In fiscal federalism literature various advantages of the provision of public benefits at State or decentralised level are pointed out. One of these is that it enables individuals to move to the States or other local jurisdictions where the collective choices as regard public benefits and taxes best suit personal interests or preferences. Individuals may 'vote by their feet'.[311] Persons who prefer public benefits of a comparatively high quality, and who are willing to contribute to the financing of such benefits by paying comparatively high taxes, may move to the States where such a pattern of public services has been chosen. Individuals with other preferences may move to States where other choices are made. In as far as social assistance benefit schemes are concerned, however, the relevance of this Tiebout-hypothesis is limited.[312] In the theory behind it, there is a nexus between the benefits that may be received and the taxes that must be paid. To put it simply, taxes may be regarded as the price that an individual is willing to pay for the benefits. In the case of social assistance benefits, however, this link between 'price' and 'product' is often largely absent. Often recipients of these benefits do not, or hardly, contribute to the funding of the benefits by paying (direct) taxes. Fiscal federalism theories teach that public benefits can only be efficiently provided if the group of the tax-paying contributors largely coincides with the group of beneficiaries.[313] In the case of redistributional programmes such as social assistance schemes this 'double identity' often does not exist.

[310] On these fiscal federalism theories see, eg Rosen, *Public Finance* (1985) ch 19; Due and Friedländer, *Government Finance* (1977) 456 *et seq*; Musgrave and Musgrave, *Public Finance in Theory and Practice* (1976) and Oates, *Fiscal Federalism* (1972).

[311] Tiebout, 'A Pure Theory of Local Expenditures' (1956) *JPolEc* 416 *et seq* and Calabresi, 'A Government of Limited and Enumerated Powers': In Defense of *United States v Lopez*' (1995) *MichLRev* 752–831, at 775–6. Cp also: Barnard, 'Regulating Competitive Federalism in the European Union?—The Case of EU Social Policy' in Shaw (ed), *Social Law and Policy in an Evolving European Union* (2000) 49–69 and Barnard, 'Social Dumping and Race to the Bottom: Some Lessons for the EU from Delaware?' (2000) *ELRev* 57 *et seq*.

[312] 312 Note, 'Devolving Welfare Programs to the States: A Public Choice Perspective' (1996) *HarvLRev* 1984–2001, at 1987.

[313] Cp Bertola *et al*, 'EU Welfare Systems and Labor Markets: Diverse in the Past, Integrated in the Future' in Bertola *et al*, *Welfare and Employment in Europe* (2000) 23–122, at 90 and Scholsem, 'A Propos de la Circulation des Etudiants: Vers un Federalisme Financier Européen?' (1989) *CDE* 306–23, at 309–10.

In a federal setting where social assistance benefit schemes are provided at State or decentralised level, freedom of movement may affect the funding of the individual States' schemes. Potentially, the free movement of persons in need of such benefits might even be a threat to social assistance schemes throughout the entire federal entity. Consider the following, oversimplified, model.

State A is grouped together with several other States in federal entity X. State A has to decide on the level of its benefits. If it opts for comparatively high benefits, and thus for comparatively high taxes, State A will encounter the problem that it may attract persons from other States who are in need of such benefits. The higher the level at which benefits are set, the greater the magnetic effect on 'needy' individuals from other States. The more 'free-riding' benefit recipients that come from other States, the greater the pressure on the funding of the benefit scheme. Should the inflow of non-contributing benefit recipients become quite considerable, State A might have to choose either to lower benefit levels or to raise tax-rates. If State A were to choose the latter option, the danger exists that tax-paying citizens would move to other States which might again lead to a reduction in tax revenues. In the end, State A might be forced to lower its benefits anyway. At the outset, State A might therefore decide to set the level of its benefits lower than the benefit level in neighbouring State B in the hope that 'free-riders' from other States would move to B. If State A were indeed to make that choice, it would indirectly increase the magnetic effect of States B's benefit scheme. This State would be faced with the same problems that State A had initially encountered and State B might therefore decide to decrease its benefits to a level lower than in State C in the hope that 'free riders' would go to that State. C might respond similarly and try to shift the burden to State D. A domino effect could occur. The fear of becoming a welfare magnet might trigger competition between States each lowering their benefits in the hope that other States would 'take care of the poor'. This competition might result in 'a race to the bottom' which could lead to a reduction in welfare benefit levels throughout the entire federal entity X.

9.2.2 A Race to the Bottom in the European Community?

The above is a theoretical model. The introduction of a general right to freedom of movement in a federal-like entity such as the European Community would not necessarily result in a 'race to the bottom'. The model is based on a number of assumptions, which would not necessarily materialise in practice. This particularly holds true for the assumption that the 'poor' are mobile. If they were given the right, would the economically inactive European Union citizens be likely to move to other States in order to collect higher benefits? Member States with the comparatively high benefit levels would answer the question in the affirmative, but there are reasons to believe that the number of free riders would not be so great as to seriously affect the funding of the benefit schemes. In the late 1950s, Member States also feared that the introduction of a free movement of workers would trigger considerable labour movement. Experience has demonstrated, however, that this movement has never been considerable.[314] Social, cultural and linguistic obstacles have prevented, and still prevent, many Community citizens from working in other Member States. It does not seem unrealistic to assume that the same would hold true for the future beneficiaries of a general right of residence.

Further, if in the United States, a country where citizens are generally more mobile than in the European Community, no conclusive evidence has been put forward as to the existence of social tourism, then one is inclined to conclude that the possible introduction of a general right of residence in the European Community would not lead to an excessive inter-State flow of free-riding social assistance recipients.

Furthermore, one may assume that in deciding whether or not to move to other Member States, European Union citizens in need of social assistance benefits would consider the geographical distance to States with higher benefits. In the United States the differences between welfare benefit levels in neighbouring States are often quite considerable, but in the European Community the differences between neighbouring States appear comparatively small. For instance, it does not seem very likely that the differences in benefit levels in the Benelux countries will trigger social tourism. Significant differences exist between the northern and the southern Member States. Social tourism is largely a 'north-south' problem and one doubts whether many of the 'southern' citizens of the Union would be willing to move 'all the way to the north'.

It could be, and it indeed has been,[315] argued that there are no strong financial objections to a general right of residence and that such a right could 'simply' be recognised without there being a need to take any protective measures for the benefit of the more generous Member States. However, there are also reasons why one should be careful and not wholly ignore the objections to the introduction of a general right of residence.

First, the accession of Eastern European States to the Community could possibly trigger social tourism. Benefit levels between the Eastern European Countries and many of the current Member States differ and benefit schemes of countries like Germany and Austria might have a magnetic effect on the 'needy' citizens of Poland, Hungary, etc.

Second, even it could be demonstrated that European Union citizens are not likely to become 'free-riders', the funding of Member States' social assistance schemes might be put under pressure. The funding of the schemes is not affected

---

[314] See, eg Muus, A Study on the Expected Effects of Free Movement for Legally Residing Workers from Third Countries within the European Community, in Curtin *et al*, Free Movement for non-EC-Workers within the European Community (1997) 5–28; Penninx and Muus, No Limits for Migration after 1992?—The Lessons of the Past and a Reconnaisance of the Future, in: IM (1989) 373–88 and Werner, 'Post-war Migration in Western Europe' (1986) IM 543–57.

[315] Von Wilmowsky, 'Zugang zu öffentlichen Leistungen anderer Mitgliedstaaten' (1992) *ZfaöR* 231–76, at 259 and Schulz (1997) n 40 above, at 339.

because a Community citizen has the intention of obtaining benefits, but because a State may have to grant benefits to a larger number of persons. Also 'needy' Community citizens who primarily move to other Member States in order to look for employment, to live closer to family members or friends, or who wish to live in a better climate, may increase the pressure on social assistance schemes. Many of the objections against a general right of residence would probably not exist if it could be shown that migration of 'needy' Community citizens was more or less in balance. This, however, seems unlikely. For various reasons, and the level of social assistance benefits is only one, some Member States will be more attractive than others and the former are likely to bear a heavier burden than the latter.

Third, the race to the bottom theory is not based on the assumption that social tourism actually occurs, but on the mere fear that it might occur.[316] In the model described in the previous sub-section, States do not lower their benefit levels once they have actually been confronted with an influx of free riders from other States. They lower benefit levels in advance in an attempt to discourage free riders from coming. The lowering of benefits in the 'race to the bottom' is often a preventive act on the part of States trying to be on the safe side.

Finally, even if it could be established that Member States would not lower benefit levels in order to deter free riders from coming or taxpayers from leaving, one cannot exclude the possibility that fear of movement may prevent Member States from increasing benefits. The possible introduction of a general right of residence might not be likely to trigger a total 'race to the bottom', but it might hamper a 'race to the top'.

It may not be very likely that the 'poor', if given the right, will move in such great numbers as to upset social assistance schemes, but the possibility cannot be wholly ruled out that the introduction of a general right of residence may have implications for the funding of social assistance schemes of some Member States. At least in considering the legislative options for realising a general right of residence, one must be realistic and assume that progress can probably only be made when some protective measures are taken to the benefit of the more generous States.

9.3 Legislative Options

9.3.1 Introduction

If the Community legislator were to study whether, and if so, how, a general right of residence could possibly be realised, it might consider several alternatives. As regards some of these one can be rather brief. For instance, one could

---

[316] Bennet, 'The Threat of the Wandering Poor: Welfare Parochialism and its Impact on the Use of Housing Mobility as an Anti-Poverty Strategy', *FordLJ* (1995) 1207 *et seq.*, at 1216–17.

explore the possibilities of setting up a common social assistance benefit scheme.[317] No doubt, such a scheme could pave the way for a general right of residence but any attempt to develop such a scheme is probably fruitless. One can assume that Member States are not willing to transfer the powers and financial resources necessary for establishing such a common scheme to the Community institutions.[318] Another alternative that is probably not feasible would be to reduce the differences between benefit levels in the various Member States or to even harmonise benefit levels.[319] This option would tackle the problem of social tourism at its core, but benefit levels simply differ too much. Member States with comparatively high benefit levels will not be willing to lower their benefits to a level that would be acceptable to States with lower benefits.[320]

Realistically, therefore, it can be assumed that a possible general right of residence must be realised in a Community where the task of establishing social assistance benefit schemes is carried out at Member State level and where benefit levels differ considerably.

[317] Fiscal federalism theories teach that redistributional programmes such as social assistance or welfare schemes cannot be efficiently organised at local or state level. For as long as freedom of movement exists, local governmental entities may serve as welfare magnets and a 'race to the bottom' may occur. Redistributional programmes should therefore be put in place at Federal or central level. See, eg: Grewal, *Economic Criteria for the Assignment of Functions in a Federal System, in: Advisory Council for Inter-Governmental Relations—Towards Adaptive Federalism* (1981) at 27 and Buchanan, *Who Should Distribute What in a Federal System, in: Hochman and Peterson, Redistribution Through Public Choice* (1974).

In setting up a common scheme, several alternatives could be considered. A'benefit scheme could be established for which the Community is wholly responsible and which would either wholly substitute or supplement the current national benefit schemes. One could also study the possibility of establishing a programme comparable to the American TANF programme (the former AFDC) under which the Community would incite the Member States to develop new, or to improve existing, benefit schemes by making available grants which would cover a large part of the expenditure.

Furthermore, one can imagine a common benefit scheme which would only apply to the 'needy' Europeans who wish to, or have decided to, establish residence in another Member State and draw inspiration from Professor Pieters' proposals to develop a so-called 'thirteenth country social security system' for migrant workers. Pieters, *Sociale Zekerheid na 1992: Eén over Twaalf* (1989) and Pieters and Vansteenkiste, *The Thirteenth State—Towards a European Community Social Insurance Scheme for Intra-Community Migrants* (1993).

[318] Cp Poiares Maduro, 'Europe's Social Self: 'The Sickness Unto Death'' in Shaw (ed), *Social Law and Policy in an Evolving European Union* (2000) 325–49, at 339.

The Community has taken some initiatives to encourage Member States that do not yet have a social assistance scheme to develop such a scheme. See Council Recommendation on Common Criteria concerning Sufficient Resources and Social Assistance Protection Systems (Recommendation 92/441, OJ 1991 C 163). See also: Coussins, 'The EC Recommendations on Social Protection: A Case Study in EC Social Policy' (1993) *SPA* 286 *et seq.* No financial resources are made available, however, for the Member States concerned and the Recommendation does not confer enforceable rights upon individuals.

Finally, mention may be made of the idea of introducing something like a 'European Social Snake' aimed at avoiding radical (downward) changes in social security schemes. Busquin, 'De Sociale Slang en het Europees Programma ter Bestrijding van Armoede' (1990) *BTSZ* 557 *et seq*

[319] See, eg Bertola *et al* (2000) n 313 above, at 105–8; Atkinson, *Poverty in Europe* (1998) and Bean *et al, Social Europe: One for All?* (1998).

[320] Peterson and Rom have proposed a common welfare standard for the United States. Peterson and Rom (1990) n 229 above, ch 5. The feasibility of their proposal seems slim though.

9.3.2 Compensation Mechanisms

In order to overcome the various objections of Member States, one could consider the possibility of setting up some kind of system whereby States that receive a comparatively high number of 'needy' persons from other Member States are compensated for the benefits they grant to such persons.[321] Two options seem to be available.

The first entails a system where the host State would be reimbursed by the State from which the migrant had moved. Such a compensation mechanism would have regard to the fact that the flow of 'needy' Community citizens in different directions is unlikely to be in balance and that the financial burden would ultimately be borne by States which are most likely to have received taxes from the persons concerned and which benefit from the reduction in the number of persons to whom they have to pay social assistance benefits.[322] The main[323] problem, however, with such a 'paying back system' is that it might in the end work out unfavourably for Member States with comparatively low benefit levels. They would be forced to bear the costs of benefits that are higher than the ones made available 'at home'. The funding of their minimum subsistence benefit schemes could be affected. Politically, compensation mechanisms under which the State of origin has to reimburse the 'new' host State do not seem feasible.[324]

In the alternative, one could consider setting up a mechanism under which the 'net-importers' of persons in need of minimum subsistence benefits would be

---

[321] See also: Vonk (1990) n 3 above, at 473.

[322] The introduction of such a reimbursement mechanism has been considered in the past. When the European Commission submitted to the Council in 1989 a proposal for a directive on the right of residence for students, it proposed to grant to students the right to receive social security benefits in the host State on condition that the State of origin reimbursed the host State upon the latter's request. See Art 1(3) of the proposal for a Council directive on the right of residence for students. OJ 1989 C 191. On this proposal see also Taschner (1993) n 93 above, at 433. Due to some Member States' fears that the costs would not be paid back by the State of origin, the Council has never adopted the Commission's proposal. O'Leary (1996) n 93 above, at 120.

Furthermore, in a memorandum which was presented by the Spanish government during the 1990–1991 Intergovernmental Conference it was proposed to grant Community citizens an unlimited right to move and reside freely and to adopt legislation that would lay down 'provisions to ensure a fair distribution of the resulting burden on the Member States, particularly in the area of social protection'. See the Spanish Memorandum on European Citizenship as published in eg, Cornett, *The Treaty of Maastricht* (1993) at 156.

[323] Another problem as regards such 'paying-back schemes' concerns the duration of the duty to reimburse the host State. A duty that is limited to a rather short period of time of for instance three months might be acceptable to Member States, but the same does not hold true for longer periods of reimbursement. Furthermore, to who should the duty to refund the host State apply? Should this duty only exist as regards Member States' own nationals who have moved elsewhere? Or should residence be taken as the starting-point and, if so, can a Member State also be obliged to refund the host State if the persons concerned hold the nationality of that State? Should the duration of the period during which the persons concerned have lived and paid taxes in the State in question, be considered as a relevant factor?

[324] Vonk (1990) n 3 above, at 469.

reimbursed by the Community. A special Community fund could be set up for this purpose.[325] The problem, however, is that such a common 'pay-back-system' does not eliminate the problem of social tourism. Persons in need of benefits would still have an incentive to move to States where benefits are relatively high. The total costs of benefits granted within the Community are likely to increase. Who will bear these costs? The main beneficiaries of such a Community reimbursement scheme would be the States with comparatively high benefits and ultimately such a scheme would require the 'net-exporting' States with the lower benefit levels to bear the extra financial burden. The latter are likely to resist. They may prefer to invest in their own benefit schemes instead of compensating other States. Ultimately, the problems concerning a Community reimbursement scheme are comparable to those relating to schemes under which the State of origin would have to pay the bill.

9.3.3 Right to Export Benefits

The afore mentioned options would allow for a general right of residence which would encompass a right to claim social assistance benefits from the moment beneficiaries establish residence in another Member State. The chances of realising such a 'full' right of residence through legislative means seem slim. Realistically, efforts need to be focussed on less far-reaching solutions.

A first option could possibly consist of reconsidering the exportability of minimum subsistence benefits. This option would not guarantee that 'needy' Community citizens are in all cases able to meet the financial means requirements and to establish residence in other Member States, but it would promote freedom of movement. By comparison with a reimbursement scheme where the State of origin has to bear the costs, the exportability of benefit schemes has the advantage that States with comparatively low benefits would not be obliged to pay more than they would if beneficiaries had stayed at home.

Various obstacles would have to be overcome though. A first one concerns the duration of the right to export benefits. Under Article 10 of Regulation No 1408/71 no time limit exists. The duration of the exportability basically coincides with the duration for which national laws guarantee entitlement to benefits. In order to increase the chances of having a proposal for the exportability social assistance adopted, one might therefore consider a right to export social assistance benefits for a limited period of time. One could think of a solution comparable to the one that exists for unemployment benefits. Article 69 of Regulation No 1408/71 allows for the export of unemployment benefits for a

---

[325] In the United States plans for introducing a federal 'charge back' were considered in the 1950s. The Federal government would reimburse the States for the expenses of welfare granted to newcomers during the first year. After that year, States would be fully financially responsible for welfare. The plan, however, has never become law. Mandelker (1955) n 222 above, at 364–5.

period of three months.[326] In fact, it may be considered rather 'odd' that a person who has been unemployed for a relatively short period of time may seek work in another Member State and continue to receive unemployment benefit, whilst a person who has been unemployed for a much longer period of time, has lost entitlement to unemployment benefit and become dependent on social assistance benefits, does not have any right to export his benefit.

Further questions arise as regards the level of the benefit and the cost of living in other Member States. These costs may very well be lower than in the State which would have to pay benefits. In *Lenoir* and *Snares* the Court explicitly stated that eligibility for 'benefits closely linked with the social environment' of Member States may be made conditional upon a residence requirement. Yet, in order to avoid Member States being obliged to pay social recipients 'more than they would need', Member States could be allowed to limit the level of their benefits to the level applied in the State to which a Community citizen has moved or to the cost of living there.[327] Obstacles to a limited right to export social assistance benefits need not be insurmountable, but in the light of the saga surrounding the export of mixed minimum subsistence benefits,[328] one may question the feasibility of introducing such a right.

9.3.4 Durational Residence Requirements

The legislator could further consider the option of replacing the financial requirements now contained in the 1990 residence directives by a single provision which would allow Member States to make eligibility for social assistance benefits conditional upon fulfilment of minimum periods of residence. Various alternatives seem to be available. During the time that Member States might apply durational residence requirements, Community citizens could be denied a right to claim benefits in the host State. As described in Section 8, this option applied in the United States in the period between the judgments in *Edwards* (1941) and *Shapiro* (1969). The main disadvantage is that 'needy' Community citizens would still be deterred from moving elsewhere. In order to partly overcome this obstacle, one could consider a relatively short durational residence requirement of, for instance, only two or three months. Also, one could choose the 'two-tier-benefit policies' comparable to those which some of the American States have applied in recent years. Thus, during the waiting-period a right to a benefit could be granted which only consists of a certain percentage of the

---

[326] See, eg Case 139/78 *Coccioli* [1979] ECR 991 and Joined Cases 41/79, 121/79 and 796/79 *Testa* [1980] ECR 1979. The Commission has proposed to the Council to extend the duration of the exportability of unemployment benefits. See COM(95) 734 def, COM(98) 779 final and Pennings, *Introduction to European Social Security Law* (1998) at 190–1.

[327] Cp Case C–237/94 *O'Flynn* [1996] ECR I–2617, 28–9 (payment for costs of funerals abroad) and Case C–158/95 *Kohll* [1998] ECR I–1931, 26 (reimbursement of costs of medical care received in other Member States).

[328] s 5.

benefits in the host State or the benefit could be limited to the level of benefits received in the State from which they have moved. Possibly, the 'waiting-period option' could be combined with one of the alternatives discussed before. Thus, for the duration of the waiting-period in the new host State, the State from which the person concerned had moved could be obliged to allow the export of benefits. Alternatively, 'needy' persons who have moved from one State to another could be given a right to obtain benefits but during an initial period the State of origin would be obliged to reimburse the host State.

The above options seem to strike a fair balance between the aim of promoting freedom of movement for Community citizens and the need to safeguard the funding of minimum subsistence schemes. The waiting-period options would lower hurdles for the non-economically active Community citizens who wish to establish residence in other States, whilst providing the Member States with a means of protecting themselves against social tourism. Yet, the feasibility of the 'waiting-period option' also seems minimal. The fact that the right to reside would not include a right to obtain social assistance benefits seems to be at odds with the policies and responsibilities of most Member States to guarantee all residents, where necessary, minimum means for subsistence. Furthermore, waiting-period requirements are at odds with the obligations, which many Member States have accepted under international agreements and treaties. For instance, Article 1 of the European Convention of Social and Medical Assistance stipulates that the Contracting Parties must ensure that nationals of the other State parties who are lawfully residing within their territory and who are without sufficient resources, shall be entitled to social assistance under the same conditions as the States' own nationals.

9.3.5 Conclusions

If the Community legislator were to consider how a general right of residence might possibly be realised or worked on, it might consider one of the above alternatives. Yet, the purport of the discussion may be clear. Due to the fear of social tourism, and constant concerns about the financing of social security and assistance schemes, Member States do not some eagerly to make any progress. They pay lip service to but do not seem willing to take definite steps towards realising a genuine right of residence for all Union citizens.[329] The issue does not rank high on the agenda of the political Community institutions. In fact, it is not even on the agenda. If the first initiatives must be taken by the political Community institutions, one should not expect that much progress will be made

---

[329] Illustrative are the results of the recent summit in Nice. In the provisional text of the Treaty of Nice Art 18 EC is proposed to be altered. The current Art 18(2) will be amended in that the provisions necessary for facilitating the rights to move and reside freely mentioned in Art 18(1) EC shall no longer be adopted by Council by unanimity. In the proposed new Art 18(3), however, it is expressly stated that Art 18(2) EC shall not apply to provisions on inter alia social security or social protection.

in the near future. Therefore, if one wishes to move towards a genuine freedom of movement, one might explore judicial options.[330]

9.4 Judicial Options

Prior to the coming into force of the Treaty on European Union, the Court of Justice did not seem to dispose of legal tools which it could have used to make a contribution to the realisation of a general non-economic right of residence for Community citizens. The EC Treaty only provided for functional residence rights intended to facilitate the right to work in other Member States (Article 39) and the right of establishment (Article 43).[331] The adoption of Directive No 90/364 on a general right of residence was not required by any Treaty provision. It was a voluntary act. Nothing prevented the Community legislator from making the right of residence subject to a financial means requirement.

The Treaty on European Union, however, has put the general right of residence in a new and different perspective. A European citizenship has formally been established (Article 17 EC) and it is in this capacity that nationals of Member States now enjoy 'the right to move and reside freely within the territory of the Member States' (Article 18(1) EC). Articles 17 and 18 EC are not merely symbolic provisions. *Martínez Sala, Elsen* and *Grzelczyk* demonstrate that the provisions may have legal force. More specifically, the rulings indicate that (*i*) the general right to reside is now a Treaty-based right; (*ii*) that Union citizens lawfully residing in the territory of other Member States can rely on Article 12(1) EC in order to claim social benefits, including minimum subsistence benefits, under the same conditions as the nationals of the host State, (*iii*) that having recourse to social assistance does not automatically lead to the loss of residence and (*iv*) that Article 18(1) EC may be relied upon by Union citizens in order to challenge national rules which hamper the right to establish residence in other Member States.

The Court has thus been willing to use Article(s 17 and) 18 as tools for strengthening the status of Union citizens. Could the Court possibly go one step further and interpret the provisions on Union citizenship as to restrict the conditions for obtaining the right to reside in other Member States? The wording of Article 18(1) EC may warrant judicial restraint,[332] but the provision does now

---

[330] Cp O'Leary (1996) n 93 above, at 144–5.

[331] The introduction of the requirement of 'effective and genuine work' for obtaining the status of Community worker (see s 3.1.3) suggests that the Court has indeed rejected the view that Art 39 EC can serve as the legal basis for a general non-economic right of residence. Van der Mei, 'The Elusive and Exclusive Concept of Union Citizenship, A Review Essay' (1998) *MJ* 391–402, at 397.

[332] In the drafters' view, any progress was to be made by the Community legislature. Art 18(2) EC provides that the Council, acting unanimously and in accordance with the co-decision procedure, may adopt provisions aimed at facilitating the exercise of free movement rights. The provisional text of the Treaty of Nice approved by the Intergovernmental Conference proposes to alter Art 18(2). The new Art 18(2) states that if 'action by the Community should prove necessary to

constitute the source of the right to reside and this might have implications for the legality of the financial means requirement laid down in national laws.[333] The rights guaranteed by Article 18(1) EC are fundamental rights which, having been put on 'on a par with other rights central to Community law',[334] must be construed broadly and which can only be subjected to limitations and conditions which do not affect the core of the right.[335]

National rules which make the right to reside conditional upon the possession of sufficient financial means are intended to protect the financial stability of social assistance schemes. This is a legitimate and compelling Member State interest that deserves protection under Community law. Yet, is it really necessary to deny needy Community citizens the right to establish residence in another Member State in order to protect the States' financial interests? The examination of American constitutional law on cross-border access to welfare benefit schemes has demonstrated that there are alternative ways in which States' interests can be safeguarded. In particular, the financing of benefit schemes could be protected by rules which make eligibility conditional upon a minimum period of residence in the State. The case law of the Court of Justice does not wholly exclude the possibility that waiting-period requirements might be upheld under Article 12(1) EC. Waiting-period requirements that are only imposed on nationals of other States constitute direct discrimination on grounds of nationality and are prohibited. Waiting-periods applied to both nationals and non-nationals, however, could possibly escape the classification of a prohibited indirect discrimination for reasons of nationality where it can be demonstrated that they are necessary to safeguard the financial stability of social assistance schemes.[336]

attain this objective' and 'the Treaty has not provided the necessary powers', the Council may adopt measures in accordance with the co-decision procedure. The Council will no longer have to act unanimously. Art 18(2) EC, however, does not apply to provisions 'on passports, identity cards, residence permits or any other such document or to provisions on social security or social protection' (Art 18(3)).

[333] To be sure, Art 1 of Dir 90/364 cannot be considered as being incompatible with Art 18(1) EC. The Art is drafted in positive terms; it states that Member States shall grant the right to reside to nationals of Member States who have sufficient financial resources (and are insured for medical care). The Art does not oblige Member States to refuse residence to persons are not able to provide for themselves. The power to deny residence to such persons derives from national law, not Community law. The question to be addressed therefore is whether national rules or measures which make residence conditional upon the possession of sufficient resources are compatible with Art 18(1) EC.

[334] Report from the Commission on Citizenship of the Union. COM(93) 702 final at 5.

[335] Opinion of Adv Gen Cosmas in Case C–378/97 *Wijsenbeek* [1999] ECR I–6207, 97.

[336] To be sure, in its case law on the free movement of workers the Court has consistently held that durational residence or employment requirements are contrary to Art 39 EC and Art 7(2) of Reg 1612/68. See s 3.1.3 and 3.2.3. This does not necessarily mean that the same requirements applied to non-economic residents also run counter to Art 12(1). In the context of the free movement of workers the Court has had regard to the financial interests of the host States by making the status of worker and, thus the right of residence and the right to equal treatment under Art 7(2) of Reg 1612/68, conditional upon the requirement of 'effective and genuine' work. In the field of the free movement of workers there was no need to uphold waiting-period requirements. The requirement of 'effective and genuine' work, however, cannot be applied to non-economic residents and it could thus be argued that host States do need waiting-period conditions in order to secure their financial interests.

Nonetheless, waiting-period requirements do not seem a serious alternative to the current financial means requirement. First, such requirements sit uneasily with the case law of the Court. In the context of the free movement of workers the Court has given due regard to the social assistance interests of the Member States. The Court has not done so by allowing States to discriminate against workers and their family members who have established residence in their territory, but rather by entitling States to refuse residence to workers who do not perform 'effective and genuine work'. More generally, the case law suggests that Member States can no longer protect their welfare state interests by making distinctions between lawful residents. These interests must be protected by using the remaining immigration powers. Translated to non-economic residents, this would imply that the social assistance interests of Member States must be secured by limitations on the right to reside rather than by exceptions to the right to equal treatment.

Second, international instruments such as the previously mentioned European Convention of Social and Medical Assistance do not seem to allow Member States to apply such durational residence requirements. Article 1 of the Convention expressly provides that the Contracting Parties must ensure that nationals of the other State parties who are lawfully residing within their territory and who are without sufficient resources, are entitled to social assistance under the same conditions as the States' own nationals. The principles enshrined in international instruments such as the European Convention must be regarded as general principles of Community law, which are protected by Community law.[337] The precise contours of the Court's 'human rights review' of Member State actions are still quite unclear,[338] but it would be rather 'odd' if the Court were to condemn the financial means requirement for the right to reside on the ground that they can secure their financial interests by a 'prohibited' alternative.

If waiting-periods, and as one may assume exportability of social assistance,[339] are no serious options, then there only seems one judicial option left for

---

[337] Ch 2, s 7 (n 237).

[338] Craig and de Búrca, *EU Law—Text, Cases & Materials* (1998) at 318.

[339] 339 The question could be raised, however, whether Art 18(1) EC precludes national rules limiting the export of social assistance. The rulings in *Martínez Sala* and *Grzelczyk* demonstrate that *Lair* and *Brown* have been overruled in the sense that one can no longer claim that Community citizens can be denied social benefits on the grounds that social policy does not as such fall within the scope of the Treaty. Further, the judgment in *Elsen* (2000) shows that Community citizens can invoke Art 18(1) EC against their own State in order to challenge national rules which are disadvantageous to Community citizens who wish to exercise their non-economic free movement rights. Case C–135/99 *Elsen* [2000] ECR I–10409, 34–6.

Nonetheless, it does not seem very likely that the Court would accept a right to export social assistance benefits on the basis of Art 18(1) EC. In fact, the judgment in *Snares* strongly suggests that the Court has already ruled out that option. It may be recalled that the Court was asked in this case whether the Community legislator has exceeded its powers in the field of the free movement of workers by inserting Art 10a in Reg 1408/71. The Court answered in the negative. Some additional observations of the Court suggest that the Court would have ruled similarly if the national court had asked whether Art 10a is compatible with Art 18.EC. The Court recognised that Community

extending the free movement rights of 'needy' Community citizens: the 'simple' invalidation of the financial means requirement. Against the conclusion that the requirements are incompatible with Article 18(1) EC two basic objections could be made.

The first is that it is too 'risky' to grant the 'poor' a right of residence without giving the Member States some kind of legal tool for protecting themselves against 'social tourism'. On the basis of the discussion of the American jurisprudence on the freedom of movement for persons in need of welfare benefits in Section 9, one could question whether there is any real risk. In *Saenz v. Roe* (1999) the Court concluded that welfare waiting-period requirements are unconstitutional. This conclusion formally rested on the Citizenship Clause of the Fourteenth Amendment which does not 'allow for . . . degrees of citizenship based on the length of residence', but in its ruling the Court clearly indicated that it also saw no 'economic need' for the requirements. As argued in Section 9.2.2, there are reasons to believe that European citizens are not so likely to move in large numbers to other States and that, even if they did appear more mobile than expected, it could be questioned whether the funding of the 'net-importers' of 'needy' Union citizens would be seriously affected. If, as the Supreme Court calculated in *Saenz*, an among 'needy' Americans a quite popular State as California could secure the funding of its benefit systems by reducing benefits by 72 cents per month, then it does not seem wholly unrealistic to conclude that a possible invalidation of the financial means requirements in the European Community would not disrupt the financing of the benefit schemes of the more generous European Member States. Certainly, the possibility cannot be excluded that some States will lower, or refuse to increase, benefits because they fear an influx of free-riding social assistance recipients. Yet, is a mere fear a good enough reason for denying the less well off Union citizens the fundamental right to move to other Member States? Furthermore, if social tourism were to occur and if States were indeed to respond by increasing taxes, taxpayers might decide to move elsewhere and this may again be a reason for States to choose the option of lowering benefit levels. Yet, would this not be a reason to impose limits on the free movement rights of these taxpayers rather than on the right of those in need of social assistance benefits?[340] There is no guarantee that

citizens could be refused a right of residence in another Member State if they, contrary to the requirement laid down in Art 1 of Dir 90/365 on a right of residence for pensioners, did not receive a pension. The non-exportability of mixed benefits could have the effect of diminishing the financial means of persons like Mr Snares. According to the Court, however, this was only the result of the differences between national social security systems. Case C–20/96 *Snares* [1997] ECR I–6057, 55. *Snares* concerned a Community provision applying to mixed benefits, but the encore given by the Court would seem to imply that the Court is not willing to accept that national rules making eligibility for minimum subsistence benefits conditional upon residence in the national territory run counter to Art 18(1) EC. This provision, so it seems, does not require the exportability of social benefits. Cp O'Leary (1996) n 93 above, at 131.

[340] Cp Fox Piven, 'The Race Among the States in Welfare Benefits: A Comment' (1998) *Publius* 39–43.

social tourism will not occur. The recognition of a general, unconditional right to reside for all Union citizens could incite some citizens to move to other States for the sole purpose of collecting higher benefits. Yet, in the light of the American and previous European experiences, one doubts whether the number of free riders would be so great as to seriously affect social assistance schemes. The problems concerning welfare migration or social tourism seem far more symbolic than real.

A second objection to the conclusion that the financial means requirements are inconsistent with Article 18(1) EC, is that it ignores the intentions of the drafters of the Treaty.[341] By expressly stating that the free movement rights are 'subject to the limitations and conditions laid down in this Treaty and by the measures adopted to give it effect', the drafters had made it patently clear that Article 18(1) EC was not inserted in the Treaty with a view to bringing about substantive changes in the free movement regime. So far the question of the compatibility of the financial means requirements with Article 18(1) EC has never been addressed by the Community judiciary, but recent judgments suggest that the will of the drafters indeed constitutes a serious, and perhaps insurmountable, obstacle.

The Court of First Instance, for example, has already accepted the validity of the health insurance requirement mentioned in Directive No 90/364. In response to a claim by the former wife of Member State national employed by the European Community that the impossibility of obtaining sickness insurance in a Member State constitutes a restriction on her right to move freely, the Court held in *Kuchlenz-Winter* (1997) that Article 18 EC expressly provides that the right to reside is subject to the conditions and limitations laid down in secondary legislation. From Directives No 90/364 and No 90/365 it would clearly follow that persons who are not in active employment must have sickness insurance in order to claim a residence right.[342]

The recent judgment in *Kaba* (2000) suggests that the Court of Justice holds a similar view. In this case the Court was asked to determine whether Article 7(2) of Regulation No 1612/68 objected to a United Kingdom rule according to which spouses of United Kingdom nationals and persons who are 'settled' in the country, could apply for indefinite leave to remain under more favourable conditions than EEA nationals who have been issued a residence permit valid for five years. The Court answered that Member States are entitled to rely on any objective difference there may be between their own nationals and those of other Member States when they lay down the conditions under which leave to remain must be granted to spouses of such persons. The Court reached this conclusion because, as Community law stands at present:

---

[341] See, eg Kovar-Simon, 'La Citoyenneté européenne' (1993) *CDE* 284 *et seq*, at 295–300; Dollat, *Libre Circulation des Persones et Citoyenneté européenne: Enjeux et Perspectives* (1998) at 133 and the Opinion of Adv Gen La Pergola in Case C–356/98 *Kaba* [2000] ECR I–2623, 51–64.

[342] Case T–66/95 *Kuchlenz-Winter* [1997] ECR II–637, 47.

'The right of nationals of a Member State to reside in another Member State is not unconditional. That situation derives . . . from . . . Article 8a of the EC Treaty (now, after amendment, Article 18 EC) which, whilst granting citizens of the Union the right to move and reside freely within the Member States, expressly refers to the limitations and conditions laid down in the Treaty and by the measures adopted to give it effect'.[343]

The issue was not directly addressed by the Court, but the above observations do suggest that, at least in the near future, the Court is not likely to overrule the intentions of the drafters[344] by holding that financial means requirements, especially where they are applied as a condition for establishing residence in another Member State, are incompatible with Article 18 EC.

9.5 Conclusions

The conclusion to be drawn at the end of this section, and chapter, is one of disappointment. The financial means requirements contained in the 1990 residence directives for the non-economically active who are not able to provide for themselves imply a *de facto* denial of the right to reside in other Member States. From the perspective of Union citizenship such a denial is problematic, but chances that the situation will improve in the near future seem slim. The Community legislator is not likely to work on the issue at all and a judgment such as *Kaba* casts doubt as to whether the Court is willing to make a contribution. In the light of the wording of Article 18 EC, and the intentions of its drafters, it would not be incomprehensible, but it would be somewhat disappointing if the Court were to remain passive. In *Edwards*, *Shapiro* and *Saenz* the American Supreme

---

[343] Case C–356/98 *Kaba* [2000] ECR I–2623, 30. On *Kaba* see Peers, 'Dazed and Confused: Family Members' Residence Rights and the Court of Justice' (2001) *ELRev* 76–83.

[344] Cp also: *Baglieri* (1993) in which the Court was asked to interpret Art 14, which provides for the adoption of measures aimed at progressively establishing the internal market by 31 December 1992. In a Declaration annexed to the Final Act adopting the Single European Act it is expressly stated that the date of 31 December 1992 'does not create an automatic legal effect'. In answering the question whether Art 14 EC imposes on Member States from that date onward an obligation to admit persons who have been subject to compulsory insurance in another Member State to voluntary affiliation to their social security schemes, the Court held that such an obligation presupposes the harmonisation of social security legislation within the Community. Case C–297/92 *Baglieri* [1993] ECR I–5211, 16–17. Even though the Court did not refer to the Declaration, it would seem that the Court, just like Adv Gen Jacobs (Opinion of Adv General Jacobs in Case C–297/92 *Baglieri* [1993] ECR I–5211, 12), did not wish to interpret Art 14 EC in a way which runs directly counter to the intentions of the drafters.

Furthermore, in *Wijsenbeek* the Court was asked whether Arts 14 and 18 EC preclude national legislation that requires persons entering national territory to present a passport. The Court held that even if Community citizens were to enjoy a right to freedom of movement under Art 14 or Art 18 EC, they do not have a right to move freely and unconditionally within the Community. For as long as national immigration, visa and asylum policies have not been harmonised, Member States remain free to carry out identity checks at the internal frontiers of the Community in order to establish whether a person is a Community citizen having the right to move freely. Case C–378/97 *Wijsenbeek* [1999] ECR I–6207, 42–3.

Court assumed responsibility for strengthening the notion of United States citizenship, the right to freedom of movement and the legal status of the 'poor' by obliging the States to admit 'the free-riding poor' for residence and to grant them, upon arrival, welfare benefits. By doing so the Supreme Court expressly overruled Congress which had allowed States to deny 'newcomers' welfare benefits during an initial period of time because it was not persuaded that welfare waiting-periods were really necessary for protecting States' welfare interests. The legal and political settings in which the subject of freedom of movement for the 'poor' must be placed may differ, but from an economic-political perspective the issues concerning the 'wandering poor' on both sides of the Atlantic are in essence quite similar.[345] The problems of welfare migration and social tourism are not as serious as they are often presented and, for this reason, one might question whether there is a need to fully respect the intentions of the drafters of the Treaty on European Union on this point. The realisation of a general freedom that would also enable the 'poor' to reside in the Member State of their choice indeed may not be a task for the Court, and it is no doubt safer to configure Community law on freedom of movement as if the 'poor' were wholly mobile,[346] but it would be quite embarrassing if the Community as a whole, which claims to pursue social objectives and has formally introduced a common citizenship, is not able to solve a problem which seems more symbolic than real. When taken seriously, Union citizenship ought to be developed in such a way that both the 'rich' and the 'poor' can enjoy the rights that come with it.

---

[345] It has been argued that the 'sink or swim together' adagio in the United States does not hold true for the European Community. The realisation of a general right of residence for all Union citizens would first require the adoption of legislative measures concerning social security at Community level. Schrauwen, 'Annotation *Martínez Sala*' (1999) *SEW* 426–30, at 430. In *Baglieri* (1993) (see n 344 above) the Court indeed drew such a conclusion in relation to social insurance benefits (and Art 14 EC), but given the unlikelihood of excessive social tourism, one could question whether there is a need for such measures as regards social assistance benefits (and Art 18(1) EC).

[346] Cp Bertola *et al* (2000) n 319 above, at 105.

4

Health Care

The European Community's goal of realising a free movement of persons inevitably raises questions about the degree to, and the conditions under, which beneficiaries can obtain medical care in other Member States.

On the one hand, one might expect Community law to provide for quite extensive cross-border health care rights. The risk of becoming sick or a victim of an accident can occur at any moment and at any place, and health care is of such tremendous importance for health and life, that Community citizens might be deterred from exercising their free movement rights if these did not encompass a right to obtain the necessary medical facilities. Indeed, access to medical care in other Member States would seem to be a prerequisite for a free movement of persons that is practical and relevant. In reverse, freedom of movement might be crucial for medical reasons. By going to other States patients placed on waiting lists may be able to obtain the care they need 'on time,' residents of border regions could obtain treatment at a place closer to their home and the 'medical movement' abroad might enable patients to obtain types of treatment which are not available 'at home' but essential for their medical condition. Further, the costs of medical services and medicines are often so high that free movement and cross-border health care rights would lack practical meaning if Community citizens were required to bear all costs themselves. In brief, from the patients' perspective it would be 'ideal' if they could move to and claim medical benefits in any other Member State at the expense of the sickness fund or health institution they are affiliated to.

On the other hand, however, some limitations on cross-border care may be expected and required. Within the European Community, it is up to Member States to organise, finance and administer health care and insurance. If patients were wholly free to choose in which State they wish to obtain medical treatment, Member States may not be able to keep up their health systems. Member States that receive large numbers of foreign patients may be confronted with financial problems if they are not compensated in any way for the costs involved and they may face capacity problems such as waiting lists if they had to admit all foreign patients unconditionally. Further, if patients were free to shop around for medical services throughout the Community, and if Member States were obliged to bear all costs, health expenditure could increase and problems of under utilisation of health facilities 'at home' could occur.

The Community's goal of promoting freedom of movement may clash with the Member States' ability to maintain financially sound and adequate health care systems. The aim of this chapter is to explore how Community law has settled this conflict. To what extent, and under which conditions, are Community citizens and third country nationals who are publicly[1] insured in one of the Member States entitled to obtain medical benefits in other Member States? To what extent are the Member States entitled to protect their health care systems by imposing restrictions on cross-border care?

The chapter is structured as follows. Section 2 puts the subject of cross-border access to medical care in its proper context by describing (*i*) the main features of the Member States' public health care and insurance systems, (*ii*) the way States have traditionally regulated cross-border access to these systems, (*iii*) the various ways in which the European Community is involved in, or touches upon, health care and related issues and (*iv*) the main principles on which the health care provisions of EC Regulations No 1408/71 and No 574/72 are based. The subsequent section discusses the cross-border health care rights which economic residents (3.1), non-residents (3.2), non-economic residents (3.3) and third country nationals (3.4) enjoy under the afore mentioned regulations and, in as far as third country nationals are concerned, the social security provisions of the agreements that the Community and its Member States have concluded with third countries. Section 4 addresses the question whether, and to what extent, beneficiaries of the free movement of persons can claim additional health care rights under the Treaty's common market provisions. The fourth section is devoted to the judgments of the Court of Justice in the *Decker, Kohll* and *Geraets-Smits and Peerbooms* cases, which have provoked much debate in health care and insurance circles. The background to the cases, the judgments themselves as well as their possible implications are examined. Section 5 discusses the degree to which American constitutional law entitles individuals covered by public health care or insurance systems to acquire in other States medical treatment at the expense of the public insurer. Can the European Community learn some lessons from the United States as to how cross-border access to medical care is best regulated? The chapter will end with some concluding and evaluating observations (section 6).

2 HEALTH CARE AND THE EUROPEAN COMMUNITY

2.1 Health Care and Health Insurance Systems of the Member States

In economic terms medical care and products may be regarded as commodities which could be supplied by private actors operating in a purely commercial

---

[1] This study does not discuss cross-border health care rights of patients who are privately insured for health care. It is estimated, however, that approximately 95% of the European Union population is covered by a public health (insurance) system. Hermesse and Lewalle, *L'Accès aux Soins en Europe—Quelle Mobilité du patient?* (1993).

market. Not one of the Member States, however, has chosen to fully entrust the supply of medical care to the market and its principles of *laissez-faire* and free competition. Governments regulate and subsidise the health care sector, many of them have made insurance for medical care mandatory by law and in many Member States health care facilities are provided by State institutions. Apart from the fact that the private provision of medical care is not necessarily the most cost-efficient,[2] public intervention has been considered necessary for reasons of 'social justice.'[3]

First, governments have taken measures in order to ensure that medical benefits meet minimum quality requirements. Medic(in)al products can be marketed only when they meet health, safety and efficacy standards. Admission to health professions is made conditional upon the possession of diplomas which often can only be obtained after rather lengthy training and education and in pursuing their professions, doctors, pharmacists, nurses, etc. are bound to observe rules of professional conduct.

Secondly, governments have intervened in the market in order to ensure that all persons, including those living in the least populated regions, have access to doctors and hospitals at a place not too far from their home (geographic accessibility). For this purpose, comprehensive establishment and capacity policies have been developed in each of the Member States.

Third, medical care should be available for all persons regardless of their economic status (financial accessibility). Governments in each of the Member States have established public or collective health care and insurance systems to which the vast majority of the population is compulsorily affiliated. The systems

---

[2] See, eg: Hyman, *Public Finance—A Contemporary Application of Theory to Policy* (1999) ch 9 and Barr, *The Economics of the Welfare State* (1998) ch 12.

[3] Governments in all Member States have taken responsibility for ensuring that all 'members of society', regardless of their place of residence or economic status, have access to adequate health care. This responsibility has found legal recognition in a right to health care which is set forth in the constitutions and or legislation of most Member States (Leenen *et al*, *Trends in Health Legislation in Europe* (1986) at 5–7) as well as international human rights instruments (see, eg: Art 25 of the Universal Declaration of Human Rights, Art 12 of the International Covenant on Economic, Social and Cultural Rights and Art 11 of the European Social Charter; see also: Toebes, *The Right to Health as a Human Right in International Law* (1999) and Roscam Abbing, *International Organizations in Europe and the Right to Health Care* (1979)). See also: Hermans, 'Patients' Rights in the European Union—Cross-Border Care as an Example of the Right to Health Care' (1997) *EJPH* 11–17.
A number of specific policy objectives derive from this right to health care: 1. Adequacy and equity in access—all citizens should have access to at least a basic minimum of health care; 'equal treatment for equal need' must be the starting-point as regards publicly funded health services. 2. Income protection—patients should be protected from health care payments which could form a catastrophic threat to their income or wealth; health care payment should be related to the individuals' ability to pay. 3. Macro-economic efficiency—health expenditures should consume an appropriate fraction of the gross domestic product. 4. Micro-economic efficiency—considering the macro-economic limits, health outcome and consumer satisfaction should be as high as possible. 5. Freedom to choose health care providers. 6. Appropriate autonomy for health care providers. See also: Hurst, 'Reforming Health Care in Seven European Nations' (1991) *HA* 1–10, at 8–9.

of the Member States differ considerably,[4] but a distinction can be made between social insurance systems and national health services.

Social health insurance schemes can be found in the 'old' Member States now located in the geographical center of the Community, ie, the Benelux countries, Germany and France. In these countries the law determines the categories of persons who are compulsorily insured, the insurance premiums to be paid, the benefit package and the rules governing the administration of the systems. Often the whole population is compulsorily insured (eg, Belgium, France, the Netherlands for exceptional medical costs), but in some States (eg, Germany, the Netherlands for normal medical costs) only, albeit large, parts of the population are covered by the insurance schemes. The level of the premiums is usually income-related and calculated on the basis of the total yearly expenditure. The administration of the insurance systems is often integrated into the general social security system and entrusted to local (semi-)public bodies such as sickness funds.

Among the social health insurances a further distinction can be made between systems based on the principle of reimbursement and systems based on the benefits-in-kind principle. In States where the former principle is applied (eg, Belgium, Luxembourg), health insurance laws state that patients are entitled to the payment of the costs of medical care. Patients have to pay the doctor, therapist, etc. themselves and, upon presentation of a receipt, they are afterwards reimbursed by their sickness fund. In Member States which have opted for the principle of benefits-in-kind (eg, the Austria, Germany, the Netherlands) beneficiaries are entitled to obtain medical benefits from health practitioners who are directly paid by the competent health insurance institutions. Apart from possible co-payments, patients are not confronted with a medical bill.

The national health services, which exist in, eg, the United Kingdom, Ireland and most of the southern Member States, are not based on an insurance model in the technical meaning of the term. Traditionally, they are characterised by funding out of the public purse and public delivery of care in accordance with the principle of benefits-in-kind. Usually, the funding of national health services

---

[4] In spite of the numerous differences, there is a clear tendency towards convergence of the systems. Palm *et al*, *Implications of Recent Jurisprudence on the Co-ordination of Health Care Protection Systems* (2000) at 19 and Recommendation 92/442 of the European Council on the convergence of the objectives of social protection policies (OJ 1992 L 245).

For more detailed descriptions of the systems of the Member States see, eg: Jacobs and Goddard, *Social Health Insurance Systems in European Countries—The Role of the Insurer in the Health Care System: A Comparative Study of Four European Countries (2000)*; Palm *et al* (2000) above, at 14–24; Jakubowski and Busse, *Health Care Systems in the EU—A Comparative Study* (1998); van Kemenade, *Health Care in Europe 1997* (1997); Hermans *et al*, *Health Care in Europe after 1992* (1992); De Klein and Collaris, *The Choices in Care: A European Problem?* (1991); Casparie *et al*, *Competitive Health Care in Europe* (1990) Vreugdenhil and De Bruine, *Gezondheidszorg in Europa—Structuur en Financiering van de Gezondheidszorg in enkele Europese Landen* (1990); Schneider *et al*, *Gesundheitssysteme im internationalen Vergleich* (1989); De Klein and Collaris, *Sociale Ziektenkostenverzekeringen in Europees Perspectief* (1987) and Abel-Smith and Maynard, *De Organisatie, Financiering en Kosten van de Gezondheidszorg in de Europese Gemeenschap* (1978).

has a closed-end character. The oldest system is the British National Health Service, which is indeed largely funded out of tax-revenues and offers medical services to almost the entire population. The systems of the other countries are based on comparable concepts but they are often less universal in the sense that the benefit packages differ for various categories of beneficiaries. Generally, national health systems are more centralised than social insurance systems.

In all States, regardless of the specific form of their health care system, governments have regulated the prices of medical treatment and products and limited the benefits that the insured can obtain at the expense of the sickness fund or the health institution they are affiliated to. The basic, and from a medical perspective necessary, types of treatment are included in the insurance packages, whilst more 'luxurious' types of treatment such as cosmetic plastic surgery, dentistry and physiotherapy, are, depending on cost or price, often excluded. As regards medic(in)al products, some States use positive lists mentioning the products which can be received at the expense of the insurer. In other States negative lists exist that state the products the costs of which are not reimbursable.

Generally, patients are free to choose the doctor they wish to be treated by. In some cases, however, this choice has been limited. In the Netherlands, for instance, the insured can only choose among the health providers with whom their sickness fund has concluded a contract. If patients wish to obtain care from a non-contracted health provider, they must ask their sickness fund for a prior authorisation. Further, in some Member States general practitioners are subject to quota regulations which imply that they can only register and treat a defined number of patients. General practitioners, who have reached their quota, must refer new patients to other general practitioners. Furthermore, in some Member States such as the Netherlands and the United Kingdom patients can only obtain medical treatment from specialists established in hospitals upon referral by a general practitioner. In such States, general practitioners serve as gatekeepers who steer patients to the appropriate specialists and prevent trivial complaints being dealt with by specialists.[5]

In all Member States health care is in principle a public affair, but in recent years private elements have become increasingly important. First, private health insurers have entered the market offering persons not covered by social insurance systems (eg, self-employed persons, employees with a high income or certain categories of civil servants) the possibility of insuring themselves for health care or enabling patients to obtain insurance for health services which are not covered by the basic packages (eg, dental care). Private insurance differs from social insurance in that private insurers operate on a commercial basis in mutual competition with each other. In addition, governments intervene less in the private insurance sector. Premiums are not always fixed by law, they may be related to the individual risk of the insured and private insurers may be entitled to refuse to accept certain persons.

---

[5] Barr (1993) n 2 above, at 311 (as regards the United Kingdom).

Secondly, in many Member States there is an increase in the number of private institutions offering usually rather specialised health services which are not made available under the national public health care systems. Such institutions often operate wholly outside public health care systems. Third, in recent years private elements have increasingly been introduced within public health systems themselves. Health care systems are characterised by a rapid growth in costs.[6] In order to maintain health care systems, reforms are constantly under consideration by all Member States. The (proposed) reforms differ from State to State and have to be viewed in the context of the existing systems,[7] but a distinction can be made between 'macroeconomic' and 'micro-economic' reform plans.[8] The former concern the more general measures aimed at controlling the total expenditure of health care systems, whilst the latter involve efforts to improve quality of care and efficiency, to shift part of the costs onto patients and to introduce competition and free-market elements into the systems. Through competition providers and insurers should be encouraged to work more efficiently. The proposed reforms do not intend to achieve full competition but merely a form of what is called 'managed competition.' Competition should increase but only within limits set by governments.[9] Providers and insurers may have to work with fixed or limited budgets, but governments retain the task of controlling the price of health services, to ensure the quality of the facilities and to safeguard the (equal) accessibility of health care.

2.2 Conditions of Access

Member States' health care and insurance systems are based on the principle of territoriality. Two premises follow from this principle. First, health care is only accessible to lawful residents regardless of nationality.[10] In principle, non-residents and undocumented residents are excluded. This premise is not fully effectuated in all cases. For instance, visitors from other States who become ill or are the victim of an accident on the national territory are usually offered the

---

[6] There are many reasons for this. Among the most important ones are the ageing of the population (ie the older people get the more vulnerable they become to chronic diseases such as cancer, heart disease, rheumatism, etc), developments in medical technology (which increase the number of health services to be provided as well as the price of the services) and the growing number of unemployed and disabled people. De Klein and Collaris (1986) n 4 above, at 93–109.

[7] For an overview of the current reforms in the various Member States see, eg: Kirkman-Liff, 'Stelselwijzigingen in Enkele Andere Landen'in Elsinga and van Kemenade, *Van Revolutie naar Evolutie* (1997) ch 7 and Langer, 'Probleme der Koordinierung beim Public/Privat-Mix von Gesundheitsleistungen' (1999) *ZSR* 716–34.

[8] Van Kemenade (1997) n 4 above, at 170–1.

[9] Cp Palm *et al* (2000) n 4 above, at 23–4.

[10] Cp von Maydell, 'Treatment of Third Country Nationals in the Member States of the European Union and the European Economic Area in Terms of Social Law' in *Commission of the European Communities/Departemento de Relações Internacionais e Convenções de Segurança Social, Social Security in Europe—Equality Between Nationals and Non-Nationals* (1995) 139–54, at 148–9.

care necessary to protect their health or life, whilst persons who have not resided in the State territory for a minimum period of time are often denied access to certain, usually rather expensive, types of treatment.[11]

The second premise entails that residents should obtain medical care from providers established on the national territory. In principle, the costs of medical care received abroad must be paid by the patients themselves. As a rule, sickness funds and health institutions only pay the 'foreign medical bill' (*i*) in cases of medical emergencies occurring abroad,[12] (*ii*) when an agreement to this effect has been concluded with the State or the health institution in question or (*iii*) when they have given patients prior authorisation for obtaining treatment abroad. In principle, no right to obtain such permission for treatment abroad exists. States are free to pursue their own 'authorisation policies' and, although differences exist,[13] such policies are generally very restrictive. Authorisation for treatment abroad is a rarely given privilege.

For the purposes of the subject of this chapter, it is significant to establish why Member States apply the territoriality principle and, in particular, why they are reluctant to bear the costs of medical treatment which their 'own' patients have obtained abroad. At the risk of oversimplification, three reasons can be given.

First, the territorial limitation of the right to obtain medical benefits is seen as a guarantee of quality. Each Member State has established its own minimum requirements as to the education of doctors, nurses, pharmacists, etc.; hospitals can only operate when they meet certain quality criteria and medic(in)al products must satisfy health, safety and efficacy standards before they can be marketed. Member States would not be able to guarantee the quality of medical care if patients were free to obtain medical care and/or products in other States where different standards are applied.

Secondly, if patients could freely decide in which State they wish to obtain medical care and products, many of them might wish to obtain care and

---

[11] In the United Kingdom, for instance, access to health care is based on residence, but only persons who have resided in the United Kingdom for more than a year are regarded as residents under the laws and regulations governing the National Health Service. The Netherlands has applied comparable rules. Persons who have established residence in the Netherlands have during the first twelve months no right to various expensive types of intramural care in case they were already receiving, or could have foreseen that they would be in need of, such forms of treatment the moment they establish residence in the Netherlands. See also: Jorens, *De Rechtspositie van niet-EU-onderdanen in het Europese Socialezekerheidsrecht* (1997) at 242–3.

[12] Such cases of medical emergency are often regulated in bi- or multilateral agreements that impose on the host State an obligation to give the necessary care and on the State of residence or insurance a duty to reimburse the expenses incurred. See, eg: Art 21(1) of the 1972 European Convention on Social Security and Art 4(1) of the 1980 European Agreement concerning the Provision of Medical Care during Temporary Residence. On the latter agreement see, eg: Creutz, 'The European Agreement Concerning the Provision of Medical Care during Temporary Residence' (1985) *ISSRev* 38–45 and Schreiber, 'Europese Overeenkomst betreffende het Verlenen van Geneeskundige Verzorging bij Tijdelijk Verblijf' (1981) *Info RIZIV* 199–203.

[13] For an overview see, eg: Palm *et al* (2000)n 4 above, at 46–65 and Kesteloot *et al*, 'The Reimbursement of the Expenses for Medical Treatment Received by 'Transnational' Patients in EU-countries' (1995) *HP* 43 *et seq*.

products which they cannot obtain at home, which are not covered by their insurance package or which are far more expensive than the benefits available at home. If the insured were to have the right, they might shop around for the most expensive types of care and products. The Member States' autonomy in deciding the types of treatment and products the costs of which they wish to bear could be affected and, because of higher costs of foreign medical care and products,[14] sickness funds may be unable to pay the medical bills out of the health contributions they receive.

Lastly, medical care must be obtained 'at home' in order to protect the infra-structure of health care systems. Member States not only determine which types of treatment should be available in the national territory. They also decide how many of the various facilities must be present. For each number of inhabitants, a certain number of general practitioners must be available and in order to offer adequate care, a specific number of hospital beds must be present. The number of facilities must be adequate. Under capacity, as reflected in waiting lists, must be avoided. At the same time, there should not be too many facilities. Overcapacity implies an unnecessary waste of financial and human resources. In order to determine over a longer period of time how many facilities must be made available, States need to know how many patients will make use of their care systems. If patients were free to choose treatment in other Member States, adequate capacity planning 'at home' would be virtually impossible.

2.3 Health Care and the Common Market

Within the European Community it is up to the Member States to organise, finance and administer health care and health insurance.[15] Community institu-tions do hold certain powers in the field of public health[16] but these do not

---

[14] The prices of medical products and services in the various Member States differ considerably. See, eg: Euzeby, 'Le Financement de la Protection sociale dans les pays de la CEE: Problèmes et Perspectives' in X, *Quel Avenir pour l'Europe sociale: 1992 et Après* (1990) 133 *et seq* and Euzeby, 'Financement de la Protection sociale, Efficacité économique et Justice sociale' (1997) *RMC* 253 *et seq*.

[15] Cp Case C–158/96 *Kohll* [1998] ECR I–1931 at 17–18 and Case C–70/95 *Sodemare* [1996] ECR I–3422 at 27. See also the Resolution of the Council and the Ministers for Health, meeting within the Council of 11 November 1991 concerning fundamental health policy choices (91/C 304/05—OJ 1991 C 304) in which it is emphasised that 'it is a matter for the Member States to determine the organ-isation and funding of health-care systems and to make fundamental health policy choices'.

[16] Public health policy is primarily concerned with preventive measures aimed at improving the health of the population or avoiding sickness and illness. For a discussion on the meaning of the term public health and related concepts see in particular Berg, *Gesundheitsschutz als Aufgabe der EU* (1997) at 40–77.

Prior to 'Maastricht', the EEC Treaty did not provide for specific Community powers in the field of public health. Issues concerning public health did arise, however, in various substantive policy areas such as environmental policy and social policy. See also: van der Mei and Waddington, 'Public Health and the Treaty of Amsterdam' (1998) *EJPH* 129–54 and Berg (1997) above.

Since the mid-1970s, and especially the mid-1980s, the Council and the 'Ministers of Health Meeting within the Council' have also taken measures solely and directly aimed at promoting or

entitle them to intervene in the internal organisation of the national health care and insurance systems. Article 152(5) EC, as inserted by the Amsterdam Treaty, explicitly provides that Community action in the field of public health shall fully respect the responsibilities of the Member States with regard to the organisation and delivery of health services and medical care.[17] This is not to say that health care and health insurance are free from Community involvement. The mere fact that health care and insurance have not been brought within the ambit of the Treaty does not free the national rules in these areas from the limits imposed by Community law, and common market rules in particular. The territoriality of health care and insurance schemes may conflict with the free movement and competition provisions of the EC Treaty. Indeed, virtually all 'actors' in the health sector (insurance organisations, providers of care, governments, pharmaceutical companies, patients, etc.) may benefit

protecting public health. Typical examples are the action programmes 'Europe against Aids' (OJ 1991 L 175) and 'Europe against Cancer' (OJ 1992 C 289). See also: Berg (1997) above and Massart-Pierard, 'Vers une Politique Commune de la Sante?' in Massart-Pierard (ed) *L'Europe de la Santé. Hasard et and ou Nécessité?* (1988) at 27 *et seq.*

The various initiatives have ultimately led to an amendment of the Treaty. The Treaty on European Union added the raising of 'the quality of life' to the list of Community objectives in Art 2 EC, it included in Art 3 EC the phrase that the activities of the Community 'shall include . . . a contribution to the attainment of a high level of health protection' (sub o) and it inserted an Art 129 which empowered the Community institutions to develop a common public health policy. The common measures and activities were aimed at supporting and coordinating the national public health policies and they oblige the Community institutions, within their own 'spheres of influence', to consider public health requirements and issues. On Art 129 EC see Verwers, 'Towards a New EC Health Policy?' in *European Public Health Association, Uniting Public Health in Europe* (1992) 11–14.

In response to the BSE crisis and other food related issues such as the concerns about the sale of genetically modified soya and American beef treated by hormones, the Treaty of Amsterdam has reformulated the public health provision (renumbered as Art 152) entirely. The aims of the Community in the field have been defined more broadly and powers have been extended, even though Art 152 EC is still imbued with the notion of subsidiarity. On the implications of 'Amsterdam' for public health policy see Barents, *Het Verdrag van Amsterdam in Werking* (1999) 203–10; van der Mei and Waddington (1998) above and Roscam Abbing, 'Volksgezondheid in het Verdrag van Amsterdam—Een Beknopte Analyse' (1998) *NTGR* 75–80.

On the European Union's role in the field of public health see Communication from the Commission to the Council, the European Parliament, the Economic and Social Committee and the Committee of the Regions—Proposal for a Decision of the European Parliament and of the Council adopting a programme of Community Action in the Field of Public Health (2001–2006) (COM(2000) 285 final; Belcher, *The Role of the European Union in Healthcare* (1999) 16–46 and Closon *et al*, 'Public Health Policy in the European Community' in Holland and Mossialos (eds), *Public Health Policies in the European Union* (1999) 49–67.

[17] Further, Art 152(4) EC expressly excludes the power to harmonise the laws and regulations of the Member States with a view to pursuing public health objectives. Case C–376/98 *Germany v Parliament and Council* [2000] ECR I–8419 at 77. On this case, in which the Court annulled Council Dir 98/43 on the approximation, regulations and administrative provisions of the Member States relating to advertising and sponsorship of tobacco products, and the question to what extent Art 95 EC can be used for harmonisation measures aimed at protecting public health, see, eg: Hervey, 'Up in Smoke? Community (Anti-)Tobacco Law and Policy' (2001) *ELRev* 101–25; Mortelmans and Ooik, 'Het Europese Verbod op Tabaksreclame: Verbetering van de Interne Markt of Bescherming van de Volksgezondheid?' (2001) *AA* 114–30 and Barents, 'De Tabaksrichtlijn in Rook Opgegaan' (2000) *NTER* 327–33.

from, or have to consider limits imposed by, the law governing the common market.[18]

First, medicines,[19] medical equipment and medical products[20] constitute goods for the purposes of Articles 28 (formerly 30) EC. Consequently, once they have been lawfully marketed in one of the Member States, medic(in)al products ought to be freely saleable throughout the Community. The free trade objective, however, is not absolute. National rules that make the marketing of medical products subject to quality, safety and efficacy requirements can be justified on the basis of Article 30 (formerly 36) EC when, and in as far as, necessary for protecting the health and life of humans and for as long as no harmonisation measures have been adopted at Community level.[21] Furthermore, Article 30 EC, in principle,[22] does not object to the application of national health insurance rules that determine which products will be or will not be reimbursed by public insurers. In *Duphar* (1984) the Court accepted that Member States may adopt rules intended to govern 'the consumption of pharmaceutical products in order to promote the financial stability of their health care insurance schemes' and that

---

[18]　A comprehensive overview of the impact of the common market rules in the health care and insurance fields would go far beyond the scope of this section. For more detailed discussions as to where common market rules and health care may 'meet' see, eg: Hollmann, 'Der Einfluss der EG auf das Gesundheitswesen der Mitgliedstaaten' (1998) *ZIAS* 180–214; Dommers, 'An Introduction to European Union Health Law' (1997) *EJHL* 19–41; ter Kuile, *Onzekerheden over de Invloed van Gemeenschapsrecht op de Nationale Gezondheidszorg* (1997); Hermans, *Europese Unie en de Gezondheidszorg—De Gevolgen van de Eenwording voor de Nederlandse Gezondheidszorg* (1994); Roscam Abbing, 'Patiënt en Gezondheidszorg in het Recht van de Europese Gemeenschap (1993); du Pré and Sevinga, De Gemeenschap en de Gezondheidszorg: een Terreinverkenning' (1990) *SEW* 350–78 and ter Kuile, 'Nationale Gezondheidszorg en Gemeenschapsrecht' (1989) *TvG* at 275–91.

[19]　See, eg: Case 238/82 *Duphar* [1984] ECR 523;Case 215/87 *Schumacker* [1989] ECR 617 and Case C–320/93 *Ortscheit* [1994] ECR I–5243.

[20]　Case C–120/95 *Decker* [1998] ECR I–1831.

[21]　In particular for medicinal products, a whole set of harmonisation measures has been adopted. In order to ensure the twin goals of protecting public health and bringing about freedom of movement for medical products Community institutions have, since the mid-1960s adopted various harmonisation measures. See Dir 65/65 (OJ Engl Spec Ed 1965–1966 at 20—harmonisation of national rules concerning authorisation for medical products); Dir 75/318 (OJ 1975 L 147—harmonising national requirements for supporting documents to be included with an application for authorisation); Dir 75/319 (OJ 1975 L 147—mutual recognition of authorisation decisions; the so-called multi-state and consultation procedures); Dir 83/570 (OJ 1983 L 332—European standard summary of product characteristics) and Dir 87/21 (OJ 1987 L 15—procedure for abridged application).

In 1995 the multi-state and consultation procedures were replaced by a decentralised (Dir 93/93, OJ 1993 L 214—obligation to grant authorisation unless there is a risk to public health) and a centralised procedure (Dir 2309/93, OJ 1993 L 214—common authorisation granted by the European Agency for the Evaluation of Medicinal Products). See also: Gardner, 'The European Agency for the Evaluation of Medicines and European Regulation of Pharmaceuticals' (1996) *ELJ* 48–82 and Broekmans *et al*, 'Europees Geneesmiddelenbeleid in Ontwikkeling' in Roscam Abbing and van Berkestijn, *Gezondheidsbeleid in Europa* (1995) 109–27.

On the free movement of medicines see also: Geddes, 'Free Movement of Pharmaceuticals within the Community: The Remaining Barriers' (1991) *ELRev* 295 *et seq*; Hancher, 'The European Pharmaceutical Market: Problems of Harmonisation' (1990) *ELRev* 9 *et seq* and Hancher, 'Creating the Internal Market for Pharmaceutical Medicines—An Echternach Jumping Procession' (1991) *CMLRev* 821 *et seq*.

[22]　But see: s 4.3.6.3.

States 'may, in order to limit costs, prepare limitative lists excluding certain medical products from the reimbursement scheme in their sickness laws.'[23]

Further, health care providers such as doctors, nurses and pharmacists can benefit from provisions on the free movement of persons and services. These professionals are entitled to take up employment, to establish themselves as self-employed persons and to provide medical services in other Member States.[24] The medical professions are subject to detailed professional rules and strict educational requirements, which vary from State to State and, thus, may act as a brake on the exercise of free movement rights by medical professionals.[25] Many of these barriers, however, have been surmounted by directives on the mutual recognition of diplomas.[26] Private hospitals, clinics and private (health) insurance companies

---

[23] Case 238/82 *Duphar* [1984] ECR 523 at 16 and Case C–249/88 *Commission v Belgium* [1989] ECR I–1275 at 31. The same principle applies to medical and hospital treatment. Case C–157/99 *Geraets-Smits and Peerbooms* [2001] ECR I–5473, 87. No harmonisation measures have been adopted for such reimbursement rules. The same holds true for national rules on the pricing of medical products. The absence of harmonisation of these rules has triggered the phenomenon of 'parallel imports'. On parallel imports and the rights of trade-mark holders to prevent marketing by others of medicinal products see, eg: Case C–201/94 *Ex Parte: Smith and Nephew Pharmaceuticals Ltd* [1996] ECR I–5819; Case 215/87 *Schumacker* [1989] ECR 617; Case C–347/89 *Eurim-Pharm* [1991] ECR I–1747; Case C–320/93 *Ortscheit* [1994] ECR I–5243; Joined Cases C–427/93, C–429/93 and C–436/93 *Bristol-Myers Squibb* [1996] ECR I–3457 and Case C–379/97 *Upjohn* [1999] ECR I–6927. For a summary of the relevant case law see the Opinion of Adv Gen Jacobs in Case C–443/99 *Merck* [2002] ECR I–0000, 15–53.

[24] See, eg: Case 246/80 *Broekmeulen* [1981] ECR 2311; Case 96/85 *Commission v France* [1986] ECR 1475 and Case 131/85 *Gül* [1986] ECR 1573. See also: Oosterman-Meulenbeld, 'Quality Regulation on Professional Health Care Practitioners in the European Community' (1993) *LIEI* 61 et seq.

[25] See, eg: the recent ruling in *Mac Quen* (2001) in which the Court held that Member States are under Art 43 EC entitled to protect public health by reserving the right to carry out eyesight-examinations to professionals holding specific qualifications, such as ophthalmologists, to the exclusion of opticians who are not qualified as medical doctors. Case C–108/96 *Mac Quen* [2001] ECR I–837.

[26] From the early Community years, it has been recognised that the existence of different national educational systems, each issuing their own diplomas and qualifications, constituted an obstacle to the free movement of persons. The Community legislator has therefore taken various initiatives aimed at the mutual recognition of diplomas.

Initially, Community institutions followed a 'vertical approach' which implied that separate mutual recognition directives were developed for separate professions. Among the first professions for which measures were adopted were doctors (the original Dirs 75/362 and 75/363—OJ L 167) (see also: Wägenbauer, 'La libre Circulation des Médicins dans la Communauté européenne—Problèmes actuels' (1976) *CDE* 707–35)—and the current Dir 93/16—OJ 1993 L 165), nurses (Dirs 77/452 and 77/453—OJ 1977 L 176), dentists (Dirs78/686 and 78/687—OJ 1978 L 233), veterinarians (Dirs No 78/1027 and 78/1028—OJ 1978 L 362—see Wägenbauer, 'L'Europe des Vétérinaires' (1979) *RTDE* 653–63), midwives (Dirs80/154 and 80/155—OJ 1980 L 33) and pharmacists (Dirs 85/432 and 85/433—OJ 1985 L 253—see, eg: Kraus, *Niederlassungsfreiheit der freien Berufe in der Europäischen Gemeinschaft unter besonderer Berücksichtigung der Apotheker* (1989)).

The adoption of these directives, however, proved to be a slow and time-consuming process partly because Member States insisted on first harmonising the educational systems before agreeing to the mutual recognition of diplomas. In the wake of the Community's initiatives to create the Internal Market by the end of 1992, another approach to the mutual recognition of diplomas was adopted. The goal of the mutual recognition of diplomas was no longer pursued on a sector-by-sector basis. Dir 89/48 established a general system for the recognition of diplomas (OJ 1989 L 19) and Dir 92/51 introduced a second general system for the recognition of professional education and training to supplement Dir 89/48 (OJ 1992 L 209). These 'horizontal' directives are based on the

can in principle benefit from Articles 43 and 49 EC. Member States, however, are entitled to impose certain conditions on the exercise of such companies' activities. In principle, national licence systems for the establishment of health care institutions are consistent with Community law provided they are applied without distinctions based directly or indirectly on nationality[27] and, as the Court held in *Sodemare* (1997), Member States are entitled to make the admission of private companies in 'social welfare systems of a health care nature' subject to the condition that they are non-profit making.[28]

Further, by virtue of Articles 39(3), 46 (formerly 56) and 55 (formerly 66) EC Member States are entitled to limit the exercise of free movement rights

starting-point that higher education diplomas awarded on the completion of professional education and training of at least three years' duration should in principle be recognised in another Member State when the holder wishes to obtain access to a certain profession in that Member State.

On the Community measures on the mutual recognition of diplomas with special reference to health professionals see, eg: Roscam Abbing, 'Quality of Medical Practice and Professional Misconduct in the European Union' (1997) *EJHL* 273–8; Roscam Abbing, 'The Right of the Patient to Quality of Medical Practice and the Position of Migrant Doctors within the EU' (1997) *EJHL* 347–60; du Pré, 'Public and Private Harmonisation of Vocational Training Qualifications in the EC: The Case of Denturists' (1996) *EJHL* 273–93; Schneider, *Die Anerkennung von Diplomen in der Europäischen Gemeinschaft* (1995), in particular 99–160; Oosterman-Meulenbeld (1993) n 24 above; Hurwitz, *The Free Circulation of Physicians within the European Communities* (1990) and van der Mijn, Kansen en Bedreigingen voor Beroepsbeoefenaren bij een Vrije Europese markt, (1989) *T v G* 305–15.

Furthermore, the aforementioned obstacles have been partly surmounted by the Court of Justice which has given a broad interpretation of the prohibitions contained in the Arts 39 (formerly 48), 43 (formerly 52) and 49 (formerly 59) E(E)C. See, eg: Case C–340/89 *Vlassopoulou* [1991] ECR I–2357; Case C–319/92 *Haim I* [1994] ECR I–425; Case C–234/97 *Fernández de Bobadilla* [1999] ECR I–4773 and Case C–238/98 *Hocsman* [2000] ECR I–6623. In these cases the Court recognised that individual Member States are in principle entitled to prescribe the knowledge and qualifications needed in order to pursue a certain occupation or to obtain access to further education, and that they, for this purpose, may require the possession of certain qualifications. The Court added, however, that the authorities of Member States to whom an application has been made by a Community national for authorisation to practice a profession must take into consideration all diplomas, certificates and other evidence of formal qualifications of the person concerned and his relevant experience by comparing the specialised knowledge and abilities so certified and that experience with the knowledge and qualifications required by national rules.

[27] Harmonisation directives have not been adopted. It should be pointed out, however, that the transnational establishment of health institutions and the provision of medical services in other Member States has so far been relatively rare. Ter Kuile (1989) n 18 above at 284. Private health insurers have to observe the three non-life insurance directives. Dir 73/239 (OJ 1973 L 228); Dir 88/357 (OJ 1988 L 172) and Directive 92/49 (OJ 1992 L 228). These directives regulate technical insurance matters like solvability and liquidity requirements, competition, the possibility of operating an insurance company in other Member States, the protection of consumers, etc. Art 54 of Dir 92/49 provides that Member States in which private health insurance serves as a partial or complete alternative to health cover provided by the statutory social security system may require that those insurances comply with the specific legal provisions adopted by that State to protect the 'general good'. See also: Hamilton, 'Interne Markt en (Aanvullende) Ziektekostenverzekeringen' (2001) *NTGR* 37–48 and Withers, 'The Concept of General Good in European Jurisprudence' in Alliance Nationale des Mutualités Chrétiennes/Association Internationale de la Mutualité, *Competition and Solidarity—Can They Co-exist in Europe's Health Care Systems?* (1997) 91–7.

[28] Case C–70/95 *Sodemare* [1997] ECR I–3395 at 32.

on grounds of inter alia public health. According to Article 4 of Directive No 64/221,[29] restrictions on entry to or residence in the territory of another Member State can only be justified on public health grounds as regards (contagious) diseases or disabilities which are listed in an Annex to Directive No 64/221.[30] The exception, however, cannot be relied upon on for economic ends[31] or to exclude the public health sector from the free movement regime.[32]

Health professionals, hospitals and health insurers[33] may further be subject to limitations imposed by the competition rules contained in Articles 81 (formerly 85) and 82 (formerly 86) EC when, or in as far as, they can be classed as undertakings for the purposes of these Treaty provisions. The case law of the Court of Justice, and the judgment in *Poucet and Pistre* (1993) in particular, indicate that health care actors must be regarded as undertakings when they perform economic activities rather than activities embodying a notion of 'solidarity.'[34] Generally, health care providers and insurers do perform economic activities and this implies that they are in principle prohibited from concluding

---

[29] OJ 1963/1964 (Spec.Ed.), at 117.

[30] If, however, a disease or disability manifests itself after a first residence permit has been granted it cannot justify expulsion or a refusal to renew the said permit. Art 4(2) of Dir 64/221. The diseases are listed under two headings. The first concerns the contagious diseases which are listed in International Health Reg 2 of the World Health Organisation as being subject to quarantine. These include tuberculosis of the respiratory system in an active state or showing a tendency to develop; syphilis; other infectious diseases or contagious parasitic diseases if they are the subject of provisions for the protection of nationals of the host country. The second category contains diseases and disabilities that can justify exclusion or expulsion on the grounds of public policy or public security such drug addiction, profound mental disturbance, manifest conditions of psychotic disturbance with agitation, delirium, hallucinations or confusion.

In the literature it has been debated whether Member States are entitled to restrict the free movement rights of persons infected by the HIV-virus or suffering from AIDS. See, eg: Carlier and Schiffino, *The Free Movement of Persons with HIV/AIDS* (2000) at 32–48; Hendriks, 'The Right to Freedom of Movement and the Unlawfulness of AIDS/HIV Specific Travel Restrictions from a European Perspective' (1990) *NJIL* 86 *et seq*; Pais Maçedo van Overbeek, 'AIDS/HIV Infection and the Free Movement of Persons within the European Community' (1990) *CMLRev* 791–824 and Dworkin and Steyger, 'Aids Victims in the European Community and the United States: Are They Protected from Unjustified Discrimination?' (1989) *TexILJ* 295–329.

[31] Art 2 of Dir 64/221. The mere fact, however, that besides objective reasons based on public security or public health economic objectives are aimed at, does not necessarily exclude the possibility of relying on the exception. Cp Case 72/83 *Campus Oil* [1984] ECR 2727 at 36 and Case C–158/96 *Kohll* [1998] ECR I–1931 at 50–1. See also: s 4 of this chapter.

[32] Case 131/85 *Gül* [1986] ECR 1573 at 17 and Case C–158/96 *Kohll* [1998] ECR I–1931 at 46.

[33] Arts 81 and 82 EC are concerned with the conduct of undertakings, not with the laws and regulations of the Member States. However, the two Articles, read in conjunction with Art 10 EC, require Member States to refrain from introducing or maintaining in force measures which may render ineffective the competition rules applicable to undertakings. Case C–70/95 *Sodemare* [1997] ECR I–3395 at 41.

[34] Joined Cases C–159/91 and C–160/91 *Poucet and Pistre* [1993] ECR I–637. See also: Hermans *et al*, 'Zorgverzekeraars en Uitvoeringsorganen Sociale Zekerheid: Ondernemingen in het Licht van het EG-Recht' (1996) *SMA* 227–38.

agreements[35] or, where they hold a dominant position in the market, from abusing that position when this could affect trade between the Member States and distort competition.[36]

[35] It is only in recent years that the implications of the competition rules for the health care sector have become apparent. See, eg: the recent ruling in *van der Woude*. The case concerned an employee of a health care institution whose employment contract was governed by a collective labour agreement relating to medical treatment for the hospital sector. By virtue of this agreement Mr van der Woude was affiliated to a specific supplementary health insurance scheme, but he wished to be insured under another scheme which provided for lower insurance premiums and a broader insurance package. Mr van der Woude claimed that his employer should also contribute to the costs of supplementary insurance if he switched to the other scheme. The national court which had to decide the case was of the view that the employer could only be required to make such contributions when the relevant provisions of the collective labour agreement were void and it asked the Court of Justice whether these provisions were compatible with Arts 81 and 82 EC. The Court, applying and largely following its conclusions in Case C–67/96 *Albany* [1999] ECR I–5751 (see also: Gyselen, 'Annotation *Albany*' (2000) *CMLRev* 425–48 and Loozen, 'CAO's, Bedrijfspensioenen en het EG-Mededingingsrecht' (1999) *NTER* 274–84) concluded that agreements by employers to make fixed financial contributions to the costs of supplementary health insurances are not in principle covered and prohibited by Art 81(1) EC. Case C–222/98 *van der Woude* [2000] ECR I–7111 at 32. See also: Joined Cases C–180/98 to C–184/98 *Pavlov* [2000] ECR I–6451 and Loozen, 'Mededinging—Pavlov en van der Woude: Meer dan een Pavlov-Reactie' (2000) *NTER* 301–7.

Another case in which the Court was asked how competition rules must be applied in the health care sector was *Ferlini* (2000). The case involved a civil servant of the European Commission who was working in Luxembourg and affiliated to the common health insurance scheme for European civil servants (RCAM). For the delivery of his wife in a Luxembourg hospital Mr Ferlini was charged an amount which was higher than the tariff that was applied to persons covered by the Luxembourg public health insurance scheme. The national court had asked the Court of Justice to determine whether the decision of a hospital association that fixes scales of fees for hospital care for persons who are not affiliated to the national social security scheme, which are higher than those applied to residents who are affiliated to the national scheme, was prohibited by Art 80(1) EC. The Court decided the case solely under the heading of Art 12(1) EC, but in his Opinion in *Ferlini* Adv Gen Cosmas did address the competition provisions. He answered the preliminary question in the affirmative provided the national court could establish that the decision of the hospital association could affect intra-Community trade significantly. Opinion Adv Gen Cosmas of 21 September 1999 in Case C–411/98 *Ferlini* [2000] ECR I–8081 at 105–35. On Ferlini see, eg: van der Steen, 'Horizontale Werking van de Vier Vrijheden en van het Discriminatieverbod van Artikel 12 EG' (2001) *NTER* 4–9 and s 4.5 below.

On the importance of the competition rules for the health care sector see also: Bosco, *Are National Social Protection Systems under Threat? Observations on the Recent Case Law of the Court of Justice* (2000); Hervey, 'Social Solidarity: A Buttress Against Internal Market Law?' in Shaw (ed), *Social Law and Policy in an Evolving European Union* (2000) 31–47; Pieters, *De Nederlandse Zorgverzekering in het Licht van het Recht van de EG—Onderzoek naar de Verenigbaarheid van het Nederlandse Zorgstelsel met het Recht op Vrij Dienstenverkeer en het Europese Mededingingsrecht* (1999); Ballon and Pieters, *Het Europese Kartelrecht en de Ziekenfondsen* (1997); Pieters and van den Bogaert, *The Consequences of European Competition Law for National Health Policies* (1997) and du Pré, 'Klein Duimpje en de Nederlandse Ziektekostenverzekeringen' (1993) *SR* 138–41.

[36] Furthermore, also Dir 89/665 on the co-ordination of laws, regulations and administrative provisions relating to the application of review procedures to the award of public supply and public works contracts may have implications for the health care and insurance sectors. See, eg: Case C–76/97 *Tögel* [1998] ECR I–5357; van der Bend, 'Aanbestedingsrecht in de Gezondheidszorgsector—Verdient het Aanbestedingsrecht in de Gezondheidszorgsector meer Zorg?' (1999) *NTG* 359–69; Hermans and Buijsen, 'Aanbesteden van Medisch-Specialistische Zorg' (2000) *SR* 286–92 and Scheiffers, 'Openbare Aanbesteding van Zorgcontracten' in Essers and Scheiffers (eds), *Grensoverschrijdende Zorg—Marktwerking vs. National Zorgbewaking* (2000) 33–8.

For an application of (the exemption of Art 13 concerning exemptions for activities in the public interest of) the Sixth Dir 77/388 on the harmonisation of the laws of Member States relating to

2.4 Regulations No 1408/71 and No 574/72: Objectives and Basic Principles of the Rules on the Coordination of Health Care and Health Insurance Schemes

Just like the other actors in the health care and insurance sectors, patients may enjoy certain rights under the common market rules or the general provisions on freedom of movement and equal treatment. For instance, in *Luisi and Carbone* (1984) the Court held that Articles 59 (now 49) *et seq.* EC encompass a right to move to other Member States in order to receive services and the Court explicitly added that 'persons receiving medical treatment' must be regarded as recipients of services.[37] Further, in *Cowan* (1989) the Court held that when 'Community law guarantees a natural person the freedom to go to another Member State the protection of that person from harm in the Member State in question, on the same basis as the nationals and persons residing there, is a corollary of that freedom of movement.'[38] This observation, it could be argued,[39] implies a right to obtain emergency treatment for 'Community travellers.'

Until recently,[40] however, the general provisions on the free movement of persons, services and nondiscrimination did not seem to have much practical significance for patients. From the early Community years, Community institutions had recognised that a genuine freedom of movement not only requires that Community citizens who become in need of medical treatment during a temporary or more permanent stay in another Member State are entitled to obtain the required care. Such persons should also have the right to have the medical bill paid by the sickness fund or the health institution they are affiliated to. A mere right to equal treatment in other Member States did not seem to impose on the State where an individual is insured an obligation to pay 'foreign' medical bills. Special measures were deemed necessary in order to ensure that Community citizens retain insurance cover when moving to other Member States. For this purpose, the Community legislator adopted as far as back as in 1958 Regulations No 3 and No 4, which contained rules intended to co-ordinate the national health insurance schemes.[41] In the early 1970s, the regulations of 1958 were

turnover taxes to natural persons active in the health sector see, eg: Case C–216/97 *Gregg and Gregg* [1999] ECR I–4947.

[37] Joined Cases 286/82 and 26/83 *Luisi and Carbone* [1984] ECR 377 at 10 and 16. Cp also the ruling in *GB-INNO-BM* (1990) in which the Court held that a 'free movement of goods requires, particularly in frontier areas, that consumers resident in one Member State may travel freely to the territory of another Member State to buy goods' (and thus medic(in)al products: APvdM) 'under the same conditions as the local population'. Case C–362/88 *GB-INNO-BM* [1990] ECR I–667 at 8.

[38] Case 186/87 *Cowan* [1989] ECR 195 at 17.

[39] Cp O'Leary, 'The Principle of Equal Treatment on Grounds of Nationality in Art 6 EC— A Lucrative Source for Member State Nationals?' in O'Leary and Tiilikainen (eds), *Citizenship and Nationality Status in the New Europe* (1998) 105–36, at 112.

[40] See also: s 4.

[41] On the health care and insurance provisions of the original 1958 regulations see, eg: Troclet, *Europees Sociaal Recht—Institutioneel Kader, Rechtsinstrumenten, Sociale Problemen en hun Oplossing* (1971) 293–8.

replaced by the currently still[42] applicable Regulations No 1408/71 and No 574/72. The former regulation sets out the social security rights that beneficiaries enjoy, whilst the latter regulation contains the administrative rules governing cooperation between the social security institutions of the competent State and the 'providing' State.

In order to guarantee that beneficiaries of the free movement of persons are entitled to gain access to medical care at the expense of their health institution in other Member States, two sets of rules must be considered. The first consists of the rules laid down in Articles 13 *et seq.* of Regulation No 1408/71, which determine the State in which beneficiaries are insured. The so-called competent State is in principle the State where beneficiaries are employed. It is in the competent State that health contributions must be paid and it is the legislation of this State that determines which persons are insured, and the conditions under which they are insured.

The second set of rules is contained in Articles 18-36 of Regulation No 1408/71 (Title III—Chapter 1: 'Sickness and Maternity Benefits') and the accompanying provisions of Regulation No 574/72. The regulations' health care provisions are quite difficult to read, but they are based on two relatively simple principles. First, in all cases in which Regulation No 1408/71 provides for a right to obtain 'benefits in kind,' ie medical treatment, nursing, medicines, etc.,[43] in

---

[42] But see, s 3.7. On the two regulations in general see, eg: Keunen, *Schets van het Europees Socialezekerheidsrecht—Europese Coördinatieregels inzake Sociale Zekerheid* (2001); Pennings, *Introduction to EC Social Security Law* (2000); White, *EC Social Security Law* (1999); Voogsgeerd, *Vrij Verkeer en Sociale Zekerheid (1999); van Raepenbusch, Le Sécurité sociale des Personnes qui Circulent à l'Intérieur de la Communauté économique européenne* (1991); Jorens, *Wegwijs in het Europees Sociale Zekerheidsrecht* (1992) and, briefly, ch 2, s 6 of this book.

[43] In Arts 18–36 of Reg 1408/71 medical care and medical products are referred to as 'benefits in kind'. In addition, the Articles apply to 'cash benefits'. The fact that Arts 18–36 apply to both types of benefits is explained by the fact that they are often subject to the same legislation under national law. Keunen (2001) n 42 above, at 137. The co-ordination rules contained in Reg 1408/71 for the two types of benefits, however, differ considerably. For this reason it is significant to distinguish the concepts of 'benefits in kind' and 'cash benefits'.

Neither one of the terms is defined in the Regulation, but the case law provides for some clarification. In *Jordens-Voster* (1980) the Court indicated that it is of no relevance under what type of legislation the benefits are offered. Rights to medical care offered under national legislation relating to invalidity benefits must be regarded as 'benefits in kind' for the purposes of Arts 18–36 of Reg 1408/71. Case 69/79 *Jordens-Voster* [1980] ECR 75 at 8. Further, the term 'benefits in kind' may also consist of direct payments or the reimbursement of costs for medical treatment, medicines, etc; 'cash benefits' are designed to compensate for a worker's loss of earnings through illness. Case 61/65 *Vaassen* [1966] ECR 257 at 278. Payments that are intended as a contribution to the financing of insurance, however, do not fall within the meaning of the term 'benefits in kind'. Case 103/75 *Aulich* [1976] ECR 697 at 7 and Case C–73/99 *Movrin* [2000] ECR I–5625 at 41. There is an 'inherent contradiction between the concept of contribution and that of benefit. The first is a condition precedent to the creation of a right, the second presupposes the existence of a right'. Opinion of Adv Gen Gand in Case 33/65 *Dekker* [1965] ECR 901, at 909.

More recently, the Court was asked in *Molenaar* (1998) whether certain benefits made available under the German Care Insurance Law (*Pflegeversicherungsgesetz*) were to be regarded as cash benefits or as benefits in kind. The law was introduced to cover the costs of care needed by persons who are dependent on assistance from other persons in the performance of their daily routine. The benefits provided under the law could be provided, at the choice of the recipient, either in the form

other Member States, the costs must be paid by the institution to which beneficiaries have paid health premiums.[44] As a rule, this is the so-called competent institution. The institution of the 'providing State,' as follows from Article 36(1) of Regulation No 1408/71, shall be fully refunded[45] by the

of care dispensed by authorised bodies or in the form of a monthly allowance (the so-called *Pflegegeld*) which enables recipients to choose the form of aid they consider most appropriate to their condition. It was argued that the care allowance was aimed at allowing recipients to cover the payment of medical expenses and that it constituted a 'surrogate' of benefits in kind. Cp Bokeloh, 'Export von Pflegeleistungen innerhalb der Europäischen Union,' in *Zentrum für Europäischen Wirtschaftsrecht, Die Krankenversicherung in der Europäischen Union* (1997) 115–62, at 135–7. The Court did not agree. After it had referred to the fact that the *Pflegegeld* was granted period-ically, that it was fixed independently of the actual costs incurred and that recipients enjoyed free-dom in using the allowance, the Court concluded that the 'care allowance . . . takes the form of financial aid which enables the standard of living of persons requiring care must be improved as a whole, so as to compensate for the additional expense brought about by their condition'. The *Pflegegeld* was thus to be regarded as a cash benefit. Case C–160/96 *Molenaar* [1998] ECR I–1545 at 34–6.

On *Molenaar* see also: de Gans, 'Comment on *Molenaar*', (1999) *RZA* 252–60; Gassner, 'Pflegev-ersicherung und Arbeitnehmerfreizügigkeit' (1998) *NZS* 313–18; Koch, 'Die Entscheidung des EuGH zum Leistungsexport des Pflegegeldes vom 5. März 1998 (Rs C–160/96)' (1998) *ZFSH* 451–4 and van der Mei, 'Het Arrest Molenaar: Export van het Persoonsgebonden Budget?' (1998) *USZ* 407–12.

In response to the *Molenaar* judgment the Administrative Commission has adopted Decision 175 of 23 June 1999 (OJ 2000 L 47) replacing Decision 109 of 18 November 1977 (OJ 1978 C 125) in which the term 'benefits in kind' was defined more precisely.

Benefits such as the *Pflegegeld* do not necessarily have to be classed as sickness benefits. Where such benefits are linked to eg, old-age pensions they might have to be classed as old-age pensions. See Opinion of Adv Gen Alber in Case C–215/99 *Jauch* [2001] ECR I–1901 at 104. Disagreeing with its Adv Gen, however, the Court concluded in *Jauch* that the Austrian equivalent of the German *Pflegegeld* was also to regarded as a sickness benefit. Case C–215/99 *Jauch* [2001] ECR I–1901 at 35.

[44] Cp Stiemer, 'Sickness Insurance—Viewpoint of the EU-Member States' in Jorens and Schulte (eds), *Coordination of Social Security Schemes in Connection with the Accession of Central and Eastern European States* (1999) 225–53, at 228.

[45] Art 36 forms part of a section headed 'Reimbursement between Institutions'. The purpose of the provision is to make clear the financial consequences that flow from the fact that benefits in kind have been provided by the institution of one Member State on behalf of the institution of another Member State, so far as the relations between the institutions are concerned. Case C–389/99 *Rundgren* [2001] ECR I–3731 at 60–2. Art 36 does not confer rights to reimbursement upon insured persons. Case C–368/98 *Vanbraekel* [2001] ECR I–5363 at 54–6.

Art 36(2) of Reg 1408/71 provides that settlement takes place on the basis of production of proof of actual expenditure or lump sum payments. The specifics concerning reimbursement are worked out in further detail in Arts 93–5 of Reg 574/72. The starting-point is that the competent organ has to pay the actual costs of the care that is provided, ie, the tariffs applied by the providing institution, which are determined on the basis of the accounting of the institution that has provided the benefits. If the costs of the individual benefits do not follow from the accounting, reimbursement takes place on a lump sum basis. The lump sum is determined on the basis of all available information. The Administrative Commission assesses the grounds used to calculate lumps sums and fixes their amount. Decision 109 of 18 November 1977 (OJ 1978 C 125). For a more detailed description of the reimbursement rules see Stiemer (1999) n 44 above, at 240–1.

Finally, Art 36(3) authorises two or more Member States to waive reimbursement between their institutions, with the result that the repayment obligation is not enforced. The mere fact, however, that States have made use of Art 36(3) is of no consequence for purposes of interpreting Arts 18–36. Case C–389/99 *Rundgren* [2001] ECR I–3731 at 64.

competent institution.[46] Secondly, medical care is in all cases to be provided in accordance with the legislation of the State where the benefits are provided as though beneficiaries were insured under that legislation.[47] In the light of the first principle, one might possibly have expected that benefits in kind would also be provided in accordance with the legislation administered by the competent institution. However, such a rule would imply that the institution of the providing State has to apply the legislation of other Member States with which it is not likely to be familiar. For practical reasons the drafters of the Regulations have opted for the rule that medical care must be delivered in accordance with the legislation of the providing State.[48]

As a result of the two rules, movement to other Member States may work out favourably or unfavourably for the insured.[49] In cases where medical benefits are obtained in a Member State other than the competent State, it is of no relevance whether or not a given type of treatment or medic(in)al product is covered by the insurance package of the competent State. The competent institution has to pay for all benefits included in the package of the 'providing State.' For instance, frontier workers who are living in State A where dental care is covered by the applicable legislation, are entitled[50] to have the dental bill paid by the insurance institution in State B even if dental care is not covered by the legislation of State B. Frontier workers, however, who are insured in that same State A and who reside in the competent State B, are not entitled to have the bill paid even though they are in fact paying health contributions for dental care.

---

[46] Where several institutions of the same Member State can be regarded as the competent institution, it is for national law to determine how reimbursement will be provided. Cp Case 818/79 *Allgemeine Ortskrankenkasse Mittelfranken* [1980] ECR 2729 at 10.

[47] This second principle only applies to 'benefits in kind'. Cash benefits must be provided in accordance with the legislation of the competent institution and are thus exportable. In the *Molenaar* and *Jauch* cases (n 43 above), which both concerned workers residing outside the competent State, this (would have) implied that the workers could enjoy the care allowances. See also: van der Mei (1998) n 43 above, 407–12.

One of the most controversial issues as regards cash benefits concerns the medical examination of beneficiaries who are staying outside the competent State. According to Art 18 of Reg 574/72 it is in principle the institution of the State where the persons in question are staying that is responsible for the investigation. The results of the investigation must be sent to the competent institution, which has the right to have the persons concerned re-examined by a doctor of that institution's choice. If the competent institution does not make use of this right, it is bound in fact and in law by the findings of the institution of the place where the persons concerned reside as regards the commencement and the duration of the incapacity to work. Case 22/86 *Rindone* [1987] ECR 1339 at 15. The person concerned cannot be required to return to the competent State to undergo examination there. *Ibid*, at 22. Art 18 is also applicable where the sickness benefits must be paid by the employer. Case C–45/90 *Paletta I* [1992] ECR I–3423 at 23. The competent institution, however, is not bound by the findings of an institution in another Member State where it can prove that Art 18 has been abused. Case C–206/94 *Paletta II* [1996] ECR I–2357 at 28. See also: van der Steen, 'Controle bij Ziekte in het Buitenland' (1996) *NTER* 176–8 and Neumann-Duesberg, 'Krankenversicherung' in Schulte and Zacher, *Wechselwirkungen zwischen dem europäischen Sozialrecht und dem Sozialrecht der Bundesrepublik Deutschland* (1991) 83–109, at 96–102.

[48] Keunen (2001) n 42 above, at 146 and the Opinion of Adv Gen Jacobs in Case C–451/93 *Delavant* [1993] ECR I–1545.

[49] Bokeloh (1997) n 43 above, at 156.

[50] s 3.1.2.

Furthermore, it is of no relevance whether the price of medical benefits in other States is higher than the prices in the competent State. In all cases, the competent institution must fully reimburse the institution of the 'providing State' for the costs it has incurred. Thus, frontier workers who have received in the State of residence medical care which is far more expensive than the care offered in the competent State, are entitled to have the entire bill, which is calculated on the basis of the tariffs applicable in the 'providing State,' paid by their insurance body.[51]

The various rights to obtain, at the expense of the competent institution, medical benefits in Member States other than the competent State are conditional upon fulfillment of administrative formalities.[52] These formalities differ but generally consist of an obligation upon beneficiaries to request a certified statement (one of the so-called E-forms)[53] from the competent institution, which indicates that they are indeed insured for medical care, the period during which medical benefits may be obtained in other Member States and/or the types of benefits for which the institutions is willing to pay the costs. The statement must be submitted to the competent health institution in the host Member State,

---

[51] In reverse, the movement of insured patients to other Member States may also work out favourably or unfavourably for the competent institution. Where beneficiaries are entitled to receive benefits in kind in a State where the costs of medical care are higher than at home or where more or other types of treatment are included in the insurance package, health expenditure could, especially where expensive types of treatment delivered in hospitals are concerned, be considerably higher than if treatment is, or would have been, obtained 'at home'. The drafters of the Regulations have recognised this. Art 17(6) of Reg 574/72 obliges the institution of the providing State, in the event of hospitalisation, to notify within three days, the competent institution of the date of entry to the hospital, the probable duration of the hospitalisation and the date of leaving the hospital. The same institution also has to notify the competent institution in advance of any decision relating to the grant of certain expensive types of treatment. The Administrative Commission has stated that the competent institution must be notified in the case of enlisted types of treatment (eg, surgical appliances, dental prostheses, accommodation and treatment in sanatoria, etc) and for types of treatment from which the costs are expected to exceed a certain fixed amount. Decision 135 of 1 July 1987 (OJ 1987 C 281) as amended by Decision 171 of 9 December 1998 (OJ 1999 L 143). In cases of medical urgency the institution of the place of residence has to inform the competent institution immediately. In order to enable the competent institution to exercise some control over its expenditure, this institution is given the right to make a reasoned objection within fifteen days. Art 17(7) Reg 574/72. The competent institution cannot object on the sole ground that a certain type of treatment is not covered by its own insurance package. Decision 121 of the Administrative Commission of 21 April 1983 (OJ 1983 C 193).

[52] But see: Art 34 of Reg 574/72 which provides for a number of cases in which reimbursement can take place when the required formalities have not been fulfilled.

[53] In order to effectuate social security and cross-border health care rights different E-forms must be used. The aim of the various certificates differs and it is therefore quite difficult to draw any definite conclusions about the legal value of the various forms. Cp Opinion of Adv Gen Lenz in Case C–425/93 *Calle Grenzshop Andresen* [1995] ECR I–269 at 56–7. The Court has indicated, though, that the legal value of the E-forms must be determined in the light of Art 39–42 EC. Case 93/81 *Knoeller* [1982] ECR 951 at 9. In the light of the 'good faith provision' contained in Art 10 EC, it could be argued that the health insurance institutions of the State to which a Community worker or citizen has moved to must presume the correctness of the information and data stated on the certificates. However, the institutions concerned remain free to verify the content of the certificates. The E-forms do not provide irrebuttable proof. Cp Case C–202/97 *Fitzwilliam* [2000] ECR I–883 at 46–59 (concerning premium duties in the case of the posting of workers) and Case C–102/91 *Knoch* [1992] ECR I–4341 at 50–4 (unemployment benefits).

which then possesses the information necessary for reimbursement by the competent institution. Upon fulfillment of all formalities, beneficiaries can obtain care as though they were insured in the State in question. They are subject to the same access conditions (eg, referral by general practitioners), the same form of payment (reimbursement or benefits in kind) and payment of own contributions as patients insured under the legislation of the State concerned.[54]

3 CROSS-BORDER ACCESS TO HEALTH CARE ON THE BASIS OF THE COMMUNITY RULES ON THE COORDINATION OF HEALTH CARE AND HEALTH INSURANCE SCHEMES

Having put the subject of this chapter in its proper context, the discussion can now proceed with an examination of the cross-border health care rights of the various categories of beneficiaries of the free movement of persons. This section examines the cross-border health care rights that beneficiaries of the free movement of persons enjoy under the Community's rules on the coordination of health insurance schemes. For Community citizens, the most important coordination rules are contained in EC Regulations No 1408/71 and No 574/72.[55] Most third country nationals will have to rely on the social security rules contained in the agreements that the Community and the Member States have concluded with the countries of which they hold the nationality.

3.1 Economic Residents

For the purposes of this book, the category of economic residents has been defined as consisting of all Community citizens and their family members who stay or reside in other Member States by virtue of Articles 39 (formerly 48) or 43 (formerly 52) E(E)C.[56] The discussion below is confined to the beneficiaries of the free movement of workers under Regulations No 1408/71 and No 574/72, the basic assumption being that the self-employed falling within the ambit of Article 43 EC enjoy the same cross-border health care rights.[57]

3.1.1 Work-Seekers

Article 39 EC confers upon all Community citizens the right to move to, and to stay for 'a reasonable period of time' in the territory of, other Member States

[54] Palm (2000) n 4 above, at 133. For details of the reimbursement procedures and formalities see Stiemer (1999) n 44 above.

[55] For other descriptions of the Regulations' health care provisions see, eg: Stiemer (1999) n 44 above and Schoukens, *Coördinatiebepalingen inzake Gezondheidszorg: het Communautaire Recht* (1994).

[56] On the category of 'economic residents' see also: ch 2, s 2.

[57] For the purposes of clarity and convenience the discussion in this section is further based on the assumption that all categories to be dealt with fall within the personal scope of Reg 1408/71.

in order to seek employment.[58] During this period, work-seekers can rely on Article 25(1) of Regulation No 1408/71 in order to claim medical benefits in accordance with the legislation of the host State at the expense of the institution they are insured with. The conditions to be met for obtaining medical care are quite strict. This right is only granted to wholly unemployed persons who are entitled to unemployment benefits in the competent State and who have made use of the right to export such benefits as guaranteed by Article 69 of Regulation No 1408/71. The exportability of unemployment benefits, and thus the right to obtain medical care, is limited to a maximum period of three months.[59] Community citizens who are only partially unemployed, who have not become or are no longer entitled to unemployment benefits, who do not satisfy the formalities for exporting such benefits or who continue to seek work after the three month period has expired, cannot benefit from Article 25.[60] Such work-seeking Community citizens can only claim medical benefits in the State concerned as 'non-residents.'[61]

3.1.2 Employed Workers

Community citizens who have been successful in their search for employment obtain the right to establish residence in the host State when the work they have found is 'effective and genuine.'[62] By virtue of Article 13 of Regulation No 1408/71 such workers are in principle insured in the State of employment and in case they do decide to establish residence in that State, they can, where necessary, invoke the nondiscrimination provision contained in Article 3 in order to

---

[58] Case C–292/89 *Antonissen* [1991] ECR I–745 at 21 and Case C–271/91 *Tsiotras* [1993] ECR I–2925 at 13–14.

[59] In order to become entitled to export unemployment benefits wholly unemployed workers must (*i*) before their departure have been registered in the competent State as persons seeking work for at least four weeks and (*ii*) register as persons seeking work in the State where they go to. See also: Art 69 of Reg 1408/71 and, for the administrative details, Art 83 of Reg 574/72. In order to effectuate the right to medical care, unemployed work-seekers must submit to the health institution in the State where they are looking for work form E 119 which, upon their request, has been issued by the competent institution. See also: Art 26 of Reg 574/72. If the persons concerned do not return to the competent State before the expiry of the period of three months, they shall lose 'all entitlement' to unemployment benefits (see, eg: Joined Cases 41/79, 121/79 and 796/79 *Testa* [1980] ECR 1979) and thus the right to obtain medical benefits in the State concerned. In cases of *force majeur*, the three month period may be extended by the competent institution (Art 25(4) of Reg 1408/71), even when the request for doing so is made after the afore mentioned period (Case 139/78 *Coccioli* [1979] ECR 991). The sickness fund of the Member State where the persons concerned are looking for work must inform the competent institution that it considers it necessary to extend the three-month period. On the basis of, inter alia, a report from the examining doctor, the competent institution can then make a decision as to the extension of the three month period. Art 26(6) of Reg 574/72. The Commission has proposed to extend this period up to six months. s 3.6.2.

[60] Art 25 is not applicable to wholly unemployed persons who resume a part-time professional or trade activity. Such persons are considered as employed persons for purposes of Arts 18–36 of Reg 1408/71. Decision 156 of 7 April 1995 (OJ 1995 L 249).

[61] s 3.2.

[62] Case 53/81 *Levin* [1983] ECR 1035. ch 2, s 2.2.

claim access to health care in, and under the same conditions as the nationals of, the host State. Article 18 obliges the institution in the State of residence whose legislation makes the acquisition, retention or recovery of entitlement to benefits conditional upon the completion of insurance or employment periods, to take into account the periods which have been completed under the legislation of another Member State. For the rest, Articles 18–36 do not contain any other provision applying to such workers. From the perspective of the coordination mechanism, this standard situation is largely an internal affair. No cooperation between health insurance institutions in different Member States is necessary to guarantee such workers access to health care in the Member State of residence.[63]

Such cooperation between health insurance institutions is necessary in order to ensure that workers who reside in a Member State other than the one in which they are employed, can obtain medical benefits in the State of residence. Article 19 of Regulation No 1408/71 provides that such workers are entitled to obtain medical care in the State of residence as though they were insured there. The care is provided in accordance with the legislation of the State of residence; the costs are borne by the competent institution.[64] Workers residing in a Member State other than the competent State can also claim medical benefits in the latter State. Frontier workers, ie, workers who return as a rule daily or at least once a week to the country of residence,[65] enjoy this right under

---

[63] To be sure, co-operation is necessary in order to implement the aggregation rule of Art 18. In order to benefit from this rule, workers must submit a form E 104 to the competent institution, which specifies the periods of insurance completed under the legislation to which they were last subject. At the request of the workers, the form is issued by the institution to whose legislation they were last subject. If no form is submitted, the competent institution must obtain it from the 'other' institution. Art 16 of Reg 574/72. Waiting periods are usually rather short and form E 104 therefore only has to relate to the most recent completed periods of insurance. European Commission, *Compendium of Community Provisions on Social Security* (1995) at 430.

For an application of Art 18 see, eg: *Tessier* (1978). The case concerned a French national who had been an *au pair* in the United Kingdom and who had received treatment during her stay under the National Health Service. On her return to France, she again received medical treatment. Her sickness fund refused to bear the costs on the ground that she had not been employed and insured for the minimum period required by French law. The Court ruled that if Ms Tessier could be classed as a worker, ie, if it could be established that she had been paying social security contributions in the United Kingdom, she could rely on Art 18 of Reg 1408/71 in order to have the periods of insurance in the United Kingdom taken into account by the French institution. Case 84/77 *Tessier* [1978] ECR 7.

In *Klaus* the Court further ruled that periods of insurance fulfilled in other Member States must also be taken into account in cases where the competent institutions, on the basis of national law, are entitled to refuse sickness benefits to persons whose illness or disability already existed at the commencement of the insurance. Case C–482/93 *Klaus* [1995] ECR I–3551.

On Art 18 see also: Case 150/82 *Coppola* [1983] ECR 43 and Case C–111/91 *Commission v Luxembourg* [1993] ECR I–817.

[64] In order to become entitled to medical benefits in the State of residence, workers must request a form E 106 from the competent organ which testifies that they are insured and submit this form for registration to the health institution in the State of residence. Art 17(1) of Reg 574/72.

[65] Art 1(b) of Reg 1408/71.

Article 20.[66] Other non-resident workers[67] can rely on Article 21.[68] Read together, Articles 19, 20 and 21 thus guarantee both categories of workers a right to choose in which of the two States they wish to obtain medical care.[69]

Further, Article 22(1)b provides that workers who have become entitled to benefits chargeable to the competent institution and who are authorised by that institution to transfer their residence to another Member State, are entitled to claim benefits in the latter State. In such cases, authorisation may be refused only if it is established that the movement of the persons concerned would be prejudicial to their health or the receipt of treatment.

3.1.3 Unemployed Workers

Community citizens who have found but later lose employment may retain the right to reside in the host State.[70] For as long as they indeed continue living there, they retain the right to obtain medical care. As workers, the partially, intermittently or wholly unemployed remain covered by Regulation No 1408/71.[71] They continue to be insured for medical care[72] and can rely on Article 3 or Article 19 in order to claim medical benefits in the State of residence at the expense of the competent institution.[73]

The loss of employment may have implications for workers who, during their employment, were residing outside the competent State. By virtue of Article 25(2) of Regulation No 1408/71, wholly unemployed frontier workers as well as wholly unemployed non-frontier workers who were residing in a Member State other than the competent State and who have decided to search for (new) employment in the State of residence, remain entitled to medical benefits in the

---

[66] This provision aims to avoid unnecessarily long work stoppages. Keunen (2001) n 42 above, at 149 and Schoukens (1992) n 55 above, at 22.

[67] Examples are: commercial travellers, persons working in more than one Member State, workers in embassies and consulates who have opted for the legislation of the country of origin and workers in frontier undertakings subject to the legislation of the country where the undertaking has its registered office, but residing and working in the neighbouring State. European Commission (1995) n 63 above, at 430.

[68] This right is guaranteed even if the worker has already received medical care for the same sickness in the State of residence. Art 21(1), second sentence of Reg 1408/71. Art 21(4) states that workers who reside outside the competent State and who wish to transfer their residence to this State, can receive medical benefits there even if, before the transfer of residence, they have already obtained medical benefits chargeable to the competent institutions.

[69] For frontier workers one exception exists. Such workers do have the right to receive medical care in both the State of residence and insurance, but they can, according to Art 19 of Reg 574/72, only obtain medic(in)al products in the State where they have 'chosen to go to the doctor' and where the products have been prescribed.

[70] See also: ch 2, s 2.2.2.

[71] Art 1(a) *juncto* Art 2 of Reg 1408/71.

[72] The partially unemployed remain insured in the State of employment. The wholly unemployed, however, are by virtue of Art 13(2)(f), as interpreted by the Court in Case C–275/96 *Kuusijärvi* [1998] ECR I–3443, subject to the legislation of the State in whose territory they reside.

[73] Cp Schoukens (1994) n 55 above, at 29–30.

State of residence as though they had been insured there during their last employment.[74] The two categories no longer have the right, however, to claim medical benefits in the State in which they used to be employed.[75]

3.1.4 Pensioners

3.1.4.1 *Introduction*

Community citizens who have definitively ended their working career because of old-age or permanent incapacity for work, lose the right to reside as a worker in the host State and they can no longer benefit from the health care provisions of Regulations No 1408/71 and No 574/72 as described so far.[76] Community law, however, does not leave such Community citizens empty handed. They may continue to live in the State of (former) employment by virtue of the so-called right to remain[77] and Articles 26–34 of Regulation No 1401/71 contain a detailed set of rules governing the health care and insur-

---

[74] However, wholly unemployed non-frontier workers who were residing in a Member State other than the competent State and who have decided to seek new employment in the State of residence, cannot benefit from Art 25(2) when they have already become entitled to unemployment benefits in the competent State. In such circumstances the persons concerned can only claim medical benefits as work-seekers under Art 25(1) (s 3.1.1). Art 25(2) *juncto* Art 71(1)(b)(ii) of Reg 1408/71.

[75] Art 25(2) of Reg 1408/71 refers to Art 71(1)(a)(ii) which stipulates that wholly unemployed frontier workers shall receive unemployment benefits in the State of residence. Art 71(1)(a)(ii) has exclusive effect. Case 1/85 *Miethe* [1986] ECR 1837 at 10–12. For as long as wholly unemployed frontier workers do not return to or establish residence in the State in which they used to work, the State of residence acts as though it were the competent State (Case C–131/95 *Huijbregts* [1996] ECR I–1409 at 24) and it is only in this State that they can claim unemployment benefits. Since Art 25(2) explicitly refers to Art 71(1)(a)(ii), it may be assumed that the same holds true for medical benefits. Non-frontier workers who were residing in a Member State other than the State of employment can choose in which of the two States they wish to claim unemployment benefits when they become wholly unemployed by making themselves available to the employment services in one of these States. The State they have chosen must be regarded as the competent State. The wholly unemployed who choose the State of former employment retain the right to claim medical benefits in the State of residence (Art 19 of Reg 1408/71) and the competent State (Art 21), but those who make themselves available to the employment services in the State of residence are subject to the legislation of, and can only claim medical benefits, in that State (under Art 25(2) of Reg 1408/71).

[76] Persons who have ceased all activity and have become entitled to a pension do not necessarily loose their status of employed persons under Reg 1408/71. Yet, for the purposes of the health care provisions they do seem to loose that status when they are covered by the pensioners provisions. Keunen (2001) n 42 above, at 144. Under these provisions the term 'employed persons' has a more restrictive meaning than the definition given in the general provision of Art 1 of the Regulation. Stiemer, 'Ziekte en Moederschap—Arbeidsongevallen en Beroepsziekten' in Pieters, *Europees Sociale Zekerheidsrecht—Commentaar* (1989) 69–88, at 75 and Stiemer (1999) n 44 above, at 230. See, eg: Art 34(2) of Reg 1408/71, which provides that Art 27–33 do not apply to pensioners who are entitled sickness or maternity benefits by virtue of the pursuit of vocational activities and that such persons, for the purposes of the chapter on sickness and maternity benefits, must be regarded as workers.

[77] Ch 2, s 2.2.2.

ance rights of pensioners.[78] These rules have a double purpose. They intend to ensure that pensioners (*i*) retain their right to medical care in the State of residence[79] and (*ii*) cannot be obliged to pay health contributions in more than one Member State.[80]

3.1.4.2 *Pension Applicants*

In many Member States, health insurance for pensioners is linked to the receipt of a pension. In practice quite some time may pass between the application for and the actual grant of a pension[81] and this could bring about the result that pension claimants who have ceased to be insured in the last competent State, would not be entitled to medical care at all. Article 26 of Regulation No 1408/71 therefore provides that during the period of application, applicants are entitled to health care in the Member States of residence provided they are entitled to such benefits under the legislation of the State of residence or by virtue of the legislation of another Member State if they were residing there. During this period, the costs of the health services are borne by the institution of the Member State that has received health insurance contributions or, in the absence of such an institution, the institution of the State of residence. Ultimately, however, the costs will have to be borne by the institution, which after the pension is awarded, will receive the health contributions.[82]

3.1.4.3 *Pensioners Receiving Pensions from one Member State Only*

As regards retired workers who are entitled to one or more pensions[83] under the legislation of a single Member State, and who have actually been granted the pension(s), various situations must be distinguished. The first involves pensioners

---

[78] Arts 37–51 of Reg 1408/71 on invalidity, old age and death pensions do not contain provisions for medical benefits 'in kind'. Co-ordination problems concerning such benefits must be dealt with under Art 18–36 of Reg 1408/71 and the accompanying provisions of Reg 574/72. Case 69/79 *Jordens-Voster* [1980] ECR 75 at 7. Arts 52–63 of Reg 1408/71 concerning workers who have become the victim of accidents at work or suffer from occupational diseases, do contain provisions for medical 'benefits in kind'. These are, however, virtually identical to the rules contained in Arts 18–36 and, for this reason, they will not be discussed separately in this chapter. For a brief description see Schoukens (1992) n 55 above, at 45–6.

[79] Cornelissen, 'The Principle of Territoriality and the Community Regulations on Social Security (Regulations 1408/71 and 574/72)' (1996) *CMLRev* 439 *et seq*, at 463.

[80] Cp Stiemer (1989) n 76 above, at 84. See also: *Rundgren* (2001) where the Court held that the purpose of Arts 27, 28 and 28a is to identify (*i*) the institution responsible for providing pensioners with sickness benefits and (*ii*) the institution responsible for bearing the costs. Case C–389/99 *Rundgren* [2001] ECR I–3731, 44.

[81] This is particularly true when a right to a pension exists in more than one Member State. De Groot, 'De Wettelijke Verzekering van Geneeskundige Verzorging en Ziekengeld binnen het Kader van de EEG-Verordeningen' in Boot *et al*, *Europees Sociaal Verzekeringsrecht* (1978) 91–110, at 101.

[82] If necessary, financial settlement takes place. See also: Art 26(2) and (3) Reg 1408/71. In order to receive medical care pension claimants must have registered themselves with the institution of the State of residence by use of form E 120, which is issued by the Member State responsible for the medical benefits.

[83] Where pensioners receive two pensions under the legislation of a single Member State, they will be treated as though they were only receiving one pension in that State. Art 34(1) of Reg 1408/71.

who are residing in the territory of the State concerned. Articles 26–34 of Regulation No 1408/71 do not contain any specific provisions for this situation. The pensioners in question are subject to the legislation of that State and they can 'simply' rely on the general nondiscrimination provision of Article 3 of Regulation No 1408/71 in order to claim medical benefits under the same conditions as the nationals of the State concerned at the expense of the institution of that State.[84]

The second situation concerns pensioners who receive a pension from one Member State but who reside in another where they are not entitled to medical benefits. Article 28 of Regulation No 1408/71 provides that such pensioners are entitled to obtain medical benefits in the State of residence as though they were residing in the State offering the pension.[85] The costs are borne by the institution of the 'pension State.'[86] Article 28 fulfils the same role as Article 19.[87] Both Articles grant persons who reside in a Member State other than the one in which they pay health premiums a right to gain access to medical care in the State of residence. Frontier workers, for instance, are during their working-career entitled to health care in the State of residence on the basis of Article 19; after their career they enjoy this right under Article 28.[88]

Pensioners who receive a pension from only one Member State but who are residing in a State where health insurance is based on residence are entitled to claim medical benefits in the latter State. Article 28a of the regulation indicates, however, that where the pensioner resides in the territory of a Member State under whose legislation the right to receive benefits in kind is not subject to conditions of insurance or employment, 'nor is any pension payable,' the costs are borne by the State responsible for the pension provided the pensioners would have been entitled to benefits in that State if they were residing there.

In *Rundgren* (2001) the Court was asked to clarify the meaning of the expression 'nor is any pension payable.' The case concerned a Swedish national who received a Swedish pension, who lived in Finland and who was required to pay in the latter State contributions for the national State pension and sickness insurance. Mr Rundgren submitted that he could not be required to pay contributions since he only received a Swedish pension and had not applied for a pension in Finland. The Finnish government argued that the expression 'pension payable' refers to a theoretical entitlement to a pension, given by the national legislation of the Member State concerned, even if the person concerned has not applied for the pension. The Court did not agree. Article 28a aims to ensure that Member States whose legislation confers a right to benefits in kind merely by

---

[84] Where necessary, such pensioners may also rely on Art 18 in order to have periods of insurance, employment or residence taken into account by the competent institution.

[85] Art 28(1)a of Reg 1408/71.

[86] Art 28(2)a of Reg 1408/71.

[87] Case 69/79 *Jordens-Voster* [1980] ECR 75 at 12.

[88] Pensioners who wish to claim benefits under Art 28 or 28a must register with the institution of the State of residence by submitting form E 121. See also: Art 29 of Reg 574/72.

virtue of residence in the State territory without imposing conditions of insurance or employment, are not penalised for doing so. Under the system established by Articles 27, 28 and 28a the institution that has to bear the costs of medical benefits in kind will always be an institution of a Member State competent in respect of pensions. The connection thus established between the competence to provide pensions and the obligation to bear the costs of benefits in kind, so the Court held, leads to the conclusion that that obligation is incidental to an actual competence in respect of pensions. Therefore, the costs of benefits in kind cannot be borne by the institution of a Member State that has only a hypothetical competence in respect of pensions.[89] Thus, because the Finnish authorities were not responsible for bearing the costs of benefits in kind of Mr Rundgren, they could not impose any duty to make contributions on him.[90]

3.1.4.4 *Pensioners Receiving Pensions from More than One Member State*

Also as regards retired workers who have worked in various Member States as a result of which they have become entitled to pensions under the legislation of more than one Member State,[91] various situations must be distinguished. The first involves pensioners who receive pensions from the institutions of more than one State, one of which is the State of residence and who are entitled to medical benefits in that State. In the absence of any coordination rules, such pensioners might be obliged to pay health contributions in more than one State and the institution of more than State might be obliged to bear the costs of medical care. Article 27 provides that such pensioners can claim health care benefits in the

---

[89] That interpretation was borne out of Art 33(1) which provides that the institution responsible for payment of a pension is authorised to make deductions from the pension actually paid by it in order to cover the costs of inter alia medical benefits. Where Member States are obliged to pay the costs of medical benefits in kind on the basis of one of the pensioner provisions discussed above, they are entitled to deduct health insurance contributions from pensions. Art 33(1) of Reg 1408/71. If no such obligation exists, no contributions can be deducted. Case 275/83 *Commission v Belgium* [1985] ECR 1097. Art 33 constitutes the 'application of a more general principle according to which a pensioner cannot be required, because he resides in the territory, to pay compulsory insurance contributions to cover benefits payable by an institution of another Member State'. Case C–140/88 *Noij* [1991] ECR I–387 at 14; Case C–389/99 *Rundgren* [2001] ECR I–3731 at 53 and Opinion of Adv Gen Alber in Case C–347/98 *Commission v Belgium* [2001] ECR I–3327 at 63. The prohibition following from Art 33 only applies to statutory pensions, not to supplementary pensions established by industrial or collective agreements. Case 275/83 *Commission v Belgium* [1985] ECR 1097; Case C–57/90 *Commission v France* [1992] ECR I–75; Case C–253/90 *Commission v Belgium* [1992] ECR I–531 and Case C–302/98 *Sehrer* [2000] ECR I–4585 at 26.

[90] Case C–389/99 *Rundgren* [2001] ECR I–3731 at 45–57.

[91] For most types of benefits the two EC regulations apply the so-called integration method. Under this method beneficiaries who have worked in, or have become entitled to benefits under the legislation of, more than one Member State, will receive a benefit in or at the expense of only one State. For long-term benefits such as invalidity or old-age pensions this method could have far-reaching financial implications, and in order to avoid these, the regulations prescribe in most cases the partial pension method which implies that pensions are awarded to beneficiaries on the basis of the rules of more than one Member State. See further the literature referred to in n 43.

State of residence as though they were solely receiving a pension in that State.[92] The second situation concerns pensioners who receive pensions from two or more States other than the State of residence. Where they have no claim to medical benefits under the legislation of the State of residence, Article 28(1) guarantees that pensioners can claim medical benefits in the State of residence. The costs are borne by the institution of the State where the pensioners have been insured for the longest time,[93] provided the pensioners would be entitled to medical benefits if they were residing there. Community citizens who remain living in the State of employment after retirement thus retain insurance cover and the right to claim medical benefits in that State. Retired workers who live in a Member State other than the one in which they were most recently employed no longer have a right to claim medical benefits in that State as though they were still working there. The health care and insurance rights of pensioners are exclusively governed by Article 26–34 and these Articles do not contain any provision comparable to Articles 20 and 21 of Regulation No 1408/71.[94] The right to choose between the competent State and the State of residence, which such persons enjoyed when they were still in employment, is lost.[95]

The recent judgment in *Sehrer* (2000) demonstrates that not all situations are covered and governed by the Regulations' pensioners provisions. The case concerned a German national who lived in Germany and used to work there as a miner. Since reaching the age of 60, he had received a statutory retirement pension in Germany as well as a supplementary retirement pension from an association for miners. Because Mr Sehrer had also worked as a miner in France, he received in addition a supplementary pension, which was based on a French collective labour agreement. When the competent German authority learnt of Mr Sehrer's French supplementary pension, it demanded payment of arrears of sickness insurance contributions from him on the basis of the gross amount

---

[92] The main purpose of Art 27 is to prevent the competent institution of the State of residence, which is compelled to pay sickness benefits, from relieving itself from that obligation on the ground that the person concerned is entitled to a benefit under the legislation of another Member State. Case 103/75 *Aulich* [1976] ECR 697 at 5.

[93] See Art 28(2) Reg 1408/71 which further indicates that where pensioners have been subject to the legislation of different Member States for equal periods of time, the Member State to whose legislation they were last subject must bear the costs. Pensioners who receive pensions from two or more States and who reside in a State where health insurance is based on residence, can claim medical benefits there, but, as follows from Art 28a, the costs are in this situation borne by the institution of the 'pension State' where the pensioners have been insured for the longest time.

[94] The Commission, however, has proposed to grant retired frontier workers a right to obtain medical care in the State in which they used to work. See also: s 3.6.2.

[95] In practice, however, this does not have very serious implications for retired frontier and other non-residents workers. Art 31 of Reg 1408/71 grants pensioners during a temporary stay in a Member State other than the one in which they reside, the right to obtain medical benefits in accordance with the legislation applicable there. See also: s 3.2.1. Further, pensioners can benefit from Art 22(1)(b) which states that workers who have become entitled to benefits chargeable to the competent institution and who are authorised by that institution to transfer their residence to another Member State, are entitled to claim benefits in the latter State. Stiemer (1999) n 44 above, at 232.

of the French pension. In doing so, however, the German authority did not take into account the fact that sickness insurance contributions had already been deducted in France. In determining whether the law applied by the German authority was compatible with Community law, not one of Regulation No 1408/71's health care provisions for pensioners could be applied. From Article 1(j) of the regulation it follows that benefits granted by industrial agreements do not fall within the scope of the Regulation with the result that Mr Sehrer, for the purposes of the regulation, was deemed to draw a retirement pension under the legislation of a single Member State (ie, Germany) only. The regulation's health care provisions for pensioners, however, only cover situations where pensioners draw pensions under the legislation of two or more Member States or situations where they draw a pension under the legislation of a single Member State but are not entitled to medical benefits in the country of residence.[96] This did not imply, however, that the German rules in question were compatible with Community law. The Court concluded that Germany, by not taking into account the fact that sickness insurance contributions had been deducted in France, had applied a rule which unlawfully hampered the exercise of free movement rights and violated Article 39 EC.[97]

3.1.5 Family Members

Community citizens who make use of the free movement rights guaranteed by Article 39 EC are entitled to be accompanied by their spouse, their (grand)children who are under the age of 21 years or dependent and their dependent (grand)parents.[98] A genuine free movement of workers which is relevant and practical requires that these family members are also entitled to medical care in the Member State in which they stay or reside. Family members[99] staying or residing in the competent State can rely, where necessary, on Article 3 of Regulation No 1408/71 in order to claim care under the same conditions as the nationals of the host State. For family members staying or residing in Member States other than the competent State Regulation No 1408/71 contains several specific provisions. Article 19(2) of Regulation No 1408/71 grants family

---

[96] Case C–302/98 *Sehrer* [2000] ECR I–4585 at 25–7.

[97] *Ibid*, at 33–6.

[98] Ch 2, s 2.3.

[99] For the purposes of Reg 1408/71, family members are defined as the persons who are defined or recognised as family members or designated as a member of the household by the legislation where benefits are provided for. Art 1(f) of Reg 1408/71. Where, however, the legislation in question regards as members of the family or members of the household only persons living under the same roof as the principal beneficiary, this condition is considered satisfied if the persons concerned are mainly dependent on that person. Where the legislation of a Member State does not enable members of a family to be distinguished from other persons to whom it applies (i.e. in Member States where the right to benefits is based on residence—Stiemer (1999) n 44 above, at 229), the term 'member of the family' has the meaning given to it in Annex I(A) to Reg 1408/71.

members[100] of frontier workers and other workers residing outside the competent State, the right to obtain medical care in the State of residence.[101] Article 25(3) of Regulation No 1408/71 provides for similar rights for family members of work-seekers, wholly unemployed frontier workers and the wholly unemployed non-frontier workers who were residing in a Member State other than the competent State and who have decided to seek (new) employment in the State of residence.[102] Furthermore, Articles 26, 27, 28 and 28a,[103] all of which intend to ensure that pension claimants and pensioners are subject to the health

[100] It had always been assumed that family members could only benefit from Art 19(2) when they were also defined or recognised as family members by the legislation of the State of residence. Stiemer (1999) n 44 above, at 229. The ruling in *Delavant* (1995) indicates that this view is no longer correct. *Delavant* concerned a French national who was employed in France and lived with her husband and two children in Germany. Mrs Delavant requested a declaration from the German sickness fund that her children would be entitled to medical care at the expense of the sickness fund. This request was refused. The sickness fund referred to Art 1(f) of Reg 1408/71, which defines family members as persons who are defined as family members under the legislation under which benefits are provided for. The fund subsequently applied the German law under which children could only be co-insured (free of charge) in cases where the income of the spouse of the insured person does not exceed a fixed maximum. Mr Delavant's income exceeded that maximum. This practice of the German sickness fund basically meant that family members of frontier workers such as Mrs Delavant must qualify as family members under the legislation of both the competent State (*in casu* France) and the residence State (*in casu* Germany) in order to benefit from Art 19 of the regulation. The Court, however, concluded that Art 1(f) of Reg 1408/71 does not deal with conditions for insurance and that the question whether or not family members meet requirements for health insurance cover must be determined by the legislation of the competent State alone. Case C–431/93 *Delavant* [1995] ECR I–1545 at 18–19.

On *Delavant* see van der Steen, 'Medische Zorg voor Gezinsleden van Grensarbeiders' (1995) NTER 121–2. The European Commission intends to correct *Delavant*. It has proposed that the Regulation must be amended in order to define family members, for the purposes of sickness and maternity benefits, as persons with derived rights and who are defined or recognised as family members or designated as members of the household by the legislation of the State of residence. Art 7(e) of the proposal to simplify Reg 1408/71. COM(1998) 779 final.

[101] The right is only granted to family members who have no right to medical benefits under the legislation of the State where they reside. The second sentence of Art 19(2) indicates that this requirement does not apply to family members who reside in a Member State where the right to obtain medical care is only conditional upon residence (eg, Finland, Denmark). If, however, the spouse or the person looking after the children pursues a professional or trade activity in that State, the requirement does apply. The second sentence of Art 19(2) reflects the basic principle underlying the Regulations that the Member State, which receives the health contributions, must also pay the 'medical bill'. European Commission (1995) n 63 above, at 430.

[102] These rights are granted provided the employed persons themselves meet the conditions for entitlement to medical benefits in the State responsible for the costs of the unemployment benefits. Art 25(3) of Reg 1408/71.

[103] Art 29 further contains a special provision for the family members of pensioners who do not reside in the same Member State as the pensioners do. Such family members can claim medical benefits in the State in which they reside. The costs are borne by the institution of the State in which the pensioner resides or when the pensioner has been insured for the longest time. Art 29(1)a (as amended by Reg 1223/98—OJ 1998 L 168), which further adds that where the family members reside in the competent State, the costs are borne by the competent institution. Family members who decide to move to the State where the pensioner resides can claim medical benefits even if they have already received benefits for the same case of sickness before transferring residence. Art 29(2)a of Reg 1408/71.

insurance of one Member State only and can claim access to medical care in the State of residence, apply equally to their family members.[104]

Most family members who are residing in a Member State other than the competent State only have a limited possibility of obtaining benefits in the competent State. Family members of workers residing outside the competent State and who do not return daily or weekly to this State, can also claim medical benefits in the competent State during a stay there.[105] Family members of frontier workers, however, have, according to the second sentence of Article 20 of Regulation No 1408/71, only such a right (*i*) in 'urgent' cases,[106] (*ii*) when the Member States concerned, or the competent institutions of these States, have reached an agreement to this effect[107] or, in the absence of such an agreement, (*iii*) when the competent institution has given prior authorisation.[108]

3.2 Non-Residents/Travellers

All Community citizens enjoy the right to cross intra-Community borders and to stay for a limited period of time in the territory of other Member States.[109] Regulations No 1408/71 and No 574/72 contain several provisions that confer upon such 'Community travellers' cross-border health care rights. A distinction is to be made[110] between beneficiaries who become in need of medical treatment and/or medic(in)al products during a stay in another Member State and beneficiaries who move to other Member States for the purpose of obtaining medical benefits.

---

[104] In order to implement the cross-border health care rights of family members several administrative formalities have to be fulfilled. Generally, the duty to request the certified statements from the competent institution and to use these for registration with the institution where the family members reside is imposed on the worker. When family members do not reside in the same State as the worker, it is up to them to fulfill the formalities. See, eg: Art 30 of Reg 574/72.

[105] Art 21(2) of Reg 1408/71. Where these family members reside in the territory of a Member State other than the one in whose territory the worker resides, medical benefits obtained in the competent State must be paid by the health institution of the State where they reside. Art 21(2), second sentence.

[106] The Administrative Commission has stated that urgent cases are present whenever medical treatment cannot be postponed without endangering the life or health of the person concerned. Decision 116 (OJ 1983 C 193).

[107] France and Belgium have concluded such an agreement that entitles families of frontier workers to gain access to health care in the state of insurance. Hermesse and Lawalle (1991) n 1 above, in the section on Belgium.

[108] For the family members of pensioners see Art 31 of Reg 1408/71. The Commission has proposed, however, to grant family members of frontier workers as well as family members of pensioners the same choice that frontier workers enjoy. s 3.6.2.

[109] Ch 2 s 4.

[110] But see: n 133.

3.2.1 Emergency Treatment

Article 22(1)a *juncto* Article 22a[111] of Regulation No 1408/71 confers upon all Community citizens 'whose medical condition necessitates immediate benefits during a stay in the territory of another Member State' the right to obtain medical benefits. Also in these E 111 cases[112] the benefits are provided in accordance with the legislation of the visited State and the costs are borne by the competent institution.[113] Article 22(1)a can only be relied upon in cases of 'emergency', ie cases in which, in the view of the doctor in the State of the

---

[111] Initially, Art 22(1)a was merely intended to apply to workers from the southern Member States working in one of the northern Member States and who became in need of medical care during a vacation in their State of origin. Creutz, 'Accord européen Concernant l'Octroi des Soins médicaux aux Personnes en Séjour temporaire' (1985) *RISS* 42–9. In practice, however, the application of Art 22(1)a has never been restricted to the State of origin and the provision had often already been applied to all persons covered by a public health (insurance) scheme. Art 22(1) of Reg 1408/71 merely speaks of (self-)employed persons, but in 1996 Art 22a was inserted which has extended the scope of Art 22(1)a (and c—see s 3.2.2 below) to all persons holding the nationality of a Member State who are insured under the legislation of a Member State. See also: Decision 174 of the Administrative Commission of 20 April 1999 (OJ 1999 L 047).

Family members also enjoy the right offered by Arts 22(1)a (see Art 22(3)) and Art 22(a). For the purposes of Art 22(1) the term 'family members' is defined by the State of residence. Art 1(f) of Reg 1408/71. For the purpose of applying Art 22(1)a to family members referred to in Art 19(2) who reside in the territory of a Member State other than the one in whose territory the worker resides, 'benefits in kind' are to be provided by the institution in the visited place on behalf of the institution of the Member State in whose territory the family members are residing. Art 22(3), second sentence, under a.

[112] In order to receive benefits in kind under Art 22(1)a beneficiaries must before departure to another Member State request from their insurance institution form E 111 which states that they are entitled to obtain 'emergency care' and the duration for which they may do so. Upon arrival in the visited State, form E 111 must be submitted to the insurance institution of the State concerned which may then issue a national document for use in that country. If no E 111 form is submitted, the institution of the visited State shall obtain it from the competent institution. Art 21 of Reg 574/72 and Decision 74 of the Administrative Commission (OJ 1973 C 75). In case the E 111-formalities are not fulfilled, the expenses shall, upon beneficiaries' application, be refunded by the competent institution in accordance with the rates administered by the institution of the visited place which shall supply the competent institution with the necessary information about such rates. Art 34(1) and (2) of Reg 574/72. The competent institution may effect reimbursement of expenses incurred in accordance with the rates it administers provided that it (*i*) is possible to make a refund in accordance with these rates, (*ii*) the expenses do not exceed a level set by the Administrative Commission (500 Euro—Decision No 161—OJ 1996 L 083) and (*iii*) beneficiaries agree to this. The amount of reimbursement shall never exceed the amount of the expenses actually incurred. Art 34(4) of Reg 574/72.

In practice, the administrative formalities often lead to difficulties. See, eg, Hermans, 'Access to Health Care and Health Services in the European Union: Regulation 1408/71 and the E 111 Process' in Leidl (ed), *Health Care and its Financing in the Single European Market* (1998) 324–43 and Hermans, 'Gezondheidszorg bij Tijdelijk Verblijf over de Grens: Toepassing Verordening 1408/71 (E111) in de Europese Praktijk' (1996) *SR* 343–8. Discussions have been held about the possible introduction of a European health care card, which would minimise the cumbersome and inefficient administrative current procedures. See, eg, Hermans (1996) above, at 347; Neumann-Duesberg (1991) n 47 above, at 94–5 and Bloch, 'Auswirkungen des Europäischen Binnenmarktes aud die gesetzliche Krankenversicherung' (1989) *BB* 2405–10, at 2408–9.

[113] This institution also determines the duration of the period during which medical benefits can be obtained.

visit,[114] treatment cannot be postponed without endangering the life or health of the Community citizen concerned.[115] Once the medical urgency is over, the providing State is entitled to send the patient[116] back to the State of residence for further treatment.[117]

3.2.2 Authorised Treatment

Article 22(1)c *juncto* Article 22a[118] of Regulation No 1408/71 grants all publicly insured Community citizens who have been authorised by the competent institution to go to the territory of another Member State in order to receive medical treatment, the right to obtain medical care.[119] The prior authorisation for treatment in another Member State is given by means of form E 112[120] which states (*i*) that the person[121] concerned is authorised to receive a given type of medical

---

[114] Jorens (1992) n 42 above, at 96–7 and Hermans (1998) n 112 above, at 337. The duty of the institution of the providing State to notify the competent institution in cases of hospitalisation or the grant of certain expensive types of treatment and the possibility for the competent institution to make a reasoned objection (n 51 above) must in emergency cases during a temporary stay abroad be done immediately. Art 21(2) of Reg 574/72.

[115] Decision 135 of the Administrative Commission (contained in European Commission (1995) n 63 above, at 293–5) at points 4 and 5. See also: Neumann-Duesberg, 'Defizite, Probleme und Perspektiven bei der Umsetzung des Europäischen koordinierenden Sozialrechts—Verordnungen Nr 1408/71 und Nr 574/72—Leistungen bei Krankheit und Pflegebedürftigkeit' in Schulte and Barwig, *Freizügigkeit und Soziale Sicherheit—Die Durchführung der Verordnung Nr.1408/71 über die soziale Sicherheit der Wanderarbeitnehmer in Deutschland* (1999) 89–108, at 96. Art 22(1)a requires 'confirmation of a pressing medical need' for benefits which encompass 'benefits in kind needed forthwith'. Case C–206/94 *Paletta* [1996] ECR I–2357 at 20.

[116] Some beneficiaries can obtain medical care more easily. Beneficiaries who are staying in another Member State for a relatively long period of time but who have not established residence in that State (eg, posted workers), can, according to Art 22c, obtain medical benefits whenever their medical condition so requires. Art 31 further holds that pensioners are entitled to treatment during a stay in a State other than the one in which they reside, when treatment becomes necessary. See also: Hermans (1998) n 112 above, at 337.

[117] For instance, beneficiaries who are suffering from sudden dental pain during a temporary stay in another Member State are entitled to the necessary treatment. This treatment may consist of the grant of painkillers or the removal of teeth, but not dental prostheses. Langer (1999) n 7 above, at 720.

[118] n 111 above.

[119] Art 22(1)c is intended 'to allow an insured person, authorised by the competent institution to go to another Member State to receive there treatment appropriate to his condition, to receive sickness benefits in kind, on account of the competent institution but in accordance with the provisions of the legislation of the State in which the services are provided, in particular where the need for the transfer arises because of the state of health of the person concerned, without that person incurring additional expenditure'. Case C–120/95 *Decker* [1998] ECR I1831 at 28 and Case C–158/96 *Kohll* [1998] ECR I–1931 at 26. Authorisation can be granted to individual insured persons as well as to a group of persons. Neumann-Duesberg (1999) n 115 above, at 97.

[120] In each State a request for treatment abroad has to be made by the specialist or the hospital treating the patient. The next step involving the actual grant of the authorisation, however, differs considerably. See also: Palm *et al* (2000) n 4 above, at 46–65 and Kesteloot *et al* (1995) n 13, above at 48–9.

[121] Family members also enjoy the right afforded by Arts 22(1)c (see Art 22(3)) and Art 22(a). For the purposes of Art 22(1)c the term 'family members' is defined by the State of residence. Art 1(f) of Reg 1408/71. For the purpose of applying Art 22(1)c to family members referred to in Art 19(2) (i.e. family members residing outside the competent State) who reside in the territory of a Member State other than the one in whose territory the worker resides, the required authorisation shall be issued by the institution of the Member State in the State of residence. Art 22(3), second sentence, under (b).

treatment and (*ii*) the period for which he is so entitled. The form has to be submitted to the institution in the visited State which, as the Court ruled in *Pierik II* (1979), is upon presentation of the form under the duty to provide the health services concerned.[122] The competent institution must fully refund the institution in the State where care has been provided on the basis of the tariffs applicable in that State.[123]

Member States are free to authorise any type of treatment considered to be effective for the sickness or the disease the persons concerned suffer from. It is of no relevance whether or not the medical benefits are covered by the legislation administered by the competent institution.[124] Of much greater importance is the question when authorisation is to be given. In other words, in which cases does the Regulation give insured persons the right to go to another Member State in order to obtain medical treatment at the expense of their insurance institution? The answer is found in Article 22(2) of Regulation No 1408/71. This provision states that authorisation for treatment in other Member States may not be refused where the treatment in question (*i*) is among the benefits provided for by the legislation of the Member State on whose territory the person concerned resides, and (*ii*) where the patient, taking account of his current state of health and the probable course of the disease, cannot be given the treatment in question within the time normally necessary for obtaining this treatment in the Member State of residence.

The Community legislator inserted the current Article 22(2) in 1981 in response to the judgments of the Court of Justice in the two *Pierik* cases. The cases concerned a Dutch national who worked, lived and was insured in the Netherlands and who had gone to Germany in order to receive hydrotherapy treatment. Upon her return to the Netherlands, Mrs Pierik asked for the costs she had incurred to be refunded. The insurance institution refused reimbursement on the ground that hydrotherapy treatment was not among the types of treatment covered by the Dutch health insurance. Mrs Pierik started legal proceedings. The Dutch court that had to decide upon the case in last resort, referred several questions to the Court of Justice relating to Article 22(2) of Regulation No 1408/71. At the time, this provision stipulated that authorisation for treatment abroad could not be refused 'where the treatment in question cannot be provided for the person concerned within the territory of the Member State in which he resides.' In *Pierik I* (1978) the Court held that the:

'Duty laid down in the second subparagraph of Article 22(2) to grant authorisation required in Article 22(1)(c) covers both cases where the treatment provided in another Member State is more effective than that which the person concerned can receive in

---

[122] This is so even if, under the legislation that it administers, the institution does not have a duty but merely a power to grant the services. Case 182/78 *Pierik* [1979] ECR 1977 at 15–16.

[123] Art 36(1) of Reg 1408/71.

[124] Case 117/77 *Pierik* [1978] ECR 825 at 15–16. Cp also: Case C–368/98 *Vanbraekel* [2001] ECR I–5363 at 31.

the Member State where he resides and those in which the treatment in question cannot be provided on the territory of the latter State.'[125]

The Court's interpretation of Article 22(2) seemed to imply that patients would also have the right to obtain authorisation for types of treatment which are deliberately excluded from the national insurance package on medical, medical-ethical or financial grounds. In *Pierik II* (1979) the Court confirmed that this was indeed the case:

> 'It emerges from the provisions and the essential aims of Article 22 that it was the intention of the regulation to give medical requirements a decisive rôle in the decision of the competent institution to grant or refuse the aforesaid authorisation by providing generally and unreservedly in the second subparagraph of Article 22(2) that authorisation may not be refused `where the treatment in question cannot be provided for the person concerned within the territory of the Member State in which he resides' . . .. Thus . . . when the competent institution acknowledges that the treatment in question constitutes a necessary and effective treatment of sickness or disease from which the person concerned suffers, the conditions for the application of the second subparagraph of Article 22(2) of Regulation No 1408/71 are fulfilled and the competent institution may not in that case refuse the authorisation referred to by that provision and required under Article 22(1)(c).'[126]

From the patients' perspective, the two *Pierik* judgments were to be welcomed. The Court had come close to recognising a free movement of patients. In principle, patients could still be required to seek and obtain medical treatment in their State of residence, but in cases where other types of treatment or better treatment would be available in other Member States, patients were entitled to obtain authorisation for and thus to receive, at the expense of the competent institution, such types of treatment. Medical requirements were said to be decisive for this right.

From the Member States' perspective, however, the two judgments were problematic. Patients were granted the right to obtain forms of treatment not included in their 'own' insurance package as well as 'foreign' types of treatment, which might have been far more expensive than offered 'at home.' The competent institutions, as the Court explicitly held in *Pierik I*, were obliged to pay the 'foreign medical bill' in full.[127] The Member States' autonomy in deciding which types of treatment are eligible for reimbursement and their ability to keep health expenditure under control seemed to have been affected. In addition, the judgments might have triggered an uncontrollable and unpredictable inter-State flow of patients, which could cause capacity problems both in the providing and the competent State.

In the Member States' view, the Court had not given sufficient regard to their health care and insurance interests. They decided to alter the regulation. In 1981

---

[125] *Ibid*, at 22.
[126] Case 182/78 *Pierik II* [1979] ECR 1977 at 12–13.
[127] Case 117/77 *Pierik I* [1978] ECR 825 at 26.

the initial Article 22(2) was replaced by the current Article 22(2).[128] The 'leg-islative correction' of the *Pierik* judgments was drastic. The wording of Article 22(2) is cumbersome but does make clear that patients do not have the right to obtain authorisation for types of treatment which are not included in their own insurance package. Further, patients do not seem entitled to rely on Article 22(2) with a view to circumventing waiting lists in the State of residence.[129] They may only have a right to obtain authorisation in cases where postponement of treat-ment would be 'medically unacceptable.'[130] In all other cases authorisation may be refused.[131] In practice, it generally is refused. Authorisation is only given in exceptional cases.[132] By replacing Article 22(2) the Member States made it patently clear that the decision whether a patient can move abroad in order to obtain care, at the expense of the sickness fund, is made by them and not by the patients themselves.[133]

[128]   OJ 1981 L 275.

[129]   Bieback, 'Krankheit und Mutterschaft' in Eichenhofer (ed) *Reform des Europäischen koor-dinierendes Sozialrechts* (1993) 55–73, at 64.

[130]   Kesteloot (1995) n 13 above, at 46.

[131]   Cornelissen (1996) n 79 above, at 464.

[132]   The 'authorisation policies' of Member States differ. Palm *et al* (2000) n 4 above, at 46–64 and Kesteloot *et al* (1995) n 13 above, at 47. Some Member States, such as the United Kingdom, only meet their basic obligations under Art 22(2) of Reg 1408/71. Authorisation for treatment is granted where waiting-periods appear to be 'too long', but authorisation is in principle refused in all other cases. A number of other Member States make more use of their freedom to send patients abroad. A Member State like Luxembourg gives authorisation for hospital treatment in other Member States relatively often. Other Member States such as Denmark, Germany, Greece, Ireland, the Netherlands and Portugal grant authorisation for types of treatment not available in their own country. This often concerns 'new' types of treatment the effectiveness of which is recognised, but which have not yet been developed or been made available in these countries. In some (of these) countries, however, authorisation is granted only for such types of treatment. Apparently, then, not all Member States comply with Art 22(2). For persons living in border regions, some countries grant authorisation more easily. Belgium, for instance, has allowed residents of frontier regions to obtain medical care within a radius of up to 25 kilometres provided that there is no similar establishment in Belgium that is closer. COM(90) 561 at 11 and De Buyser, 'Grensoverschrijdende Gezondheidszorg' in Jorens, *Grensarbeid—Sociaalrechtelijke and Fiscaalrechtelijke Aspecten* (1997) 129–60, at 145–6.

[133]   In the view of the drafters of the Regulation Art 22(1)a was supposed to cover cases where the need for treatment occurred abroad and was not, or could not have been, foreseen at the moment the persons concerned decided to travel to another Member State. Art 22(1)c was intended to apply to cases in which the need for medical treatment was or could be foreseen. It concerns cases where patients are sent abroad in order to receive medical care. This distinction, however, is not entirely reflected in the text of Art 22. Art 22(1)a stipulates that beneficiaries are entitled to obtain treatment when their 'condition necessitates immediate treatment' during a stay in the territory of another member State. The wording of Art 22(1)a leaves room for the view that it can also be relied upon by persons who know in advance that they will come to need medical treatment. This may be at odds with the objective of and the intentions of the drafters of Art 22(1)a, but at least in some cases one has to assume that patients can indeed rely on that provision if they know in advance that they will come to need treatment. An overly restrictive interpretation of Art 22(1)a 'would cause a significant obstacle to the free movement of persons whose conditions necessitates continuous and regular medical treatment such that they will be likely to require immediate benefits in the event of a stay in the territory of another State'. Decision 163 of the Administrative Commission (OJ 1996 L 241). The Administrative Commission has stated that patients in need of kidney dialysis (Decision 123—OJ 1984 C 203) and oxygen therapy (Decision 163—OJ 1996 L 241) can rely on Art 22(1)a in other Member States, and it could be argued that the same holds true for patients in need of treatment dur-ing pregnancy (see, eg, Neumann-Duesberg (1999) n 112 above, at 98) and those suffering from other

3.3 Non-Economic Residents

The third category of beneficiaries of the Community provisions on the free movement of persons which has been identified for the purposes of this book consists of so-called non-economic residents. It concerns Community students, pensioners and the residual category of 'other' Community citizens whose right to reside in other Member States is [134] based on Article 18(1) EC and set out in

chronicle diseases and needing other forms of treatment. In other cases, one might be more hesitant to accept that patients who know in advance that they will be in need of treatment can invoke Art 22(1)a of the Regulation. Art 22(1)a could possibly be abused. Consider the following example, taken from a Dutch newspaper article (NRC Handelsblad, 25 September 1993).

A German woman living in a small German village close to the Dutch border was suffering from a worn-out hip. Surgery was necessary. The woman wished to be operated on in Winterswijk, a Dutch village just across the German-Dutch border, in order to enable her family members to visit her regularly in hospital. Unfortunately, the *Krankenkasse*, the German sickness fund, was not willing to finance the surgery in the Netherlands. Nevertheless, the woman agreed with the Dutch hospital that she would be admitted on a Saturday in order to be operated on two days later. On the Saturday concerned the woman had herself driven to the market in Winterswijk where she laid down in the market square and called for help. With a fictitious accident she was transported to the Dutch hospital. Two days later she was given a new hip. The *Krankenkasse* had to pay the costs of the surgery. In case of accidents abroad 'the EC regulation' would oblige the sickness fund to pay the costs of the received treatment.

The newspaper message provides an example of a case which should have been dealt with as an Art 22(1)c case but which was handled as an Art 22(1)a case. Yet, the conclusion was correct that the *Krankenkasse* had to reimburse the health care provider in the Netherlands. Even though the Regulation itself is silent on the issue, it is to be assumed that it is in principle up to health care providers to decide whether or not a particular case is an emergency. Jorens (1992) n 42 above, at 96–7. Similar 'tricks' could possibly be played with Art 25. The unemployed who wish to obtain a certain type of treatment which is either not covered by their insurance or who wish to avoid waiting-lists could register with an employment office in another member State, export their unemployment benefit and claim medical benefits in the State concerned as though they were insured in that Member State. It is hard to establish how often Arts 22(1)a and 25 are used in the way described above, but given the fact that doctors and other health care providers are often self-employed and thus often likely to be interested in increasing their income by accepting more patients, the possibility cannot be excluded that it happens quite often.

The question could be raised whether the competent institutions must in all such cases bear the costs. Neither Reg 1408/71 nor Reg 574/72 contains a provision which could free the competent institution from the obligation to pay the bill and in the light of the Community's goal of promoting freedom of movement, the basic assumption must be that institutions must presume the correctness of the views of health care providers in other Member States. By analogy with the case-law of the Court on determination of sickness for the purposes of the grant or payment of cash benefits (*Paletta* cases—see n 46 above) or the medical examinations of applicants or recipients of invalidity (Arts 40 and 51 of Reg 574/72—see, eg: Case C–279/97 *Voeten* [1998] ECR I–8293), however, one cannot exclude the possibility that the competent institutions can refuse payment in cases where they can prove that Art 22(1)a has been 'abused'. Difficulties concerning the demarcation of emergency cases and authorisation cases have also arisen in *Agnello*, a Luxembourg case. The case concerns a French frontier worker in Luxembourg. After an accident, he transported his spouse to a Belgian hospital for emergency treatment. Afterwards he asked for the E 111 form. The form was refused on the ground that the accident had not taken place in Belgium. Mr Agnello started legal proceedings and called upon the Luxembourg court to refer the case to the Court of Justice. The court refused to do so, however, on the ground that the E 111 form could be issued retroactively. The sickness fund in question has appealed that decision in Luxembourg. Palm *et al* (2000) n 4 above, at 82.

[134] See especially: ch 3, s 4.3.

further detail in Directives No 93/96, No 90/365 or No 90/364.[135] As regards the cross-border health care and insurance rights of these categories, a distinction is to be made between pensioners and 'other' Community citizens, on the one hand, and students, on the other hand.

3.3.1 Pensioners and 'other' Community Citizens

Regulations No 1408/71 and No 574/72 have never been drafted with the category of non-economic residents in mind. At the time of drafting, Community law merely provided for a free movement of workers and self-employed persons. The category of non-economic residents did not yet 'exist.' Until recently,[136] Article 2 of Regulation No 1408/71 defined the personal scope to include employed or self-employed persons 'who are or have been subject to the legislation of one or more Member States' and 'who hold the nationality of one of the Member States.' This did not, and does not, imply, however, that non-economic residents are necessarily excluded from the scope of the regulations' application. In fact, in many cases they will be able to benefit from the provisions contained in Regulation No 1408/71.

The definitions of the term worker differ for the purposes of Article 39 EC and the social security regulations. Article 1(a) of Regulation No 1408/71 defines employed persons as persons who are 'insured, compulsorily or on an optional continued basis' by one of the branches of a social security scheme for employed persons as well as persons who are compulsorily insured under a social security scheme for all residents or for the whole population if such persons can be identified as employed persons by virtue of the manner in which a social security scheme is administered or financed. This definition is much broader than the definition of worker for the purposes of Article 39 EC which requires in particular that Community citizens meet the threshold requirement of 'effective and genuine work.'[137] Many part-time workers will not be able to meet this requirement. As regards the right of residence they will have to rely on Directive No 90/364. The requirement of 'effective and genuine work,' however, does not apply under Regulation No 1408/71. Part-timers who perform merely 'marginal and ancillary' activities can be classed as workers for the purposes of the social security regulation.[138] By virtue of Article 13 *et seq* they will be insured in the State concerned and be entitled to claim medical care there under the same conditions as the nationals of the host State. Moreover, many Community citizens who would like to establish residence in other Member States without taking up employment there will be covered by the social security regulations because as workers they are subject to the legislation in the State of origin (or another

---

[135] Ch 2, s 3.
[136] See also: s 3.3.2.
[137] Case 53/81 *Levin* [1982] ECR 1035 at 17. See also: ch 2, s 2.2.4.
[138] Cp eg: Case 2/89 *Kits van Heijningen* [1990] ECR I–1755.

Member State). A change of private residence does not lead to the loss of the status of worker in the State of employment under Regulation No 1408/71 and such non-economic residents can rely on Article 19 of Regulation No 1408/71 in order to claim medical benefits in the State of residence. Furthermore, pensioners covered by residence Directive No 90/365 will also be regarded as pensioners for the purposes of Article 26–34 of Regulation No 1408/71. As a result, they are entitled to obtain medical benefits in the State of residence. In sum, the vast majority of the pensioners, the residual category of 'other' Community citizens as well their family members is publicly insured in one of the Member States and this entitles them to all rights and benefits discussed in section 3.1 and Section 3.2.

3.3.2 Students

Much of what has been said above could also apply to the specific category of Community students, ie, Community citizens who have made use of the opportunity guaranteed by Articles 12, 149 and 150 EC to study in other Member States.[139] By performing part-time jobs in the evenings or at weekends students may acquire the status of worker for the purposes of Regulation No 1408/71 and, in this capacity, they may benefit from the various health care provisions of the two social security regulations. The Community legislator has recognised, however, that the coordination rules for workers and their family members do not in all circumstances provide students and their family members with sufficient health insurance cover. For instance, many students could merely benefit from the health care provisions of Regulations No 1408/71 and No 574/72 in their capacity as family members. This meant that students who participate in the *Socrates/Erasmus* programme[140] and who do not establish residence, ie, the place where they have the permanent or normal centre of their interests,[141] in the State of their studies could only rely on Article 22(1)a of Regulation No 1408/71 in order to claim treatment in cases of medical emergency. Otherwise, they could, at least in theory, be required to return to their country of origin in order to obtain treatment. Furthermore, in a number of Member States specific health insurance schemes for students exist. Sometimes such schemes merely provide insurance for students studying at a national educational institution with the result that students following courses or training in other Member States could be without insurance cover or be forced to insure themselves with 'quite expensive' private insurers.[142] Also, such schemes may

---

[139] Ch 2, s 3 and, more extensively, ch 5, s 4.

[140] Ch 5, s 4.9.

[141] Cp Case C–90/97 *Swaddling* [1999] ECR I–1073 at 29–30.

[142] In a recent proposal for a Recommendation of the European Parliament and of the Council, the European Commission has included a provision (numbered as 2(c)) which calls upon Member States to take appropriate measures so that students who have private health insurance can transfer the advantages of this insurance to the host country. COM(1999) 708 final.

apply compulsorily to foreign students, which could imply that such students might have to pay health insurance contributions in more than one State.

With a view to promoting the free movement of students, the Community legislator inserted Article 22c into Regulation No 1408/71 in 1997 which entitled students to rely on Article 22(1)a 'for any condition necessitating benefits during the stay in the territory' of the State where they are studying.[143] Further, in 1999 the legislator adopted Regulation No 307/1999 which has extended the personal scope of Regulation No 1408/71 in its entirety to students[144] and has inserted new provisions specifically governing the cross-border health care rights of students. Article 34a provides that some of the provisions applying to (self-)employed persons (and their family members), and which have been discussed in Section 3.2 and Section 3.3, are to be applied by analogy to students and their family members.[145] Article 34b has replaced the aforementioned Article 22c.

The new health care and insurance provisions for students are quite difficult to fathom mainly because Regulation No 307/1999 has not introduced rules for determining the State in which students are insured.[146] Community students can be insured in the State of origin and/or the State of the studies. Students who are (only) insured in the State of origin and who have kept their residence there can, where necessary, rely on Article 3 of Regulation No 1408/71 in order to claim medical benefits under the same conditions of the nationals of that State.[147] According to Article 34b, such students have the right to rely on Article 22(1)a in the State where they study for any condition necessitating benefits during their stay. The right to medical treatment is thus not limited to emergency situ-

---

[143]   The Article was inserted by Reg 1290/97 (OJ 1997 L 176).

[144]   Art 2 of Reg 1408/71 has been amended and now provides that besides (self-)employed persons, students who are or have been subject to the legislation of one or more Member States also fall within the scope of the Regulation. The newly inserted Art 1(ca) of Reg 1408/71 defines a student as 'any person other than an employed or self-employed person or a member of his family or survivor within the meaning of this regulation who studies or receives vocational training leading to a qualification officially recognised by the authorities of a Member State, and is insured under a general social security scheme or a special social security scheme applicable to students'

[145]   Besides the provisions which will be discussed below these concern Art 23 (calculation of cash benefits), Art 24 (special rules for substantial benefits in kind), Art 35 (not discussed in this Chapter) and Art 36 (reimbursement by the competent institution).

[146]   The new health care and insurance provisions for students do not prevent double health insurance. In the preamble to Reg 307/1999 it is stated that it 'is desirable, as far as possible, to prevent' students 'from being subject to a double levy of contributions, or acquiring dual rights to benefits', but, due to 'the specific nature of the situation relating to students' no agreements could be reached on specific conflict rules. See the eighth recital of the preamble to Reg 307/1999. The Member States represented in the Council have not been able to agree on rules determining the applicable legislation. The additional rights that the two new provisions confer upon students and their family members have only been guaranteed since 1 May 1999. See (the new) Art 95d(1). This does not apply to the rights guaranteed by Art 18 of Reg 1408/71 (see Art 95d(2)) and illnesses that already existed on the said date (Art 95d(3)).

[147]   In addition, such students can benefit from Art 18 of Reg 1408/71 (which by virtue of Art 34a applies by analogy to students) in order to have their periods of insurance or residence fulfilled in other States taken into account where the legislation of the State concerned makes entitlement to benefits conditional upon fulfillment of such periods.

ations. All medical products or services, which may be medically required are included. *De facto*, students who are insured and residing in the State of origin can choose in which of the two States they wish to 'go to the doctor.' Students who are insured in the State of origin but who have decided to establish residence in the State of their studies do not seem to have such a choice. In the State where they study and reside, they can claim 'full access' to medical care under Article 19 which, as Articles 34a states, applies by analogy to students. Article 34a, however, does not refer to Articles 20 and 21 and this would seem to imply that students cannot claim under Regulation No 1408/71 medical benefits in the competent State during a stay. On the basis of national law such students may possibly claim medical benefits in the competent State, but Regulation No 1408/71 does not seem to entitle them to challenge national rules which preserve medical benefits for insured students who are studying at a national educational institution.[148] Students who are only insured in the State where they study can benefit from Article 3 of Regulation No 1408/71 when they wish to claim medical care in that State.[149] Students, who do not reside in the State where they are insured and study, can benefit from Article 19 of Regulation No 1408/71 in order to get medical care and products in the State of residence.[150]

3.3.3 Right to Reside and the Health Insurance Requirement

The right of residence of pensioners, students and 'other' Community citizens as well as the family members of these categories, is conditional upon the requirement that the persons concerned are 'covered by sickness insurance in respect of all risks in the host Member State.'[151] This requirement has been introduced in order to avoid non-economic residents becoming a burden on the public purse of the host State. Neither the directive nor any of the prepatory documents[152] clarify the precise meaning of the requirement. It seems unlikely, however, that many

---

[148] Art 34a states that Arts 22(1)a and c (as well as the provisions contained in Art 22(3) (family members) and Art 22(2) (right to authorisation)) apply by analogy to students and their family members. These provisions, however, can only be relied upon in order to claim emergency treatment or authorised treatment in a Member State other than the State of insurance. Remarkably, then, students can rely on the aforementioned provisions in 'third' Member States, but not in the State where they are insured. Possibly, however, students can challenge national rules that preserve medical benefits for insured students who are studying at a national educational institution under Arts 12 and/or 18 EC.

[149] Where necessary, Art 18 of Reg 1408/71 can be relied upon.

[150] There is no specific health care provision which entitles students who are insured, but who have decided not to establish residence, in the State where they study, to claim medical care in that State. Neither Arts 20 and 21 nor Art 34b of the Regulation, which only applies in State other than the competent State, can be relied upon. It would seem, however, that such non-resident students can invoke Art 3 in order to challenge possible residence requirements contained in the State of insurance.

[151] Arts 1(1) of the Dirs 93/96, 90/365, 90/364.

[152] The Commission's proposal of 1979 for a general right of residence (see ch 2 s 3.1) did not contain a condition as regards health insurance. In the negotiations on the 1979 proposal the issue of health insurance does not seem to have come up. The condition appears for the first time in the Adonnino Report of 1985. See EC Bull.Suppl.7/85 at 14. The report indicates that the health

Community citizens will encounter serious difficulties in meeting this requirement. The majority of the beneficiaries of the three 1990 directives is publicly insured for medical care and covered by Regulations No 1408/71 and No 574/72. As workers, pensioners, students or family members, they will be able to benefit from Articles 3, 13 and/or the health care provisions in order to claim medical benefits in the State of residence. Further, the principle that all beneficiaries, regardless of the State where they are insured, have the right to obtain medical benefits in the State of residence in accordance with the applicable legislation, guarantees that non-economic residents are insured 'in respect of all risks in the host Member State.'[153] Furthermore, the two regulations ensure that the costs of medical care are (to be) fully reimbursed by the institution to which beneficiaries have paid their health contributions and this would seem to guarantee that the persons concerned will not become a burden on the host State's public purse.[154]

insurance requirement was introduced in order to avoid beneficiaries becoming an unreasonable burden on the public purse of the host State, but nowhere does it explain the precise meaning of the requirement. In its proposals for the three Directives on the right of residence the Commission has followed the recommendations of the Adonnino-report, but the precise contours of the insurance condition are again not elucidated in the proposals (or the text of the adopted directives).

[153] For another view see the Opinion of Adv GenGeelhoed in Case C-413/99 *Baumbast*, pending, at 116.

    Taken literally, the requirement that beneficiaries must be insured for 'all risks in the host State' could be interpreted to imply that the persons concerned must be insured for all risks including eg, dental care, cosmetic plastic surgery and co-payments even in cases where such types of benefits and payments are excluded from the legislation in the host State. The mere fact, however, that certain types of medical benefits are to be wholly or partially paid by patients already guarantees that patients receiving such benefits, regardless of their nationality, will not become a burden on the public purse. The literal interpretation of the requirement of insurance for 'all risks' runs counter to the purpose of the health insurance requirement. Therefore, it would seem more logical to read the requirement to imply that non-economic residents must, in principle, be insured for the same risks as the nationals of the host State in a comparable situation. Van Nuffel, 'Een Bijna Algemeen Verblijfsrecht in de Europese Gemeenschap' (1990) *SEW* 887-993, at 900. This interpretation of the insurance requirement also seems to be consistent with the definition of the financial means requirement contained in particular in Dir 90/364 which sets the level of resources below which Member States grant social assistance benefits to their own nationals as the criterion to be applied in determining whether or not nationals of other Member States possess sufficient financial resources.

[154] This is not to say that problems regarding the health insurance requirement cannot arise. For instance, students who are covered by a special scheme applicable to students which does not allow them to obtain medical benefits outside the State of origin may still be forced to enrol in a rather expensive private insurance scheme in order to acquire the right to reside in the State of the studies. See also: Martin and Guild, *Free Movement of Persons* (1996) at 211. Furthermore, the requirement may pose problems for Community citizens falling outside the scope of Reg 1408/71 such as the privately insured. Such Community citizens will have to ensure that their insurance in the State of origin covers treatment for 'all risks' in the State where they intend to reside or, when this is not the case, insure themselves (additionally) in the State of their planned residence. The Directives do not specify what type of insurance is required and it may thus be assumed that both private and public health insurance may suffice for satisfying the requirement. Cp *Report from the Commission to the Parliament and Council on the Implementation of Directives 90/364, 90/365 and 93/96—Right of Residence* (1998) at 11. Neither do the directives indicate where a person must be insured. The only condition is that Community citizens and their family members must be insured for all risks which may occur on the territory of the State of residence. As regards private insurance it may thus be assumed that an insurance contract with any private insurer established in one of the Member States suffices as long as all risks in the Member State of residence are covered. See also: Langer (1999) n 7 above, at 721–2.

3.4 Third Country Nationals

Third country nationals do not enjoy the right to freedom of movement within the Community[155] and they are (therefore also) excluded from the personal scope of Regulations No 1408/71 and No 574/72.[156] In principle, nationals of third countries can only claim the cross-border health care rights that the social security regulations confer upon family members. This does not imply, however, that Community law has nothing to offer to third country nationals who wish to claim medical benefits in one of the Member States. They may possibly enjoy certain rights under the cooperation or association agreements that the Community and its Member States have concluded with third States. For the purposes of this book three (sets of) agreements have been selected: the Agreement creating the European Economic Area (hereafter: the EEA Agreement), the Maghreb agreements (concluded with Morocco, Algeria and Tunisia) and the Association Agreement with Turkey.

3.4.1 EEA Nationals

In order to promote a continuous and balanced strengthening of trade and economic relations between the European Community and its Member States, on the one hand, and Norway, Iceland and Liechtenstein, on the other hand, the EEA Agreement has extended the scope of the four common market freedoms to the nationals and territories of the three EEA countries mentioned. As a result, EEA nationals can benefit from the provisions on the free movement of (self-)employed persons and they enjoy, under the services provisions, the right to travel freely throughout the EEA.[157] In addition, the application of the three non-economic residence directives of 1990 has been extended to EEA nationals.[158]

As to cross-border health care rights, one can be relatively brief. Article 29 EEA largely reproduces Article 42 (formerly 51) EC and by virtue of Annex VI to the Agreement, Regulations No 1408/71 and No 574/72 are also applicable in the European Economic Area. Basically, the EEA Agreement has extended the scope of the right to equal treatment in social security matters, the rules for determining the applicable legislation as well as the health care provisions contained in Article 18–36 of Regulation No 1408/71 and the corresponding provisions of Regulation No 574/72 to all EEA nationals. As a result, the nationals of

---

[155] Case C-378/97 *Wijsenbeek* [1999] ECR I-6207 at 43.

[156] Art 2 of Reg 1408/71. To be sure, stateless persons and refugees are covered by the regulation when they are residing within the Community and can be classed as a worker or a self-employed person.

[157] Ch 2, s 4.

[158] See also: ch 2, s 3.

Norway, Iceland and Liechtenstein enjoy in all eighteen States the rights that have been discussed in Section 3.2 and Section 3.3 of this chapter.[159]

3.4.2 Turkish Nationals

The 1963 EEC–Turkey Association Agreement, the Additional Protocol of 1970 and the various decisions adopted by the EEC-Turkey Association Council do not confer upon Turkish workers a right to freedom of movement within the Community or between Turkey and the Community.[160] Access by Turkish nationals to the labour market and territory of Member States is in principle governed by national immigration laws.[161] However, Turkish workers and their families who have been admitted by one of the Member States do enjoy certain social security rights under Decision No 3/80 of the EEC–Turkey Association Council. This Decision on the application of social security schemes to the benefit of Turkish workers provides for a right to equal treatment in social security matters (Article 3) and a right to export certain benefits (Article 6). It also extends the application of most rules determining the applicable legislation contained in Articles 13 *et seq.* of Regulation No 1408/71 to Turkish workers (Article 9) and the Decision states that virtually all health care provisions contained in Regulation No 1408/71 apply by analogy to Turkish workers.[162]

At first glance, it would thus seem that Turkish workers enjoy quite extensive health insurance protection in the Member State that they have been admitted to. Nonetheless, significant limitations exist. It may be recalled[163] that the Court was asked in *Taflan-Met* (1996)[164] to determine (*i*) whether, and if so, when, Decision No 3/80 had come into force and (*ii*) whether the provisions of the Decision could be relied upon by Turkish workers in court. Uncertainty as to the binding force existed because the decision did not contain any provision on its

---

[159] Sakslin, 'The Agreements on the European Economic Area' in Jorens and Schulte (eds), *European Social Security Law and Third Country Nationals* (1998) 399-417, at 410-11. To be sure, in Opinion 1/91 the Court of Justice held that the fact that two international instruments are identically worded does not necessarily mean that they have the same legal effect. The context of a rule determines its legal effect. Opinion 1/91 [1991] ECR I-6079. On this point see Zuleeg, 'International Instruments on Equal treatment in Social Security Matters' in *Commission of the European Communities/Departemento de Relações Internaçionais e Convençóes de Segurança Social, Social Security in Europe—Equality between Nationals and Non-Nationals* (1995) 89–101, at 93–4. It seems very unlikely, however, that any of the provisions governing the cross-border health care rights are to be interpreted more restrictively as regards EEA nationals.

[160] Ch 2, s 5.3.

[161] Case C–210/97 *Akman* [1998] ECR I–7519 at 50.

[162] By virtue of Arts 10 and 11 of Decision 3/80, Arts 18–36 of Reg 1408/71 apply by analogy to Turkish workers (and their families). Art 25(1) (right of work-seekers to obtain medical benefits in the State where they seek employment—s 3.1.1) and Art 25(2) (which states that wholly unemployed frontier workers as well as the wholly unemployed non-frontier workers who were residing in a Member State other than the competent State and who have decided to seek (new) employment in the State of residence, shall receive medical benefits in the State of residence as though they had been insured there during their last employment—s 3.1.3) of Reg 1408/71 do not apply to Turkish workers.

[163] Ch 3, s 6.3.

[164] Case C–277/94 *Taflan-Met* [1996] ECR I–4085.

coming into force and the Commission's proposal for a regulation implementing Decision No 3/80 within the Community has never been adopted by the Council. The Court concluded that the decision was supposed to have come into force on the day the decision was adopted, ie, 19 September 1980.[165] In the Court's view, however, the provisions of Decision No 3/80 could not be relied upon in court. In reaching this conclusion the Court drew a comparison with Regulation No 1408/71 and it's implementing Regulation No 574/72. The main principles set forth in the former Regulation could only have been given practical effect because of the procedures and formalities contained in the latter Regulation. The coming into force of Regulation No 574/72 was seen as a prerequisite for the enforcement of the rights enshrined in Regulation No 1408/71. Decision No 3/80, however, is not yet accompanied by an implementing legislative measure comparable to Regulation No 574/72. As long as such a measure has not been adopted, the Court held that the provisions of Decision No 3/80 could not have direct effect.[166] In *Sürül* (1999), however, the Court has nuanced the conclusions drawn in *Taflan-Met*. The Court held that the reasoning which had led it to conclude in *Taflan-Met* that the provisions of Decision No 3/80 do not have direct effect, must apply by analogy to all other provisions which require additional measures for their application in practice. The Court ruled, however, that technical or administrative problems do not arise in relation to the nondiscrimination provision of Article 3(1) of the decision. This Article can be directly invoked in national courts.[167]

Translated to the provisions relevant for access to medical benefits, *Taflan-Met* and *Sürül* seem to imply that Turkish workers can only benefit from those provisions which are not dependent for their practical application on any implementing measures or the fulfilment of administrative formalities. As a rule, Turkish workers (and their family members) will live in the State of employment and insurance. There they can, where necessary, rely on Article 3 of Decision No 3/80 in order to claim access to health care under the same conditions as the host State's nationals. Turkish workers do not have the right to have periods of insurance, residence or employment they might have fulfilled in other Member States taken into account by the competent institution. Article 18 of Regulation No 1408/71 is to be applied to Turkish workers but is conditional upon fulfilment of various administrative formalities for its implementation.[168]

---

[165] *Ibid,* at 21.

[166] *Ibid,* at 31–7.

[167] Case C–262/99 *Sürül* [1999] ECR I–2685 at 58–74.

[168] As regards the relatively small group of Turkish workers who are residing in a Member State other than the one of insurance, *Taflan-Met* and *Sürül* seem to lead to a 'quite odd' result. The workers seem able to benefit from Arts 20 and 21 of Reg 1408/71, which apply by analogy with Art 11 of Decision 3/80 to Turkish workers and which do not make the right to claim medical benefits in the competent State conditional upon any formalities, in order to gain access in the State where they are insured. Yet, they do not seem entitled to claim medical care in the State of residence. Implementation of Art 19 of Regulation, which has been held to apply by analogy to Turkish workers, is conditional upon fulfillment of a cooperation between health insurance institutions.

Turkish workers also do not seem to have any right to claim medical benefits in Member States other than the State of residence or insurance. Article 25(1), which confers upon work-seekers the right to obtain medical care in the Member State where they seek work, is excluded from the health provisions which are according to Article 11 of Decision No 3/80, to be applied by analogy to Turkish workers. The rights of non-residents to emergency and authorised treatment (Article 22(1)a and c) are for all practical effects dependent on the exchange of one of the E-forms.

3.4.3 Maghreb Nationals

The cooperation and/or Euro–Mediterranean agreements which the European Community and its Member States have concluded with Morocco, Algeria and Tunisia do not provide for a free movement of workers between the Community and these countries or a freedom of movement for Maghreb nationals between the Member States.[169] However, the Agreements do contain a number of provisions that confer upon Maghreb nationals rights in the field of labour and social security law. Article 41(1) of the cooperation agreement with Morocco, as now replaced by Article 65 of the Euro–Mediterranean Agreement of 2000, confers upon Moroccan nationals the right to equal treatment in the field of social security. The second paragraph grants Moroccan nationals the right to aggregation of insurance, employment or residence periods for various social security benefits among which rights to obtain health care. Article 42 of the cooperation agreement (now Article 67 of Euro–Mediterranean Agreement) states that the Cooperation Council shall adopt measures to implement the principles set out in Article 41. A decision equivalent to Decision No 3/80 of the EEC–Turkey Association Council, however, has not been adopted.[170] Similarly phrased provisions are contained in Articles 39 and 40 of the 1978 Cooperation agreement with Algeria and Articles 65 and 67 of the 1998 Euro–Mediterranean agreement with Tunisia.

From the judgments in *Kziber* (1991)[171] and *Krid* (1995),[172] as discussed in chapter 3,[173] it follows that the provisions guaranteeing equality of treatment in the field of social security produce direct effect and that the term social security in these provisions must be understood 'by means of analogy with the identical concept in Regulation No 1408/71'. In the State where they are employed, insured and residing Maghreb nationals thus have the right to be treated equally

---

[169] Ch 2, s 5.3.

[170] Recently, however, a proposal for social security measures has been made in the context of the Euro-Mediterranean agreements with Morocco (<http://europa.eu.int/eur-lex>).

[171] Case C–18/90 *Kziber* [1991] ECR I–199. On this judgment see, eg: Vonk, 'Het HvJEG-arrest in de zaak Kziber—Een Levenskus voor de Slapende Paragrafen in de EG-samenwerkingsovereenkomsten' (1991) *MR* 149–51.

[172] Case C–103/94 *Krid* [1995] ECR I–719 at 23–4.

[173] Ch 3, s 6.2.

as regards health insurance and access to medical care just as the nationals of the host State. Apart from the right to equal treatment, the three agreements do not offer Maghreb nationals any other rights in the fields of health care and insurance. In the absence of any implementing decisions, and by analogy with the *Sürül* judgment, it may be assumed that Maghreb nationals cannot benefit from aggregation rules and the provisions guaranteeing health care rights to persons staying or residing in a Member State other than the State of insurance.

3.5 Patient Mobility

For a proper understanding of the Community rules on the coordination of health insurance schemes it is useful to see how they are applied in practice and how much use is actually made of the cross-border health care rights. For this purpose, a study conducted by the Association Internationale de la Mutualité (AIM) is of particular interest.[174]

The AIM-study first of all demonstrates that the costs of cross-border health care constitute only a very small percentage of the total health care expenditure of Member States. The percentage is on the average between 0.3 per cent and 0.5 per cent.[175] Furthermore, virtually all cross-border health care takes place among the original six Member States. The study makes a calculation of the global claims and debts of each Member State,[176] and it appears that about 90 per cent of the total claims costs of cross-border health care within the Community is in the hands of Belgium, France, Germany, and Italy. These four are the main providers of cross-border health care. Together with Luxembourg and the Netherlands, these countries are also responsible for 90 per cent of the total debts of care provided under Regulations No 1408/71 and No 574/72. The health care system of France appears to be the most popular. It takes on 49 per cent of the total claims. Italy, being responsible for about 36 per cent of the total debts, is the main debtor. The concentration of movement between the 'old' six may, as the authors of the study explain, not come as a real surprise. Belgium, France, Germany, Luxembourg and the Netherlands are all located in the geographical heart of the Community and these Member States have more experience in applying the coordination mechanism set up by Regulations No 1408/71 and

---

[174] Hermesse and Lawalle (1991) n 1 above. For updates of the study see Hermesse, Lewalle and Palm, 'Patient Mobility within the European Union' (1997) *EJPH* 4–10 and Palm *et al* (2000) n 4 above, at 38–44.

[175] Only Luxembourg spends a relatively high percentage (5%) of its health care expenditures on care abroad. Due to the low number of inhabitants and tax-payers, and the therefore limited finances available for health care, Luxembourg seems to have opted for allowing its residents to be treated in other Member States instead of developing a comprehensive health care system within the country itself.

[176] The claims relate to the costs of care given by each Member State to persons insured in another country, whilst the debts concern the costs for health care enjoyed by their 'own' insured in another Member State.

No 574/72 than the 'newer' Member States in the 'outer-ring' of the Community. The authors of the study further suggest that the fact that the 'old' Member States have an insurance-based health care system rather than national health services may be a reason for their greater involvement in cross-border care.

Of the three main cross-border health care situations (emergency treatment, authorised treatment and 'frontier workers') authorised treatment abroad is responsible for the largest percentage (about 60 per cent) of the costs of cross-border health care. This is explained by the fact that authorisation for treatment abroad is usually given for specific diseases. It usually concerns rather specialised and expensive types of treatment. Because of these costs, the number of authorised treatments is, by comparison with other forms of cross-border health care, relatively low. France is by far the most popular Member State to which patients of other Member States are sent. The reasons why France attracts so many patients from other Member States could be geographical in nature, but those conducting the study state that it is more likely that the high quality of the French health care system (in particular with respect to kidney, heart and liver transplants) constitutes the main reason. The quality of the French system is probably also one of the reasons why the French authorities hardly give any authorisations to French patients for treatment abroad. Italy and Luxembourg appear to be the Member States that are the least strict in granting authorisation for treatment abroad. This attitude probably results from the limitations of the health care systems in the two countries. In general, it might have been expected that countries with a less developed health care system would give authorisation for treatment abroad rather frequently. This, however, does not appear to be true. Apparently, these countries choose to invest in the development of their national health care system rather than to send their patients abroad.[177]

As regards health care provided in emergency cases during a temporary stay abroad, it is noticeable that tourist countries like Spain, Portugal, Italy and Greece are only responsible for a low proportion of the total claims for 'emergency care.' Tourists appear reluctant to take advantage of the health care systems in these countries. Emergency treatment on the basis of Article 22(1)a of Regulation No 1408/71 is above all provided by Member States, and in particular France, in the geographical centre of the Community. This conclusion may, in as far as France is concerned, not come as a surprise since it is one of the most popular tourist countries within the Community. With respect to the Netherlands, Belgium and Germany, however, the conclusion surprises somewhat. The authors of the AIM-study explain the high percentage of the costs of emergency care of Article 22(1)a by referring to the comparatively high quality and costs of the health care systems in these Member States and the fact that these States absorb quite high numbers of work-related movements.

Cross-border treatment of persons living in frontier regions is the most frequent but also the cheapest. The costs of health care granted to frontier work-

---

[177] See also: n 132 above.

ers in the Member States of their residence constitute a small percentage of the total expenditure. The treatment concerned mostly consists of regular and relatively cheap types of treatment. Most of the health care provided under Article 19 of Regulation 1408/71 takes place between the Member States in the geographical centre of the Community. Germany and Luxembourg appear to be the countries that have to pay the most for health care of frontier workers in the State of residence.[178]

3.6 Initiatives to Extend Cross-Border Health Care Rights

3.6.1 *The Call for an Extension of Cross-Border Health Care Rights*

The rules and principles governing cross-border access to health care that have been described in this section are virtually as old as the Community itself. Regulations No 1408/71 and No 574/72 have only been in existence since the early 1970s but their health care provisions are based on the same principles as their equivalents in the original Regulations No 3/58 and No 4/58. On the one hand, it has always been recognised that Community citizens who become in need of medical care while staying or residing in another Member State should have the right to obtain the required treatment and to have the bill paid by their insurance institution. On the other hand, however, from the beginning it has been equally undisputed that Community citizens should not have a right to travel to other Member States for the sole purpose of obtaining medical treatment at the expense of the

---

[178] The study also shows that the formalities and procedures are in practice not always fully applied. Member States and the competent health institutions often consider the procedures to be too cumbersome, too complicated and/or too expensive. This particularly holds true for the E 111 formalities for emergency treatment. Due to the frequency and relatively low costs of emergency treatment many Member States do not require (all) the formalities to be fulfilled. Emergency treatment is simply given and financial settlement often takes place on the basis of a flat rate payment. Many Member States even waive the recovery of the costs of emergency treatment. They may do this unilaterally, but flat rate payment and the waiving of the claims for the costs, are more often based on bi- or multilateral conventions or agreements with other Member States or health care institutions. Other forms of financial settlement or the waiving of claims, are also common as regards the costs of treatment given to beneficiaries living in frontier regions. In many Member States (eg Belgium, the United Kingdom and Spain) the E 111 formalities are not considered to be of much practical value and it has been suggested that the E 111 formalities should be abolished altogether. In other Member States, however, the formalities are deemed necessary for bureaucratic reasons. Furthermore, due to a lack of information, language problems, the immediacy of the medical treatment or the fact that the institution to which form E 111 has to be submitted is often too far away, many insured persons do not fulfill the required formalities. In order to avoid the administrative formalities many Community citizens even appear to take out private travel insurance when travelling abroad. Rambags, 'Samenloop Ziekenfondsverzekering (EG-verordeningen 1408/71 en 574/72) en Reisverzekering' (1988) *De Beursbengel* 448 *et seq*. On the practice of the E 111 formalities see further the references in n 112. With respect to authorised treatment, however, the formalities are fully applied and recovery takes place on the basis of actual expenditures. This is explained by the fact that E 112 treatment usually concerns rather specialised and expensive types of medical treatment. Moreover, the number of times authorisation is given is, at least in comparison to emergency treatment and 'frontier treatment', rather low.

institution they are insured with. In essence, access to medical care has traditionally been seen as a territorially limited right; those who wish to benefit from the
medical services available in other States have to bear the costs themselves. The
only time that the Court of Justice did touch upon the basic principles governing
the cross-border access to health care (*Pierik* cases), the Member States repaired
the situation quickly (by amending Article 22(2) of Regulation No 1408/71).[179]

Since the late 1980s, early 1990s, however, the territorial limitation of the
right to obtain medical care has increasingly been debated and criticised. The
health care provisions of Regulations No 1408/71 and No 574/72 have been
classed as being 'too restrictive' and no 'longer appropriate to today's requirements.'[180] The criticism has been threefold.[181] First, the territorial limitation of
the right to gain access to medical care has been said to give insufficient regard
to the interests of patients. For instance, residents of frontier regions often have
to go to hospitals which are relatively far away from their homes, whilst, if it
were not for the existing legal obstacles, they could be treated in hospitals 'just
across the border.' Furthermore, because of waiting lists, many beneficiaries
have to wait for quite some time before they can get treatment, whilst, if given
the right, they could be treated immediately or much sooner in another Member
State. Secondly, the rules on cross-border access to health care have been
claimed to obstruct an efficient use of the health care facilities in the Union. In
some Member States there is a shortage of various types of treatment, whilst in
other States surpluses of the same or comparable types of treatment exist. An
increased cross-border use of health care facilities could possibly bring these
shortages and surpluses more into balance. This would stimulate a more
efficient use of the existing medical facilities and prevent, at least partly, an
unnecessary waste of resources. Third, the exclusion of third country nationals
from Regulations No 1408/71 and No 574/72 has increasingly been felt as an
omission. Even though they fall outside the Community's free movement
regime, third country nationals do in practice move from one State to another
and since, as a rule, they pay health contributions under the same conditions as
the nationals of the host State in whose territory they reside, it has increasingly
been felt unjustified to deny them the benefits of the coordinator rules and the
provisions on cross-border access to health care in particular.[182]

In response to the above criticism and desires, several initiatives have been
taken in order to promote the cross-border access to, and use of, health care
facilities. Two strategies have been followed. The first is the 'legislative strategy'
which consists of extending health care rights by amending the provisions of

---

[179]   s 3.3.2.

[180]   COM(94) 333 at IV.12.

[181]   Van der Mei, 'Cross-border Access to Medical Care Within the European Union: Some
Reflections on the Judgments in *Decker* and *Kohll*' (1998) *MJ* 277–97, at 278–9.

[182]   See, eg: the Explanatory Memorandum of the Commission for its proposal to amend
Reg 1408/71 with a view to extending the personal scope of the regulation to third country nationals. COM(97) 561 final.

Regulation No 1408/71. The second method consists of a 'contractual strategy' under which cross-border care is promoted through the conclusion of agreements between insurers and providers in different States.

3.6.2 Legislative Strategy

The Commission has submitted to the Council several proposals for amending the health care provisions of Regulations No 1408/71 and No 574/72. Most useful for purposes of this discussion is the Commission's 1998 proposal for the simplification of the two social security regulations.[183] In this proposal various earlier and more specific proposals for amending health care provisions have been clustered.

For a proper understanding of the proposed changes to medical 'benefits in kind,' it is to be pointed out that the Commission has proposed to extend the personal scope of the Regulation considerably. In the envisaged new Article 1 it is stated that the regulation shall apply to 'persons who are or have been subject to the social security legislation of one or more Member States, as well as the members of their family and to their survivors.' The term 'persons' indicates that the personal scope will be extended as to include (*i*) not only (self-)employed persons and students but also all insured persons including those who are no longer, or have never been, economically active and (*ii*) third country nationals.[184]

---

[183] COM(1998) 779 final. On this proposal see Eichenhofer, 'How to Simplify the Co-ordination of Social Security' (2000) *EJSS* 229 *et seq*; Pennings and Essers, 'Het Voorstel van de Europese Commissie tot Vereenvoudiging van Verordening 1408/71' (2000) *SMA* 512–25 and Sakslin, 'Social Security Co-ordination—Adapting to Change' (2000) *EJSS* 169–87.

[184] To be sure, the proposal does not intend to confer any free movement rights upon third country nationals. It merely intends to offer nationals of third countries who have acquired the right to stay or reside in a(nother) Member State under (inter)national law, the social security protection guaranteed by the regulation. On this point, the 1998 proposal is largely based on an earlier Commission proposal of 1997. COM(1997) 561 final. On the background of the proposal(s) to include third country nationals in the scope of the social security regulations see Verschueren, 'The Commission's Proposal to Extend Regulation (EEC) No 1408/71 to Third Country Nationals' in Jorens and Schulte (eds), *European Social Security Law and Third Country Nationals* (1998) 187–208; Jorens, *De Rechtspositie van Niet-EU-Onderdanen in het Europees Socialezekerheidsrecht* (1997) Ch VI; Verschueren, 'EC Social Security Coordination Excluding Third Country Nationals: Still in Line with Fundamental Rights after the *Gaygusuz* Judgment?' (1997) *CMLRev* 991–1017 and Altmaier and Verschueren, 'The Extension of the Scope of Regulation 1408/71 to Nationals of Non-member Countries' in *Commission of the European Communities/Departemento de Relações Internaçionais e Convenções de Segurança Social, Social Security in Europe—Equality Between Nationals and Non-Nationals* (1995) 245–61.

A second proposed amendment to the general provisions relevant to cross-border access to health care concerns the simplification of the rules for determining the applicable legislation. In the proposed new Art 8 it is explicitly stated that persons are subject to the legislation of one Member State only. Persons who are pursuing a professional activity in a Member State are subject to the legislation of that State, whilst beneficiaries not pursuing such an activity are assigned to the legislation of the State where they reside. The latter category, however, only covers persons who have ceased all activity. Those who are only temporarily inactive, and who have become entitled to social security benefits (sickness or unemployment) by virtue of a professional activity are treated as though they were still active.

The proposed chapter on 'Sickness and Maternity' consists of thirteen Articles numbered as Articles 14–26. They are based on the same principles as the current Articles 18–36.[185] Thus, (*i*) medical benefits are in all cases provided in accordance with the legislation where they are provided and (*ii*) the costs are to be borne by the institution of the State where beneficiaries have paid health contributions.[186] The proposed new Article 14 provides that 'persons' who are insured for medical care and who reside in the territory of a Member State other than the competent State shall receive medical benefits 'in kind' in the State of residence as though they were insured there. The wording of Article 14 largely coincides with the wording of the current Article 19. The main difference is that third country nationals are also offered the right in question. The envisaged new Article 15 provides that all persons residing outside the competent State can also obtain benefits in the competent State. All persons who, for whatever reason, are staying in the competent State will be granted an automatic right to medical benefits there.[187] The substantive differences with the current provisions are (*i*) that frontier workers and other workers residing outside the competent State will retain the right to choose in which of the two States (ie, State of residence or the competent State) they wish to obtain medical benefits when they become wholly unemployed or retire and (*ii*) that the family members of all 'persons' residing outside the competent State will be given such a choice.[188]

Articles 16 and 17 contain provisions applying to persons who are temporarily present in Member States other than the competent State. Article 16 replaces the current Articles 22(1)a and 22a and provides for the general rule that insured persons visiting other Member States 'shall receive immediately necessary benefits in kind.' The main difference with the current provisions is that third country nationals travelling within the Community will also be able to benefit from the right to emergency treatment. Article 17 contains special rules for various groups of persons who are staying temporarily in other Member States for a specific purpose. Persons pursuing (self-)employed activ-

---

[185] The proposed chapter no longer contains a specific aggregation rule for health benefits as is the one now contained in Art 18 (see s 3.1.2). Art 4 of the proposed regulation provides for a general aggregation rule to be applied to all benefits covered by the regulation.

[186] As with the current Art 36 of Reg 1408/71, the proposed Art 26 lays down the rule that the costs of medical benefits in kind provided by the institution of one Member State on behalf of another shall give rise to 'full reimbursement'.

[187] Explanatory Memorandum of the Commission, COM(1998) 779 final, at 8.

[188] In addition, this choice is proposed to be granted to recipients of 'pre-retirement benefits' (and their family members). These benefits are proposed to be included in the material scope of the regulation. See Arts 2(i) and 7(s) of the proposal. The inclusion of these benefits builds on earlier proposals of the Commission (OJ 1980 C 169 and COM(95) 735 def) in which it was proposed to bring early retirement pensions within the scope of Reg 1408/71 and to offer recipients of such benefits a right to claim medical benefits in kind in the State of residence and, where applicable, the competent State.

ities outside the competent State (eg, seconded workers), students and work-seekers are entitled to claim medical benefits in the State concerned as though they were residing there. Article 17 does not seem to grant the categories concerned more extensive rights than they enjoy under the current provisions. The main difference is that they no longer have to fulfil the E 111-formalities but rather the formalities for persons residing outside the competent State. As regards the work-seekers, it is to be noted that the duration of the right to export unemployment benefits, and the accompanying right to claim medical benefits, is extended to a period of six months in principle.[189] Furthermore, the proposed new Article 18 provides that persons who have been authorised by the competent institution to go to the territory of another Member State to receive the treatment appropriate to their condition shall receive the benefits in kind there. Apart from the extension to third country nationals no significant changes are envisaged. The second sentence of Article 18, which states the situations in which authorisation must be accorded, is phrased differently but does not seem to be broader scope than the second sentence of the current Article 22(2). Finally, the pensioner provisions will be simplified considerably. The central health care provision for pensioners is contained in Article 20 of the proposal which provides that recipients[190] of one or more pensions and members of their families shall receive medical benefits in kind in the State where they reside.[191]

As to the chances that the 'legislative strategy' will soon lead to changes, one cannot be too optimistic.[192] The regulations can only be amended when all Member States agree to this.[193] The entire redrafting and simplification of the regulations[194] will probably be the subject of difficult and lengthy discussions in the Council. Experiences with previous Commission proposals aimed at extending

---

[189] See Art 17(3). This provision refers to Art 50 which grants work-seekers the right to export their unemployment for a maximum period of six months in principle. The Commission's proposal of 1998 builds as regards work-seekers on earlier proposals of 1980 (COM(80) 312 final) and 1996 (COM(95) 734 def.).

[190] Art 22 states that Art 20 shall apply *mutatis mutandis* to pension claimants.

[191] The main substantive difference with the current provisions concerns the question who is to bear the costs in cases where pensioners receive pensions from more than one Member State. The current rule that the costs is borne by the institution of the Member State where pensioners have been insured for the longest time, is proposed to be replaced by the rule that the costs shall be divided among the Member States paying a pension proportional to the period completed in each State (Art 20(2)).

[192] Cp Pennings and Essers (2000) n 183 above, at 524.

[193] EC Treaty Art 42.

[194] Art 72 of the proposal states that the regulation shall come into force upon the adoption and coming into force of a regulation which will lay down the procedures for implementing the regulation. The 1998 proposal does not include a proposal for an equivalent of Reg 574/72 nor has a separate proposal for an implementing regulation been submitted to the Council.

health care rights[195] suggest that the Member States are not 'too eager' to accept significant changes.[196]

[195] In 1995, for instance, the Commission had already submitted to the Council a proposal which was aimed at (*i*) granting family members of frontier workers, former frontier workers and family members of the latter the right to receive treatment in the competent State and (*ii*) extending the personal scope of Arts 22(1)a and c to all persons who are publicly insured in one of the Member States regardless of their nationality. The proposal did not seem to have far-reaching implications. The experiences with frontier workers, who already have a right to gain access to care 'on both sides of the border', suggest that granting the three categories mentioned a right to choose a doctor across the border would hardly, if at all, affect health care funding and capacity planning. Cp Hermesse and Lewalle (1993) n 1 above. Further, in practice virtually all Member States already apply the rules concerning emergency and authorised treatment in other Member States to all persons insured under their system regardless of their nationality. Nonetheless, the Commission's proposal was largely rejected. The Council was willing to extend the scope of Art 22(1)a and c but it explicitly preserved the rights to emergency and authorised treatment to 'persons who are nationals of the member States' so as to exclude third country nationals. The formal argument for rejecting the proposal concerned an alleged lack of powers on the part of Community. This argument was not persuasive however. Cp Pieters, 'Enquiry into the Legal Foundations of a Possible Extension of Community Provisions on Social Security to Third Country Nationals Legally Residing and/or Working in the EU' in *Commission of the European Communities/Departemento de Relações Internaçionais e Convenções de Segurança Social, Social Security in Europe—Equality Between Nationals and Non-Nationals* (1995) 189–243. The proposal to grant family members of frontier workers, former frontier workers and their family members the right to obtain care on 'both sides of the border' was wholly rejected.

[196] For this reason it is understandable that the Commission has never sent a specific proposal for altering Art 22(1)c and/or Art 22(2) of the Regulation to the Council and that Art 18, second sentence, as proposed in the 1998 proposal is basically identical as the current Art 22(2). The feasibility of any such amendment simply seemed minimal.

In the literature some authors have discussed the possibility of extending the scope of Art 22(2) or partially abolishing prior authorisation rules. Neumann-Duesberg, for instance, has considered whether the requirement of prior authorisation might not be abolished entirely. Abolition could have positive aspects. In particular, increased cross-border use of health care facilities could guarantee a more efficient use of facilities in States where overcapacity exists. In the view of this author, the main obstacle to the abolition of the requirement is that the competent institutions are obliged to fully reimburse the costs of treatment obtained in other States. The costs of medical facilities differs widely in the various States and an increased inter-State flow of patients would lead to considerable financial problems. The 'poorer' Member States especially could have difficulties in maintaining their systems financially if they were obliged to bear the full costs of treatment the insured receive in the 'richer' States. In order to stimulate cross-border use of medical care, one would therefore have to consider a limitation of the prior authorisation requirement for some specific types of treatment that should be carefully checked in order to avoid medical tourism. Neumann-Duesberg (1991) n 47 above, at 92–3.

Bieback has claimed that a distinction is to be made between forms of treatment which are included in the insurance package of the competent State and forms of care which are not. As to the latter, he argued that prior authorisation rules should be maintained in order to avoid social tourism. Bieback, 'Soziale Sicherung für den Fall der Krankheit und Mutterschaft' in *Europäisches Sozialrecht—Bundestagung des Deutschen Sozialrechtsverbandes e.V. 9.bis11.Oktober 1991* (1992) 51–69, at 60. With respect to the 'included' forms of treatment, however, Bieback considered the second requirement contained in Art 22(2) superfluous because it would hardly leave any room for the patients' right to receive medical services in other States (*Luisi and Carbone*). In his view, the condition should be deleted or replaced by a provision which would oblige the competent institution to grant authorisation for 'included products' in all cases unless this would be detrimental to the health of the patient concerned. Bieback (1993) n 126 above, at 64. Bieback recognises, however, that the competent institution should have the right to refuse authorisation in cases where the grant of such authorisation would lead to a disproportional increase in health expenditure. A second best solution would, in his view, therefore be to request the Administrative Commission to draw up lists

3.6.3 *Contractual Strategy*

In addition to these legislative initiatives, attempts have been made to extend cross-border access to, and use of, medical facilities by concluding, or promoting the conclusion of, agreements between health care providers and health insurance institutions in different Member States. Some agreements have already been concluded. One of the most well known examples concerns a 1978 agreement between Dutch and Belgian health institutions. The number of medical facilities in the Dutch regions of Zeeland Flanders and West-Brabant is insufficient and other facilities in the Netherlands are difficult to reach due to geographical obstacles. Under the 1978 agreement residents of these Dutch regions are given the right to obtain treatment in a number of Belgian hospitals.[197] Further, in recent years some projects have been started which are aimed at extending the cross-border health care rights of patients living in border regions by promoting the conclusion of more cross-border agreements.[198] The strategy followed in the context of these projects, which have mainly been carried out by health institutions and Member States in the geographical heart of the Union,[199] is comparable. The first step involves the exchange of information

(comparable to the lists referred to in eg, Art 17(7) of Regulation 574/72) mentioning the types of treatment for which authorisation must be given.

Furthermore, at an AIM-seminar held in Bruges in 1991 it was proposed to abolish the requirement of prior authorisation for the costs of medical treatment except the costs of hospitalisation and that a list could be drawn up which would contain types of treatment which could be subject to a financial ceiling. Hermesse *et al*, *Gezondheidsbescherming in de Europese Gemeenschap* (1991) at 36.

[197] On the case of Zeeuws-Vlaanderen see in particular Rombouts, *Grensoverschrijdende Gezondheidszorg? Een Onderzoek naar de Huidige en Toekomstige Mogelijkheden en Knelpunten van Grensoverschrijdende Gezondheidszorg* (1990); Van Tits and Gemmel, *Een Grensoverschrijdende Verkenning van Belangen. Ziekenhuiszorg in Zeeuwsch-Vlaanderen en Belgisch Vlaanderen* (1995); Van Tits and Gemmel, *Haalbaarheidsonderzoek Samenwerkingsnetwerk Ziekenhuizen in de Euregio Scheldemond* (1995) and De Buijser (1996) n 132 above, at 135–6. Further, there is a border agreement between Dutch health insurance institutions and a German hospital in Aachen under which victims of car-accidents can be sent directly to the Aachen hospital. Besides a French-Belgian agreement which entitles all members of frontier workers' families access to health care on either side of the border, there is an agreement between a French health institution and a Belgian hospital which allows pregnant women resident in Halluin to obtain treatment in the maternity s of the Mennin hospital in Belgium. Similar arrangements are made for the use of a Belgian child guidance centre. Further, a bilateral agreement has been concluded between the United Kingdom and Ireland that regulates the financing of cross-border care between the two countries and extends rights to gain access to care across the border for certain categories of persons. Palm *et al* (2000) n 4 above, at 66.

[198] Most projects concern specialised medical practices such as cardiology, traumatology, paediatrics, radiotherapy, etc. Palm *et al* (2000) n 4 above, at 67.

[199] Quite a few projects have been carried out in border-regions between the Netherlands, Belgium and Germany. See, eg: Grunwald and Smit, *Grensoverschrijdende Zorg—Zorg op Maat in de Euregio Maas-Rijn; Evaluatie van een Experiment* (1999); Hofmann and Kocks, 'Freier Zugang zu Gesundheitsleistungen im Grenzgebieten—Grenzüberschreitendes Projekt in der Euregio Maas and Rhein' (1998) *ZFSH/SGB* 306 *et seq*; Godry, 'Krankenbehandlung ohne Grenzen— Anmerkungen zu einem Modellprojekt im niederländischen-deutschen Grenzgebiet' (1997) *ZFSH/SGB* 416 *et seq*; Ros and van der Zee, *Grensoverschrijdende Zorg—Vooronderzoek naar de Haalbaarheid van een Experiment in een Grensgebied betreffende Verruiming van Mogelijkheden voor Grensoverschrijdend Zorgverkeer—Uitgevoerd door het NIVEL in opdracht van de*

regarding the types of treatment for which shortages and surplus exist on the both sides of the border. Communication between health institutions across the border is to be intensified before the second step is taken which involves the drafting of lists of types of treatment for which agreements can be concluded. Upon agreement of the list and conclusion of the contract, patients can then be referred to health care providers across the border.

The projects aim to explore the possibility of promoting cross-border health care within the current legal framework. The EC Regulations' provisions and the principles on which these are based are not proposed to be altered. Thus, medical care is in all cases to be delivered in accordance with the legislation of the 'providing State' and the institution of the State of insurance has to fully reimburse the health institution of the providing State. It is not planned to adjust national laws and regulations either. In fact, the initiatives are merely aimed at promoting more flexible authorisation policies. For a limited period of time form E 112 will be given more easily or automatically.

There have been some successes,[200] but it seems unlikely that the contractual method will lead to a significant extension of cross-border health care rights throughout the Community. The initiatives are taken in a few border regions only and the approach followed in these regions is characterised by caution. Member States only allow their sickness funds or providers to conclude cross-border agreements when there is a guarantee that health expenditure will not increase and that the accessibility and infrastructure of their national care systems is not in any way affected. Just like the legislative method, the contractual method for extending cross-border access to health care is ultimately based on an assumption of the voluntary cooperation of the Member States (or their health institutions) and experience so far suggests that Member States are only willing to cooperate when inter-State patient flow can be kept fully under control.

Ziekenfondsraad (1996) and Bijzondere Euregionale Commissie Grensoverschrijdende Zorg, *Zorg Dichtbij oòk over de grens—Advies over Grensoverschrijdende Zorg in de Euregio Maas-Rijn* (1994). See also the project in the Euregion Rhine and Meuse which involves cooperation between German sickness funds and a hospital in Nijmegen (the Netherlands) regarding the opportunities for persons insured in Germany to obtain specialised types of treatment such as heart surgery and radiotherapy. Lottman and van der Wilt, *Eindrapportage Project Grensoverschrijdende Zorg in de EU-Region Rijn and Waal* (1999) and *Nationaal Ziekenhuisinstituut/Deutsche Krankenhausinstitut, Grensoverschrijdende Gezondheidszorg—Duits-Nederlandse Samenwerking in de Gezondheidszorg in de Euregio Rijn-Waal* (1995). See also: Hermans and den Exter, *Cross-Border Alliances in Health Care: International Cooperation between Health Insurers and Providers in the Euregio Meuse-Rhine*, available on: <http://www.mefst.hr/cmj/1999/4002/400219.htm> and Palm *et al* (2000) n 4 above, at 67–70.

[200] For a brief overview of the first experiences and results of the various projects see, eg: Brouwer, *Het Nederlandse Gezondheidszorgstelsel in Europa—Een Economische Verkenning* (1999) at 53–66.

3.7 Conclusions

The goal of Regulations No 1408/71 and No 574/72 is to co-ordinate national health care and insurance schemes in such a way that Community citizens who travel to, or establish residence in, other Member States retain health insurance cover. On the basis of the discussion in this section, the conclusion can be drawn that the regulations largely meet this objective. The vast majority of Community citizens falls within the personal scope of Regulations No 1408/71 and No 574/72 which guarantee a right to emergency treatment in any Member State beneficiaries may visit, a right to obtain care in the State where they (seek) work and, above all, a right to claim access to medical care in the Member State in whose territory they reside. Apart from possible co-payments, beneficiaries are entitled to have the medical bill paid by the institution they are insured with or affiliated to.

This section has also demonstrated, however, that Regulations No 1408/71 and No 574/72 do not meet the specific objective in all respects. Basically, the regulations only grant cross-border rights to persons who become in need of medical care *during* a temporary or more permanent stay in another Member State. The possibilities of travelling to other States in order to obtain medical benefits are limited. As interpreted by the Court in *Luisi and Carbone*, Article 49 EC does entitle Community citizens to travel to other Member States for the purpose of obtaining medical treatment, but a right to have the costs reimbursed only exists when sickness funds have given prior authorisation. Apart from the few cases mentioned in Article 22(2), Regulation No 1408/71 does not provide for a right to obtain such authorisation. Formally a free movement of patients may thus exist, but because of the limited scope of Article 22(2) and the rather restrictive national authorisation policies, this freedom of movement does not seem to have much practical relevance for most Community citizens.

For a long time, it was undisputed that it should be for Member States (or their sickness funds) to decide whether patients were entitled to move to other Member States for medical purposes. In order to protect the funding of health insurance schemes and to protect the infrastructure of medical care systems, Member States claim they need to control or regulate the inter-State flow of patients. In principle, this view is still held today, but in recent years the territorial limitation upon the right to gain access to health care has been criticised and questioned. Among Member States as well as in health care and health insurance circles, there is a growing awareness that cross-border access to health care may promote the accessibility of medical care in border regions and, albeit to a much lesser extent, that an extension of cross-border rights may help to solve waiting lists and other capacity problems. Yet, the legislative and contractual attempts to overcome the current territorial obstacles have so far not been very successful. The health care provisions of Regulation No 1408/71 are not likely to be fundamentally amended in the near future and the method of promoting cross-border access to medical care by concluding cross-border agreements between health insurers and health care providers seems too cumbersome and too time-consuming to expect a significant extension of cross-border health care rights throughout the Community in the short term. Both the legislative and the contractual method require the voluntary cooperation of Member States and, used as they are to the principle of territoriality and as much as they fear medical tourism, the Member States only seem willing to cooperate on condition that expenditure does not increase and that the infrastructure of their care systems is wholly safeguarded.

4 CROSS-BORDER ACCESS TO HEALTH CARE ON THE BASIS OF THE TREATY PROVISIONS GOVERNING THE COMMON MARKET

4.1 Introduction

Until the mid-1990s Member States regarded the health care provisions of Regulations No 1408/71 and No 574/72 as a self-contained regime which, free from any other obligations imposed by Community law, exclusively governed the degree to which, and the conditions under which, Community citizens must be awarded cross-border health care rights.[201] That national health insurance rules could possibly be contrary to, or that Community citizens could possibly derive additional cross-border health care rights from, the Treaty provisions governing the common market was either denied or simply not recognised.[202]

On the one hand, this was not wholly incomprehensible. From the early Community years, cross-border access to health care had been strictly regulated and application of private rules governing the common market to the still predominantly public health sector seems 'risky'. On the other hand, however, the above view of the two social security regulations was surprising. Even a brief survey of the jurisprudence of the Court of Justice demonstrates that health care and health insurance rules are not wholly immune to the limitations imposed by the Treaty's common market rules and that obedience to secondary legislation does not guarantee compliance with the Treaty itself.[203] In particular, prior authorisation rules seemed hard to compare with the rules and principles governing the free movement of goods and services. As stated in sections 2.3 and 2.4, Articles 28 and 49 EC entitle Community citizens to move to other Member

---

[201] Palm (2000) n 4 above, at 105; Neumann-Duesberg (1999) n 112 above, at 92 and the observations of various Member States' governments in the *Decker* and *Kohll* proceedings.

[202] Leibfried and Pierson, 'Halbsouveräne Wohlfahrtsstaaten—Soziale Sicherung in der europäischen Mehrebenen-Politik' (1997) *BDIP* at 45.

[203] Cp eg: Leingärtner, 'Diskussionsbeitrag zur Kritik and der Rechtsprechung des EuGH in den Rechtsachen C–160/96, C–120/95, C–158/96, Molenaar, Decker u. Kohll aus der Sicht der Lesitungsberechtigten' in Schulte and Barwig (eds), *Freizügigkeit und Soziale Sicherheit—Die Durchführung der Verordnung Nr.1408/71 über die soziale Sicherheit der Wanderarbeitnehmer in Deutschland* (1999) 117–21, at 118.

States in order to obtain medical goods[204] and services[205] and it is settled case law that national rules which hamper freedom of movement are, in the absence of justification, incompatible with the free movement rules.[206] Further, the prohibitions of Articles 28 and 49 EC are not absolute. National rules which hamper free movement of goods or services may possibly be justified under Articles 30 (formerly 36) and 46 (formerly 56) EC or the so-called 'rule of reason'. The Court of Justice may promote freedom of movement but this is not to say that it does not keep an eye on the Member States' health care interests.

In the light of existing case law, and suggestions made in the literature,[207] it was in fact quite remarkable that until the mid-1990s no questions had been submitted to the Court on the compatibility of prior authorisation rules with the Community rules on the free movement of goods and services.[208] This finally happened though in 1995 and 1996 when the *Decker* and *Kohll* cases were referred to the Court.

4.2 *Decker* and *Kohll*

4.2.1 Facts

Both *Decker* and *Kohll* were Luxembourg cases. Except in cases of emergency treatment in the event of an accident or illness occurring abroad, insured persons could under the Luxembourg health insurance rules only obtain treatment abroad with the prior consent of their sickness fund. Authorisation could only be given for medical benefits which were covered by the Luxembourg rules and on

---

[204] Medic(in)al products constitute 'goods' for purposes of Art 28 EC (formerly 30 EC—Case 238/82 *Duphar* [1984] ECR 523 and Case 215/87 *Schumacker* [1989] ECR 617) and the 'free movement of goods requires, particularly in frontier areas, that consumers resident in one Member State may travel freely to the territory of another Member State' to buy (medical) goods 'under the same conditions as the local population' (Case C–362/88 *GB-INNO-BM* [1990] ECR I–667 at 8).

[205] Medical care must be classed as a service in the sense of Art 50 EC (Case C–159/90 *Grogan* [1991] ECR I–4685) and Art 49 entitles 'persons receiving medical treatment' to move to other Member States in order to receive medical services (Case 286/82 *Luisi and Carbone* [1984] ECR 377 at 16).

[206] Ch 2, s 7.3.

[207] These suggestions were especially made in the German literature. See, eg: Steindorff, 'Dienstleistungsfreiheit im EG-Recht' (1983) *RIW* 831–9 and von Maydell, 'Erbringung von Sozialleistungen (insbesondere im Gesundheitswesen) und Marktfreiheit' in von Maydell and Schnapp (eds), *Die Auswirkungen des EG-Rechts auf das Arbeits- und Sozialrecht der Bundesrepublik—Unter besonderer Berücksichtigung der neuen Bundesländer* (1992) 25–43. See also: van der Mei, 'Patients' Access to Cross-Border Care and Insurance Cover' in *Alliance Nationale des Mutualités Chrétiennes/Association Internationale de la Mutualité, Competition and Solidarity—Can They Co-exist in Europe's Health Care Systems?* (1997) 68–75 and Mavridis, 'Le Citoyen européen Peut-il se Faire Soigner dans l'Etat de son Choix?' (1996) *DS* 1086–93.

[208] van der Mei, The European Court of Justice and the Co-ordination of Health Insurance Schemes, in: Association Internationale de la Mutualité/ European Institute of Social Security, Health Care without Frontiers within the European Union—Free Movement of Goods and Services in the Health Care Sector (1999) at 18–25, at 18 (citing Jorens).

production of a written request from a doctor established in Luxembourg indicating that the treatment in question could not be carried out in Luxembourg.

In *Decker* the legality of these prior authorisation rules was challenged by a Luxembourg national and resident who had purchased a pair of spectacles with corrective lenses from an optician in Arlon, Belgium. Mr Decker's request to be reimbursed for the cost was rejected by the Luxembourg sickness fund on the ground that he had not asked for prior authorisation. Mr Decker challenged that decision in a Luxembourg court, which referred the case to the Court of Justice asking whether the prior authorisation rules were compatible with the Treaty provisions on the free movement of goods.[209]

Kohll concerned a Luxembourg resident who had requested authorisation for the treatment of his daughter by an orthodontist in Trier, Germany. The request was rejected on the ground that the treatment in question was not urgent and could have been obtained in Luxembourg itself. Mr Kohll appealed that decision and the competent court submitted a preliminary question to the Court concerning the validity of the Luxembourg prior authorisation rules under the provisions of the EC Treaty on the free movement of services.[210]

4.2.2 Application of Articles 28 and 49 EC to Medical Benefits

Before the Court could examine whether prior authorisation rules hamper freedom of movement, and if so, whether, they could be justified, it had to ascertain that such rules can be reviewed under Articles 28 and 49 EC. Various governments represented in the proceedings before the Court had denied this. The rules would fall wholly outside the scope of the free movement provisions.

The first reason for this would be that the contested rules concerned social security. Reference was made to case law in which the Court had ruled that it is for Member States, and not the Community, to organise social security systems[211] and to lay down rules governing access to the systems.[212] The argument

---

[209] In *Decker* the Luxembourg Court submitted the following question to the Court: 'Is Article 60 of the Luxembourg Social Insurance Code, under which a social security institution of Member State A refuses to refund to an insured person, who is a national of Member State A, the cost of spectacles with corrective lenses, prescribed by a doctor established in member State A but purchased from an optician in Member State B, on the ground that all medical treatment outside Member State A must be authorised in advance by the above social security institution, compatible with Arts 30 and 36 of the EC Treaty in so far as it penalises in general the importation by private individuals of medicaments or, as in this case, spectacles from other Member States?'

[210] In *Kohll* the preliminary questions were as follows: '1. Are Arts 59 and 60 of the Treaty establishing the EEC to be interpreted as precluding rules under which reimbursement of the cost of benefits is subject to authorisation from the insured person's social security institution if the benefits are provided in a Member State other than the State in which that person resides? 2. Is the answer to the first question different if the aim of the rules is to maintain a balanced medical and hospital service accessible to everybody in a given region?'

[211] See, eg: Case C–70/95 *Sodemare* [1996] ECR I–3422 at 27 and Case 238/82 *Duphar* [1984] ECR 523 at 6.

[212] See, eg: Case 110/79 *Coonan* [1980] ECR 1445 at 12 and Case C–349/87 *Paraschi* [1991] ECR I–4501 at 5.

was not persuasive. It is established case law that in areas, which have not been brought within the ambit of the Treaty, Member States must also observe the limitations imposed by the rules governing the free movement of goods, services and persons.[213] Social security, as Advocate General Tesauro put it in his Opinion in *Decker* and *Kohll*, does not constitute 'an island beyond the reach of Community law'.[214] In both judgments the Court confirmed that Community law does not detract from the Member States' powers to lay down the conditions of insurance and entitlement to benefits, but that in exercising these powers, Member States must comply with Community law, and Articles 28 and 49 EC in particular.[215]

A second reason as to why the contested Luxembourg rules would not be caught by Articles 28 and 49 EC was that these rules would be fully consistent with Article 22 of Regulation No 1408/71. By challenging national prior authorisation rules the validity of this Community provision would indirectly be called into question. The Luxembourg rules were indeed fully consistent with Article 22 of the Regulation, but as could have been expected, the Court did not accept this argument either. Article 22(1) applies to situations in which insured persons have received prior authorisation from the competent institution, but the provision does not regulate situations where such authorisation is not granted. Both in *Decker* and *Kohll* the Court concluded that mere compliance with a provision of secondary Community law does not remove national rules from the obligations resulting from provisions of primary Community law.[216]

4.2.3 Restrictive Effects of Prior Authorisation Rules

Having established that the Luxembourg rules could be reviewed under the free movement provisions, the Court proceeded with the question whether the rules

---

[213] In fact, there is not a single policy area or area of law in which Member States and their institutions can ignore the principles of non-discrimination and freedom of movement See, eg: Case C–279/93 *Schumacker* [1995] ECR I–225 (tax law) and Case C–226/97 *Lemmens* [1998] ECR I–3711 (criminal law). Some governments had also referred to the judgment in *Poucet and Pistre* in which the Court had indicated that social security institutions may fall outside the scope of the Treaty's competition rules (Arts 80 and 81 EC) in as far as they pursue non-economic activities in furtherance of a public task. Joined Cases C–159/91 and C–160/91 *Poucet and Pistre* [1993 ECR I–637. Cp also: Case C–244/94 *Federation Francaise des Societes d'Assurance* [1995] ECR I–4013. The Court did not even see a need to respond to the argument. The fact that health insurance institutions may possibly be partly exempt from the competition rules does not imply that the legislation and rules applying to them are free from the obligations resulting from the Treaty provisions on the free movement of goods and services.

[214] Opinion of Adv Gen Tesauro in Case C–120/95 *Decker* and Case C–158/96 *Kohll* [1998] ECR I–1831 at 17.

[215] Case C–120/95 *Decker* [1998] ECR I–1831 at 25 and Case C–158/96 *Kohll* [1998] ECR I–1931 at 21. On this point see in particular the Opinion of Adv Gen Fennelly in Case C–70/95 *Sodemare* [1997] ECR I–3398 at points 23–30.

[216] Case C–120/95 *Decker* [1998] ECR I–1831 at 30 and Case C–158/96 *Kohll* [1998] ECR I–1931 at 28. In fact, provisions of secondary law themselves must be in conformity with the Treaty itself and, in case they are not, they can be invalidated by the Court of Justice. See, eg: Case 41/84 *Pinna I* [1986] ECR 1.

hampered cross-border movement of goods and services. In *Decker* some Member States had argued that the Luxembourg authorisation rules did not have the purpose or effect of restricting the free movement of goods. The rules did not prohibit the import of spectacles, they did not influence the possibility of purchasing them outside the national territory and they did not prohibit Luxembourg opticians from importing spectacles and corrective lenses from other Member States. The authorisation rules would merely lay down the conditions for the reimbursement of medical expenses. In *Kohll* similar arguments were expressed as regards the freedom to provide and receive medical services. The Court rejected the arguments. In *Decker* it observed that the rules at issue encouraged persons insured under the Luxembourg social security scheme to purchase their spectacles from opticians established in Luxembourg rather than in other Member States. While the national rules at issue in the main proceedings did not deprive insured persons of the possibility of purchasing medical products in another Member State, they did make reimbursement of the cost incurred in that Member State subject to prior authorisation, and denied such reimbursement to insured persons who have not obtained that authorisation. Such rules were to be categorised as a barrier to the free movement of goods since they encouraged insured persons to purchase those products in Luxembourg rather than in other Member States. The rules were liable to curb the import of spectacles assembled in those States.[217] In *Kohll* the Court stated that while the Luxembourg rules did not deprive insured persons of the possibility of approaching a provider of services established in another Member State, they did deter insured persons from approaching providers of medical services established in another Member State and they did constitute, for them and their patients, a barrier to the freedom to provide services.[218]

4.2.4 *Justification of Prior Authorisation Rules*

The most difficult questions the Court had to answer, concerned the possible justification of prior authorisation rules. The Court considered three grounds for justification.

4.2.4.1 *Quality of Medical Benefits*

A first suggested justification concerned the protection of public health. The 'protection of health and life of humans' is mentioned in Article 30 (formerly 36) EC as a ground on which national rules which hamper the free movement of goods could possibly be justified. Article 46 (formerly 56) EC allows Member States to lay down rules for the special treatment of foreign nationals on grounds of 'public policy, public security or public health'. Luxembourg had argued that medical products must be supplied by professionals such as

---

[217] Case C–120/95 *Decker* [1998] ECR I–1831 at 34–6.
[218] Case C–158/96 *Kohll* [1998] ECR I–1931 at 34.

pharmacists and opticians who are authorised by law to pursue their profession and who, due to their rather lengthy training, guarantee that the products and services provided are of sufficient quality. If medical products such as spectacles are supplied in another Member State, supervision to ensure that this has been carried out properly would be called into question or even impossible. Similarly, the quality of medical services provided by doctors in other Member States could only be ascertained at the time a request for treatment abroad is made.

The Court was not persuaded. In *Decker* it observed that the conditions for taking up and pursuing regulated professions have been the subject of Community legislation.[219] As a result, the purchase of a pair of spectacles from an optician established in another Member State provided guarantees equivalent to those afforded on the sale of a pair of spectacles by an optician established in the national territory.[220] In *Kohll* the Court held that Article 46 does not permit Member States to exclude the public health sector, as a sector of economic activity and from the point of view of freedom to provide services, from the application of the fundamental principle of freedom of movement. After referring to several directives which coordinate or harmonise the conditions for taking up and pursuing the profession of doctor and dentist, the Court concluded that

> 'doctors and dentists established in other Member States must be afforded all guarantees equivalent to those accorded to doctors and dentists established on national territory, for the purposes of freedom to provide services'.[221]

In both cases the Court concluded that prior authorisation rules such as the ones applicable in Luxembourg could not be justified on grounds of public health in order to ensure the quality of medical products and services supplied in other Member States.

4.2.4.2 *Financial Stability of Health Insurance Schemes*

A second suggested justification for prior authorisation rules concerned the control of health expenditure. As stated in Section 2.2, the prices and costs of medicines, medical products and medical care differ considerably in the various Member States. If the Member States and/or their sickness funds were obliged to reimburse the cost of all medical benefits obtained in other Member States, they might be confronted with higher expenditure and this could possibly affect the financial stability of their insurance schemes. The requirement of prior authorisation was claimed to be the only effective and the least restrictive means for controlling expenditure on health and balancing the budget of health insurance systems.

At first glance, this suggested justification seemed to pose a quite delicate problem for the Court. The need to preserve the financial stability of health insurance schemes is an interest that is worthy of protection by Community law.

---

[219] For the relevant directives see n 26 above.
[220] Case C–120/95 *Decker* [1998] ECR I–1831 at 42–3.
[221] Case C–158/95 *Kohll* [1998] ECR I–1931 at 46–8.

In *Duphar* (1984) the Court had already recognised that 'Community law does not detract from the powers of the Member States . . . to adopt . . . provisions intended to govern the consumption of pharmaceutical products in order to promote the financial stability of their health care insurance schemes'.[222] In *Duphar*, however, the Court had recognised the preservation of the financial stability of health insurance schemes as a general interest for purposes of the so-called rule of reason.[223] It is settled case law that this judicially created exception can only be relied upon in order to justify non discriminatory rules. Prior authorisation rules, however, seem to be discriminatory. Articles 30 or 46 EC did not seem to leave room for prior authorisation rules either. These Treaty provisions do not wholly exclude the possibility of applying discriminatory rules, but the Court has consistently held that these two provisions can only be invoked in defence of non-economic aims.[224]

Nonetheless, the problem was not as difficult as it seemed. In fact, Mr Decker and Mr Kohll themselves presented the solution to solve the problem to the Court. The former had referred to the fact that as regards spectacles the Luxembourg rules provided, at the material time, for a flat-rate reimbursement that was fixed independently of the cost actually incurred. The mere fact that spectacles were purchased in another Member State would thus not lead to an increase in expenditure. For dental care the Luxembourg rules did not provide for a flat-rate reimbursement, but Mr Kohll claimed that expenditure would not increase, and that the financial stability of the Luxembourg insurance scheme would not be affected, when he, as requested, were reimbursed in accordance with the rates applicable in Luxembourg.

The Court approved of the line of reasoning followed by Mr Decker and Mr Kohll. It accepted that the maintenance of the financial stability of health insurance schemes may be a justification ground for purposes of the so-called rule of reason. Aims 'of a purely economic nature' cannot justify a barrier to the fundamental principle of the free movement of goods and services', but it 'cannot be excluded that the risk of seriously undermining the financial balance of the social security system may constitute an overriding reason in the general interest capable of justifying a barrier of that kind'.[225]

The Luxembourg rules could not pass the test. In *Decker* the Court concluded that 'reimbursement at a flat rate of the cost of spectacles and corrective lenses purchased in other Member States has no effect on the financing or balance of the social security system'.[226] In *Kohll* the Court held that 'reimbursement of the

[222]   221 Case 238/82 *Duphar* [1984] ECR 523 at 16.

[223]   Ch 2, s 7.3.

[224]   As regards goods see, eg: Case 238/82 *Duphar* [1984] ECR 523 at 23 and Case 7/61 *Commission v Belgium* [1961] ECR 317 at 329. As regards services, see Joined Cases 62 and 63/81 *Seco SA* [1982] ECR 223 at 236–7 and Case C–17/92 *Fedicine* [1993] ECR I–2239 at 16 and 21.

[225]   Case C–120/95 *Decker* [1998] ECR I–1831 at 39 and Case C–158/96 *Kohll* [1998] ECR I–1931 at 41.

[226]   Case C–120/95 *Decker* [1998] ECR I–1831 at 40.

cost of dental treatment provided in other Member States in accordance with the tariff of the State of insurance has no significant effect on the financing of the social security system'.[227]

The fact that Article 22(1) of Regulation No 1408/71 prescribes that medical benefits must be provided in accordance with the social insurance rules of the 'other' Member States, and that Article 36(1) obliges the competent institution to pay the 'medical bill' fully, could not alter this conclusion. Article 22(1) of Regulation No 1408/71, the Court ruled, is intended

> 'to allow an insured person, authorised by the competent institution to go to another Member State to receive there treatment appropriate to his condition, to receive sickness benefits in kind, on account of the competent institution but in accordance with the provisions of the legislation of the State in which the services are provided, in particular where the need for the transfer arises because of the state of health of the person concerned, without that person incurring additional expenditure'.[228]

Article 22, however, is not intended to 'regulate and hence does not in any way prevent the reimbursement by Member States, at the tariffs in force in the competent State, of the cost of medical products purchased in another Member State', in cases where no prior authorisation has been given.[229]

4.2.4.3 'A Balanced Medical and Hospital Service Open to All'

In *Decker* the Court finally concluded that the Treaty provisions on the free movement of goods preclude the application of national rules under which social security institutions refuse to reimburse to an insured person on a flat-rate basis the cost of a pair of spectacles with corrective lenses purchased from an optician established in another Member State, on the ground that prior authorisation is required for the purchase of any medical product abroad.[230]

In *Kohll*, however, the Court had to consider an additional argument that had been raised in defence of the prior authorisation rules in question. According to the various governments represented in the proceedings before the Court, prior authorisation rules would be necessary to protect the infrastructure of health care systems. In order to provide adequate care, Member States must ensure that there are enough doctors, medical facilities and hospital beds available on their territory. Waiting lists and other problems of under capacity imply a limitation on the accessibility of the health care system and must be avoided. At the same time, the number of available doctors, facilities and beds should not be too large. Overcapacity implies an unnecessary waste of human and financial resources. Capacity planning, so it was argued, would be virtually impossible if patients were free to choose in which State they wished to obtain medical treatment.

---

[227] Case C–158/96 *Kohll* [1998] ECR I–1931 at 42.

[228] Case C–120/95 *Decker* [1998] ECR I–1831 at 28 and Case C–158/96 *Kohll* [1998] ECR I–1931 at 26.

[229] *Ibid*, at 29 and 27 respectively.

[230] Case C–120/95 *Decker* [1998] ECR I–1831 at 46.

Member States would need the power to control, to a certain extent, where patients can obtain medical care and prior authorisation rules would be the only effective means for protecting the infrastructure of their health care systems.[231]

Especially in as far as intramural care is concerned this argument seemed to have force. In fact, the Court seemed to have no other choice than to accept that the protection of the infrastructure of health care systems could be a ground on which certain national rules could be justified. The Court indeed did so, but it was forced to be creative. In order to protect the infrastructure of their health care systems, Member States need to make a distinction between patients consulting health providers abroad and patients going to providers established in the national territory. Discriminatory measures are required to avoid possible problems of over- or under capacity. Therefore, the rule of reason did not seem an option. The same seemed to hold true for Article 56 (now 46) EC. This provision does not necessarily exclude discriminatory rules, but can only be relied upon in defence of non-economic ends.

The Court found the following solution. Although the objective of 'maintaining a balanced medical and hospital service open to all' is intrinsically linked to the method of funding the social security system, the Court held that it may

> 'fall within the derogation on grounds of public health under Article 56 of the Treaty, in so far as it contributes to the attainment of a high level of health protection. [ ] Article 56 of the Treaty permits Member States to restrict the freedom to provide medical and hospital services in so far as the maintenance of a treatment facility or medical service on national territory is essential for the public health and even the survival of the population'.[232]

The fact that Member States may under certain conditions restrict the freedom to provide and receive medical services did not imply that the Luxembourg prior authorisation rules could be justified. Neither one of the parties in the proceedings before the Court had shown that the rules at issue were necessary to provide a balanced medical and hospital service accessible to all or that the rules were indispensable for the maintenance of an essential treatment facility or medical service on national territory.[233]

In conclusion, the Court held that the Treaty provisions on the free movement of services preclude national rules which make the reimbursement, in accordance with the scales of the State of insurance, of the cost of dental treatment provided by an orthodontist established in another Member State, conditional upon the prior authorisation of a social security institution.[234]

---

[231]   Cp Hermesse and Lewalle (1993) n 1 above.
[232]   Case C–158/96 *Kohll* [1998] ECR I–1931 at 50–1.
[233]   *Ibid*, at 52.
[234]   *Ibid*, at 54.

4.2.5 Conclusions

It may not have been possible to predict the outcome of the *Decker* and *Kohll* rulings with mathematical precision, but virtually all conclusions drawn by the Court did derive from principles developed in earlier case law.[235] The rulings could be regarded as a normal evolution of the Court's jurisprudence on the free movement of goods and services. From a health care and insurance perspective, however, it seemed more appropriate to class the two rulings as a revolution.[236] Under the regime of Regulations Nos 1408/71 and 574/72 it is for Member States to decide whether and when patients can go to other States in order to obtain, at the expense of their sickness funds, medical products or care. Member States

---

[235] For comments on, and analyses of, the two judgments see, eg: Sieveking, 'The Significance of the Transborder Utilisation of Health Care Benefits for Migrants' (2000) *EJML* 143–55; Becker, 'Brillen aus Luxemburg und Zahnbehandlung in Brüssel—Die Gesetzliche Krankenversicherung im europäischen Binnenmarkt' (1998) *NZS* 359–64; Hamilton, 'Annotatie *Decker-Kohll*' (1998) *TvG* 394–7; Hermans *et al*, 'Zorg in het Buitenland: Gevolgen voor Patiënten en Zorgverzekeraars' (1998) *Staatscourant* 5; Jorens, 'Annotatie *Decker-Kohll*' (1998) *RZA* 303–9; van der Mei, 'Grensoverschrijdende Toegang tot de Gezondheidszorg in de Europese Gemeenschap' (1998) *USZ* 462–71; van der Mei, '*Decker* and *Kohll*: Op Weg Naar een Vrij Verkeer voor Patiënten in de Europese Gemeenschap?' (1998) *SR* 187–96; van der Mei (1998) n 178 above, von Maydell, 'Wenn Schutzzäune fallen . . . Das Kohll-Decker-Urteil des Europäischen Gerichtshofes (EuGH) hat Fragen Aufgeworfen: Gefährdet die Grenzöffnung die Deutschen Krankenversicherung? Oder verheisst der Richterspruch mehr Markt im Gesundheitswesen?' *GuG* 3; Neumann-Duesberg, 'Kohll-Decker-Urteile 'Die EuGH-Position ist Angreifbar' (1998) *GuG* 22–7; Novak, 'EG-Grundfreiheiten und Europäisches Sozialrecht' (1998) *EuZW* 366–9; du Pré, 'Het EG-Verdrag door een Ziekenfondsbrilletje' (1998) *SMA* 364–76; van Raepenbusch, 'La libre Choix par les Citoyens européens des Produits médicaux et des Prestataires de Soins, Conséquence sociale de Marché interieur' (1998) *CDE* 683–97; Schulz-Weidner, 'Rechtliche Entwicklungen bei Krankenkassenleistungen im Ausland' (1998) *KrV* 241–5; Sendler, 'Europäisches Gesundheitswesen Offensiv Gestalten' (1998) *KrV* 285–90; Spiegel, 'Der EuGH Als (Wiederentdecktes) Feindbild' (1998) *SS* 665–8; van der Steen, 'Vergoeding van Medische Zorg over de Grens: Alleen bij Toestemming Vooraf?' (1998) *NTER* 159–63; Tomscheid, 'EG-Binnenmarkt rüttelt an den nationalen Sozialversicherungssystemen' (1998) *KrV* 246–50; Wismar and Busse, 'Freedom of Movement Challenges European Health Care Scenery' (1998) *Eurohealth* 13–15; Brouwer (1999) n 197 above; Cabral, 'Cross-border Medical Care in the European Union—Bringing Down a First Wall' (1999) *ELRev* 387–95; Cath, 'Vuurwerk of Veenbrand? Decker en Kohll Spoken door Europa (1)' (1999) *MC* 466–7; Cath, 'Blijft het Tobben of Onstaat er Iets Moois? Decker en Kohll Spoken door Europa (2)' (1999) *MC* 468–71; Kanavos, 'Cross Border Health Care in Europe—European Court Rulings Have Made Governments Worried' (1999) *BMJ* 1157–8; Mavridis, 'Une Libéralisation des Soins de Santé—Un premier Diagnostic après les arrêts CJCE Kohll et Decker' (1999) *DS* 172–5; Nourissat, 'Quand Panacée Rejoint Europe ou Comment la Cour de Justice Consacre la Liberté des Soins dans la Communauté' (1999) *SJ* 10002; Pieters, *De Nederlandse Zorgverzekering in het Licht van het Recht van de Europese Gemeenschap* (1999); Roscam Abbing, 'Editorial: Public Health Insurance and Freedom of Movement within the European Union (Cases Kohll and Decker)' (1999) *EJHL* 1–6; Steinmeyer, 'Der Zugang zu Leistungen der Kranken- und Pflegeversicherung der EU-Bürger—Veränderte rechtliche Dimensionen (Vertragsfreiheiten)' (1999) *ZSR* 735 *et seq*; Stuyck, 'Annotatie *Decker* and Kohll' (1999) *SEW* 259–62; Callens, 'De Arresten Kohll en Decker: Implicaties voor Grensoverschrijdende Zorg' in Essers and Scheiffers (eds), *Grensoverschrijdende Zorg—Marktwerking vs. National Zorgbewaking* (2000) 11–13, en Linders, 'De Arresten Kohll en Decker: Impact op de Tariefstelling in de Gezondheidszorg' in Essers and Scheiffers (eds), *Grensoverschrijdende Zorg—Marktwerking vs. National Zorgbewaking* (2000) 14–18.

[236] Van der Mei (1999) n 207 above, at 18 and van der Mei, 'The Kohll and Decker Rulings: Revolution or Evolution?' (1999) *Eurohealth* 14–16.

and/or their sickness funds can pursue their own authorisation policies and regulate cross-border care in accordance with national needs and interests. *Decker* and *Kohll*, however, indicated that prior authorisation rules are at odds with the Treaty provisions on the free movement of goods and services. Prior authorisation seemed no longer necessary in order to have the costs of cross-border care reimbursed; the rulings suggested that the decision whether or when to go to other Member States for medical treatment could not only be made by sickness funds but by the patients themselves too. The rulings did not call into question the validity of Article 22(1)c of Regulation No 1408/71 and they thus did not abolish the prior authorisation procedure. *Decker* and *Kohll* did introduce, however, an alternative procedure under which reimbursement of the costs of cross-border care is not a privilege granted by sickness funds but rather a judicially enforceable Treaty-based right of patients that can only in some cases and under certain conditions be limited.

Decker and *Kohll*, however, did not imply that patients had acquired an unconditional right to choose in which Member State they wish to obtain medical care. First, much more than in the *Pierik* judgments,[237] the Court had an eye for the health care interests of Member States.[238] The Luxembourg authorisation rules could not withstand judicial scrutiny, but the Court did accept that Member States are entitled to impose restrictions on the free movement of medical benefits when, and in as far as, necessary for securing the financial stability of health insurance schemes and/or 'maintaining a balanced medical and hospital service open to all'. Second, the scope of the *Decker* and *Kohll* rulings was far from clear. The conclusions drawn by the Court seemed partially linked to the facts of the case and the specific features of the Luxembourg health insurance system. Many Member States strongly opposed to the application of the private principles governing the common market to social health care and insurance systems and they therefore tried to interpret the two rulings as restrictively as possible.[239]

Decker and *Kohll* triggered extensive debates about their precise meaning and implications. Did the rulings also have implications for hospital care, benefits in kind systems and patients placed on waiting lists?[240] How should the economic

---

[237] s 3.3.2.

[238] Cp Keunen (2001) n 42 above, at 160.

[239] For an overview of the views of the Member States and the various actors in the health care scene see in particular Palm *et al* (2000) n 4 above, at 82–107. See also: Gobrecht, 'National Reactions to Kohll and Decker' (1998) *Eurohealth* 16–17; Ministerie van Volksgezondheid, *Welzijn en Sport, De Gevolgen van de Arresten Kohll en Decker voor het Nederlandse Stelsel van Ziektekostenverzekeringen (1998); Union des caisses de Maladie, Avis officiel aux Assurés des Caisses de Maladie (1998); Standpoint of the Executive Committee of the Association of Dutch Health Insurers. . . . Following the Decisions of the Court of Justice of the European Communities in the Decker and Kohll Cases* (1998) and Ziekenfondsraad, *Grensoverschrijdende Zorg: Arresten Decker en Kohll* (1998).

[240] For an extensive list of unresolved questions see Palm *et al* (2000) n 4 above, at 105. For comment on the implications of *Decker* and *Kohll* for private health insurances (in the Netherlands) see Ingelse, 'Verplichting tot Vergoeding van in andere Lid-Staten Gemaakte Ziektekosten: Decker en Kohll in Nederland' (2000) *SMA* 208–11.

objectives of the free movement provisions be reconciled with the Member States' social objectives in the fields of health care and health insurance? Because of the significance of these issues, it was inevitable that new cases would be put to the Court in which the Court would be asked to clarify the scope and precise meaning of the *Decker* and *Kohll* rulings. The first cases in which the Court was asked to do so were *Geraets-Smits and Peerbooms* (2001) and *Vanbraekel* (2001).

4.3 *Geraets-Smits and Peerbooms*

4.3.1 *Facts*

Geraets-Smits and Peerbooms concerned the Dutch health insurance scheme. This scheme is based on the principle of benefits in kind. Unlike the Luxembourg insurance rules, the Dutch rules do not confer upon the insured a right to be reimbursed for the medical bills that they themselves have paid to providers. Insured persons are entitled to obtain medical benefits in kind and, apart from possible own contributions, free of charge. Providers are directly paid by sickness funds.

With a view to effectuating the principle of benefits in kind, sickness funds in the Netherlands must conclude contracts with health care providers that have been recognised by the Minister of Health.[241] In these agreements the contracting parties must agree on inter alia the nature and extent of the parties' mutual obligations and rights, the categories of care to be provided and the quality and effectiveness of the care. The agreements do not apply to the scales of charges for health care, which are governed exclusively by the Law on the scales of charges for health care. The sickness funds are free to enter into agreements with any care provider, subject to a twofold reservation. First, sickness funds must conclude contracts with institutions based in the area they operate in and, second, they can only conclude contracts with providers who have been authorised to provide care.

Insured persons must obtain medical benefits from one of the providers with whom their sickness fund has concluded a contract. In principle, sickness funds are under no obligation to pay the costs of medical benefits provided by non-contracted providers. Non-contracted care must be paid by the patients themselves. This is different only where sickness funds, upon the request of the patients, or their doctors, have given their prior authorisation. Such permission for non-contracted medical benefits may be given when two conditions are met. First, the types of treatment for that authorisation is requested, must be capable of being regarded as qualifying benefits under Dutch legislation. These include

---

[241] For a more detailed description of the Netherlands public health insurance rules see Pieters (1999) n 35 above, at 31–58.

'medical and surgical assistance' to be provided by a general practitioner or specialist, the extent of which is determined in accordance with 'what is normal in the professional circles concerned'. Second, in granting authorisation it must be determined whether the treatment is necessary for the medical treatment of the insured person.

The validity of these prior authorisation rules was challenged in *Geraets-Smits and Peerbooms* by two patients. The first was a patient suffering from Parkinson's disease who had asked for reimbursement of the costs of treatment in a clinic in Kassel, Germany. Mrs Geraets-Smits' request was denied on the grounds that satisfactory and adequate treatment for Parkinson's disease was available in the Netherlands, that the specific clinical treatment in Kassel provided no additional advantage and that there was therefore no medical necessity justifying treatment in that clinic.

The second patient was a Dutch national who, after a traffic accident, had lapsed into a coma. He was taken to a hospital in the Netherlands and then transferred in a vegetative state to a university clinic in Innsbruck, Austria. In this clinic Mr Peerbooms was given a special type of therapy which in the Netherlands was used only experimentally. The therapy proved successful. Mr Peerbooms regained consciousness. His sickness fund, however, refused to bear the cost on the ground that the coma treatment in Austria was not regarded as a benefit qualifying for reimbursement under the Dutch insurance rules. Moreover, even if the treatment in question would have been regarded as normal within the professional circles, the sickness funds argued that the treatment, in relation to the facilities offered in the Netherlands, had no additional medical value.

In order to be able to make a decision in the two cases before it, the competent Dutch court asked the Court of Justice whether national rules which make the reimbursement of the cost of medical care provided by a 'foreign' doctor or hospital with whom the sickness fund has not concluded an agreement subject to prior authorisation hamper the free movement of services as guaranteed by Articles 49 and 50 EC and, if so, whether such rules can be justified by the objectives which benefits-in-kind systems aim to achieve.[242]

---

[242] Similar questions have been raised and referred to the Court of Justice in Case C–385/99 *Müller-Fauré and van der Riet*. Like *Geraets-Smits and Peerbooms*, this case concerns two patients who challenged the Dutch prior authorisation rules for non-contracted care. The first patient was in need of quite extensive dental treatment. Being dissatisfied with the treatment given by Dutch dentists, Mrs Müller-Fauré decided to seek the required dental treatment in Germany whilst on holiday there. Her request for reimbursement of the costs was rejected on the ground that the Dutch legislation is based on the principle of benefits-in-kind and that a right to be reimbursed for the costs can only be given in exceptional cases. No emergency situation in the sense of Art 22(1)a of Reg 1408/71 existed and there was in the view of the sickness fund 'no need' for Mrs Müller-Fauré to be treated by a provider with whom the fund has not concluded an agreement.

Mrs van der Riet was a patient who had requested authorisation for an arthroscopy in a Belgian hospital because such an operation could be performed much sooner than in the Netherlands. Ms van der Riet was refused authorisation on the ground that sufficient facilities were available in the Netherlands and that the waiting period was not considered unacceptably long. The questions submitted to the Court by the Central Raad van Beroep largely overlap with those raised in *Geraets-Smits and Peerbooms*.

4.3.2 Application of Articles 49 and 50 EC to Hospital Care

Before addressing the question of whether the prior authorisation rules under challenge unlawfully restrict the free movement of services, the Court had to ascertain that Mrs Geraets-Smits and Mr Peerbooms could actually benefit from Article 49 EC. More specifically, the Court had to ascertain that the hospital services they had received could be regarded as services for the purposes of Community law.

Article 50 EC provides that services shall be considered 'services' within the meaning of the Treaty when they are 'normally provided for remuneration'. In the proceedings before the Court, several governments had argued that hospital services cannot be regarded as 'services', particularly when they are provided in kind and free of charge. In doing so, the governments in question referred to the Court's ruling in *Humbel* (1988)[243], in which the Court had held that courses taught at publicly funded educational institutions cannot, in principle, be classed as services for the purposes of Articles 49 *et seq.* EC. The essential characteristic of the remuneration, so the Court had reasoned, lies in the fact that 'it constitutes consideration for the service in question, and is normally agreed upon between the provider and the recipient of the service'. In the case of courses provided under national educational systems, which as a rule are funded from the public purse, that characteristic was considered to be absent. In establishing or maintaining national educational systems States do not seek to be engaged in gainful activity. Rather, by doing so, States are fulfilling their duties towards their own population in the 'social, cultural and educational fields'.[244] Transposing *Humbel* to the health care sector, the governments in question argued that there would be no remuneration within the meaning of Article 50 EC, where patients receive hospital care without having to pay for themselves or where all or part of the amount they pay, is reimbursed to them.

The governments in question received support from two Advocates General. In his opinion in *Vanbraekel* (2001) Advocate General Saggio interpreted *Humbel* as to imply that the Treaty provisions on the free movement of services cannot be applied to public benefits which, on the one hand, constitute an integral part of public health systems in as far as these are established and organised by the State and, on the other hand, are funded out of the public purse.[245] In *Geraets-Smits and Peerbooms* Advocate General Ruiz-Jarabo Colomer concluded that the two applicants in the cases could not be regarded as recipients of services. Since Mrs Geraets-Smits and Mr Peerbooms had relied on Article 49 EC in order to have the costs of treatment paid by their sickness fund, the

---

[243] Case 263/86 *Humbel* [1988] ECR 5365. See also: Case C–109/92 *Wirth* [1995] ECR I–6447.

[244] Case 263/86 *Humbel* [1988] ECR 5365 at 17–19. The fact that pupils or their parents must sometimes pay teaching or enrolment fees was not considered to be of any relevance in this regard. See also: the Opinions of Adv Gen Slynn in Case 293/83 *Gravier* [1985] ECR 1425 at 602–4 and Case 263/86 *Humbel* [1988] ECR 5365 at 5377–80.

[245] Opinion of Adv Gen Saggio in Case C–368/98 *Vanbraekel* [2001] ECR I–5363 at 19–22.

Advocate General considered whether the legal relationship of insured persons with their sickness funds could be defined in terms of the provision of services in the sense of Article 50. He concluded that no such classification could be made. In the Netherlands general practitioners are not paid for the individual treatments or consultations of patients registered with them. They are paid a fixed amount for every patient regardless of whether or not patients actually make use of the practitioners' services.[246] Contracted hospitals are paid on a treatment-by-treatment basis, but the payments by sickness funds do not necessarily cover the actual costs of medical benefits. On the basis of the specific way in which tariffs for hospital care are calculated, the Advocate General held that these must be seen as a means of fixing hospitals' yearly budgets. Therefore, the payments that sickness funds make to health care providers could not be classified as remuneration for the purposes of Article 50 EC.[247]

The Court, however, did not support the above arguments. Disagreeing with Advocate General Saggio, the Court held that it is settled case law that 'medical activities fall within the scope of Article 60 EC Treaty, there being no need to distinguish in that regard between care provided in a hospital environment and care provided outside such an environment'.[248]

Further, the Court rejected the arguments of Advocate General Ruiz-Jarabo Colomer that hospital services provided in the context of benefits in kind systems cannot be classed as a service within the meaning of Article 50 EC. First, it did not see how the argument could be relevant to the cases of Mrs. Geraets-Smits and Mr. Peerbooms who had obtained medical care in other States, had paid the bill themselves and had asked for reimbursement of the costs incurred. Medical services provided in Member States other than the State of insurance and paid for by the patients themselves, so the Court ruled, do not cease to fall within the scope of the Treaty provisions on the free movement of services merely because the legislation in the State of insurance is based on the principle of benefits in kind.[249] Second, the mere fact that hospital care is financed directly by sickness funds on the basis of agreements and preset scales of fees could not remove such care from Articles 49 and 50 EC. Article 50 EC does not require that services are paid for by those for whom they are performed[250] and the payments made by Dutch sickness funds to health care providers, albeit set at a flat rate, constitute, according to the Court, the consideration for hospital services and unquestionably represent remuneration for hospitals.

[246] See also: Langer (1999) n 7 above, at 538.
[247] Opinion of Adv Gen Ruiz-Jarabo Colomer in Case C–157/99 *Geraets-Smits and Peerbooms* [2001] ECR I–5473 at 41–9.
[248] Case C–157/99 *Geraets-Smits* [2001] ECR I–5473 at 53. The Court's conclusion was not as obvious as it was presented. In support of its conclusion the Court referred to the rulings in *Luisi and Carbone, Grogan* and *Kohll*. Not one of these cases, however, concerned medical care provided in public hospitals and in not one of the judgments had the Court expressly indicated that such care is actually to be regarded as a service for the purposes of Arts 49 and 50 EC.
[249] *Ibid*, at 55.
[250] *Ibid*, at 57 (citing Case 352/85 *Bond van Adverteerders* [1988] ECR 2085 and Joined Cases C–51/96 and C–191/97 *Deliège* [2000] ECR I–2549).

4.3.3 *Restrictive Effects of Prior Authorisation Rules for Non-Contracted Care*

Having established that the hospital services received by Mrs Geraets-Smits and Mr Peerbooms fell within the scope of Articles 49 and 50 EC, the Court proceeded by determining whether the prior authorisation rules under challenge restricted freedom of movement. The Court recalled that Article 49 EC precludes application of national rules that have the effect of making the provision of services between the Member States more difficult than the provision of services within one Member State.[251] The Dutch government had argued that its legislation had no such effect because both the rules governing the conclusion of contracts between sickness funds and health care providers and the rules governing authorisation for non-contracted care, would not make any distinction between providers established on Dutch territory and 'foreign' providers.

The Court could not agree. First, it held that Dutch sickness funds will mainly strike contractual arrangements with hospitals in the Netherlands and that, with the exception of hospitals in frontier regions, it seems unlikely that a significant number of foreign hospitals would ever enter into agreements with Dutch sickness funds. Therefore, the requirement of obtaining prior authorisation mainly applies to hospitals situated outside the Netherlands.[252]

Secondly, the Court considered the rules applicable to authorisations for non-contracted care to be discriminatory in nature. As regards the first requirement, namely that the proposed treatment must be 'normal in the professional circles concerned, it held that by its very essence such a condition is liable to lead to refusals of authorisation.[253] The second requirement, ie that the treatment must be necessary for the medical condition of the persons concerned, applied equally to non-contracted providers established in the Netherlands and non-contracted foreign providers. Dutch case law, however, demonstrates that in determining the necessity for treatment abroad the medical facilities available in the Netherlands are taken into consideration and that a 'medical necessity' is only considered to be present if adequate treatment cannot be obtained without undue delay in contracted hospitals in the Netherlands. The Court held that the requirement by its very nature will severely limit the circumstances in which authorisation can be obtained.[254]

4.3.4 *Justification of the Prior Authorisation Requirement*

The Court proceeded by considering whether the prior authorisation rules under challenge could possibly be justified. After having recalled that national

---

[251] *Ibid*, at 61.
[252] *Ibid*, at 66–8.
[253] *Ibid*, at 63.
[254] *Ibid*, at 64.

health care or insurance rules can be justified when they are necessary for safeguarding the financial stability of social security schemes or maintaining a 'balanced medical and hospital service open to all', the Court recognised that intramural care, by comparison with extramural care, undoubtedly shows certain distinct characteristics. According to the Court, the 'number of hospitals, their geographical distribution, the mode of their organisation and the equipment with which they are provided, and even the nature of medical services which they are able to offer, are all matters for which planning must be possible'.[255] Under a contract system, such as the one existing in the Netherlands, this kind of planning meets a variety of concerns. First, it seeks to achieve the aim of ensuring that there is sufficient and permanent access to a balanced range of high-quality hospital treatment. Secondly, planning assists in meeting a desire to control costs and to prevent, as far as possible, any wastage of financial, technical and human resources. Such wastage, the Court held, is all the more damaging because it is generally recognised that the hospital care sector generates considerable costs and must satisfy increasing needs, while the financial resources that may be made available for health are limited, whatever the mode of funding applied. From those perspectives, a requirement that 'the assumption of costs .. of hospital treatment provided in another Member State must be subject to prior authorisation appears to be measure which is both necessary and reasonable'.[256]

Looking at the Dutch system, the Court held that it is clear that, 'if insured persons were at liberty, regardless of circumstances, to use the services' of non-contracted hospitals, whether they were situated in the Netherlands or in another Member State, 'all the planning which goes into the contractual system in an effort to guarantee a rationalised, stable, balanced and accessible supply of hospital services would be jeopardised at a stroke'.[257]

4.3.5 *Justification of Conditions for Granting Prior Authorisation*

Thus, Community law does not preclude a system of prior authorisation for intramural care. This did not imply, however, that Member States and their sickness funds are wholly free in applying prior authorisation rules. The Court did require that the conditions attached to the grant of authorisation are needed to safeguard the financial stability of social security schemes or to maintain a 'balanced medical and hospital service open to all'.

4.3.5.1 *'Normal in the Professional Circles Concerned'*

As regards the first requirement contained in the Dutch law, namely that medical services must be regarded as 'normal in the professional circles concerned',

---

[255] Case C–157/99 *Geraets-Smits* [2001] ECR I–5473 at 76.
[256] *Ibid*, at 80.
[257] *Ibid*, at 81.

the Court began by recalling its own holding in *Duphar* (1984)[258] that it is not in principle incompatible with Community law for Member States to establish, with a view to achieving their aim of limiting costs, limitative lists excluding certain products from reimbursement. According to the Court, the same principle must apply to medical and hospital treatment. In principle, Community law does not have the effect of requiring a Member State to extend the list of medical services paid for by its social insurance system.[259]

The Court added, however, that lists of medical preparations and types of treatment that are excluded from reimbursement, must be drawn up in accordance with objective criteria, without reference to the origin of the products. In order for a prior authorisation scheme to be justified, it must, in any event, be based on objective, non discriminatory criteria which are known in advance, in such a way as to circumscribe the exercise of the national authorities' discretion, so that it is not used arbitrarily. Further, such an authorisation a scheme must likewise be based on a procedural system which is easily accessible and capable of ensuring that a request for authorisation will be dealt with objectively and impartially within a reasonable time and refusals to grant authorisation must be capable of being challenged in judicial or quasi-judicial proceedings. [260]

The Dutch insurance rules are not based on a pre-established list of treatment. Rather, the Dutch legislator has opted for leaving it to the sickness funds to determine which types of treatment are reimbursable in accordance with the criterion 'normal in the professional circles concerned'. That criterion, the Court explained, is open to a number of interpretations. It could refer to what is considered 'normal' only in the Netherlands medical circles or, alternatively, to what is considered 'normal' according to the state of international medical science and medical standards generally accepted at international level. The Court held that in refusing authorisation for foreign treatment, only 'an interpretation on the basis of what is sufficiently tried and tested by international medical science' can be regarded as objective standards. To 'allow treatment habitually carried out on national territory and scientific views prevailing in national medical circles to determine what is or is not normal will not offer those guarantees and will make it likely that Netherlands providers of treatment will always be preferred in practice'.[261] If, however, the condition that treatment must be regarded as 'normal in the professional circles concerned' is tried and tested by international medical science, and applied without distinction to treatment provided on the national territory and treatment provided abroad, refusals to offer authorisation are justified in view of the need to ensure the financial stability of sickness insurance schemes and to maintain an adequate,

---

[258] Case 238/82 *Duphar* [1984] ECR 523.
[259] The fact that a particular type of treatment is covered or not covered by the insurance schemes of other Member States is irrelevant in this regard. Case C–157/99 *Geraets-Smits* [2001] ECR I–5473 at 53 at 87.
[260] *Ibid*, at 89–90.
[261] *Ibid*, at 96.

balanced and permanent supply of hospital care on the national territory.[262] In applying the afore mentioned requirement, national authorities must take into consideration all the relevant information, including existing scientific literature and studies, the authorised opinions of specialists and the fact that the proposed treatment is covered or not covered by the health instance scheme of the State where treatment is provided.[263]

4.3.5.2 *Necessity of Treatment*

The second requirement for the award of authorisation, ie that medical services must be necessary for the patients' treatment, formally applies to both non-contracted providers established in the Netherlands and non-contracted foreign providers. Practice, however, demonstrates that authorisation for treatment abroad is often only considered necessary when appropriate treatment cannot be provided, without undue delay, in the Netherlands. In this respect, no distinction is drawn between whether the treatment could be provided by a contracted estab-lishment or by a non-contracted establishment. The Court accepted that the requirement concerning the necessity of the treatment can be justified under Article 49 EC, provided that authorisation is refused only 'when the same or equally effective treatment can be obtained without undue delay' from a con-tracted establishment. National authorities 'have regard to all the circumstances of each specific case' and 'take due account not only of the patient's medical con-dition at the time when the authorisation is sought but also of his past record'.[264] Such a condition, the Court explained, 'can allow an adequate, balanced and per-manent supply of high-quality hospital treatment to be maintained on the national territory and the financial stability of the sickness insurance scheme to be assured'.[265] If contracted providers could not be given priority, the consequent outflow of patients 'would be liable to put at risk the very principle of having con-tractual arrangements with hospitals' and, consequently, 'undermine all the plan-ning and rationalisation carried out in this vital sector in an effort to avoid the phenomena of hospital overcapacity, imbalance in the supply of hospital medical care and logistical and financial wastage'.[266] The Court added, however, that once it is clear that medical care cannot be provided by a contracted provider, it is not allowed to make any distinction between non-contracted hospitals established on the national territory and non-contracted hospitals in other Member States.

4.3.6 *Comments*

Some of the Court's observations and conclusions in *Geraets-Smits and Peerbooms* may be tied to the specific features of the Dutch health insurance sys-

---

[262]   Case C–157/99 *Geraets-Smits* [2001] ECR I–5473, at 97.
[263]   *Ibid*, at 98.
[264]   *Ibid*, at 103–4.
[265]   *Ibid*, at 105.
[266]   *Ibid*, at 106.

tem, but it is plain that the judgment has implications for other Member States too. The Court has sought to provide clarification as regards a number of issues that had been debated in the 'post-*Kohll* discussions'.[267]

4.3.6.1 *Intramural Care and Extramural Care*

A first issue concerns the application of Article 49 and 50 EC to hospital care.[268] *Kohll* concerned medical care provided by a dentist operating outside a hospital infrastructure and the ruling did not clearly indicate whether and, if so, to what extent, the Court's conclusions regarding the compatibility of prior authorisation rules with Article 49 EC could be extended to intramural care.[269]

Prior to *Geraets-Smits and Peerbooms*, it had been widely recognised that application of Article 49 EC to medical services could affect intramural care more than for extramural care. Views differed, however, on how, and the extent to which, Community law ought to have regard to the specific features of hospital services.

On the one hand, it had been argued that prior authorisation rules would be compatible with Community law whenever they are applied to medical services provided in hospitals. Prior authorisation rules could be validly applied to care provided by, or in, foreign hospitals either because hospital services could not be classified as a service within the meaning of Article 50 EC[270] or because the rules could, in all circumstances, be justified as being necessary for protecting hospital infrastructures.[271] Advocates of this 'institutional approach' did not

---

[267] For a first comment on the ruling see van der Mei, 'Zorg over de Grens: Het Arrest *Geraets-Smits and Peerbooms*' (2001) *USZ* 852–6.

[268] See, eg: Belcher (1999) n 16 above, at 70–1; Schutyser, 'Round Table: Positions and Reactions of the Private Actors' in *Association Internationale de la Mutualité/European Institute of Social Security, Health Care without Frontiers within the European Union—Free Movement of Goods and Services in the Health Care Sector* (1999) 63–5, at 64 and *Union des Caisses de Maladie* (1998) n 237 above.

[269] In fact, in *Kohll* the Court seemed to have carefully avoided making any definite statements about intramural care. The preliminary question the Luxembourg court had sent to the Court was drafted in general terms of 'benefits' and 'medical services'. See n 209 above. In its judgment the Court delimited the issue under consideration by holding that the dispute before the national court concerned treatment provided by an orthodontist established in another Member State, outside 'any hospital infrastructure' (Case C–158/96 *Kohll* [1998] ECR I–1931 at 29) and in its final conclusion the Court held that the provisions on free movement of services preclude national rules that make the reimbursement of the costs of dental treatment provided by an orthodontist conditional upon the prior authorisation of sickness fund (*Ibid*, at 54).

[270] See, eg: the Opinion of Adv Gen Saggio in *Vanbraekel* as discussed in s 4.3.2 and the views expressed by various governments in the *Geraets-Smits and Peerbooms* proceedings.

[271] See, eg: the Opinion of Adv Gen Tesauro in *Decker* and *Kohll*. In considering whether the Luxembourg prior authorisation rules could be justified as being necessary for maintaining 'a balanced medical and hospital service open to all', Adv Gen had made a clear distinction between extramural and intramural care. As regards the former, Tesauro recognised that in the absence of prior authorisation rules patient mobility could increase especially in border-regions. He did not expect, however, that the accessibility of medical services in border regions would be affected. Patient movement was not likely to be 'one-way' and the possibility of applying their own reimbursement rates would enable States to secure the funding of medical services. According to the Adv Gen this would be quite different as regards the hospital infrastructure. The location and the number of hospitals is determined by forward-planning and the cost of one person's stay in a hospital cannot be

reject cross-border access to hospital care as such. They fully recognised that it could be of invaluable importance for handling, for instance, waiting list problems. In their view, however, cross-border access to hospital care should not be enforced by application of Articles 49 *et seq.*, but rather be promoted by inciting the Member States to pursue more flexible and generous authorisation policies in accordance with the rules and procedures of Regulations No 1408/71 and No 574/72.[272]

On the other hand, *Kohll* had been, and indeed could very well have been, interpreted as to imply that prior authorisation rules for intramural care could run counter to Article 49 EC. The Court had held that 'Article 56 EC permits Member States to restrict the freedom to provide medical and *hospital* services' (*ital*: APvdM) in so far as the maintenance of a treatment facility or medical service on national territory 'is essential for the public health and even the survival of the population'. This clearly suggested that hospital services must be regarded as services for the purposes of Community law and that prior authorisation rules for such services are in principle to be regarded as being incompatible with Article 49 EC. Advocates of this view did not lose sight of the specific implications that cross-border movement of patients could have for intramural care. They suggested a 'functional approach' according to which the specific features of hospital care would be taken into consideration when applying on a case-by-case basis the justification tests of the rule of reason and/or Article 56 EC.

In *Geraets-Smits and Peerbooms* the Court did not adopt either one of these approaches fully, but the Court's solution comes closer to the institutional than to the functional approach. The Court rejected the institutional approach in that it did not accept that prior authorisation rules are valid when, and just because, they are applied to medical services provided within hospital institutions. Articles 49 and 50 EC apply to both extramural and intramural care; prior authorisation rules for hospital care are not in all cases justified. However, the Court did consider the distinction between intramural and extramural care to be relevant. The Court referred to the 'very distinct characteristics' of intramural care and it considered prior authorisation requirements to be necessary and reasonable measures for keeping hospital costs under control and ensuring sufficient and permanent access to a balanced range of high-quality hospital treatment. In principle, prior authorisation requirements for hospital care are justified. Article 49 EC does not entitle Community citizen to approach on their initiative hospitals in other Member States and to submit the medical bill to

separated from the cost of a hospital as a whole. If large numbers of patients were to move across borders to avail themselves of hospital services, hospitals in the State from which they moved could be under utilised. Tesauro did not fear that the freedom to choose one's doctor and hospital, would lead to an 'uncontrolled and uncontrollable flow of patients', but he did consider prior authorisation rules for intramural care essential for upholding adequate hospital services. Opinion of Adv Gen Tesauro in Cases C–120/95 *Decker* and C–158/96 *Kohll* [1998] ECR I–1831 at 58–60.

[272]   See, eg: the Opinion of Adv Gen Ruiz-Jacabo Colomer in Case C–157/99 *Geraets-Smits and Peerbooms* [2001] ECR I–5473 at 75–80.

their sickness fund. The decision whether insured persons can go to other Member States in order to obtain, at the expense of their sickness fund, hospital care is, in principle made by sickness funds, not by patients themselves. *Geraets-Smits and Peerbooms* implies that cross-border access to hospital care remains governed by the rules and procedures contained in Regulation No 1408/71 and Regulation No 574/72, the main difference being that insured persons may be entitled to get authorisation in a greater number of cases than the few falling within the ambit of Article 22(2) of Regulation No 1408/71.

The reasoning which led the Court to the conclusion that prior authorisation requirements are in principle justified does not seem applicable to extramural care. Read together, *Kohll* and *Geraets-Smits and Peerbooms* thus suggest that courts, when judging the compatibility of authorisation rules with Article 49 EC, must make a distinction between the two types of care. When applied to hospital care, courts must assume prior authorisation rules to be lawful; it is up to insured persons to demonstrate that a refusal to grant authorisation or to reimburse the costs of foreign care will not affect the financial stability of care schemes or the State's capacity to maintain medical facilities. When applied to extramural care prior authorisation rules are assumed to be unlawful, unless Member States or their sickness fund can demonstrate that the interests just mentioned would be affected. In practice, however, it may not be so easy to distinguish extramural and intramural care.[273] For instance, should vaccinations for foreign travels given by doctors in a hospital be classed as intramural care? Do patients actually have to be hospitalised in order for their treatment to be classed as hospital care or does it suffice that the treating doctor works for, or is based in, a hospital? Are the services provided by or in a hospital's emergency department to be regarded as intramural care? Are the services offered in nursing homes to be classed as intramural care?

4.3.6.2 *Contracted Care versus Non-Contracted Care*

A second issue that had been discussed in the post-Decker/Kohll debates concerned benefits in kind systems.[274] The Luxembourg insurance scheme is based on the principle of reimbursement and neither in *Decker* nor in *Kohll* had the Court made any specific comments about systems based on the principle of benefits in kind. Many Member States that have chosen a benefits in kind system therefore claimed that the Court's rulings had no, and if nonetheless so, only minimal, implications for them.[275] Many of these Member States also argued that the common market rules could not preclude application of their authorisation rules because medical care offered within the context of their

---

[273] Cp Pieters (1999) n 35 above, at 85.
[274] See, eg: Gobrecht (1998) n 238 above, at 16 and Neumann-Duesberg, 'Grenzüberschreitenden Behandlungsleistungen—Die Praxis der gesetzlichen Krankenversicherung' in *Zentrum für Europäisches Wirtschaftsrecht, Grenzüberschreitende Behandleistungen im Binnenmarkt* (1998) 21–38.
[275] n 238 above.

schemes would not constitute services for the purposes of Article 50 EC. Since under benefits in kind schemes medical care is offered free of charge, there would be no remuneration in the sense of Article 50 EC.

As could have been expected, the Court rejected the argument. First, the Court did not see why medical benefits received in other Member States cannot be classed as a service just because the Member State under whose legislation patients are insured, has internally chosen for delivery of care in accordance with the principle of benefits in kind. Second, the mere fact that persons insured under a benefits in kind scheme do not have to pay health care providers themselves does not necessarily imply that no remuneration is paid. The remuneration required by Article 50 EC can be paid by third parties such as sickness funds.[276] In principle, Articles 49 and 50 EC thus apply to both reimbursement systems and benefits in kind systems.

The core of the Dutch government's concerns, however, did not relate to the benefits in kind principle as such but rather to contracting scheme that it had established in order to implement the principle. The Dutch government had claimed that if the use of non-contracted providers would have to be put on a par with the use of contracted providers, health care providers would no longer have an interest in cooperating in the contracting scheme. Prior authorisation rules for non-contracted care would be necessary to avoid the collapse of the Dutch system. The Court agreed. Member States would only be able to keep hospital expenditure under control and to ensure sufficient and permanent access to a balanced range of hospital services, when they can properly plan the number of hospitals, their geographical distribution, the mode of their organisation, etc. The Netherlands has chosen to largely entrust this planning to sickness funds who, by entering negotiations with, and by concluding contracts with, individual care providers, are to ensure that insured persons have access to the medical services they are entitled to by law. If, so the Court explains, insured persons were at liberty to use the services of non-contracted hospitals, 'all the planning which goes into the contractual system in an effort to guarantee a rationalised, stable, balanced and accessible supply of hospital services would be jeopardised at a stroke'.[277] In principle, Member States and their sickness funds are entitled to require from patients insured under their laws to obtain medical treatment in or from contracted hospitals and to refuse reimbursement when patients have decided to be treated in non-contracted hospitals. If contracted providers could not be given priority, the consequent outflow of patients would 'undermine all the planning and rationalisation carried out' in the hospital sector and possibly cause problems of overcapacity, imbalances in the supply of hospital medical care, etc.[278]

---

[276] Case C–157/99 *Geraets-Smits and Peerbooms* [2001] ECR I–5473 at 55–8.
[277] *Ibid*, at 81.
[278] *Ibid*, at 106.

Member States' health care systems have been developed as territorially closed systems. *Geraets-Smits and Peerbooms* demonstrates that Community law does not so much object to the closed nature but rather to the territoriality of the schemes. Contracting systems which steer insured persons to contracted providers seem to be compatible with Community law, provided two conditions are met. First, when contracting health care providers Member States and/or their sickness funds must treat foreign providers and national providers equally. Applications for contracts of foreign providers cannot be rejected on ground of the providers' nationality or place of establishment.[279] Secondly, when applying prior authorisation rules for non-contracted care no distinction can be made between providers on the national territory and providers established in other Member States.

It is doubtful whether the Court's conclusions regarding contracting systems and the justification of prior authorisation rules can be extended to extramural care. The Court spoke of the 'very distinct characteristics' of hospital care and the entire explanation as to why prior authorisation rules are justified, seemed applicable to intramural care only. Planning may be relevant for extramural care too, but the financial and infra-structural implications of a possible increase in the number of patients seeking treatment elsewhere are not likely to be so serious as to demand prior authorisation requirements. In principle, therefore, it would seem that such requirements cannot be lawfully imposed and that sickness funds can only refuse or limit payment of the costs of 'foreign' extramural care when they can demonstrate that payment will affect the financial balance of health insurance schemes or the capacity of providers to deliver adequate services.[280]

4.3.6.3 *Included and Excluded Medical Benefits*

Under the coordination regime of Regulation No 1408/71 insured persons are only entitled to get authorisation for reimbursement of the costs of medical

---

[279] Cp Case C–70/95 *Sodemare* [1997] ECR I–3395. National rules, such as the one contained in the Dutch insurance legislation, which require from sickness funds to conclude contracts with providers established within the area or region they operate in, seem hard to compare with Community law. Cp Palm (2000) n 4 above, at 125–7. Further, when pursuing their contracting policies Member States and their sickness funds must comply with the Community rules on public procurement. See, eg: Case C–76/97 *Tögel* [1998] ECR I–5357.

[280] It does not seem wholly impossible to demonstrate such a need. Consider the Dutch rules on general practitioners. Sickness funds pay general practitioners a fixed amount for every patient registered with them. It is of no relevance whether some patients consult the general practitioner more often than others or that some patients do not consult the general practitioner at all during a given year. See Opinion of Adv Gen Ruiz-Jarabo Colomer in Case C–157/99 *Geraets-Smits and Peerbooms* [2001] ECR I–5473 at 45. Where patients inform their sickness funds in advance that they do not wish to be registered with a general practitioner that has been contracted by this fund and that they prefer to receive treatment from a non-contracted practitioner in another Member State, the sickness fund does not seem to have strong arguments for refusing reimbursement. This may be different, however, where patients who have registered with a general practitioner wish to obtain treatment from a non-contracted practitioner based in another Member State. Sickness funds, so it could be argued, cannot be required to pay to twice.

products and services that are covered by the legislation of the Member State in whose territory they reside.[281] In the discussion on *Decker* and *Kohll* it was generally assumed that patients could neither derive a right to be reimbursed for non-covered benefits from Article 49 EC.[282] The power to define the material scope of health care and insurance schemes and to determine which benefits are and which benefits are not reimbursable, would be part of the States' autonomy in these fields. Only the application of the criteria applied in deciding which medical benefits are and which medical benefits are not reimbursable would be subject to to compliance with Community law.[283]

In *Geraets-Smits and Peerbooms* the Court endorses this view. It is for the legislation of each Member State to organise social security and to determine the conditions for entitlement to benefits. Community law, as the Court had already held in *Duphar* (1984), does not prohibit Member States to establish, with a view to achieving their aim of limiting costs, limitative lists excluding certain medical products from reimbursement and this same principle must apply to medical and hospital treatment. 'It follows', so the Court held, 'that Community law cannot in principle have the effect of requiring from a Member State to extend the list of medical services paid for by its social insurance system.'[284] Member States are entitled to establish their own insurance package and to make reimbursement of non-covered benefits subject to requirement of prior authorisation provided (*i*) reimbursement lists are drawn up in accordance with objective, non discriminatory criteria which are known in advance, (*ii*) prior authorisation schemes are easily accessible and capable of ensuring an objective and impartial handling of request of for authorisation within a reasonable period of time and (*iii*) that refusals to grant authorisation can be challenged in judicial or quasi-judicial proceedings.

Member States are thus entitled to make reimbursement of the costs of medical products or services that they have chosen not to include or to exclude subject to prior authorisation by sickness funds which, in principle, do not seem obliged to give such authorisation. One might therefore be tempted to conclude that *Geraets-Smits and Peerbooms* does not add anything to Article 22(2) of Regulation No 1408/71. This, however, is not necessarily the case. Because of the constantly and rapidly changing developments in the medical sciences circles many Member States have entrusted part of the task to define insurance packages to health professionals by using open criteria such as 'adequate and appropriate' or 'what is normal in the professional circles concerned'. *Geraets-Smits and Peerbooms* demonstrates that the Court accepts such open criteria provided they are not interpreted in accordance with views in national medical circles

[281] Art 22(2) Reg 1408/71.

[282] See, eg: the views expressed by the various governments in *Geraets-Smits and Peerbooms* and Langer (1999) n 7 above, at 540.

[283] Palm (2000) n 4 above, at 123 and the view expressed by the European Commission in *Geraets-Smits and Peerbooms* (Report for the Hearing, at 67–8).

[284] Case C–157/99 *Geraets-Smits and Peerbooms* [2001] ECR I–5473 at 87.

only. In order to avoid protective interpretations to the benefit of providers on the national territory, the Court demands that such criteria are interpreted on the basis of international standards. The Court did not define 'international standards'. It spoke of types of treatment which are tried and tested by international medical science and held that national authorities, when applying the criteria, must take into consideration all the relevant information, including existing scientific literature and studies, the authorised opinions of specialists and the fact that the proposed treatment is covered or not covered by the health instance scheme of the State where treatment is provided.

It is not entirely clear what the Court requires from national authorities and how much weight must be given to the various factors. Should a new form of treatment be tried and tested in more than one Member State or does it suffice that the quality, safety and efficacy of a new type of treatment that has been developed, tried and tested in a single clinic is not questioned or contested by other medical scientists? In medical circles, is there at all such a thing as an international standard? For every specialist who is willing to state that a given new type of treatment is sufficiently tested and tried, one probably can find a scientist who is willing to state the opposite. Medical scientists, and in particular those who have been contracted or hired by sickness funds, may not always be willing to recognise the progress that scientists in other Member States have made. The Peerbooms case is illustrative. At the time, Mr Peerbooms requested authorisation for treatment in Innsbruck, neuro stimulation therapy for persons who had fallen into a coma was only used experimentally in the Netherlands. The Dutch sickness fund, acting upon an advisory opinion of medical consultant, refused authorisation arguing that there was no scientific evidence of the effectiveness of the neuro stimulation therapy and that adequate treatment could have been obtained from a contracted provider based in the Netherlands. A neurologist who was appointed by the court in Roermond, however, concluded that the treatment in Innsbruck was appropriate and adequate. In such a situation, whose medical opinion should be decisive? In order to avoid patients becoming the victim of disputes and rivalry between scientists, and by analogy with the Court's observation in *Decker* and *Kohll* that 'doctors and dentists established in other Member States must be afforded all guarantees equivalent to those accorded to doctors and dentists established on national territory', it could be argued that the international standard is met whenever a given type of treatment is considered to be appropriate and adequate in the State where it is developed and provided, unless the sickness fund in question can demonstrate that the treatment in question, in relation to the facilities available under the own health system, has no additional medical value.

4.3.6.4 *Waiting Lists*

Article 22(2) of Regulation only confers upon insured persons a right to obtain authorisation for treatment in another Member States where, taking account of their current state of health and the probable course of their disease, the treatment in question cannot be given within the time normally necessary in the Member State of residence. Apart from cases in which postponement of treatment would be medically unacceptable, Article 22(2) does not seem to entitle patients to circumvent waiting lists.[285]

Upon reading *Kohll*, however, the question could have been raised whether patients placed on a waiting list can possibly rely on Article 49 EC in order to receive, within a shorter period of time, the required treatment in another Member State.[286] Prior authorisation rules hamper the free movement of services and it seemed far from easy to explain that, or why, authorisation rules are needed to ensure the financial stability of their health insurance schemes or to maintain 'a balanced medical and hospital service open to all'. That patients placed on waiting lists may seek treatment in Member States where costs of treatment are higher than 'at home' did not seem to affect the financial stability of insurance schemes. After all, the Court had expressly indicated that Member States, where necessary, are entitled to limit reimbursement of treatment obtained abroad up to the maximum provided under their own legislation. Further, the fact that patients may seek treatment abroad rather than at home does not necessarily imply that medical services or facilities for which waiting lists exist cannot be maintained. On the contrary, if more patients would decide to seek treatment abroad, waiting lists are likely to become shorter and the accessibility of the health care system in the State of the patients' residence would seem to improve. Indeed, cross-border movement of patients may be seen as a means for solving waiting list problems.[287]

Geraets-Smits and Peerbooms demonstrates that insured persons can indeed invoke Article 49 EC in order to circumvent waiting lists, but that the conditions under which they can do so are much stricter than *Kohll* suggested.

First, waiting lists usually exist for types of treatment that are provided in, or by, hospitals and this implies that Member States and their sickness funds are entitled to make reimbursement of the costs of cross-border medical care subject to the grant of prior authorisation. Article 49 EC does not entitle insured persons placed on waiting lists to freely shop around in the 'common health care market' and to obtain, at the expense of their insurance institution, treatment from, or in, any foreign hospital that is able to provide the necessary treatment within a shorter period of time than providers in the State of residence.

---

[285] s 3.2.2.

[286] See, eg: Palm *et al* (2000) n 4 above, at 110 and Cath, 'Europa en Vrij Verkeer—Consequenties voor de Zorgsector' (1999) *PhW* 1779–80.

[287] *Kohll* suggested that even the disappearance or elimination of a given treatment facility or medical service would not be a sufficient ground for justification under Art 46 EC. The ruling suggested that this provision would only allow for restrictions on the free movement of services as regards the maintenance of medical services or facilities which are *essential* for the public health of the population. The judgment did not precisely indicate what was meant by this, but it has been argued that the maintenance of a given facility or service on the national territory could not be regarded as 'essential' for public health when patients, at a place close to their place of residence, can obtain treatment for a certain disease in another Member State. See Brouwer (1999) n 199 above, at 24.

Secondly, the Court concluded that authorisation can be refused 'when the same or equally effective treatment can be obtained without undue delay' from a contracted establishment, provided national authorities 'have regard to all the circumstances of each specific case'.[288] *Geraets-Smits and Peerbooms* thus indicates that Member States can demand from insured persons to make use of the health care facilities that have been developed and made available for them. In order to ensure adequate planning and rationalisation in the hospital sector and to avoid overcapacity and imbalances in the supply of medical care, Member States are thus entitled to give priority to providers operating within their insurance scheme. The resources and facilities 'at home' must be fully used, before the question of a possible right to treatment by a non-contracted provider in another Member State has to be addressed.

Geraets-Smits and Peerbooms does not clearly indicate what must be understood by 'undue delay'. This criterion, however, seems to be broader than the criterion used in Article 22(2) of Regulation No 1408/71. First, Article 22(2) stipulates that in determining whether or not authorisation will be granted or refused, national authorities must take account of the insured person's current state of health and the course of his or her disease. In *Geraets-Smits and Peerbooms*, however, the Court imposed on national authorities the duty to take into consideration not only the current but also the past medical record of the insured person requesting authorisation.

Further, the criterion of 'undue delay' might, in certain circumstances, serve as a legal weapon for patients who wish to challenge waiting lists by claiming authorisation for treatment abroad. Article 22(2) of the regulation does not seem to have such potential. The criterion 'within the time normally necessary' for giving treatment seems to have a subjective meaning in the sense that it refers the health care system and facilities available in the State of residence. The time that patients are placed on a waiting list must, so it seems, be regarded as time which is normally necessary for providing the treatment in question. The term 'undue delay' used by the Court in *Geraets-Smits and Peerbooms* does not refer to the facilities available in the State of residence. It leaves room for an interpretation according to which the mere fact of being placed on a waiting list for a given type of treatment does in itself constitute a factor to be taken into consideration when interpreting 'undue delay'.

Neither in *Kohll* nor in *Geraets-Smits and Peerbooms* did the Court make any statements on the implications of cross-border care for the States where patients move to. The 'patient-importing' States may be confronted with capacity problems. Waiting lists might occur or become longer as a result of an influx of foreign patients. The accessibility of the health care system for the population of the host States might be affected. Can these States impose restrictions on the rights of 'foreign' patients? Can they give preferential treatment to their 'own' resident patients? If the observations of the Court in *Kohll* and *Geraets-Smits*

---

[288] *Ibid*, at 103–4.

and Peerbooms are taken literally, the questions must be answered in the negative. After all, the 'maintenance' of essential medical services or facilities is only endangered in cases of overcapacity, whilst waiting lists are rather reflections of undercapacity. The maintenance of the medical services in question is not threatened. Rather, there is a demand for more facilities. It should be recognised, however, that the two cases did not deal with the problems faced by the States where patients move to. The observations of the Court on Article 46 EC were drafted with the 'sending' States in mind and do not give sufficient regard to the interests of, and they are arguably not to be literally applied to, the receiving States. As significant as the right of patients to move to and to obtain medical services in other States may be, it does not seem desirable to interpret the right so broadly as to have the practical effect of limiting the right of the residents of the State concerned to obtain medical care. It is submitted that in cases where waiting lists exist, and in particular where these are *de facto* caused by cross-border patient mobility, some form of preferential treatment of residents over non-residents ought to be justified under Article 46 EC.

4.3.6.5 *Conclusions*

Geraets-Smits en Peerbooms raises new questions, but the judgment has taken away much of uncertainty caused by *Decker* and, in particular, *Kohll*. Prior authorisation rules are in principle justified when applied to hospital care, contracting schemes are in principle 'euro-compatible'[289] and Community law does not require sickness funds to bear the costs of medical benefits that are not covered by the legislation they implement. Member States are free to organise health care and insurance in the way they deem appropriate and demand from insured persons to make use of the facilities that they have made available for them. *Geraets-Smits and Peerbooms* basically implies that cross-border access to non-contracted hospitals and 'non-covered' medical benefits is not, as many had feared after the *Decker* and *Kohll* rulings, fully subjected to the economically determined Treaty provisions on the free movement services. Rather, cross-border access to such medical services remains regulated by the rules and procedures of Regulations No 1408/71 and No 574/72. Article 49 EC has only additional value in the sense that it *de facto* extends the scope of Article 22(2) of Regulation No 1408/71.

4.4 *Vanbraekel*

4.4.1 *Introduction*

Since 28 April 1998, the day on which the rulings in *Decker* and *Kohll* were delivered, two procedures are available for Community patients who wish to

---

[289] Palm (2000) n 4 above, at 130.

travel to another Member State in order to receive, at the expense of their insurance institution, medical treatment. The first concerns the authorisation procedure set out in Article 22 of Regulation No 1408/71. The grant of the E 112 form entitles insured persons to receive treatment in another Member State in accordance with the legislation applicable there as though they were insured in that State. Apart from possible own contributions, the insured do not have bear the costs. Patients are entitled to have the health care provider paid by the competent institution in the State concerned (benefits in kind systems) or to be reimbursed by this institution for the bill they themselves have paid to the provider (reimbursement systems). Subsequently, the institution in the State where treatment has been provided, can ask the patients' sickness fund for reimbursement of the costs it has incurred.[290] The second procedure is the one introduced by *Decker* and *Kohll*. Under this procedure no authorisation is awarded. The procedure applies to patients who, on their own initiative, have approached a foreign provider, who have paid the provider themselves and who, upon return, ask their own insurance organ for reimbursement of costs as though these had been incurred in the State of insurance. Under this procedure patients are not administratively integrated in the host State's health insurance schemes; the costs are reimbursed as if treatment had been performed in the State of residence.[291]

The distinction between the two procedures, as *Decker* and *Kohll* demonstrate, is relevant where the tariffs for medical goods and services in the 'other' State are higher than in the State of residence. Where authorisation has been granted and all E 112 formalities have been fulfilled, sickness funds must fully reimburse the competent institution in the 'other' State for the costs incurred. The difference between the amount reimbursable under the legislation of the 'other' State and the maximum amount payable under the legislation of the insurance, must be paid by the patients' sickness funds. Under the *Decker/Kohll* procedure, however, the difference in question may have to be paid by the patients themselves. With a view of ensuring the financial stability of their sickness insurance schemes, sickness funds are entitled to apply their own reimbursement rates and to limit reimbursement up to the maximum amount provided for under their own legislation.

What rules and tariffs, however, must be applied where tariffs in other Member States are lower than in the State of residence or insurance? Are sickness funds entitled to limit payment up to the actual costs incurred or are patients entitled to claim from their insurance organ the difference between the lower foreign amounts and the higher amounts payable in the State of insurance? In answering these questions, should any distinction be made between Regulation No 1408/71's authorisation procedure and the '*Decker/Kohll* procedure'? Further, what rules must be applied when sickness funds are

---

[290] Art 36(1) of Reg 1408/71.
[291] Palm (2000) n 4 above, at 33.

obliged by Community law or national law to award prior authorisation but have failed or refused to do so? Which reimbursement rates must be applied when sickness funds have decided to award authorisation *a posteriori*? Such questions were addressed by the Court in its judgment in *Vanbraekel*, which was delivered on the same day as the ruling in *Geraets-Smits and Peerbooms*.

4.4.2 Facts

Vanbraekel involved a Belgian national, Mrs Descamps, who in 1990 had sought authorisation from her Belgian sickness fund to undergo surgery in a hospital in Paris. According to the relevant Belgian rules, medical care provided in foreign hospitals could only be refunded when the treatment concerned had an additional medical value which had been established by a doctor or physician with academic credentials. Mrs Descamps' request for authorisation was refused on the ground that she had not submitted the required opinion of a doctor practising in a national university institution. Despite being refused authorisation, Mrs Descamps went ahead with the operation in France and she subsequently claimed reimbursement of the costs of that treatment in court. During the proceedings, which were after the death of Mrs Descamps continued by her husband, Mr Vanbraekel, and their six children, it was ultimately established that the treatment in the Paris had had additional medical value. The initial refusal to reimburse authorisation was unfounded and the court held that the sickness fund had to pay for Mrs Descamps treatment. This, however, did not end the dispute between the Vanbraekels and the sickness fund. The two parties could not agree on the basis of which tariffs the costs of Mrs Descamps treatment in Paris were to be reimbursed. The Vanbraekels claimed that the fund had to reimburse in accordance with the rates applicable in Belgium which were higher than the ones applied in France. The sickness fund only wanted to reimburse on the basis of the lower French tariffs. In order to be able to decide in the case the Belgian court decided to stay the proceedings in order to ask the Court of Justice whether reimbursement was to take place on the basis of the Belgian or the French legislation.

4.4.3 Judgment of the Court

In answering the question the Court first considered the health care provisions of Regulation No 1408/71. Article 22 entitles insured persons who have obtained authorisation for treatment in another Member State to obtain that treatment, at the expense of their sickness fund, in accordance with the legislation applicable in that other State. In such cases, Article 36 of Regulation No 1408/71 obliges the insured person's sickness fund to fully reimburse the competent institution in the 'providing' State on the basis of the tariffs applicable in that State. The Court added that 'both the practical effect and the spirit' of Article 22 of Regulation No 1408/71 require that where it is established that an initial refusal to grant authorisation was held to be unfounded, the person in question is entitled 'to be reimbursed directly by the competent institution by an amount to that which it would ordinarily have borne if authorisation had properly been granted in the first place'.[292]

Subsequently, the Court went into the question whether the Vanbraekels could possibly claim extra reimbursement to cover the difference between the amount reimbursable under the Belgian legislation and the amount payable under French legislation. According to the Court, such a claim could not be made under Article 22 of Regulation No 1408/71. Article 22 is not intended to regulate reimbursement at the tariffs applicable in the State of insurance. That provision neither prevents nor requires that insured persons are reimbursed for extra reimbursement covering the difference between the higher tariffs in the State of insurance and the lower tariffs in the State where treatment has been received.[293]

The Court then considered whether an obligation to provide additional reimbursement might arise under Article 49 EC. After having recalled that Article 49 precludes the application of national rules which have the effect of making the provision of services between Member States more difficult than the provision of services purely within one Member State,[294] the Court observed that there is no doubt that the fact that a person has a lower level of cover when he receives treatment in another Member States than when he receives treatment 'at home', may deter, or prevent, that person from receiving services in other Member States. The question to be answered therefore was whether reimbursement of 'foreign' care at a rate lower than care obtained in the State of insurance could be justified by the need to safeguard the financial stability of insurance schemes or the goal of maintaining a balanced medical and hospital service open to all. In the Court's view, neither one of these two overriding reasons could justify the refusal to reimburse Mrs Descamps in accordance with the higher Belgian rates. The national court had recognised that Mrs Descamps should have been awarded prior authorisation. In such circumstances, the Court concluded, it cannot be claimed that payment of additional reimbursement is liable to jeopardise the maintenance of a balanced medical and hospital service open to all in the State of insurance. Furthermore, since such additional payment does not impose any additional financial burden on the sickness fund scheme in the competent State, the Court held that it could not be argued that such payment has a significant effect on the financing of the health insurance scheme in that State.[295]

---

[292] Case C–368/98 *Vanbraekel* [2001] ECR I–5363 at 34.

[293] *Ibid*, at 36–7.

[294] *Ibid*, at 44. In *Vanbraekel* the Court confirmed *Geraets-Smits and Peerbooms'* conclusion that medical services provided within hospitals fall within the scope of Arts 49 and 50 EC.

[295] *Ibid*, at 51–2.

4.4.4 Comments

In response to the *Decker* and *Kohll* rulings, commentators had already warned that the existence of two procedures for reimbursement of medical costs could complicate the administrative management of cross-border access to care.[296] *Vanbraekel* seems to complicate matters further. Besides situations in which sickness funds have granted prior authorisation (E 112 cases) and those in which the funds have not given authorisation (*Decker-Kohll*), situations must be distinguished in which it has been established that prior authorisation has not but should have been given and those in which authorisations have been granted *a posteriori* (*Vanbraekel*).

Where the costs of care in other States are higher, sickness funds which have given an insured person prior authorisation for treatment in another Member State are obliged by Article 36 of Regulation No 1408/71 to fully reimburse the institution of that other State. The tariffs applicable in the latter State must be applied.[297] In case insured persons have not asked for authorisation or when such permission has been lawfully refused, no obligation to reimburse sickness funds in other States exists. Sickness funds may be required to reimburse insured persons, but they are free to limit reimbursement up to the maximum provided for under their legislation.[298] The remaining part must be paid by the patients themselves. *Vanbraekel* indicates that where authorisation has been granted *a posteriori* or where it has been established by the sickness fund itself or by a court decision that a request for authorisation has been unlawfully rejected, the sickness fund in question must reimburse the insured persons directly by an amount equivalent to that it would have had to pay in case authorisation had been properly granted in the first place.[299] Thus, patients who have asked for, and who are on the basis of Community law or national law indeed entitled to, authorisation for treatment abroad, are entitled to have the costs borne by the institution they are affiliated to regardless of the fact whether or not the authorisation has actually been awarded. The latter fact is only relevant for the question to whom the amount involved must be transferred. Where prior authorisation has been given, the competent institutions have to pay the institutions in the State where treatment has been provided on the basis of Article 36 of Regulation No 1408/71. In the alternative case, the amount involved must be paid to the insured persons on the basis for Article 22 of the regulation.

Where the costs of medical care in other Member States are lower than in the competent State, the competent institutions must in principle bear the costs up to the maximum provided under their own legislation. When the competent institution has granted prior authorisation for treatment in another Member

---

[296] See, eg: *Palm* (2000) n 4 above, at 132.

[297] Case C–368/98 *Vanbraekel* [2001] ECR I–5363 at 32–3.

[298] Case C–120/95 *Decker* [1998] ECR I–1831 at 40 and Case C–158/96 *Kohll* [1998] ECR I–1931 at 42.

[299] Case C–368/98 *Vanbraekel* [2001] ECR I–5363 at 34.

State, it must refund the institution in that State for the costs it has incurred on the basis of Article 36 of Regulation No 1408/71 and pay the remaining amount to the insured persons on the basis of Article 49 EC. In situations where insured persons are entitled to but have failed to ask for authorisation or where they have unlawfully been refused prior authorisation, Article 49 EC orders the competent institutions to pay the entire amount, calculated under the rules they apply, to insured persons.[300]

The Court's conclusion in *Vanbraekel* that insured persons who have obtained medical treatment in another Member State where the costs are lower than in the State of insurance are entitled to additional reimbursement must be welcomed. At first glance, the conclusion seems somewhat surprising. The Court observed that 'there is no doubt' that a lower level of insurance cover for treatment in another Member State than for treatment 'at home' may deter of even prevent insured persons from seeking treatment in another Member State. Where the costs of care in other Member State are higher than in the State of insurance, there indeed seems to be no doubt that insured persons may be deterred from seeking treatment abroad. This is less obvious, however, where costs in other States are lower. This particularly holds true for persons insured under a benefits in kind scheme who are not confronted with medical bills and often will have no idea about the costs of their treatment. Be that as it may, the Court's conclusion must be welcomed because it promotes cross-border access to health care without imposing any additional financial burden on Member States and their sickness funds. One of the main obstacles to cross-border care concerns the fact that costs of travelling are often not covered. Even when patients know that the medical bills for foreign treatment will be paid, they may decide not to seek treatment abroad because of the travel and hotel costs they and those accompanying them may incur. The right to 'additional reimbursement', as recognised in *Vanbraekel*, may help many patients to overcome this financial burden.

4.5 Ferlini

The cases discussed in the previous sections demonstrate that Community citizens who, at the expense of their sickness fund, wish to obtain medical care in a Member State other than the one in which they reside cannot only rely on Regulations No 1408/71 and No 574/72 but also on the Treaty provisions on the free movement of goods and services. Another recent ruling, *Ferlini*, shows that Community citizens may also enjoy cross-border health care rights under Article 12(1) EC, which prohibits within the scope of application of the Treaty any discrimination on grounds of nationality.

Ferlini involved an official of the European Commission who was residing in Luxembourg and affiliated to the Joint Sickness Insurance Scheme for officials

---

[300] *Ibid*, at 53.

of the European Communities. In 1989 his wife gave birth at a Luxembourg hospital. Mr Ferlini received an invoice in an amount which was approximately 70 per cent more than the fee which was applicable to persons who are insured under the Luxembourg insurance for sickness and childbirth. The amount Mr Ferlini was required to pay was calculated on the basis of scales applicable to persons who are not affiliated to the national insurance scheme, which were fixed unilaterally and on a uniform basis by all Luxembourg hospitals within the 'Luxembourg Hospitals Group'. Ferlini refused to pay the sum and challenged the invoice in court. In his view, the scales applied to him were contrary to inter alia the principle of equality. The national court adjourned the proceedings in order to ask the Court of Justice whether Articles 39 and 12 EC preclude application of the Luxembourg scales of fees for persons not affiliated to the national social security scheme.

The Court commenced by recalling that Article 12(1) EC applies independently only where no specific rules prohibiting discrimination are applicable. The Court observed that Mr Ferlini fell outside the scope of Regulation No 1408/71 and that scales of fees for medical care cannot be regarded as condition of work within the meaning of Article 39(2) EC or Article 7(1) of Regulation No 1612/68. Further, in the Court's view these scales could neither be regarded as social advantages for the purposes of Article 7(2) of Regulation No 1612/68. The Court has given a particularly broad definition of the term 'social advantages' as to cover all benefits granted to national workers because of their worker status of by virtue of their residence in the State concerned. Yet, Mr Ferlini could not benefit from Article 7(2) because the Court reasoned that Mr Ferlini merely sought equal treatment in the fixing of scales for medical care. He did not claim any advantage consisting of payment by the host State of a flat rate to reimburse maternity expenses.[301] Consequently, the Court had to answer the question relating to the alleged discrimination on the basis of Article 12(1) EC. In doing so, the Court stated that discrimination can only exist of the application of different rules to comparable situations or application of the same rule to different situations. The Luxembourg government had argued that officials of the European Communities such as Mr Ferlini would not be in a comparable situation to Luxembourg nationals affiliated to the Luxembourg social security scheme because they would neither pay taxes nor social security contributions in Luxembourg. The Court rejected the argument by briefly stating that Mr Ferlini was not claiming any social security benefit in Luxembourg.[302] Mr Ferlini found himself in a situation comparable situation and was according to the Court victim of indirect discrimination on grounds of nationality because the higher scales of fees which were applied to him affected non-nationals more than Luxembourg nationals. In the absence of any suggested ground for justification, the Court concluded that Article 12(1) EC had been violated.[303]

[301]   Case C–411/98 *Ferlini* [2000] ECR I–8081 at 45.
[302]   *Ibid*, at 54.
[303]   *Ibid*, at 60.

Ferlini demonstrates that Article 12(1) EC may play a safety-net role for Community citizens seeking medical treatment in other Member States. In situations where Community citizens cannot claim any rights under Regulation No 1408/71, the provisions on the free movement of workers or Article 49 on the free movement of services, Article 12(1) EC can possibly be relied upon. As will be shown in the next Section, this conclusion may be particularly relevant for patients who wish to obtain treatment in a foreign hospital run by a national health service.

4.6 National Health Services

Decker, Kohll, Geraets-Smits and Peerbooms , *Vanbraekel* and *Ferlini* all concerned social health insurances. Do these judgments have any, and if so what, implications for national health services?[304] On the basis of the ruling in *Humbel,* in which the Court concluded that education cannot be classed as a service in the sense of Article 50 EC when it is mainly funded out of the public purse,[305] one might be tempted to conclude that the judgments only have minimal implications for national health services which are for the main part funded from tax-revenues. Such a conclusion, however, may be too premature. The conclusions drawn in *Humbel* cannot be automatically transposed to the health care sector. In the field of public education, the State usually acts both as the provider and the funder of the benefits offered. The State does not receive any substantial payment or compensation for the cost incurred by students, their parents or another 'actor'. Generally, the relationship between public educational institutions and their students indeed seems to lack the necessary economic character. That relationship, however, may very well be economic in nature when the courses offered to students by public schools or universities are mainly funded from sources other than tax-revenues[306] or, possibly, when students attend courses at independently operating private schools which are subsidised by the State.[307] More in general, in the case of bi-partite provider-recipient relationships under which the State itself acts as the provider, the 'public/private funding distinction'[308] may indeed constitute the main, and perhaps the decisive,

---

[304] See, eg: Baeyens, 'Free Movement of Goods and Services in Health Care: A Comment on the Cases Decker and Kohll from a Belgian Point of View' (1999) *EJHL* 373–83, at 379; McConn, 'Round Table: Positions and Reactions of the Public Actors' *Association Internationale de la Mutualité/ European Institute of Social Security, Health Care without Frontiers within the European Union—Free Movement of Goods and Services in the Health Care Sector* (1999) 39–40 and Langer (1999) n 7 above, at 538.

[305] See the previous section.

[306] For instance, the post-graduate courses or facilities which public universities offer are usually funded out of tuition fees or alternative private funds. The possibility cannot be excluded that such courses may constitute services in the sense of Art 50 EC.

[307] Cp Schulz, *Freizügigkeit für Unionsbürger* (1996) at 159–60.

[308] O'Leary, *The Evolving Concept of Community Citizenship—From the Free Movement of Persons to Union Citizenship* (1996) at 75.

criterion for determining the economic character of activities performed. However, *Geraets-Smits and Peerbooms* demonstrates that the same does not hold true where the State provides benefits which are paid by a third party or when it funds benefits which are provided by third parties.

If this interpretation of *Humbel* is accepted and transposed to national health services, then one could first of all conclude that the four judgments do have implications for the prior authorisation rules which national health service institutions themselves apply. Indeed, the Court's observation in *Geraets-Smits* that medical services provided in one Member State do not cease to fall within the scope of the Treaty merely because the patient in question is insured under an insurance scheme based on the principle of benefits in kind, can be extended to national health services. The relationship between patients affiliated to a national health service and providers established in another Member State may very well be defined in terms of the provision of services.[309] In principle, there do not seem to be persuasive reasons why patients covered by national health services should enjoy less cross-border health care rights than patients subject to a social health insurance.

Furthermore, medical care offered in States where national health services exist, does not necessarily have to fall outside the scope of Article 50 EC. Under most national health services medical care was initially both State-provided and State-funded, but reforms in recent years have largely separated the provision and the funding of medical care. Usually, medical treatment is still ultimately paid for out of the public purse, but the care itself is increasingly provided by hospitals and general practitioners operating on an independent and (semi-) commercial basis.[310] The relationship between national health service institutions and 'their' patients may not necessarily be classifiable in terms of the provision of services, but the relationship between private health care providers and their patients in a Member State such as the United Kingdom, be they established in the United Kingdom or another Member State, might very well be economic in nature.[311]

Further, *Humbel* does not necessarily imply that Community law has no implications for medical benefits offered by or in national health service institutions. The judgment does not exclude the possibility that such medical benefits

---

[309] The fact that medical benefits which eg, British patients obtain in other Member States are ultimately funded out of taxes rather than insurance premiums does not imply that the relationship of these patients with foreign providers is non-economic in nature. Cp Case 344/87 *Bettray* [1989] ECR 1621 at 15 (holding that the status of Community worker for the purposes EC Treaty of Art 39 can also be acquired when the remuneration is largely provided by subsidies from public funds).

[310] For instance, the District Health Authorities in the United Kingdom were initially supposed to provide medical care themselves, but today they are above all entrusted with the task of purchasing for their residents medical care from the most efficient hospitals. See Barr (1998) n 2 above (ch 12) and Palm (2000) n 4 above, at 113.

[311] Cp Eichenhofer, 'Dienstleistungsfreiheit und reier Wahrenverkehr als Rechtsgrundlagen fuer Grenzueberschreitenden Behandlungsleistungen' in *Zentrum fuer Europaeisches Wirtschaftsrecht, Grenzueberschreitenden Behandlungsleistungen im Binnemarkt* (1998) 231 *et seq*, at 14–15 and Hervey (2000) n 35 above, at 42.

can be defined as services. The medical benefits which these providers offer to their 'national' patients are largely funded out of the public purse and, hence, do not seem to constitute services. However, when the benefits are offered to foreign patients this conclusion is not entirely obvious. In this regard, education and health care differ. At present, no Community rule or mechanism exists which imposes on the State from which students move a duty to bear the true economic cost of the education which students receive in other States. The relationship between public universities and foreign students seems to lack an economic character because there is no third party which can be required to pay the cost or, in terms of Article 50 EC, the remuneration. In the area of health care, however, such compensation or reimbursement mechanisms do exist. All Member States can be required to pay the cost of the care which 'their' patients have obtained in other Member States under the regime of Regulation No 1408/71 and all States have developed their own authorisation policies.[312] In cross-border situations, medical benefits offered by national health services do seem 'normally provided for remuneration' and it could be argued that sickness funds hamper free movement of services whenever they refuse to pay for the cost of care offered by national health services in other Member States.

Furthermore, even if medical benefits offered by national health services do not fall within the scope of Articles 49 and 50 EC, they are not necessarily excluded from Community law in general. In *Humbel* the Court ruled that students cannot rely on Articles 49 and 50 EC in order to claim admission to public universities or schools in other States, but in *Gravier* (1985) and subsequent judgments the Court concluded that students do have such a right under Articles 12 *juncto* Articles 149 and 150 EC.[313] Read together, *Gravier* and *Humbel* suggest that access to education is covered by the Treaty and that the Court has merely chosen to deal with questions concerning the cross-border access to public and private education under different legal headings.[314] When these conclusions from the educational case law are transposed to the health care sector, and *Ferlini* would seem to indicate that they can indeed be transposed, it could be argued that Article 12 EC entitles Community citizens to gain access to health care in other Member States in cases where Article 49 cannot be relied upon.[315] If so, patients could possibly further claim that a refusal to bear the cost of care obtained from national health service institutions hampers the right to obtain health care in other States.

---

[312] One could object and claim that in cases where the patients' sickness funds refuse to grant authorisation and to pay the medical bill issued by national health service institutions or doctors, the latter cannot be seen as a 'remunerated' providers of services and that for this reason prior authorisation rules cannot be said to violate Art 49 EC. Yet, if this were correct, Member States could unilaterally define the Community concept of services by 'simply' granting or refusing a right to reimbursement.

[313] Case 293/83 *Gravier* [1985] ECR 593. See also: ch 5, s 4.

[314] Van der Mei, 'The Elusive and Exclusive Concept of Union Citizenship, A Review Essay" (1998) *MJ* 391–402, at 396.

[315] Cp Case C–411/98 *Ferlini* [2000] ECR I–8081 at 62.

4.7 Third Country Nationals

A first glance, *Decker* and *Kohll* do not seem to have implications for persons who do not hold the nationality of one of the Member States. Community law, as it stands at present, does not confer upon third country nationals the right to travel to other Member States.[316] This is not to say, however, that the rulings have no significance for them.[317] Two points can be made.

First, in order to establish 'an area of freedom, security and justice', Articles 61 and 62 EC confer upon the Council the task of, and the powers for, adopting the measures necessary for the abolition of border controls. Once these measures are adopted within five years after the entry into force of the Treaty of Amsterdam on 1 May 1999, third country nationals will fall within the scope of Community law and enjoy the right to travel freely within the Community. This will not automatically entitle third country nationals to take up employment, to establish a company or to provide services in other Member States. The relevant Community provisions expressly preserve these rights for Community citizens.[318] Article 49 EC, however, does not contain a nationality requirement for service recipients and it could thus be argued that, in the near future, third country nationals will be able to claim the same cross-border health care rights as Community citizens.[319]

Secondly, the fact that Community law does not yet confer upon third country nationals a right to travel across intra-Community borders does not necessarily mean that third country nationals who have acquired a right to enter other Member States under national or international law cannot benefit from the *Decker* and *Kohll* rulings. Reference may be made to the 1998 judgment of the Court in *Martínez Sala*. It may be recalled[320] that Ms Martínez Sala was a Spanish national who lived in Germany and who claimed a right to equal treatment as regards child-raising allowances under Article 12 EC. Ms Martínez Sala did not seem to fall within the scope of the Treaty provisions on the free movement of workers and, as a recipient of a social assistance benefit, she did not meet the financial means requirement laid down in Directive No 90/364. Ms Martínez Sala resided in Germany by virtue of an international agreement to which both Germany and Spain were parties. The German government argued that she could not rely on Article 12 EC because she would fall outside the personal scope of Community law. The Court disagreed. As a Community citizen lawfully residing in the territory of another Member State, she fell within the Treaty provisions on European citizenship and this, so the Court ruled, sufficed

---

[316]   Ch 2, s 5.

[317]   Cp also: Nickless, 'Kohll and Decker: A New Hope for Third Country Nationals' (1999) *Eurohealth* 20–2.

[318]   Art 39 EC *juncto* Art 7(1) of Reg 1612/68 (right to take up employment, Art 43 EC (right of establishment) and Art 49 (right to provide services) EC.

[319]   Cp Guild, *European Community Law from a Migrant's Perspective* (2000) at 41–2.

[320]   See in particular ch 2, s 4 and ch 3, s 4.3.

for reliance on Article 12 EC as regards all benefits falling within the material scope of Community law.[321]

Admittedly, *Martínez Sala* concerned a Community citizen residing in another Member State; the case did not concern, and the Court did not make any comments on, third country nationals who are merely travelling to other Member States. Yet, the judgment does indicate that Community law not only protects the legal status of persons who are staying or residing in other Member States by virtue of Community law itself. It could be argued that in deciding on the legality of prior authorisation rules applied to third country nationals, national courts must include in their considerations the fact that such persons may have acquired the right to enter a Member State on the basis of national law or international agreements. A duty to consider this 'acquis non-communautaire' could possibly imply that national courts cannot deny third country nationals the right to rely on Article 49 EC on the ground that they have no right to enter other Member States.[322] Certainly, *Martínez Sala* does not compel such a particularly, and probably indeed overly, broad interpretation of Article 49 EC. Yet, from a health care perspective much can be said for it. The reasons why third country nationals still do not enjoy a right to travel freely within the Community are different from, and do not seem in any way related to, the motives for applying prior authorisation rules. The right to travel is denied in order to protect the immigration and related policies of the host States, whilst prior authorisation rules are applied in order to protect the health care and insurance interests of the State where patients are insured. For the latter State it does not seem relevant whether patients are admitted to other States by virtue of Community law, national law or international law. Why would third country nationals who are insured, and pay premiums, under the same conditions as the nationals of the State of insurance and which have lawfully entered, and obtained medical benefits in, other Member States be denied reimbursement of the costs incurred?[323]

---

[321] Case C–85/96 *Martínez Sala* [1998] ECR I–2691 at 61–2.

[322] On a possible duty of national courts to use this 'acquis non-communautaire' see, eg: also the Opinion of Adv Gen Cosmas in Case C–378/97 *Wijsenbeek* [1999] ECR I–6207 at 107–16.

[323] In fact, one could even go one step further and claim that all third country nationals established in the Community are at present already entitled to rely on Art 49 EC in order to claim the right to move to and receive medical services in other Member States. Cp Hatzopoulos (2000) n 24 above 7, at 58–9; Kapteyn and Verloren van Themaat, *Introduction to the Law of the European Communities* (1998) at 751 and Hatzopoulos, 'Annotation *Svensson*' (1996) CMLRev 569–88, at 575. Some, although not conclusive, support for this view seems to have been given in *Svensson* where the Court held that Luxembourg had violated Art 49 EC by making the grant of an interest rate subsidy in respect of housing subject to the condition that the loan had been obtained from credit institutions established in Luxembourg. The Court did not attach any importance to the fact that the plaintiffs were third country nationals. Unlike Adv Gen Elmer, the Court was of the view that the plaintiffs did have standing under Community law. Case C–484/93 *Svensson* [1995] ECR I–3955. In the absence of a nationality requirement in Art 49 EC and any compelling economic objections, why should equally insured third country nationals not be entitled to benefit from *Decker* and *Kohll*? It is doubtful, however, whether the argument has much chance of being accepted in the near future. The wording of Art 49 EC may not exclude the possibility that third country nationals residing within the Community can be classed as recipients of (medical) services, but Art 1 of Dir 73/148 (OJ 1973 L 172) does state that Member States are merely obliged to abolish

4.8 Conclusions

The judgments discussed in this section have made it patently clear that the initial, and long-held, assumption that cross-border access to health care would fall into a legal 'vacuum, hermetically sealed from the impact of the European Single Market'[324] no longer stands. Patients can claim cross-border health care rights not only under Regulations No 1408/71 and No 574/72, but also under the Treaty provisions on freedom of movement and non discrimination.

This section has demonstrated, however, that the significance of these Treaty provisions is not as great as one might have thought upon reading *Decker* and *Kohll*. These rulings left room for the suggestion that cross-border access to medical care would be fully subjected to the economic rules governing the common market and that patients, in principle, could move to other States in order to obtain, at the expense of their sickness fund, health care services. The judgments suggested that patients could freely choose between the rules and procedures of Regulation No 1408/71, which basically guarantee that the costs incurred are paid by patients' sickness funds, and the *Decker/Kohll* procedure, which could possibly be used in order to obtain medical care at a place closer to patients' home, to receive medical care that is not available in the State of residence or to circumvent waiting lists. *Geraets-Smits and Peerbooms* shows that the Treaty provisions on the free movement of services are applicable to, in principle, all forms of medical care and to any type of health care system, but the ruling demonstrates that the *Decker/Kohll* procedure does not constitute a genuine alternative for the 1408/71-procedure. The patients' choice is limited. The *Decker/Kohll* procedure is essentially limited to medic(in)al products and extramural medical services that are covered by the legislation in which the insured reside. Cross-border access to hospital care and 'non-covered care' remains in principle governed and regulated by the authorisation rules and procedures of Regulations Nos 1408/71 and 574/72. For such forms of medical care Article 49 EC only has additional significance in that it may confer upon insured persons the right to obtain authorisation in a larger number of cases than Article 22(2) of Regulation No 1408/71 does (*Geraets-Smits and Peerbooms*) or a right to reimbursement where authorisation has been given *a posteriori* or been unlawfully refused (*Vanbraekel*).

---

restrictions on the free movement rights of 'nationals of the Member States wishing to go to another Member State as recipients of services'. No similar provision for third country nationals exists and the Court has never held that a similar obligation vis-à-vis third country nationals can be read in Art 49 EC. In fact, in *Wijsenbeek* (1999) the Court seems to have rejected such an obligation where it held that Member States are still entitled to require from persons who wish to cross their borders to present a valid passport as provided for by inter alia Dir 73/148 in order to establish whether the person concerned is a Community citizen having the right to move freely among the Member States or a third country national not having that right. Case C–378/97 *Wijsenbeek* [1999] ECR I–6207 at 43.

324 Belcher (1999) n 16 above, at 116.

5 THE UNITED STATES

The main aim of this book is to examine the degree to which European Community law entitles individuals to move to and to claim access to public services in other Member States. The Community, however, is still a relatively young and inexperienced organisation which can learn from other federal or federal-like entities in determining how cross-border access to public benefits can be best regulated. For this purpose, this book investigates how American constitutional law, and where relevant, federal law have sought to reconcile the constitutional guarantees of freedom of movement and equality of treatment with the need to safeguard the quality of public services.[325] This section examines the United States' rules and principles governing the degree to which individuals can seek access to medical care in other States.

5.1 The American Health Care System

The United States has a vast and complex health care system which differs in many respects from, and is far more costly than,[326] the European systems.[327] The American system is fragmented. It consists of numerous subsystems which serve different categories of persons and in which various public and private 'actors' play a role in the delivery, funding and organisation of medical care. Its complexity and the differences between it and the European countries are caused, and explained, by the fact that the American system is essentially a private system based on the market model. In the United States health care has always been, and still is, seen as the prime responsibility of the individual rather than the State or society.[328] In the European Community approximately 95% of

---

[325] Ch 1, s 3.3.

[326] The American health care system is the most expensive in the world. In 1995 about 13% of the gross domestic product (GDP) was spent on health care, whilst the European Community's Member States spent on average approximately 8–9% of their GDP on health care. Shi and Singh, *Delivering Health Services in America—A Systems Approach* (1998) at 449.

[327] For more extensive descriptions of the United States health care system(s) see, eg: Verbelen, *The United States' Health Care System. Invisible Hand, Visible Effects* (1995); Furrows *et al*, *Health Law—Cases, Materials and Problems* (2000); Neipp, *Das Gesundheitswesen der USA: Ein Vorbild für die Gesetzliche Krankenversicherung?* (1988) and Williams and Torrens, *Introduction to Health Services* (1984).

[328] The Federal Constitution does not confer upon Congress or the States an obligation to provide health care facilities, to pay for individuals expenses or to protect health. *Maher v Roe*, 432 U.S. 464 (1977) at 469–70. See also: eg Capron, 'United States of America' X, *The Right to Health in the Americas* (1989) 498–520. If an individual has no access to care because a State has not provided medical benefits, that problem stems, according to the Supreme Court, from his own indigence and not from any failure on the part of the State. Parmet, 'Regulation and Federalism: Legal Impediments to State Health Care Reform' (1993) *AJLM* 121–44, at 124 and Parmet and O'Connell, 'Rehnquist's Road to Serfdom: The Ominious Message from *Rust v Sullivan*' (1992) *AP* at 94 *et seq*. State constitutions or statutes may contain a right to health care or some kind of duty for States to provide medical care for the poor, but such rights or duties are not enforceable. Dowell, 'State and Local Government Responsibilities to Provide Medical Care for the Poor' (1988–1989) *JLH* 1–45.

the population is covered by a public health care or insurance scheme.[329] In the United States this holds true for only 25 per cent of the population. About 60 per cent is privately insured;[330] 15 per cent of the American population is without sufficient health insurance cover.[331]

In the United States, governments have only taken 'health care responsibility' for indigents, the elderly and other people with no ties to the employment market who are not able to get access to adequate care. For this purpose, governments have subsidised and established hospitals, taken various initiatives to ensure that indigent patients have access to at least emergency care[332] and developed public

---

[329] n 1.

[330] Private health insurance is usually connected to employment, but can take quite different forms. Many employers insure their employees with Health Maintenance Organizations (HMOs) which act both as providers and insurers of medical care. The basic idea is that payments made by the employer (and/or employees) entitle the insured to a comprehensive range of services which must be obtained from one of the providers participating in the HMO and which include in particular many preventive services such as check-ups which help the insured to maintain their health (hence, the name 'health maintenance' organisation). Preferred Providers Organizations (PPOs) are quite similar to HMOs. PPOs are arrangements in which a group of care providers offers care to the insured employees who are encouraged but not obliged to use preferred providers.

[331] See, eg: Bovbjerg and Kopit, 'Coverage and Care for the Medically Indigent: Public and Private Options' (1986) IndLRev 857 et seq and Davis and Rowland, 'Uninsured and Undeserved: Inequities in Health Care in the United States' (1983) MMF Quart 157 et seq.

The group of the uninsured comprises about 35 million people and mainly consists of (young) part-timers working for relatively small firms whose income is too high for Medicaid eligibility but too low for the payment of private insurance premiums. The uninsured are likely to become a burden on the public purse. Non-profit making hospitals often do provide the uninsured with (emergency) care and recoup the costs by increasing the fees the insured have to pay, whilst the uninsured who have been forced to pay high medical bills themselves may be faced with financial problems so serious that they become eligible for Medicaid. In addition to continuously rising health care costs, this large group of uninsured persons has been the main reason why various health care reform plans have been proposed and debated in the last two decades. On the various proposals see, eg: White, Competing Solutions—American Health Care Proposals and International Experience (1995) and Marmor, Understanding Health Care Reform (1994).

The most well known proposal is the one which President Clinton introduced to Congress in 1993. This proposal for a Health Security Act aimed at guaranteeing universal access and controlling expenditure. On this proposal see White (1995) above, ch 9 and Verbelen (1994) n 327 above, at 60–2. So far these plans have not led to structural changes, which secure universal coverage for all United States citizens and legal residents.

[332] Two initiatives are worth mentioning here. The first concerns the Hill-Burton Act of 1946, which provided federal grants for the construction of public and non profit hospitals. Rosenblatt, 'Health Care Reform and Administrative Law: A Structural Approach' (1978) YaleLJ 243 et seq. Hospitals built with Hill-Burton grants would have to render medical services to all persons residing within the 'territorial area' (the so-called community service obligation) and to provide 'a reasonable volume of services unable to pay (the so-called free care obligation).

The second initiative involves the Emergency Medical Treatment and Active Labour Act (EMTALA) which amended the Social Security Act to prohibit the practice of 'patient dumping', i.e. the practice of hospitals to refuse to provide emergency care to patients, or to transfer unstable patients to public hospitals, on the ground the patients' inability to pay. On this practice see, eg: Dallek, 'Health Care for Undocumented Immigrants: A Story of Neglect' (1980) ClearinghouseRev 407–14. EMTALA restricts transfers of unstable patients, requires hospitals to provide appropriate medical screening examination aimed at determining whether or not a medical emergency exist and to provide emergency care. Kamoie, 'EMTALA: Reaching Beyond the Emergency Room to Expand Hospital Liability' (2000) JHL 25–55.

health insurance schemes. Most important are the Medicare and Medicaid programmes, which Congress established in 1965.

Medicare is governed by Title XVIII of the Social Security Act. It is a Federal programme which finances medical care for persons of 65 and over as well as disabled persons who are receiving insurance benefits under other titles of the Social Security Act. The programme provides for hospital insurance (Part A) and supplementary insurance (Part B). Part A, which is mainly financed by a tax on employees' income, offers protection against the cost of hospital care and home care for a defined period of time. Part B provides insurance for physician and non-hospital care which is subject to payment of monthly premiums. This insurance is optional but virtually all beneficiaries covered by Part A have chosen to enroll in Part B. Medicare is administered by the Federal government, it is based on rules and criteria which in principle apply universally throughout the country and it entitles beneficiaries to obtain care from any provider participating in the programme.

Medicaid was established, and is governed, by Title XIX of the Social Security Act. The programme provides for federal grants which are intended to encourage States to offer medical care to indigents and other low-income individuals. Today, all States operate Medicaid programmes. By law, the Federal Medical Assistance Percentage cannot be more than 83 per cent and not less than 50 per cent of the total amount States spend. The States have to pay the remaining part themselves. Within quite broad federal guidelines, States are free to lay down their own eligibility standards, to define their 'own' insurance packages and to set the rates of payments made to health care providers. In order to receive federal funding, however, States are required to include certain individuals in their programmes such as recipients of the Federal welfare programme TANF (the former AFDC) and SSI.[333] States have the option of providing Medicaid coverage to other groups such as the 'medically needy', ie persons whose income exceeds the 'normal' eligibility standards for Medicaid but who might be confronted with medical bills so high that the amount of money they can spend on the normal cost of living would *de facto* fall below the stated Medicaid standards.[334] Title XIX of the Social Security Act requires that States offer a number of basic facilities to beneficiaries such as hospital care, nurses and midwives services and laboratory facilities. States can also obtain federal funding for certain optional services such as prescribed drugs and dental care.

---

[333] See also: ch 3, s 8.1. Under the original Medicaid rules individuals who received AFDC benefits were automatically eligible for Medicaid. The Personal Responsibility and Work Opportunities Act (PRWORA) of 1996 has eliminated the AFDC programme and replaced it by the Temporary Assistance for Needy Families (TANF) programme. However, families who met the original AFDC eligibility criteria have remained eligible for Medicaid. On the impact of PRWORA on Medicaid see also: Schneider, 'The Impact of Welfare Reform on Medicaid' (1998) *Publius* 161–74.

[334] See, eg: Loue, 'Access to Health Care and the Undocumented Alien' (1992) *JLM* 271–332, at 287 and McGinnis, 'Undocumented Aliens' Right to Medicaid after *Plyler v Doe*' (1984) *FordILJ* 83–117, at 89–90.

In principle, beneficiaries are entitled to obtain the services from any provider which has chosen to participate in Medicaid and has concluded a contract with the State for this purpose. States are free to set the reimbursement rates but, in doing so, they must ensure that a sufficient number of providers joins the programme so that the 'needy' are entitled to medical care to an extent comparable to other residents of the States. The differences among the Medicaid programmes of the several States are considerable. The quality and number of the services offered, the groups of beneficiaries covered and the income eligibility levels vary from State to State.[335] In addition to a Medicaid programme, most States have established medical programmes for indigents who do not qualify for Medicaid. Such State programmes are not funded by the Federal government and wholly governed by State law.

The American health care system differs in so many respects from the European systems that a comparative analysis of the degree to which American constitutional law and European Community law entitle individuals to gain access to public medical care in other States must necessarily be limited in scope. The private health care and insurance sectors fall outside the scope of this chapter and the federally funded and administered Medicare programme is of no relevance. The conflict between the 'free movement interest' and the 'health care and insurance interests' of individual States only arises as regards public health care programmes which American States have made available for the 'poor'. The discussion below will therefore be confined to Medicaid and other public health care programmes which States have chosen to put in place.

5.2 Residents

The diversity among States' Medicaid and other public health care systems may provide an incentive for the poor to move to States with comparatively generous and well-developed systems.[336] Some States have been aware of this. They have attempted to decrease the magnetic effect of their systems by making eligibility for public medical care programmes conditional upon fulfilment of durational residence requirements. The constitutionality of waiting-period requirements for public health care schemes not covered by Medicaid[337] was

---

[335] For a more extensive description of the Medicaid programme see, eg: Coughlin and Holahan, *Medicaid since 1990: Costs, Coverage and the Shifting Alliance between the Federal Government and the States* (1994).

[336] Stone, 'Why States Can't Solve the Health Care Crisis' (1992) *AP* 51 *et seq*, at 51 and Bobinski, 'Unhealthy Federalism: Barriers to Increasing Health Care Access for the Uninsured' (1990) *UCDavisLRev* 255–348, at 271.

[337] The requirements are not imposed as regards Medicaid programmes. The Social Security Act does not allow States to apply waiting-period requirements. See 42 USC 1396a(b)3 (prohibiting 'any citizenship requirement which excludes any citizen of the United States') and HCFA State Medicaid Manual, s 3230.3.

considered by the American Supreme Court in *Memorial Hospital v Maricopa County*[338] (1974). The case involved Henry Evaro, an indigent suffering from a chronic asthmatic and bronchial illness, who had moved from New Mexico to Arizona. One month after his arrival in Arizona, Evaro had a severe respiratory attack and he was sent to Memorial Hospital, a non-profit-making private hospital, for treatment. Pursuant to an Arizona statute, the hospital notified the county, Maricopa, that it had in its charge an indigent who might qualify for county care. The hospital requested that Evaro be transferred to the county's public hospital and claimed reimbursement of the costs of the care it had given to him. Maricopa county would probably have responded positively had it not been for an Arizona statute which stated that only those indigents who had resided in the county, and thus within the State, for at least twelve months were eligible for free non emergency care.[339]

In reviewing the Arizona durational residence requirement the Court first had to establish the appropriate standard of review.[340] In *Shapiro v Thompson* (1969) the Court had concluded that one-year waiting-period requirements for welfare benefits are subject to strict scrutiny. Such requirements penalise the constitutional right to travel and any classification which does so, is unconstitutional unless shown to be necessary to promote a compelling governmental interest.[341] It was not certain, however, whether durational residence requirements for non emergency medical care were to be classed as a penalty on the right to travel. In a footnote in *Shapiro* the Court had explicitly held that it had not yet expressed its view on the test to be applied to durational residence requirement in fields other than welfare[342] and the Court had already accepted that tuition waiting-period requirements in the field of higher education were not subject to strict scrutiny.[343] In *Memorial Hospital* the Court decided to class the waiting-periods being challenged as a 'penalty':

'Whatever the ultimate parameters of the Shapiro penalty analysis (. . .), it is at least clear that medical care is as much `a basic necessity of life' to an indigent as welfare assistance. [. . .] The right of interstate travel must be seen as ensuring new residents the same vital government benefits and privileges in the States to which they migrate as are enjoyed by other residents'.[344]

---

[338] *Memorial Hospital v Maricopa County*, 415 U.S. 250 (1974).

[339] The fact that the durational residence requirement was imposed by the county rather than the State was not considered a relevant factor: 'Appellant Evaro has been effectively penalized for his interstate migration, although this was accomplished under the guise of a county residence requirement. What would be unconstitutional if done directly by the State can no more readily be accomplished by a county at the State's discretion'. *Memorial Hospital v Maricopa County*, 415 U.S. 250 (1974) at 256.

[340] See also: ch 2, s 8.4.

[341] *Shapiro v Thompson*, 394 U.S. 618 (1969) at 634. On *Shapiro* see ch 2, s 8.5 and ch 3, s 8.4.

[342] *Ibid*, n 21.

[343] See especially: *Vlandis v Kline*, 412 U.S. 441 (1973). See also: ch 5, s 8.4.

[344] *Memorial Hospital v Maricopa County*, 415 U.S. 250 (1974), at 259–61.

Having established that strict scrutiny was to be applied,[345] the Court considered a number of arguments which the county of Maricopa had raised in defence of the requirements in question. The first concerned the preservation of the quality and the fiscal integrity of the medical care programme. In the absence of a waiting-period requirement, so the County argued, any indigent sick person could seek admission to its hospital. The facilities in the hospital were apparently 'the newest and most modern' and a large influx of 'free-riding' indigents would cause long waiting-periods and put pressure on the funding of the programme. The Court could not agree. To the extent that the waiting-period was intended to 'inhibit the immigration of indigents generally, that goal is constitutionally impermissible'. In as far as the goal is to 'deter only those indigents who take up residence . . . solely to utilize . . . new and modern public medical facilities, the requirement at issue is clearly overinclusive'.[346] Citing *Shapiro* the Court held the class of barred newcomers to be all-inclusive, 'lumping the great majority who come to the State for other purposes with those who come for the sole purpose of collecting higher benefits'. An indigent 'who considers the quality of public hospital facilities in entering the State is no less deserving than one who moves into the State in order to take advantage of its better educational facilities'.[347] Maricopa County had further argued that it should be able to protect long time residents because of their contributions to the community, particularly through the past payment of taxes. The Court rejected the argument by quoting *Shapiro* where it had already held that the Equal Protection Clause prohibits such an apportionment of state services.[348] The County further defended the waiting-period by arguing that the requirement would be necessary for public support for the development of modern and effective medical facilities. Even if waiting-period did not deter migration, voters would believe that waiting-periods protected them from low income families being attracted to the county hospital. The Court was not persuaded of this: 'A State may not employ an invidious discrimination to sustain the political viability of its programs'.[349] In conclusion, the Court held that the County had not met the

---

[345] The fact that Arizona had not participated in the Medicaid could not alter this conclusion. *Memorial Hospital v Maricopa County*, 415 U.S. 250 (1974) at 261.

[346] *Ibid*, at 263–4.

[347] *Ibid*, at 264. The Court added that it is also 'useful to look at the other side of the coin- at who will bear the cost of indigents' illnesses if the County does not provide the needed treatment. For those newly arrived residents who do receive at least hospital care, the cost is often borne by private non profit hospitals . . . many of which are already in precarious financial straits. . . . When absorbed by private hospitals, the costs of caring . . . must be passed on to paying patients and 'at a rather inconvenient time'—adding to the already astronomical costs of hospitalisation which bear so heavily on the resources of most Americans. . . . The financial pressures under which private non-profit hospitals operate have already led many of them to turn away patients who cannot pay or severely limit the number of indigents they will admit. . . . And, for those indigents who receive no care, the cost is, of course, borne by their own suffering'.

[348] *Ibid*, at 266.

[349] *Ibid*. The arguments that the waiting-period could be justified because they would serve as a test of bona fide residency, would prevent fraud and that they would be necessary for budget predictability were also rejected by the Court. *Ibid*, at 267–9.

burden of showing a compelling state interest and that the waiting-period was in violation of the Equal Protection Clause.

It does not seem very likely that the conclusions drawn by the Court in *Memorial Hospital* are affected by the more recent decision in *Saenz v Roe* (1999). It may be recalled that in *Saenz* the Court abandoned *Shapiro*'s penalty-on-the-right-to-travel analysis and that it developed a new legal framework under which durational residence requirements must be reviewed under the Privileges and Immunities Clause of the Fourteenth Amendment. The standard of review to be applied under this Clause is more categorical than the one applied in *Shapiro*, but, according to the Court, it is 'surely no less strict'. No certainty exists, but there do not seem to be any good reasons for assuming that in *Saenz* the Court has moved away from *Memorial Hospital* or that it is considering doing so.[350]

From the moment they establish residence in another State, United States citizens thus have the right to benefit from the public health care programmes and facilities available there under the same conditions as that States' long-term residents. Provided they meet the financial and other eligibility criteria for Medicaid and other public health programmes, and apart from possible own contributions, they are in principle under no obligation to pay the 'medical bill'.

5.3 Non-Residents

The States' Medicaid and other public health care systems for the poor are based on the principle of territoriality. The basic assumptions are that only residents are eligible for medical services and that beneficiaries can only claim medical care in the State of residence.[351] A few exceptions appear to exist, however. Residence normally implies physical residence in a State *plus* an intention to remain there for a certain period of time.[352] For Medicaid purposes, however, mere physical presence in a State may in some cases suffice in order to be classed as a resident. Beneficiaries may choose their 'Medicaid residence'. For instance, an individual who resides in one State but seeks employment or temporarily works in another can choose the latter State as his State of residence for Medicaid purposes. Also, the spouse of an employed person working in State B who is residing in State A may choose residence in either one of the two States.[353] Furthermore, a State can arrange for an individual to be placed in an institution located in another State. The 'arranging' State 'retains responsibility' for the individual concerned and this includes cases where a State has initiated placement in another State because it lacks a sufficient number of appropriate

---

[350] Ch 2, s 8.5.2.
[351] HCFA State Medicaid Manual, s 3230.
[352] Ch 2, s 8.3.
[353] HCFA State Medicaid manual, s 3230.3 B.

facilities to provide services to its residents.[354] Generally, treatment in another State, however, is a privilege, not a right.[355]

The question arises, however, whether the 'poor' possibly can claim cross-border medical rights under the Constitution. Are residence requirements for public health care or insurance programmes constitutional?[356] More specifically, are such requirements consistent with the Privileges and Immunities Clause of Article IV § 2 of the Constitution which insures a 'citizen of State A who ventures into State B the same privileges which the citizens of State B enjoy'.[357]

The only case in which the Supreme Court has ever commented on the relevance of the Clause to health care rights is *Doe v Bolton*[358] (1973). The case concerned a Georgia Statute which made the right to abortion subject to a number of conditions one of which concerned the residence of the mother in the State. The residence requirement was held to be unconstitutional. The requirement, the Court ruled,

> 'is not based on any policy of preserving State-supported facilities for Georgia residents, for the bar also applies to private hospitals and to privately retained physicians. There is no intimation, either, that Georgia facilities are utilized to capacity in caring for Georgia residents. Just as the Privileges and Immunities Clause . . . protects persons who enter other States to ply their trade, . . . so must it protect persons who enter Georgia seeking the medical services that are available there. . . . A contrary holding would mean that a State could limit to its own residents the general medical care available within its borders. This we could not approve.'[359]

Doe concerned non-residents using their own financial resources to obtain medical care. The case did not involve publicly funded care. Nonetheless, in *Doe* the Court implicitly seems to have said that medical services must be regarded as 'fundamental' for the purposes of the Privileges and Immunities Clause of

---

[354] HCFA State Medicaid manual, s 3230.3 D. Finally, in cases where other States are not interested in concluding 'interstate agreements', States can allow individuals who are physically present in the State to be classed as residents of the State by having 'open agreements'. *Ibid*, s 3230.5.

[355] States can further conclude agreements with other States to resolve cases of disputed residence or for other reasons. Such agreements, which can pertain to one or more individuals, supersede general residency rules. The basic idea is that a State agrees to provide Medicaid services to (an) individual(s) physically residing in their territory but who for Medicaid purposes is (or are) still (a) resident(s) of another State.

[356] The Equal Protection Clause does not seem to prohibit such requirements. *Shapiro*, *Memorial Hospital* and *Saenz* merely concerned durational residence requirements, not 'simple' residence requirements. Strict scrutiny is only to be applied in cases where States discriminate among State residents 'because of the timing of their migration'. *Attorney General of New York v Soto-Lopez*, 476 U.S. 898 (1986) at 904. Discrimination against non-residents is merely reviewed under the rational relation test. See ch 2, s 8.4. Residence requirements for access to public health care are neither subject to a 'heightened level' of judicial scrutiny because they discriminate on grounds of wealth or because of special importance attached to health care. See *Maher v Roe*, 432 U.S. 464 (1977) at 469–70 and Mariner, 'Access to Health Care and Equal Protection of the Law: The Need for a New Heightened Scrutiny' (1986) *AJLM* 345–80.

[357] *Paul v Virginia*, 75 U.S. (8 Wall.) 168 (1869) at 180–1.

[358] *Doe v Bolton*, 410 U.S. 179 (1973).

[359] *Ibid*, at 200.

Article IV § 2. If correct, this would imply that residence requirements for public health care are unconstitutional unless a State can demonstrate that they are 'substantially related' to the furtherance of a State interest.[360] *Doe* suggests that the preservation of the quality and the fiscal integrity of public health care programmes constitute such 'substantial' interests and it could thus be argued that States are not obliged to give all non-residents 'full' access to their programmes. The 'substantial relation test' to be applied under the Privileges and Immunities Clause, however, does not seem to allow States to deny access to care in all circumstances. For instance, a refusal to grant non-residents emergency care would seem incompatible with the Clause.[361] Neither *Doe* nor any other decision of the Supreme Court, however, provides guidance in determining the precise degree to which States must offer residents of other States access to medical care or whether they can be constitutionally obliged to bear the costs of care which beneficiaries have obtained in other States.[362]

5.4 Aliens

A third category of persons which has often been discriminated against by States in the fields of health care and insurance consists of aliens. Depending on their immigration status, aliens have been denied equal access to medical care. Often, they have only been given a right to emergency care. The Supreme Court has never ruled on the constitutionality of State rules for public medical care containing alienage classifications.[363] In order to establish the validity of such rules under the Constitution, the general constitutional rules and principles governing the status of the various categories of aliens (permanent residents, non-immigrants and undocumented aliens) as developed in fields other than public medical care must be considered.

5.4.1 Permanent Residents

Up until the early 1970s courts subjected State rules which made eligibility for social or public benefits conditional upon United States citizenship to the lenient rational relation test reasoning that States had a 'special public interest' in

---

[360] See also: ch 2, s 8.6.1.

[361] Also, States which deny access to public care programmes which are financed through payroll taxes to resident-workers on the ground that they reside in another State might violate the Privileges and Immunities Clause. See Parmet (1993) n 327 above, at 130–1.

[362] State rules which deny non-residents access to publicly funded health care programmes or services do not seem to run counter to the Commerce Clause (ch 2, s 8.6.2). In 1945 Congress enacted the McFarran-Ferguson Act which exempts 'the business of insurance' from review under the Commerce Clause. Publicly funded care can probably benefit from this exemption. See Parmet (1993) n 327 above, at 127 who states that public health care may also be immune to Commerce Clause inquiries by virtue of the market participant doctrine (ch 2, s 8.6.1).

[363] On the differences between alienage classifications and nationality classifications see ch 2, n 410.

favouring United States citizens over aliens.[364] In 1971, however, the Supreme Court considerably strengthened the legal status of aliens, and in particular those who have acquired permanent resident status, in *Graham v Richardson*.[365] In this case the Court was asked whether the Equal Protection Clause prevents States from making welfare benefits conditional upon the possession of United States citizenship or, in the case of aliens, residence in the United States for a specified number of years. The Court held that alienage classifications were subject to strict scrutiny. Referring to *Shapiro v Thompson*, the Court held that since States cannot preserve the fiscal integrity of their welfare programmes by making distinctions between State citizens, they may neither do so by treating United States citizens and aliens differently. As citizens, resident aliens pay taxes and they contribute to the economic growth of a State and for this reason there is no 'special public interest' in tax revenues to which aliens have contributed on an equal basis with residents.[366]

Memorial Hospital means for medical care what *Shapiro* means for welfare and eligibility for Medicaid is in most cases conditional upon receipt of welfare benefits. Therefore, the conclusions drawn in *Graham* as regards welfare benefits can be transposed to the field of health care. As a result, States do not seem entitled to deny aliens access to public health care on the ground that they lack United States citizenship or that they have not resided in the United States for a given number of years.

This conclusion seems to be inconsistent with the Federal rules for Medicaid eligibility. Congress allows States to deny aliens full Medicaid coverage for the first five years of their residence in the United States.[367] Congress itself is entitled to discriminate against aliens when it provides public benefits such as those covered by the Medicare programme. Federal alienage classifications, as the Court ruled in *Mathews v Diaz* (1976), are merely subject to rational relation review.[368] Does this imply that States can 'hide behind' Congress and, in

---

[364] See also: ch 2, s 8.7.1 and ch 3 s, 8.6.1.

[365] *Graham v Richardson*, 404 U.S. 365 (1971).

[366] *Ibid*, at 376.

[367] HCFA State Medicaid Manual s 3211.6. This conclusion only applies to aliens who entered the United States on or after 22 August 1996. Aliens who on that date were lawfully residing in the United States and who met the conditions for Medicaid eligibility, continue to be entitled to the benefits.

[368] *Mathews* concerned a number of aliens who had been lawfully admitted to the United States and who attacked federal provisions which made enrolment in the Medicare programme for aliens of 65 years or older conditional upon permanent residence or residence for a minimum period of five years in the United States. The Court did not have much difficulty in upholding the provisions being challenged. Aliens do enjoy a right to equal treatment (under the due process Clause of the Fifth Amendment—see ch 2, n 422), but this in no way implies that the Federal government is obliged to treat aliens in all respects equally with United States citizens. Congress, the Court held, may very well decide to deny claims of aliens 'to share in the bounty that a conscientious sovereign makes available to its own citizens and some of its guests' and it may make distinctions among aliens according to length of residency. Since the relationship between the United States and aliens has been committed to the political branches of the Federal government and since there is no constitutional duty to provide aliens with welfare or health care, the Court was reluctant to question the decision of Congress. The Court decided to employ mere rational relation scrutiny and in doing so

spite of the limitations imposed by the Equal Protection Clause, deny aliens Medicaid services? *Graham* strongly suggests that they cannot do so. In this case it was argued by the defendant States that the alienage classifications being challenged for welfare benefits could be upheld because they would be fully compatible with the rules laid down by Congress. The Court rejected the argument. It admitted that Congress has broad powers to determine the conditions under which aliens are admitted to the United States, but it denied that the classifications had actually been authorised by Congress. Moreover, even if this had been the case, Federal rules could not have prevented the discrimination against aliens. Congress, the Court concluded, does not have the power to authorise individual States to violate the Equal Protection Clause.[369] Consequently, *Graham* seems to imply that States cannot deny full Medicaid coverage to permanent resident aliens and that the Federal provisions which authorise the States to do so are invalid.[370] The fact that States granting Medicaid to aliens during the first five years of their residence may not be able to receive Federal funding, and thus may have to bear the financial burden themselves, does not seem to affect this conclusion. Fiscal concerns, as *Graham* indicates, cannot justify discrimination against resident and taxpaying aliens.

5.4.2 Non-Immigrants and Undocumented Aliens

In *Graham* the Court considered alienage classifications as suspect for the purposes of equal protection analysis. This would seem to imply that any alienage discrimination is subject to strict scrutiny and, thus, probably unconstitutional. This, however, is not the case. Subsequent case law indicates that the protection offered by the compelling State interest test is largely preserved for permanent resident aliens and that discrimination against non-immigrants and undocumented aliens is subject to a lower level of scrutiny.[371] This is particularly relevant for medical care. Generally, aliens who are only temporarily staying in the

---

it rejected the view that the five-year residence requirement was not rationally related to the goal of maintaining the fiscal integrity of the Medicare programme because aliens must pay premiums and federal taxes. The Court expressly denied that the decision in *Graham* would compel another conclusion. That case concerned State rather than Federal statutes and the relationships of aliens with individual States differ from the relations which aliens have with the Federal government. Congress does hold the power to exercise control over travel across the borders of the United States, but the Constitution does inhibit every State's power to restrict travel across State borders. Moreover, a division by a State of the category of persons who are not citizens of that States into subcategories of United States citizens and aliens has no apparent justification, whereas a comparable classification by the Federal government is a routine and normally legitimate part of its business. *Mathews v Diaz*, 426 U.S. 67 (1976) at 17–20.

[369] *Graham v Richardson*, 404 U.S. 365 (1971) at 382.

[370] Chang, 'Immigrants under the New Welfare Law: A Call for Uniformity, A Call for Justice' (1997) *UCLALRev* 205 *et seq*, at 266 and X, 'Welfare Reform: Treatment of Legal Immigrants' (1997) *HarvLRev* 191 *et seq*, at 1193–994.

[371] Ch 2, s 8.7.

United States and undocumented aliens are not eligible for full medical care coverage under public programmes. They are only entitled to emergency care.[372]

The jurisprudence of the Supreme Court does not provide much guidance as to whether , and under which conditions, State rules excluding foreign students, temporary workers, visitors or other aliens covered by the heterogeneous group of non-immigrants are constitutional. The decision in *Toll v Moreno* (1982) demonstrates that State alienage requirements are unconstitutional in cases where the Federal immigration authorities have explicitly or implicitly indicated that non-immigrant aliens should be treated equally.[373] *Toll*, however, does not indicate which of the equal protection tests must be applied to rules which discriminate against non-immigrants where the Federal authorities allow but do not oblige States to grant such aliens public benefits. The same holds true for State rules which deny undocumented aliens full public health care coverage.

The leading case on the legal status of this category is *Plyler v Doe*[374] (1982). In reviewing a Texas policy under which undocumented school-age children were denied access to free public education under the Equal Protection Clause, the Court held that undocumented aliens are entitled to equal protection from the laws, but that their undocumented status does prevent them from being treated as a suspect class. The Court did not limit itself to mere rational relation review because the case involved, on the one hand, undocumented children who could 'affect neither their parents' conduct nor their own status' and, on the other hand, concerned education which was not just 'some' governmental benefit. The statute in question could only be upheld if Texas could show a 'substantial state interest'. The Court held that a concern for the preservation of resources was in itself not such a substantial interest. Texas had to have stronger justification grounds. Texas claimed that it was entitled to protect itself from an influx of illegal immigrants who might move to the State for educational purposes alone. The Court did not deny that States, in spite of the exclusive federal control of external borders, had some power to deter the influx of illegal aliens

---

[372] For the purposes of Medicaid, an emergency medical condition is defined as a 'medical condition (including labour and delivery) manifesting itself by acute symptoms of sufficient severity (including severe pain) such that the absence of immediate medical attention could reasonably be expected to result in (a) placing the patient's health in serious jeopardy, (b) serious impairment to bodily functions, or (c) serious dysfunction of any bodily organ or part. HCFA State Medicaid Manual, s 3211.11. States which offer emergency care to undocumented aliens may be eligible for Federal funding under the Balanced Budget Act. See also: Schlosberg, *Not-Qualified Immigrants' Access to Public Health and Emergency Services After the Welfare Law* (<http://www.healthlaw. org/pubs/19980112immigrant.html>).

See also: California's Proposition 187 which excludes undocumented aliens from all medical services except for emergency services ordered by Federal law and which provides for a procedure under which the providers are obliged to notify inter alia the United States immigration authorities of an aliens apparent illegal status. See also: Schuler, 'Equal Protection and the Undocumented Immigrant: California's Proposition 187' (1996) *BCTW LJ* 275–312, at 277 in particular.

[373] *Toll v Moreno*, 458 U.S. 1 (1982) at 12–13.

[374] *Plyler v Doe*, 457 U.S. 202 (1982). On *Plyler* see, eg: Hull, 'Undocumented Alien Children and Free Public Education: An Analysis of *Plyler v. Doe*' (1983) *UPittLRev* 431 *et seq* and ch 5, s 8.5.3.

in order to protect the States' economy or other traditional State interests,[375] but it found no evidence that Texas' interests were actually affected. The dominant incentive for illegal entry was, as the Court said, the availability of employment. Only few, if any, illegal immigrants would come to Texas or the United States in order to gain access to education. Charging 'tuition to undocumented children constitutes a ludicrously ineffectual attempt to stem the tide of illegal immigration'.[376]

The value of *Plyler* as a precedent in terms of medical care is uncertain.[377] The decision does not indicate which of the equal protection tests must be applied when reviewing State rules which deny aliens access to all medical care other than emergency services. It would seem, however, that even if an intermediate standard of review were to be applied, States might be able to demonstrate a need for excluding undocumented aliens 'full' access to medical care. Illegal immigration may not be induced by the educational opportunities for children, but access to adequate medical care may very well constitute an incentive for such migration.[378]

5.5 Lessons for the European Community?

In comparison with the 'American' sections in the chapters on minimum subsistence benefits and public education, this section has been relatively short. The reasons are not hard to find. First, unlike the European systems, the American health care system is predominantly private in nature. The comparative analysis of the rules and principles governing cross-border access to public health care in the United States has necessarily been limited to Medicaid and other health care systems States have developed for the poor. Secondly, the degree to which American law confers upon individuals a right to gain access to public medical care in other States is quite limited. The Constitution and the Federal Medicaid rules do not require from the States much more than to grant (*i*) public health insurance and care to United States citizens and permanent resident aliens residing within their borders and (*ii*) to give non-residents, non-immigrant aliens and undocumented aliens emergency care under the same conditions as their American residents. In particular, publicly insured patients do not have the right to move to other States for medical purposes nor to have the medical bill paid by the institution they are insured with or affiliated to. By comparison with European Community law, American law on cross-border access to public health care has not been very well developed. No federal rules coordinating the States' public health care systems exist; hardly any case law on cross-border

---

[375] *Ibid*, at 228 and in particular n 23.
[376] *Ibid*, at 228.
[377] *Ibid*, at 243 (Burger, CJ dissenting).
[378] Cp Schuler (1996) n 371 above, at 309. For another conclusion see McGinnis (1984) n 333 above, at 99–109.

access to health care exists. Basically, for the European Community there is not much to be learned from the limited American experience. The reverse would rather seem to hold true.

6 CONCLUSIONS

In the course of the last decades, European Community law on the free movement of persons has proven to be quite dynamic. More and more beneficiaries have been included in the free movement regime and the rights of the various categories have been extended considerably.[379] This dynamism, as Chapter 3 has demonstrated, has had significant changes for the Member States' rules governing the access to their territories and minimum subsistence benefits schemes. Community law still does not entitle all Union citizens to establish residence in other Member States and to claim minimum subsistence benefits there, but the legal status of the 'poor' has been strengthened considerably since the early 1960s. The same can hardly be said for the legal status of the 'sick'. Community law governing the access to health care in other Member States has proven to be quite static. Until recently, the cross-border access to health care was considered to be exclusively governed by the provisions of Regulations No 1408/71 and No 574/72 and the main principles on which these provisions are based have never been fundamentally altered. In brief, just as three decades ago, the regulations confer upon Community citizens rights to obtain medical care during a temporary or more permanent stay in another Member State, but the regulations do not entitle patients to go to other States in order to obtain medical care. In recent years, the situation has changed in that it has become clear that patients can also derive cross-border health care rights from the Treaty provision on freedom of movement and non discrimination. However, case law, and the ruling in *Geraets-Smits and Peerbooms* in particular, demonstrates that the practical significance of the Treaty provisions should not be exaggerated. Cross-border access to hospital care and medical care that is not covered by patients' insurance package remains primarily governed and regulated by the authorisation rules and procedures of Regulations Nos 1408/71 and 574/72. Within the European Community, the right to gain access to health care is still, in principle, a territorially limited right.

---

[379] Ch 2.

5

Education

The 1957 Treaty of Rome did not confer upon European Community institutions specific powers for the development of a common educational policy. The Treaty did not mention any educational rights for the employed and self-employed beneficiaries of the free movement of persons and a free movement of students was not provided for. The word 'education' could not even be found in the EEC Treaty. In the view of the drafters, education was, and would remain, a policy area to be governed by Member States. More than four decades later, this premise still stands. Article 149(1) of the current EC Treaty stipulates that the Community shall fully respect 'the responsibility of the Member States for the content of teaching and the organisation of education systems and their cultural and linguistic diversity.' Article 149(4) EC expressly adds that Community institutions are not empowered to harmonise the national rules governing educational systems.

The mere fact, however, that the Treaty now contains such protective clauses demonstrates that things have changed over the years. From the early years, the Community institutions have recognised that education and training are closely linked to, and of the utmost importance for, the European integration process. An efficiently functioning common market requires a well trained and qualified labour force and a genuine free movement of workers can only be realised when Community citizens, both before and during their working-life, have the possibility of acquiring in other Member States the knowledge, skills and qualifications necessary for performing work there.[1] Since the early 1960s, Community institutions have therefore entered the fields of vocational training and education. Initially, the Community's role was still rather modest, but since the judgments of the Court of Justice in *Gravier*[2] (1985) and *Commission v Council (Erasmus)*[3]

---

[1] See, eg: 'Council Decision of 2 April 1963 laying down general principles for implementing a Common Vocational Training Policy (63/266/EEC)' *Council of the European Communities—General Secretariat, European Educational Statements* (1987) at 199–202.

[2] Case 293/83 *Gravier* [1985] ECR 593. See also: s 4.1.

[3] Case 242/87 *Commission v Council (Erasmus)* [1989] ECR 1425. See also: s 2.3.

(1989), and subsequent Community practice, the Community's role in the area can no longer be ignored.[4] Today, the Community institutions hold significant pow-

[4] Community law and policy on education have attracted considerable attention in the doctrine. See, eg Shaw, 'From the Margins to the Centre: Education and Training Law and Policy' Craig and De Búrca, *The Evolution of EU Law* (1999) 555–95; van der Ven, 'De Europese Unie en de Nederlandse Studiefinanciering' in *De Staat van de Studiefinanciering* (1999) 37–61; Field, *European Dimensions—Education, Training and the European Union* (1998); Shaw, 'The Nature and Extent of `Educational Rights' under EC Law' (1998) *JSWFL* 203 *et seq*; Vermeulen and Kuijer, *Toegang tot het Onderwijs binnen de Europese Unie—Juridische Aspecten van de Toegang tot Onderwijsvoorzieningen voor Middelbaar en Hoger Onderwijs voor EG-migranten en Derdelanders binnen de Europese Unie in een Drietal Lidstaten* (1997); Brouwer, *De Europese Gemeenschap en Onderwijs: Geschiedenis van de Samenwerking en het Communautair Beleid op Onderwijsterrein* (1996); André de la Porte and Zegveld, *Mobiliteit van Studenten binnen de Europese Unie* (1996); O'Leary, *The Evolving Concept of Community Citizenship—From the Free Movement of Persons to Union Citizenship* (1996) ch 5; van der Ven, *Onderwijsrecht en Onderwijsbeleid in Nederland en de Europese Unie—Ontwikkelingen voor Hoger Onderwijs na Maastrich*t (1996); Frazier, *L'Education et la Communauté européenne* (1995); McMahon, *Education and Culture in European Community Law* (1995); Beckedorf and Henze, 'Neuere Entwicklungen in der Bildungspolitik der Europäischen Gemeinschaft' (1993) *NVwZ* 125–30; De Witte, 'Higher Education and the Constitution of the European Community' in Gellert (ed), *Higher Education in Europe* (1993) 186–202; Leenknegt, 'Onderwijs en de Europese Integratie' (1993) *S&W* 50–5; Thiele, 'Die Rechtssprechung des Gerichtshofs der Europäischen Gemeinschaften zum Recht auf Gleichbehandlung von EG-Ausländern beim Zugang zu Bildungseinrichtungen und auf Studiefinanzierung' (1993) *ZfRV* 185–97; Van Gerven and van den Bossche, 'Freedom of Movement and Equal Treatment for Students in Europe: An Emerging Principle?' in Schermers *et al* (eds), *Free Movement of Persons in Europe: Problems and Experiences* (1993) 405–26; Verbruggen, 'Toegang tot het Onderwijs en Studiefinanciering' (1992–1993) *TOO* 282–90; De Witte, 'The Influence of European Community Law on National Systems of Higher Education' in Pertek (ed), *General Recognition of Diplomas and Free Movement of Professional* (1992) 73–88; De Witte, 'Het Europees Onderwijsrecht' in *Europa en het Onderwijs* (1992) 13–44; Oertzen, *Bildung und Berufsausbildung in den Europäischen Gemeinschaften—Eine Analyse der Kompetenzgrundlagen und der subjektiven Rechte im Rahmen des EWG-Vertrages* (1992); van der Ven, 'Naar een Europese Studiefinanciering?' (1992) *NTOR* 156–66; Wimmer, 'Freedom of Movement for Students under Community Law' (1992) *ELSA* 53–68; Watson, 'Wandering Students: Their Rights under Community Law' in Curtin and O'Keeffe (eds), *Constitutional Adjudication in European Community and National Law* (1992) 79–88; Curall, 'Bildung und Ausbildung im Recht der Europäischen Gemeinschaft' (1991) *RJB* 139–61; De Blois, 'Europees Gemeenschapsrecht en Onderwijs' (1991) *SEW* 513–37; Hartley, 'Free Movement of Persons' Green *et al*, *Legal Foundations of the Single European Market* (1991) ch 13; Shaw, 'Vocational Training and Education in the European Community' (1991) *EBLRev* 279–82; Schweitzer, 'Bildungspolitik und EWG-Vertrag—Eine Bestandsaufnahme' (1991) *ZfRV* 14–25; Verschueren, 'De Buitenlandse Student' in van Hoestenberghe (ed), *Studentenrecht* (1991) 259–72; von Wittkowski, *Die Rechtsprechung des Europäischen Gerichtshofs zur Freizügigkeit und Gleichbehandlung von Angehörigen der EG-Mitgliedstaaten hinsichtlich des Besuchs von Ausbildungsstätten und deren Auswirkung für die Bundesrepublik Deutschland* (1991); Curall, 'Education Rights under the EC Treaty' in *Mobility of People in the European Community* (1990) 13–32; De Witte, 'Recht op Onderwijs zonder Grenzen?' (1990) *JF* 535–49; Fuchs, 'Bildung ohne Grenzen' (1990) *DV* 245–6; Hennis, 'Access to Education in the European Communities' (1990) *LJIL* 35–44; Lenz, 'Zuständigkeiten und Initiativen der Europäischen Gemeinschaft im Bereich des Bildungswesen' in EG-Forum, *Beilage zu IBW-Heft* (1990) 183–208; Lichtenberg, *Freizügigkeit und Bildungswesen in der Europäischen Gemeinschaft an der Schwelle zum Gemeinsamen Binnenmarktes, in: Festschrift für Ernst Steindorff* (1990) 1269–86; Sieveking, 'Bildung im Europäischen Gemeinschaftsrecht' (1990) *KritV* 344–73; Waegenbauer, 'Die Einbeziehung der Hochschulen in den Europäischen Integrationsprozess' (1990) *ER* 135–42; Conrad, 'Die Rechtsprechung des Gerichtshofs der Europäischen Gemeinschaften auf dem Gebiet des Bildungswesen' (1989) *WissR* 97–110; Crijns, 'EG-recht en Onderwijs' (1989) *NTOR* 23–41; De Witte (ed), *European Community Law of Education* (1989); Flynn, 'Vocational Training in

ers in the field of education and a common educational policy does now exist. Further, in pursuing national policies regarding admission to their educational systems Member States must observe the limitations imposed by Community law.[5] In principle, Member States are still entitled to lay down the conditions for access, but in so doing they must respect the rights that Community law confers upon nationals and residents of other (Member) States.

This chapter examines the degree to which, and the conditions under which, Community law entitles individuals to gain access to education in other Member States.[6] Are individuals entitled to gain access to education and, if so,

---

Community Law and Practice' (1989) *YEL* 59–85; Felmer, 'Gemeinschaftsrecht und Nationales (Aus-)bildungsrecht' (1989) *RJB* 175 *et seq*; Gilliams, 'Van 'Gravier' tot 'Erasmus': Over de Bijdrage van het Hof van Justitie tot de Uitbouw van een Europees Onderwijsbeleid' (1989–1990) *RW* 494–504; Gould, 'Equality of Access to Education' (1989) *MLRev* 497 *et seq*; Hartley, 'La libre Circulation des Etudiants en Droit communautaire' (1989) *CDE* 325 *et seq*; Isaac, 'L'Enseignement supérieur et le Champ d'Alication du Traité CEE' in Philip (ed), *L'Enseignement supérieur et la Dimension européenne* (1989) 11–18; Lenz, 'Die Rechtsprechung des Europäischen Gerichtshofs im Bereich des Bildungswesen' (1989) *EA* 125–34; Lonbay, 'Education and Law: The Community Context' (1989) *ELRev* 363–87; Maresceau, 'Komt Toegang tot het Onderwijs ook Binnen de Werkingssfeer van het EEG-Verdrag?'in *Liber Amicorum Van Den Bogaert* (1989) 165–85; Traversa, 'L'Interdiction de Discrimination en Raison de la Nationalité en Matière d'Accès à l'Enseignement' (1989) *RTDE* 45–69; Avenarius,'Zugangsrecht von EG-Ausländern im Bildungswesen der Bundesrepublik Deutschland' (1988) *NZfV* 385–93; Drijber, 'Gelijke Behandeling van Studenten uit de EEG—Zijn er nog Grenzen?' (1988) *NJB* 22–9; Meade, 'Free Movement of Students: Access to Higher Education in another Member State' (1988) *MR* 260–3; Hochbaum, 'Politik und Kompetenzen der Europäischen Gemeinschaften im Bildungswesen' (1987) *BayV* 481–90; Sieveking, 'Europäisierung der Bildungspolitik?' (1987) *ZAR* 99–108 and Neave, 'The Role of Education in European Integration' (1986) *IP* 277–84.

[5] In *Casagrande*, for instance, the Court held that 'although educational training and policy is not as such included in the spheres which the Treaty has entrusted to the Community institutions, it does not follow that the exercise of powers transferred to the Community is in some way limited if it is of such a nature as to affect the measures taken in the execution of a policy such as that of education and vocational training'. Case 9/74 *Casagrande* [1974] ECR 773 at 12. Also, in *Gravier* the Court held that 'although educational organization and policy are not as such included in the spheres which the Treaty has entrusted to the Community institutions, access to and participation in courses and apprenticeship, in particular vocational training, are not unconnected with Community law'. Case 293/83 *Gravier* [1985] ECR 293 at 19.

[6] This chapter only discusses the cross-border rights which Community law confers upon the recipients of education (pupils, students) to the exclusion of the rights offered to the providers (teachers, professors, schools, etc).

Teachers and professors may be classed as workers for the purposes of Art 39 EC. See, eg: Case 44/84 *Hurd* [1986] ECR 29 (teachers of 'European schools'); Case 66/85 *Lawrie-Blum* [1986] ECR 2121 (trainee teachers); Case 33/88 *Allué* [1989] ECR 1591 (university lecturers) and Case C–4/91 *Bleis* [1991] ECR I–5627 (teachers in secondary education).

Their employment does not fall within the scope of the public service exception of Art 39(4). See, eg: Case 66/85 *Lawrie-Blum* [1986] ECR 2121 at 27–8; Case 33/88 *Allué* [1989] ECR 1591 at 7 and Case C–4/91 *Bleis* [1991] ECR I–5627 at 7.

National rules which impose, in respect of recruitment of teachers in private schools, more stringent conditions on non-nationals (Case C–123/94 *Commission v Greece* [1995] ECR I–1457 at 6), which contain certain limits on the (duration of) employment contracts of lecturers in foreign languages but not on the contracts of other lecturers (Case 33/88 *Allué I* [1989] ECR 1591 at 19; Joined Cases C–259/91, C–331/91 and C–332/91 *Allué II* [1993] ECR I–4309 at 21; Case C–272/92 *Spotti* [1993] ECR I–5185 21 and Case C–90/96 *Petrie* [1997] ECR I–6527 at 57) or which limit the taking into account of previous periods of work spent in other Member States for the purposes of

does this also include a right to claim student grants? To what extent can Member States restrict admission of non-nationals and non-residents to their educational institutions with a view to securing the organisation and/or funding of their systems? How has Community law settled the conflict[7] between the aims of promoting freedom of movement and securing equality of treatment, on the one hand, and the need to protect the education systems of Member States, on the other hand?

The chapter is structured as follows. Section 2 puts the subject of cross-border access to education in its proper context by describing (*i*) the main features of the national educational systems, (*ii*) the ways in which Member States have traditionally regulated cross-border access to their systems and (*iii*) the evolution and main principles of the common educational policies. The subsequent four Sections deal with the educational rights of economic residents (3), non-residents (or Community students) (4), non-economic residents (5) and third country nationals (6).[8] After a brief summary and evaluation (section 7), the chapter then continues with an analysis of American constitutional law on cross-border access to education (section 8). As described in chapter 2, the American Constitution provides for a general right to freedom of movement which encompasses a right to equal treatment in other States. Does this imply a right to study in other States, and if so, under what conditions must students be admitted? The analysis of American law on cross-border access to education partly provides the basis for Section 9 in which Community law will be evaluated and in which the question is addressed whether, and if so, how, Community rules governing cross-border access to education could possibly be improved or adjusted.

---

determining the pay of (contractual) teachers (Case C–195/98 *Österreichischer Gewerkschaftsbund* [2000] ECR I–10497 at 51 and 56) may be in breach of Art 39(2) EC.

National rules which require from teachers to possess a certain level of knowledge of the national language, however, may be compatible with Art39 EC. See Case 379/87 *Groener* [1989] ECR 3967 at 15–19. On *Groener* see also s 4.7 below.

In addition, Community citizens can rely on Arts 43 and 49 EC in order to establish private schools (Case 147/86 *Commission v Greece* [1988] ECR 1637—also indicating that the establishment of private schools does not fall under the public authority provision of Art 45 (formerly 55) EC) or to provide in other Member States educational services of a private nature (cp Case 263/86 *Humbel* [1988] ECR 5365).

Further, providers of education can benefit from the social security rules of Reg 1408/71. See, eg: Case 33/88 *Allué* [1989] ECR 1591 (exclusion of lecturers of foreign languages from social security regimes may constitute a discrimination contrary to Art 3 of Reg 1408/71); Case C–216/89 *Reibold* [1990] ECR I–4163 (unemployment benefit for university lecturers participating in exchange programs) and Case C–102/91 *Knoch* [1992] ECR I–4341 (*idem*).

See also: Case 44/84 *Hurd* [1986] ECR 29 (Member States which tax teachers of 'European schools' for their income funded out of the Community budget violate the 'loyalty provision' contained in Art 5 (now 10) EC) and Case C–407/98 *Abrahamsson* [2000] ECR I–5539 (compatibility of positive action rules for women in university rules with Art 2(4) of Dir 76/207 on equal treatment for men and women).

[7] On the conflict between the 'free movement interest' and the 'public benefit interest' in general, see ch 1, s 2.

[8] See also: ch 1, s 3.1 and ch 2, ss 2 up to 5.

2 EDUCATION AND THE EUROPEAN COMMUNITY

2.1 Educational Systems of the Member States

Within the European Community it is for Member States to organise, administer and finance their educational systems. States are free to do so in accordance with their social, religious and cultural norms and traditions. In spite of the numerous differences among the educational systems,[9] a number of common characteristics can be detected. A first common feature is that the educational systems are all largely public in nature. In economic terms, education may be regarded as a commodity or service which, in principle, could be provided by private actors operating in a commercial market. Not one Member State, however, has chosen to fully entrust the provision of education to the market principles of *laissez-faire* and undistorted competition. The market mechanism is not necessarily the most cost-efficient and it does not guarantee 'socially just' results.[10] In particular, the private market does not guarantee that all 'members of society,' regardless of their socioeconomic status and place of residence, can gain access to adequate education. In order to make education financially and geographically accessible to all members of society,[11] governments in each of the Member States have intervened in, and largely removed education from, the private market by establishing public[12] schools and universities.

Furthermore, Member States' systems are all divided into pre training, primary and secondary education and higher education. In secondary education and higher education a distinction is often made between general education and vocational training. The former type of education is aimed at increasing knowledge

---

[9] For more detailed descriptions of the educational systems of the Member States See, eg: European Commission, *Strukturen der algemeinen und beruflichen Bildung in den Mitgliedstaaten der Europäischen Gemeinschaft* (1991); Müller-Solger, *Bildung und Europa—Die EG-Förderungsmassnahmen* (1993); Teichler, *Europäische Hochschulsysteme—Die Beharrlichkeit vielfältiger Modelle* (1990) and Ortelius, *The Database on Higher Education in Europe* (<http://ortelius.unifi.it/index2.html>).

[10] See, eg: Barr, The Economics of the Welfare State (1998) ch 12 and Le Grand *et al*, The Economics of Social Problems (1993) ch 3.

[11] Governments are under an obligation to promote the availability and accessibility of education. This obligation has found legal recognition in, and results from, the right to education which is enshrined in various international human rights instruments. See, eg: Art 26 of the Universal Declaration on Human Rights, Art 2 of the First Protocol to European Convention on Human Rights and Fundamental Freedoms and Art 13 of the International Covenant on Economic, Social and Cultural Rights. Next to this 'social aspect', the right to education contains an aspect of freedom which entails the right to choose a specific form of education and the right to establish educational institutions. See also: Leenknegt, *Vrijheid van Onderwijs in Vijf Europese Landen—Een Rechtsvergelijkend Onderzoek naar de Gemeenschappelijke Beginselen op het Gebied van Onderwijs in België, Duitsland, Engeland, Frankrijk en Nederland* (1997) and, in particular, Coomans, *De Internationale Bescherming van het Recht op Onderwijs* (1992).

[12] Private education has historically played a relatively modest role, even though the number of private educational organisations which enter the market without any public financial support has increased in recent years.

and cultural awareness or developing 'the mind in a general manner,'[13] whilst vocational training is said to be more directly aimed at preparing students for specific professions. The distinction, however, is not clear-cut. General secondary and higher education may also prepare students for specific jobs, whilst vocational training courses also contain many elements which are 'general' in nature.

Among the various types of education, higher education is the one on which Member States spend most of their resources. The sums that Member States make available for higher education differ considerably. States such as the Netherlands, Germany and Denmark spend significantly more than the southern Member States do.[14] Noticeable is Luxembourg's low spending, which is explained by the absence of a university system in the country. Also, the degree to which governmental responsibilities and powers regarding the organisation, funding and administration of higher education are divided between the central government and local government varies. The degree of decentralisation is relatively high in the United Kingdom and federal States such as Belgium and Germany, whilst in Member States such as the Netherlands and the Scandinavian countries the autonomy and powers of local government entities, such as municipalities, school districts, etc., are comparatively limited.

In order to make education, and higher education in particular, financially accessible to all members of society, many States have developed student financial aid systems.[15] These systems are intended to provide students with the financial means they need for bearing the costs of the studies (tuition fees, study materials, etc.) and/or their maintenance (housing, travel expenses, etc.). A distinction can be made between direct and indirect student financial aid schemes. Direct aid consists of student grants and loans that are awarded to the students themselves. Some Member States, such as Austria and Belgium, only provide grants, whilst other countries, such as Denmark and Germany, provide both grants and loans. The Scandinavian States and the Netherlands[16] have devel-

---

[13] Cp the Opinion of Adv Gen Slynn in Case 239/85 *Commission v Belgium* [1988] ECR 305 at 337.

[14] For some figures, see, eg: Kaiser *et al*, *Public Expenditure on Higher Education— A Comparative Study in the Member States of the European Community* (1992). See also: O'Leary (1996) n 4 above, at 166–8.

[15] Oosterbeek, 'An Economic Analysis of Student Financial Aid Schemes' (1998) *EJE* 21–9, at 21–2. For an overview of the systems, see, eg: Vossensteyn, *Mobiliteit en Studiefinanciering— Studiefinancieringsarrangementen van 16 West-Europese Landen voor het Volgen van een Volledig Hoger Onderwijsprogramma in het Buitenland* (2000); Vossensteyn, *Access: Selection and Affordability—A Comparative Analysis of the Barriers in Higher Education in Nine Western European Countries* (1997); van Vught and Vossensteyn, 'De Toekomst van het Nederlandse Stelsel van Studiefinanciering in Europees Perspectief' in Cohen *et al*, *Expertbijdragen, Scenario's en Achtergrondinformatie—Een Bundeling Bijdragen ten Behoeve van het College Toekomst Studiefinanciering* (1997) 31–44; Vossensteyn, 'Studiefinanciering in Internationaal Perspectief' (1996) *THOM* nr.5; Hulst, *Studiefinanciering in Zes Europese Landen* (1995); Ulleroe, *Le Budget de l'Etudiant et son Financement en Europe* (1994) and Oijen *et al*, *International Comparative Study of Financial Assistance to Students in Higher Education* (1990).

[16] See, eg: Roorda, 'Het Vormgeven van de Rust; of: De Teloorgang van de Wet op de Studiefinanciering' (1994) *NTOR* 2–16.

oped relatively generous direct aid schemes. For a significant part, student grants are awarded irrespective of the parents' income and they cover a substantial part of the costs of the studies and maintenance. Greece, Ireland and the United Kingdom have also developed direct aid schemes, but these schemes are wholly based on the financial strength of parents and student grants are, in comparison with the Scandinavian and the Dutch ones, rather small. Indirect student financial aid, which is offered in countries like Austria, Belgium, France, Germany, Portugal and Spain, consists of family benefits or tax benefits that are granted to students' parents. Indirect aid is usually flanked by modest direct aid schemes that are only accessible for students whose parents' income, taking into account various forms of indirect aid, falls below a certain level.

2.2 Conditions of Access

The power of Member States to organise and administer their educational systems includes the power to lay down the conditions for admission to these systems.[17] A distinction can be made between 'internal' and 'external' conditions of access. The former concern conditions that apply to all persons who wish to be admitted to educational institutions. It concerns, eg, requirements that pupils or students have finished preparatory training, have obtained certain diplomas, language and age requirements, duties to pay tuition and enrolment fees, etc. The external conditions of access are those which specifically apply to nationals and/or residents of other States.

Educational admission policies have traditionally been based on the principle of territoriality. Public education is generally open for all persons who are lawfully[18] residing in the territory of the State. In principle, the nationality of legal residents is of no relevance to the right to be admitted. Nationality is relevant, however, as regards non-resident students who merely move to another State in order to pursue education. Nationals of the State in question are generally admitted as though they were residing in their 'own' State, whilst non-nationals are often refused admission and the required residence permit. For non-resident foreigners admission is not a right. It is a privilege, which often has only been granted to students from former colonies and been made subject to a maximum number of students or a percentage of the total student body.

Many of the 'educational' cases that have come before the Court of Justice, and which will be discussed in this Chapter, concerned Belgium. A good understanding of these cases requires some insight into the rather unique Belgian

---

[17] For more detailed descriptions see, eg: De Jonghe and Dillo, *Access to Higher Education* (1991); Mohr, *Studentenhandboek* (1990) and Ortelius, n 9 above.

[18] In recent years governments in the various Member States have taken initiatives to exclude illegal residents from welfare state services including education. As regards the Netherlands see, eg: Coomans, 'Recht op Onderwijs, Ook voor `Illegale' Vreemdelingen' (1996) *MR* 57–60.

admission policies.[19] The uniqueness of these policies lies in the fact that traditionally they have never been aimed at excluding foreign students from their educational institutions. A 1971 law stated that the Belgian State would contribute to the funding of universities in accordance with the number of enrolled students regardless of their State of origin. From the early 1970s, however, the number of foreign students grew considerably and this increased the pressure on the financing of the educational system. The Belgian authorities did not decide to limit access by foreign students by imposing quota regulations. Rather, they did so by imposing on foreign students a duty to pay an additional tuition fee, the so-called *Minerval*. Neither foreign students nor their parents can be required to contribute to the funding of public education through the payment of (income) taxes and it was therefore felt justified to ask from them to pay part of the cost of their education. Students whose parents lived in Belgium, Luxembourg students and students from countries with which Belgium had concluded certain development agreements were excluded from the duty to pay the additional fee. The level of the *Minerval* was set at a minimum of 50 per cent of the fixed cost per student of a given study. Furthermore, it was decided that once the number of foreign students at a given higher education institution exceeded a quota of 2 per cent, all other foreign students would only be taken into account for funding by the Belgian State if they had paid the *Minerval*. Students, who were not taken into account for funding, could be refused admission.

National student financial aid schemes have traditionally been based on the principles of territoriality and nationality. In most States, student grants are awarded to nationals and non-nationals who are residing on the national territory. Non-nationals must already live on the national territory the moment they commence studying and some States require non-nationals to have lived on their territory for a minimum number of years. Non-nationals who merely come to the State for educational purposes are not eligible. Such non-nationals may live on the national territory during their studies, but they are not regarded as residents for the purposes of student grant schemes. Further, with the exception of the Scandinavian States, Member States only give grants and loans to students who are enrolled at public schools and universities established on their territory. As a rule, on the basis of national law student grants are not exportable.[20]

2.3 The Common Educational Policy

Education may primarily be a matter for Member States, but this is not to say that the Community has no role to play in the field. On the contrary, Articles

[19] For more detailed information on the Belgian policies and regulations see, eg: Verbruggen, n 4 above, at 39–42. See also: van der Mei, 'Nogmaals: Inschrijvingsgelden voor EG-Studenten' (1995) *NTOR* 202–8, at 202 and Joris and Veny, 'Bijkomende Inschrijvingsgelden voor Buitenlandse Studenten—Welke Wetgeving is van Toepassing?' (1988) *RW* 735–40.

[20] For an overview of the national rules governing entitlement to student grants for foreign studies see especially, Vossensteyn (2000) n 15 above.

149 and 150 EC (prior to the coming into force of the Treaty of Amsterdam: Articles 126 and 127) empower the Community institutions to act in the fields of education and vocational training respectively and significant common policies in these fields have been developed. Before commenting on the two Articles and the nature of the Community's activities in the fields, a brief history is in order. The insertion of Articles 149 and 150 EC by the Treaty on European Union was 'no accident,' but rather the 'natural culmination'[21] of a series of events and activities since the early Community years. Some historical knowledge is required for a good understanding of the two Articles and the Community rules on cross-border access to education.

The word 'education' may not have been mentioned in the EEC Treaty, but the drafters were aware of the importance of education and training for the Community and the establishment of a common market. They recognised that a free movement of, in particular self-employed, persons could not be realised without adopting measures for the mutual recognition of diplomas and therefore conferred upon the Community institutions the powers necessary for adopting such measures.[22] More important for the purposes of this book was

---

[21] Jones, 'Humanresourcen, Bildung, Ausbildung, Jugend' (1992)—Speech delivered on 20 February 1992, quoted in Schink, *Kompetenzweiterung im Handlungssystem der Europäischen Gemeinschaft: Eigendynamik und Policy Entrepreneurs* (1993) at 118.

[22] Art 47 EC (formerly 57 E(E)C). The Community legislator has adopted various directives on the mutual recognition of diplomas. Initially, a 'vertical approach' was followed which implied that separate mutual recognition directives were developed for specific professions such as doctors (Dirs No 75/362 and 75/363 (OJ L 167) as replaced by the current Dir 93/16 (OJ 1993 L 165)), nurses (Dirs No 77/452 and 77/453—OJ 1977 L 176), dentists (Dirs No 78/686 and 78/687—OJ 1978 L 233), veterinarians (Dirs No 78/1027 and 78/1028—OJ 1978 L 362), midwives (Dirs No 80/154 and 80/155—OJ 1980 L 33), pharmacists (Dirs No 85/432 and 85/433—OJ 1985 L 253) and architects (Dir 85/384 (OJ 1985 L 223) as replaced by Dir 85/614 (OJ 1985 L 376) and Dir 8617 (OJ 1986 L 71). For lawyers see also: Dir 77/249 (OJ 1977 L 78); Dir 98/5 (OJ 1998 L 77) and Case C–168/98 *Luxembourg v Parliament and Council* [2000] ECR I–9131 (dismissing action for annulment of Dir 98/5).

The adoption of these vertical directives proved to be a slow and time-consuming process partly because Member States insisted in most cases on first harmonising the educational systems before agreeing on the mutual recognition of diplomas. In the wake of the Community's initiatives to create the Internal Market by the end of 1992, another approach to the mutual recognition of diplomas was adopted. The goal of the mutual recognition of diplomas was no longer pursued on a sector-by-sector basis. Dir 89/48 established a general system for the recognition of diplomas (OJ 1989 L 19) and Dir 92/51 introduced a second general system for the recognition of professional education and training to supplement Dir 89/48 (OJ 1992 L 209). These 'horizontal' directives are based on the starting-point that higher education diplomas awarded on the completion of professional education and training of at least three years' duration should in principle be recognised in another Member State when the holder wishes to obtain access to a certain profession in that Member State.

Besides the Community legislator, the Court has contributed to decreasing the diploma obstacles to freedom of movement through its interpretation of Arts 39 (formerly 48), 43 (formerly 52) and 49 (formerly 59) E(E)C. In the absence of harmonisation, Member States are entitled to prescribe the knowledge and qualifications needed for admission to a certain occupation or education and, for this purpose, Member States may require the possession of certain qualifications. However, the Court has interpreted the afore mentioned Treaty provisions so as to impose on Member States an obligation to take into consideration all diplomas, certificates, experience obtained or acquired in other Member States, to cp these with the requirements laid down by their national rules and, where equivalence is established, to admit the persons concerned to the profession in question. See, eg: Case C–340/89 *Vlassopoulou* [1991] ECR I–2357; Case C–319/92 *Haim I* [1994] ECR I–425; Case

Article 128 EEC which empowered the Council to lay down 'general principles' for implementing a common vocational training policy.[23] The Article reflected a lack of ambition on the part of the drafters.[24] The wording of Article 128, as well as the fact that the general principles could be adopted without consultation of the European Parliament and by a simple majority of votes in the Council, indicated that the common vocational training policy was not envisaged to be developed by the adoption of legally binding measures.[25]

In 1963 the Council fulfilled its task of formulating the general principles for implementing a common vocational training policy by adopting Decision No 63/266.[26] In furtherance of the goals set in the Decision, the Council and the 'Ministers of Education meeting within the Council' adopted from the early 1970s various legally non-binding conclusions and recommendations.[27] Legislative measures, which could possibly have been based on the 'common market provision' of Article 100 EEC (now 94 EC) and/or the 'safety net clause' of Article 235 EEC (now 308 EC), were rarely adopted. Even though the Commission had sought to extend Community powers,[28] the predominant view during the 1960s and 1970s was that the common vocational training policy should be limited to providing general orientations or guidelines.[29] The Commission could not do much more than to promote the voluntary coopera-

---

C–234/97 *Fernández de Bobadilla* [1999] ECR I–4773 and Case C–238/98 *Hocsman* [2000] ECR I–6623.

On professional recognition of diplomas see, eg: van Nuffel, 'Het Algemeen Stelsel van Erkenning van Diploma's' (1996) *SEW* 371–80; Schneider, *Die Anerkennung von Diplomen in der Europäischen Gemeinschaft* (1995) (with numerous references to other literature); Pertek, *L'Europe des Diplomes et des Professions* (1994); Pertek, 'Free Movement of Professionals' (1992) *YEL* 293–324 and Laslett, 'The Mutual Recognition of Diplomas, Certificates and other Evidence of Formal Qualifications in the European Community' (1990) *LIEI* 1–66.

[23] Art 128 EEC Treaty read: 'The Council shall, acting on a proposal from the Commission and after consulting the Economic and Social Committee, lay down general principles for implementing a common vocational training policy capable of contributing to the harmonious development both of the national economies and of the common market'.

[24] Flynn (1989) n 4 above, at 60.

[25] Rather, the 'general principles' of Art 128 were probably supposed to function as guidance for the Commission which was entrusted to promote cooperation between the Member States in matters relating inter alia to 'basic and advanced vocational training' (Art 118 EEC) and which, by administering the European Social Fund (ESF), was to promote the employment opportunities of workers through 'vocational training and retraining' (Art 125 EEC). See also: Wohlfarth *et al*, *Die Europäische Wirtschaftsgemeinschaft—Kommentar zum Vertrag* (1960) at 386.

[26] n 1 above.

[27] For an overview see *Council of the European Communities—General Secretariat, European Educational Policy Statements* (1987). The measures did not only concern vocational training but also education in general.

[28] In its first proposal for the general principles in 1963, for instance, the Commission had stated that it should also have the possibility of acting in the field of general education and that it 'needed' the power to adopt legally binding measures. The Council, however, disagreed. See Schink (1993) n 21 above, at 39 and Hochbaum (1987) n 4 above, at 485.

[29] Hochbaum, 'The Federal Structure of Member States as a Limit to Common Educational Policy: The Case of Germany' in De Witte, *European Community Law of Education* (1989) 145 *et seq*, at 154.

tion of the States and educational institutions in vocational training and educational projects by providing financial incentives.

Even though through this 'facilitating approach'[30] some progress was made, a genuine vocational training policy had not been developed by the early 1980s. With the launching of the project of a 'Peoples' Europe'[31] and plans to create an internal market within the Community, however, the absence of a common policy in the field of education was increasingly felt as an omission. In particular, the European Commission and the European Parliament called for an extension of the Community's powers in the fields of vocational training and education. In 1985 these two institutions received considerable support from the Court of Justice. In *Gravier* the Court held, after referring to Article 128 and a number of Community 'soft-law' measures concerning access to vocational training, that the common vocational training policy referred to in Article 128 was gradually being established and that the conditions for access to vocational training fell within the scope of the Treaty and, consequently, that any discrimination based on nationality was prohibited by Article 7 EEC (now 12 EC).[32]

In *Gravier* the Court had laid down the legal foundations for a free movement of students within the Community. More generally, however, the decision seemed to imply that Article 128 was a Treaty provision which, at least through the operation of Article 7 EEC, could have legal force. The Commission was quick to see the potential implications and read *Gravier* in such a way as to imply that Article 128 EEC could constitute the legal basis for the adoption of legislative measures. It decided to base the proposal for the *Erasmus* programme solely on Article 128. In its judgment in *Commission v. Council (Erasmus)* (1989) the Court endorsed the Commission's reading of Article 128 EEC and *Gravier*. In the Court's view, the task of implementing the common vocational training policy was one for the Member States and the Community institutions working in cooperation. From 'an interpretation of Article 128 based on that conception,' it followed that the Council was indeed 'entitled to adopt legal measures providing for Community action in the sphere of vocational training and imposing corresponding obligations of cooperation on the Member States.'[33]

For the Commission, the *Erasmus* judgment opened unique opportunities. In order to have proposals for legislative measures adopted, there was no longer a

---

[30] Neave, *The EEC and Education* (1984) at 96.

[31] See the second report of the 'Adonnino Committee' (EC Bull. Suppl. 7/85) at point 5.

[32] Case 293/83 *Gravier* [1985] ECR 293 at 23–6. See also: s 4.1.

[33] Case 242/87 *Commission v Council (Erasmus)* [1989] ECR 1425 at 11. See also: Case 56/88 *United Kingdom v Council (Petra)* [1989] ECR 1615 and Joined Cases C–51/89, C–90/89 and C–94/89 *United Kingdom v Council (Comett II)* [1991] ECR I–2757. On the *Erasmus* judgment see, eg: Classen, 'Bildungspolitische Förderprogramme der EG—Eine kritische Untersuchung der vertragsrechtlichen Grundlagen' (1990) *EuR* 10–19; Gilliams (1989) n 4 above, at 394–504; Schmidt-'Räntsch, Erlass von Förderprogrammen durch den Rat der EG aufgrund Art.128 EWGV' (1989) *NJW* 3071–2 and Lenaerts, 'Erasmus: Legal Basis and Implementation' in De Witte, *European Community Law of Education* (1989) 113–26 (written before the judgment itself).

need to reach the unanimity in the Council as required by Articles 100 (now 94) and 235 (now 308) of the Treaty. A simple majority would suffice for adopting binding measures on the basis of Article 128. In addition, the Commission could also partly conquer the field of education in general because the Court appeared willing to give a very broad definition of the term 'vocational training.' Many forms of education, which had traditionally been classed as general education, were considered to be covered by the term 'vocational training.'[34] The Commission did not hesitate to make use of the new opportunities. Within a relatively short period of time a wide range of measures were taken. Various educational programmes were created[35] which, being governed by the Commission, were intended to encourage the voluntary participation of educational institutions of higher education.

Within a relatively short time a European vocational training policy was established. As significant as the various measures may have been, however, this development did not proceed without debate and criticism. On the one hand, it was claimed that education should no longer be approached from a purely economic perspective. In spite of the broad meaning given to the concept of vocational training, the desire was expressed that the Community should also be involved in general education so that due regard could be given to the personal, social and cultural aspects of education and training.[36] On the other hand, some Member States, such as the United Kingdom and Germany,[37] feared that their autonomy in the field of education was affected. It had been the Court, a Community institution without democratic legitimation, which, without the Member States' consent, had empowered the Council to adopt legislation by simple majority and without a need to consult the European Parliament. The limits of Community powers were not clearly delimited. The fear of an ever extending Community educational policy, which would increasingly affect national education systems, was more and more expressed.[38]

Ultimately, these desires and concerns have led to an amendment of the Treaty. The 1992 Treaty on European Union added a new Article 3(p), which states that the activities of the Community shall include 'a contribution to education and training of quality and to the flowering of the cultures of the Member States.' Article 3(p) was worked out in further detail by Articles 126 and 127 EC (now 149 and 150 EC) which replaced the old Article 128 of the EEC Treaty.[39]

[34] On the definition of the term 'vocational training' see also: s 4.2.

[35] Roughly speaking, a distinction could be made between mobility programmes and research and technology programmes. De Witte (1993) n 4 above, at 192. For an overview of the various educational programes see Müller-Solger *et al* (1993) n 9 above.

[36] Verbruggen (1991–1992) n 4 above, at 131.

[37] Read: the *Länder*.

[38] Van der Mei, 'Vrij Dienstenverkeer in de EG' (1994) *NTOR* 102–7, at 106–7 and Verbruggen (1991–1992) n 4 above, at 138.

[39] For more detailed descriptions of Arts 126 and 127 EC see, eg: Lenaerts, 'Education in European Community Law' (1994) *CMLRev* 7–41; van der Ven, 'Europees Onderwijsrecht na Maastricht' (1994) *NTOR* 140–52; Lenaerts, 'Het Onderwijs in het Europees Recht na 'Maastricht'' (1992–1993) *TOO* 264–81; Bergreen, 'Das Bildungswesen nach Maastricht—Auswirkungen der

The two Articles provide for a more defined balance of powers governing coop-eration between Member States and the Community in the fields of education and vocational training. They are based on the principle that Member States hold the primary responsibility of establishing, organising and governing edu-cational systems. The Community's role is merely complementary and supple-mentary in nature. Its activities should bring about a 'European added value.'[40]

Article 149 deals with general education; Article 150 concerns vocational training. In the field of general education the Community shall contribute to the development of quality education and, if necessary, support and supplement Member States' action by the adoption, in accordance with the co-decision pro-cedure, of 'incentive measures' and recommendations. The Community shall encourage mobility of students and teachers, promote cooperation between educational establishments, encourage the development of distance learning, etc. In the field of vocational training the Community is entitled to develop a vocational training policy which shall support and supplement the actions of Member States. More specifically, under Article 150 Community action shall aim to facilitate adaptation to industrial changes, improve vocational training in order to facilitate vocational integration and reintegration into the labour market, etc. Community action, which includes legislative measures, is aimed at an intermediary function between education, industrial life and the labour mar-ket.[41] In both fields the Community in principle is not entitled to meddle in the substance of education.[42] Paragraphs 4 of Articles 149 and 150 EC emphasise the protection of the national autonomy in the field of education by stating that the Community shall take 'incentive measures' excluding any harmonisation of the laws and regulations of the Member States. Community action will continue

Beschlüsse von Maastricht auf den Bildungsföderalismus' (1992) *RJB* 436 *et seq*; Dittmann and Fehrenbacher, 'Die Bildungdrechtliche Harmonisierungsverbote (Art.126 Abs.4 EGV, Art.127 Abs.4 EGV) und ihre Bedeutung für die nationale Bildungshoheit' (1992) *RJB* 478 *et seq*; Dohms, 'Die Kompetenz der EG im Bildungsbereich der algemeinen Bildung nach Artikel 126 EGV' (1992) *RJB* 451 *et seq* and Lane, 'New Community Competences under the Maastricht Treaty' (1993) *CMLRev* 939–79.

[40] In exercising their powers, the Community institutions have to act in accordance with the prin-ciple of subsidiarity laid down in Art 5 (formerly 3b) EC. The second sentence of this Articles reads: 'In areas which do not fall within its exclusive competence, the Community shall take action, in accordance with the principle of subsidiarity, only if and in so far as the objectives of the proposed action cannot be sufficiently achieved by the Member States and can therefore, by reason of the scale or effects of the proposed action, be better achieved by the Community'. On the importance of the subsidiarity principle for the fields of education and vocational training see also: De Groof and Friess, 'Opportunities for a European Educational Policy' (1997) *EJELP* 9–17 and Leenknegt, 'Europees Onderwijsrecht en Subsidiariteit' in Bekkers *et al* (eds), *Subsidiariteit en Europese Integratie—Een Oude Wijsheid in een Nieuwe Context* (1995) 93 *et seq*.

[41] Cohen, 'Europa en het Onderwijs(recht)' Postma (ed), *Europa en het Onderwijs* (1992) 21–42, at 36.

[42] But see: Art 149(2) EC which states that the Community shall aim at developing a European dimension in education. According to the third paragraph of Arts 149 and 150 the 'Community and the Member States shall foster cooperation with third countries and the competent international organizations'. See also: Gori, External Relations in Community Education and Vocational Training Policies' (1998) *MJ* 25–51.

to take the form of providing financial incentives for educational institutions, which are invited to participate in the cooperation prescribed or proposed by the Community.[43]

In response to the insertion of Articles 149 and 150, the Council rearranged the various educational programmes. These are now clustered under two general programmes: *Socrates* and *Leonardo da Vinci*.[44] The former covers all programmes which are intended to implement Article 149; the latter programme implements Article 150.[45] Even though the line of demarcation between Articles 149 and 150 is not crystal clear,[46] the Community powers are defined more clearly since the coming into force of the Treaty of Maastricht and much of the initial criticism has faded away. Therefore, it may not come as a surprise that the Treaties of Amsterdam and Nice have introduced no significant substantive changes. Apart from the renumbering of Articles 126 and 127 as Articles 149 and 150 EC, 'Amsterdam' has only added a new phrase in the preamble to the EC Treaty which provides that the contracting parties are 'determined to promote the development of the highest possible level of knowledge for their peoples through a wide access to education and through its continuous updating.'[47] The Treaty of Nice, which is still waiting for ratification, has not altered the Treaty rules relevant to education. The Charter of Fundamental Rights of the

[43] Leanerts (1993) n 39 above, at 279.

[44] Mention may further be made of the Youth for Europe Programme (Decision 818/95—OJ 1995 L 87) that aims to contribute to the educational progress of young people by facilitating exchanges, encouraging youth action at local level and facilitating the access of disadvantaged young people into the programme's activities as well as the European Voluntary Service for Young People which offers young people the opportunity of spending a period of time in another country and of getting involved in local projects as volunteers so that they 'broaden their horizons, . . . familiarise themselves with a different social and cultural environment and develop self-confidence' (European Commission, European Voluntary Service—available on<http/: europa.eu.int/comm/education/volunt/index.html>).

[45] *Socrates* covers *Erasmus* and *Lingua* as well as the more recent programme *Comenius* which deals with Community action in the areas of primary and secondary education. *Leonardo* concerns Art 150 and covers inter alia *Comett* and *Petra*. See also: Hermans, 'The Socrates Programme: From Negotiation to Implementation' (1997) *EJELP* 19–39 and van der Mei, 'EG-Recht en Onderwijs' (1993–1994) *JBOO* 17–26. On the future of the common educational policy and recent initiatives see, eg: Mitchell, 'EU Cooperation in Higher Education and Training: New Challenges and Recent Progress' (1996) *EJVT* 43–54; van der Mei, 'EG-Recht en Onderwijs' (1995–1996) *JBOO* 17–25 and Education, *Training and Youth—A New Generation of Programmes* (2000–2006) (available on <http://europa.eu.int.comm/education/newprogr/index.html>).

[46] Arts 149 and 150 EC do not define the terms 'education' and 'vocational training'. This is as such remarkable since the powers of the various Community institutions in the two fields differ. The definition the Court has given to the term 'vocational training' in the 'old' Art 128 cannot be used to demarcate the scope of Arts 149 and 150. University training was covered by the Court's definition of 'vocational training', but it is now (also) covered by Art149 EC. Difficult questions regarding the proper legal basis may therefore arise. Lenaerts (1993) n 39 above, at 273–5. Ultimately, it will be for the Court to draw the proper borderline between Arts 149 and 150 EC, but, with Lenaerts, it can be argued that Art 149 is the basic provision on which Community action is in principle to be based and that Art 150 complements Art 126 whenever specific vocational training aspects are involved. Art 149 is the *lex generalis,* Art 150 the *lex specialis.* Lenaerts (1993) n 39 above, at 273.

[47] The proposal to add this observation was made by the British Prime Minister Blair and relates to the reformulated Art 136 (the former Art 117) of the EC Treaty on social policy. See Barents, *Het Verdrag van Amsterdam* (1997) at 37.

European Union, which was adopted at the Nice summit, provides in Article 14 for a right to education and to have access to vocational and continuing training that includes the possibility of receiving free compulsory education. In the near future, however, this right to education is unlikely to bring about significant changes. The Charter does not establish new powers. It does not modify current powers and tasks of the Union[48] and its legal status still needs to be determined.

3 ECONOMIC RESIDENTS

3.1 The Community's Power to Grant Educational Rights to Workers and their Family Members

The drafters of the original EEC Treaty did not pay much, if any, attention to the question whether Community law should confer upon workers[49] a right to gain access to education in the Member State of employment.[50] Education was, and would remain, a national affair.[51] In the drafters' view, it would be entirely up to the Member States to determine whether beneficiaries of Article 48 EEC (now 39 EC) would be admitted to their educational institutions, and if so, the conditions under which, they would be admitted. The Community institutions which had to realise the free movement of workers during the 1960s, however, recognised that a genuine free movement of workers could not be realised without granting workers and their family members educational rights.[52] Article 7(3) was included in Regulation No 1612/68 which states that Community workers shall 'by virtue of the same right and under the same conditions as the national workers, have access to training in vocational schools and retraining centres.'

---

[48] Art 51 of the Charter.

[49] For the purposes of this book the category of economic residents has been defined so as to consist of all Community citizens and their family members who stay or reside in another Member State on the basis of Art 39 or Art 43 EC. See ch 2, s 2. The self-employed beneficiaries of Art 43 EC will not be dealt with separately. As noted in ch 2, s 2.4, this book is based on the assumption that, at least in as far as cross-border access to public benefits is concerned, the self-employed and their family members enjoy the same rights as workers and their family members do. Cp Case C–337/97 *Meeusen* [1999] ECR I–3289 at 26–30.

[50] In the so-called Val Duchesse documents (ch 2, n 12) this author did not find any document which indicates, or even suggests, that the Member States' delegations had paid attention to educational rights for workers.

[51] Hartley (1991)n 4 above, at 175.

[52] For instance, the European Commission and Parliament had expressed concern about the low level of training of, at the time in particular Italian, migrant workers. In order to increase employment opportunities, migrant workers should have the right to gain access to vocational training schools in both the State of origin and the State of employment. See, eg: *Verslag namens de Sociale Commissie nopens de Resultaten van de Studiereizen in de Landen van de Gemeenschap ter Bestudering van Bijzondere Vraagstukken in Verband met het Vrije Verkeer van Werknemers, Europees Parlement Zittingsdocumenten* 1963–1964, Document 118, January 1964 and Boni, *Freizügigkeit und Integration—Struktur und integrationspolitike Bedeutung der Arbeitsmarktverflechtung zwischen den Mitgliedstaaten der Europäischen Wirtschaftsgemeinschaft* (1976) 133–4.

As regards family members, it was stipulated in the preamble to Regulation No 1612/68 that all obstacles to the integration of the worker's family in the host State's society had to be eliminated. Such integration requires children of Community workers to go to school. Article 12 was included in the Regulation which provides that the:

> 'children of a national of a Member State who is or has been employed in the territory of another Member State shall be admitted to that State's general educational, apprenticeship and vocational training courses under the same conditions as the nationals of that State, if such children are residing in its territory. Member States shall encourage all efforts to enable such children to attend these courses under the best possible conditions.'

Politically, the inclusion of Article 7(3) and Article 12 did not raise many problems during the Council negotiations in the 1960s. Legally, however, the inclusion of the two provisions was not wholly uncontroversial. The policy area of education had not been brought within the ambit of the Treaty. The question had been raised whether the Council was at all empowered to grant educational rights upon Community workers and their family members.[53] In 1974 the German government raised this point in the proceedings before the Court in *Casagrande* in support of its view that it could not be obliged to make student grants available to children of Community workers. The Court did not accept the argument:

> 'Although educational and training policy is not as such included in the spheres which the Treaty has entrusted to the Community institutions, it does not follow that the exercise of powers transferred to the Community is in some way limited if it is not of such a nature as to affect the measures taken in execution of a policy such as that of education and training.'[54]

The Community institutions thus had not overstepped the limits of their powers by including in Regulation No 1612/68 provisions granting educational rights. *Casagrande* indicates that the Community is entitled to grant educational rights in as far as this is necessary for the realisation of the free movement of workers. In order to grant these rights no substantive educational powers are required; the functional power to take measures with a view to realising the free movement of workers suffices.[55]

---

[53] See, eg: Knolle, 'Freizügigkeit der Arbeitnehmer—Zur Verordnung Nr.15 der Europäischen Wirtschaftsgemeinschaft' (1961) *BArbBl* 674–9, at 677.

[54] Case 9/74 *Casagrande* [1974] ECR 773 at 12.

[55] De Witte, 'The Scope of Community Powers in Education and Culture in the Light of Subsequent Practice' in Bieber and Ress (eds), *The Dynamics of EC-Law* (1987) 261–81. *Casagrande* is a typical example of a case which indicates that in determining the material scope of the right to equal treatment of workers the functional criterion of promoting freedom of movement must be applied. See also: ch 2, s 2.2.3.

3.2 Community Workers

3.2.1 Admission to Education

The drafters of Regulation No 1612/68 regarded education primarily as a form of training for improving the labour skills of workers. This explains why Article 7(3) of the regulation merely speaks of a right to attend vocational schools and retraining centres. The Court has interpreted Article 7(3) accordingly. In *Lair* (1988) the Court held that an educational institution cannot be regarded as a vocational school in the sense of Article 7(3) just because some vocational training is provided. The concept of vocational school 'is a more limited one and refers exclusively to institutions which provide only instruction either alternating with or closely linked to an occupational activity, particularly during apprenticeship.'[56] Generally, universities do not fulfill this condition.

The rather limited scope of Article 7(3) does not imply, however, that Community workers are not entitled to have access to universities and other types of 'general' education. Workers do have such a right under Article 7(2) of Regulation No 1612/68 which provides for a right to be treated equally with the host State's nationals as regards 'social advantages.' In the view of its drafters, Article 7(2) would not cover educational rights,[57] but in *Lair* the Court held that this provision entitles a Community worker 'in the same way as national workers to all advantages available to such workers for improving their professional qualifications and promoting their social advancement.'[58] Access to any form of education may improve workers' qualifications and contribute to the integration of workers into the host State's society. Even though the Court has never said so explicitly, it may be assumed that all[59] forms of education not covered by Article 7(3) can be regarded as 'social advantages' in the sense of Article 7(2) of the Regulation.[60]

---

[56] Case 39/86 *Lair* [1988] 3161 at 23.

[57] De Witte (1989–1990) n 4 above, at 539 and O'Keeffe, 'Equal Rights for Migrants: the Concept of Social Advantages in Art 7(2), Reg 1612/68' (1986) *YEL* 93–123, at 95.

[58] Case 39/86 *Lair* [1988] ECR 3161 at 22. See also: Case 235/87 *Matteucci* [1988] ECR 5589 at 11.

[59] Possibly, an exception can be made for those forms of education that are directly related to, and intended to prepare individuals for, certain posts in the public services which are covered by Art 39(4) EC. On the public service exception see ch 2, s 7.1.

[60] See also: Van Gerven and van den Bossche (1993) n 4 above, at 410. As regards the access to education, Art 7(2) thus fulfils a safety-net role vis-à-vis Art 7(3). Cp the Opinion of AdvGen in Case 39/86 *Lair* [1988] ECR 3161 at 3187–8.

In a proposal for amending Reg 1612/68 the Commission has included a new Art 7(3) which reads: 'A worker who is a national of a Member State shall, by virtue of the same right and under the same conditions as nationals workers, have access to all levels of education and university or other vocational training and to vocational rehabilitation, retraining and further training'. OJ 1998 C 344 at 9; COM(98) 394 final. The text of the proposed Art 7(3) indicates that the Commission intends to make this provision the one and only education clause for Community workers. The proposed Art 7(3) must be seen as a codification of the case law.

3.2.2 Student Grants

3.2.2.1 Grants for Studies in the State of Employment

Community workers' right to gain access to education under the same conditions as the nationals of the host State logically implies that workers must be treated equally as regards the payment of tuition fees, the recognition of diplomas and the application of *numerus clausus* regulations. These are all issues directly linked to access to education. This link is less obvious as regards student grants, especially in as far as these cover the cost of maintenance. Grants may facilitate access, but they are not in all cases, or for all persons, a prerequisite for attending courses. The question whether Community workers can claim student grants was submitted to the Court in the aforementioned case of *Lair* (1988). Ms. Lair was a French national who, after having worked in Germany, was studying at the University of Hannover. The German authorities had refused Ms. Lair a grant on the ground that she had not resided and been employed in Germany for a minimum period of five years as required by German law. She challenged the refusal claiming that the requirement in question was at odds with Article 7(2) of Regulation No 1612/68. The Court reiterated that the concept of social advantages in Article 7(2) covers all benefits, which 'whether or not linked to a contract of employment,' are 'granted to national workers primarily because of their status as workers or by virtue of the mere fact of their residence on the national territory.' It follows, the Court held, that Community workers are entitled 'in the same way as national workers to all the advantages available to such workers for improving their professional qualifications and promoting their social advancement.'[61] Student grants were classed as a social advantage[62] and the durational residence and employment requirement in question was held to be incompatible with Article 7(2). Member States, the Court concluded, cannot 'unilaterally make the grant of social advantages in Article 7(2) conditional upon the completion of a given period of occupational activity.'[63] Thus, from the moment they take up employment and establish residence in another Member State, Community workers can gain admission to education and claim student grants under the same conditions as the nationals of that State.[64]

---

[61] Case 39/86 *Lair* [1988] ECR 3161 at 21–2.

[62] It could be argued that Community workers who have started studying at a vocational training school covered by Art 7(3) of Reg 1612/68 can claim equal treatment as regards student grants under this provision. If one of the conditions under which national workers can attend a vocational training course is that they obtain a student grant, then such a grant can be regarded as one of the conditions Art7(3) refers to. See, eg: Opinion of Adv Gen Slynn in Case 39/86 *Lair* [1988] 3161 at 3185–6. The Advocate General made reference to the *Casagrande* judgment in which the Court had held that the similar phrase 'under the same conditions' in Art 12 of Reg 1612/68 also applied to student grants. Case 9/74 *Casagrande* [1974] ECR 773 at 8. See also Van Gerven and van den Bossche (1993) n 4 above, at 411.

[63] Case 39/86 *Lair* [1988] ECR 3161 at 42.

[64] The durational residence and employment requirement at issue in *Lair* only applied to non-Germans. The requirement thus constituted direct discrimination on grounds of nationality. By analogy with the Court's case law on the validity of durational residence requirements for social

3.2.2.2 *Grants for Studies Abroad*

With the exception of the Scandinavian States, Member States usually make entitlement to student grants subject to the condition of being enrolled at a recognised educational institution on the national territory. The drafters of Regulation No 1612/68, who had primarily been concerned with the legal status of workers in the State of employment, had not intended to outlaw such conditions. Nonetheless, workers may have a right to student grants for studies outside the territory of the State of employment. Consider *Matteucci* (1988).[65] Ms Matteucci was an Italian national who was residing and working as a teacher in rhythmics in Belgium. In order to take a singing and voice-training course in Berlin, she applied for one of the scholarships that Germany and Belgium had made available for each other's nationals under a cultural agreement. The competent Belgian institution, however, refused to forward Ms Matteucci's name to the German authorities on the ground that eligibility for the scholarships was restricted to German and Belgian nationals. In the light of the aim of Regulation No 1612/68 to promote integration of workers and their family into the host State, one might have thought that the refusal of the Belgian institution did not run counter to Article 7(2). The Court, however, concluded that the provision had been violated. Article 7(2) lays down a general rule:

> 'which imposes responsibility in the social sphere on each Member State with regard to every worker who is a national of another Member State and established in its territory as far as equality of treatment with nationals is concerned. Consequently, where a Member State gives its nationals the opportunity of pursuing training provided for in another member State, that opportunity must be extended to Community workers established in its territory.'[66]

In *Matteucci* the Court merely condemned the nationality criteria contained in the cultural agreement between Belgium and Germany. It did not express its view on the legality of national rules that preserve student grants for students who follow courses on the national territory. Therefore, the ruling did not imply that workers had acquired a right to export student grants.

---

security and social assistance benefits (see, eg: Case C–326/90 *Commission v Belgium* [1992] ECR I–5517, Case C–111/91 *Commission v Luxembourg* [1993] ECR I–817 and ch 3, n 54), it may be assumed that durational residence or employment requirements which must be satisfied by both nationals and non-nationals constitute indirect discrimination on grounds of nationality.

[65] Case 235/87 *Matteucci* [1988] ECR 5589.

[66] *Ibid*, at 16. In the proceedings before the Court the French government had argued that such agreements fall within the cultural sphere to which the Treaty would not apply. The Court rejected this argument by ruling that the refusal to grant such a benefit may jeopardise the Community right to equal treatment and that the 'application of Community law cannot be precluded on the ground that it would affect the implementation of a cultural agreement between two Member States'. *Ibid*, at 14.

3.2.3 *Frontier Workers*

On the basis of national law non-nationals are often only eligible for student grants when they have taken up residence in the territory of the State concerned. *Matteucci* did not preclude application of such requirements. Ms Matteucci lived in Belgium. The ruling merely indicated that temporary presence in another State for educational purposes does not affect workers' residence status in the State of employment and their right to integrate in that State's society. Frontier workers, however, have chosen not to reside in the State of employment and to become a 'full member' of that State's society. Does this imply that such workers can be denied student grants?

So far, the Court has never addressed the issue. Existing case law demonstrates that frontier workers can invoke Article 7(2) of Regulation No 1612/68, but it does not guarantee that frontier workers can actually claim grants in the State of their employment. In *Meints* (1997) the Court accepted that a former frontier worker, who had been denied a special unemployment benefit in the State of employment on grounds of his residence in another Member State, could rely on Article 7(2) of Regulation No 1612/68. The Court rejected the argument concerning integration into the host State's society by referring to a phrase in the preamble to Regulation No 1612/68 according to which the right to freedom of movement must be enjoyed 'without discrimination by permanent, seasonal and frontier workers.' Article 7(2), the Court concluded, provides without any reservation for equality of treatment as regards social advantages, and thus can be relied upon by workers who have not taken up residence in the State of employment.[67]

Meints, however, concerned a social advantage that was granted to workers because of their objective status as workers. General education and student grants for such education[68] are advantages that are granted by virtue of residence. Can such benefits be classified as social advantages for non-resident workers?[69] *Meeusen* (1999) suggests that they can. In this case, which will be discussed in further detail in section 3.3.2, the Court concluded that a child of a frontier worker could invoke Article 7(2) in the State where one of her parents was employed (*in casu* the Netherlands) in order to claim student grants for studies in the State where she and her parents lived (Belgium). The Court did not

---

[67] Case C–57/96 *Meints* [1997] ECR I–6689 at 50–1.

[68] It is undisputable that frontier workers are entitled to be admitted to educational institutions in the State of employment. The right to be admitted to vocational training derives from Art 7(3) of Reg 1612/68, which does not contain a residence requirement. The right to be admitted to courses of general education can be based on Art 7(2) or, in the unlikely event that it could not, on Art 12(1) EC *juncto* Arts 149 and 150 EC. See also: s 4.2. Further, frontier workers, as one may assume, can claim student grants for vocational training on the basis of Art 7(3) of Reg 1612/68. See ns 62 and 68 above.

[69] Cp Sewandono, *Werknemersverkeer en Gezinsleven* (1998) at 226; van der Mei, 'De Rechtmatigheid van Woonplaatsvereisten voor Bestaansminimumuitkeringen onder het EG-Recht' (1999) *SMA* 451–9, at 458 and Lhernould, 'Avantages sociaux et Egalité de Traitement—Une nouvelle Etape dans la Jurisprudence de la CJCE' (1999) *DS* 938–9.

seem to attach any importance to the distinction between benefits linked to employment and advantages granted by virtue of residence. It must be noted, however, that the child in question could only claim a student grant in the Netherlands because the Dutch legislator had decided that Dutch nationals, including those residing outside the Netherlands, could receive a grant for studies at the Belgian university she was attending. *Meeusen* demonstrates that frontier workers cannot be denied advantages that are granted by virtue of residence on grounds of their nationality, but the ruling does not clarify whether they can be denied such benefits on the ground that they do not reside in the State of employment. Read together, *Meeusen* and *Meints* may suggest that frontier workers can claim in the State of employment student grants for general education followed in that, or another, Member State, but there is no certainty. So far, the Court has never held that residence requirements for student grants and other advantages granted by virtue of residence, which are applied to nationals and non-nationals alike, run counter to Article 7(2) of Regulation No 1612/68. Frontier workers cannot be discriminated against for reasons of their nationality, but so far the Court has never obliged Member States to treat non-resident workers as though they were residents.

3.2.4 *Status of Community Worker*

Community provisions on the free movement of workers provide for equal treatment rights in virtually all educational matters. Enjoyment of these rights, however, is conditional upon the possession of the status of Community worker.

The Court has given quite a broad interpretation of the concept of Community worker. The mere fact that Community citizens have moved to another State for educational purposes does not imply that they cannot be classed as Community workers.[70] Further, the Court has given due regard to the emergence of new 'flexible' forms of labour. The status of worker can be obtained by students who work part-time during evenings or weekends. The fact that work is performed on the basis of 'on-call contracts'[71] or through temporary employment agencies, is no obstacle. Even trainees and interns, who usually work for educational purposes, may be classed as Community workers.[72] In addition, the Court has accepted that Community workers can retain their

---

[70] Case 53/81 *Levin* [1982] ECR 1035 at 21.

[71] Case C–357/89 *Raulin* [1992] I–1027 at 10.

[72] Case 66/85 *Lawrie-Blum* [1986] ECR 2121 at 19 and Case C–3/90 *Bernini* [1992] ECR I–1071. The fact that internships are part of students' education and that they are often regarded as preparation for the actual pursuit of an occupation, does not exclude the possibility of interns attaining the status of Community worker. Trainees can obtain this status despite the fact that their productivity is often rather low, that they work only a few hours a week and that they receive a relatively low remuneration. Case 66/85 *Lawrie-Blum* [1986] ECR 2121 at 15 and 19–20. The Commission has proposed to codify this case law by including stagiaires (or interns) in Arts 1 of Reg 1612/68 and Dir 68/360. See COM (1998) 394 def, Explanatory Memorandum, at 10.

privileged status when they have ceased working and commenced studying. In *Lair* the Court held that Community workers who have voluntarily given up their employment in order to study can retain their worker status on condition that there is 'some continuity between the previous occupational activity and the course of the study; there must be a relationship between the purpose of the study and the previous occupational activity.'[73] As regards workers who have become

---

[73] Case 39/86 *Lair* [1988] ECR 3161 at 37. In subsequent case law the Court has confirmed this conclusion. See, eg: Case 197/86 *Brown* [1988] ECR 3205 at 26; Case C–357/89 *Raulin* [1992] ECR I–1027 at 21 and Case C–3/90 *Bernini* [1992] ECR I–1071 at 19.

In *Bernini* the Court specified that in assessing the link between the previous occupational activity and the subject of the study, national courts have to consider the 'various factors which are useful in that assessment, such as the nature and the diversity of the activities pursued and the duration of the period between the end of those activities and the commencement of the studies'. Case C–3/90 *Bernini* [1992] ECR I–1071 at 19. In his Opinion in *Raulin* Adv Gen Van Gerven proposed interpreting the requirement of continuity broadly. Studies, which improve the position of workers in the 'sector of activity' in which they are employed, would provide proof of sufficient continuity, even if, as a result of such studies, workers are able to gain access to higher or more specialised posts in that sector. The continuity, however, should not be interpreted too broadly. Opinion Adv Gen in Case C–357/89 *Raulin* [1992] ECR I–1027 at 1047. On this point see also: van den Bossche, 'Elders Gaan Studeren op Andermans Kosten?' (1992) *NJB* 792–7, at 795.

The Court does not require studies to commence immediately following the ending of the occupational activity. A 'certain period of time' may have elapsed. Case C–3/90 *Bernini* [1992] ECR I–1071 at 21.

Further, *Grzelczyk* (2001) suggests that the above-mentioned relationship between work and studies is not required in all cases. The case concerned a French student who was studying sports at the University of Louvain, Belgium. During the first three years of his studies Mr Grzelczyk was able to provide for himself by the income earned from various small jobs. In the fourth and final year, however, he was no longer able to combine his studies and employment. Since his parents were not able to maintain him, Mr Grzelczyk applied for a social assistance benefit in Belgium. His application was rejected on the ground that social assistance benefits could only be awarded to Belgian nationals and Community citizens falling within the ambit of Reg 1612/68. The national court which has to decide the case asked the Court of Justice, *inter alia*, whether denying Mr Grzelczyk the requested benefit is compatible with Articles 12 and 18 EC. The Belgian court had not included the provisions on the free movement of workers in its preliminary questions because it assumed that Mr Grzelczyk did not fulfill the criteria for treatment as a worker. Adv Gen Alber, however, and probably also the Court, however, had doubts about that assumption. In his Opinion Adv Gen Alber did consider whether Mr Grzelczyk could possibly still be classed as a worker in the sense of Art 39 EC. In principle, loss of employment leads to the loss of the status of worker (cp Case C–85/96 *Martínez Sala* [1998] ECR I–2691 at 32) but, under reference to *Lair* and *Brown* the Adv Gen stated that the status of worker and the right to invoke Art7(2) of Reg 1612/68 can be retained when a worker gives up employment in order to commence study which is substantially related to the nature of the work that he was last engaged in. From the information given by the national court it did not become clear whether Mr Grzelczyk satisfied the requirement of a link between his work and his studies. Adv Gen Alber, however, did not deem thmust be decisive. *Lair* and *Brown* concerned Community citizens who had first worked and subsequently embarked on a study. In such cases a link between the work and the studies needs to be established in order to avoid 'real students' claiming student grants. In the Adv Gen's view, the case of Mr Grzelczyk was different because he had been working and studying at the same time. In such cases, Alber did not consider it necessary to insist on a link between studies and work. Opinion of Adv Gen Alber in Case C–184/99 *Grzelczyk* [2001] ECR I–6193 at 98–101. In its judgment the Court seemed to approve the Adv Gen's reasoning and conclusions. Because the national court had limited its question to Articles 12 and 18 EC, the Court did not deem it necessary to go into the question whether Grzelczyk could retain worker status. The Court expressly added, however, that it was for the national court to determine, in the light, in particular, of the Opinion of the Adv Gen whether or

involuntarily unemployed, the Court stated in *Lair* that such continuity or relationship is not required if the person concerned is 'obliged by conditions in the job market to undertake occupational training in another field of activity.'[74]

The definition of the term Community worker, however, is not infinitely broad. The case law suggests that the Court has carefully wished to avoid that Article 39 EC could *de facto* serve as the legal basis for a free movement of students.[75] For the purposes of Article 39 EC, studies do not constitute economic activities.[76] Further, in order to acquire the status of Community worker and the rights linked to it, students must perform work that can be regarded 'effective and genuine.' The Court has never specified how many hours must be worked, but it could be argued that a Community citizen must work approximately 50 per cent of 'normal' working hours.[77] In practice, it may be quite

not the facts and circumstances of the case are such as to permit Mr Grzelczyk to be regarded as a worker for the purposes of Community law. Case C–184/99 *Grzelczyk* [2001] ECR I–6193 at 18.

Community citizens who lose the status of worker and subsequently return to, or continue to reside in, another Member State, retain the right to rely on Art7 (2) of Reg 1612/68 in order to claim benefits which are intrinsically linked to the objective status of worker (Case C–57/96 *Meints* [1997] ECR I–6689—special unemployment benefits and Case C–349/97 *Paraschi* [1998] ECR I–4501—incapacity for work benefits). However, such workers cannot claim rights or benefits granted by virtue of residence in the (former) host State. See Case C–33/99 *Fahmi* [2001] ECR I–2415 at 47 (student grants). In *Fahmi* the Court seems to have rejected the argument of Adv Gen Alber who had concluded that (children of) former workers who have returned to their State of origin remain entitled to tax-funded benefits, such as student grants, where the persons concerned (*i*) receive a pension from the State of employment and (*ii*) pay taxes in respect of such a pension in that State; Case C–33/99 *Fahmi and Esmoris Cerdeiro-Pinedo Amado* [2001] ECR I–2415 at 79.

[74] Case 39/86 *Lair* [1988] ECR 3161 at 37. This observation of the Court is not free from criticism. Firstly, as argued ch 2, s 2.4, Community workers who become involuntarily unemployed do not necessarily lose their right to reside as a worker in the host State. Arguably, they retain the right to equal treatment under Art 39 and Reg 1612/68. Secondly, the observation of the Court that workers who have become unemployed against their will and who are not forced by conditions in the labour market to undertake training in another field of activity, suggests that such workers lose entitlement to 'social advantages'. As regards workers who are still lawfully residing in the host State, however, this conclusion seems no longer correct. In *Martínez Sala* (1998) the Court held that all Community citizens who lawfully reside in the territory of another Member State enjoy under Art 12 a right to equal treatment which covers inter alia all benefits which can be classed as social advantages in the sense of Art 7 (2) of Reg 1612/68. See Case C–85/96 *Martínez Sala* [1998] ECR I–2691 at 63 as confirmed in Case C–184/99 *Grzelczyk* [2001] ECR I–6193 at 32.

[75] See also: van der Mei, 'The Elusive and Exclusive Concept of Union Citizenship, A Review Essay' (1998) *MJ* 391–402, at 397–8.

[76] See, eg: Case 66/77 *Kuyken* [1978] ECR 2311 and Case 238/83 *Meade* [1984] ECR 2631. *Kuyken* concerned a Belgian national who had followed a course of study in the Netherlands. On completion of his studies, Mr Kuyken returned to Belgium where he applied for a special unemployment benefit for young workers who have just completed their studies. The benefit was denied on the ground that Kuyken had not studied in school recognised by the Belgian State. The national court which was to rule upon the case asked the Court of Justice whether the refusal to grant the benefit was compatible with Community law on the free movement of workers. The Court concluded that neither Art 48 (now 39) E(E)C nor Reg 1408/71 prohibit such a denial because students who have never been employed fall outside the personal scope of the relevant provisions. Case 66/77 *Kuyken* [1978] ECR 2311 at 23.

[77] Jørgensen, *Union Citizens—Free Movement and Non-Discrimination* (1996) at 31.

difficult for full-time students to meet this threshold requirement for obtaining the status of worker and the rights linked to it.[78]

Further, the possibility of retaining the status of worker having given up employment for educational purposes was merely accepted by the Court in *Lair* because this would correspond with current developments in labour markets. The Court said that continuous careers are no longer so common and occupational activities are frequently interrupted by periods of training or retraining.[79] The possibility of retaining the status of Community worker was not recognised in order to enable 'real students' to obtain the status of worker through relatively short jobs, to give up this work once the studies begin and to claim as a Community worker student grants under Article 7(2) of Regulation No 1612/68. In *Brown* the Court concluded that in 'such circumstances, the employment relationship, which is the only basis for the rights deriving from Regulation 1612/68, is merely ancillary to the studies to be financed by the grant.'[80] Community law does not cover 'abuses' of the status of Community worker.[81]

3.3 Children of Community Workers

3.3.1 Admission to Education

Article 12 of Regulation No 1612/68 confers upon children of Community workers who are residing in the territory of the host State the right to gain access to 'general educational, apprenticeship and vocational training courses' under the same conditions as nationals of the host State. The Court has interpreted this provision to apply to the admission[82] to all[83] forms of education.[84]

---

[78] The *Bernini* judgment indicates that it will often be quite difficult for trainees to satisfy the criterion of 'effective and genuine' work. The Court held that in assessing whether or not interns perform such work, one does not have to take into account the number of hours during which trainees still have to familiarise themselves with the work. Case C–3/90 *Bernini* [1992] ECR I–1071 at 16. In *Bernini* Adv Gen Van Gerven suggested that the ten weeks which an intern from a technical school worked at a furniture factory was too short. Opinion of Adv Gen Van Gerven in Case C–3/90 *Bernini* [1992] ECR I–1071 at 11–12. In *Brown*, however, the Court held that a student who had entered a 'pre-university industrial training' relationship with an employer of eight months, which consisted of a three-month introduction course and five months of employment, could be classed as a Community worker. Case 197/86 *Brown* [1988] ECR 3205 at 23.

[79] Case 39/86 *Lair* [1988] ECR 3161 at 38.

[80] Case 197/86 *Brown* [1988] ECR 3205 at 27.

[81] Case 39/86 *Lair* [1988] ECR 3161 at 37–8.

[82] In practice, children of workers who wish to attend schools or universities in the host State often encounter problems concerning the academic recognition of diplomas or other qualifications obtained in the State of origin. By means of analogy with Community rules on professional recognition s 4.5), it could be argued that Member States and educational institutions are obliged to consider foreign diplomas, to compare these to national diplomas and, when equivalence is established, to recognise the diplomas. As a result, educational institutions could be prevented from requiring children to take additional exams or re-sit a school year before they are granted access to education at the same level as that which they had attained in their country of origin. Stalford, 'Transferability

cont./

Article 12 refers in rather general terms to 'children of workers.' In *Gaal* (1995) it was argued, however, that 'independent' children, ie, children who are not financially supported by the parent-worker,[85] could not claim educational rights under Article 12. The case concerned a Belgian child who had lived in Germany for many years where his father had obtained the status of Community worker. In 1989 the child applied for a student grant for a one-year period of study in the United Kingdom. The grant was denied on the ground that Gaal was over 21 and no longer a dependent child. After the death of his father he received an orphan's allowance and Gaal was not dependent on his mother. Article 10 of Regulation No 1612/68 grants children of Community workers the right to reside with the worker in the State of employment only when they are younger than 21 years or when they are dependent upon the worker. The close relationship between Articles 10 and 12, so it was argued by the German authorities, would imply that children can only invoke Article 12 when they satisfy the conditions laid down in Article 10. The Court disagreed. The concept of child in Article 12 is not limited by an age limit or a requirement of being dependent on the worker. To make the right to invoke this provision subject to these two conditions would be contrary to both the letter and the spirit of Article 12.[86]

of Educational Skills and Qualifications in the European Union: The Case of EU Migrant Children' in Shaw (ed), *Social Law and Policy in an Evolving European Union* (2000) 243–58, at 247.

[83] See, however, n 59. The same would seem to apply to family members.

[84] Joined Cases 389 and 390/87 *Echternach* [1989] ECR 723 at 29. The fact that certain types of education are not explicitly mentioned is caused by the difficulty of detailing all possible forms of education. Case 76/72 *Michel S.* [1973] ECR 457 at 15. Art 12 only applies to children who are residing in the State where the worker is employed. This does not mean, however, that children who have not established residence in that State cannot claim access to education. The ruling in *Meeusen* (s 3.3.2), in which the Court held that 'non-resident' children who are dependent on the worker can rely on Art 7(2) in order to claim student grants in the State of employment, does not seem to leave room for any conclusion other that that such children can also claim access to education under this provision. Independent children residing outside the State of employment can claim access to all forms of education under Art 12 (1) EC. See also: s 4.

[85] The Court has never really indicated when children or other family members must be regarded as dependants of a worker. In *Lebon* the Court indicated that in order to be classed as a dependent family member the person concerned must be 'factually supported' by the worker. Case 316/85 *Lebon* [1987] ECR 2811 at 13–14. The Court did not indicate what the worker's support should consist of, but, arguably, this support has to be valuable in financial terms. Otherwise, and if for instance 'moral support' would suffice, the requirement of dependency for relying on Art 7(2) would have no practical significance. Cp also *Bernini* where the Court held that benefits can only be regarded as a social advantage for the worker where the worker continues to support the family member. Case C–3/90 *Bernini* [1992] ECR I–1071 at 25. Art 10 of Reg 1612/68 suggests that children below the age of 21 are in all cases assumed to be dependants of the worker. If indeed so, this would imply that the requirement of financial support only applies to children of 21 years and older and other family members.

[86] Case C–7/94 *Gaal* [1995] ECR I–1031 at 23–31. On *Gaal* see Denys, 'Het Begrip Kind' (1995) *NTER* 115–16; van der Mei, 'Kinderen van EG-werknemers: Het Recht op Onderwijs en Studiefinanciering' (1995) *NTOR* 211–17; Szczekalla, 'EuGH: Begriff des 'Kindes' in Art.12 Verordnung (EWG) Nr.1612/68' (1995) *EuZW* 670–2 and White, 'Children and Right to Education under Article 12 of Regulation 1612/68' (1995) *ELRev* 501–7.

3.3.2 *Student Grants*

3.3.2.1 *Grants for Studies in the State of Employment*

The second sentence of Article 12 provides that 'Member States shall encourage all efforts to enable . . . children to attend . . . courses under the best possible conditions.' The sentence suggests that the drafters of Regulation No 1612/68 had not intended to confer upon children a legally enforceable right to claim student grants in the host State. Nonetheless, children do have such a right. In *Casagrande* (1974) the Court held that the first sentence of Article 12, which states that children can participate in education 'under the same terms as the citizens' of the host State, must be interpreted to apply to all 'general measures intended to facilitate educational attendance'[87] including student grants. In *Echternach* (1989) the Court specified that the status of a child of a Community worker implies that 'children must be eligible for study assistance from the State in order to make it possible for them to achieve integration in the society of the host country.'[88]

3.2.2.2 *Grants for Studies Abroad*

The drafters of Article 12 had only considered the situation in which the children live together with the parent-worker in the State of employment and claim

---

[87] Case 9/74 *Casagrande* [1974] ECR 773 at 9. See also: Case 68/74 *Alaimo* [1975] ECR 109 at 5; Joined Cases 389 and 390/97 *Echternach* [1989] ECR 723 at 33 and Case C–308/89 *di Leo* [1990] ECR I–4185 at 9.

[88] Joined Cases 389 and 390/87 *Echternach* [1989] ECR 723 at 35. In addition to the right to equal treatment in educational matters children of Community workers enjoy special rights with respect to language education. These rights are granted by Dir 77/486 on the education of children of migrant workers. OJ 1977 L 199. The Directive can be seen as an implementation of the second sentence of Art 12 of Reg 1612/68 according to which Member States must encourage all efforts to enable children of Community workers to attend educational courses under the best possible conditions. The Court ruled that this sentence 'is intended to encourage special efforts, to ensure that the children may take advantage on an equal footing of the education and training facilities available'. See Case 9/74 *Casagrande* [1974] ECR 773 at 8. The Directive obliges Member States to promote the teaching of (*i*) the (or one of the) official language(s) of the host State and (*ii*) 'the mother tongue and culture of the country of origin'. The aim is to promote not only the integration of children of migrant workers into the host State, but also their possible future re-integration in the Member State of origin. The Directive orders the Member States to adopt special educational measures for children of Community workers in order to compensate certain 'cultural handicaps' which such children may have when they reside in a Member State other than their own. Member States cannot restrict themselves by extending their existing educational policy to children of Community workers; special programmes have to be set up for them. Member States have to take 'affirmative action' in order to avoid material inequality between children of national workers and Community workers. Most probably, however, the rights mentioned in the Directive cannot be enforced in the national courts. The terms used in the provisions of the Directive seem too vague in order for the provisions to have direct effect. This conclusion is unfortunate particularly because of the difficulties which exist with regard to the implementation of the directive. On this directive see Cullen, 'From Migrants to Citizens? European Community Policy on Intercultural Education' (1996) *EJFL* 109–29; Domhof, 'Untersuchung zur Entstehung der Richtlinie des Rates der Europäischen Gemeinschaften von 25.7.1977 über die schulische Betreuung der Kinder von Wanderarbeitnehmern' in X (source unknown) (1979) and Wittek, 'Eine Europäische Dimension von Ausländerpolitik—Zur Richtlinie der EG vom 25.7.1977': (1982) *RJB* 40–50.

access to education, and student grants for studies, in that State. On a number of occasions, however, the Court has been confronted with cases which deviated from this standard situation. These cases concerned children of workers who had asked for grants for studies outside the State of employment. The Court has held that children of workers can indeed rely on Community law in order to transfer student grants abroad and, step by step, it has extended the possibilities for doing so.

A first case in which the issue arose was *di Leo* (1990). The case involved an Italian national who was living in Germany with her Italian father who had acquired the status of Community worker there. On account of the *numerus clausus* applied in medical faculties at German universities, Ms di Leo was unlikely to gain admission to a German medical faculty and she therefore decided to study medicine at the University of Sienna in Italy. In 1987 she applied for an educational grant in Germany. The German authorities denied her application because, according to the German laws applicable at the material time, grants for studies outside the national territory could only be granted to German nationals who were habitually residing in Germany. In 1988 the German law was amended as to include in its scope children of Community workers provided such children were not studying in the Member State of which they are nationals. The latter condition was introduced in order to prevent abuses which could occur where children would claim grants in both Germany and the State of origin. Ms di Leo contested the refusal by invoking Article 12 of Regulation No 1612/68. In the proceedings before the Court, the German Government argued that Ms di Leo could not rely on Article 12 because this provision explicitly requires children to reside in the State where the parent-worker is employed. The Court could not agree. The requirement contained in Article 12:

'is designed to restrict equal treatment as regards the advantages referred to in that article solely to the children of Community workers who reside within their parents' host country. However, it does not mean that the right to equal treatment depends on the place in which the child concerned pursues his studies.'[89]

The Court also rejected another argument of the two Governments according to which studies outside the territory of the host State would not contribute to the integration of the worker and his family in the society of the host State. If:

'such integration must be successful, it is essential for the child of a Community worker who resides with his family in the host Member state to have the opportunity to choose a course under the same conditions as a child of a national of that State.'[90]

This interpretation of Article 12 was not, according to the Court, any different for children of workers who study, or wish to study, in the Member State of which they hold the nationality.[91]

---

[89] Case C–308/89 *di Leo* [1990] ECR I–4185 at 12.
[90] *Ibid*, at 13.
[91] *Ibid*, at 16.

Di Leo did not imply that the residence criterion in Article 12 had lost its meaning. The judgment implied for children what *Matteucci* meant for Community workers: temporary presence in another State for educational purposes does not affect the right to claim, as a resident of the host State, equal treatment as regards student grants. The *di Leo* judgment did indicate, however, that Article 12 can only be invoked by children who actually reside in the State of employment prior to commencing studies in another State.[92] Subsequent cases, however, demonstrate that children who do not reside in the State where the worker is employed prior to their studies can claim equal treatment as regards student grants for 'foreign' studies under Article 7(2) of Regulation No 1612/68. In *Bernini* (1992) the Court was faced with the case of an Italian student residing in Italy who had embarked on architectural studies at the University of Naples. She applied for a student grant in the Netherlands where her Italian father was working and living. Her request was denied. The Netherlands Law on Study Finance did provide for the possibility of receiving a grant for architectural studies at the University of Naples, but this possibility was reserved for Dutch students and foreign students residing in the Netherlands. The Dutch court which had to rule upon the case asked the Court of Justice whether the provisions of the Netherlands law under challenge were compatible with Article 7(2) of Regulation No 1612/68. The Court answered the question in the negative. The Court confirmed earlier judgments in cases such as *Deak*[93] (1984) and *Lebon*[94] (1987) by holding that the principle of equal treatment embodied in Article 7(2) is also directed towards family members in the descending line who are dependent on the Community worker. Unlike Article 12, Article 7(2) does not contain a residence requirement and this led the Court to the conclusion that if a national rule 'imposes no residence requirement on the children of national workers, such a condition may neither be imposed on the children of Community workers.'[95]

Thus, the dependent children of workers do not have to reside in the Member State where the parent-worker is employed in order to claim student grants for studies outside that State's territory.[96] *Bernini*, however, did not imply that all non-resident children hold such a right. Ms Bernini's father was resident in the Netherlands and the ruling could be interpreted as to mean that children residing and studying in another Member States can merely claim benefits under Article 7(2) because this promotes the integration of the parent-worker into the host State. *Meeusen* (1999),[97] however, demonstrates that Article 7(2) can also

[92] Cp the Opinion of Adv Gen Darmon in Case C–308/89 *di Leo* [1990] ECR I–4185 at 24.

[93] Case 94/84 *Deak* [1985] ECR 1873 at 24.

[94] Case 316/85 *Lebon* [1987] ECR 2811 at 13.

[95] Case C–3/90 *Bernini* [1992] ECR I–1071 at 28. Family members may invoke Art 7(2) in their own right. *Ibid*, at 26.

[96] Van den Bossche (1992) n 73 above, at 796.

[97] Case C–337/97 *Meeusen* [1999] ECR I–3289. On *Meeusen* see, eg: van der Mei, 'Annotation *Meeusen*' (1999) *USZ* 687–8; Mortelmans, 'Annotation *Meeusen*' (1999) *AA* 841–8 and van der Steen, 'Studiefinanciering ook voor Kinderen van Grensarbeiders' (1999) *NTER* 210–15.

be relied in cases where both the student child and the worker reside outside the territory of the State of employment. The case concerned a Belgian student whose Belgian parents were working in the Netherlands but had kept their private residence in Belgium. The child, who resided in and studied chemistry in Antwerp, could not claim a student grant in Belgium and she therefore decided to apply for a student grant in the Netherlands. Dutch students were entitled to student grants for studies at universities in the Netherlands as well as a number of foreign educational institutions which, for the purposes of the student grant scheme, had been put on a par with Dutch educational institutions. The Antwerp Institute for Chemistry was among these institutions. Ms Meeusen's application was denied, however, on the ground that she did not possess Dutch nationality and did not reside in the Netherlands. That Ms Meeusen herself did not live in, and studied outside, the Netherlands could not, because of *Bernini*, be a reason for refusing her the grant. The Dutch government, however, interpreted *Bernini* as to mean that Article 7(2) can only be relied upon because, and when, this may help to promote the integration of the workers themselves into the host State's society. This *rationale* could not be extended to Ms Meeusen whose parents had chosen not to reside, and thus not to integrate, into the State of employment. The Court did not agree. It rejected the 'integration-argument' by holding that the preamble to Regulation No 1612/68 expressly stipulates that frontier workers also enjoy the right not to be discriminated against. Nowhere does Article 7(2) indicate that the right to equal treatment as regards social advantages can be made conditional upon workers' residence in the State concerned and this, so the Court concluded, implied that:

> 'in a situation where national legislation . . . does not impose any residence requirement on the children of national workers for financing of their studies, such a requirement must be regarded discriminatory if it is imposed on the children of workers who are nationals of other Member States?'[98]

The Court's interpretation of Article 7(2) in cases as *Bernini* and *Meeusen* seems quite broad. On the basis of national law, non-nationals can only claim student grants when they are both residing and studying in the national territory. Children as Ms Meeusen, however, who have never lived in the State where they claim grants, who do not study there and whose sole link with that State is that they are dependent on a worker who is merely employed there, are nevertheless entitled to claim student grants.

In a number of respects, however, *Bernini* and *Meeusen* are limited in scope. First, the rulings do not imply that children of Community workers enjoy an independent right to obtain student grants for studies in other Member States. Ms Bernini and Ms Meeusen could only claim a student grant because Dutch students studying at the same universities they were attending were entitled to obtain a grant under Dutch law. The Court only condemned the nationality

---

[98] *Ibid*, at 23.

criteria contained in the Dutch rules. It did not express its view on the compatibility of national rules restricting student grants to students who are following courses at a recognised educational institution on the national territory with Article 7(2) of Regulation No 1612/68.[99]

Second, Bernini and *Meeusen* do not exclude the possibility that children of frontier workers can still be denied student grants in the State of employment on the ground that they do not live in that State's territory. *Meints* indicates that residence requirements may run counter to Article 7(2), but, as stated in section 3.2.3, the Court has so far never held that this provision precludes residence requirements for student grants and other benefits granted by virtue on the national territory.

Third, the judgments in *Bernini* and *Meeusen* do not seem to be relevant for independent family members. It is settled case law that children and family members of workers can rely on Article 7(2) of Regulation No 1612/68 only when the rights or benefits they claim can be regarded as social advantages for the workers themselves. This is only the case for dependants of the worker.[100] Children who are not dependent on the worker can rely on Article 12 of the Regulation (*Gaal*) in order to claim student grants for studies both within and outside the host State when they, before beginning their studies, are residing in that State (*di Leo*). Independent children who do not reside in the State of employment cannot, as children of Community workers, claim educational rights under Regulation No 1612/68. They are in a position akin to the category of Community students whose educational rights will be examined in Section 4. Arguably, it is only in this capacity that independent children who are residing in a State other than the one in which the worker is employed, can claim educational rights.

3.3.3 Status of Child of a Community Worker

All rights discussed above are granted to persons holding the status of a child of a Community worker. On a number of occasions the Court has been confronted with cases in which it was asked whether this status could be relied upon. The problem in most of these cases did not so much concern the family relationship with the parent-worker. Rather, the question was whether the parent could still be classed as a Community worker, and thus whether the child could still be regarded as a child of a Community worker.

In *Humbel* (1988),[101] for instance, the Court was faced with the case of a French national who had acquired the status of worker in Luxembourg, but who had sent his son to school in Belgium. Mr. Humbel challenged the school fee, the so-called *Minerval*, which he had to pay for his son. Since the fee was

---

[99] In the recent case of *Fahmi and Esmoris Cerdeiro-Pinedo Amado* (2001) the Court was asked to rule on the legality of such rules, but the Court avoided going into the issue. See also: s 9.3.

[100] Case 316/85 *Lebon* [1987] ECR 2811. See also: ch 2, s 2.3.

[101] Case 263/86 *Humbel* [1988] ECR 5365.

not imposed on Belgian nationals, Mr Humbel claimed that the *Minerval* was based on a discriminatory rule and therefore at odds with Article 12 of Regulation No 1612/68. The Court rejected his argument: 'Article 12 of the regulation lays obligations only on the Member State in which the migrant worker resides.'[102] In other words, from *Humbel* it follows that children can only be regarded as children of a Community worker in the State where the parent holds the status of Community worker.[103]

In *Brown* (1988) the question arose whether a child who was born after his parents had returned to the country of origin could derive any rights from Article 12 in the Member State where one of the parents had worked. The Court answered that Article 12 'grants rights only to a child who has lived with his parents or either one of them in a Member State whilst at least one of his parents resided there as a worker.'[104] Children who are born after the parent has lost[105] or given up the status of worker do not acquire the status of family member of a Community worker. As a result, they cannot invoke Article 12 of the Regulation.

Brown left room for the conclusion that a child who had once lived with a Community worker in the State of employment, could always return to this State and invoke Article 12 even if the parent-worker has already returned to the State of origin. *Echternach* (1989) demonstrates, however, that such an interpretation of Article 12 is incorrect. One of the children who invoked Article 12 in this case was a German national who was born and had lived with his parents in the Netherlands when his German father was working there. The family had returned to Germany, but the child could not continue his studies there because the Dutch qualifications he had acquired were not recognised there. The child therefore returned to the Netherlands for the purpose of completing his studies. The Dutch authorities refused his application for a student grant. The Court

---

[102] *Ibid*, at 24–5.
[103] Arguably, a person as Mr Humbel can invoke Art 12 EC in order to challenge discriminatory enrolment fees to be paid for children attending schools in another Member State. See also: ss 4.1 and 4.2.
[104] Case 197/86 *Brown* [1988] ECR 3205 at 30.
[105] Children may also lose the status of child of a worker, and the right to claim educational rights under Art 12 or Art 7(2), as a result of the parent-worker's death. Children who are entitled to remain in the host State permanently by virtue of Reg 1251/70 (ch 2, ss 2.2 and 2.3) retain the right to equal treatment on the basis of Art 7 of this reg. See, eg: Case C–7/94 *Gaal* [1995] ECR I–1031. As regards children who do not meet the criteria for the right to remain more difficult questions could arise. It could be argued that they retain the right to reside, and the right to rely on Art12 or 7(2), for as long as the residence card given to them remains valid. Cp ch 2, s 2.2.4. Upon expiry of the residence card, however, it would seem that children holding the nationality of one of the Member States will have to bring themselves within one of the other categories of beneficiaries of the free movement of persons (ie ,worker, student or a non-economic resident). For children who only hold the nationality of a third country the death of the parent-worker could lead to loss of the right to reside. As regards third country family members who lose their status as a result of a divorce the Commission has proposed to grant them a residence right and corollary rights (Art 10(4) of the proposed new Reg 1612/68—COM(1998) 394 def), but the proposal does not refer to third country family members who lose their status as a result of death.

ruled, however, that the child could rely on Article 12 of the Regulation. A genuine integration of the worker and his family in the society of the host country can only be achieved if children of workers have the possibility of going to school and pursuing further education in order to be able to successfully complete that education.[106] The judgment did indicate, however, that children do in principle lose the status of child of a Community worker at the time the worker returns to the Member State of origin. This would seem to imply that a child cannot rely on Article 12 in order to commence, as a child of a Community worker, new studies and claim student grants in the State where the worker used to be employed.[107]

3.4 Other Family Members of Community Workers

Spouses, grandchildren and grandparents may enjoy the right to join the worker in the State of employment under Article 10(1) of Regulation No 1612/68,[108] but they cannot benefit from Article 12. This provision only applies to children of Community workers. The exclusion from Article 12 does not imply that these family members cannot claim any educational rights in the State where the Community worker is employed. As to the family members who are dependent on Community workers, one may assume that they, on the basis of Article 7(2) of Regulation No 1612/68, are entitled to gain access to education and student grant schemes under the same conditions as nationals of the host State.[109] *Lair* indicates that access to all forms of education and student grants constitutes a social advantage[110] and, as follows from *Lebon*, when given to dependent

---

[106] On this judgment see, eg: Mortelmans, 'Annotation *Echternach*' (1989) *SEW* 736–47 and Defalque, 'Annotation *Echternach*' (1989) *JT* 426 *et seq*. This right to complete educational courses logically includes a right to reside in the State concerned for the period in question. See Opinion of Adv Gen Geelhoed in Case C–413/99 *Baumbast*, pending, at 84. Geelhoed goes even one step further by concluding that the right to complete an education also includes a right of residence for the parent taking care of the child. This right can be based on Art 12. Since the parents' right is derivative in nature, however, it can be limited for the period that the child needs for completing his education and be ended when the parents ceases to be caretaker of the child. *Ibid*, at 92–4.

[107] In his Opinion in *Fahmi and Esmoris Cerdeiro-Pinedo Amado* Adv Gen Alber proposed that this conclusion should be modified as regards children of workers who have returned to their State of origin and who (*i*) are in receipt of a pension from the State of employment and (*ii*) pay taxes in respect of such a pension in the latter State. In Alber's view, such workers (and, presumably, children of workers—APvdM) retain the right to rely on Art 7(2) in order to claim student grants in the State of former employment (for studies in the State of origin and, as one may assume, the State of former employment—APvdM). Opinion of Adv Gen Alber in Case C–33/99 *Fahmi* [2001] ECR I–2415 at 79. The Court, however, seems to have rejected this view. Case C–33/99 *Fahmi* [2001] ECR I–2415 at 47.

[108] See ch 2, s 2.3.

[109] The judgment in *Forcheri* (1983) (s 4.1) suggests that family members will have to rely on Arts 12, 149 and 150 EC in order to claim educational rights. *Forcheri*, however, was decided before the Court developed the rule that (dependent) family members can claim rights under Art 7(2) of Reg 1612/68 and it may assumed that the Court today would decide cases concerning educational rights of (dependent) family members under Reg 1612/68.

[110] s 3.2 above.

family members, this benefit may be regarded as a social advantage for the workers themselves.[111] The legal status of dependent family members in the field of education thus seems identical to that of dependent children examined in section 3.3.[112]

Until recently, the legal status of family members who are not dependent on the Community worker was more difficult to determine. The difficulties did not so much concern access to education itself. As will be shown in Section 4, on the basis of Article 12(1) EC *juncto* Articles 149 and 150 EC, all Community citizens have the right to gain access to education in other Member States.[113] The uncertainty about the rights of independent family members related to the question whether, or to what extent, they can claim student grants in the State where the worker is employed. Independent family members can invoke Article 12 EC in that State, but, as will be shown in Section 4.3, the Court ruled in *Lair* (1988) that this provision only applies to student financial aid in as far as it is intended to cover tuition and enrolment fees.[114] In as far as they cover maintenance cost, grants would fall outside the scope of Article 12 EC and this seemed to imply that independent family members only have a limited right to claim student grants. The judgment in *Martínez Sala* (1998), however, already suggested that the Court had moved away from *Lair*. As stated earlier in this book,[115] in this judgment the Court ruled that (*i*) all benefits which can be classed as a social advantage in the sense of Article 7(2) of Regulation No 1612/68 also fall within the material scope of Article 12(1) EC and (*ii*) that all Community citizens lawfully established in another Member State can rely on Article 12(1) EC. More recently, in *Grzelczyk* (2001), the Court has ruled that Union citizens who have exercised the rights to move and reside freely as conferred by Article 18 EC can rely on Article 12 EC in order to claim social assistance benefits. The Court explicitly indicated that *Lair* could no longer alter that conclusion.[116] *Martínez Sala* and *Grzelczyk* do not seem to leave room for any conclusion other than that Member States are no longer entitled to refuse 'full' student grants to family members residing on their territory. Like dependent family members, independent family members are entitled to equality of treatment as regards grants for studies in the host State and for studies outside that State, where they reside there prior to their studies. In addition, family members who are dependants of the worker but who do not reside in the State where the worker is employed,

---

[111] Case 316/85 *Lebon* (1987) ECR 2811 at 13.

[112] The same could be said to apply to family members who are not covered by Art 10(1) of Reg 1612/68 but who have been admitted by virtue of Art 10(2).

[113] See also: *Forcheri* (1983) in which the Court held that spouses of Community workers who have lawfully installed themselves with the worker in the State of employment can rely on Art 7 EEC (now 12 EC) in order to claim access to education under the same conditions as nationals of the host State. Case 152/82 *Forcheri* [1983] ECR 2323 at 17–18.

[114] Case 39/86 *Lair* [1988] ECR 3161 at 14–15. See also: Case 197/86 *Brown* [1988] ECR 3205 at 17–18.

[115] See especially: ch 2, s 3.3 and ch 3, s 4.2.

[116] Case C–184/99 *Grzelczyk* [2001] ECR I–6193 at 34–6.

would seem entitled to claim grants for studies outside that State where, and under the same conditions as, nationals are given such a right. For the reasons stated in Section 3.3.2, however, it is doubtful whether independent family members enjoy the same right. Until the Court provides further clarification no definitive conclusions can be drawn, but it is submitted that unlike dependence and residence, the specific family relationship between a worker and a family member should not make a difference in determining the educational rights of family members.[117]

3.5 Conclusions

The drafters of the Treaty of Rome may not have granted educational rights to workers and their family members, but, in the course of the last four decades, the legal status of the two categories in educational matters has been strengthened considerably. The political Community institutions took the first step by including Article 7(3) and 12 in Regulation 1612/68. Further steps have been taken by the Court which has appeared willing to give quite a broad interpretation of the concept of Community worker and Articles 7(2) and 12 of Regulation No 1612/68. Basically, Community workers and their (dependent) family members must be treated equally in the field of education in virtually all respects. They may even enjoy educational rights when they do not reside in the State of employment or when they wish to study in another State.

The Court, however, has not given an infinitely broad interpretation of the relevant provisions. By laying down the requirement of 'effective and genuine' activities for obtaining the status of worker and by prohibiting abuses of that status of worker, the Court has prevented all the educational rights and benefits linked to the status of Community worker and family member of a Community being 'too easily' obtained by Community citizens who are in fact 'real' students. The educational rights guaranteed by Article 39 and specified in Regulation No 1612/68 are functional rights that are aimed at facilitating the free movement of workers. They do not constitute independent rights for Community citizens to study and claim student grants in other Member States.[118]

---

[117] Arguably, the same conclusions can be drawn as regards the family members mentioned in Art 10(2) of Reg 1612/68 who have been admitted for residence on the basis of national law. In *Martínez Sala* the Court referred to Community citizens lawfully residing in other Member States. Lawful residence may derive from national law or international law. Fries and Shaw, 'Citizenship of the Union: First Steps in the European Court of Justice' (1998) *EPL* 533–59, at 547.

As regards family members who do not hold the nationality of one of the Member States the situation would seem more complicated. As regards third country nationals who hold a right of residence under Community law it may safely be assumed that they also come within the personal scope, but it is far from certain whether the same holds true for third country family members who have been admitted on the basis of national law. The Commission has proposed to extend the scope of Arts 12 and 7(2) to all family members who have been admitted to the State of employment by virtue of Art 10 of Reg. COM(1998) 394 fin.

[118] Van der Mei (1998) n 75 above, at 397–8.

4 COMMUNITY STUDENTS

In 1984 Françoise Gravier contended before the Court of Justice that if the concept of the European Community had any real meaning, it should enable all students to move to educational institutions in other Member States.[119] Ms Gravier's call for a free movement of students was not new. From the early years, Community institutions had frequently recognised the promotion of student mobility as one of the main objectives of the common vocational training policy referred to in Article 128 of the EEC Treaty.[120] Ms Gravier's assertion was of course not motivated by the policy objectives that the Community institution had had in mind. The immediate reason for her contention was that she wished to challenge the *Minerval*, the additional enrolment fee she had to pay as a foreign student in Belgium.[121] Ms Gravier was a 'real' student. She could not claim to be a Community worker or a family member of a Community worker.[122] She argued, however, that she could invoke the principle of nondiscrimination in her

[119] Opinion of Adv Gen Slynn in Case 293/83 *Gravier* [1985] ECR 593 at 595.

[120] In particular, such mobility could contribute to the realisation of a genuine free movement of workers within the Community. In Decision 63/266 the Council stated that every person should be able to receive 'adequate training, with due regard for freedom of choice of occupation, place of training and place of work'. In a Resolution of the Ministers of Education meeting within the Council of 6 June 1974 it was held that cooperation in the field of education should be aimed at encouraging 'the freedom of movement and mobility of teachers, students and research workers, in particular by the removal of administrative and social obstacles to the free movement of such persons and by the improved teaching of foreign languages'. Two years later, in the Resolution of 9 February 1976 comprising an action programme in the field of education, the Council and the Ministers called for a discussion to develop a common policy on the admission of students from other Member States to higher education institutions and for proposals designed to eliminate obstacles to mobility of students. In 1980 the Education Committee (which was set up by the action programme just mentioned) presented a general report on how such policies were to be developed. In this report, which was approved by the Council and the Ministers for Education, a wide range of ideas and proposals were made which included inter alia the notion that Member States should treat students from other Member States equally with respect to the application of *numerus clausus* regulations and tuition fees. On 2 June 1983 the Council and the Ministers adopted a conclusion specifically dealing with the promotion of mobility in the field of higher education. The Resolution called upon the States to support student mobility within the Community by asking for flexibility with respect to the academic recognition of diplomas and by entrusting the European Commission to grant schemes for the support of joint study programmes with the aim of intensifying academic mobility. Furthermore, in a 'Solemn Declaration on European Union' the Heads of State or Government agreed to promote exchanges of teachers and students. All the above documents are contained in Council of the European Communities-General Sectretariat, European Educational Statements (1987).

[121] On the *Minerval* see s 2.2.

[122] In the 1960s the Social Committee of the European Parliament had already studied the possibility of applying the regulation of the free movement of workers to young persons who go to other Member States for the purpose of attending courses. Yet, due to the expected 'legal difficulties' the Committee did not advise including such young persons in the regulation. (European Parliament Documents 1963–1964, 25 maart 1963, Document 7, Rapporteur Rubinacci). Also in the literature it had been suggested that Art 39 EC could possibly serve as the legal basis for a free movement of students. See, eg: Steindorff, 'Ausbildungsrechte im EG-Recht (1983) *NJW* 1231–3. Yet, as described in s 3.2.3, the Court has not taken up these suggestions.

capacity of recipient of (educational) services. Gravier's argument would not succeed. In the *Gravier* judgment (1985) the Court did not even consider it.[123] One might therefore have expected that Community law would leave Ms Gravier with empty hands. The possibility of reading into the Treaty a free movement of students seemed to have been exhausted and the Commission's draft directive of 1979 on a general right of residence, which would have implied a free movement of students,[124] had not yet been adopted by the Council. Nonetheless, Ms Gravier won her case. The Court ruled that she could in her capacity as a national of a Member State invoke the principle of nondiscrimination contained in Article 7(1) (now: Article 12(1)) EC in order to gain access to educational institutions in other States.[125] In *Gravier* the Court laid down the legal foundations for a free movement of students within the European Community.

Gravier heralded a series of judgments in which the Court was asked to clarify what the free movement of students precisely entails. This Section describes and analyses the case law of the Court and aims to establish the conditions under which Community citizens who cannot benefit from the provisions described in the previous Section, can gain access to education in other Member States. For a proper understanding of Community law on the subject, however, it is useful first to go back into history and to consider why, and how, the Court created the free movement of students.

4.1 Judicial Creation of a Free Movement of Students

The establishment of the principle of a free movement of students is generally ascribed to the Court's ruling in *Gravier*. A description of this judgment alone, however, does not suffice for understanding why and how the Court realised a free movement of students within the European Community. *Gravier* had been foreshadowed[126] by *Forcheri* (1983)[127] and, strictly speaking, the Treaty based principle of a free movement of students was only finalised in *Raulin* (1992).[128]

---

[123] See also: s 4.8.

[124] Ch 2, s 3.1.

[125] Case 293/83 *Gravier* [1985] ECR 593. On *Gravier* see, eg: Flynn, 'Gravier: Suite de Feuilleton' in De Witte, *European Community law of Education* (1989) 95–112; Arnull, 'Of Strip Cartoonists, Vets and Gunsmiths' (1988) *ELRev* 260 *et seq*; Oppermann, *Europäisches Gemeinschaftsrecht und Deutsche Bildungsordnung—Gravier und die Folgen* (1987); Schermers, 'De Minerval voor Buitenlanders' (1986) *AA* 37–40; Timmermans, 'Annotatie *Gravier*' (1986) *SEW* 86–94; Foblets, 'Extra-Collegegeld voor Buitenlandse Studenten aan Belgische Universiteiten?' (1985) *JF* 535–44 and Steiner, 'Annotation *Gravier*' (1985) *CMLRev* 348–52.

[126] Flynn (1989) n 4 above, at 62.

[127] Case 152/82 *Forcheri* [1983] ECR 2323. On *Forcheri* see Moore, 'Article 7 of the Treaty of Rome Bites' (1985) *MLRev* 452–9 and Starkle, 'Extension du Principe de Non-Discrimination en Droit communautaire au Ressortissant d'un Etat membre licitement Installé dans un autre Etat membre' (1984) *CDE* 672 *et seq*.

[128] Case C–357/89 *Raulin* [1992] ECR I–1027. On this judgment see, eg: O'Keeffe, 'Annotation *Raulin*' (1992) *CMLRev* 1215–28 and van den Bossche (1992) n 73 above.

The creation of the free movement of students is best described as a three-step process.

4.1.1 Forcheri

Forcheri involved the wife of an Italian national who was working for the European Commission in Brussels. Mrs Forcheri attended a course at an educational institution that trained students to become social workers. Unlike Belgian nationals, she was required to pay the additional enrolment fee known as the *Minerval*. Mrs Forcheri was not entitled to an exemption from the *Minerval* on the ground that such a privilege was only granted to students whose spouses were in paid employment and paid taxes to the Belgian Treasury. Officials of the European Community are not taxable in Belgium. The Belgian court which had to decide the case called upon the Court of Justice to determine whether the duty to pay the Minerval was consistent with the principle of nondiscrimination as embodied in the Articles 7 EEC (now 12 EC), 48 EEC (39 EC) and Article 12 of Reg 1612/68.

The Court first referred to Article 7 EEC and observed that the Belgian rule under consideration was clearly discriminatory in nature. The Court was of the opinion that the issue brought before it was whether the payment of the *Minerval* fell within the scope of the Treaty. In other words, did access to educational courses, and in particular those concerning vocational training, fall within the scope of the Treaty? At the outset, the Court stated that EC officials fall within the personal scope of the Treaty on a dual basis by reason of their post within the Community and by virtue of Article 48 EEC. As regards the material scope, the Court quoted some of the statements in the preamble to Reg 1612/68, Article 128 of the EEC Treaty and Council Decision No 63/266[129] in which the general principles for implementing a common vocational training policy were laid down. This enabled the Court to conclude that:

'although it is true that educational and vocational training policy is not as such part of the areas which the Treaty has allotted to the competence of the Community institutions, the opportunity for such kinds of instruction falls within the scope of the Treaty.'[130]

Consequently, if a Member State:

'organises educational courses relating in particular to vocational training, to require of a national of another Member State lawfully established in the first Member State an enrolment fee which is not required of its own nationals in order to take part in such courses constitutes discrimination by reason of nationality, which is prohibited by Article 7 of the Treaty.'[131]

---

[129] s 2.3 above.
[130] Case 152/82 *Forcheri* [1983] ECR 2323 at 17.
[131] *Ibid*, at 18.

By ruling that the opportunity for educational and vocational training courses fell within the scope of the Treaty the Court established the principle of equal access to education and vocational training in other Member States. The Court concluded that this principle could be invoked by nationals of the Member States who are 'lawfully established' in another Member State. The principle of equal access was, however, formulated in such a broad way that the question arose[132] whether the principle could possibly also be relied upon by Community citizens without a pre-existing right of residence. This question was submitted to the Court in *Gravier*.

4.1.2 Gravier

Françoise Gravier was a young French woman whose normal residence was in France. She had been admitted to the Academie Royale des Beaux-Arts in Liège, Belgium, to study the art of strip cartoons. The academy charged all students a registration fee of 10.000 Belgian Francs a year. In addition, Ms Gravier had to pay an extra enrolment fee, the *Minerval*, of about 25.000 Belgian Francs, which students of Belgian nationality were not required to pay. Her application for exemption from this enrolment fee was rejected. After she refused to pay the fee and was denied enrolment, Ms Gravier brought an action before a Belgian court claiming that the Minerval was discriminatory and contrary to Community law. The national court, which obviously had read the Court's judgment in *Forcheri*, asked the Court whether EC nationals who move to another Member State for the sole purpose of following courses in an institution offering instruction, in particular, to vocational training fell within the scope of the Treaty.

In resolving the issue the Court of Justice first defined the nature of the problem. The Court delimited the issue under consideration by stipulating that:

> 'although educational organisation and policy are as such not included in the spheres which the Treaty has entrusted to the Community institutions, access to and participation in courses of instruction and apprenticeship, in particular vocational training, are not unconnected with Community law.'[133]

The Court illustrated this by referring to Articles 7 and 12 of Reg 1612/68, Article 128 of the Treaty and Council Decision No 63/266. It further referred to a number of Council resolutions and guidelines which showed that the Community institutions had given particular attention to access to vocational training and its improvement throughout the Community. The Court stated that the:

> 'common vocational training policy referred to in Article 128 of the Treaty is thus gradually being established. It constitutes, moreover, an indispensable element of the

---

[132] O'Leary, 'The Principle of Equal Treatment on Grounds of Nationality in Art 6 EC— A Lucrative Source for Member State Nationals?'in O'Leary and Tiilikainen (eds), *Citizenship and Nationality Status in the New Europe* (1998) 105–36, at 118.

[133] Case 293/83 *Gravier* [1985] ECR 293 at 19.

activities of the Community, whose objectives include inter alia the free movement of persons, the mobility of labour and the improvement of the living standards of workers.

Access to vocational training is in particular likely to promote free movement of persons throughout the Community, by enabling them to obtain a qualification in the Member State where they intend to work and by enabling them to complete their training and develop their particular talents in the Member State whose vocational training programmes include the special subject desired.'[134]

The Court concluded that it:

'follows from all the foregoing that the conditions of access to vocational training fall within the scope of the Treaty.'[135]

Subsequently, the Court applied this conclusion to the facts of the case under consideration:

'The imposition on students who are nationals of other Member States, of a charge, a registration fee or the so-called `minerval' as a condition of access to vocational training, where the same fee is not imposed on students who are nationals of the host Member State, constitutes discrimination on grounds of nationality contrary to Article 7 of the Treaty.'[136]

The Court's holding implied that not only Community citizens with a pre-existing right of residence, but all Community citizens, regardless of their nationality and State of residence, could invoke the principle of equal access to vocational training in other Member States.

4.1.3 Raulin

The fact that all Community citizens were granted the right to gain access to vocational training in other States did not yet imply that the Court had formally established a free movement of students within the Community. In *Gravier* the Court had not explicitly stated that students also have a right to reside in other Member States for the duration of their studies. The Commission, however, drew the rather logical[137] conclusion that the right to gain access to vocational training also includes the right to stay in the Member State concerned and it submitted to the Council a proposal for a directive in which the conditions for exercising this Treaty-based right were worked out.[138] In *Raulin* the Court confirmed the Commission's interpretation of *Gravier* by holding that the right

---

[134] *Ibid*, at 23–4.

[135] *Ibid*, at 25.

[136] *Ibid*, at 26.

[137] Cp van Gerven and van den Bossche (1993) n 4 above, at 424. In *Gravier* the Court did not deal with the issue of the right to reside probably because the Belgian authorities had granted Ms Gravier such a right during the proceedings. Case 293/83 *Gravier* [1985] ECR 593 at 6–8.

[138] The Council adopted the proposal as Dir 90/366. On this Directive, which has now been replaced by Dir 93/96, and the right of residence for students see s 4.4.

to equal treatment regarding the conditions of access to vocational training does not only apply

> 'to the requirements laid down by the educational establishment in question, such as enrolment fees, but also to any measure that may prevent the exercise of that right. It is clear that a student admitted to a course of vocational training might be unable to attend the course if he did not have a right of residence in the Member State where the course takes place.'[139]

In *Raulin* the Court thus took the final necessary step for the establishment of the principle of a free movement of students. After it had read into Article 7 *juncto* Article 128 EEC the principle of equal access to vocational training in *Forcheri* for all Community citizens 'lawfully established' in another Member State and had extended this principle to all Community citizens in *Gravier*, the Court finalised a Treaty based free movement of students in *Raulin* by concluding that Article 7 EEC also confers upon students a right of residence for the duration of the studies. After the amendments of the Maastricht Treaty and the renumbering of the Treaty of Amsterdam, the free movement of students is now based on, and governed by, Articles 12, 149 and 150 EC.

4.1.4 Comments

From the perspective of promoting student mobility, the establishment of a free movement of students was of course to be welcomed. In just a few judgments the Court had achieved more than the political Community institutions had been able to do in the two previous decades. From a legal perspective, however, the above discussed judgments were rather curious. Even at first glance it is clear that the Court read much more into Articles 7 and 128 EEC than the drafters of the provision had ever envisaged. Had the Court not reached, or even crossed, the limits of its powers of interpretation? The 'Article 7-Article 128 construction' was first applied in *Forcheri*. In light of *Casagrande*, in which the Court had accepted that the Community may also enter the field of education in as far as necessary to promote the free movement of workers,[140] the conclusion seemed rather obvious that Mrs Forcheri could not be required to pay the *Minerval* which, in the Court's own words, was 'so clearly discriminatory in nature.' The problem, however, was that neither Article 48 EEC nor Reg 1612/68 mentioned educational rights for spouses of Community workers. Thus, in order to reach the desired conclusion, the Court had to fill a gap in the provisions on the free movement of workers. The Court chose Articles 7 and 128 EEC for this purpose. This choice may have been innovative but the Court's conclusion that a spouse of a Community worker cannot be discriminated against in educational matters did fit within the Community's objectives in the

---

[139] Case C–357/89 *Raulin* [1992] I–1027 at 34.
[140] s 3.1.

field of the free movement of persons. The same cannot be said for the conclusion drawn in *Gravier*. In this judgment the Court did not recognise unwritten educational rights for persons who already fell within the personal scope of the free movement of persons as guaranteed by Community law. In *Gravier* the Court recognised an independent right for all Community citizens to study in other Member States. One might have expected that this fundamentally different and potentially much further reaching conclusion would have been supported by a different and more extensive justification. Remarkably, however, the reasoning in *Gravier* did not add much to the one the Court had followed in *Forcheri*. In *Gravier* the Court did explain more extensively the importance of a free movement of students,[141] but in support of the conclusion that the Treaty guarantees such a freedom the Court did not do much more than refer to the Council Decision of 1963 and a number recommendations and conclusions adopted by the Council and the Ministers of Education meeting within the Council. From neither one of the measures mentioned by the Court, however, could the conclusion be drawn that the Council and the Member States had envisaged, let alone taken, concrete legally binding measures aimed at promoting student mobility. In fact, the various resolutions did not do more than to call upon and incite the Member States to voluntarily promote student mobility.[142]

It may very well be that the common vocational training policy was 'gradually being established,' but this policy had not yet been developed as far as to include a legally enforceable right for all Community citizens to study in other Member States.[143] The vocational training policy the Court saw, was nothing but a *fata morgana*.[144] The right to study in other Member States had not, as the reasoning in *Gravier* seemed to suggest, already been established by the political Community institutions. Rather, it was the Court itself that created this right and included Community students in the free movement regime.

---

[141] Case 293/83 *Gravier* [1985] ECR 593 at 19.

[142] Interestingly, the Court did not refer to a 1976 Resolution comprising an action programme in the field of education (see n 120 above, at IV14(a)) which merely spoke of arranging a 'discussion . . . on the question of developing a common policy on the admission of students from other Member States'. Cp also Timmermans (1986) n 125 above, at 92.

[143] Furthermore, the Community institutions had only adopted conclusions, recommendations, etc. Even though one may dispute whether, or to what extent, such soft-law measures have legal force (see, eg: Oertzen (1992) n 4 above, at 46–67 and van Crayenest, 'La Nature juridique des Résolutions sur la Co-opération en Matière d'Education' in De Witte, *European Community Law of Education* (1989) 127 *et seq*), it is clear that the Member States when adopting these measures, had not intended to transfer to the Community their powers to grant or refuse non-nationals access to their educational systems. On the contrary, if they had wished to do so, they would probably have adopted legally binding measures on the basis of Art 100 EEC (94 EC) or Art 235 EEC (308 EC). The fact that they chose instead soft-law measures suggests that the Member States represented in the Council only wished to promote student mobility on a voluntary basis free from any legal restraints imposed by the Community.

[144] Opperman, *Von der EG-Freizügigkeit zur gemeinsamen europäischen Ausbildungspolitik? Die 'Gravier'-Doktrin des Gerichtshofs der Europäischen Gemeinschaften* (1988) at 23.

4.2 Scope of the Free Movement of Students

As revolutionary as it may have been, the judicial creation of a free movement of students did not automatically mean that many students could actually take up studies in other Member States. The practical relevance of the newly created freedom would first of all depend on the meaning to be given to the term 'vocational training' in Article 128 EEC. If the term were to be interpreted in accordance with the meaning it traditionally has under the national laws of the Member States, or the meaning which the Court itself has given to the concept of 'vocational school' in Article 7(3) of Reg 1612/68,[145] the practical impact of *Gravier* would have been relatively limited. Basically, the right to study in other Member States would then only be guaranteed to students who follow forms of education and training which are aimed at preparing students for a particular profession or type of work. In particular, a free movement for university students would not be guaranteed.

In *Gravier*, however, the Court had already indicated that the concept of vocational training was to be determined within the realm of Community law rather than national law. The Court had held that:

> 'any form of education which prepares for a qualification for a particular profession, trade or employment or which provides the necessary training and skills for such a profession, trade or employment is vocational training, whatever the age and the level of training of the pupils or students, and even if the training programme includes an element of general education.'[146]

The definition given by the Court was still rather vague, but did indicate that many types of education which are normally not considered as vocational training under national laws or regulations, could also fall within the scope of Article 128 EEC and the free movement of students. The important question whether university studies are covered had not yet been answered in the *Gravier*. That question came before the Court in *Blaizot* (1988).[147] The case concerned a number of veterinary students who were studying at a university in Belgium and who claimed that they were entitled to repayment of the *Minerval*, which they had paid prior to the judgment in *Gravier*. In support of their claim the students reasoned that university studies constituted 'vocational training' in the sense of Article 128 EEC. The Belgian authorities objected by arguing that such studies would essentially be academic in nature and that they would not directly prepare a person for a certain profession.[148] The Court agreed with the students. University studies are not necessarily excluded from Article 128. On the contrary, university studies generally fulfill the criteria laid down in *Gravier*.

---

[145] s 3.2.1. above.
[146] Case 293/83 *Gravier* [1985] ECR 593 at 30.
[147] Case 24/86 *Blaizot* [1988] ECR 379.
[148] The argument of the Belgian government was not necessarily without force. Cp eg: Watson, 'Annotation *Gravier*' (1987) *CMLRev* 89–97, at 95.

According to the Court, this was only different for certain courses which are intended for persons wishing to increase their general knowledge rather than prepare themselves for an occupation.[149]

From the case law the conclusion can be drawn that Community citizens have the right to gain access in other Member States to all forms of education with the exception of primary and secondary education[150] and courses that are essentially aimed to 'increase knowledge or cultural awareness or `develop the mind'.'[151] Somewhat oversimplified, it can be concluded that the Court had recognised a free movement of students, but not a free movement of pupils. This, however, does not necessarily imply that Community law does not provide for a right to get equal access to primary and secondary education in other Member States. On the contrary, it probably does. The judgments mentioned above were all based on the 'old' Article 128 EEC. This provision has been replaced by the Articles 126 and 127 EC, now renumbered as Articles 149 and 150 EC.[152] By analogy with *Gravier* it can be argued that education in general has been brought within the scope of the Treaty and that the principle of equal access to education in other Member States now applies to all forms of education.[153] Community law does not only provide for a free movement of students, but also for a free movement of pupils.

---

[149] Case 24/86 *Blaizot* [1988] 379 at 20. See also: Case 197/86 *Brown* [1988] ECR 3205 at 10 and Case 242/87 *Commission v Council (Erasmus)* [1989] ECR 1425 at 25. This conclusion indicated that the Court had rejected the so-called 'teachers-argument' which implied that a course in, for instance, ancient Arabic literature could be classed as vocational in nature because it would prepare students for the profession of teacher in ancient Arabic literature. Flynn (1989) n 4 above, at 71.

In *Blaizot* the Court further held that the fact that university education is sometimes divided into two stages of which only the second would prepare for a qualification for a particular profession, can not be taken in account for the purposes of Art 128. Access to the second stage is usually dependent on completion of the first stage, so that the two stages must be regarded as single. It is not possible to make a distinction between one stage which does constitute vocational training and a second which does not. Case 24/86 *Blaizot* [1988] ECR 379 at 21. In *Humbel* the Court specified that the 'various years of a study programme ...must be considered within the framework of the programme as a whole, . . . provided that the programme forms a coherent single entity and cannot be divided into two parts, one of which does not constitute vocational training while the other does'. Case 263/86 *Humbel* [1988] ECR 5365 at 12.

[150] Primary and secondary education cannot be classed, as one may conclude from the Court's judgment in *Humbel* (1988), as 'vocational training'. Case 263/86 *Humbel* [1988] ECR 5365 at 12.

[151] Opinion of Adv Gen Slynn in Case 293/85 *Commission v Belgium* [1988] ECR 305 at 337.

[152] s 2.3.

[153] See also: Vermeulen and Kuijer (1997) n 4 above, at 23; Devroe and Wouters, *De Europese Unie* (1995) at 511 and van der Mei, 'Vrij Dienstenverkeer in de EG en Toegang tot het Onderwijs' (1994) *NTOR* 102–7, at 107. Further support for this view can be found in the *Martínez Sala* ruling in which the Court held that all benefits (and thus all forms of education—see s 3.2.1) which can be classed as a social advantage for the purposes of Art 7(2) of Reg 1612/68 fall within the scope of Community law and thus the material scope of Art 12 EC. Case C–85/96 *Martínez Sala* [1998] ECR I–2691 at 57.

4.3 Student Grants

4.3.1 Lair *and* Brown

In *Gravier* the Court had held that the 'conditions of access to vocational train-ing' fall within the scope of the Treaty. Quota regulations for foreign stu-dents[154] and tuition and enrolment fees are obviously covered,[155] but does the

---

[154] See, eg: the judgment in *Commission v Belgium* (1988). It may be recalled (s 2.2.) that Belgium introduced in the mid-1970s a new financing system for higher education according to which the amount of government funding was made dependent upon the number of registered students. Foreign students were only taken into account in as far as they did not exceed two percent of the total number of Belgian students. The Belgian State was not financially responsible for other foreign students and the principals of educational establishments institutions were entitled to refuse to enroll students who are not taken into account for funding. In the Commission's view the Belgian legislation was in breach of Arts 7 and 128 EEC and it initiated an infringement procedure against Belgium under Art 169 EEC (now Art 226 EC). The Court ruled that the Belgian legislation had the direct effect of excluding students from other Member States from vocational training once the 2% quota had been reached. The legislation constituted a direct discrimination on grounds of national-ity contrary to Art 7 EEC (Art 12 EC). Case 42/87 *Commission v Belgium* [1988] ECR 5445 at 8. The ruling in *Commission v Belgium* (1988) demonstrates that the Court strictly observes whether Member States act in accordance with the principle of nondiscrimination embodied in Art 12 EC and that it does so even if significant changes in the organisation and funding of educational systems must be made. The judgments further show that the distinction between 'conditions of access' (which fall within the scope of the Treaty) and 'educational organisation and policy' (falling within the domain of the Member States) is rather fluid.

In response to the judgment in *Commission v Belgium* (1988) the Flemish community brought its legislation into conformity with Community law. The Walloon community, however, did not do so with the result that in 1994 Belgium was again convicted for not having obeyed Community law. Case 47/93 *Commission v Belgium* [1994] ECR I–1593. On the latter judgment see Nihoul, 'Le Minerval Réclamé aux Etudiants communautaires en Belgique' (1994) *JdT* 705–12 and van der Mei (1995) n 19 above.

[155] Shortly after *Gravier*, the Belgian legislator had made an attempt to limit the possibility of stu-dents reclaiming the fees paid prior to *Gravier*. The law governing the *Minerval* was amended as to imply that fees charged between 1 September 1976 and 31 December 1984 could not be refunded. An exception was made for Community students who had started legal proceedings before 13 February 1985, the day the judgment in *Gravier* was delivered. In the view of the European Commission the Belgian law was after the amendment of 21 June 1985, still incompatible with Art 7 of the EEC Treaty. The Commission started an infringement procedure against Belgium. The Court concluded, however, that the time limits fixed by the Commission in the pre-litigation procedure were too short and it dismissed the Commission's action as being inadmissible. Case 293/85 *Commision v Belgium* [1988] ECR 305 at 20.

The same issue was later addressed by the Court in *Barra* (1988) and *Blaizot* (1988). In both cases the Belgian government had argued that the Court should restrict the temporal effect of *Gravier* because this judgment constituted 'a new development in Community law' the effects of which would lead to a 'complete financial catastrophe'. In *Barra*, which concerned students all of whom pursued technical and vocational studies at a Technical Institute in Liège, the Court refused to do so. Such a temporal restriction could only be made 'in the judgment ruling upon the interpretation sought'. Since the Court had in *Gravier* not restricted the effect of the judgment, it could not do so in *Barra*. Case 309/85 *Barra* [1988] ECR 355 at 13–14. In other words, it was too late for such a tem-poral restriction. *Gravier* applied *ex tunc*.

In its judgment in *Blaizot*, which was delivered on the same day, the Court was willing to some-what decrease the financial burden on Belgium. As stated above in s 4.2, the case concerned univer-sity students. The Court recalled that a common vocational training was gradually being established and that it was only on the basis of that development that it became possible to regard university

same hold true for student grants? As noted earlier, grants may facilitate access, but they are not in all cases, or for all persons, a prerequisite for attending courses. Due to its significance, the question was bound to be submitted to the Court and, two years after *Gravier*, this indeed happened in *Lair* (1988) and *Brown* (1988). Both cases concerned Community citizens who had moved to other Member States and, after a brief period of employment, had embarked on university studies. Ms Lair and Mr Brown had applied for a student grant but their requests were refused. If they could not be regarded as a Community worker for the purposes of Article 39 EC and Reg 1612/68, could they possibly rely on Article 12(1) EC in order to challenge the refusal to offer them student grants?

On legal grounds it could have been argued that Community students have a right to claim student grants in the State of their studies. First, as regards Community workers and their family members, the Court had already indicated that the right to gain access to education under the same conditions as the host State's nationals includes the right to equal treatment as regards student financial aid.[156] Second, in some of the *soft-law* measures the Council and the 'Ministers of Education meeting within the Council' had adopted, reference was made to student grants and scholarships.[157] By analogy with the line of reasoning in *Gravier*, it could thus be argued that student financial aid would also fall within the scope of the Treaty.

On political-economic grounds, however, arguments could be made in support of the opposite view. If Member States, and especially those with more developed student financial aid systems, were obliged not only to admit students from other States to their schools and universities, but to award them student grants too, such Member States might attract many students from other States where no, or less developed, student grant systems exist.[158] The ability of the 'more generous' States to maintain student grant systems, and possibly their entire educational systems, could be affected.

---

studies as 'vocational training'. The Court, however, said that in particular the attitude of the Commission, which had changed its opinion on the classification of university studies as 'vocational training',might have led the Belgian authorities to consider that its legislation on the *Minerval* was in conformity with Community law. In such circumstances pressing considerations of legal certainty required the effect of the ruling in *Blaizot* to be limited in time. University funding should not retroactively be thrown into confusion and unforeseeable consequences for the proper functioning of universities should be avoided. The Court concluded that Art 7 EEC (now 12 EC) could not be relied upon by university students who wished to reclaim the fees paid unnecessarily prior to the date of the *Blaizot* judgement. An exception was made for students who had already started proceedings prior to the judgement. Case 24/86 *Blaizot* [1988] ECR 379 at 31–5. In as far as university studies are concerned, *Gravier* thus applied only *ex nunc*.

[156] ss 3.2.2 and 3.3.2.

[157] See, eg: Resolution of the Council and the Ministers of Education meeting within the Council of 9 February 1976 Comprising an Action Programme in the Field of Education. OJ 1976 C 38, at point 14.

[158] Compare the observations of the government of the United Kingdom in Case 39/86 *Lair* [1988] ECR 3161.

The question whether Article 7 EEC (now 12 EC) would also apply to student financial aid was thus quite delicate. Legal arguments supporting an affirmative answer did not seem to lead to an economically and politically desirable result.[159] In *Lair* and *Brown* the Court settled the issue as follows:

> 'It is only to the extent to which assistance of that kind is intended to cover registration and other fees, charged for access to education that by virtue of the judgment in Gravier it falls, as relating to conditions of access to vocational training, within the scope of the Treaty and that consequently the prohibition of discrimination on grounds of nationality laid down by Article 7 of the EEC Treaty is applicable.
>
> Subject to that reservation, it must be stated that at the present stage of development of Community law assistance given to students for maintenance and for training falls in principle outside the scope of the EEC Treaty for the purposes of Article 7. It is, on the one hand, a matter of educational policy, which is not as such included in the spheres entrusted to the Community institutions . . . and, on the other, a matter of social policy, which falls within the competence of the Member States in so far as it is not covered by specific provisions of the EEC Treaty.'[160]

The Court thus chose the 'political solution.' The thrust of *Lair* and *Brown* is that the Court wished to avoid imposing on Member States an obligation to offer student grants to students from other Member States which could put their student grant schemes, and possibly even their entire educational systems, in jeopardy.[161]

4.3.2 Martínez Sala *and* Grzelczyk

The outcome of *Lair* was thus understandable, but the legal reasoning which led the Court to its conclusion fit uneasily with the case law on the free movement of persons.[162] In *Lair* and *Brown* the Court held that maintenance grants do not

---

[159] Cp von Wilmowsky, 'Zugang zu öffentlichen Leistungen anderer Mitgliedstaaten' (1992) *ZfaöR* 231–77, at 243–6.

[160] Case 39/86 *Lair* [1988] ECR 3161 at 14–15. See also: Case 197/86 *Brown* [1988] ECR 3205 at 17–18.

[161] Cp Arnull, *The General Principles of EEC Law and the Individual* (1990) at 37. The distinction between the cost of maintenance and tuition fees was necessary in order to avoid a conflict with *Gravier*. If the Court had denied students the right to equal treatment as regards student grants in as far as they cover tuition fees, a discrimination as regards the fees would *de facto* have been present.

In *Raulin* the Court was asked whether Art 7 EEC (12 EC) also applies to study finance systems which make no distinction between the costs of access to courses and maintenance costs. According to the Dutch government, any attempt to break down the basic student grant would be artificial and alien to the basic philosophy of the Dutch study finance legislation, which was to make a contribution towards the students' maintenance costs. The Dutch system would be an instrument of social policy falling outside the scope of the Treaty. The Court rejected the argument reasoning that the Dutch grants were made up of various elements including the cost of access to courses. In order to guarantee students from other Member States equal treatment with regard to grants covering tuition fees, the Court obliged Member States to determine which part of the grants covered the costs of admission. Case C–357/89 *Raulin* [1992] ECR I–1027 at 27–8.

[162] Cp O'Leary (1998) n 132 above, at 108; von Wilmowsky (1991) n 159 above, at 243–6 and von Wittkowski (1991) n 4 above, at 82 *et seq*.

come within the ambit of the Treaty because the Member States' powers in the substantive fields of social and educational policy had not been transferred to the Community. This 'transfer-of-powers approach' was similar to the one the Court had applied in *Gravier*, but at odds with the way in which the Court had traditionally determined the material scope of the right to equal treatment of the beneficiaries of the free movement of workers. In cases such as *Casagrande* the Court had ruled that beneficiaries of Article 39 EC enjoy equality of treatment when, and in as far as, this is necessary for promoting freedom of movement.[163] In *Lair* the Court did apply this functional approach to Community workers, but it did not do so as regards Community students. Ever since *Casagrande* the Court has continued to apply a functional line of reasoning in the context of the free movement of workers[164] and persons.[165] In fact, it was only in cases concerning rights to student grants for Community students that the Court continued to apply the 'transfer-of-powers' approach.[166]

In *Lair* and *Brown* the Court had indicated, however, that at that 'stage in the development of Community law,' maintenance grants fell outside the scope of Article 12(1) EC. Two more recent judgments suggest, however, that Community law has evolved and that maintenance grants are now no longer categorically excluded from the nondiscrimination rule and that the Court has wholly abandoned the 'transfer-of-powers approach.' In the first case, *Martínez Sala* (1998), the Court ruled that (*i*) all benefits which can be classified as a social advantage in the sense of Article 7(2) of Reg 1612/68 fall within the material scope of Article 12(1) EC and (*ii*) that all Community citizens who are lawfully established in another Member State can rely on Article 12(1) EC.[167] Maintenance grants constitute social advantages for the purposes of Article 7(2) (*Lair*) and Community students are entitled, for the duration of their studies, to reside in the host State (*Raulin*). *Martínez Sala* did not involve Community students but the ruling did already suggest students can rely on Article 12(1) EC in order to claim equal treatment as regards maintenance grants.

This conclusion is confirmed by *Grzelczyk* (2001).[168] The case involved a French student who was studying sports at the University of Louvain, Belgium. During the first three years of his studies Mr Grzelczyk defrayed his own costs of maintenance, accommodation and studies by taking on various minor jobs and by obtaining credit facilities. In the fourth and final year, however, he was no

---

[163] In order to facilitate freedom of movement for workers, Community law may cross the boundaries of policy areas which have as such not (yet) been brought within the ambit of Community law. See ch s 3.1.

[164] See, eg: Case C–18/95 *Terhoeve* [1999] ECR I–345.

[165] See, eg: Case 186/87 *Cowan* [1989] ECR 195 and Case C–43/95 *Data Delecta* [1996] ECR I–4661.

[166] See, eg: Case C–357/89 *Raulin* [1992] ECR I–1027 and Case C–3/90 *Bernini* [1992] ECR I–1071.

[167] Case C–85/96 *Martínez Sala* [1998] ECR I–2691 at 57–61.

[168] Case 184/99 *Grzelczyk* [2001] ECR I–6193. See also: van der Mei, 'Freedom of Movement and Financial Aid for Students: Some Reflections on *Grzelczyk* and *Fahmi and Esmoris Cerdeiro Pinedo Amoris*' (2000) *EJSS* 181–207.

longer able to combine his studies with employment. Since his parents were unable to bear the costs of his maintenance, Mr Grzelczyk applied for a minimum subsistence allowance, the so-called *minimex*. Initially, the competent authority awarded Mr Grzelczyk the *minimex*, but it later withdrew the allowance on grounds of his nationality. According to Belgian legislation, persons not possessing Belgian nationality were only eligible for a minimum subsistence allowance when they come within the scope of EC Reg 1612/68 on the free movement of workers. Mr Grzelczyk, so the Belgian authorities argued, was not a worker but a student. Was the refusal to grant Mr Grzelczyk the *minimex* compatible with Articles 12(1) and 18(1) EC? In answering the question the Court commenced by stating that a student of Belgian nationality who found himself in exactly the same circumstances as Mr Grzelczyk would have been entitled to receive a social assistance benefit. Mr Grzelczyk was discriminated against on grounds of his nationality. Since Article 12(1) EC prohibits discrimination on grounds of nationality only within the scope of application of the Treaty, the core question to be answered was whether Mr Grzelczyk was covered by Community law. Article 12 EC, so the Court held, must be interpreted in conjunction with the Treaty provisions on European Union citizenship which is 'destined to be the fundamental status of nationals of the Member States, enabling those who find themselves in the same situation to enjoy the same treatment in law irrespective of nationality'.[169] Confirming *Martinez Sala*, the Court held that Community citizens lawfully residing in the territory to another Member State can rely on Article 12 EC in all situations which fall within the scope *ratione materiae* of Community. Those situations, the Court stated, include 'those involving the exercise of fundamental freedoms guaranteed by the Treaty and those involving the exercise of the right to move and reside freely in another Member States, as conferred by Article [18] of the Treaty'.[170] Subsequently, the Court referred to the fact that it had held in *Lair* and *Brown* that, at that stage in the development of Community law, assistance given to students for maintenance fell in principle outside the scope of the Treaty. The Court stated, however, that since *Brown* a Union citizenship has been introduced, that the Treaty now contains a new chapter on education and vocational training and that the Council has adopted Directive No 93/96 on the right of residence for students. The fact that a Union citizen pursues university studies in another Member State cannot, of itself, deprive him of the possibility of relying on Article 12(1) EC.[171]

4.3.3 Comments

Although neither *Martinez Sala* nor *Grzelczyk* involved students claiming student grants, the rulings do not seem to leave room for any conclusion other than

---

[169] Case 184/99 *Grzelczyk* [2001] ECR I–6193 at 31.
[170] *Ibid*, 33.
[171] *Ibid*, at 36.

that Community students are now entitled to invoke Article 12(1) EC with a view of claiming equality of treatment as regards maintenance grants. The scope of the right to equal treatment of all Union citizens who are lawfully residing in the territory of another Member State, including Community students, must be determined in accordance with the afore mentioned 'functional approach'.The mere fact that Member States' powers concerning student grants have not been transferred to the Community institutions can be no reason for denying students the right to invoke Article 12(1) EC in order to claim grants in the host State.

That the Court has moved away from the legal reasoning which it had followed in *Lair* and *Brown* does not necessarily imply that the Court has also moved away from the political conclusion drawn in these two rulings. *Martinez Sala* and *Grzelczyk* do not necessarily imply that Member States must actually give maintenance grants to Community students. The conclusion that these students can now invoke Article 12(1) EC merely implies that they cannot be discriminated against for reasons of their nationality.[172] *Martinez Sala* and *Grzelczyk* do not object to application of national rules which make entitlement to maintenance grants conditional upon prior residence, habitual residence or domicile[173] rather than 'simple' residence in the national territory.[174] By applying such rules, Member States could reserve student grants for their own population and exclude students who have merely come to, and are only staying or

---

[172] The conclusion that Member States can no longer deny Community students maintenance grants on grounds of their nationality, can only be supported. As interpreted in *Brown* and *Lair,* Art 12(1) EC allowed Member States to give maintenance grants to their own nationals who reside abroad and who merely return home for educational reasons and to deny such grants to non-nationals who are in a comparable position. There do not seem to be sound political, economic or other reasons for allowing Member States to make such distinctions which are at odds within the fundamental status of Union citizenship which, as the Court stressed in *Grzelczyk*, requires all nationals of Member States, 'who find themselves in the same situation to enjoy the same treatment in law irrespective of nationality'.

[173] Neither residence nor domicile has a fixed meaning and it may be difficult to distinguish the two concepts. Compare the discussion in ch 3, s 5.1.5. Somewhat oversimplified, however, domicile can be classed as 'the place where a person has his/her principal establishment . . . which serves either to link a transaction to the territorial competence of an authority, or to permit contact with a person at the place where he/she is found'. Residence, by comparison, is the place 'where a natural person effectively lives . . . but which many not be his/her domicile'. Garot, 'A New Basis for European Citizenship: Residence?'in La Torre, *European Citizenship: An Institutional Challenge* (1998) 229–48, at 236.

[174] After all, Community students enjoy the right to reside in the State of the studies. As regards students who only hold the nationality of another Member State, it is rather easy to determine whether they must be regarded as domiciliaries or as mere residents. This could be done by simply refusing grants to students who have acquired a residence card under Dir 93/96 and giving such grants to non-nationals who have acquired the right to reside under Art 39 EC, Art 43 EC, Dir 90/365 or Dir 90/364. As regards, students holding their 'own' nationality some difficult issues would seem to arise, however. Mere registration as a resident would not suffice since this would entail direct discrimination on grounds of nationality. In order to determine whether or not national students are 'free-riders' who merely return from abroad for educational purposes, concepts like habitual residence or domicile may have to be applied. The American experiences, examined in section 8, demonstrate, however, that application of such definitions in practice is far from easy.

residing in, the State for educational reasons.[175] Such policies are likely to work mainly to the detriment of non-nationals and could thus possibly constitute an indirect discrimination for reasons of nationality. Arguably, however, national rules which make eligibility for full grants conditional upon domicile in the national territory may be justified as being necessary for securing the financial stability of student grant schemes.

4.4 Right to Reside

In *Raulin* the Court concluded that the right to study in other Member States encompasses a right to reside in the State concerned. In doing so, the Court confirmed the view of the political Community institutions, which shortly after *Gravier* had already drawn that conclusion and had adopted Directive No 90/366, in which the conditions under which students can establish residence in the host State were set out in further detail. These conditions are now laid down in Directive 93/96.[176]

---

[175] In order to have regard to States' financial and educational interests, there is no need to exclude grants covering maintenance costs altogether from Art 12(1) EC. *Lair*, for instance, allows Member States to give full grants to their own nationals who reside abroad and who have merely returned to their State of origin for educational reasons and to deny such grants to non-nationals who are in a comparable position. Such direct discrimination on grounds of nationality is hard to compare with the notion of Union citizenship; there seem to be no sound political, economic or other reasons for allowing Member States to make such distinctions.

[176] OJ 1993 L 317. Dir 93/96 replaced the original Dir 90/366 which was annulled by the Court in Case C–295/90 *Parliament v Council* [1992] ECR I–4193. The Commission had initially proposed that the students directive should be based on Art 7(2) (now 12(2)) of the E(E)C Treaty. OJ 1989 C 191/2. When the Council reached political agreement on this proposal in December 1989, however, it decided to base the directive on Art 235 (now 308) which only requires the Council to consult the European Parliament and only allows unanimous decision making by the Council. By choosing Art 235, the Council presumably wished to avoid a precedent for the application of Art 7(2) which allows for quality majority voting. Taschner, 'Free Movement of Students, Retired Persons and other European Citizens—A Difficult Legislative Process' in Schermers *et al* (eds), *Free Movement of Persons in Europe* (1993) 427–36, at 436. The European Parliament, however, claimed that the Directive should have been based solely on Art 7(2) of the Treaty since Art 235 can only be applied when the Treaty does not provide for the powers necessary for attaining the Community's objectives. When the Council definitively adopted the directives in June 1990 it ignored Parliament's arguments. Dir 90/366 was based on Art 235. In order to safeguard its prerogatives in the legislative procedure, the Parliament subsequently started proceedings under Art 173 (now 230) of the Treaty asking the Court to annul Dir 90/366. In its ruling the Court reiterated *Raulin* and concluded that the residence directive should indeed have been based on Art 7(2) alone. Case C–295/90 *Parliament v Council* [1992] ECR I–4193 at 18. On this judgment see O'Leary, 'Annotation Case C–295/90 *Parliament v Council*' (1993) *CMLRev* 639–51; Röttinger, 'Bedeutung der Rechtsgrundlage einer EG-Richtlinie und Folgen einer Nichtigkeit' (1993) *EuZW* 117–21; Kampf, 'La Directive 90/366/Cee relative au Droit de Séjour des Etudiants communautaires: sa Transposition en France' (1992) *RMCE* 303–17 and Kampf, 'Die 'richtige' Rechtsgrundlage der Richtlinie über das Aufenthaltsrecht der Studenten' (1990) *EuR* 397–404. On 29 October 1993 the Council adopted Dir 93/96 on the right of residence for students which is *qua* substance virtually identical to the original Dir 90/366, on the basis of Art 7(2) alone.

According to Article 1 of the Directive, Member States shall recognise[177] the right of residence for students who (*i*) are enrolled in a recognised educational establishment for the principal purpose of following a vocational training course,[178] (*ii*) assure the relevant national authority, by means of a declaration or any other equivalent means, that they have sufficient resources to avoid becoming a burden on the social assistance system of the host Member State and who (*iii*) are covered by sickness insurance in respect of all risks in the host Member State.[179] These are conditions both for obtaining and maintaining the right to reside.[180] Students are entitled to reside in the host State for the duration of their studies.[181] During this period they have the right to be accompanied by their spouse and their dependent children.[182]

---

[177] Art 1 of Dir 93/96 states that Member States 'shall recognise' the right of residence of students and not, as the first Article of the original (see previous footnote) Dir 90/366 did, that Member States shall 'grant the right of residence' to students. The change in wording was introduced in order to underline that the right of residence is based on the Treaty itself. European Commission, *Right of Residence—Report to the Parliament and the Council on the Implementation of Directivess 90/364, 90/365 and 93/96* (1999) at 6–7.

[178] This first requirement does not seem to be very controversial. One could question, however, what is meant by the phrase 'for the principal purpose' of following a vocational training course. In particular, the question could be raised whether students who have enrolled in an educational establishment must actually study. Do students who never attend classes or who consistently refuse to do exams, benefit from the right to reside in the host State as a 'student'? By analogy with the Court's definition of the concept of Community worker (ch 2, s 2.4) the argument could be made that only students who 'effectively and genuinely' study, are entitled to reside as Community students in the State in which they are enrolled at an educational establishment. Vermeulen and Kuijer have argued that students must spend at least 50% of the time normally required for their studies and that students who only exist 'on paper', cannot benefit from the residence right governed by Dir 93/96. Vermeulen and Kuijer (1997) n 4 above, at 67–8.
Furthermore, it is not entirely clear why a student must be enrolled in a 'recognised' educational establishment. A recognised educational institution may be described as a school or university which has been permitted by the Member State concerned to provide education and to issue recognised diplomas. Vermeulen and Kuijer (1997) n 4 above, at 67. Public schools and universities will generally be classed as 'recognised' institutions. Since Dir 93/96 seems primarily relevant to public education (see s 4.8), one might doubt whether the requirement of being a recognised educational establishment has much substantial meaning. Cp Martin and Guild, *Free Movement of Persons in the European Union* (1996) at 210.

[179] On this requirement see also: ch 4, s 3.3.3.

[180] Art 4 of Dir 93/96: 'the right of residence shall remain for as long as beneficiaries of that right fulfil the conditions laid down in Article 1'. In *Grzelczyk,* however, the Court stated that measures to withdraw residence permits or refusals to renew permits in no case may become the automatic consequence of having recourse to the host State's social assistance scheme. Art 4 of Dir 93/96 does indeed provide that the right of residence is to exist for as long as beneficiaries fulfil the conditions laid down in Art 1, but the sixth recital in the directive's preamble envisages that beneficiaries must not become an 'unreasonable burden' on the public finances of the host State. The Court concluded that Dir 93/96 thus accepts a certain degree of solidarity between nationals of a host Member State and nationals of other Member State, particularly if the difficulties which a beneficiary encounters are temporary. Case C–184/99 *Grzelczyk* [2001] ECR I–6193 at 43–4.

[181] Art 2 of Dir 93/96 and Case C–357/89 *Raulin* [1992] I–1071 at 39. The right of residence is evidenced by a residence card which may be limited to the duration of the course of studies or to one year where the course lasts longer. In the latter event the card shall be renewable annually. Art 2 (1) of Dir 93/96.

[182] Unlike Community workers (Art 10 Reg 1612/68), pensioners (Art 1 Dir 90/365) and the remaining category of 'other' European citizens (Art 1 Dir 90/364), students do not have the right to

The formulation of the 'financial means requirement' is rather cumbersome. Unlike the other 1990 residence directives,[183] the students directive does not state that students must possess sufficient financial means.[184] Rather, by means of a declaration, students must assure the competent national authority that they possess sufficient financial means in order not to become a burden on the host State's social assistance system. What does this mean? The drafters of Directive No 93/96 intended to reduce the burden of proof on students. Students would not have to present full proof of their financial resources. It would suffice if they could make it appear plausible to the competent national authority that they would not burden the host State's public purse.[185] Yet, how much proof is necessary? What should the declaration entail? Do national authorities have to accept a declaration that they suspect is false?[186] Furthermore, the directive nowhere indicates at what point students' financial resources must be consid-

---

be accompanied by their dependent grandchildren and dependent family members in the ascending line. Residence rights for such family members of students were not considered necessary in order to effectuate the free movement of students. Taschner (1993) n 176 above, at 433. In view of the fact that students are often not married but rather living together, one could raise the question whether a genuine free movement of students would not require a right for boy- and girlfriends to be included in the Directive. Cp House of Lords—Select Committee on European Communities, 27th Report on Student Mobility in the European Community (1989–1990) at 27. The question is not purely theoretical. In fact, in view of the judgments of the Court in Case *59/85 Reed* [1986] ECR 1283 (the right to live with an unmarried partner can be regarded as a social advantage for the purposes of Art 7(2) of Reg 1612/68) and Case C–85/96 *Martínez Sala* [1998] ECR I–2691 (the material scope of Art 12 EC covers all rights and benefits which may be regarded as social advantages), it could be argued that Community students have a right to be joined by their boy- or girlfriend in the Member States where nationals hold such a right. Cp further the Opinion of Adv Gen La Pergola in Case C–65/98 *Eyüp* [2000] ECR I–4747 6.

[183] Ch 2, s 3.2. The differences between the students directive, on the one hand, and the directives for pensioners and the residual category of 'other' Community citizens, on the other hand, is explained by the fact that the duration of students' residence is limited to the duration of their studies. Students are less likely to become a burden on the social assistance scheme of the host State. See also: Case C–424/98 *Commission v Italy* [2000] ECR I–4001 at 45 *juncto* 40 and Case C–184/99 *Grzelczyk* [2001] ECR I–6193 at 41.

[184] Students do not actually have to possess sufficient financial means. In *Commission v Italy* (2000) the Court held that Art 1 of Dir 93/96 does not contain any requirement as regards a specific level of means of subsistence. A national rule which requires from students to actually possess sufficient financial means runs counter to Art 1. Case C–424/98 *Commission v Italy* [2000] ECR I–4001 at 44–6 and Case C–184/99 *Grzelczyk* [2001] ECR I–6193 at 40.

[185] Taschner (1993) n 176 above, at 434. The formulation of the requirement is the result of a compromise reached between the Community institutions. The Council simply wished to impose the same requirements on students as on the beneficiaries of the other two 1990 residence directives. The Commission had initially proposed (OJ 1989 C 191) that students would not have to prove at all that they posses sufficient financial means. It was even proposed that students were to have a right to benefit from the host State's social security system, provided the students' Member State of origin would reimburse the host state upon request. The Council rejected the proposal. During the last Council meeting a compromise was reached the result of which is now contained Art 1 of the Directive.

[186] Cp van Nuffel, 'Een bijna Algemeen Verblijfsrecht in de Europese Gemeenschap— Commentaar op de Verblijfsrichtlijnen van 28 juni 1990' (1990) *SEW* 887–903, at 902.

ered 'sufficient.' Should the minimum subsistence level or, the often lower, amount of full student grants be considered?[187]

4.5 Recognition of Diplomas

The practical relevance of the right to study in other Member States would be minimal if the diplomas that students have obtained in the Member State of origin were not recognised in the States where they wish to continue their education. Apart from the measures that have been taken in the context of the *Socrates-Erasmus* programme,[188] the political Community institutions have so far not undertaken much activity as regards the so-called academic recognition[189] of diplomas. Legislative measures comparable to the ones adopted for professional recognition do not exist.[190] It is up to the Member States and national educational institutions to decide whether or not a diploma obtained in other Member States will be recognised. The Community is only empowered

---

[187] In order to avoid legal uncertainty, it has been suggested that it would have been better if the directive had stated that the right to reside would remain for as long as the student does not actually become a burden on the host State's social assistance system. Vermeulen and Kuijer (1997) n 4 above, at 66. One could even go further and raise the question whether the financial means requirement might be deleted altogether. See also: s 9.3.2.

[188] s 4.9 below.

[189] Academic recognition must be distinguished from the professional recognition of diplomas. The former concerns recognition for access to education, whilst the latter relates to access to employment or a profession. Zilioli, 'The Recognition of Diplomas and its Impact on Educational Policies' in De Witte, *European Community Law of Education* (1989) 51 *et seq*, at 52. On the academic recognition of diplomas see, eg: Frazier, 'L'Education et L'Union européenne' (1997) *RMC* 476–91; De Witte, 'Equivalentie van Studieperiodes en Erkenning van Diploma's' (1992–1993) *TOO* 290–6; Dalichow, 'Academic Recognition within the European Community' (1987) *EJE* 39–58 and Hagen, 'University Cooperation and Academic Recognition in Europe: The Council of Europe and the Communities' (1987) *EJE* 77–83.

Academic and professional recognition may not always be easily distinguishable. See, eg: the Communication from the Commission on recognition of qualifications for academic and professional purposes (COM(94) 596 final at 5) and De Witte (1992–1993) 293 above. De Witte mentions a number of examples covered by a 'grey zone' in which the classification (professional or academic recognition?) may be difficult. One of these concerns the so-called AIOs (Assistenten in Opleiding—'Assistants in Training') at Dutch Universities. Under Dutch law AIOs have a rather ambiguous status. On the one hand, they are assistants who pursue research and have teaching tasks in return for which they receive a (rather low) remuneration. On the other hand, AIOs are still in training and are according to Dutch law governing their status, in 'the second stage' of their university education. Should diploma requirements for access to the position of AIO be classed as academic or professional recognition? One may safely say that it concerns conditions for professional recognition. There is no doubt that AIOs perform 'effective and genuine activities' under the supervision of another person in return for which they receive a remuneration (ch 2, s 2.2.4) and that they can obtain the status of Community worker.

[190] This might be explained by the fact that various measures aimed at academic recognition have already been taken outside the framework of the Community (Dalichow (1987) n 189 above, at 39—for a short overview of the various 'extra-Community' measures see Vermeulen and Kuijer (1997) n 4 above, at 46–8) as well as the fact that the Community only holds limited powers in this field (see next footnote).

to 'encourage' academic recognition of diplomas 'by supporting and supplementing the action of the Member States through the adoption of incentive measures.'[191]

The fact that academic recognition is primarily a matter for Member States does not imply, however, that Community law is of no relevance. By analogy with the Court's jurisprudence on the professional recognition of diplomas, one may assume that Community law imposes certain limits on Member States and educational institutions.[192] In *Vlassopoulou* (1991) the Court ruled that when deciding upon an application for authorisation to practice a profession, Member States must take account of diplomas, certificates and other qualifications which have been obtained in other Member States. These 'foreign' qualifications have to be compared with national qualifications. When this comparative investigation leads to the conclusion that foreign diplomas indicate that the knowledge and/or skills of the holders are equivalent to those of evidenced by national diplomas,[193] that diploma should be recognised.[194] The same line of reasoning could be applied to academic recognition. This means that Member States and educational institutions must consider foreign diplomas, compare these to national diplomas and, when equivalence is established, recognise the diplomas.

4.6 Language Requirements

In order to be admitted to educational institutions in other Member States students must often demonstrate that they have a certain level of working know-

[191] Art 149 EC. The first paragraph of Art 149 further provides that the Community must fully respect 'the responsibility of the Member States for the content of teaching and the organization of education systems and their cultural and linguistic diversity'. It has been argued that the Community is not empowered to lay down substantive rules aimed at the mandatory recognition of educational results achieved in other Member States. Vermeulen and Kuijer (1997) n 4 above, at 43. On how the European Commission aims to encourage the Member States and educational institutions to promote the academic recognition of diplomas see, eg: Memorandum on Higher Education within the Community of 5.11.91 (COM(91) 349 fin); Communication from the Commission on the Recognition of Qualifications for Academic and Professional Purposes (COM(94) 596 final) and the Green Paper on 'Education, Training, Research: The Obstacles to Transnational Mobility (Bull.EU Supplement 5/96).

[192] See also: Vermeulen and Kuijer (1997) n 4 above, at 43–4.

[193] A right to appeal a possible negative decision must be guaranteed. Case 222/86 *Heylens* [1987] ECR 4097 at 10–13.

[194] Case C–340/89 *Vlassopoulou* [1991] ECR I–2357 at 23. While comparing the equivalence of foreign diplomas attention may only be paid to the level of knowledge and qualifications the holders presumably have, taking into account the nature and the duration of their studies or training. When it appears that there is only partial equivalence of knowledge and skills, the host State may require the persons in question to prove that they have acquired the knowledge and qualifications which they were lacking. Case C–340/89 *Vlassopoulou* [1991] ECR I–2357 at 17–19. See also: Fierstra, 'Annotation *Vlassopoulou*' (1992) *SEW* 640–9; Stein, 'Annotation *Vlassopoulou*' (1992) *CMLRev* 625–36; Lonbay, 'Picking over the Bones: Rights of Establishment Revisited' (1991) *ELRev* 507–20 and Nachbauer, 'Art.52 EWGV—Mehr als nur ein Diskriminierungsverbot?' (1991) *EuZW* 470–2.

ledge of the language of the State concerned. In principle, institutions are entitled to apply language requirements. In the field of education, Community institutions must, as Article 149(1) EC puts it, fully respect the 'cultural and linguistic diversity' of Member States. This is not to say that Member States and their educational institutions are entirely free to apply language requirements. These requirements are generally far more difficult for non-nationals to meet than for nationals of the host State. They may constitute an indirect discrimination on grounds of nationality, which would mean that Member States could only lay down language conditions required for the specific studies students wish to follow and that the level of the required working knowledge should not be disproportionally high. One may doubt, however, if the Court of Justice would apply the 'indirect discrimination test'[195] very strictly. In the case of *Groener* (1989) the Court upheld an Irish rule which required a certain level of Irish language for teaching posts even though the lessons were given in English.[196] *Groener* was decided under the provisions on the free movement of workers, but strongly suggests that the Court will leave the Member States considerable discretion in applying language requirements.[197]

4.7 Family Members of Community Students

According to Article 1 of Directive No 93/96, the spouse and dependent children have the right to accompany the Community student to the State of the studies. The question whether these family members have the right to attend educational institutions in the host State is nowhere answered in the Directive. For family members who hold the nationality of a Member State, this does not seem to have any consequences. They can claim admission to education in their own right in the State concerned on the basis of Article 12 *juncto* Articles 149 and 150 EC. Both as regards admission to education and eligibility for student grants, the legal status of these family members coincides, as may safely be assumed, with the status of the Community students themselves.

More difficult questions arise as regards family members who lack the nationality of one of the Member States. It has been argued that such family members have no right to gain access to education on the basis of Community law as long as the Community legislator has not explicitly conferred this right upon

---

[195] Ch 2, s 7.2.

[196] Case 379/87 *Groener* [1989] ECR 3967 at 15–19. See also: Mortelmans, 'Annotation *Groener*' (1989) *AA* 736–47.

[197] In practice, language requirements may seriously impede student mobility and it may therefore not come as a surprise that Community institutions aim to promote the learning of various Community languages. See the Green Paper on 'Education, Training, Research: The Obstacles to Transnational Mobility' (Bull.EU Supplement 5/96), at 26 and 30 and Resolution of the Council and the Representatives of the Governments of the Member States, Meeting within the Council of 14 December 2000 Concerning an Action Plan for Mobility.

them.[198] The argument is based on the judgment in *European Parliament v. Council* (1992) in which the Court confirmed *Raulin* by holding that Community students enjoy a right to reside in the State of the studies under Article 12 EC.[199] In response to the view advocated by the Council and the Dutch government that the original Directive No 90/366 (now No 93/96) would encompass more than a right to reside for students, and that therefore Article 235 (now 308) of the Treaty should have been the legal basis for the directive, the Court held that the measures which can be adopted on the basis of the former Article 7(2) EEC (now 12(2) EC) are not necessarily confined to the rights which follow from the first paragraph of the Article. They may also concern aspects which may be necessary for a genuine exercise of these rights. Various elements of the contested directive concern the exercise of the right to reside and the Court explicitly mentioned the residence rights conferred upon the spouse and children of the Community student.[200] In other words, according to the Court only the Community student itself can directly rely on the first paragraph of Article 12 in order to gain access to education and reside in another Member State. Family members would only enjoy the right to reside in the host State by virtue of secondary legislation.

On the basis of the judgment in *Parliament v Council* alone, one might indeed conclude that the spouse and children who lack the nationality of one of the Member States have no right to gain access to the educational system of the State where the Community student is studying as long as the Community legislator has not granted them such a right. However, the judgment in *Martínez Sala* casts doubt on this point. This judgment can be interpreted as to imply that all persons falling within the personal scope of Community law can invoke Article 12(1) EC in order to claim equal of treatment as regards all rights or benefits which fall within the material scope of the Treaty.[201] If indeed true, then the afore mentioned family members would seem to have the same educational rights as the Community students themselves. Directive No 93/96 has brought these third country family members within the personal scope of Community law and, as follows from the previous subjection, the right to be admitted to educational institutions as well as the right to claim student financial aid are covered by the Treaty's material scope. It is submitted that the legal status of third country children of Community students in the field of education is, or at least should be, identical to the status of children who hold EC-nationality without there being a need to adopt specific legislative measures for this purpose.

---

[198] Vermeulen and Kuijer (1997) n 4 above, at 38 and Wapenaar, *Personenverkeer binnen de Europese Unie—Het Communautaire Recht inzake Personenverkeer, met Bijzondere Aandacht voor de Positie van Derdelanders* (1997) at 157.
[199] Case C–295/90 *European Parliament v Council* [1992] ECR I–4193 at 18–19.
[200] *Ibid.*
[201] Ch 2, s 3.2.

4.8 Education and The Concept of Service

Prior to *Forcheri* and *Gravier*, Articles 49 (formerly 59) *et seq.* EC on the free movement of services had been suggested as the legal basis of a free movement of students.[202] In *Luisi and Carbone* (1981) the Court had held that recipients of services in the sense of Article 50 EC (60 EEC) have a right to move to and stay in other States and that 'persons travelling for the purpose of education' can be regarded as recipients of services.[203] Understandably, Françoise Gravier relied on the *Luisi and Carbone* judgment in defence of her claim that the *Minerval* was inconsistent with the Treaty. The Court, however, remained silent on Article 49 EC and the fact that the judgment in *Gravier* was decided solely on the basis of Articles 7 and 128 EEC, suggested that the Court had rejected the 'services argument.' The explanation for this had in fact already been given by Advocate General Slynn in his Opinion in *Gravier*. Article 50 EC stipulates that services shall be considered 'services' within the meaning of the Treaty when they are 'normally provided for remuneration.' In determining whether educational courses meet this requirement, the Advocate General had made a distinction between private and public education as regards the application of the Article 49 *et seq.* The former type of education is usually provided by institutions with a view to making a profit. The very purpose of such institutions in providing education is to receive remuneration. The fees, which students of private schools have to pay, are largely fixed at a level that is related to the actual economic cost of the education. Commercial criteria determine the level of the fees. The situation is different with respect to education provided by the State. The fees to be paid by students bear little relation to the true economic cost of the education. State education is largely funded from the State budget. It is ultimately the resident taxpayer who finances State education. The State does not intend to engage in economic activity or to make a profit. State education is basically a matter of social policy.[204] Three years later the Court endorsed the view of the Advocate General in *Humbel*:

> 'The essential characteristic of remuneration lies in the fact that it constitutes consideration for the service in question, and is normally agreed upon between the provider and the recipient of the service. [ ] That characteristic is, however, absent in the case of courses under the national education system. First of all, the State, in establishing and maintaining such a system, is not seeking to engage in gainful activity but is fulfilling its duties towards its population in the social, cultural and educational fields. Secondly, the system in question, as a general rule, is funded from the public purse and not by pupils or their parents.'[205]

---

[202] See, eg: Maresceau (1989) n 4 above, at 181–3.
[203] Ch 2, s 4.1.
[204] Opinion Adv Gen Slynn in Case 293/83 *Humbel* [1985] ECR 293 at 602–4.
[205] Case 263/86 *Humbel* [1988] ECR 5365 at 17–18. See also: Völker, *Passive Dienstleistungsfreiheit im Europäischen Gemeinschaftsrecht* (1990) ch 5.

The scope of Articles 49 *et seq.* is thus limited to private education; students who wish to attend public educational establishments in other Member States have to rely on Article 12 read in conjunction with Articles 149 and 150.[206]

4.9 *Erasmus/Socrates* Students

Community institutions have always stressed the importance of student mobility. The most important initiatives are those that have been taken in the context of the *Erasmus* programme.[207] The programme, which is now falling under the umbrella of *Socrates*,[208] aims to promote student mobility by a number of 'Actions.' Action 1 concerns the establishment of a European University Network under which universities in the different Member States are encouraged, by financial incentives, to conclude agreements aimed at the exchange of students and teachers. Action 2 involves making available special student grants

---

[206] The above conclusion is simply stated, but raises many more questions that are often not easily answerable. A first set of questions concerns the demarcation between private and public education. In determining whether or not education can be regarded as a service in the sense of Art 50 EC, the Court in *Humbel* seemed to have attached importance to two factors: the (public or private) source out of which education is mainly funded and the (economic or social) motives for providing education. In *Wirth* (1993), however, the Court held that 'courses given in an establishment of higher education which is essentially financed out of public funds do not constitute services within the meaning of Art 60' of the Treaty. Case C–109/92 *Wirth* [1993] I–6447 at 19. See also: van der Mei (1994) n 153 above, at 102–7. In *Wirth* the Court did not seem to attach much significance to the fact that the State may be fulfilling a 'welfare duty' towards its population. Does this imply that the 'public/private funding distinction (O'Leary (1996) n 4 above, at 75) is the sole and decisive criterion for the classification of education as a service? Does this mean that public universities must be regarded as providers of services when they offer post-graduate courses or masters-programmes which are (at least in the long run) to operate independently of any public funding? Do *Humbel* and *Wirth* imply that students attending privately established schools do not fall within Arts 49 and 50 EC when these schools are in the main financed by State subsidies? The 'line between wholly state-funded and partly state-funded services, or between services which are economic in nature and those which are provided within the context of educational and cultural policy' is far from clear (Craig and de Búrca, *EU Law—Text, Cases & Materials* (1998) at 770) and needs further clarification.

Further questions arise once it is established that a given type of education is covered by Arts 49 and 50 EC. Are private schools or universities obliged by Community law to admit non-resident students? Can admission to private colleges be made conditional upon possession of a diploma awarded by a school in the State concerned? Can non-residents be required to pay additional tuition fees? Can Art 49 EC be relied upon in cases against private schools or colleges? The article can be invoked in order to challenge rules set by private bodies which regulate certain activities in a collective manner (cp Case 36/74 *Walrave* [1974] ECR 1405 and Joined Cases C–51/96 and C–191/97 *Deliège* [2000] ECR I–6511), but does the same hold true for rules applied by individual colleges or universities? On the latter question, see van der Steen, 'Horizontale Werking van de Vier Vrijheden en van het Discriminatieverbod van Artikel 12 EG' (2001) *NTER* 4–9, at 8.

[207] Council Decision 87/327 establishing the European Community Action Scheme for the Mobility of Students (*Erasmus*). OJ 1987 L 166. On Erasmus and the legal status of Erasmus-students see, eg: Davies, *The EU Higher Education Exchange and Mobility Programmes* (1997); André de la Porte and Zegveld, 'Het Europa van de Student—Studentenmobiliteit binnen de Europese Unie' (1995) *AA* 685–93; Gazan and Oomen, 'Internationaliseringsprogramma's en het Nederlandse Hoger Onderwijs; Van Erasmus naar Socrates in de Europese Unie' (1995) *IS* 155 *et seq* and Feuchthofer, 'Europäische Förderprogramme in Bildungswesen' (1992) *RJB* 180–92.

[208] s 2.1.3 above.

for students who participate in the programme. The grants, which may be granted for a period of three up to twelve months, cover the cost of linguistic preparation for study in another Member State, travel expenditure and the higher cost of living in the host State. Action 3 concerns the European Community Course Credit System (ECTS) under which participating universities are essentially obliged to recognise periods of studies fulfilled in other Member States for the purposes of their 'own' studies. Tuition fees must be paid in the State of origin; no fees are due in the State of the temporary studies. The goal of *Erasmus* is thus limited. It only aims to promote the exchange of students who wish to pursue part of their studies 'at home' in another Member State. The programme does not aim to promote or facilitate the right of Community students to follow their entire studies in another Member State.[209]

4.10 Student Mobility

The impact which *Gravier* and its progeny have had on student mobility within the European Community is quite considerable. At the end of the 1970s, many Member States did host quite a number of foreign students, but most of these came from non-Member States and former colonies in particular.[210] Student mobility of Community citizens among the Member States was modest. Since the judgment in *Gravier*, and in particular since the establishment of the *Erasmus* programme, the mobility of European students has increased.[211] Even though the original goal of enabling ten percent of European students to follow part of their studies abroad has not been achieved, more than 500.000 students have participated in the programme in the period between 1987 and 1995.[212] The 'spontaneous' mobility of students outside the context of *Erasmus* is also quite considerable today. Even though statistics do not always make a clear distinction between *Erasmus* students and 'free-movers,' it has been estimated that for instance in the year 1993/1994 almost 100.000 Community students were registered at universities in other Member States. Three quarters of these 'free movers' were studying in the United Kingdom (37%), France (23%) and Germany (13%). A look at the net balance between incoming and outgoing students demonstrates that five Member States may be regarded as 'net-importers'

---

[209] On the experiences with the *Erasmus* programme see in particular Teichler and Maiworm, *The Erasmus Experience—Major Findings of the Erasmus Evaluation Research Project* (1997).

[210] To be sure, statistical systems monitoring student mobility and exchanges did not exist at the time. Education Institute of the European Cultural Foundation, 'La Mobilité intra-européenne des Etudiants des premier et deuxième Cycles' as quoted in Gordon and Jallade, *Student Mobility within the European Union: A Statistical Analysis* (1995) at 4.

[211] For student mobility figures see, eg: Gordon and Jallade, '"Spontaneous" Student Mobility in the European Union: A Statistical Survey' (1996) *EJE* 133–51; Gordon and Jallade (1995) n 210 above; Baligant *et al*, *Analyse economique de la Mobilité Etudiant à l'Echelle de l'Union Européenne* (1994) and De Jonge and Dillo, *Student Mobility within the European Community* (1991).

[212] Verli-Wallace, 'Le nouveau Programme communautaire "Socrates"' (1995) at *RMCUE* 518.

of students: the United Kingdom, France, Belgium, Austria and Sweden. The United Kingdom is by far the most important 'student-importer.' In 1993 and 1994 it received almost 27,000 more foreign students than it 'sends abroad.' France and Belgium had a net-balance of 8,400 and 1,800 respectively. Virtually all other Member States appear to be 'exporters of students.' Greece is the biggest exporter. The number of outgoing students exceeds the incoming number by almost 17,000. Germany (5,000), the Netherlands (3,000) and Luxembourg (2,400) are in view of the size of their populations also relatively large student exporters. Interesting are the figures about the movement of students between specific countries. The number of German students going to the United Kingdom, for instance, is almost nine times as high as the number of UK-students going to Germany. *Vis-à-vis* other countries (France, Ireland), the United Kingdom also absorbs a comparatively large number of students. Belgium receives about eight times as many Dutch students as the Netherlands receives Belgian students.

The reasons why 'free-movers' decide to study in other Member States vary. Often movement abroad is caused by shortcomings in the supply of education in the home State. Thus, in Luxembourg students move abroad simply because a university system does not exist and in Greece, Ireland and the Netherlands *numerus clausus* regulations constitute the main 'push factor.'[213] The large number of Dutch students at medical and veterinary faculties at Belgian universities, for instance, is largely explained by the fact that for such studies a *numerus clausus* is applied in the Netherlands and that the Dutch Minister of Education allows Dutch students of medicine to export their student grants when they study at certain enlisted foreign universities. Further, student mobility is often caused by the quality of education, the conditions of student life or cultural aspects in other Member States. The language of a given country appears to be one of the main criteria that students apply when making their choice of a specific country or university. The fact that Member States such as the United Kingdom and France are net-importers of students is largely explained by the fact that the languages in which the courses and studies are offered are relatively well spoken by students from other Member States,[214] whilst British and French students often lack sufficient knowledge of foreign languages.

4.11 Conclusions

From the early Community years, the Community institutions have frequently stressed the importance of promoting student mobility for the achievement of the Community's objectives, and the free movement of persons in particular.

---

[213] Gordon and Jallade (1996) n 211 above, 9.2.
[214] *Ibid* at 137.

Looking back, one must conclude that, in spite of the Member States' reluctance to cooperate, the institutions have been quite successful. Today, all Community citizens have the right to study in other Member States and student mobility has increased. This is not to say, however, that Community law on the free movement of students has remained free from criticism. The current rules are still debated. On the one hand, it is claimed that Community law does not give sufficient regard to the educational interests of in particular the Member States which 'import' more students than they 'export,' and who are thus faced with an unequal financial burden. Measures should be taken to protect or compensate the 'net-importers' of students.[215] On the other hand, however, it is generally felt that there are still (too) many obstacles to student mobility within the Community. In its 1996 Green Paper on 'Education, Training, Research: the Obstacles to Transnational Mobility'[216] the European Commission identified various legal, bureaucratic and psychological hindrances and problems which still hamper student mobility. Free movers, i.e., the students who study, or wish to study, in other Member States outside the framework of the *Socrates-Erasmus* programme, especially still appear to face many obstacles. These

---

[215] The fact that it has been the Court rather than the Council which has developed the most relevant legal rules on the free movement of students has provoked critical comments. See, eg: Hartley (1989) n 4 above, at 343; Hartley (1991) n 4 above at 192–3 and O'Leary (1996) n 4 above, at 143. It has been argued that significant and potentially far-reaching decisions such as the free movement of students should not be made by a judicial body like the Court of Justice which would not be sufficiently equipped for making such decisions. Student movements would not be likely to be in balance and the effects of the principle of a free movement of students would not be equally felt by or in all Member States. As a result, both the funding and organisation could be seriously affected by the Court's case law. O'Leary (1996) n 4 above, at 106. The Court has been accused of not having seriously addressed the possible implications of its case law and it has been suggested that it would have been better if the Court had left it 'to the Council to adopt a policy on migrant students'. No doubt such a policy would have taken more time to develop, but 'the end result would probably have been preferable from the educational point of view'. Hartley (1991) n 4 above at 192–3.

Such criticism cannot be wholly dismissed. One must be critical when a significant decision such as the establishment of a free movement of students is made by the judiciary and it indeed appears that the financial burden of a free movement of students is not equally felt by all Member States. It is submitted, however, that the above-mentioned criticism is too one-sided. From the early years, the Council and the 'Ministers of Education meeting within the Council' had frequently stated that they would promote and take common measures in the fields of education and vocational training and, in particular, that they would promote student mobility. Yet, during the first two decades they did not do much more than pay lip service to these proclaimed objectives. When cases such as *Forcheri*, *Gravier* and *Erasmus* were sent to 'Luxembourg', the Court found itself in a situation where the importance of common activities in the field of education such as promoting student mobility was increasingly recognised, but where, due to the absence of specific educational powers for Community institutions and an unwillingness on the part of Member States, no concrete measures had yet been taken. The Court's genuine motives may be hard to find, but the rulings in question suggest that the Court deliberately wished to make a breakthrough. It is not certain, but one may seriously doubt whether all the 'European achievements' could have been made if it had not been for the Court. Arguably, the positive aspects of the Community's educational activities overshadow the negative ones and one could therefore evaluate the Court's role more positively than the afore mentioned authors do.

[216] Bull.EU, Supplement 5/96. See also: COM(96) 462 final. For a comment on the Green Paper see Verbruggen, The Commission's Green paper '"Education, Training, Research: The Obstacles to Transnational Mobility": Content and Comment' (1997) *EJELP* 41–8.

include problems concerning the recognition of previously obtained diplomas and qualifications, the lack of sufficient knowledge of the language of the State of the studies and the non-transferability of student grants.[217] Thus, progress may have been made, but the conflict between the aim of promoting freedom of movement for students and safeguarding States' educational interests, has still not been settled satisfactorily.[218]

5 THE 'OTHER' NON-ECONOMIC RESIDENTS

So far little attention has been paid to the question whether, or to what extent, the 'other'[219] non-economic residents can claim access to education and student grants systems in the State in which they have chosen to reside. Directives Nos 90/365 and 90/364 do not mention any educational rights for pensioners. The residual category of 'other' Community citizens or the family members of both categories and so far the Court has never been asked to clarify the legal status of these categories in the field of education.

This, however, does not mean that non-economic residents are denied Community rights in the field of education. As persons falling within the scope of Community law, they can rely on Article 12(1) EC, read in conjunction with Article 149 and 150 EC. This entitles them to gain admission to all forms of education and, as would seem to follow from the rulings in *Martínez Sala* and *Grzelczyk*, to obtain student grants under the same conditions as the nationals of the host State.[220] As has been argued before,[221] Article 12 EC allows Member States to make eligibility for full grants conditional upon 'habitual residence' or 'domicile' in the national territory. Unlike Community students, however, beneficiaries of Directives Nos 90/365 and 90/364, as a rule, meet this requirement.

---

[217] See also: the Resolution of the Council and of Representatives of the Governments of the Member States, Meeting within the Council of 14 December 2000 Concerning an Action Plan for Mobility (OJ 2000 C 371).

[218] In s 9 some observations will be made as to how the situation could possibly be improved.

[219] For the purposes of this book the category of 'non-economic' residents consists in principle of students, pensioners and 'other' Community citizens. See ch 1, s 3. In this chapter, however, the first category was dealt with in the previous section on Community students (or non-residents). The reason for this is that, from the perspective of the conflict between promoting the free movement of persons and protecting the educational interests of Member States, Community students must be regarded as non-residents or 'outsiders'. It concerns Community citizens who move to other Member States for the sole purpose of studying and who have generally not contributed to the financing of public education through the payment of direct taxes. The same does not apply to pensioners and 'other' Community citizens; they must be regarded as (non-economic) residents. See also section 9 of the present chapter.

[220] This also would seem to hold true for the family members of pensioners or 'other' Community citizens who do not hold a nationality of one of the Member States. Cp s 4.7.

[221] s 4.3.

Further, the question could be raised whether the application for, or receipt of, student grants can possibly affect the right to reside in the host State. The financial means requirements contained in the 1990 residence directives are intended to avoid beneficiaries becoming a burden on the host State. Student grants are funded out of the public purse and it could thus be argued that the host State is entitled to end legal residence the moment a non-economic resident applies for student financial aid. However, the financial means requirements contained in the residence directives for pensioners and the residual category of Community citizens have never been included primarily with student grants in mind. The main concern of the drafters of the directives was to avoid Community citizens who are not able to provide for themselves moving to other States and claiming social assistance benefits there.[222] The Treaty provisions on European Citizenship demand a restrictive interpretation of the 'limitations and conditions'[223] to which the residence rights of the two categories may be subjected and this, so it could be argued, leads to the conclusion that application for, or enjoyment of, student grants in itself cannot be a valid reason for ending lawful residence.

6 THIRD COUNTRY NATIONALS

6.1 Introduction

Third country nationals are in principle excluded from the Community rules on the free movement of persons.[224] They only enjoy rights under these rules in as far as these rights promote the exercise of free movement rights by Community citizens. More concretely, this means that third country nationals in principle can only benefit from the rights conferred upon the family members of the various categories discussed in the previous Sections.[225] This is not to say, however, that Community law and policy have nothing to offer to third country nationals in the field of education. In particular,[226] third country nationals may enjoy

---

[222] See especially: ch 2, s 3.1 and ch 3, s 4.

[223] Art 18(1) EC.

[224] See ch 2 s 5.

[225] The benefits which derive from Directive No 77/486 (see n 88 above) are in principle preserved for children of Community workers. In a Declaration adopted at the time the Directive itself was adopted, the Council and the Member States expressed their 'political will' to include children of third country nationals in the measures taken in furtherance of this Directive. See Vermeulen/Kuijer (1997) n 4 above, at 41 (n 99). See further also the Council Resolution on the Admission of Third-Country Nationals to the Territory of the Member States of the European Union for Study Purposes, as published in Guild, *The Developing Immigration and Asylum Policies of the European Union—Adopted Conventions, Resolutions, Recommendations, Decisions and Conclusions* (1996).

[226] Further, the *Socrates/Erasmus* programme is open not only to Community citizens, but also to nationals of the three EEA countries, ten associated countries in Eastern Europe as well as Cyprus, Malta and Turkey. See European Commission, *Socrates*—Opening of the Actions of the *Socrates* programme to Certain Additional Countries (http://europa.eu.int/comm/education/socrates/new-co.html) and European Commission, Gateway to Education—*Socrates*—European

educational rights under agreements the Community and its Member States have concluded with third countries. For the purposes of this book, the Agreement on the European Economic Area (EEA), the E(E)C–Turkey Agreement and the agreements concluded with Maghreb countries have been selected for examination.

6.2 EEA Nationals

One can be relatively brief with regard to the educational rights offered to EEA nationals. The EEA Agreement has extended the scope of the Community's provisions on the free movement of workers to the nationals and territories of Norway, Iceland and Liechtenstein.[227] In addition, Directives Nos 93/96, 90/364 and 90/365 have been extended to EEA nationals and Article 4 EEA contains a nondiscriminating provision which is phrased in identical terms to Article 12(1) of the EC Treaty. As a result, EEA-nationals and their family members seem to enjoy, in each of the 15 Member States and the other two EEA States,[228] the same rights in the field of education as those which have been discussed in Sections 3 and 4 of this chapter.[229]

Community Action Programme in the Field of Education (2000–2006) (available on website just referred to) at 4. Nationals of the States concerned can only benefit from the Community's support provided under the programmes if the 'sending' or 'receiving' country is a Member State of the Community. For instance, student mobility among Cyprus and the EEA countries is not supported. See further also the definition of the term 'student' in Art 2 of the *Socrates* programme (OJ 1995 No L 87), which nowhere indicates that nationality of one of the Member States is a prerequisite for participation in the programme.

[227] See further ch 2 s 5.1.

[228] In reverse, Community citizens may enjoy these educational rights in the territory of the three countries concerned. See ch 2 s 5.2. Amongst each other, the Nordic countries have always promoted international student mobility. Foreign students, and in particular those holding the nationality of one of the other Nordic countries, have generally been admitted to education without having to pay additional tuition and enrolment fees. Further, Nordic students have been encouraged to study abroad by exporting student financial aid benefits especially for studies in one of the other Nordic countries. Denmark and Sweden have traditionally been net-importers of students, the other three States net-exporters. Initially, student mobility was largely 'spontaneous'; formal agreements between the States and/or their educational institutions aimed at regulating student movements did not exist. Since the late 1980s, however, several attempts to organise student mobility have been made. In 1988 *Nordplus* was set up. This programme allows students to follow part of their studies at home in other Nordic States and may be regarded as the Nordic equivalent of the *Socrates/Erasmus* programme. See further eg Nyborg, 'International Student Mobility: The Nordic Experience', (1996) *EJE* 193–203.

[229] To be sure, it is not wholly certain whether the right to freedom of movement for EEA students and the other economically inactive EEA nationals is based on the EEA Agreement itself. Art 4 EEA contains a non-discrimination provision which is phrased similarly to Article 12(1) EC, but 'common EEA policies' in the field of education comparable to the policies now based on Art 149 and 150 EC, do not exist. In Art 78 of the Agreement it is merely stated that the Contracting Parties shall strengthen and broaden cooperation in the framework of the Community's activities in the fields of 'education, training and youth'. Therefore, the line of reasoning followed by the Court in *Gravier* cannot be automatically transposed to the EEA. However, the possibility cannot be wholly excluded that the Court, if it were directly asked, would recognise that the right of EEA students to study in EC Member States is based on the EEA Agreement itself. See

6.3 Maghreb Nationals

Maghreb nationals are in a less privileged position than EEA nationals. The 1978 cooperation agreements concluded with Algeria, Morocco and Tunisia and the more recent Euro–Mediterranean agreements concluded with the latter two countries do not confer upon Maghreb nationals free movement rights. Provisions specifically dealing with educational rights are nowhere to be found and equivalents of Article 12(1) EC or Article 7(2) of Regulation No 1612/68 do not exist.[230] In principle, the legal status of Maghreb nationals in the field of education is governed by national law and not by Community law. It could be argued, however, that Maghreb nationals are entitled to gain access to vocational training courses. The Maghreb agreements provide for a right to equal treatment as regards working conditions, which, so it could be argued,[231] may encompass access to vocational training in the host State.[232]

eg Handoll, *Free Movement of Persons in the EU* (1996) at 323. Further, a 'common EEA citizenship' does not exist. Therefore, one cannot be wholly certain that the conclusions following from the Court's ruling in *Martínez Sala* (ie Community citizens who are lawfully established in the territory of another Member State can, as persons falling within the scope of the Treaty provisions on European Union citizenship, invoke the non-discrimination provision contained in Article 12 EC in order to claim social advantages such as 'full' student grants under the same conditions as the nationals of the host State) can be extended to EEA nationals. Strictly speaking, it could therefore still be argued that EEA students (compare s 4.4) and other economically inactive EEA nationals (s 5) can be denied student grants in as far as these cover maintenance costs (see in particular Art 3 of Dir No 93/96) by reason of their nationality.

[230] See ch 2 s 5.3.

[231] See Martin/Guild (1996) n 178 above, at 14.6 (referring to Case C–116/94 *Meyers* [1995] ECR I–2131 in which the Court held that vocational training may be regarded as a working condition for the purposes of Dir No 76/207 on the principle of equal treatment for men and women). On an extensive interpretation of this right to equal treatment as regards working conditions, one could even argue that this right to vocational training also encompasses a right to claim student grants. Compare n 62 above.

[232] In the recent *Fahmi and Esmoris Cerdeiro-Pinedo Amado* (2001) case the question arose whether Moroccan workers could possibly rely on Art 41 of the 1978 Morocco Agreement in order to claim student grants for children pursuing a study outside the host State. Art 41 offers a right to equal treatment in social security matters (para 1) and a right to receive family allowances for family members who are resident in the European Community (para 3). The concept of social security in Art 41(1) 'must be understood by analogy with the identical concept in Reg No 1408/71' (Case C–18/90 *Kziber* [1991] ECR I–199 at 25–26) and the question could be raised whether student grants can be regarded as family benefits for the purposes of Reg No 1408/71. The Court, however, avoided answering this question. The case concerned a Moroccan worker, Mr. Fahmi, who had worked in the Netherlands and who, upon return to Morocco, claimed child allowances for his son, Rida, who was studying there. The Court held that it followed both from the wording and spirit of Art 41(1) and (3), that the non-discrimination principle can only be applied to children residing within the Community. Case C–33/99 *Fahmi and Esmoris Cerdeiro-Pinedo Amado* [2001] ECR I–2415 at 57–58. It seems unlikely, however, that the student grants can be classed as family benefits for the purposes of Reg No 1408/71 or as family allowances in the sense of Art 41 of the Morocco Agreement. See further s 9.3.2.3

6.4 Turkish Nationals

The drafters of the 1963 Association Agreement between the Community (and its Member States) and Turkey, the Additional Protocol of 1970 and Decision 1/80 of the E(E)C–Turkey Association Council had not paid much attention to the legal status of Turkish nationals in the field of education.[233] The prime beneficiaries, Turkish nationals who have been admitted for employment to one of the Community's Member States, are nowhere expressly granted educational rights. Article 37 of the Additional Protocol and Article 10 of Decision No 1/80, which confer upon Turkish workers a right to equal treatment as regards remuneration and conditions of work, could possibly be interpreted as to encompass a right to gain access to vocational training courses,[234] but in the absence of an equivalent in Decision No 1/80 of Article 7(2) of Regulation No 1612/68, Turkish workers do not seem entitled to be admitted to general education or to claim student grants in the host State.

The only provision of Decision No 1/80 which expressly mentions educational rights is Article 9. It provides that Turkish children of Turkish nationals who are or have been legally employed in a Member State of the Community, must be 'admitted to courses of general education, apprenticeship and vocational training under the same educational entry qualifications as the children of nationals of the Member States.' Article 9 is phrased similarly to Article 12 of Regulation No 1612/68 and, as the latter provision, it is intended to promote the integration of the family of Turkish workers into the host Member State.[235] Therefore, one may assume that Article 9 must be interpreted, as far as possible,[236] in accordance with the principles on which Article 12 of the Regulation is based.[237] If so, Turkish children of Turkish workers would seem to have a directly enforceable right[238] to gain access to all forms of education made available in the host State.[239] However, Article 9 does not encompass a right to equal

---

[233] On these measures see further ch 2 s 5.2.

[234] Compare the observations made in s 6.2 as regards Maghreb nationals.

[235] See Martin/Guild (1996) n 178 above, at 13.76.

[236] The provisions of Decision No 1/80 are 'as far as possible' to be interpreted in accordance with the principles in the case law on Article 39 EC. See Case C–434/95 *Bozkurt* [1995] ECR I–1475 at 20 and O'Leary, 'Employment and Residence for Turkish Workers and their Families: Analogies with the Case-Law of the Court of Justice on Article 48 EC', in *Scritti in Onore di Giuseppe Federico Mancini—Volume II Diritto Dell/Unione Europea* (1998) 731–67.

[237] Peers, 'Annotation *Akman*', (1999) *CMLRev* 1027–42. Until further clarification by the Court uncertainty about the precise meaning and scope of Art 9 and the degree to which the principles developed under Art 12 can be applied to Art 9, will remain. For instance, Art 9 only speaks of Turkish children, whilst Art 12 of Reg No 1612/68 seems to apply to all children regardless of their nationality. Does this imply that children of Turkish workers who do not have Turkish nationality cannot rely on Art 9? Further, the text of Art 9 suggests that children must not only reside in the host State's territory but also be living with their parents. Does this mean that they must live under the same roof? Compare Martin/Guild (1996) n 178 above, at 13.74.

[238] Case C–210/97 *Akman* [1998] ECR I–7519 at 41 and Peers (1999) n 237 above, at 1040.

[239] See Martin/Guild (1996) n 178 above, at 13.72 and Wapenaar (1997) n 198 above, at 157.

treatment for student grants for Turkish children. Turkish children only have to be admitted to education under the 'same educational entry qualifications' and not, as Article 12 of Regulation No 1612/68 provides, under the 'same conditions.'[240] Turkish workers are entitled to claim indirect student financial aid offered in the form of family benefits for children residing with them under Decision No 3/80 on the application of social security schemes.[241] In *Sürül* (1999) the Court concluded that the equal treatment provision contained in Article 3(1) of Decision No 3/80 can be invoked in court by Turkish workers claiming family allowances.[242]

7 CONCLUSIONS

Community law on cross-border access to education has come a long way. The legal status of third country nationals in the field of education is fragmented and generally not very well developed, but as regards Community citizens considerable progress has been made. Today, all the categories of Community citizens whose legal status has been discussed in this chapter enjoy quite extensive rights in the field of education. Community workers and their (dependent) family members have a virtually unlimited right to equal treatment in educational matters. They must be admitted to any educational institution and they can claim student grants under the same conditions as nationals of the host State, even in relation

---

[240] The wording of Art 9 was intended to avoid the Court's interpretation of the previously mentioned phrase in Art 12 encompassing a right to equal treatment as regard student grants being extended to Turkish children covered by Decision No 1/80. See Peers, 'Towards Equality: Actual and Potential Rights of Third-Country Nationals in the European Union', (1996) *CMLRev* 7–50, at p 27. Further, the second sentence of Art 9 stipulates that Turkish children may be eligible to benefit from the advantages provided for by the legislation in the field of education in the host State. The use of the word 'may' suggests that the provision does not have direct effect.

[241] On Decision No 3/80 see in particular ch 3 s 6.3.

[242] Case C–262/96 *Sürül* [1999] ECR I–2685 at 74. Thus, at the present stage of Community law, the legal status of Turkish nationals in the field of education is not well developed, but the possibility cannot be excluded that improvements will be made in future years. In particular, Art 9 of the 1963 Assocation Agreement, which contains a general non-discrimination clause comparable to Art 12(1) EC, could provide a weapon for Turkish nationals who wish to challenge national rules denying them educational rights. In *Sürül* (1999), a social security case discussed in ch 3 s 6.3, Adv Gen La Pergola concluded that this provision has direct effect. The Court refrained from clarifying the legal status and scope of Art 9. It answered the preliminary questions on the basis of the equal treatment provision of Art 3 of social security Decision No 3/80 which was referred to as the 'implementation and the concrete expression, in the particular field of social security, of the general principle of non-discrimination laid down in Art 9' of the 1963 Agreement. Case C–262/96 *Sürül* [1999] ECR I–2685 at 64. These observations of the Court show resemblances with its case law on Art 12 EC which has proved to be a lucrative legal source for Community citizens. If, as one may assume, Art 9 indeed has direct effect, Turkish nationals may be able to claim additional educational rights. In the absence of a common EC–Turkey policy in the field of education and vocational training, it does not seem likely that the *Gravier* case law can by means of analogy be extended to Turkish students (Peers (1996) n 237 above, at 27), but Art 9 could possibly be relevant to Turkish workers and their family members who wish to claim educational rights including student grants (Peers, Social Security Equality for Turkish Nationals, (1999) *ELRev* 627–37, at 635).

to studies outside that State's territory. The legal status of the category of non-economic residents, ie, for the purposes of this chapter pensioners and the residual class of Community citizens covered by Directive No 90/364, has so far not been clearly defined, but they do seem to have the right to gain access to all forms of education in the host State and a right to claim student grants there. In addition, all Community citizens have a right to go to other Member States in order to take up studies and to claim student grants there in as far as these cover tuition and/or enrolment fees. The Court of Justice, the main initiator of the extension of cross-border educational rights, however, cannot be accused of having ignored the educational and financial interests of the Member States. In particular, the Court has wished to avoid that the admission of non-nationals, and non-residents in particular, would affect student grant schemes and educational systems. First, the Court has denied Community students a right to claim student grants in the State where they study in so far as these cover the costs of maintenance. Second, by making the status of Community worker conditional upon the requirement of 'effective and genuine work,' the Court has created a threshold for Community students who, through the pursuit of small jobs, may try to obtain the status of worker and to claim, in this capacity, 'full' student grants.

The Court has sought to reconcile the potentially conflicting interests of promoting freedom of movement and the need to safeguard Member States' educational interests, but the compromise it has reached is disputed. This particularly holds true for the rules governing the rights of Community students. As concluded in Section 4.11, it is claimed that Community law and policy do not give sufficient regard to the fact that some Member States receive far more students than they 'send' abroad. In one way or another, these States ought to be compensated for the burden imposed on them. It is also argued, however, that there are still too many obstacles to cross-border access to education. Due to problems concerning the recognition of their diplomas, insufficient knowledge of foreign languages and/or a lack of sufficient student financial aid, many Community citizens are still unable to take up a course of study in other Member States. In Section 9 some observations will be made as to whether, and if so, how, this conflict can be settled more satisfactorily. Before doing so, however, this Chapter proceeds with an analysis of American constitutional law on cross-border access to public education. To what extent are United States' citizens entitled to move and to gain access to public education in other States? To what extent are the American States entitled to protect themselves against 'educational tourism'? What lessons can the European Community possibly learn from the American experience?

8.1 The American Educational System: A Brief Introduction

As in the European Community, education is highly valued in the United States. In the words of the American Supreme Court, education has played a 'fundamental role in maintaining the fabric'[243] of American society and it must be regarded as a prerequisite for individuals' effective participation in political, cultural and economic life.[244] The importance attached to education has resulted in a vast and diverse educational system in which governments at local, State and Federal level as well as private institutions play a role in the delivery, organisation and/or funding of education.

The public education system, to which this Section is limited, is essentially local in character. The role of the Federal government is limited. Education is primarily a matter for individual States and the systems of each of the States are characterised by a high degree of decentralisation. In the area of higher education individual colleges and universities enjoy considerable autonomy. Government influence on the organisation of the institutions, admission policies and educational programmes is, by comparison with most European educational systems, minimal. Colleges and universities are mainly funded out of the States' budgets and, to a lesser extent, federal funds and tuition fees. In the fields of primary and secondary education, States are divided into school districts which are mandated to implement the States' educational policies. In fulfilling this task the districts enjoy considerable freedom. They control the operation and the management of the schools, often have an important say in the substance of the educational programme offered and they are responsible for a big part of the funding of the institutions. Often, the districts have their own taxation powers. The revenue from taxes (on property) covers about 50 per cent of the funding of education; the remaining parts are funded from the States' (40 per cent) and the federal budget (10 per cent).

The local funding of the public school system has resulted in large differences in the amount of money spent per pupil/student. Consequently, the quality of schools in the different districts varies. Constitutional law does not object to these differences. In *San Antonio Independent School District v Rodriguez* (1973) the Court was asked on behalf of a number of children living in 'poor districts' to rule upon the constitutionality of Texas' school funding system which was largely based on local property taxes. The Supreme Court showed deference *vis-à-vis* the State legislatures. According to the Court, the case involved 'difficult questions of educational policy,' an area 'in which this Court's lack of specialised knowledge and experience counsels against premature interference

---

[243] *Plyler v Doe*, 457 U.S. 202 (1982) at 221.
[244] *Brown v Board of Education*, 347 U.S. 483 (1954) at 493.

with the informed judgments made at the state and local levels.'[245] The Court refused to class 'wealth' as a suspect classification and did not recognise education as a fundamental right for equal protection purposes. The Court did not apply strict or intermediate scrutiny. It limited itself to rational relation review and concluded that the Texas system was not 'so irrational as to be invidiously discriminatory.'[246]

Governments at various levels, companies, trade unions as well as educational institutions themselves have often established student grant or loan programmes in order to facilitate admission to higher education. The scope of these programmes is generally rather limited, however. Eligibility is often reserved for certain categories of students and most of the grant or loan programmes cover only part of the study costs. The costs of maintenance are in principle to be borne by the students themselves who may have to take out private loans. Universally accessible public student financial aid systems comparable to the ones that have been developed in some European countries, do not appear to exist in the United States.[247]

8.2 Conditions of Access

The disparity among the educational systems of the various States may provide an incentive for students to move to and to study in other States. States have been aware of this. In their admission policies[248] they have built in safeguards intended to protect the funding and organisation of educational systems against the consequences of a possible large influx of pupils or students from other States. The measures for protecting primary and secondary education, on the one hand, and higher education, on the other hand, differ.

Admission to primary and secondary education has in many cases been made conditional upon residence in the school district; non-resident pupils have been

---

[245] *San Antonio Independent School District v Rodriguez*, 411 U.S. 1 (1973) at 42.

[246] On *Rodriguez* and 'territorial' discrimination see eg Neuman, 'Territorial Discrimination, Equal Protection and Self-Determination', (1987) *UPennLRev* 261–382. Compare also *Kadrmas* (1988) in which the Court held that there was no fundamental right to education which could trigger strict scrutiny and that the denial of free transportation to public schools to 'poor' children was not so arbitrary or invidious as to violate the Equal Protection Clause. *Kadrmas v. Dickinson Public Schools*, 487 U.S. 450 (1988).

[247] For this reason as well as the fact that there have not been relevant cases before the Supreme Court, this Section does not discuss questions concerning student financial aid. For (limited) information on student financial aid schemes in the United States see Oijen *et al* (1990) n 15 above, at 21–22 and 28.

[248] In practice, the variety of admission policies is enormous. Often, it is not the States but the universities, colleges or school districts which establish the conditions of access. For an overview of the policies governing admission to higher education, see further Hellmuth, *Residency for Tuition Purposes: A Study of the Rules in Use at the Fifty State Universities* (1981). The description of the conditions of access to public education in this section is necessarily oversimplified and merely discusses the main and most common principles on which admission policies are based. For purposes of convenience, this Section will simply speak of the States' conditions of access.

denied admission. Children are only entitled to go to school in the district (and thus the State) where they live and where their parents can be required to pay property taxes. Generally, parents who wish to send their children to schools in another district (or State) can only do so by moving to that district themselves. Children who leave their parents' house in order to go to school in another district, and who live with family members, friends, etc., are in most districts treated as non-residents who, in principle, can be denied access. In some districts cross-border admission policies are less strict. Non-residents are admitted to schools but on condition that they pay an additional tuition fee.

Such non-resident tuition fees are much more common in the field of higher education. States have allowed non-resident admission to their colleges and universities,[249] but they have all imposed on non-residents a duty to pay additional tuition fees. The argument for imposing differential tuition fees on residents and non-residents runs as follows. Residents pay taxes to the State and thus contribute indirectly to the funding of public education. Since non-residents do not contribute equally, States require non-residents to pay their 'equal share' by charging them higher tuition fees. Differential tuition policies enable States to distribute the cost of operating and supporting educational institutions more evenly between resident and non-resident students.[250] This so-called cost-equalisation argument is not based on the contributions paid during the period of the studies. The economic status of resident and non-resident students is, during this period, more or less the same. The argument relates to the situation before and after the course of study. Prior to studying, non-resident students have not resided in the State and they are more likely to leave after graduation. Prior to studying, they or their parents have not paid taxes to the State to the same degree as residents have and more so than residents, non-residents are likely to 'use' their education in other States. The higher tuition fees to be paid by non-residents compensate the States for the fact that they often do not receive the benefits of the investment they have made in educating non-residents.

For tuition purposes, States do not apply the traditional definition of residence. If they did, differential tuition policies would be ineffective. Residence normally requires physical presence within the State *plus* an intention to stay there for at least a certain period of time.[251] If States were to apply this concept for tuition purposes, they could only collect higher tuition fees from the relatively small group of 'real' non-resident students, i.e., the students who continue to live in another State during their studies. Even the students who have merely come to the State for educational purposes and who will leave upon graduation, would have to be classed as residents and be admitted at the lower in-State tuition rate. Such 'free-riding students' are strictly speaking residents of the

---

[249] To be sure, some States have occasionally limited the percentage of the total student body which may consist of non-residents. Note, 'The Constitutionality of Nonresident Tuition', (1971)*MinnLRev* 1139–62, at 1150.

[250] Note, The Constitutionality of Nonresident Tuition (1971) *ibid*, at 1147.

[251] See ch 2 s 8.3.

States and for many governmental purposes they are indeed treated as such. They have the right to vote, to register their car, etc. From the perspective of tuition policy, however, they are viewed as 'educational tourists' who should pay their 'equal share' in the funding of public education by paying higher tuition. For tuition purposes, States define residents as all students who prior to enrolment have resided or been domiciled in the State for a minimum period of time (usually one year). This definition implies that higher out-of-State tuition fees are not only to be paid by the 'real' non-residents and 'free-riders.' They are also to be paid by students who have primarily come to the State in order to work, to live with their spouses or parents and students who initially came for educational purposes but who have later decided to live and work in the State after graduation. The cost-equalisation argument does not apply to these so-called bona fide residents in the same way as it does to the 'real' non-resident and free-riding students. States claim, however, that the one-year residence requirement serves as a test of bona fide residency. One-year of residence in the State would give an indication as to the motives of students for coming to the State. From students who prior to enrolment have resided in the State for more than a year, it can be assumed that they are bona fide residents. Students who do not satisfy the durational residence requirement are likely to be 'free-riders.' Occasionally, some States have held the classification as non-residents at the moment of enrolment to be conclusive for the entire duration of the studies. Most States, however, have allowed recently arrived students to ask for a reclassification. Students are given the opportunity to demonstrate that they are or have become bona fide residents (or domiciliaries) of the State. They can submit employment contracts, evidence of registration as a voter of the State, registration of a car in the State, etc. or any other means of evidence which can demonstrate 'domiciliary intent.' Students who are able to demonstrate such intent can be reclassified; students who cannot do so, retain the status of non-resident. Students are, however, only entitled to rebut the presumption of non-residence after one year. This one-year postponement has been defended by States on the ground that recently arrived bona fide resident-students have, prior to studying, not paid taxes to the same extent as long-term residents (past-contributions-argument).[252] Furthermore, the one-year postponement rule has been said to avoid the administrative burden and cost caused by reclassification procedures on behalf of whose claims are, at the outset, unfounded.

In sum, States have traditionally imposed a duty to pay the higher out-of-state tuition fees on (*i*) the real nonresident students, (*ii*) free-riding students and (*iii*) bona fide residents who have not resided in the State in the year prior to

---

[252] The past-tax-contributions-argument explains why States generally impose durational residence requirement of *one year*. Taxes are payable annually and the payment of taxes was thought to prove that a person was living in the State for other purposes than 'securing advantages' from other taxpayers. Masters, 'Comment—Nonresident Tuition Charged By State Universities in Review', (1970) *UMKCLRev* 341–54, at 343–44 (quoting *Bryan v Regents of University of California*, 188 Cal.559, 205 P.1071 (1922)).

their studies. The first two categories usually have to pay the higher tuition fees throughout the course of their studies; the latter category can, upon proof of 'domiciliary intent,' become eligible for in-State tuition one year after their arrival in the State.

8.3 Non-Residents

8.3.1 Higher Education

Differential tuition policies for admission to higher education have never been controversial. The practice of charging non-residents higher tuition is so common and widely accepted that the Supreme Court has not once been confronted with a case in which tuition residence requirements were challenged. The case law of the Court does indicate, however, that tuition residence requirements are constitutional. In *Vlandis v Kline* (1973), a case which will be discussed in further detail in Section 8.4, the Court held that 'a State has a legitimate interest in protecting and preserving the quality of its colleges and universities and the right of its bona fide residents to attend such institutions on a preferential tuition basis.' The Court added that a State does not have to class 'students in its university system as residents, for the purposes of tuition and fees, just because they go to school there.'[253] More specifically, the Supreme Court has allowed States to apply the concept of domicile for tuition purposes which has been defined as an individual's 'true, fixed and permanent home and place of habitation.' It 'is the place to which, whenever, he is absent, he has the intention of returning.'[254]

In the more recent case *Saenz v Roe* (1999) the Court indicated that by requiring non-residents to pay additional tuition fees, States do not violate the Privileges and Immunities Clause of Article IV § 2 of the Constitution.[255] In *Saenz* the Court rejected the view that States could impose durational residence requirements for welfare benefits. One of the reasons given by the Court was that welfare benefits are consumed in the State itself and there was no danger that citizens of other States would come and establish residence 'in order to acquire some readily portable benefit, *such as . . . a college education*, that will be enjoyed after they return to their original domicile' (emphasis added).[256]

---

[253] *Vlandis v Kline*, 412 U.S. 441 (1973) at 452.

[254] *Ibid*, at 454. The concept of domicile is, as the Court itself admitted, not always easy to apply in individual cases. Students must demonstrate 'something' which shows that they are more than just 'educational tourists', but the Court has never precisely indicated what this 'something' should entail. The Court has merely given some criteria which may be considered in individual cases. These include year-round residence, voter registration, place of completing tax returns, property ownership, driver's licence, car registration, marital status, vacation employment, etc. *Vlandis v Kline*, 412 U.S. 441 (1973) at 454. The Court thus leaves the States considerable discretion in determining whether or not a student has acquired domicile status.

[255] On the Privileges and Immunities Clause see further ch 2 s 8.6.1.

[256] *Saenz v Roe*, 119 S.Ct 1518 (1999). On *Saenz* see in particular ch 3 s 8.4.4.

Tuition residence requirements for admission to higher education, and as one may safely assume primary and secondary education, are thus valid. As brief as they may be, the above observations suggest that the cost-equalisation argument, the only justification offered by the States for charging non-residents higher tuition, has been accepted by the Supreme Court.[257]

8.3.2 *Primary and Secondary Education*

In the field of primary and secondary education, residence requirements have more often been applied as a condition for admission. Non-residents have been denied admission altogether. At first glance, there does not seem to be a real need for such exclusions. The States' ability to maintain the quality of their primary and secondary schools is not likely to be affected by the admission of non-residents. As may be assumed, the inter-State mobility of pupils is relatively low. As a rule, pupils live with their parents and, usually, it is not the education of the children but rather the employment opportunities of the parents that will determine where the family will move and live. Even if families move for educational reasons, this does not seem to pose a real 'problem' because, by paying taxes, the parents contribute to the funding of the schools. *Saenz* (1999) further indicates that State statutes governing access to education are 'fundamental' for the purposes of the Privileges and Immunities Clause. In principle, States will have to demonstrate that they have a substantial reason for excluding non-residents and that there are no less restrictive means for securing their educational interests. If, however, States can maintain the quality of their higher educational institutions by charging non-residents higher tuition fees, why would they not be able to do so in the field of primary and secondary education?

Nonetheless, the judgment in *Martinez v Bynum*[258] (1982) indicates that States are constitutionally permitted to deny residents of other States admission to public schools. The case concerned an 8-year-old United States citizen, Roberto Morales, who had moved from Mexico to Texas where he lived with his sister. Roberto was a true free-rider. His sole motive for coming to Texas was to attend school there and he was planning on returning to Mexico after finishing his education. Roberto was denied free-tuition admission to the schools in Texas. A Texas Code provided that free-tuition admission to public

---

[257] Compare also *Reeves, Inc. v State* (1980) in which the Court was asked to rule upon the constitutionality of the refusal of South Dakota to sell to non-residents cement produced by a public plant. In reaching the conclusion that the refusal to sell to non-residents was constitutional the Court observed: 'The State's refusal to sell to buyers other than South Dakotans is 'protectionist' only in the sense that it limits benefits generated by a state program to those who fund the state treasury and whom the States was created to serve. Petitioners' argument apparently also would characterize as 'protectionist' rules restricting to state residents the enjoyment of *state educational institutions* . . . police and fire protection . . . Such policies, while perhaps 'protectionistic' in a loose sense, reflect the essential and patently unobjectionable purpose of state government—to serve the citizens of the state' (emphasis added). *Reeves, Inc. v State*, 447 U.S. 429 (1980) at 443.

[258] *Martinez v Bynum*, 461 U.S. 321 (1982).

schools was granted to all children who lived within the school district except for those minors who lived apart from their parents and who were merely staying in Texas in order to go to school there. In reviewing the Texas Code, the Supreme Court held that States may 'of course' require children to reside in the school district before admitting them to public schools.[259] A residence requirement:

> furthers the substantial state interest in assuring that services provided for residents are enjoyed only by residents. Such a requirement with respect to attendance at public free schools does not violate the Equal Protection Clause of the Fourteenth Amendment. . . . It does not burden or penalize the constitutional right to travel, . . . for any person is free to move to a State and establish residence there. A bona fide residence requirement simply requires that the person does establish residence before demanding the services that are restricted to residents.[260]

There was, according to the Court, a further, independent justification for local residence requirements in the public-school context. The provision of primary and secondary education is one of the most important functions of local governments. In the absence of residence requirements there was 'little doubt that the proper planning and operation of the schools would suffer significantly. . . . The State thus has a substantial interest in imposing bona fide residence requirements to maintain the quality of public schools.'[261]

States are thus indeed entitled to deny children from other States admission to their public schools. The Court merely subjected residence requirements for admission to public schools to the rational relation test of the Equal Protection

---

[259] *Ibid*, at 329.

[260] *Ibid*, at 328–29.

[261] *Ibid*, at 329–30. In a n the Court added that invalidating residence requirements 'would cause substantial numbers of inter-district transfers, which would . . . cause schools populations to fluctuate. . . . Fluctuating school populations would make it impossible to predict enrolment figures—even on a semester-by-semester basis, causing over- or-under-estimates on teachers, supplies, materials, etc. . . . The increased enrollment of students would cause overcrowded classrooms and related facilities; over-large teacher-pupil ratios; expansions of bilangual programs; the purchase of books, equipment, supplies and other customary items for support; all of which would require a substantial increase in the budget of the school districts'. *Martinez v Bynum*, 461 U.S. 321 (1982) at 329 (n 9). The Court did not wish to suggest that 'findings of this degree of specifity are necessary in every case' but they would 'illustrate the problems that prompt States to adopt regulations' such as the one contained in the Texas Code.
    The only question left, then, was whether 'free-riding' children, like Roberto Morales, were to be classed as residents for educational purposes. The Court held that States are under no obligation to do so. In order to reach this conclusion the Court did not, as it had done in the field of higher education (see s 8.3.1), rely on the concept of domicile. Instead, the Court gave a somewhat stricter definition of the term residence than the classic definition of the term. A State may not only require a pupil to be physically present in the State and to have the intention to stay there for at least some time; a State may also demand from pupils a 'present intention to remain' in the State. Pupils (or their parents) must not have any concrete plans to leave the State. Free-riders do not meet this standard. They already plan to leave the State after finishing school and thus, as non-residents, they can be denied admission to public schools. The Court itself claimed that the definition it gave of the term residence was the classic definition. This was hard to understand, however. In previous cases the Court had never indicated that an 'intention to remain' was an essential component of the residence definition. See *Martinez v Bynum*, 461 U.S. 321 (1982) at 339–41 (Marshall, dissenting).

Clause, but remained wholly silent on the Privileges and Immunities Clause. Why? The reason, it seems, is that the provision in question of the Texas Code did not contain a requirement of residence in the State but a requirement of residence in the school district. Texas residents who resided in another district were equally denied admission. In other words, the Code did not discriminate between State-residents and residents of other States, but merely between residents of the school district and residents of other districts. In *Martinez* the Court was primarily concerned with the consequences of the invalidation of these residence-in-the-district requirements. The invalidation of the residence requirements in question was not likely to cause a huge increase in the inter-State movement of pupils, but could have triggered an increased inter-district movement of pupils within the State. The distance between childrens' homes and other school districts will often be relatively short and children can return home every evening. Many parents might choose to send their children to 'better' schools in other districts. In the absence of residence-in-the-district-requirements the inter-district movement of pupils within the State could be considerable and the 'proper planning and operation of the schools' might be affected. Basically, in *Martinez* the Court upheld residence-in-the State requirements as constitutional because it did not wish to invalidate residence-in-the-district requirements.

8.4 Residents

The target group of higher out-of-state tuition fees consists of 'real' and 'free-riding' non-resident students. Yet, the so-called bona fide residents also have to pay the non-resident tuition if they have not resided in the State for at least one year prior to commencement of the studies. Up until the late 1960s, the constitutionality of tuition waiting-periods was beyond doubt. Courts merely employed rational relation scrutiny and considered the waiting-periods to be reasonably related to the legitimate purposes of cost-equalisation and 'proof of domiciliary intent.'[262] The Supreme Court decision in *Shapiro v Thompson* (1969), however, cast doubt on the validity of tuition waiting-periods. In that decision the Court invalidated waiting-period requirements for welfare benefits under the Equal Protection Clause by holding that 'any classification which serves to penalize the exercise' of the fundamental right to travel is, 'unless shown to be necessary to promote a compelling State interest, unconstitutional.'[263] Even though the Court had explicitly stated in *Shapiro* that the decision did not imply a view as to the validity of tuition waiting-periods,[264] it

---

[262] See Parent, 'Tuition Residence Requirements: A Second Look in Light of *Zobel* and *Martinez*', (1986) *IndLJ* 287–314, at 291–3; Note (1971) n 249 above, at 1147 and 1153 and Segal, Residency, Tuition and the Twelve Month Dilemma, (1969) *HoustLRev* 241–56, at 249–51.

[263] *Shapiro v Thompson*, 394 U.S. 618 (1969) at 634.

[264] *Ibid*, at 638 (n 21).

could have been, and it indeed was,[265] argued that such requirements were no longer permissible. Tuition waiting-period requirements deny 'new' residents the right to be admitted at the lower in-State tuition fee rate. The requirements thus seemed to penalise the right to travel with the result that they were to be scrutinised under the virtually insurmountable 'compelling State interest test.' Further, it seemed that the Court had not left any room for the traditional justification grounds for tuition waiting-periods. In particular, in *Shapiro* the Court had held that States cannot apportion state services among citizens according to past tax contributions[266] and that one-year waiting-period requirements cannot be justified as an 'efficient rule of thumb' for determining the residence of those who have moved to other States.[267]

In spite of their apparent strength, the above arguments have not been seen as persuasive by the Supreme Court. Shortly after *Shapiro* the Court summarily affirmed[268] the decision of a California Court in *Kirk v Board of Regents* (1969)[269] in which tuition waiting period requirements had been upheld. *Kirk* involved an Ohio resident who had moved to California in order to live with the husband that she had recently married. Three months after arrival, she enrolled in a State university where she was classified as a non-resident for tuition purposes. A State statute provided that the resident status for tuition purposes could only be acquired by students who had been bona fide residents of California for more than one year before the opening of a semester. Ms Kirk challenged the one-year waiting-period in court thereby mainly relying on *Shapiro*. The California court, however, was not willing to invalidate the tuition waiting-period and it took pains to explain why *Shapiro*'s penalty analysis did not have to be applied in tuition cases. The court stated that a tuition waiting-period did not have a deterrent effect on the right to travel. Persons such as Ms Kirk, who came to the State in order to accompany their spouses, would not take into consideration that they might have to pay higher tuition fees and the Court considered it to be absurd that a person would marry a resident of the State in order to obtain one year of higher education at a lower cost. Furthermore, the court in *Kirk* recognised the value of higher education, but it considered it not as important as welfare. Unlike welfare, education was not a 'basic necessity of life' the denial of which 'could cause great suffering and even loss of life.' In the California court's view, the requirements under challenge did not constitute a penalty on the right to travel; the requirements were not subject to strict scrutiny. In applying the less demanding rational relation test, the court in *Kirk* accepted cost-equalisation as a justification-ground for the tuition waiting-period. California has a valid interest:

[265] Note, 'Residence Requirements for Tuition: An Unresolved Dilemma', (1972) *IndLRev* 283 *et seq.* and Masters (1970) n 252 above, at 341 *et seq.*

[266] *Shapiro v Thompson*, 394 U.S. 618 (1969) at 632–33.

[267] *Ibid*, at 636–37.

[268] Summary affirmance implies that the Supreme Court, without writing a full opinion itself, agrees with a lower court in the result. *Zobel v Williams*, 457 U.S. 55 (1982) at 64 (n 13).

[269] *Kirk v Board of Regents*, 78 Cal.Rptr.260 (1969).

in providing tuition free education to those who have demonstrated by a year's residence a bona fide intention of remaining here and who, by reason of that education will be prepared to make a greater contribution to the state's economy and future. Accordingly, we hold that the regulation classifying students as residents and nonresidents for tuition purposes is not arbitrary or unreasonable and bears a rational relation to California's objective and purpose of financing, operating and maintaining its many publicly financed educational institutions . . .[270]

The fact that the decision in *Kirk* has been summarily affirmed indicates that also in the view of the Supreme Court tuition waiting-periods were valid. Summary affirmance, however, does not necessarily imply that the Supreme Court also agrees with the lower court's reasons for its decisions.[271] It seems unlikely that the Supreme Court would have approved of the California court's reasoning. In support of the view that strict scrutiny did not have to be applied, the California court placed emphasis on the deterrent effect of tuition waiting periods on the exercise of the right to travel. It was implicit in *Shapiro*, however, and this was explicitly confirmed by the Court in *Dunn v Blumstein* (1972)[272] that the degree to which travel is actually discouraged is irrelevant for equal protection analysis. In *Dunn* the Court spoke in this regard of 'a fundamental misunderstanding of the law.' Furthermore, the court in *Kirk* held that strict scrutiny did not have to be applied because education could not constitute a 'basic necessity of life.' In *Shapiro* the Supreme Court had not given any indication, however, that the importance of a given benefit or right would be decisive for the test to be applied under the Equal Protection Clause.[273]

Thus, *Kirk* indicated that tuition waiting-periods are valid, but the case left uncertain why this should be the case.[274] Three years later, however, the

---

[270] *Kirk v Board of Regents*, 78 Cal.Rptr.260 (1969) at 269.

[271] *Zobel v Williams*, 457 U.S. 55 (1982) at 64 (n 13).

[272] *Dunn v Blumstein*, 405 U.S. 330 (1972).

[273] Furthermore, it does not seem very likely that the Supreme Court agreed with the California court's response to the argument that the one-year waiting-period requirement would constitute an irrebuttable presumption of non-residence. The latter court had rejected the argument by holding that a 'student from another State . . . is classified as a nonresident because he is presumed to be in California primarily for educational purposes. If appropriate facts and circumstances arise subsequent to a student's classification as a nonresident, there is nothing in the regulation that would prevent petitioner's reclassification as a resident'. *Ibid*, at 268–69. The view that the presumption of non-residency was rebuttable only seemed correct, however, in as far as students had been bona fide residents for one year. During the waiting-period the presumption of non-residence was clearly irrebuttable. Further, the California court had suggested that the cost-equalisation-argument was invalid under the compelling state interest test, but that the argument would be valid under the rational relation test. In *Shapiro*, however, the Court had made no distinction between the two tests and it had held the past contribution rationale to be constitutionally impermissible *per se*. *Shapiro v Thompson*, 394 U.S. 618 (1969) at 632–33.

[274] After *Kirk* the Court also summarily affirmed two other decisions of lower courts which had upheld tuition waiting-period requirements. See *Starns v Malkerson*, 326 F.Supp.234 (D.Minn.1970) *aff'd mem.*, 401 U.S. 985 (1971) and *Sturgis v Washington*, (368 F.Supp.38 (W.D.Wash.1973). There is no need to discuss these decisions here in further detail because both courts followed the same line of reasoning as the court in *Kirk*. On *Sturgis* see Note, 'Durational Residence Requirements From *Shapiro* through *Sosna*: The Right to Travel Takes a New Turn', (1979) *NYULRev* 622 *et seq.*, at 652–53. On *Starns* see Note, 'State University's One-Year

Supreme Court did give a full opinion in *Vlandis v Kline* (1973)[275] in which it attempted to give some clarification as to why, in its view, tuition waiting-periods were constitutional. *Vlandis* concerned two students who upon application for admission to the university were classed as non-residents for tuition purposes. The students attacked a section of the statute which read: 'The status of a student, as established at the time of his application for admission . . . shall be his status for the *entire* period' of the studies (emphasis added). The students attacked the conclusiveness of the initial classification as non-residents for the rest of the studies. They claimed to have a constitutional right to controvert the presumption of non-residence by presenting evidence that they are, or have become, bona fide residents of the State. The Court held that the conclusive presumption of non-residence was indeed unconstitutional. Standards of due process, the Court said, require that States allow an individual the opportunity to present evidence showing that he is a bona fide resident entitled to in-state rates.[276]

Vlandis itself did not concern tuition waiting-periods and the case was decided under the Due Process Clause. The Court stated, however, that it was well aware of the special problems involved in determining the bona fide residence of students who come from out of State to attend public education. Its holding should:

> in no wise be taken to mean that Connecticut must classify the students in its university system as residents, for purposes of tuition and fees, just because they go to school there. Nor should our decision be construed to deny a State the right to impose on a student, as one element in demonstrating bona fide residence, a reasonable durational residence requirement. (. . .) We fully recognize that a State has a legitimate interest in protecting and preserving the quality of its colleges and universities and the right of its bona fide residents to attend such institutions on a preferential tuition basis. (. . .) The State can establish such reasonable criteria for in-state status as to make virtually certain that students who are not, in fact, bona fide residents of the State, but who have come there solely for the educational purposes, cannot take advantage of the in-state rates.[277]

Thus, waiting-period requirements could not be justified, as the California court in *Kirk* had held, on the basis of the cost equalisation argument. In the view of the Supreme Court, this argument 'would give rise to grave problems under the Equal Protection Clause.'[278]

Waiting Period Requirement to Attain Resident Status for Tuition Payment does not Violate Fourteenth Amendment', (1971) *AlabLRev* 147–62.

[275] *Vlandis v Kline*, 412 U.S. 441 (1973).

[276] *Ibid*, at 452.

[277] *Ibid*, at 452–54. In a n the Court explained why the provision challenged in *Vlandis* was to be distinguished from cases involving tuition waiting-period requirements. The latter type of requirements enable a student who was initially classed as non-resident for tuition purposes, to rebut the presumption of non-residence after one year by presenting evidence to show bona fide residence. In *Vlandis*, on the other hand, a student was prevented from ever rebutting the presumption of non-residence during their studies. *Ibid*, at 452 (n 9).

[278] *Vlandis v Kline*, 412 U.S. 441 (1973) at 450 (n 6).

Vlandis shows that tuition waiting-periods are in the view of the Supreme Court constitutional only when, and so far as, they serve as an objective test of bona fide residence or 'domiciliary intent.' In later cases the Court has confirmed that[279] tuition waiting-periods are constitutional, but the Court has never given any additional reasons in support of this conclusion.[280] This is unfortunate because the 'bona fide residence explanation' is hard to grasp. The Court has never held much more than that States should have the possibility of ascertaining for themselves that free-riding students do not 'dress up' as bona fide residents in order to become entitled to the lower in-State tuition fees and that States may encounter 'special problems' in determining the bona fide residence status of students. These observations merely explain why students who have not resided in the State concerned for one year prior to commencing their

[279] See eg *Zobel v Williams*, 457 U.S. 55 (1982) at 64 (n 13—holding that the one-year tuition residence requirement is 'a test of bona fide residence, not a return on prior contributions to the commonweal').

[280] In *Vlandis* the Court had explained why tuition waiting-periods are constitutional, but it did not clarify how this conclusion fitted in *Shapiro*'s penalty-on-the-right-to-travel analysis. One year after *Vlandis*, however, the Court did attempt to clarify the issue in *Memorial Hospital v Maricopa County* (1974). The case concerned durational residence requirements for non-emergency medical care. In support of the view that waiting-periods for medical care were to be subjected to the compelling State interest test the Court held that 'whatever the ultimate parameters of the *Shapiro* penalty analysis' may be, 'it is at least clear that medical care is as much a "basic necessity of life" to an indigent as welfare assistance'. *Memorial Hospital v Maricopa County*, 415 U.S. 250 (1974) at 259. As stated earlier, it seemed unlikely that the Supreme Court supported most of the reasoning of the California court, but the Supreme Court did now adopt the reasoning of the court in *Kirk* on this point. In support of its conclusion that waiting-periods for medical care did constitute a penalty, the Supreme Court made (in a footnote) reference to tuition waiting-periods and it quoted in full some observations of the court in *Kirk*: 'While we fully recognize the value of higher education, we cannot equate its attainment with food, clothing and shelter. *Shapiro* involved *the immediate and pressing need for preservation of life and health* of persons unable to live without public assistance, and their dependent children. Thus, the requirement in Shapiro could cause great suffering and even loss of life. The durational residence requirement for attendance at publicly financed institutions of higher learning do not involve similar risks. Nor was petitioner precluded from the benefit of obtaining higher education. Charging higher tuition to non-resident students cannot be equated with the granting of basic subsistence to one class of needy residents while denying it to an equally needy class of residents'. *Ibid*, at 260 (n 15). On *Memorial Hospital* see further ch 4 s 5.2. *Vlandis* and *Memorial Hospital*, read together, thus implied that tuition waiting-periods do not violate the Equal Protection Clause because it was in the view of the Supreme Court not wholly irrational to require from students, who have not yet resided for a minimum period of time in the State concerned, to demonstrate that they are bona fide residents rather than free-riding students who have merely come to the State for educational purposes.

This conclusion, however, no longer seems very relevant. Quite recently, the Court has abandoned *Shapiro*'s penalty-on-the-right-to-travel analysis in *Saenz v Roe* (119 S.Ct. 1518 (1999)). The constitutionality of durational residence requirements is now to be judged under the Privileges or Immunities Clause of the Fourteenth Amendment. The precise contours of the test to be applied under this Clause are still far from clear. The Court did not say much more than that the appropriate standard of review to be applied may be more categorical than the one applied in *Shapiro* but that the test would surely be no less strict. See further ch 2 s 8.5.2 and ch 3 s 8.4.4. *Saenz* itself concerned welfare waiting-period requirements, but the decision does indicate that the new legal framework for reviewing durational residence requirements has not altered the Court's view on the constitutionality of tuition waiting-periods. More than once the Court referred to *Vlandis* and it suggested that the 'bona fide residence argument' still stands.

studies may be presumed to be free-riders. The non-fulfilment of this one-year residence rule, however, is not the real reason why 'new' bona fide residents are temporarily denied the benefit of lower resident tuition fees. This benefit is denied because newly arrived bona fide residents can only rebut the presumption of non-residency after one year of residence within the State. It is this second durational residence requirement which temporarily withholds from bona fide residents the benefit of lower in-state tuition fees and which constitutes in fact the tuition waiting-period. Why should not all students have the opportunity to demonstrate 'domiciliary intent' directly upon arrival or at any other moment they may choose? The answer to the question whether students are free-riders or bona fide residents ultimately depends on their subjective intent and does not seem in any rational way related to the time at which students are given the opportunity to demonstrate their true intentions.

8.5 Aliens

Constitutional law on cross-border access to public education, as examined so far, applies in principle equally to aliens. Aliens can be required to pay the higher out-of-state tuition fees when they have not resided in the State for at least one year and for as long as they have not established domicile in the State. Alien children can only go to school in the State where they, together with their parents, reside. This sub-Section explores the constitutionality of alienage classifications in the field of education.[281] Do States have to grant aliens access to public education and, if so, under which conditions? Can States charge aliens higher tuition fees than United States citizens on the sole ground that they lack United States citizenship? The answers to such questions vary and depend on the immigration status of the alien and the level of the education.

8.5.1 Permanent Residents

Permanently resident aliens (or immigrants) are entitled to gain access to public education under exactly the same conditions as United States citizens. Illustrative is *Nyquist v Mauclet*[282] (1977). The case concerned a New York statute that barred resident aliens from State financial assistance for higher education. Resident aliens could only become eligible for such financial assistance once they had applied for United States citizenship. Two foreign students holding permanent residence status had applied for but were refused the assistance on the ground that they were not willing to relinquish their own nationality. In reviewing the New York statute, the Supreme Court, largely following its opinion in *Graham v Richardson*,[283] held that State classifications based on alienage

---

[281] On these classifications see ch 2 s 8.7.
[282] *Nyquist v Mauclet*, 432 U.S. 1 (1977).
[283] See ch 2 s 8.5.

are 'inherently suspect and subject to close judicial scrutiny.'[284] New York sought to justify the statute *inter alia* on the ground that its purpose was to enhance the educational level of the electorate. The Court held this to be a legitimate objective but said that the objective would hardly be frustrated by including resident aliens in financial assistance programmes. Resident aliens, the Court said, are:

> obligated to pay their full share of the taxes that support the assistance programmes. There is thus no real unfairness in allowing residents aliens an equal right to participate in programs to which they contribute on an equal basis. . . . The State is surely not harmed by providing resident aliens the same educational opportunity it offers to others.[285]

In conclusion, the statute was held to violate the Equal Protection Clause. *Nyquist* was only concerned with student financial aid for higher education but the above observation puts beyond doubt that resident aliens enjoy the right to equal treatment in all educational matters. They are 'full members of society' who contribute on the same basis to the funding of public education and who, as a result, can equally benefit from public education at whatever level. Alienage classifications which deny permanent resident aliens admission to education, impose on them higher tuition fees than United States citizens or which impose additional waiting-periods are unconstitutional.[286]

8.5.2 Non-Immigrants

Non-immigrants may sometimes enjoy similar educational rights to immigrant aliens. The decision in *Toll v Moreno*[287] (1982) shows that whenever the Federal immigration authorities (implicitly) indicate that aliens have be treated equally in educational matters, States have to act accordingly. *Toll* itself involved students holding a so-called 'G–4 visa.' This was a visa issued to employees of international organisations and their family members. G–4 visaholders were in principle non-immigrants who are generally not entitled to establish domicile in the United States. The Federal authorities had, however, made an exception for G–4 visaholders. Such persons were expressly granted the right to establish domicile. In addition, the Federal authorities had granted them important tax

---

[284] *Nyquist v Mauclet*, 432 U.S. 1 (1977) at 7. The Court rejected the argument that the New York statute was not based on alienage but would only distinguish within the heterogenous class of aliens. The Court concluded, as it had also done in *Graham*, that only aliens and not United States citizens were harmed by the statute and that the statute therefore did discriminate against aliens. *Nyquist v Mauclet*, 432 U.S. 1 (1977) at 8–9.

[285] The Court also rejected the argument brought forward by the State of New York that the statute could be justified because it offered an incentive for aliens to become naturalised. Encouraging naturalisation is not a matter for the States because immigration and naturalisation are under the exclusive control of the Federal government. *Nyquist v Mauclet*, 432 U.S. 1 (1977) at 10.

[286] See further eg Maxwell, An Aliens' Constitutional Right to Loan, Scholarship and Tuition Benefits at State Supported Colleges and Universities, (1979) *CalWLRev* 514–62.

[287] *Toll v Moreno*, 458 U.S. 1 (1982).

exemptions. The purpose of this federal policy was to induce international organisations to establish themselves and to operate in the United States. The students challenged the tuition policy of the University of Maryland. Only United States citizens and permanent resident aliens were entitled to obtain residence status, whilst all non-immigrant aliens were ineligible for such status. The latter had to pay higher tuition fees. Maryland argued that the salaries of students' parents were exempt from Maryland's income tax and that the students had to pay their 'equal share' to the funding of public education in the form of higher tuition fees. The Supreme Court rejected this view. The States could not recoup indirectly the taxes that the Federal government had expressly barred the States from collecting by requiring G–4 visaholders to pay the higher out-of-state tuition fees.[288] As a general principle, the Court stated that 'state regulation not congressionally sanctioned that discriminates against aliens lawfully admitted to the country is impermissible if it imposes additional burdens not contemplated by Congress.'[289] The Court could not conclude that Congress had ever contemplated that a State could charge G–4 visa holders higher tuition fees.[290]

Generally, however, federal immigration policy gives little guidance as to whether non-immigrants have to be treated equally in educational matters. Often, preemption analysis does not enable courts to decide upon alienage classifications in education cases. They will have to resort to equal protection analysis.[291] In general, non-immigrants enjoy a less privileged status in educational matters than immigrants do. For tuition purposes States generally treat non-immigrants as non-residents who have to pay the higher out-of-state tuition fees. The decision in *Elkins v Moreno*[292] (1978) suggests that they are indeed constitutionally entitled to do so. As in the case of *Toll*, *Elkins* involved non-immigrant students holding a G–4 visa who were suing the University of Maryland. The University classed the students as non-residents on the ground that holders of G–4 visas could not be regarded as, and could not demonstrate that they are, permanent residents. The Court did not agree. The Immigration and Nationality Act did not rule out the possibility that non-immigrants could adjust their status to that of permanent residents. The Court certified the case for decision by the State court arguing that the question whether G–4 visa holders can acquire domicile in a State was ultimately a matter of State law, not of Federal law. Even though the issue was not directly addressed in *Elkins*, the opinion of the Court did seem based on the assumption that unlike permanent residents, non-immigrants can be subjected to the higher out-of-State tuition fees.

---

[288] *Ibid*, at 16.
[289] *Ibid*, at 12–13.
[290] *Ibid*, at 17. On *Toll* see further Olivas, '*Plyler v Doe*, *Toll v Moreno*, and Postsecondary Admissions: Undocumented Adults and "Enduring Disability" ', (1986) *JLE* 19–55.
[291] See ch 2 s 8.7.3.
[292] *Elkins v Moreno*, 435 U.S. 647 (1978).

8.5.3 Undocumented Aliens

In the field of primary and secondary education States have generally offered aliens' children the right to go to school in the district in which they reside. An exception, however, has occasionally been made for children of undocumented aliens. Children must be legal residents of the State, actual residence does not suffice.

The constitutionality of such lawful residence requirements was considered by the Supreme Court in *Plyler v Doe*[293] (1982). In this case the Court was asked whether the policy of Texas according to which undocumented school-age children were denied access to free public education, violated the Equal Protection Clause. Texas contended that it simply did not have to afford the same educational benefits to undocumented aliens as it does to legal residents. The denial of access would further the State's interest in preserving its limited resources for the education of its lawful residents. In reviewing the Texas statute the Supreme Court had no difficulty in concluding that undocumented aliens are entitled to the protection offered by the Equal Protection Clause.[294] The Court did not apply strict scrutiny because undocumented children, because of their illegal status, could not be treated as a suspect class and because education, as the Court had already ruled in *Rodriguez*, does not constitute a fundamental right which is able to trigger strict scrutiny on its own.[295] The Court, however, did not wish to limit itself to mere rational relation review because the case involved, on the one hand, undocumented children who could 'affect neither their parents' conduct nor their own status' and, on the other hand, concerned education which was not just 'some' governmental benefit. The Texas statute, the Court said:

> imposes a lifetime hardship on a discrete class of children not accountable for their disabling status. The stigma of illiteracy will mark them for the rest of their lives. By denying these children a basic education, we deny them the ability to live within the structure of our civic institutions, and foreclose any realistic possibility that they will contribute in even the smallest way to the progress of our Nation.[296]

---

[293] *Plyler v Doe*, 457 U.S. 202 (1982). On *Plyler* see eg Culver, Equal Protection, 'Education, and The Undocumented Alien Child: *Plyler v Doe*', (1983) *HoustLRev* 899–918; Gerety, 'Children in the Labyrinth of *Plyler v Doe*', (1983) *UpittLRev* 379–98; Hull, 'Undocumented Alien Children and Free Public Education: An Analysis of *Plyler v Doe*', (1983) *UPittLRev* 431 *et seq.*; Lichtenberg, 'Within the Pale: Aliens, Illegal Aliens, and Equal Protection', (1983) *U PittLRev* 351–77; Perry, 'Equal Protection, Judicial Activism, and the Intellectual Agenda of Constitutional Theory: Reflections on, and Beyond, *Plyler v Doe*', (1983) *UpittLRev* 329–50; Osifchok, 'The Utilization of Intermediate Scrutiny in Establishing the Right to Education for Undocumented Alien Children: *Plyler v Doe*', (1982) *PeppLRev* 139–64 and Towler, 'Does the Constitution Guarantee a Free Public Education to Undocumented Alien Children?', (1981) *BayLRev* 637–55.

[294] The Court held that 'the protection of the Fourteenth Amendment extends to any one, citizen or stranger, who *is* subject to the laws of a State . . . That a person's initial entry into a State, or into the United States, was unlawful . . . cannot negate the simple fact of his presence within the State's perimeter . . . Given such presence . . . he is entitled to the equal protection of the laws that a State may choose to establish'. *Plyler v Doe*, 457 U.S. 202 (1982) at 215.

[295] See s 8.1.

[296] *Plyler v Doe*, 457 U.S. 202 (1982) at 223.

The Court held that the Texas statute could only be upheld if shown to further a 'substantial state interest.' In response to the contention that a State like Texas would not owe the same duty to undocumented aliens as it does to legally admitted aliens, the Court said that it was in principle for the Federal authorities to determine the legal status of aliens within the country. The Court was reluctant though to:

> impute to Congress the intention to withhold from these children, for as long as they are present in this country through no fault of their own, access to a basic education . . . and we perceive no national policy that supports the State in denying these children an elementary education. The State may borrow the federal classification. But to justify its use as a criterion for its own discriminatory policy, the State must demonstrate that the classification is reasonably adapted to the 'purposes for which the state desires to use it.[297]

In answering the question whether the Texas policy furthered a substantial state interest, the Court said that a concern for the preservation of resources standing alone can hardly justify the classification used. Texas had to come with stronger justification grounds. One of the grounds that were asserted was that Texas was entitled to protect itself from an influx of illegal immigrants. The Court did not deny that States had, in spite of exclusive federal control of external borders, some power to deter the influx of undocumented aliens in order to protect the States' economy or other traditional State interests.[298] No evidence was found, however, that Texas' interests were affected. The dominant incentive for illegal entry was, as the Court said, the availability of employment. Only few, if any, illegal immigrants would come to Texas or the United States in order to gain access to education. Charging 'tuition to undocumented children constitutes a ludicrously ineffectual attempt to stem the tide of illegal immigration.'[299]

Further, Texas had suggested that the category of illegal children would impose a burden on the State's ability to provide high quality public education. The Court responded that, even if access by some children affected the quality of the education that was provided, the State had to justify its selection of the group of illegal children as the appropriate target group for exclusion from schools. Texas could not do so because the Court said that, in terms of educational cost and need illegal children were 'basically indistinguishable' from legally resident aliens.[300]

Lastly, Texas had suggested that undocumented children were less likely than other children to remain within the State and to put their education to productive social or political use within the State. The Court responded that, even if thought to be legitimate, such an interest was difficult to quantify. Apart from the fact that many of the illegal children were likely to remain within the State,

---

[297] *Ibid*, at 223.
[298] *Ibid*, at 228 (in particular n 23).
[299] *Ibid*, at 228.
[300] *Ibid*, at 230.

the Court considered it to be clear that whatever savings might be achieved by denying illegal children an education, they are 'wholly insubstantial in light of the cost involved to these children, the State, and the Nation.'[301] In conclusion, the Statute was held to be unconstitutional.

Children of undocumented aliens thus have to be granted access to public primary and secondary education and, possibly, higher education.[302] It is doubtful whether a similar conclusion could be reached as regards undocumented aliens' themselves. In *Plyler* the Court said that 'persuasive arguments support the view that a State may withhold its beneficence from those whose very presence within the United States is the product of their own unlawful conduct' and that 'those who elect to enter our country by stealth and in violation of our law should be prepared to bear the consequences, including, but not limited to, deportation.'[303] Aliens who enter the United States illegally, can thus probably be denied access to public education.[304]

8.6 Conclusions

The main rules and principles governing cross-border access to education within the United States have hardly altered in the course of the last decades. The Supreme Court has left the States' traditional admission policies largely untouched. In the field of higher education, States are still entitled to (*i*) charge non-residents higher tuition fees, (*ii*) to class the category of so-called free-riders as non-residents for tuition purposes and (*iii*) to charge bona fide residents out-of-state tuition fees when they have not resided in the State for one year prior to their studies. The only limitations the Court has imposed on States are (*i*) that bona fide residents must be given the opportunity to rebut the presumption of non-residence after a reasonable period of time (one year) and (*ii*) that aliens who have been allowed by the Federal immigration authorities to establish domicile in the United States, must be treated equally with United States citizens. In the area of primary and secondary education, the Court has given constitutional approval to the classic policies according to which children can only go to school in the district, and thus the State, in which they reside. The sole adjustment the Court has made is that all children, including undocumented

---

[301] *Plyler v Doe*, 457 U.S. 202 (1982), at 230.

[302] Brinkac, 'Should Undocumented Aliens be Eligible for Resident Tuition Status at State Universities?', (1986) *SanDiegoLRev* 467–84, who argues that children of undocumented aliens should be eligible for the lower in-State tuition.

[303] *Plyler v Doe*, 457 U.S. 202 (1982) at 219–20.

[304] Recently, the legal status of undocumented aliens in the field of education again attracted considerable attention when Proposition 187 was passed in California. The Proposition denies undocumented aliens a variety of public benefits including public elementary and secondary education. The denial of access to public education is hard to compare with *Plyler*. See further Schuler, 'Equal Protection and the Undocumented Immigrant: California's Proposition 187', (1996) *BostCTWLJ* 275–312.

aliens' children, who actually reside in a given district/State must be admitted to schools in the district in which they reside.

Since the admission policies of the American States have largely survived constitutional challenges, it is not surprising that the subject of cross-border access to public education has never triggered many debates in the United States. The main issues that have been the subject of debate concerned the implications for the field education of decisions in other policy areas such as welfare. Nonetheless, the lack of attention paid to the subject is somewhat surprising. Some of the reasoning and conclusions of the Supreme Court are not as obvious as they appear. This not only holds true for the conclusion that tuition waiting-period requirements are constitutional,[305] but also, for instance, for judicial approval of differential tuition policies.[306] The Court has never said much more than that States must have a substantial reason for charging non-residents higher tuition fees and that differential tuition policies, 'while perhaps "protectionistic" in a loose sense, reflect the essential and patently unobjectionable purpose of state government—to serve the citizens of the state.'[307] *Saenz*, however, indicates that tuition residence requirements are subject to scrutiny under the Privileges and Immunities Clause of Article IV section 2. If the Clause's 'substantial reason test' as developed in areas other than education were actually to be applied, it might be questioned whether tuition residence requirements could withstand scrutiny. Would funding and organisation be affected if non-residents were not, or could not, be charged additional tuition fees? Arguably, this would only be the case where States are confronted with an influx of non-resident students whose numbers (far) exceed the number of residents who move to other States in order to obtain education. In particular, States which may be regarded as net-exporters of students do not seem to have any substantive reason for charging incoming students higher tuition fees.[308] Furthermore, why has the Court accepted that non-resident children can be denied admission to public schools altogether? In *Martinez* the Court merely applied rational relation scrutiny. It may not indeed be wholly arbitrary to deny children whose parents have not contributed to the funding of public education through the payment of taxes admission to schools and it may be true that 'the proper planning and operation of the schools would suffer significantly' if bona fide residence requirements were not applied. Yet, could this planning and operation not be protected by merely charging non-residents higher tuition fees or by applying

---

[305] See s 8.4.

[306] Compare Coenen, 'State User Fees and the Dormant Commerce Clause', (1997) *VdbiltLRev* 795–842, at 807 (n 60).

[307] *Reeves, Inc. v State*, 447 U.S. 429 (1980) at 443.

[308] Compare Clarke, 'Validity of Discriminatory Nonresident Tuition Charges in Public Higher Education under The Privileges and Immunities Clause', (1971) *NebLRev* 31–64 who has argued (before *Vlandis*) that a State must give 'full' equal access to non-resident students to the extent that it has surplus educational facilities. In this author's view, States have surplus facilities and for this reason there would be no need to charge non-residents higher tuition.

non-resident admission quota? Why did the Court not apply the 'rational relation test' with some 'more bite'?

More questions could be raised, but the point to be made is that the conclusions drawn by the Court in cases concerning cross-border access to public
education sit uneasily with the more general case law. Arguably, if the Court
had applied the general principles on the right to travel and the right to equal
treatment in other States[309] as developed in fields other than education, it might
have reached different conclusions. This is not so much meant as a criticism, or
as a call upon the Supreme Court to move away from some of its conclusions,
but merely intended to demonstrate that the Supreme Court has taken quite a
lax and deferential attitude *vis-à-vis* States. Why has the Court been so lenient
towards States? Why has the Court not taken an affirmative stance against discriminatory State policies as it has done in the field of welfare? Why has the
Supreme Court not been as active in the field of education as the European
Court of Justice?

It is not possible to give a single definite answer to these questions, but various factors may help to explain the Court's approach. The Court's observation
that differential tuition policies 'reflect the essential and patently unobjectionable purpose of state government—to serve the citizens of the state'[310] suggests
that the explanation for the Court's reluctance to impose limits on the States'
powers derives from the legal-political structure of the American federal Union.
In the constitutional framework, States are not viewed as 'conveniently local
administrative departments of the national government designed to assist in the
implementation of national policy.' Rather, they are seen as governmental
entities, which hold independent lawmaking powers aimed at the provision of
public benefits and services within their territory.[311] This power, so it has been
argued, not only provides the basis for the right of States to exclude non-
residents from public services when, or in as far as, this is necessary for upholding these services. The range of this lawmaking power goes even further
to provide the rule that in principle States can preserve public benefits for their
residents. Like other groups

> free to combine their members' efforts to produce collective benefits to be shared among
> the group, political communities, including states, have a prima facie justification for
> limiting distribution of their public goods to those who combined to provide them.[312]

This view of States and their constitutional position in the Federal Union, however, merely explains the Court's reluctance to impose limits on States' powers

---

[309] See ch 2 s 8.

[310] *Reeves, Inc. v State*, 447 U.S. 429 (1980) at 443.

[311] Varat, 'State Citizenship' and Interstate Equality', (1981) *UChicLRev* 487–571, at 520.

[312] *Ibid*, at 523. The 'reality of the existence of states qua states, rather than as departments of a
national government, requires a conception that the state's citizens own state-owned resources, and
that a state is not required to share its treasury with the nation at large'. Cohen, 'Equal Treatment
for Newcomers: The Core Meaning of National and State Citizenship', (1984) *ConstComm* 9–19,
at 17.

to discriminate against non-residents. It does not explain why the Court has accepted that students who are bona fide residents must submit proof of their status, and only become entitled to lower in-State tuition fees, after one year of residence nor does the above view explain why aliens who have lived in the United States for many years without having acquired permanent resident status can be required to pay higher out-of-State tuition fees.

It is hard to establish the Court's genuine motives, but the case law suggests that the Court's deferential attitude towards States is also, if not primarily, prompted by practical reasons. States' admission policies in the field of education have never been perceived as unfair, inefficient or overly protectionist. The public school systems have been subject of many debates, but criticism has primarily been focused on the disparity in the quality in the different districts/States, not on the fact that children cannot attend schools in other districts or States. The quality of education offered to children in 'poorer' districts should be improved by changes to the funding systems, not by granting such children a right to gain access to schools in other districts/States. Children should have a right to quality education in the district in which they, together with their parents, reside. Increasing the inter-district mobility of pupils has never been seen as a means of improving the quality of education of 'poor' pupils. If anything, such mobility is seen as a threat to the quality of public school systems.

The reverse seems to be the case, however, in the area of higher education. Increasing the possibility of studying at universities or colleges in other States has always been, and still is, seen as a valuable objective. It enables students to choose among a larger number of colleges, universities and courses and in this way increases the knowledge and professional skills of the American population. Where States have always attempted to discourage indigents from exercising their right to travel, they have always accepted and even promoted inter-State student mobility. They have never discouraged residents from studying in other States and have accepted that residents of other States will come to study at their State universities. Charging non-residents enables States to protect their educational systems and has never been proven to obstruct or hinder inter-State student mobility. The motive for applying waiting-period requirements may not be very persuasive, but it must be noted that, unlike welfare waiting-periods, tuition waiting-period requirements have never been imposed in order to discourage freedom of movement and they do not deny admission to education itself. Generally, differential tuition policies are considered to strike a fair balance between the national interest in inter-State student or pupil mobility and the States' interest in maintaining adequate systems of higher education. Thus, where the European Court has been faced with Member States which were quite protectionistic and reluctant to promote student mobility, the Supreme Court has never been in a position where it saw a need to take steps to ensure that individuals can move to and gain access to education in other States. A free movement of students has always existed and the opinions of the Court suggest that it simply did not wish to intervene in practices and policies which 'did not seem to bother anybody' and which did not seem to seriously obstruct any valuable constitutional goal.

9.1 Introduction

Returning to the European Community, it may be recalled that the Community has achieved much in promoting cross-border access to education in the last two decades. In the original EEC Treaty no mention was made of educational rights for workers and the free movement of students was not provided for. Today, Community law confers upon all Community citizens a right to gain access to education in other Member States and for many of them this includes a right to claim student grants in those States.

Nonetheless, Community law on cross-border access to education, as it stands today, is still debated. This particularly holds true for the category of the Community students, ie, Community citizens who move to other Member States for the sole purpose of studying there and who do not fall within the scope of the provisions on the free movement of workers.[313] On the one hand, it is claimed that Community law does not give sufficient regard to the educational and financial interests of Member States. Some Member States 'import' more students than they 'export.' The imbalances in student movements would constitute a significant burden on the resources of some Member States[314] for which they should be compensated. On the other hand, it is claimed that there are still too many obstacles to cross-border access to education. In particular, free-movers, ie, Community students who study in other Member States outside the context of the *Socrates/Erasmus* programme, still face many obstacles. The question is where to go from here. Should future activities be focussed on the protection of the educational and financial interests of Member States who receive more students than they 'send' abroad or should emphasis be placed on the promotion of student mobility? Or, ideally, is it possible to combine both efforts? Given the fact that some educational systems have a stronger magnetic effect on students than others, is it possible to alter the current legal rules with a view to increasing student mobility while giving full respect to the educational interests of Member States? Can some lessons be learned in this regard from the United States?

---

[313] See ss 4.11 and 7.
[314] O'Leary (1996) n 4 above, at 171.

9.2 Free Movement of Students versus the Protection of Educational Systems

In exploring how the conflict between the objective of promoting the free movement of students,[315] on the one hand, and the need to safeguard the educational interests of the Member States, on the other hand, could be settled more satisfactorily, one could approach the conflict from a political-economic perspective. As in the case of minimum subsistence benefits,[316] elements of theories on fiscal federalism may be of help[317]

9.2.1 Race to the Bottom Hypothesis

One of the commonly cited advantages of a federal or multi-level system of government is that it allows for a decentralised supply of public benefits. Decentralisation enables the federal entity to respond to the different preferences which citizens in the various States, or other local governmental entities, may have for public services. In every State citizen-voters can make collective choices as to what public benefits will be made available, what the 'quality' of these benefits should be, how public benefit systems must be organised and how much taxes have to be paid in order to finance these benefits. The advantages of decentralisation are particularly relevant for the organisation of education in an entity like the European Community where the financial means available for, and the views on how to organise, education differ so considerably.

Fiscal federalism theories start from the presumption that freedom of movement is guaranteed among local government entities. On the one hand, freedom of movement is positively valued. According to the so-called Tiebout-hypothesis, the right to move elsewhere enables individuals 'to vote on their feet.'[318] Individuals who prefer public benefits such as public education of a comparatively high quality, and who are willing to pay the 'price' in the form of comparatively high taxes, are able to move to a State where such a pattern has been

---

[315] In recent years (as regards the initial years see n 120) Community institutions have frequently stated that the promotion of student mobility constitutes a key role in the common educational and vocational training policies. See eg the Recommendaton of the European Parliament and of the Council of 10 July 2001 on mobility within the Community for students, persons undergoing training, young volunteers, teachers and trainers (OJ 2001 L 215); the Resolution of the Council and of Representatives of the Governments of the Member States, Meeting within the Council of 14 December 2000 Concerning an Action Plan for Mobility (OJ 2000 C 371); the Bologna Declaration on the European Space for Higher Education (http://europa.eu.int/comm/education), the Green Paper of the European Commission mentioned in s 4.11, the Council conclusions of 27 November 1992 (OJ 1992 C 336) and the Council Resolution of 24 May 1988 (OJ 1988 C 177).

[316] See ch 3 s 9.2.

[317] On theories on the economics of federalism (or fiscal federalism) see eg Hyman, *Public Finance—A Contemporary Application of Theory to Policy* (1999) ch 18; Rosen, *Public Finance* (1985) ch 19; Due/Friedländer, *Government Finance* (1977) 456 *et seq.*; Musgrave/Musgrave, *Public Finance in Theory and Practice* (1976) and Oates, *Fiscal Federalism* (1972).

[318] Tiebout, 'A Pure Theory of Local Expenditures', (1956) *JPolEc* 416 *et seq.*

selected. Others who are not willing to pay such a price, may move to States where the quality of public education and taxes are lower. On the other hand, the theories warn of the possible negative implications for the right to freedom of movement. Inter-State mobility may be a threat to the efficient supply of public benefits such as education. The social benefits of the States' investments in education may spill over to other States. Upon graduation, students may decide to work in other States and use their knowledge and skills in, and to the benefit of the economies of, other States. A full freedom of movement may even enable students to move to other States for the sole purpose of receiving education and then to leave the State once they have finished their studies. Such 'free-riding students' are neither before nor after their studies fully taxable in the States of their studies and the economies of the States concerned do not benefit from the investment made in educating these students. Fiscal federalism theories teach that public benefits can only be efficiently provided for at local level if the persons who make the collective choices are also the ones who finance and consume the benefits.[319] In the area of education, the group of consumers, i.e., the students, will often not coincide with the group of contributors, i.e., the taxpayers. In the case of free-riding students, the necessary coincidence of consumers and contributors may even be virtually absent.

Spill over effects, or negative externalities, could possibly trigger a 'race to the bottom.' Consider the following model. State A is grouped together with several other States in federal entity X. State A has to make a decision as to the nature and quality of its educational system. If State A were to opt for high quality, and thus rather expensive, education, it would have to levy high taxes. If it were to do so, State A might attract students from other States seeking high quality education. The more 'free-riding' students who come from other States, the greater the pressure on the funding of the educational system. Should the net-inflow of non-contributing benefit recipients prove to be considerable, State A might have to choose either to decrease its investment in education or to increase its tax rates. If State A were to choose the latter option, taxpaying citizens might move to other States leading to a reduction in tax revenues. In order to avoid such a situation, State A might decide in advance not to spend too much on education in the hope that 'free-riding' students from other States will move to State B. If State A did indeed choose to do so, it would indirectly increase the magnetic effect of the benefit scheme in State B. This State would be faced with problems comparable to those which State A initially encountered and State B might decide to lower educational investment to reach a level lower than that of State C in the hope that free-riders would move to C. State C might respond similarly and try to shift the burden to State D. The fear of becoming an educational magnet could trigger competition between States lowering investment in education

---

[319] Ideally, there should be a 'triple identity' of 'voters', 'contributors' and 'consumers'. See Scholsem, 'A Propos de la Circulation des Etudiants: Vers un Federalisme Financier Européen?', (1989) CDE 306–23, at 309–10.

in the hope that other States will educate students. This competition may result in a downward movement, 'a race to the bottom,' leading to a decrease in educational investment in the entire federal entity X.

9.2.2 A Race to the Bottom in the European Community?

Fiscal federalism theories teach us that when negative external effects occur, measures have to be taken to internalise these effects. Before considering what such measures might entail, the question needs to be addressed whether there is actually a need to take such measures within the European Community. The 'race to the bottom hypothesis' is based on a number of assumptions some of which do not necessarily hold true in practice, and in European practice in particular. An initial assumption is that students are mobile and that they move to the States where the best, and often the most expensive education, is offered. European students, however, do not seem as mobile as free-riders in the above described model. Mobility is severely restricted by linguistic barriers, problems concerning the recognition of diplomas and the lack of sufficient student financial aid. Also, the quality of educational systems does not seem to be the main criterion which European students apply when choosing the State in which they study. Practice demonstrates that the main criterion European students apply is knowledge of the language of the State concerned or in which the courses are taught[320] and this explains why the big language countries, i.e., the United Kingdom, France and, to a lesser extent, Belgium, especially are faced with a net-import of students.

A second assumption on which the above model of a race to the bottom is based, is that Member States actually limit investment in education in order to avoid becoming educational magnets. This assumption does not seem to hold true, however. Decisions concerning the quality of and investment in education are not primarily, or at least not solely, made on the basis of student mobility figures. There are no indications that the mentioned three countries have ever raised, or will raise, taxes or reduce educational investment in response to an influx of foreign students. Generally, States attach great importance to, and often take pride in, making available high quality education and public schools and universities are important providers of employment which play a significant economic role in the communities in which where they are established.[321]

A third assumption is that taxpayers might leave a State if, due to an expected increase in educational costs caused by an influx of foreign students, tax-rates were actually raised. Statistics or scientific proof to support this point does not seem to be available, but it is doubtful whether individuals or companies will leave the Member State in which they reside or are established when they have

---

[320] See House of Lords—Select Committee on European Communities (1998–1999) n 182 above at point 84 (Professor Teichler) and Gordon/Jallade (1996) n 211 above, at 137.
[321] von Wilmowsky (1991) n 159 above, at 265–66.

to pay more taxes in order to maintain the quality of education. For many tax-payers, high quality education, from which they themselves can also benefit, would seem to be one of those public benefits to which they are willing to contribute by paying taxes. The reverse might even be the case. Even if this were to lead to a higher tax-burden, companies might move to States with comparatively well-developed educational systems because they may need highly educated employees.

The significance of the above model for the European Community thus seems rather limited. European students are not as mobile as the Tiebout-hypothesis assumes and even if student mobility was to increase in future years, an educational race to the bottom is unlikely to occur. In fact, it could be argued that the problems which some Member States face are not caused by student mobility but rather by 'student immobility.' In the United Kingdom, for instance, it has been recognised that the imbalance in students movements, and the resulting financial burden, is not only caused by the number of foreign students attending British universities but also, if not primarily, by the small number of British students studying at foreign universities. In principle, foreign students are 'more than welcome' in the United Kingdom. Financial and educational problems do not necessarily have to be dealt with by discouraging foreign students or asking for some kind of compensation. They could just as well be tackled by encouraging more British students to study abroad.[322]

In principle, there seem to be no compelling reasons why one should not consider how student mobility could be further promoted. In Section 9.3 a few options will be discussed. Nonetheless, the relevance of fiscal federalism theories cannot be dismissed altogether. Applied to the European Community, the above described model may be seen as a warning that one cannot wholly ignore the position of States which are 'net-importers' of students while promoting student mobility. A mismatch between 'contributors' to and 'beneficiaries' of educational systems may cause funding or capacity problems for some States which may occur when initiatives for promoting student mobility prove to be successful. In Section 9.4 a few observations will therefore be made as to how the financial and/or educational interests of these States could be safeguarded.

---

[322] Compare the discussion in House of Lords—Select Committee on European Communities (1998) n 182 above, at points 64–96. The various points raised in the discussion primarily concerned *Erasmus* students and it was admitted that the problems concerning the imbalance in student movements might be somewhat different and more worrying as regards as the category of 'free-movers'. Nonetheless, the *rationale* of the argument that the problems could just as well, and preferably, be dealt with by promoting mobility of British students, would also seem to apply to free-movers.

9.3 Options for Promoting Student Mobility

9.3.1 Introduction

Community citizens who wish to study in other Member States outside the framework of the *Erasmus/Socrates* programme still face a number of obstacles. As both the Commission[323] and the Council[324] have indicated, these include, in particular, a lack of knowledge of the language in which courses are taught, problems concerning the recognition of diplomas or other qualifications acquired in the Member State of origin, the absence of a right to student grants covering the cost of maintenance and issues relating to the financial means requirement contained in Directive No 93/96.

This section does not consider how the first two obstacles could be minimised or eliminated. By promoting the teaching and dissemination of the European languages, and the 'small languages' in particular, the Community could facilitate student mobility[325] and possibly reduce the problems caused by the imbalance in student movements. Yet, in order to achieve this, the legal rules and principles governing the free movement of students do not need to be altered. The necessary policy measures will have to take the form of some kind of financial incentive for Member States which can be taken within the current legal framework. The same would seem to hold true for problems concerning academic recognition of diplomas. National rules concerning such recognition may run counter to the Treaty's free movement and nondiscriminating provisions, but they may be justified for educational reasons.[326] Rules or practices which can pass judicial scrutiny will have to be tackled by the political Community institutions that only hold the power to support and supplement 'the action of the Member States through the adoption of incentive measures.'[327] Both the language and the diploma obstacles to student mobility are intrinsically linked with the substance of education itself and will ultimately be lessened by encouraging voluntary action by Member States rather than by restricting their educational powers.

Arguably, however, the approach to be followed may differ as regards the 'student financial aid obstacle' and the financial means requirement. Student grants and other forms of financial aid do not relate directly to or affect the

---

[323] See n 216 above.

[324] See n 217 above.

[325] See Art 149(1) EC. The Community has already taken various initiatives to promote language learning within its *Erasmus*, *Comenius* and *Grundtvig* programs as well as the specific language programme *Lingua*. In addition, 2001 has been proclaimed as the European Year of Languages which is described as 'a celebration of Europe's linguistic diversity' and which promotes language learning and related skills through various activities. For an overview of the various activities see http://europa.eu.int/comm/education/languages.

[326] See s 4.5.

[327] See Art 149(1) EC. Compare also Recommendation of the European Parliament and of the Council of 10 July 2001 on mobility within the Community for students, persons undergoing training, young volunteers, teachers and trainers. OJ 2001 L 215.

substance of education itself. In order to promote the mobility of European students, one could consider tackling these obstacles by developing 'hard' legal rules.

9.3.2 Student Grants

9.3.2.1 Introduction

At the present stage of Community law, 'free movers' only have a limited right to student grants. These Community students cannot benefit from grants made available under the *Erasmus-Socrates* programme, they can only claim limited grants in the State where they study and, due to territorial restrictions contained in national laws, they usually are not entitled to transfer student grants abroad. In principle, the costs of maintenance must be borne by the students themselves or their parents and this may, for students from low-income families in particular, constitute an obstacle to studying abroad.

In order to surmount this obstacle, one could consider imposing the burden of having to bear maintenance costs on an 'actor' other than the students or their parents. The most logical candidate[328] is the State where students live prior to commencement of studies in another Member State. It is this State where taxes have usually been paid, to which students will often return upon graduation and it is this State which is most likely to benefit from the skills and knowledge obtained by the students. More specifically, one could consider the option[329] of making student grants exportable.[330]

In doing so, it is worthwhile recalling[331] that student grants are only one means of making education financially accessible. An alternative means, for

---

[328] Two alternatives could be considered. The first would be the State where students are attending a course of education. Arguably, this option should be rejected. If the host State had to bear the costs of both Community students' education and the costs of their maintenance, it might attract so many students from countries where no or less developed financial aid schemes exist, that their student grant schemes could be seriously affected. Compare the comments made in s 4.3.

A second candidate could be the Community itself. For instance, one could explore whether 'Action 2' of the *Erasmus-Socrates* programme (see s 4.9) could be extended to 'free-movers' or whether a common student financial aid scheme taking the form of a loan scheme could be established. Given the financial and administrative implications, however, it would seem that the chances of having such proposals adopted, are quite small.

[329] In the alternative, one could consider setting up some kind of reimbursement scheme under which the host State would be obliged to give Community students 'full' student grants under the same conditions as national students and which would impose on the State of origin a duty to reimburse the host State for the costs incurred. The prospects for introducing such a scheme, however, seem remote. Students might move to States with the most generous aid systems with the possible result that the total amount to be spend on student grants in the Community would increase. Ultimately, the financial burden would be imposed on the 'poorer' States which could be faced with additional expenditure. These States may not be able to bear this financial burden or prefer to spend the amounts involved in (further) developing (their) own student financial schemes.

[330] In its 1996 Green Paper on the obstacles to student mobility the European Commission took the view that there is indeed 'room for greater transferability of grants'. European Commission, Green Paper on 'Education, Training, Research' (1996) n 216 above, at 24 and 29.

[331] See s 2.1.

which quite a few Member States have opted, consists of offering financial aid to students' parents in the form of family benefits or child allowances. Regulation No 1408/71 contains various provisions which intend to co-ordinate national family benefit and child allowance schemes in order to avoid Community citizens being deterred from exercising their free movement rights because of a possible loss of such benefits or allowances.[332] The main rule is laid down in Article 73 which provides that workers subject to the legislation of a Member State are entitled to family benefits for children who are residing in the territory of another Member State. The benefits must be paid at the rate applicable in the State of employment, even when living costs in the State where the children are living, and/or studying, are lower.[333] Thus, children of workers who are subject to legislation in a Member State where financial aid for children who are studying is given in the form of family benefits, are indirectly entitled to public financial support regardless of the Member States where they reside or study. Indirect student financial aid can be exported.[334]

At the present stage of Community law, the same conclusion cannot yet be drawn as regards direct student financial aid. In cases like *Matteucci*, *di Leo*, *Bernini* and *Meeusen*[335] the Court may have extended the possibility of workers and their family members to obtain student grants for studies abroad, but in at least two[336] respects the current rules applicable to student grants are still more restrictive than the rule contained in Article 73 of Regulation No 1408/71.

First, workers and their family members are only entitled to grants for foreign studies under Article 7(2) of Regulation No 1612/68 where the host State has given its own nationals such a right. Ultimately, it is still up to the Member States to decide whether or not student grants can be transferred abroad. In principle, direct student financial aid is not exportable.

Secondly, Article 7(2) can only be invoked by those who hold the status of Community worker or family member of a Community worker in another Member State. Article 73 of Regulation No 1408/71, however, can also be relied

---

[332] Compare Case C–228/88 *Bronzino* [1990] ECR I–531 at 12. For a brief introduction to this Regulation and the implementing Regulation No 574/72 see ch 2 s 6.

[333] Case 41/84 *Pinna* [1986] ECR 1 at 23–24.

[334] The Court's ruling in *Vestergaard* suggests that Member States are neither entitled to restrict tax-benefits, which are offered in order to reduce the financial burden of studying children, to tax-payers whose children are studying at an educational institution on the national territory. In this case the Court concluded that the Danish legislation on income tax violated Art 49 EC Treaty in as far as it, for the purposes of deducting costs relating to participation in professional training, made a distinction between courses organised on the national territory and courses organised in other Member States. Case C–55/98 *Vestergaard* [1998] ECR I–741.

[335] See ss 3.2.2 and 3.3.2.

[336] Further, it may be recalled that *Bernini* and *Meeusen* do not exclude the possibility that children of frontier workers can still be denied student grants in the State of employment on the ground that they do not live in that State's territory. Residence requirements may run counter to Art 7(2), but, as stated in s 3.2.3, the Court has so far never held that this provision precludes residence requirements for student grants and other benefits granted by virtue on the national territory. On the legality of residence requirements for public benefits granted by virtue of residence on the national territory see further ch 6 s 3.

upon by workers who have never exercised their free movement rights and who wish to claim in their own State financial aid for children who are residing and studying in another Member States.[337]

The four judgments referred to, however, do show that the Community rules governing entitlement to student grants for foreign studies are evolving and that these rules show more and more resemblance to the Article 73-rule for family benefits.[338] The question arises whether this development can be taken one step further to make student grants exportable too. When indirect student financial aid can be transferred abroad, why should the same not hold true for direct student aid? The recent judgment in *Fahmi and Esmoris Cerdeiro-Pinedo Amado* (2001) demonstrates that it is indeed pertinent to raise the question.

9.3.2.2 *Fahmi and Esmoris Cerdeiro-Pinedo Amado*

Until 1986 the Netherlands offered financial aid for children who were studying in the form of child allowances. The 1962 General Law on Dependent Children's Allowances (Algemene Kinderbijslagwet—AKW) entitled insured persons to a child allowance for children who were dependent on them, aged between 16 and 27 years and who devoted the main part of their time to studies or related activities. From October 1986, however, the AKW was amended by the Law on Study Finance (Wet op de Studiefinanciering—WSF) which gave children between the ages of 18 and 27 a right to study finance consisting of a basic grant, the level of which was independent of the parents' income and the same for all students receiving a particular type of education and a supplementary grant and/or loan, the level of which varied according to parental income. The motive behind the WSF was to enable students to be financially independent of their parents, to ensure equal treatment for students and to enhance the status of students.[339] The WSF conferred the right to study finance on Dutch nationals and foreign nationals residing in the Netherlands who were studying at Dutch universities or one of the few foreign universities which, for student grant purposes, have been put on a par with Dutch educational institutions. The latter condition was imposed because the number and variety of educational facilities and courses in the Netherlands were deemed sufficient and the Netherlands Minister for Education lacked powers to impose conditions

---

[337] See eg Case C–194/96 *Kulzer* [1998] ECR I–921 at 27–31.

[338] Compare the Opinion of Advocate General La Pergola in Case C–337/97 *Meeusen* [1999] ECR I–3289 at 19. On the comparison between the rules governing family benefits and student grants see also Steinmeyer, Familienleistungen und Ausbildungsförderung, in: *Deutschen Sozialrechtsverbandes, Europäisches Sozialrecht* (1992) 169–92.

[339] Case C–33/99 *Fahmi and Esmoris Cerdeiro-Pinedo Amado* [2001] ECR I–2415 at 10. On *Fahmi* see eg van der Mei, 'Freedom of Movement and Financial Aid for Students: Some Reflections on *Grzelczyk* and *Fahmi and Esmoris-Cerdeiro Pinedo Amodo*', (2001) *EJSS* 181–207 and van der Mei, 'Vrij Verkeer van Studenten en Export van Studiefinanciering', (2001) *USZ* 606–11.

regarding the quality of education in other States.[340] The new arrangements did not become applicable with immediate effect. The WSF of 1986 contained a transitional arrangement according to which child allowances could still be obtained for children who were studying aged between 18 and 27 years. In 1996 this arrangement was amended as to limit entitlement to child allowances for student children who were already entitled to such an allowance and who continued to follow the same type of education as they had been following on 1 October 1995.

The 1996 amendment worked out negatively for Mr Fahmi, a Moroccan national, and Mrs Esmoris Cerdeiro-Pinedo Amado, a Spanish national, who had worked and lived in the Netherlands. After having become unfit for work, they both the decided to return to their State of origin. They both continued to receive an allowance for incapacity for work by virtue of which they were entitled to child allowances for their children who had returned with them. The competent Dutch social security institution, however, refused to pay allowances for the last quarter of 1996, and in the case of Mrs Esmoris also the first quarter of 1997, on the ground that the children, upon completion of their secondary education, had commenced in 1996 courses of higher education in Morocco and Spain respectively. The children no longer met the condition of the 1996 transitional arrangement for child allowances. Mr Fahmi and Mrs Esmoris appealed the decision to refuse them payment of the child allowance in a Dutch court, which decided to refer the case for preliminary ruling to the Court of Justice. In brief, the Dutch court wished to know whether the replacement of a right to child allowances for children who were studying with a right to student grants is compatible with Community law where the effect of this replacement is that persons like Mr Fahmi and Mrs Esmoris Cerdeiro-Pinedo Amado are deprived of financial aid for their student children.

The Court did not review the two-step legislative process in its entirety. It judged the old rules for child allowances and the new rules applicable to student grants separately. As regards the abolition of child allowances, the Court held that Member States are free to organise their social security systems in the way they deem appropriate and that there was nothing that indicated infringements of Community law.[341]

As regards the Dutch law on student grants, the Court made a distinction between Mr Fahmi and Mrs Esmoris. As to the claim of the former, the Court

---

[340] Kamerstukken, II 1985/86, 19 125, nr.6, at 30–31. For the latter reason, the Netherlands Minister of Education has been willing to offer student grants to nationals and residents of the Netherlands who are following studies in other Member States which have been the subject of harmonisation measures within the framework of 'vertical' directives on the mutual recognition of diplomas for, in particular, the medical professions. See n 22 above. However, studies falling within the scope of the 'horizontal' Directive No 89/48 on the mutual recognition of diplomas, which is not based on a prior harmonisation of educational systems, have not been put on a par with recognised institutions on the national territory. Stb, 1990, 660.

[341] Case C–33/99 *Fahmi and Esmoris Cerdeiro-Pinedo Amado* [2001] ECR I–2415 at 26–27.

could be rather brief. As a third country national, Mr Fahmi could not benefit from Regulation No 1408/71 on the co-ordination of social security schemes. The sole provision that he could possibly invoke, was Article 41 of the EC-Morocco Cooperation Agreement. This Article provides for a right to equal treatment in social security matters (paragraph 1) and a right to family allowances for children residing within the Community (paragraph 3).[342] The Court did not go into the question whether student grants could possibly be classified as a social security benefit or family allowance for the purposes of Article 41 of the Agreement. The purpose of the Corporation Agreement, the Court held, was to consolidate the position of Moroccan workers and their family members living with them in the host Member State. Both from the wording and the spirit of Article 41 it followed that provision can only be invoked by workers and their family members when the latter are residing within the Community.[343]

In the case of Esmoris, the Court considered whether the Dutch rule that student grants are in principle only offered to students pursuing studies within Dutch territory is compatible with Article 3 or any other provision of Regulation No 1408/71 and Article 7(2) of Regulation No 1612/68.[344] The Court rephrased the preliminary questions in order to limit them to the specific situation of the plaintiff. The Court held that pensioners like Mrs Esmoris cannot claim student grants under Regulation No 1408/71. Pensioners do not fall within the scope of Article 73 of Regulation No 1408/71. They can only rely on Article 77 which, in brief, provides that pensioners are entitled to 'family allowances' in the State where they draw a pension irrespective of the Member State in whose territory they or their children are residing. According to Article 1(u)(ii) of Regulation No 1408/71, 'family allowances' only cover benefits granted exclusively by reference to the number and, where appropriate, the age of members of the family.[345] Student grants, the Court concluded, do not fall within that definition.

Neither could Article 7(2) of Regulation No 1612/68 be of help to persons like Mrs Esmoris Article 7(2) is intended to facilitate freedom of movement by eliminating obstacles to the integration of workers and their families in the State of employment. The Court concluded that, as a general rule and except in special circumstances, the nondiscrimination rule of Article 7(2) cannot be extended to workers who, after ceasing all occupational activity in the host State, have decided to return their State of origin.[346]

---

[342] See ch 2 s 6 and ch 3 s 5.2.

[343] Case C–33/99 *Fahmi and Esmoris Cerdeiro-Pinedo Amado* [2001] ECR I–2415 at 55–57.

[344] *Ibid*, at 27. The fact that most questions submitted by the national court concerned the Dutch rules on student grants, whilst Mrs. Esmoris had started the case on the basis of the law governing child allowances, was no reason for the Court to deny admissibility. *Ibid*, at 28–29.

[345] *Ibid*, at 35.

[346] *Ibid*, at 47–51. Workers who have stopped working altogether and have decided to return to the State of origin can claim under Article 7(2) only rights or benefits which are linked to the previous occupational activity. Case C–43/99 *Leclere* [2001] ECR I–4265 at 57–58 and Case C–389/99 *Rundgren* [2001] ECR I–3731 at 34.

9.3.2.3 *Right to Export Student grants?*

In view of the specific facts of the case, there was indeed no real need for the Court to answer the question of whether national rules limiting the export of maintenance grants are compatible with Community law. The case does indicate, however, that it is pertinent to raise the question and the careful way in which the Court avoided going into the issue, suggests that the legality of such rules, at the very least, cannot be automatically assumed. Such rules might run counter to various provisions of Community law.

9.3.2.3.1 Article 73 of Regulation No 1408/71

A first provision concerns Article 73 of Regulation No 1408/71. If student grants could be classified as family benefits in the sense of Article 1(u)(i) of this regulation, virtually all Community students would be entitled to claim grants for studies in other Member States. *Fahmi* does not exclude such a conclusion. The Court concluded that student grants cannot be regarded as 'family allowances' for the purposes of Article 77 of Regulation No 1408/71, but, without being asked, it added that there was no need to determine whether grants can be classified as 'family benefits.'[347] Nonetheless, it does not seem very likely that student grants can be regarded as family benefits. Article 1(u)(i) of Regulation No 1408/71 defines 'family benefits' as 'all benefits in kind or in cash intended to meet family expenses under the legislation provided for under Article 4(1)(h).' In many Member States entitlement to student grants is made dependent on the income of parents and it could thus be argued that such grants are aimed at meeting family expenses.[348] Many benefits, however, meet family expenses, but this does not imply that they can all be classified as family benefits for that reason alone. Article 1(u)(i) provides that family benefits are all benefits in kind or in cash that intend to meet family expenses 'under the legislation provided for in Article 4(1)(h).' The latter provision includes 'family benefits.' This is not, as Advocate General Jacobs observed in *Leclere* (2001), as circular as it seems. The rider in Article 1(u)(i) simply makes clear that there is more to being a family benefit than being intended to meet family expenses.[349] The decisive factor as

---

[347] Case C–33/99 *Fahmi and Esmoris Cerdeiro-Pinedo Amado* [2001] ECR I–2415 at 35.

[348] In his Opinion in *Fahmi and Esmoris Cerdeiro-Pinedo Amado* Advocate General Alber recognised this, but he nonetheless concluded that student grants cannot be classified as family benefits. In his view, grants are intended to cover the needs of children who, as a rule, are no longer minors and are responsible for their own personal life. The commencement of studies would be the distinguishing moment at which children extricate themselves from the family relationship serving as the model family expenses. In addition, student grants are expensive benefits for which no premium duties exist and for this reason it would not be justified to extend the notion of 'family benefits' to benefits such as student grants which only indirectly compensate family expenses. Opinion of Adv Gen Alber in Case C–33/99 *Fahmi and Esmoris Cerdeiro-Pinedo Amado* [2001] ECR I–2415 at 45–46. The arguments given by Alber are not really persuasive. The distinctive moment he refers to would rather seem to be the day of graduation following which children will enter the labour market (compare Peers (1999) n 237 above) and the mere fact that student grants are 'expensive' and not premium based (compare Case C–78/91 *Hughes* [1992] ECR I–4839 at 21) would seem immaterial factors for their classification.

[349] Opinion of Advocate General Jacobs in Case C–43/99 *Leclere* [2001] ECR I–4265 at 50.

regards family benefits, as Advocate General Darmon held in *Kromhout* (1985), is the 'existence of a child in respect of whom entitlement to benefits has arisen.'[350] It concerns benefits which are granted to parents and primarily intended as a contribution in the costs of taking care and raising children. Student grants cannot be regarded as such benefits. They are offered to students themselves and primarily aimed at making education financially accessible. The possibility cannot be wholly excluded, but the chance that Community students will indeed be able to claim a right to export student grants under Article 73 of Regulation No 1408/71 would seem to be rather remote.

9.3.2.3.2 Article 7(2) of Regulation No 1612/68

National rules limiting the export of student grants may further be incompatible with Article 7(2) of Regulation No 1612/68. If Mrs Esmoris had still been working and residing in the Netherlands, would she and/or her daughter have been entitled to rely on Article 7(2) of Regulation No 1612/68 in order to claim a student grant for the daughter's studies in Spain? A genuine integration of Community workers and their families into the host State's society would seem to require that children of Community workers, just as national children, can study at educational institutions that best suit their preferences and career prospects. For linguistic and cultural reasons, however, family members of Community workers are likely to be more interested in studying in other Member States than children holding the nationality of the host State. It could thus be argued, as Advocate General Alber did in his Opinion in *Fahmi and Esmoris Cerdeiro-Pinedo Amado*, that national rules restricting the export of student grants constitute indirect discrimination on grounds of nationality[351] and that such rules can only be saved when the State applying them can demonstrate that they are necessary for, and proportional to, a legitimate public interest. On what ground, then, can the non-exportability of student grants possibly be justified?

In the proceedings before the Court in *Fahmi and Esmoris Cerdeiro-Pinedo Amado* the United Kingdom had argued that student grants could not be made exportable because they are based on the 'social-economic circumstances' of national university cities. Advocate General Alber rejected the argument reasoning that Member States can take the differences in living cost into account when determining the level of grants.[352] It is indeed hard to understand why, for this reason, student grants could not be made exportable. A possible right to export student grants might provide an incentive for children of workers to

[350] Opinion Adv Gen Darmon in Case 104/84 *Kromhout* [1985] ECR 205.

[351] Opinion of Adv Gen Alber in Case C–33/99 *Fahmi and Esmoris Cerdeiro-Pinedo Amado* [2001] ECR I–2415 at 79. Alber did go into the importance of Art 7(2) because, in his view, former workers who have returned to their State of origin would retain the right to rely on this provision in order to claim tax-funded benefits (such as student grants) when they (*i*) receive a pension from the State of employment and (*ii*) pay taxes in respect of such a pension in that State.

[352] Opinion of Adv Gen Alber in Case C–33/99 *Fahmi and Esmoris Cerdeiro-Pinedo Amado* [2001] ECR I–2415 at 83.

embark on studies in States where the costs of living are higher than at home, but Article 7(2) of Regulation No 1612/68 does not seem to oblige Member States to increase the level of student grants.[353] In reverse, children of workers may decide to study in relatively cheap States or universities. Export of grants to such States does not impose any additional burden on student grant schemes.[354]

Another argument that could be made in favour of limits on the exportability of student grants relates to the need to protect the infrastructure of educational systems. In order to provide adequate education, governments must ensure that there are enough universities, courses, libraries, professors, etc. available. Undercapacity implies a limitation on the accessibility of education and must be avoided. At the same time, the number of educational facilities should not be too large in relation to the demand. Overcapacity implies an unnecessary waste of human and financial resources. Proper capacity planning, so it could be argued, requires that States anticipate how many students will attend their universities and that the power to refuse grants for studies abroad enables them to control student movements to the extent necessary for safeguarding their educational infrastructure. This argument is not persuasive either. In times where educational funding is increasingly put under pressure, where class- and lecture-rooms are overcrowded and where it is increasingly difficult to provide adequate housing and other student-related facilities, it is hard to understand how a possible increase in the number of students studying abroad could possibly affect the quality and accessibility of national universities and schools. Rather, it would seem that the recognition of a right for children of workers to export student grants could contribute to improving the quality and accessibility of educational systems on the national territory.[355]

The strongest argument that can be made in favour of rules limiting export of grants concerns the quality of education. The main[356] reason why the Dutch legislator decided in 1986 to limit the export of student grants was that the Minister of Education lacks powers to impose conditions regarding the quality of education in other States. In *Fahmi and Esmoris Cerdeiro-Pinedo Amado* Advocate General Alber was of the opinion that student grants primarily aim to enable

---

[353] Such a rule may be indirectly discriminatory (compare Case 41/84 *Pinna* [1986] ECR 1 at 23–24), but, by analogy with the Court's reasoning in cases as *Decker*, *Kohll* (see ch 4 s 4.2 and *O'Flynn* (see ch 2 s 7.2), it would seem that Member States can limit payment of grants up to the maximum paid to students attending education on the national territory.

[354] Compare Case C–368/98 *Vanbraekel* [2001] ECR I–5363 at 52.

[355] Admittedly, the States hosting the students might encounter some infrastructure problems, but this does not seem a good enough reason for the State of origin to justify the non-exportability of student grants. Compare the comments made in ch 4 s 4.3 . . . On the question what protective measures might be available for the States receiving the students, see s 9.4.

[356] As noted above, the other argument made in support of the decision to limit the export of student grants was that there were enough educational facilities and courses available in the Netherlands itself. In a Community where a right to freedom of movement for students is guaranteed, however, this cannot in itself be a ground for the justification of rules limiting the export of student grants.

students to qualify for a certain profession and that, for this reason, it would indeed be legitimate to finance only studies that meet certain quality norms. Alber referred to Directive No 89/48[357] which obliges Member States to recognise diplomas awarded in other Member States for the purposes of access to regulated professions. Within the scope of this directive, education provided in the Member States is presumed to meet the required quality standards. By virtue of Article 4 of this directive, however, Member States are allowed to impose additional requirements on the holders of foreign diplomas when the matters covered by, and the duration of, 'foreign' education substantially differ from national requirements. The Advocate General concluded that Member States, which offer student grants for national studies which prepare students for certain professions, can justify the refusals of student grants for foreign studies when they subject the holders of foreign diplomas to the additional requirements mentioned in Article 4 of Directive No 89/48.[358]

The central thesis of the Advocate General that Member States are entitled to make the award of student grants conditional upon the pursuit of studies which meet certain quality standards would seem in order.[359] However, his conclusion that Member States are entitled to refuse student grants in cases where foreign studies do not wholly meet the educational standards applied at home, is open to dispute. Alber's reasoning seems based on the presumption that students, upon graduation, will return to and take up a profession in their national territory. Although many may do so, it must be recognised that children of workers who have decided to study in the State of origin have the right, and may very well decide, to work in that State and that, as a rule, the diplomas they have acquired will suffice for admission to professions there. Why would the quality standards applied in the State offering the grants have to serve as the sole standard of reference? In a Community where freedom of movement for students, workers and self-employed persons is legally guaranteed, it would seem far more logical to conclude that Community workers and their children workers who have chosen to study in the State of origin are also entitled to grants when the school or university they attend, meets the quality standards applied in that State. Further, children of Community workers are entitled to study, and after graduation to work, in any Member State and it could thus be argued that, for student grant purposes, all educational institutions which, in the Member State where they are established, are permitted to issue diplomas which suffice for admission to professions in that State or any other Member State must be presumed to provide 'sufficient quality.' In other words, it could be argued that the

---

[357] OJ 1989 L 19.

[358] Opinion of Adv Gen Alber in Case C–33/99 *Fahmi and Esmoris Cerdeiro-Pinedo Amado* [2001] ECR I–2415 at 80–87.

[359] Further, his conclusion that not only the 'vertical directives' on the recognition of in particular medical diplomas, but also the 'horizontal' Directive No 89/48 can limit the powers of the Member States to refuse student grants for studies in other Member States, implies a significant extension of the possibility of exporting grants.

refusals to offer student grants for studies in other Member States are only justifiable in the few cases where children have decided to study at educational institutions whose diplomas are not recognised for admission to professions in any of the Member States.

From the perspective of the Community's objective of promoting freedom of movement for workers and integration of workers' families into the host State, it seems wholly immaterial whether financial aid for children studying in other Member States is granted in the form of student grants or in the form of family benefits. From the Member States' perspective, there do not seem to be any sound or compelling reasons as to why the basic premises concerning direct and indirect student financial aid for children studying in other Member States ought to be different. Arguably, the substantive principle embodied in Article 73 of Regulation No 1408/71 that children who are residing and/or studying in other Member States are for the purposes of entitlement to family benefits to be treated as though they were residing and/or studying within the national territory, can in principle be extended to Article 7(2) of Regulation No 1612/68 in relation to student grants to the benefit of both the workers and their children.

9.3.2.3.3 Article 12(1) EC

The conclusion that national rules limiting the export of student grants are at odds with Article 7(2) of Regulation No 1612/68 implies a break with the long-held assumption that Member States are in principle free to determine whether, and the conditions under which, they offer student grants for studies in other Member States. In one significant respect, however, the conclusion is still limited in scope. It only applies to children of Community citizens who have taken up employment and/or established residence in another Member State.[360] For the vast majority of Community students, whose parents have never exercised their free movement rights and who live in their own Member State prior to the commencement of studies in another Member State, the above observations and conclusions are of no relevance. They cannot invoke Article 7(2) against their own State. Regulation No 1612/68 merely aims to promote a free movement of workers, not a free movement of students.

Recent case law, however, leaves room for the suggestion that Community students can invoke Article 12(1) against their own Member State in order to claim student grants for studies in other Member States. The argument to be made is not that Community students should be entitled to invoke Article 12(1) EC in order to avoid Member States treating their own nationals less favourably than non-nationals. In principle, Community law does not object to such

---

[360] Arguably, however, the conclusion that student grants are exportable can be extended to all Community citizens and their family members who are lawfully residing in the territory of another Member State. Workers can also rely on Art 7(2) of Reg No 1612/68, independent children of workers can claim the right to export grants under Art 39 (or 12(1) EC), the self-employed and their children can do so on the basis of Art 43 EC (see ch 2 s 2.4) and non-economic residents and their children can invoke Art 12(1) EC for this purpose (compare ch 2 s 3.3).

reverse discrimination.[361] Rather, the argument that can be made, is that national rules limiting the export of student grants unlawfully and unnecessarily restrict the Community right to study in other Member States. *Martinez Sala* and *Grzelczyk* demonstrate that *Lairs* conclusion that Community students cannot invoke Article 12(1) EC in order to claim maintenance grants no longer stands. Further, the case law reveals that Community law may also preclude the application by the State of origin of rules which hamper the right to work,[362] establish a company[363] or live[364] in other Member States. In principle, there do not seem to be any sound reasons why this case law cannot be extended and applied to the free movement of students. If correct, it could be argued that national rules limiting the export of student grants can only be upheld under Article 12(1) EC when it can be demonstrated that they are necessary for, and proportional to, a legitimate public interest.[365]

Bearing in mind the observations made above in relation to Article 7(2) of Regulation No 1612/68, it can be questioned whether rules limiting the exportability of grants can be justified under Article 12(1) EC. As said, arguments relating to the quality of education in other Member States are only persuasive where foreign diplomas afford no entitlement to admission to professions in one of the Member States and such rules do not seem to be truly necessary for securing educational infrastructures or the financial stability of student grant schemes. One could object and claim that a possible right to export student grants for all Community students would encourage recipients upon graduation to work in other Member States and that Member States would not be able to receive the benefits from the educational investment they have put into these persons. In a Community where a free movement of workers and self-employed persons is guaranteed, however, such an argument is not persuasive and should be rejected.

Further, the objection could be made that exportability of grants would open the door for 'abuse.' Community citizens living in States where no student grants schemes exist, could seek to establish residence in another Member State where generous student grant schemes are available and, after a brief period of time, claim grants for their studies in the State of origin or another Member State. It could be argued that Member States ought to be entitled, as some indeed have done, to make the right to student grants for studies in other Member States conditional upon a minimum period of previous residence on the national territory. Community law, however, does not seem to leave room for such requirements. When applied to nationals of other Member States only, such durational residence requirements constitute direct discrimination on grounds of nationality. When applied to nationals and non-nationals they must be regarded as indirect discrimination, which implies that such rules might be justified when demon-

---

[361] See ch 2 s 7.4.
[362] See eg Case C–18/95 *Terhoeve* [1999] ECR I–345.
[363] Case 81/87 *Daily Mail* [1988] ECR 5483.
[364] Judgment of Case C–135/99 *Elsen* [2000] ECR I–10409.
[365] Compare C–55/94 *Gebhard* [1995] ECR I–4165 at 37.

strated to be necessary for a legitimate public interest. It is doubtful whether such a need can be demonstrated. Member States are entitled to make maintenance grants conditional upon (habitual) residence in their territory and that requirement seems to be a sufficient protection against possible abuses.[366]

To summarise, there do not seem to be compelling reasons as to why the conclusion drawn above as regards children of Community workers cannot be extended to all Community students. It is submitted that refusals to offer student grants for studies in other Member States should only be justified under Article 12(1) EC in the few instances where students have decided to study at educational institutions whose diplomas are not recognised for admission to professions in any of the Member States.[367]

---

[366] See Vossensteyn (2000) n 15 above, at 62. Compare *Swaddling* (1999) in which the Court held that the length of a person's residence cannot be regarded as an intrinsic element of the concept of (habitual) residence. The question whether or not a person can be regarded as a resident must be answered on a case-by-case basis in accordance with various factors such as the person's family situation, the reasons which led him to move, the fact that a person is in stable employment and the length and continuity of residence. Case C–90/97 *Swaddling* [1999] ECR I–1075 at 30.

[367] The possible recognition of a right to export student grants would raise several questions about possible overlaps of rights to claim student financial aid and how this might be prevented. In the absence of anti-cumulation rules, a right to export grants could mean that students might be able to receive financial compensation for tuition and enrolment fees in both the State where they study and the State of origin. Further, students whose parents have taken up employment in another Member State might be able to obtain maintenance grants in two or even more States. A student who resides and studies in State A and whose father works in State B, may have a right to get a grant in State A and, on the basis of Art 7(2) of Reg No 1612/68, in State B. If the mother were working in State C, the student might possibly be able to claim financial aid there too and if the student in question would decide to live in State D, he or she might even be able to obtain (partial) grants in four States.

Such overlap of student grants could be avoided in various ways. Compare T.M.C. Asser Instituut, *Studiefinanciering buiten Nederland in het Licht van de Europese Jurisprudentie* (2000) 37–41. First, Member States could unilaterally adopt and apply anti-cumulation rules on the basis of which grants are reduced or denied in cases where students are entitled to receive grants in other States. Compare van der Steen (1999) n 97 above, at 214. This unilateral method for combatting overlaps may be problematic, however. Member States are not always fully informed about the laws and regulations concerning student grants in other States and there might be the risk of students falling between two stools where both States involved claim to be entitled to apply their anti-cumulation rules.

An alternative way in which overlaps could be avoided is to promote the conclusion of agreements among the Member States in which the contracting parties would lay down rules determining which State is to pay a grant. Community law does not object to such agreements provided they respect the rights which students enjoy under Community law. Case 235/87 *Matteucci* [1988] ECR 5589 at 19.

Arguably, however, the best method would be to develop priority rules for student grants comparable to those contained in Reg No 1408/71 for family benefits. Art 76 of Reg No 1408/71 and Art 10 of the implementing Reg No 574/72 contain various rules which seek to avoid overlap in entitlements to family benefits in cases where a child's parents work and/or live in different Member States. In brief, the priority rules determine which State is to pay family benefits and they entitle other States to suspend payment up to the level paid in the assigned State where a right to family benefits may exists on the basis of national law or Reg No 1408/71. Without elaborating on the numerous and detailed questions which would have to be addressed in developing priority rules for student grants, one could consider bringing grants within the scope of Reg No 1408/71 and inserting a basic provision comparable to Article 73 which would in principle entitle students to student grants in the Member State where they habitually resided prior to commencement of their studies. In addition, a provision could be included which would entitle this State to suspend payment up to the amount that students are entitled to grants covering tuition fees in the State

9.3.3 *Right to Reside and the Financial Means Requirement*

In considering how the legal status of Community students could be improved, some comments are finally to be made on the conditions that students must fulfil in order to reside in the State of their studies. According to Article 1 of Directive No 93/96, students must (*i*) be sufficiently insured for medical care and (*ii*) assure the relevant national authorities that they have sufficient resources to avoid becoming a burden on the social assistance system of the host Member State. The formulation of the latter requirement is far from clear.[368] In order to avoid legal uncertainty, it has rightly been suggested that it would have been better if the Directive had stated that the right to reside remained as long as the student do not actually become a burden on the host State's public purse.[369] One could, however, go one step further and ask whether the financial means requirement cannot be deleted altogether.

In *Raulin* (1992) the Court held that the residence right of students is not granted unconditionally. As a corollary of the right to nondiscriminatory access to education, the right of residence is confined to what is necessary to allow the student to study in other Member States.[370] Consequently, the right may be limited to the duration of their studies and be made subject to conditions deriving from the legitimate interests of the host Member State 'such as the covering of maintenance cost and health insurance' to which the principle of non-discriminating was said not to apply.[371] The reasoning of the Court was not persuasive.[372] In *Lair* the Court had held that student grants covering maintenance costs fall outside the scope of Article 12(1) of the Treaty because such grants are matters of 'educational policy, which is not as such included in the spheres entrusted to the Community institutions' and 'social policy, which falls within the competence of the Member States.'[373] On the basis of these observations one would had to conclude that not only student grants but also social assistance benefits fell outside the scope of Article 12(1) EC. The exclusion of maintenance grants and social benefits from the scope of Community law, however, seemed to support the view that there is no need to make students' residence conditional

---

where they study. Where entitlement to maintenance grants exists in more than one State, one could consider a provision comparable to Art 76 of Reg No 1408/71 that would establish the rule that maintenance grants are in principle to be paid by the State where the student resided prior to taking up studies in another Member State. For situations in which students would have a right to grants in two Member States other than the one in which they lived before their studies, one could further draw inspiration from Art 10(3) of Reg No 574/72 and establish a rule that the State with the highest maintenance grants is to pay such grants and be given the right to be reimbursed by the 'other' State for half of the sum involved.

[368] See s 4.5.
[369] Vermeulen/Kuijer (1997) n 4 above, at 66.
[370] Case C–357/89 *Raulin* [1992] ECR I–1027 at 39.
[371] *Ibid*, at 38.
[372] Compare O'Leary, 'The Social Dimension of Community Citizenship', in: Rosas and Antola (eds), *A Citizens' Europe—In Search of a New Order* (1995) 156–81, at 174–76.
[373] Case 39/86 *Lair* [1988] ECR 3161 at 14–15.

upon fulfilment of the financial means and health insurance requirements. Why should Community students have to make it plausible that they will not become a burden on the host State's public purse, when they were not entitled to claim student grants or social assistance benefits there in any event? The protection of the financial stability of student grant and social assistance schemes is a legitimate interest that deserves protection under Community law, but if students cannot gain access to these schemes, this interest would not seem to be affected.

The rulings in *Martínez Sala* and *Grzelczyk* do not have to change the picture. Community students are now entitled to invoke Article 12(1) EC in order to claim equal treatment as regards maintenance grants and social assistance benefits. This conclusion, however, merely implies that Member States can no longer refuse social assistance and grants to Community students on the ground that they are nationals of other States. Member States are still entitled to exclude full-time students from their social assistance schemes, to require from social assistance recipients to look, or to be available, for full-time work or to make eligibility for maintenance grants and social assistance benefits conditional upon habitual residence or domicile in the national territory.[374] Abolition or invalidation of the financial means requirement is not likely to have many, if any, financial implications for the host State.[375] The opposite might even hold true. The administrative costs of enforcing the requirement[376] could be saved. *Raulin* still stands, but it is submitted that the duty imposed on students to persuade immigration authorities that they will not become a public burden constitutes an unnecessary burden on their Community right to study in other Member States.

9.4 Options for Protecting the Educational Interests of the Member States

As stated in Section 9.2, student mobility is unlikely to trigger an educational 'race to the bottom' within the Community. Arguments for promoting student mobility further are more persuasive than calls for compensating or protective

---

[374] See s 4.4 of this chapter and ch 3 s 6.

[375] Indeed, there are no signs that students have, or will, become a burden on the social assistance schemes of host States. In a report to the Parliament and Council on the implementation of the 1990 residence directives the Commission stated that it had asked the Member States how many students had become a burden on their social assistance schemes since the implementation of the directives and what steps had been taken in response. None of the Member States provided any data. This may not come as a real surprise. As a rule, students will not be able to claim benefits because they may not be able to meet substantive criteria for benefit entitlement such as being obliged to look for and accept (full-time) work. Compare also the Opinion of Advocate General in Case 424/98 *Commission v Italy* [2000] ECR I–4001 at 28. Admittedly, the above does not necessarily imply that no students have obtained social assistance benefits, but the States' responses do strongly suggest that the issue does not have much practical relevance.

[376] Compare Hoepelman, 'Het Verblijfsrecht van Studenten uit EU-Staten: De Praktijk aan een Nederlandse Universiteit', Fernhout (ed), *Dertig Jaar Vrij Verkeer van Werknemers* (1999) 103–16.

measures for the (few) Member States that are net-importers of students. Nonetheless, the problems that these States may face cannot be wholly ignored. An increase in student mobility could also increase the imbalances in student movement and this may cause (additional) financial or capacity problems for the net-importers. How can such problems possibly be avoided or minimised?

9.4.1 Reimbursement Mechanisms

In response to concerns about the imbalances in student movement and the unequal financial burdens imposed on some Member States, it has been suggested that student mobility could be better promoted by requiring Member States to pay the true economic cost of the education which their nationals and/or residents receive abroad.[377] Such reimbursement systems have been expected to produce the dual effect of encouraging governments to improve the quality of their educational courses as an element of educational 'competition,' while guaranteeing the quality of national education by not subjecting it to an open-ended and undetermined influx of foreign students.[378] In developing such a scheme, one might draw inspiration from chapter 4 and consider setting up a reimbursement scheme comparable to the one established by Regulations Nos 1408/71 and 574/72 for cross-border health care rights.[379] Reimbursement schemes seem appealing because they take into consideration the fact that student movement within the Community is not in balance. They relieve the net-importers of students of the unequal financial burden they bear and the schemes impose this burden on the States where taxes have been paid by the students (or their parents) and where they may (or are likely) to return to upon graduation.

Nonetheless, the feasibility and, arguably desirability, of reimbursement mechanisms scheme is questionable. The core problem is that such schemes compel States to repay the costs incurred by other Member States. They would be required to invest in the educational systems of other States. Since students may move to States with more expensive educational systems, such reimbursement mechanisms would imply that the 'poorer' Member States are required to

---

[377] O'Leary (1996) n 4 above, at 189–90; Kampf, 'La Directive 90/366/CEE relative au Droit de Séjour des Etudiants communautaires: Sa Transposition en France', (1992) *RMC* 307 *et seq.*, at 317; Hartley (1991) n 4 above, at 193 and Scholsem (1989) n 317 above, at 318.

[378] O'Leary (1996) n 4 above, at 189–90. Such ideas for a repayment system to the benefit of student importing countries show similarities with the ideas for introducing a student voucher system, which being guided by the principle that 'money will follow the student', would enable students to choose in which of the Member States they wish to study at the expense of their 'own' State. Undervisnings Ministeriet, *A Short Presentation of the Danish Presidency's Main Themes in Education* (1993).

[379] See ch 4 s 3. See also the Opinion of Adv Gen Slynn in *Humbel*: 'The analogy with health care is striking since, although Community nationals by and large are entitled to medical care throughout the Community, that entitlement is underpinned by a complex system designed to determine which State should ultimately bear the cost of treatment. It is to my mind unfortunate that no such system for education throughout the Community exists'. Case 263/886 *Humbel* [1988] ECR 5365 at 5380.

reimburse the richer Member States. Educational expenses of the poorer States would increase and it is likely that these States would prefer to invest in the development of their own educational systems. The Nordic countries have been working on a repayment scheme but so far they have not been successful.[380] If the Nordic States are unable to reach agreement on such a scheme, then in view of the much bigger differences in public expenditure on public education among the Community's Member States, one may doubt whether a system in which the State of origin has to 'pay the educational bill' is viable.[381] In the alternative, one might consider setting up a fund at Community level out of which the 'net-importing' States would be reimbursed. The chances of having such a fund approved by the Member States may be somewhat greater, but still seem to be minimal. In whatever way such a common reimbursement fund might be financed, it can probably only operate effectively if richer Member States were the net-recipients and poorer States the net-contributors. The latter, as one might expect and arguably should respect, would be unwilling to cooperate.

9.4.2 *Differential Tuition Policies*

If it is neither feasible nor desirable to impose the cost of education of free-riding students on either the Community or the Member State of origin, then one could consider protecting the educational interests of the student importing countries by allowing them to apply differential tuition policies comparable to those applied by American States or universities.

[380] As stated above in n 228, the Nordic countries (Iceland, Norway, Sweden, Finland and Denmark) have always promoted international student mobility. In 1991 the 'Cooperation Programme for Higher Education in the Nordic Countries' was adopted in which the five States agreed to further promote student mobility and competition among educational institutions with a view to improving the quality of education. In 1994 an additional agreement on admission to higher education was signed in which Nordic students were not only granted several equal treatment rights, but in which the five States also indicated that the promotion of student mobility should be planned in gradual stages. Thus, on a temporary basis quotas for Nordic students were envisaged and the Nordic States declared their intention to reach a mutual agreement on the settlement of the costs of education. More concretely, it was intended that the State of origin should bear the cost of the education which their 'free-moving' students, ie students who study outside *Nordplus*, receive in other Nordic States. Even though the total cost involved did not seem exhorbitant, it has appeared quite difficult to reach agreement on establishing a reimbursement scheme. It was intended that such a scheme would only be set up for a limited group of studies, but no agreement could be reached on the selection of these studies. In addition, States have been unable to agree on the possibility of student-sending countries limiting the number of students on behalf of whom they have to bear the educational costs. Partial reimbursement from a special Nordic fund has been considered as an alternative, but such a fund has not yet been set up. See further eg Nyborg (1996) n 228 above, at 193–203.
[381] See also van der Mei (1998) n 75 above, at 400. The possibility cannot be excluded that a reimbursement system will act as a brake on mobility within the EU. The cost incurred by mobile students, might encourage the 'poorer' Member States to 'keep their nationals at home'. Baligant *et al*, 'Economic Analysis of Student Mobility on a European Scale', as quoted in Nyborg (1996) n 228 above, at 202. Furthermore, in the field of health care Member States may have set up a reimbursement scheme, but it is precisely as regards patients who would move to other States for the sole purpose of obtaining benefits that Member States have always opposed a duty of reimbursement. See ch 4 s 3.3.

In order to do so, it is first necessary to look again at *Gravier* and to ascertain whether the Court has not already ruled out the possibility of pursuing such policies. When the Belgian legislator introduced the *Minerval* in early 1970s, it seemed inspired by American differential tuition policies. The *Minerval* was introduced in order to ensure 'a certain financial stability' of the educational system.[382] Foreign students had to compensate for the fact that their income is not taxable and that they cannot be required to contribute to the education they enjoy in Belgium. In *Gravier* the Court did not go into this 'taxpayer argument.' It merely concluded that the inequality of treatment inherent in the *Minerval* rules constitutes discrimination on grounds of nationality. The Court's silence on the 'taxpayer argument' has been understood to imply that the Court also rejected the *rationale* behind the *Minerval* and that this, for practical reasons, would have been a correct decision for the Court.[383] During their studies foreign students pay indirect taxes and they or their parents may before or after their studies work and be taxed in the State concerned. Also, not all residents pay taxes, but they can nonetheless benefit fully from public education.[384] The relationship between the paying of taxes and the right to benefit from education funded out of the tax revenues would be too confusing to make a connection between the taxes paid and the rates for tuition.

With respect, this interpretation of *Gravier* is not wholly persuasive. First, under Belgian legislation Belgian students did not have to pay the *Minerval*. The law governing the *Minerval* was partly based on nationality criteria and thus constituted direct discrimination on grounds of nationality. The question whether the Belgian rules could be justified was not, and did not have to be, addressed by the Court. Second, the above reading of the 'tax-payer-argument' does not seem based on a correct reproduction of the arguments for pursuing differential tuition policies. Neither the Belgian authorities nor any of the American States have ever claimed that the amount of tuition to be paid should be calculated on the basis of the taxes which have been, are or will be paid. In the logic behind differential tuition policies there is no scope for non-resident students to prove that they have in the past paid 'more than enough' taxes. Such policies are not based on the principle of *juste retour*. As part of redistributive policies, they are based rather on a notion of residence or membership. As a class, non-residents have not contributed to the funding of public education through the payment of taxes and, as a class, they cannot benefit from the lower tuition rate for residents.

In *Gravier* the Court did not express a view on the *rationale* behind the *Minerval*. The question whether national rules which, without making any distinction on grounds of nationality, impose higher fees on students who have merely come to the Member State concerned for educational reasons, remains

---

[382] See the Opinion of Adv Gen Slynn in Case 293/83 *Gravier* [1985] ECR 593, at 596.
[383] Timmermans (1986) n 125 above, at 91.
[384] Compare also von Wilmowsky (1991) n 159 above, at 256 (n 91).

in principle unanswered. In his Opinion in *Gravier* Advocate General Slynn suggested that such rules might be compatible with Article 12 EC where he held that there 'is force in the argument that it is not discriminatory to require those who do not contribute directly or indirectly to the common weal to make some contribution.'[385] In practice, such rules would primarily work to the detriment of nationals from other Member States and they may therefore constitute indirect discrimination on grounds of nationality. However, differential tuition fees could possibly escape the prohibition enshrined in Article 12(1) EC where it can be demonstrated that they are necessary for, and proportional to, the legitimate financial and educational interests of the Member States.[386] As regards Member States which are structurally faced with a net-import of European students, and which set the non-resident tuition fees at such a rate as to cover the marginal cost of foreign students, it could be argued that there is indeed force in the 'taxpayers' argument.' Whereas other alternatives, such as non-resident quotas, directly restrict or hinder admission to universities, differential tuition policies merely make admission more expensive. If States were to calculate non-resident tuition fees in such a way as to cover the total cost of education offered to non-resident students, student mobility would not impose additional pressure on their educational budget and they would possess the funds to cope with possible capacity problems. With 'non-residents completely paying their own way,' Member States could spend whatever amount they wished to educate their own 'citizens and . . . accommodate non-residents at the same time.'[387]

Nonetheless, differential tuition policies also have clear disadvantages. If States were to have the right to charge non-resident students higher tuition fees, they could set the fee at a rate which exceeds the marginal cost of the education offered to non-resident students. In theory, they could shift part of the burden of funding resident students on to non-resident students. Moreover, differential tuition policies would enable Member States to regulate or to control the admission of students from other Member States. Tuition fees for non-resident students could even be made so high that not a single student would consider studying in the Member State concerned. In other words, there is no guarantee that the power to charge higher tuition fees on non-resident students will not be excessively used or even abused. In the United States no 'abuses' have been reported, but this does not mean that these could not occur in the European Community. Member States have no experience of differential tuition policies and, more than the American States, they have always expressed concerns about

---

[385] Opinion of Adv Gen Slynn in Case 293/83 *Gravier* [1985] ECR I–593 at 604.

[386] See van der Mei (1994) n 19 above, at 206–7.

[387] Paraphrasing Note, 'The Constitutionality of Nonresident Tuition' (1971) n 249 above, at 1150–51. Furthermore, the mere fact that non-resident students have to pay higher tuition fees than resident students does not have to affect student mobility. The threshold for studying in another State where 'free-riders' have to pay 2000 Euro and domiciled students only 1000 Euro, is much lower than in a State where all students have to pay 3000 Euro. The degree to which student mobility is hampered does not depend on a difference between the fees to be paid by the various students, but on the question of how much tuition must be paid.

the impact of student mobility on their systems of higher education. Differential tuition policies would seem to require some form of supervision as to how the power to charge higher tuition fees to non-residents will be used. The possibility cannot be wholly excluded, but in view of the judicial reluctance to second-guess economic choices, one may doubt whether differential tuition policies have a good chance of being accepted.[388]

9.4.3 *Quantitative Restrictions*

If reimbursement schemes and differential tuition policies are neither feasible nor desirable, one might consider the alternative of allowing Member States that are net-importers of students to impose limits on the number of students they admit to their universities. The lawfulness of quotas would seem to depend on the criteria applied. *Numerus clausus* regulations which limit the number of student places on the basis of social need would seem in order,[389] whilst the opposite holds true for rules limiting the number of students on the basis of nationality. The question to be addressed is whether Member States, with a view to protecting their educational interests, are permitted to adopt rules limiting the number of non-residents, i.e., students who prior to the commencement of their studies resided in other Member States, that will be admitted to their universities.

At first glance, the prospect of having such rules accepted by the Court or the Council seems very remote. The rules would seem to hamper student mobility far more than differential tuition policies do and they may even be regarded as a *de facto* denial of the right to study in other Member States once the fixed number has been reached. Nonetheless, one cannot wholly exclude the possibility that such quantitative restrictions, albeit in exceptional circumstances, might be compatible with Community law. Restrictions on the number of non-residents that will be admitted could possibly escape the classification of a prohibited indirect discrimination on grounds of nationality where it can be proven

---

[388] Furthermore, the policies would also raise some questions as to who must be regarded as a resident for tuition purposes. The *rationale* behind differential tuition policies demands that Community students must beregarded as non-residents. The mere fact that they enjoy under Article 12(1) EC *juncto* Dir No 93/96 a right to reside in the State of their studies cannot suffice. As regards Community students who hold the nationality of another Member State no difficult issues arise. Those who reside as Community students in the State concerned can be classed as non-residents, whilst the nationals of other Member States whose right to reside is based on Art(s) 39 (or 43) EC or one of the other two 1990 directives can claim to be residents for the purposes of tuition policy. Administrative problems comparable to the ones American States and universities confront, could arise as regards national students who have returned from abroad. Should they be treated as non-residents or as residents? How can they prove that they are not free-riders who have merely returned for educational purposes?

[389] Oertzen (1992) n 4 above, at 225 and Verbruggen (1992) n 4 above, at 61. In *Bertini* (1986) the Court still suggested that the Council could possibly introduce quantitative limitations (Joined Cases 98, 162 and 258/85 *Bertini* [1986] ECR 1885 at 11), but in view of Article 149(4) (prohibition of harmonisation of educational laws and regulations) this would seem doubtful.

that they are necessary for maintaining the quality and accessibility of educational systems. It does not seem wholly impossible that such evidence could be provided. A substantial influx of students from other Member States could have implications for the funding and infrastructure of educational systems. Such an influx could cause overcrowded lecture rooms, affect professor-student ratios or limit housing and other student-related facilities. States that decided to expand educational facilities might face problems of overcapacity if in subsequent years the number of enrolments was to drop. Such problems, which might affect the quality and/or funding of higher education, could be avoided if States were entitled to control and limit numbers of students.[390] It could be argued that some form of preferential treatment of residents, might be necessary for maintaining adequate educational systems. For instance, due to *numerus clausus* regulations applicable in the Netherlands, many Dutch students have decided to study in Belgium. Dutch students are even encouraged to do so by 'their own' Minister of Education who has allowed them to export student grants when they embark on certain studies at Belgian universities. As a result, in some Flemish faculties more than 50% of the students is Dutch. In such situations, would it not be desirable to allow Belgium or the Flemish community to impose certain limits on access of students from the Netherlands? In Belgium much importance has traditionally been attached to freedom of choice in the field of education, but, as a result of *numerus clausus* applied in the Netherlands, the Flemish community may be forced to take certain measures which might consist of the introduction of *numerus clausus*. The Court may not be easily persuaded, but it is submitted that Member States should be entitled to limit the number of non-residents that will be admitted to their education systems in cases where such measures are needed in order to guarantee a 'balanced educational system open to all'[391] or *de facto* force them to adopt measures which inflict upon their autonomy in the field of education.

9.5 Conclusions

The main rules and principles governing cross-border access to education, and the free movement of students in particular, were developed in the mid and late 1980s. The Court, the main initiator, has made a significant contribution to achieving the goal of promoting the free movement of persons by conferring

[390] Compare Varat, 'State Citizenship' and Interstate Equality, (1982) *ChicLRev* 487 *et seq.*, at 553–54.

[391] Indeed, a comparison may again be made with health care. In *Kohll* the Court took into consideration the impact which patient mobility might have on the infrastructure of medical and hospital services by allowing the States to impose restrictions on the free movement of services which are necessary for protecting a 'medical and hospital service open to all'. ch 4 s 4.2.4. *Kohll* was primarily concerned with States from which patients move, but as stated in ch 4 s 4.3, it could be argued that the possibility of imposing restrictions on the free movement of patients is also, if not above all, relevant to the 'receiving' State.

upon Community citizens quite extensive educational rights. At the same time, the Court has taken into consideration the educational interests of Member States in particular by allowing them to preserve 'full' student grants for those who are domiciled or working within the national territory. The way the Court has attempted to strike a balance between the free movement goal and States' educational interests has not gone without criticism, but the main rules developed by the Court seem to be widely supported. This is not to say that Community law on cross-border access to education is wholly satisfactory. As the Commission indicated in its 1996 Green paper on educational mobility there are still quite a lot of obstacles that may dissuade students from studying in other Member States. The Commission itself has taken various initiatives to decrease or eliminate many of these obstacles, but one cannot wholly exclude the possibility that the Court may have to assist. Such judicial help could be particularly welcome with attempts to promote the transferability of student grants.

6

Conclusions

1 INTRODUCTION

In the course of the last four decades, European Community law has increasingly imposed restraints on Member States' powers to regulate access of non-nationals to their territories and welfare state services. In the late 1950s, when the Community was established and the foundations of the current welfare states were laid down, Member States were still largely sovereign to control immigration and to determine whether, when and the conditions under which, non-nationals were accorded access to their public services.[1] For non-nationals access to public benefits was most often a privilege, not a right. Today, nationals of the Member States enjoy, as citizens of the European Union, a whole set of legally enforceable rights which entitle them to enter, reside in and gain access to public services in other Member States. This book has shown, however, that the gates to the national territories and welfare states[2] have not been opened completely. Community law on freedom of movement and nondiscrimination has not been construed so broadly as to enable Union citizens to freely 'shop around' for public services. Member States still hold significant powers to protect themselves against 'welfare tourism' and to secure the funding and/or organisation of their benefit systems. In each of the three fields discussed in this book, Community law governing cross-border access to public benefits entails a compromise between the competing interests of promoting freedom of movement and protecting public services.

Standing back from the more detailed issues, which have already been addressed and the concrete questions which arise in individual cases, this final chapter will draw certain horizontal comparisons and consider how Community law has sought to reconcile the previously mentioned competing interests. The aim is to explore whether Community law provides for some more general rules or principles, which must be applied when answering questions on cross-border access to public services, which, no doubt, will continue

---

[1] Cp Leibfried and Pierson, 'Semi Sovereign Welfare States: Social Policy in a Multitiered Europe' in Leibfried and Pierson, *European Social Policy—Between Fragmentation and Integration* (1995) 43–77, 50.

[2] Cp Entzinger, 'De Andere Grenzen van de Verzorgingsstaat—Migratiestromen and Migratiebeleid' in Engbersen, *Zorgen in het Europese Huis—De Grenzen van Nationale Verzorgingsstaaten* (1994) 142–72.

to arise in future years.[3] In doing so, three categories of persons will be dealt with: residents, non-residents and third country nationals. The first category is discussed in section 2 and consists, for the purposes of this Chapter, of all Union citizens who are lawfully residing in the territory of another Member State. Section 3 considers non-residents which include frontier workers and, above all, Union citizens who merely travel to other Member States without relocating their economic base or private residence. Section 4 considers the legal status of third country nationals staying or residing within the Community.

2 RESIDENTS

2.1 Introduction

Community law confers residence rights upon various categories of Union citizens and each of these enjoys legal protection against discriminatory treatment in other Member States. The conditions under which residence rights can be exercised still differ from category to category, but as regards the legal status in the host State of those who have exercised the right, a comparable development can be detected. In brief, Community law has gradually been heading in the direction, and, arguably, can be interpreted as already having reached the point, of guaranteeing all Union citizens the right to gain access to virtually all public benefits under the same conditions as the nationals of the host State from the moment they establish residence in another Member State until the day they voluntarily give up or are involuntarily deprived of their status of lawful resident. Under certain conditions, Member States are still empowered to refuse, or end, residence of nationals of other Member States, but the case law suggests that they are no longer entitled to protect the funding and/or organisation of their public benefit systems by making distinctions among Union citizens lawfully residing within their borders on grounds of nationality or length of residence. Union citizenship may not yet give entitlement to a general and unconditional right of residence, but it does guarantee 'full and equal membership' of the welfare state for all those citizens who have established residence in another Member State. This membership status may be labelled 'denizenship,' a concept which has been used to describe the status of non-nationals who have acquired secure or permanent resident status and who enjoy the same rights as do nationals with the exception of political rights such as the right to vote and stand as a candidate in elections.[4]

---

[3] The main focus will be on the general provisions governing freedom of movement and equality of treatment. The more specific rules and principles of the social security Regs 1408/71 and 574/72 are not the subject of analysis.

[4] See, eg: Hammar, *Democracy and the Nation State: Aliens: Denizens and Citizens in a World of International Migration* (1990) 12–13; Layton-Henry, 'Citizenship or Denizenship for Migrant Workers' in Layton-Henry (ed), *The Political Rights of Migrant Workers in Western Europe* (1990) 186–95, 188 and Brubaker, 'Membership without Citizenship: The Economic and Social Rights of Non-Citizens' in Brubaker, *Immigration and the Politics of Citizenship in Europe and North America* (1989) 145–62.

2.2 Community Workers

The roots of this development are found in the case law on the free movement of workers. In the late 1960s, when it formally realised the free movement of workers the Council spoke in the preamble to Regulation No 1612/68 of a 'fundamental right' which can be exercised in 'freedom and dignity,' can improve workers' 'living and working conditions' and which may help to promote their 'social advancement.'[5] These promising goals were not supported by the grant of an extensive set of rights in the substantive part of the Regulation. Besides rights directly concerning the taking up of employment,[6] workers were not given much more than a right to equal treatment with respect to vocational training,[7] trade union activities,[8] fiscal advantages[9] and social advantages related to employment[10] and housing facilities.[11] Workers were supposed to provide for themselves through full-time work and if they were unable to generate sufficient financial means due to sickness, incapacity for work or unemployment, they could claim benefits under the Community rules on the coordination of social security schemes. In the view of the Community legislator, equality of treatment was to be guaranteed in the fields of labour law and social security law, but entitlement to residence-based benefits such as social assistance, general education and student grants was, and would remain, regulated by national law. Workers were primarily seen as 'economic agents' who were offered some social protection but were not viewed as fully-fledged and equal members of the host States' society and welfare state.

Since the mid-1970s, however, the Court of Justice has assumed responsibility for promoting freedom of movement for workers. The Court has largely filled the gap between the intentions proclaimed in the preamble and the concrete provisions contained in the substantive part of Regulation No 1612/68. Two issues have been particularly relevant.

The first concerns the concept of Community worker. Unemployment and changing patterns in the labour market have led to new forms of labour, such as on-call contracts, part-time work and homework, which are for many persons the main, if not the sole, possibility of making a living and improving their living conditions. The emergence of these new forms of labour has encouraged, and in fact compelled,[12] the Court to recognise that 'flexible' workers, even

---

[5] Third and fifth recitals of the preamble to Reg 1612/68.

[6] Arts 1–6 of Reg 1612/68.

[7] Art 7(3) of Reg 1612/68.

[8] Art 8 of Reg 1612/68.

[9] Art 7(2) of Reg 1612/68.

[10] The notion of 'social advantages' was probably understood to cover only employment related issues. O'Keeffe, 'Equal Rights for Migrants: The Concept of Social Advantages in Article 7(2), Regulation 1612/68' (1986) *YEL* 93–123, 95.

[11] Art 9 of Reg 1612/68.

[12] O'Leary, 'The Principle of Equal treatment on Grounds of Nationality in Article 6 EC—A Lucrative Source for Member State Nationals?' in O'Leary and Tiilikainen (eds), *Citizenship and Nationality Status in the New Europe* (1998) 105–36, 116.

when their income is 'lower than what is considered to be the minimum required for subsistence,'[13] can benefit from the free movement provisions.[14]

The second issue concerns the notion of 'social advantages' in Article 7(2) of Regulation No 1612/68. The broad definition the Court has given of this notion not only implies an extension of the scope of the right to equal treatment. It also reflects a change in perception. The concept not only covers benefits granted to national workers 'primarily because of their status of workers,' but also benefits which are offered 'by virtue of the mere fact of residence' in the territory of the host State.[15] Workers are thus not only viewed and to be treated as members of the work force, but, indeed, also as residents who, as members of the host State's welfare state, must be offered access to virtually all[16] public services available in the host State.[17]

The Court has recognised, however, that the concept of worker and the notion of social advantages cannot both be interpreted too broadly. The Member States' legitimate concerns about the funding of their welfare state facilities, required some safeguard to be included into the free movement regime. The Court has not

---

[13]   Case 53/81 *Levin* [1982] ECR 1035, 15.

[14]   *Ibid*, (part-time workers) and Case C–357/89 *Raulin* [1992] ECR I–1027 (on-call contracts).

[15]   Case 207/78 *Even* [1979] ECR 2019, 22. In a proposal for amending Reg 1612/68 (COM (1998) 394 def) the Commission has proposed replacing the current Art 7(2) by a provision which reads that a 'worker who is a national of a Member State shall enjoy the same financial, fiscal, social, cultural and other advantages as nationals workers'. The reference to 'other advantages' suggests a significant extension of the scope of the right to equal treatment. See, eg: Sewandono, 'Het Commissievoorstel tot Wijziging van Verordening (EEG) nr.1612/68: Meer Bescherming van Familie- en Gezinsleven en Meer Gelijke Behandeling' in (1999) *SEW* 284–90, 287. On the face of it, the proposed new Art 7(2) leaves room for the suggestion that political rights such as the right to vote and stand as a candidate in elections or other rights typically linked to possession of the nationality of the host State might be covered. This, however, is not the intention. The proposal does not intend to more than to codify the case law of the Court. COM (1998) 394 def, Explanatory Memorandum 15. In its explanatory memorandum the Commission refers to various advantages such as those concerning leisure activities and this might possibly be understood to imply that the notion of 'other' advantages is intended as the codification of a ruling such as the one in Case C–334/94 *Commission v France* [1996] ECR 1307.
   Further, in the proposed Arts 7(1) and 7(2) the phrase 'in the territory of another Member State' can no longer be found. In the Explanatory Memorandum this change is not explained, but it might be understood as a codification of *Matteucci* (1988) in which the Court held that whenever a Member State offers its own nationals residing within the national territory benefits to be enjoyed outside that territory (*in casu* student grants) it is obliged to offer such rights under the same conditions to Community workers. Case 235/87 *Matteucci* [1988] ECR 5589 16.

[16]   Only certain benefits linked to military service (Case C–315/94 *De Vos* [1996] ECR I–4117, 22) or benefits for war veterans (Case 207/78 *Even* [1979] ECR 2019, 23) are excluded.

[17]   The fact that benefits fall within, or derive from, policy areas which have not been brought within the ambit of the Treaty is of no significance. It is settled case law that in areas still falling within their domain, Member States must also obey the Community principles of freedom of movement and non-discrimination. See, eg: Case 65/81 *Reina* [1982] ECR 33, 15 (demographic policy) and Case C–279/93 *Schumacker* [1995] ECR I–225, 21–4 (tax law). The scope of the right to equal treatment of workers is determined by a functional criterion, which means that equality of treatment must be guaranteed in as far as it may facilitate freedom of movement and the integration of the worker in the host State's society. See ch 2, s 2.2.3.

chosen[18] the option of allowing Member States to apply rules which make entitlement to benefits conditional upon minimum period of residence or employment.[19] Rather, the Court has opted to impose a threshold for obtaining the status of Community worker and the accompanying right to reside. This status can only be obtained by Community citizens whose work in another Member State can be considered 'effective and genuine.' Those whose activities are merely 'marginal and ancillary' do not obtain the status of Community worker and the right to reside.[20] Basically, the Court seems to have established the rule that

---

[18] Cp Steiner, 'The Right to Welfare: Equality and Equity under Community Law' (1987) *ELRev* 477 *et seq*, 41 and Hailbronner, 'Die Neuere Rechtsprechung zum EG-Freizuegigkeitsrecht' (1988) *ZAR* 3–13, 6.

[19] Waiting-period requirements applied to non-nationals only, constitute direct discrimination on grounds of nationality and are consequently prohibited. Case 249/83 *Hoeckx* [1985] ECR 982, 23–4 and Case 39/86 *Lair* [1988] ECR 3161, 42. Further, the court has held that durational residence requirements applied to nationals and non-nationals alike constitute indirect discriminations on grounds of nationality. Case C–111/92 *Commission v Luxembourg* [1993] ECR I–817, 10 and Case C–326/90 *Commission v Belgium* [1992] ECR I–5517, 3.

To be sure, it could still be argued that waiting-period requirements applied to both nationals and non-nationals can possibly be justified on the ground that States, in order to protect the funding of their benefit schemes, should be entitled to reserve social benefits for those who for a given period of time have contributed to the funding of benefits by making tax-contributions. So far, the Court has never gone into such a 'past contributions argument'. However, because of the protection offered by the requirement of 'effective and genuine work', one may doubt whether waiting-period requirements can be said to be necessary for, and proportional to, the public interest of safeguarding the financial stability of public benefit systems.

Further, national rules which make entitlement to certain benefits covered by Reg 1408/71 conditional upon minimum periods of insurance or employment are not necessarily outlawed. The regulation prescribes that the competent institutions must take periods of insurance or employment in other Member States into account as if these were fulfilled under their own legislation (see, eg: Arts 18 (sickness and maternity benefits) and 67 (unemployment benefits)), but where this aggregation does not suffice for meeting the minimum period requirement, benefits can still be denied for the remaining period. Such waiting-period requirements cannot be circumvented by relying on Art 7(2) of Reg 1612/68. This regulation, as its Art 42 indicates, does not affect the regime of Reg 1408/71. It could possibly be argued that Community citizens who, even with help of the aggregation rules, are unable to meet eligibility criteria concerning minimum periods of insurance or employment, can claim benefits under Arts 39 and/or 12 EC on the ground that the criteria constitute indirect discrimination on grounds of nationality. Chances of the argument being accepted, however, seem slim.

[20] Case 53/81 *Levin* [1982] ECR 1035, 17. It is of course hard to know the Court's true motives, but it would indeed seem that the Court has deliberately chosen to take into consideration Member States' welfare state interests through the interpretation of the notion of worker rather than by accepting the legality of durational residence or employment requirements or by making enjoyment of right under Art 39 EC conditional upon the motive of workers (Case 53/81 *Levin* [1982] ECR 1035, 16). The concept of worker may not be defined by reference to national law (Case 53/81 *Levin* [1982] ECR 1035, 11), but the three requirements of work, remuneration and subordination, which the Court has laid down (Case 66/85 *Lawrie Blum* [1986] ECR I–2121, 17), do indicate that the Court itself has been inspired by national definitions of the concept of worker. The requirement that work must also be 'effective and genuine', however, cannot, at least to the knowledge of this author, be found in the labour laws of any of the Member States. The work performed by Community citizens whose jobs are according to the Court to be considered as 'marginal and ancillary' may very well be economic in nature and, as a rule, part-time workers are seen and treated as workers under national labour laws. The 'new' and 'unique' requirement that work must be 'effective and genuine' for the purposes of Art 39 EC has been established by the Court itself and it is hard to find any other explanation than that this was done in defence of the Member States' welfare state interests.

Member States can only protect their welfare state interests by refusing residence to nationals of other Member States whose work cannot be regarded as 'effective and genuine,' but that Community citizens who meet that requirement must be admitted for residence and be treated as 'equal members' of their society[21] and welfare state from the moment they actually exercise that right.

2.3 Family Members of Community Workers

In the preamble to Regulation No 1612/68 the Council had stated that freedom of movement requires (*i*) the right for workers to be joined by family members and (*ii*) the elimination of obstacles to the integration of the family into the host country.[22] The first point was taken seriously by the Community legislator. Article 10(1) confers the right to reside on quite a broad group of family members including the workers' spouse, their children below the age of 21 and other family members in the descending and ascending line who are dependent on the worker.[23] The second point concerning the family's integration into the host

---

[21] In this regard it may further be pointed out that the Commission has proposed to insert in Reg 1612/68 a new Art 1a which provides that within the scope of the Regulation 'all discrimination on grounds of sex, racial or ethnic origin, religion, belief, disability, age or sexual orientation shall be prohibited'. This proposed provision must be set against the background of Art 13 EC, which was inserted by the Treaty of Amsterdam and which confers upon the Council the power to take appropriate action to combat discrimination based on the same grounds as those mentioned in the proposed new Art 1a of Reg 1612/68. On Art 13 EC see, eg: Bell, 'Equality and Diversity: Anti-Discrimination Law after Amsterdam', in Shaw (ed), *Social Law and Policy in an Evolving European Union* (2000) 157–70; Barnard, 'Article 13: Through the Looking Glass of Union Citizenship' in O'Keeffe and Twomey (eds), *Legal Issues of the Amsterdam Treaty* (1999) 375–94; Bell, 'The New Article 13 EC Treaty: A Sound Basis for European Anti-Discrimination Law?' (1999) *MJ* 5–23; Waddington, 'Testing the Limits of the EC Treaty Article on Non-Discrimination' (1999) *IndLJ* 133–51; Barents, *Het Verdrag van Amsterdam in Werking* (1999) ch 7 and Bell and Waddington, 'The 1996 Intergovernmental Conference and the Prospects of a Non-Discrimination Treaty Article' (1996) *IndLJ* 320–6.

[22] Fifth recital of the preamble to Reg 1612/68.

[23] The Commission has proposed to amend Art 10(1) and to offer the right to reside to (*i*) 'any person corresponding to a spouse under the legislation of the host Member State', (*ii*) descendants and (*iii*) ascendants of the worker and the spouse as well as (*iv*) any other family member of the worker or spouse 'who is dependent on the worker or is living under his roof in the Member State whence he comes'. COM(1998) 394 def.

The first point concerning 'quasi-spouses' is a codification of the judgment in Case 59/85 *Reed* [1986] ECR I–1283. On this point, the proposal has been critically commented upon in the literature. See, eg: Sewandono (1999) n 15 above, 285. It has been suggested that Art 10 should also include partners who are put on a par by the legislation of the State of origin. See, eg: Sewandono, *Werknemersverkeer en Gezinsleven* (1998) at 296–8 and Carlier, 'Proportionality and Citizenship in relation to the Free Movement of Persons' in Carlier and Verwilghen, *Thirty Years of Free Movement of Workers in Europe* (2000) 41–57, 53. See also Jesserun d'Oliveira, 'Vrijheid van Verkeer voor Geregistreerde Partners in de Europese Unie' (2001) *NJB* 205–10 and Elman, 'The Limits of Citizenship: Migration, Sex Discrimination, and Same-Sex Partners in EU Law' (2000) *JCMS* 729–49. The Commission's proposal is understandable, however. As desirable and necessary as it may be to promote equal treatment of unmarried partners (of the same sex) and to facilitate freedom of movement for them, in a European Community where views and policies on such issues in question still differ, one must be critical of a rule which would impose on some States the views developed in others.

State's society, however, seems to have been less relevant to the legislator. Regulation No 1612/68 only mentions a right to pursue employed activities (Article 11)[24] and, for children, a right to gain access to education (Article 12) in the host State. The status of family members was deemed to derive from the status of the workers themselves. Family members would only have the right to reside in the State of employment when, and for as long as, the workers live there and, apart from the two rights mentioned in Articles 11 and 12, they could not claim any other rights in their own capacity.[25] In more practical terms, family members could join the worker, but they would either have to provide for themselves through the income earned from work or be taken care of by the worker. They were not supposed to become a burden on the host State.

Step by step, however, the Court has strengthened the legal status of family members and developed a legal framework which may actually help them to integrate, in their own right, into the host State. Apart from the fact that the Court has interpreted Article 12 as to provide a full right to equal treatment for both dependent and independent[26] children in the field of education,[27] two steps have been particularly relevant. The first concerns dependent family members. Even though Article 7(2) of Regulation No 1612/68 only refers to workers, the Court has held that dependent family members, regardless of their nationality,[28] can also invoke[29] this provision in order to claim equality of treatment as regards 'social advantages.'[30] By invoking Article 7(2) dependent family members of Community workers can claim all rights and benefits which the host State's nationals enjoy in the capacity of workers[31] or by virtue of residence[32] in

---

[24] The Commission has proposed to alter Art 11 as to explicitly entitle family members (holding the nationality of only a third State) the right to pursue self-employed activities too. COM(1998) 394 def.

[25] The derived status of family members was also reflected in the common social security rules. Art 1(f) of Reg 1408/71 defines family members as persons who are defined or recognised as family members by the legislation of the host State. This was understood to imply that family members could only claim derived rights (ie, rights which are under national law specifically offered to, or for, family members such as family allowances and co-insurance for health care) under the Reg to the exclusion of 'personal rights' (ie, rights which are granted to beneficiaries in their capacity as workers, residents or nationals). Under the regime of Reg 1408/71, the latter were reserved for the workers themselves.

[26] Case C–7/94 *Gaal* [1995] ECR I–1031.

[27] See also: ch 5, s 3.3.

[28] See, eg: Case 94/84 *Deak* [1985] ECR 1873.

[29] Art 7(2) Reg 1612/68 cannot only be relied upon by workers who are claiming benefits for, or on behalf of, their family members (see, eg: Case C–310/91 *Schmid* [1993] ECR I–3011, 26), but also by the family members themselves (see, eg: Case C–3/90 *Bernini* [1992] ECR I–1072, 26).

[30] Family members qualify only indirectly for equal treatment under Art 7(2). Benefits constitute 'social advantages' only when they can be regarded as social advantages for the workers themselves. Case 317/85 *Lebon* [1987] ECR 2811, 12. Even though the Court has never ruled so explicitly, it may be assumed that this right to equal treatment under Art 7(2) cannot only be enjoyed by the family members mentioned in Art 10(1) of Reg 1612/68, but also by those who have been admitted for residence by virtue of Art 10(2).

[31] Cp Case 94/84 *Deak* [1985] ECR 1873 (concerning special unemployment benefits for work-seekers).

[32] See, eg: Case C–3/90 *Bernini* [1992] ECR I–1071 (concerning student grants).

the national territory.[33] Dependent family members are not to be put on a par with the family members of nationals of the host State. Rather, they must be treated equally with these nationals themselves.[34]

The second step, arguably, has been taken in *Martínez Sala* (1998) and *Grzelczyk* (2001). It concerns family members who are not or no longer dependent on the worker. From these cases it follows that Union citizens who have exercised their right to freedom of movement and have lawfully established residence in the territory of another Member States can invoke Article 12(1) EC in order to claim a right to equal treatment in, in principle, any policy area.[35] Neither *Martínez Sala* nor *Grzelczyk* concerned family members, and in the former ruling the Court confirmed that only dependent family members can rely on Article 7(2) of Regulation No 1612/68, but both rulings do not seem to leave room for any conclusion other than that independent family members who hold the nationality of a Member State[36] can invoke Article 12(1) EC in order to claim equal treatment as regards virtually all public benefits from the moment[37] they establish residence in the host State.[38]

---

[33] Until recently (n 40 below), Art 7(2) was particularly relevant for family members in the field of social security law. As stated in n 25, in the view of the Community legislator, family members would only enjoy derived rights under Reg 1408/71 to the exclusion of 'personal rights'. This view was approved by the court. Case 40/76 *Kermaschek* [1976] ECR 1669 7. In many cases, however, the court has held that family members could claim such 'personal rights' under Art 7(2) of Reg 1612/68. See, eg: Case C–310/91 *Schmid* [1993] ECR I–3011, 13.

[34] To be sure, in *Taghavi* (1992) the court held that the Iranian spouse of an Italian worker could not rely on Art 7(2) in order to claim an invalidity allowance in Belgium because spouses of Belgian workers could not claim such an allowance either under the applicable law. Case C–243/91 *Taghavi* [1992] ECR I4401, 11. *Taghavi*, however, fit uneasily into the case-law (see, eg: Verschueren, 'Het Arrest Taghavi en de Tegemoetkoming voor Gehandicapten aan niet-EG-Familieleden van EG-Werknemers' (1993) *MR* 74–5) and the ruling in *Schmid* (1993), in which the court wholly ignored *Taghavi* and, concluded that the child of a Community worker could claim in Belgium a disability allowance under Art 7(2) even though the family members of Belgian workers could not claim such an allowance either, suggests that the conclusion drawn in *Taghavi* no longer stands. See also: ch 3, s 3.2. The Commission also seems to share this view. In its 1998 proposal for amending Reg 1612/68 (COM(1998) 394 fin) it has inserted an Art 10(3) which states that all family members entitled to live in a Member State under Art 10(1) or 10(2) 'shall be entitled to all financial, tax, social, cultural or other advantages available to *nationals*' (*ital*: APvdM).

[35] Case C–85/96 *Martínez Sala* [1998] ECR I–2681, 57–61 and Case C–184/99 *Grzelczyk* [2001] ECR I–6193, 32.

[36] Arguably, independent family members who only hold the nationality of non-Member States also enjoy a right to equal treatment as regards virtually all public benefits. In *Martínez Sala* the Court only spoke of Union citizens who are lawfully residing in the territory of another Member State, but it seems indisputable that third country family members who have exercised the right to reside guaranteed by Art 10(1) of Reg 1612/68 fall within the personal scope of Community law, and thus, Art 12(1) EC. The legal position of family members who have been admitted to the State of the workers' employment by virtue of Art 10(2) of Reg 1612/68 is not wholly clear. They can rely on Art 7(2) of the Reg, but it is not certain whether they can, in their own capacity, claim rights under Art 12(1) EC.

[37] National rules which make eligibility of non-nationals for social benefits conditional upon a minimum period of residence constitute direct discrimination on grounds of nationality (Cp Case 7/75 *Mr and Mrs F* [1975] ECR 679, 17) and, as concluded in ch 3, s 3.2.2, one may assume that waiting-period requirements applicable to non-national and nationals alike constitute indirect discrimination on grounds of nationality.

[38] One may object and claim that the conclusion that all family members are entitled to claim 'social advantages' may increase pressure on the financial budgets of social assistance and other

The immigration status of family members may still be dependent on the status of the workers,[39] but the same no longer seems to hold true for the rights they enjoy upon arrival in the host State's territory.[40] Once, and for as long as, they lawfully reside there, family members must be treated as equal members of that State's society. For the Member States, the message following from the case law, and *Martínez Sala* and *Grzelczyk* in particular, is the same as in the case of the workers. Member States can only protect their welfare state interests by using their remaining immigration powers. They are no longer entitled to do so by applying discriminatory rules governing access to their welfare states.

2.4 Non-Economic Residents

Migrant workers and their family members may always have been seen as a potential threat to the welfare state, but this holds even more true for the economically inactive nationals of other States. In the early 1990s, Member States, as members of the Council, promoted European citizenship by recognising a general right of residence (Directive No 90/364) and, one year later, they were even willing to formally establish a Union citizenship (Article 17 EC) and to 'constitutionalise' the right of residence (Article 18 EC).

The Member States made it patently clear, however, that the economically inactive should not become a burden on the host States' welfare state systems, and social assistance schemes in particular.[41] The afore mentioned directive provides that the non-economically active are only entitled to reside in another Member State when, and for as long as, they are able to provide for themselves and are sufficiently insured for health care. The wording of Article 18(1) EC indicates that the provision was not intended to bring about any substantive

public benefits systems. One could also argue, as the German government had done in the *Lebon*-proceedings (ch 3, s 3.2.2) that workers, by temporarily giving financial support to family members, enable these family members to obtain the right to reside and to claim social advantages in their own right. There are no indications, let alone any proof, however, that such abuses occur in practice. From the perspective of protecting the welfare state interests of the host States, the *Lebon*-rule is over inclusive and, arguably, there is no need to adhere to it. Also, the Commission does not see a need for the rule. It has proposed to insert a new Art 10(3) in Reg 1612/68 which directly (Explanatory Memorandum—COM(1998) 394 def 13) confers upon family members a right to equal treatment as regards 'financial, tax, social, cultural or other advantages' (cp fn 15 above).

[39] Case C–356/98 *Kaba* [2000] ECR I–2623. See also: Blake, 'Family Life in Community Law: The Limits of Freedom and Dignity' in Guild, *The Legal Framework and Social Consequences of Free Movement of Persons in the European Union* (1999) 7–17, 8.

[40] The willingness of the Court to strengthen the status of family members, and to regard them as equal members of the host State's society, is further demonstrated by the ruling in *Cabanis-Issarte* (1996) in which the Court (largely) abandoned the distinction between personal rights and derived rights (see n 33 above). Case C–87/94 *Cabanis-Issarte* [1996] ECR I–2097, 30–44.

[41] In the words of Tomuschat: 'The main gist . . . is clear. A person who is not actively involved in economic life must take care of his or her vital necessities in a manner congruent with taking his or her own responsibility, without enjoying the right to rely on public funds of the State of residence'. Tomuschat, 'Annotation *Martínez Sala*' (2000) *CMLRev* 449–57, 455.

changes in the free movement regime. The right to reside freely is subject to the 'limitations and conditions' laid down in the Treaty and secondary legislation.[42]

By inserting Articles 17 and 18 EC in the Treaty, however, Member States did provide the Court with two legal tools which it could use for strengthening the legal status of the non-economically active. *Martínez Sala* and *Grzelczyck* (2001)[43] demonstrate that the Court is indeed willing to make use of these new tools. In *Martínez Sala* the Court ruled that nationals of a Member State who are lawfully residing in the territory of another Member State fall within the scope of the Treaty provisions on European citizenship and that they, in this capacity, can rely on Article 12(1) EC in order claim equal treatment as regards all rights and benefits covered by Regulations No 1408/71 and No 1612/68.[44] The Court seemed to have established the rule that all Union citizens are entitled to gain access to welfare state benefits under the same conditions as nationals of the host State when, and for as long as, they lawfully reside in that State. Until recently, one could still have objected to this interpretation of *Martínez Sala* and have argued that one cannot, and should not read into a single judgment which might have been confined to the rather unique facts of the case,[45] which was not extensively reasoned, seemed to run counter to the intentions of those who drafted the Treaty and which has not been free from criticism.[46] The judgment of the Court in *Grzelczyk*, however, confirms the suggested reading of *Martínez Sala*. The Court accepted that Community students can invoke Article 12(1) EC in order to claim equal treatment as regards social assistance, provided their residence in the host State is lawful. Article 12(1), the Court held, must be read in conjunction with Article 18(1) EC, which provides for free movement rights subject to conditions laid down in the Treaty and secondary legislation.[47] Read together, *Martínez Sala* and *Grzelczyk* imply that Member States still hold the power to refuse 'needy' economically inactive nationals of other Member States residence on their territory, and to end lawful residence when such persons become an unreasonable burden on their social

---

[42] Further, even though the Member States may have been aware of the fact that non-economic residents were to be admitted to their educational institutions (see ch 5, s 4) and that some of them could possibly benefit from certain provisions of Reg 1408/71 (ch 2, s 6), they had not included in the 1990 residence directives or the Treaty on European Union any provision offering beneficiaries additional protection against discriminatory treatment in, or by, the host States. EC Treaty Art 17(1) provides that Union citizens shall enjoy the rights accorded by the Treaty, but the insertion of this provision was not intended as an extension of rights. In fact, the only provision which did say something specific about the legal status of the non-economically active in the territory of another Member State, Art 3 of Dir 93/96, expressly denies students a right to obtain maintenance grants in the host State.

[43] Case C–184/99 *Grzelczyk* [2001] ECR I–6193. See ch 3, s 4.3.

[44] Case C–85/96 *Martínez Sala* [1998] ECR I–2691, 57–61.

[45] O'Leary, 'Putting Flesh on the Bones of European Union Citizenship' (1999) *ELRev* 68–79, 77; Bulterman, 'Annotation to *Bickel*' (1999) *CMLRev* 1325–34, 1329 and Fries and Shaw, 'Citizenship of the Union: First Steps in the European Court of Justice' (1998) *EPL* 533–59, 558.

[46] For criticism on the ruling see, eg: Becker, 'Freizügigkeit in der EU—Auf dem Weg vom Begleitrecht zur Bürgerfreiheit' (1999) *EuR* 522–33 and, especially, Tomuschat (2000) n 41 above.

[47] Case C–184/99 *Grzelczyk* [2001] ECR I–6193, 37.

assistance schemes, but that Member States which do not make use of this power must grant the persons concerned social assistance and other welfare state services under the same conditions as their own nationals.

2.5 Residence

The conclusion that lawful residence in the territory of another Member State provides the basis for a right to equal treatment as regards access to public services does not necessarily mean that all Union citizens who are living in another Member State can actually enjoy all such benefits. Member States are entitled to make enjoyment of certain benefits such as social assistance and maintenance grants conditional upon 'habitual residence' in the national territory. The notion of 'habitual residence' can be equated with 'domicile,' which has a more comprehensive meaning than residence. Residence can be described as the place where a person effectively lives. Domicile is the place where a person has his principal establishment. A person can have more than one place of residence, but only one domicile. Domicile is a legal concept which, for the purposes of the laws or benefits in question, links an individual to specific legal order to avoid the person concerned being entitled to benefits or being subject to duties in more than one State.[48] In most cases residence and domicile will coincide, but this is not necessarily the case as regards students, teachers participating in exchange programmes, pensioners and other persons having ties with more than one Member State. Community law is based on the assumption that social assistance or maintenance grants in one Member State only[49] and this implies that as regards such multi-based persons a choice must be made between the States they have ties with. The ruling in *Swaddling* (1999) demonstrates that the concept of habitual residence or domicile must be determined by taking into account the person's family situation, the reasons which led him to move to another State, the length and continuity of residence, the stability of employment and his intentions 'at it appears from all the circumstances.'[50] General rules cannot be given, but application of these various factors will often lead to the conclusion that students, for instance, cannot be regarded as 'habitual residents' of the State where they study and that they, in spite of the *Grzelczyk* ruling, will not be able to claim social assistance or maintenance grants in that State.

[48] See, eg: Garot, 'A New Basis for European Citizenship: Residence?' in La Torre (ed), *European Citizenship: An Institutional Challenge* (1998) 229–48 and Corson, 'Reform of Domicile Law for Application to Transients, Temporary Residents and Multi-Based Persons' (1981) *ColJLSP* 327–64.

[49] Ch 3, s 5 and ch 5, s 4.3.

[50] Case C–90/97 *Swaddling* [1999] ECR I–1075, 30 (in relation top Art 10a of Reg 1408/71).

2.6 Conclusions

Community law can be interpreted as to have reached the point of guaranteeing all Union citizens a right to equal treatment as regards access to virtually[51] all welfare state services from the moment they lawfully establish residence in the territory[52] of another Member State on the basis of Community law, international law or national law until the moment they voluntarily give up, or involuntarily lose, their lawful resident status. Member States are no longer entitled to protect their welfare state interests by making any distinctions between nationals and non-nationals or 'recently arrived' and 'long-term' residents. Member States must protect their interests by using their remaining immigration powers. Union citizenship gives entitlement to a 'full and equal membership' of the welfare state in the State of lawful residence.

In spite of the progress which has been made, European Community law has not yet evolved as far as American constitutional law has. It still does not provide for an unlimited and unconditional right to reside freely and, unlike United States citizens, European Union citizens can still be denied political rights such as the right to vote and stand as a candidate in national elections. Nonetheless, the reason why, and the degree to which, Community law and American law protect citizens who have established residence in another State against discriminatory treatment in social-economic matters have become quite similar.

Durational residence requirements, the main legal instruments which American States have used to protect their welfare state interests, have been condemned by the Supreme Court.[53] In *Shapiro* (1969) the Court classed such requirements as unconstitutional penalties on the constitutional right to travel,[54] but the main concern of the Court has never been that waiting-period requirements actually deter or burden the exercise of the right to travel. The problem with such requirements is that they make a distinction between two categories of persons who both hold citizenship of the State wherein they reside. In *Saenz v Roe* (1999) the Court made clear that it is a privilege of United States citizenship to establish residence in any State and, from the moment this is actually done, to claim an equality of rights with every other State citizen.[55] The Court formally still spoke of this right to equal treatment with other State citizens as a component of the right to travel, but it in fact wholly separated the

---

[51] n 16.

[52] The mere fact that Community citizens who have established lawful residence in another Member State have a right to equal treatment as regards public benefits does not necessarily mean that such benefits can only be enjoyed within the territory of the State concerned. When the host State offers its own nationals who are not residing in the national territory, it must give the benefits in question to nationals of other Member States under the same conditions. See, eg: Case 235/87 *Matteucci* [1987] ECR 5589 and Case C–337/97 *Meeusen* [1999] ECR.

[53] To be sure, there is one exception: tuition waiting-period requirements. See also: ch 5, s 8.4.

[54] Ch 2, s 8.5.1.

[55] Ch 2, s 8.5.2.

right to freedom of movement and the right to equal treatment.[56] Durational residence requirements discriminate against United States citizens who have completed their 'interstate travel' and acquired citizenship in their new State. As fundamental as the right to reside freely among the various States may be for United States citizens, it is in fact merely a means for choosing State citizenship and it is in this capacity that they are entitled to 'full' equality of treatment. The comparison with the ruling of the Court of Justice in *Martínez Sala* may not be perfect but is nonetheless striking. The Court did not attach any importance to the (source of) right to freedom of movement (itself). It simply held that Mrs Martínez Sala, as a Union citizen lawfully residing in the territory of another Member State, could claim equality of treatment with the nationals of the host State. Community law may not entitle Union citizens to citizenship of, and all political rights in, the Member State where they reside, but those who have established residence in another Member State have acquired a kind of membership status which could be labelled 'European Union Denizenship.'

3 NON-RESIDENTS

3.1 Introduction

From a historical perspective, the above conclusions regarding the legal status of Union citizens lawfully residing in the territory of another Member State are no doubt revolutionary. Four decades ago, Member States offered non-nationals only, if at all, access to (most) public benefits after a minimum period of residence or employment, and they could even end residence once non-nationals became in need of (social assistance) benefits. Today, States are obliged to grant nationals of other Member States access to public benefits under the same conditions as their own nationals from the moment they establish residence within their borders and the possibility of expelling non-nationals has been severely restricted.

Viewed from the perspective of the welfare state, however, the conclusions drawn in Section 2 cannot be said to be so revolutionary. Member States may be obliged to grant 'unanticipated and costly'[57] benefits to non-nationals, but they still hold the power to deny residence to economically inactive and 'needy' nationals of other Member States, they can still levy taxes on Union citizens working and residing within their territory and, given the low mobility rates, the conclusions of the previous section are not likely to jeopardise welfare state benefits. In essence, Community law, as discussed above, merely implies an attack on the nationality principle, not on the territoriality principle. The case law, culminating in *Martínez Sala* and *Grzelczyk*, has evolved as to provide for

---

[56] Cp *Saenz v Roe*, 119 S.Ct. 1518 (1999), Chief Justice Rehnquist, dissenting.
[57] Steiner (1985) n 18 above, 41.

a territorially defined form of membership which is in line with, and in fact only strengthens, the notions of equality and solidarity on which welfare states are internally based. Welfare states have largely been 'de-nationalised,' but the conclusions drawn in Section 2, do not imply a 'de-territorialisation' of public benefit systems.

The territoriality of the welfare state is questioned, however, when the attention is shifted to the category of non-residents. For the purposes of this section, non-residents include frontier workers, other workers who have decided not to establish residence in the State of employment and Union citizens who travel to other Member States without relocating the centre of their economic and private interests. It is only when one considers the status and cross-border rights of non-residents that the tension between the goal of guaranteeing freedom of movement and safeguarding welfare state interests fully comes to the surface. Territoriality entails various things, but, above all, it means that public benefits are in principle preserved for persons working and residing within the State borders. Only such persons can be required to contribute their equal share to the funding of public benefit schemes and, as 'members,' gain access to these schemes. If States were obliged to share all public benefits with non-residents welfare state services would be put in jeopardy.[58] At the same time, however, it is clear that freedom of movement and Union citizenship would be nothing but empty notions if non-residents could be denied access to all public benefits on the sole ground that they are 'non-contributors.' A right to freedom of movement, which is practical and relevant, requires enjoyment of certain public services and access by non-residents does not in all cases have to affect the funding or organisation of benefit schemes.

This section seeks to establish whether Community law provides some general rules which may help to separate benefits that can be preserved for residents from those to be shared with non-residents. This is not an easy task. Written Community law reveals little and the relevant Court judgments are so small in number, and they often concerned such unique and different factual constellations, that it is quite difficult to draw general conclusions. Nonetheless, it is possible to distill some principles or rules from Community law.

For instance, Member States are no longer entitled to protect their welfare state interests by using their immigration powers. As regards residents the Court has prohibited States from applying discriminatory rules to Union citizens residing within their territory and has only allowed them to protect their welfare state services by using immigration powers. As to the non-residents, the situation is the reverse. Upon production of a passport or identity card, all nationals of other Member States must be admitted to the national territory.[59] Member

---

[58] Ch 1, s 2.
[59] Joined Cases C–286/82 and 26/83 *Luisi and Carbone* [1984] ECR 377, 16; Case C–68/89 *Commission v the Netherlands* [1991] ECR I–2637, 13 and Case C–274 *Bickel* [1998] ECR I–7637, 15.

States can only protect their systems by applying discriminatory rules in the substantive policy area concerned.

The discussion below focuses on the rules and principles that must be applied when reviewing the legality of the two main discriminatory criteria which have traditionally been used by Member States in order to exclude non-residents from their public benefits systems: nationality and residence.

3.2 Frontier Workers

The main provision available for frontier workers and other workers who have decided not to establish residence in the State of employment is Article 7(2) of Regulation No 1612/68. Are Member States entitled to deny equal treatment as regards 'social advantages' to workers and family members on the ground that they have not established residence in the national territory?

In support of the view that States indeed have such a right several arguments have been brought forward. In *Meints* (1997), for instance, some governments had argued that national rules which make entitlement to social benefits (*in casu* special unemployment benefits) do not run counter to Article 7(2) because this provision would not provide for the possibility of exporting benefits. Further, in *Meeusen* (1999) it was argued that frontier workers and their children cannot claim non-discrimination under Article 7(2) because this provision primarily aims to promote the integration of the worker's family in the host State. Frontier workers, however, have voluntarily chosen not to reside, and thus not to fully integrate, in the State of employment and, for this reason, they would not be able to claim the full benefits of Article 7(2). The Court, however, has rejected these arguments. Both in *Meints* and in *Meeusen* the Court referred to the preamble of Regulation No 1612/68 which explicitly states that the right to freedom of movement must be enjoyed 'without discrimination by permanent, seasonal and frontier workers.'[60]

Another argument that could be made is that frontier workers and their family members do not enjoy a right to equal treatment as regards all social advantages. It is settled case law that the concept of social advantages covers all rights and benefits which are granted to national workers 'primarily because of their status of workers' or 'by virtue of the mere fact of . . . residence' in the territory of the host State. Frontier workers are workers and it is nothing but logical that they, as follows from *Meints*, can rely on Article 7(2) in order to challenge rules that deny them employment-related benefits on grounds of their nationality or the fact that they reside in another Member State. It is less obvious, however, why workers who have decided not to transfer their private residence to the State of employment should also enjoy a right to nondiscrimination as regards benefits that are granted by virtue of residence. Why would non-residents be

---

[60] Case C–57/96 *Meints* [1997] ECR I–6689 50–1.

entitled to residence-based benefits just because they work in the State concerned? *Meeusen*, in which the Court accepted that a child of a frontier worker could claim nondiscrimination as regards student grants in the State of the parent's employment, demonstrates that frontier workers and their families can claim residence-based benefits under Article 7(2).[61] Ms Meeusen, however, could only claim a student grant because the law on student grants in the State of employment did not require from children of national workers to reside or study in the national territory. In other words, *Meeusen* merely implies that frontier workers cannot be denied student grants and other benefits granted by virtue of residence for reasons of their nationality. Neither in *Meeusen* nor in any other judgment, however, has the Court expressed its view on the compatibility of residence requirement for residence-based benefits with Article 7(2) of Regulation No 1612/68. In sum, frontier workers cannot be discriminated against on grounds of their nationality, but so far the Court has never obliged Member States to treat such non-resident workers as though they were residents.

3.3 Travellers

3.3.1 Nationality Requirements

The most[62] important Treaty provision available to 'Community travellers' who wish to challenge rules denying them access to public benefits on the ground that they lack the nationality of the State they visit, is Article 12(1) EC. Within the scope of application of the Treaty, the provision prohibits any discrimination on grounds of nationality. The prohibition is strict. Once it is established that Article 12(1) is applicable, nationality criteria are in principle prohibited. Thus, in order to establish whether Article 12(1) can be relied upon, it must be determined whether the situation of Union citizens seeking access to public services in another State falls within the ambit of Community law. Two conditions must be met. First, the Union citizens themselves must fall within the scope of the provision. No problems seem to arise here. All Union citizens enjoy the right to travel to other States and those who exercise the right fall within the scope of Community law. Second, it must be established that Article 12(1) EC can also be relied upon in relation to the desired benefit. On this point, interpretation problems have arisen. In determining the scope of the right to equal treatment, the Court has followed different approaches or methods, which may lead to different answers to the question whether or not a given right or benefit is covered by Article 12(1) EC.

---

[61] Case C–337/97 *Meeusen* [1999] ECR I–3289.

[62] Besides Art 12(1), Union citizens travelling to other States may rely on Art 49 EC in order to challenge nationality requirements. See, eg: Case C–20/92 *Hubbard* [1993] ECR I–3777, 14 and Joined Cases C–62 and 63/81 *Seco* [1982] ECR 223, 8.

In the first judgments in which the provision was applied independently, the Court made the answer to the question whether or not a given right or benefit falls within the ambit of Article 12(1) EC dependent on the degree to which the powers in the substantive policy area concerned have been transferred to the Community. Thus, in *Gravier* (1985), after having referred to various measures which the Member States and the Community institutions had taken in the field of vocational training, the Court concluded that access to such training falls within the scope of the Treaty.[63] Following a similar line of reasoning, the Court concluded in *Lair* (1988) that Article 12 EC does not extend to student grants covering the costs of maintenance since such grants were considered as matters of educational and social policy falling with the domain of the Member States.[64]

In later cases, however, the Court did not adopt such a 'transfer of powers approach.'[65] In *Cowan*, for instance, the Court ruled that a recipient of services could rely on Article 12(1) in order to claim financial compensation for victims of crimes even though the powers in the area concerned (criminal law) were still in the hands of the Member States. The Court ruled that whenever Community law guarantees a natural person the right to go to another Member State the 'protection of that person from harm in the Member States in question, on the same basis as that of nationals and persons residing there is a corollary of that freedom of movement.'[66] In subsequent cases such as *Commission v. Spain* (1994), *Data Delecta* (1996) and *Bickel* (1998) the Court followed a similar line of reasoning as regards the rights to gain access to public museums,[67] courts[68] and to use minority languages in court proceedings.[69] The powers in the respective areas remained in the hands of Member States but this did not free them from the obligation not to apply rules which 'discriminate against persons to whom Community law gives the right to equal treatment or restrict the fundamental freedoms guaranteed by Community law.'[70] In these cases the Court followed a 'functional approach' in determining the material scope of Article 12(1) EC comparable, if not similar, to the one it had applied in the context of the free movement of workers. Under this approach, equality of treatment must be guaranteed when, and in as far as necessary for, guaranteeing an effective or practical and relevant free movement of persons. It is of no relevance whether, or the extent to which, powers in a given substantive policy area have been transferred to the Community.

---

[63] Case 293/83 *Gravier* [1985] ECR 293, 19–25.

[64] Case 39/86 *Lair* [1988] ECR 3161, 14–15.

[65] In fact, this approach has only been applied in educational cases. See also: Case C–357/89 *Raulin* [1992] ECR I–1027 and Case C–3/90 *Bernini* [1992] ECR I–1071.

[66] Case 186/87 *Cowan* [1989] ECR 195, 17.

[67] Case C–45/93 *Commission v Spain* [1994] ECR I–911.

[68] Case C–43/95 *Data Delecta* [1996] ECR I–4661; Case C–323/95 *Hayes and Hayes* [1997] ECR I–1711 and Case C–122/96 *Saldanha* [1997] ECR I–5325.

[69] Case C–274/96 *Bickel* [1998] ECR I–7637.

[70] See, eg: Case 43/95 *Data Delecta* [1996] ECR I–4661, 12.

Cowan and the other cases just mentioned suggest that the material scope of Article 12(1) EC must be determined in accordance with the functional method initially developed in the context of the free movement of workers. This did not automatically imply, however, that the right to equal treatment of non-residents reaches as far as the equivalent right of workers. In a case like *Cowan* the Court spoke of the right to equal treatment as a 'corollary' of the right to freedom of movement. As regards workers residing in the State of employment, the right to be treated equally in socioeconomic matters can indeed be said to be a corollary of, or a prerequisite for, their rights to work, reside and integrate in the host State's society. The same cannot be said, as regards non-residents. A possible right to claim social assistance benefits or admission to education in other Member States does not logically follow from the right to travel. Certainly, a right to equal treatment as regards social and educational benefits could promote, and indeed trigger, mobility, but the rulings in cases such as *Cowan* and *Data Delecta* do not necessarily imply that the Court has recognised such a right to equal treatment. The right to travel was not perceived as a concomitant of the right to equal treatment. Only the reverse held true.

Nonetheless, the more recent rulings in *Martínez Sala* (1998) and *Grzelczyk* (2001) suggest that Community citizens do hold the right to move to other States in order to claim access to virtually all public services under the same conditions as the nationals of those States. In the former case the German Government had argued that it was not obliged by Community law to grant a child-raising allowance to an economically inactive Spanish national residing within its borders. The allowance Ms Martínez Sala had applied for fell outside the material scope of Article 12(1) EC and she herself was not covered by the personal scope of the Treaty. The Court did not agree. As regards the material scope of Article 12 EC, it held that the child-raising allowance in question falls within the scope of both Regulation No 1408/71 and Article 7(2) of Regulation No 1612/68 and this implied, according to the Court, that the allowance 'indisputably' fell within the scope of Community law.[71] In addition, the Court held that Ms Martínez Sala, as a national of a Member State who was lawfully residing in the territory of another Member State, fell within the personal scope of the Treaty provisions on European Citizenship. Article 17(2) attaches to the status of citizen of the Union the rights and duties laid down by the Treaty, including the right laid down in Article 12 not to suffer discrimination on grounds of nationality.[72] In *Grzelczyk* the Court basically confirmed *Martínez Sala* by holding that Union citizens who are lawfully residing in the territory of another Member States can rely on Article 12(1) EC in all situations which fall within the scope *ratione materiae* of Community law. Those situations include, so the Court held, those exercising 'the right to move and reside freely in another Member State, as conferred by Article 18 EC.'[73]

[71] Case C–85/96 *Martínez Sala* [1998] ECR I–2691, 57.
[72] 60–5 above.
[73] Case C–184/99 *Grzelczyk* [2001] ECR I–6193, 32–3.

The two rulings suggest that the material scope of Article 12(1) EC must be determined in accordance with the same criteria as, and that it reaches as far as, the scope of the right to equal treatment of workers.[74] All Community citizens fall within the personal scope of Community law and all those who exercise the right to freedom of movement come within the material scope of Community law, and Article 12 EC. Consequently, *Martínez Sala* and *Grzelczyk* can be interpreted to imply that all Community citizens who travel to other Member States can gain access there to virtually all public services, including, eg, social assistance benefits, education and student grants schemes, under the same conditions as the nationals of the host State. Put differently, the rulings can be interpreted as to imply that Member States are no longer entitled to deny social benefits to Community citizens residing outside their territory for reasons of their nationality.

Admittedly, one cannot be wholly certain of this conclusion. Both *Martínez Sala* and *Grzelczyk* concerned residents, not non-residents. Yet, it is submitted that such a conclusion should be drawn. Certainly, Community citizens who merely travel to other Member States should not be entitled to claim social assistance benefits there.[75] The exclusion of non-residents would indeed seem a *sine qua non* for securing the financial stability of social assistance benefit schemes.[76] Similarly, virtually anyone would agree that Community students should have no right to claim full student grants in the State where they have taken up their studies. A duty to admit non-residents to both education itself and student grant systems, could put the funding of the grant systems at least in jeopardy. However, the conclusion that the scope of Article 12(1) EC is broad enough to cover virtually all social and educational benefits does not imply that non-residents must actually be accorded such benefits. That conclusion merely means that States cannot deny benefits to non-residents on ground of their nationality. When applied equally to nationals and non-nationals, national rules which make access to public benefits conditional upon residence in the State territory can avoid being classed as a prohibited indirect discrimination by reason of nationality when they are necessary for, and proportional to, the legitimate goal of maintaining public services. As long as welfare state tasks are primarily carried out at Member State level distinctions between residents and non-residents are in many cases a 'must' for protecting public benefit systems. Residence serves as one of the main criteria for tax or premium duties and it may therefore possibly also be applied as a criterion for determining entitlement to benefits. Nationality, however, is not a common criterion for imposing duties of

---

[74] In fact, it would seem that the *scope ratione materiae* of Art 12(1) EC has been extended so far that the application of the non-discrimination principle depends almost exclusively on the *scope ratione personae* of Community law. Maduro, 'Europe's Social Self: "The Sickness unto Death"', in Shaw (ed), *Social Law and Policy in an Evolving European Union* (2000) 325–49, 336.

[75] Cp Schockweiler, 'La Portée du Principle de Non-Discrimination del'Article 7 du Traité CEE' (1991) *RDE* 3 *et seq*, 24 and Steiner, 'Recipients of Services—Some More Equal than Others' (1985) *ELRev* 348 *et seq*, 352.

[76] Cp von Wilmowsky, 'Zugang zu öffentlichen Leistungen anderer Mitgliedstaaten—Das Integrationskonzept des EWG-Vertrages in der Leistungsverwaltung' (1991) *ZfaöR* 231–81, 258.

contribution and, arguably, it cannot, or at least should not, serve as a condition for entitlement to social benefits.[77] In *Martínez Sala* and *Grzelczyk* the Court did not make a direct link between free movement rights and the right to equal treatment. According to the Court, the latter right correlates to, and follows from, the combined status of Union citizen and lawful resident of another Member State. The same conclusion can be drawn as regards 'Community travellers.' Arguably, their right to equal treatment is not primarily granted in order to facilitate or promote the right to travel. All nationals of Member States have acquired the status of Union citizen and it is the corollary of that status not to be discriminated against in 'non-political matters' by any other Member State on the ground that this status has not been acquired by virtue of the nationality of that Member State.[78]

3.3.2 Residence Requirements

It follows from the foregoing that Member States are no longer entitled to protect their welfare states against an influx of residents from other States who may be in need, or who come for the sole purpose, of obtaining public benefits by refusing them entry to the national territory or by denying them benefits on grounds of their nationality. The proper legal tool to be used is the residence requirement.[79] In assessing the compatibility of residence requirements for enti-

---

[77] *Lair*, for instance, allows States to offer maintenance grants to nationals who have never lived in the national territory, and to deny such grants to economically inactive Union citizens who are living within the national territory. Arguably, there is no need, and no room, for such direct discriminations based on nationality. See also: ch 5, Ss 4.3, n 175.

[78] Further, in rulings in cases such as *Data Delecta* (1996) the Court held that Member States are prohibited, also in areas (still) falling within their domain from discriminating 'against persons to whom Community law gives the right to equal treatment' *or* restricting 'the fundamental freedoms guaranteed by Community law'. The right to equal treatment is thus not only linked to the right to freedom of movement but also to Union citizens who, according to Art 17(2) EC, 'enjoy the rights conferred by this Treaty' including the right not to be discriminated against on grounds of nationality (Case C–85/96 *Martínez Sala* [1998] ECR I–2691, 61).

[79] The view that residence rather than nationality requirements are the proper legal tools for protecting welfare state interests finds further support from another observation of the Court in *Martínez Sala*. The Court expressly stated that 'persons genuinely seeking work must also be classed as a worker'. Case C–85/96 *Martínez Sala* [1998] ECR I–2691, 32. Since *Antonissen* (1991) it is settled case-law that Community citizens have the right to enter and to stay for a 'reasonable period of time' in the territory of another Member State in order to seek work (Case C–292/89 *Antonissen* [1991] ECR I–745, 21), but in *Lebon* (1987) the Court held that work-seekers could not be regarded as workers entitled to claim equal treatment as regards social advantages under Art 7(2) of Reg 1612/68 (Case 316/85 *Lebon* [1987] ECR 2811, 26). The fact that work-seekers are now classed as workers does not seem to leave room for any conclusion other than that work-seekers can rely on Art 7(2) of Reg 1612/68. Compare O'Leary (1999) fn 12 above, 76. That conclusion, however, does not imply that Member States are now actually obliged to offer work-seekers access to all 'social advantages'. Work-seekers merely enjoy a right to stay in the State concerned; they have not acquired the right to establish residence there. *Martínez Sala* would seem to imply that work-seekers can still be denied access to benefits on the ground that they are not resident; the ruling merely seems to imply that they can no longer be denied benefits on the ground that they lack the nationality of the State where they seek work. On this point see also van der Steen, 'De Europese Burger Krijgt Handen en Voeten' (1998) *NTER* 163–6, 165.

tlement or access to public benefits with Community law two provisions must be considered: Article 49 EC and Article 12(1) EC.

3.3.2.1 *Article 49 EC*

If Françoise Gravier's claim[80] that she could invoke the principle of non-discrimination in her capacity as recipient of educational services in order to challenge the tuition fee which she as a foreign student was required to pay had been successful, Article 49 EC could have been a particularly lucrative source for European citizens who wish to avail themselves of public services in other States. Article 49 EC provides for a right to go to other States for the sole purpose of receiving services[81] and, more than once, the Court has held that national rules which make the right to provide or receive services conditional upon establishment or residence in the national territory imply the very negation of the free movement of services.[82] Such rules can only be upheld in the few instances in which they are necessary to protect public policy, security or health.[83] Basically, if Françoise Gravier's argument had been accepted, the Court would have come close to recognising a right to freely 'shop around' for public benefits.

Clearly, the drafters of the Treaty provisions on the free movement of services never intended, and the provisions simply cannot be interpreted as, to create such 'unique' opportunities for Community citizens. As part of the common market rules, the provisions are based on the assumption that States are not entitled to intervene in the private market with a view to favouring their own nationals or residents at the expense of non-nationals and non-residents. Such 'selfish intents'[84] frustrate the functioning of the market mechanism. By their nature, residence requirements are at odds with a common market for commercial services. The same does not hold true for public services. In many cases, residence requirements are a 'must' for maintaining welfare state services. Member States' ability to maintain public services partly depends on their capacity to exclude residents of other Member States. To some degree, welfare states must be allowed to be selfish. The rules and principles governing free movement of services do not seem to have sufficient regard to the specific public nature of such services. These rules and principles do not seem to leave enough room for the application of residence requirements in cases where these are actually needed for protecting public services.

The Court has recognised this. First, it has limited the scope of Articles 49 *et seq*. Article 50 EC defines 'services' as services which are 'normally provided for

---

[80] Ch 5, s 4.

[81] See, eg: Case C–274/96 *Bickel* [1998] ECR I–7637, 15.

[82] See, eg: Case C–222/95 *Parodi* [1997] ECR I–3899, 31; Case 39/75 *Coenen* [1975] ECR 1547 7 and Case 33/74 *van Binsbergen* [1974] ECR 1299, 11.

[83] Case C–288/89 *Mediawet I* [1991] ECR I–4007 11 and Case C–352/85 *Bond van Adverteerders* [1988] ECR 2085, 32–4.

[84] Gergen, 'The Selfish State and the Market' (1988) *TexLRev* 1099–153.

remuneration.'[85] In *Gravier* the Court still remained silent on Articles 49 and 50 EC but three years later the Court explained in *Humbel* (1988) that the 'essential characteristic of remuneration lies in the fact that it constitutes consideration for the service in question,' and that it 'is normally agreed upon between the provider and the recipient of the service.'[86] Such a characteristic was considered to be absent in the case of courses offered under national educational systems because (*i*) in establishing and maintaining such systems States are not seeking to engage in gainful activity but are rather fulfilling duties towards their population in the social, cultural and educational fields and (*ii*) such public educational systems are, as a rule, funded from the public purse.[87] More in general, *Humbel* seems to imply that in the case of bipartite provider-recipient relationships, under which the State itself acts as the provider, services do not constitute services in the sense of Article 50 EC when they are mainly funded out of tax revenues are provided.[88] As regards such bipartite relationships, the 'public/private funding distinction'[89] constitutes the main, and often decisive, criterion for determining whether or not a given benefit can be classed as a service in the sense of Article 50.

Second, where Article 49 EC does apply to public services,[90] the Court does not always apply the traditional tests for justification strictly. The Court does not always apply the justification tests as strictly as it does in commercial cases. For instance, in its case law the Court has always held that the public policy, health and security exception contained in Article 46 EC cannot be relied upon

[85] Joined Cases C–286/82 and 26/83 *Luisi and Carbone* [1984] ECR 377, 9.

[86] Case 263/86 *Humbel* [1988] ECR I–6447, 17.

[87] The fact that pupils, students and/or their parents may have to pay enrolment or tuition fees could not alter that conclusion. *Ibid*, 16–18.

[88] See also Case C–109/92 *Wirth* [1993] ECR I–6447, 19.

[89] O'Leary, *The Evolving Concept of Community Citizenship—From the Free Movement of Persons to Union Citizenship* (1996) 75.

[90] For public services, Art 49 EC is particularly relevant where third parties play a role in the provision, financing and/or organisation of public services. Privatisation processes have largely eroded the traditional picture of the welfare state in which the State itself provides services to its population. In order promote efficiency and to reduce bureaucracy, governments have called in third parties to provide, organise, regulate and/or administer public benefits. These third parties, which may be responsible for managing their own budget and often operate quite independently of the State organ that installed, or contracted, them, may provide services in the sense of Art 50 EC. For instance, where public institutions (eg, national health service institutions) fund services which are performed by private actors (eg, general practitioners) operating on independent and/or commercial basis, the relationship between that private actor and the recipient (ie, the patient) of the publicly funded service could very well be economic in nature. Further, the remuneration mentioned in Art 50 EC does not necessarily have to be paid by the recipient himself. Payment by a third party may suffice. Joined Cases C–51/96 and C–191/96 *Deliège* [2000] ECR I–0000, 56 and Case 352/85 *Bond van Adverteerders* [1988] ECR 2085, 16. This could for instance imply that services offered by a public institution (eg, hospital) can be classed as services when these services are paid for by a third party (eg, sickness funds). In such triangular settings it would seem that each of the three bi-lateral relationships involved must be judged separately. This conclusion seems particularly relevant for cross-border access to public services. From *Geraets-Smits and Peerbooms*, for instance, it follows that the specific features of the relationship between the State or its emanations (eg, sickness funds) and individual citizens (insured persons) are of no relevance for the classification of the relationship which those citizens may have with (health care) providers in other States.

for economic reasons. In *Kohll*, however, the Court held that although the objective of 'maintaining a balanced medical and hospital service open to all' is intrinsically linked to the method of funding the social security system, it may 'fall within the derogation on grounds of public health under Article 46 of the Treaty, in so far as it contributes to the attainment of a high level of health protection.' Article 46 EC, the Court ruled, 'permits Member States to restrict the freedom to provide medical and hospital services in so far as the maintenance of a treatment facility or medical service on national territory is essential for the public health and even the survival of the population.' Further, a ruling as *Geraets-Smits and Peerbooms* shows that the Court does not always require strict application of the necessity and proportionality tests. Patient mobility has never been high and it simply does not seem very likely that the funding or infrastructure of health care systems would ever be affected as a result of inter-State patient flows. Yet, the Court did accept a national rule according to which patients could be denied reimbursement of the costs for treatment by a foreign non-contracted health care provider when similar or comparable treatment can be obtained from a contracted provider.[91] The mere risk that health care systems could be affected seemed sufficient to uphold the rules under challenge in the case. *Kohll* and *Geraets-Smits and Peerbooms* concerned national rules restricting reimbursement of the costs of medical care which residents have obtained in other States. The cases did not involve, and the Court did not make any specific comments on, rules restricting access of non-residents to public benefits. Nonetheless, the rulings do show that the Court, when interpreting the economic free movement rules, is sensitive to Member States' concerns regarding the protection of welfare state services and that social objectives in a policy area as health care may serve as a buttress against the potentially damaging effects of common market law.[92]

3.3.2.2 *Article 12*

3.3.2.2.1 Introduction
Where Article 49 EC does not apply, Community travellers can invoke Article 12(1) EC in order to challenge national rules denying them access to or enjoyment of public services on the ground that they do not reside in the State concerned. Residence requirements constitute indirect discrimination on grounds of nationality, and are thus incompatible with Article 12(1), unless the State applying the requirements can demonstrate that they are necessary for, and proportional to, the legitimate public interest of protecting the financial stability and/or maintaining public benefit schemes.

When one starts searching the case law for substantive rules or principles which indicate when, or under which conditions, residence requirements for

---

[91] Ch 4, s 4.3.
[92] Hervey, 'Social Solidarity: A Buttress Against Internal Market Law?' in Shaw (ed), *Social Law and Policy in an Evolving European Union* (2000) 31–47.

entitlement to public services are permissible under Article 12(1), one finds that there is not much of substance to go by. Virtually all cases decided under the heading of Article 12(1) concerned national rules containing nationality criteria. There is only one exception: *Bickel* (1998). The case concerned a decree of the Italian Province of Bolzano which conferred upon the minority of the German-speaking citizens of the province the right to use their own language in relations with the judicial and administrative authorities in the province. An Austrian lorry driver and a German tourist who had no knowledge of Italian, claimed that they should also be entitled to use the German language in legal proceedings which had been brought against them. After having established that the right requested could enhance the exercise of the right to move freely within the Community,[93] the Court held that the Bolzano residence requirement mainly affected nationals of other Member States and that the requirement therefore 'can be justified only if it is based on objective considerations independent of the nationality of the persons concerned and is proportionate to the legitimate aim of the national provisions.' The Bolzano decree could not pass the test. It was argued that the aim of the rules being challenged was to protect the ethno-cultural minority residing in the province. The Court held this to be a legitimate aim, but it could not see how this aim would be undermined if a right of German-speaking nationals of other Member States to have their proceedings conducted in German would not, as the referring Italian court had expressly indicated, bring about additional complications or costs for courts.[94]

For the purposes of this discussion, not much can be learnt from *Bickel*. The judgment does not teach much more than that in cases where the non-residents' access does not in any serious way threaten the maintenance of public services, non-residents must be accorded access. Indirectly, however, *Bickel* raises a significant question: are all residence requirements for the enjoyment of public services indeed prohibited unless a justification can be demonstrated? The procedural threshold for the indirect discrimination test is low. Union citizens merely have to state that a residence requirement is likely to affect them more than the nationals of the State concerned and, by doing this, they can impose on the State concerned the burden of proving that there is actually a need for denying them benefits. Do Community citizens actually have such a right? Can States actually be required to explain and justify the exclusion of non-residents from any public service? Does Article 12(1) confer upon Community citizens the right to travel to other States for the sole purpose of collecting public benefits? Does Community law, in principle, confer upon Community citizens the right to choose the welfare state regime they prefer or is it based on the premise that Member States, in principle, can preserve welfare state services for their residents?

---

[93] Case C–274/96 *Bickel* [1998] ECR I–7637, 16–18.
[94] *Ibid*, 27–30.

In the absence of any other directly relevant judgment of the Court or any other concrete guidance provided by Community law, it is worthwhile taking a brief look at American constitutional law and consider how the United States Supreme Court has answered such questions and whether it has developed substantive rules or principles determining the legality of residence requirements for entitlement to public benefits.

3.3.2.2.2 The Prima Facie Illegality Residence Requirements

Under the Privileges and Immunities Clause of Article IV § 2 of the Constitution, the main constitutional provision under which discrimination against non-residents in non-economic matters must be reviewed,[95] the American Supreme Court has developed a 'substantial relation test,' which resembles the indirect discrimination test applied by the European Court of Justice. In brief, this test implies that residence requirements are unconstitutional unless the State concerned can demonstrate that the requirements are substantially related to the protection of a substantial State interest.[96] At first glance, it would thus seem that American States can indeed be required to explain and justify any rule denying non-residents access to their public services. A closer look at the Supreme Court's jurisprudence, however, suggests that this does not necessarily hold true. Most cases decided under the Privileges and Immunities Clause concerned State rules governing the pursuit of commercial activities and the Court has suggested that the substantial relation test does not, or does not always, have to be applied when reviewing State rules governing access to public rights or benefits. Illustrative is *Reeves, Inc v. State* (1980) in which the Court was asked to rule upon the constitutionality of the refusal of South Dakota to sell to non-residents cement produced by a public plant. In reaching the conclusion that the refusal to sell to non-residents was constitutional the Court observed that the:

> 'State's refusal to sell to buyers other than South Dakotans is 'protectionist' only in the sense that it limits benefits generated by a state program to those who fund the state treasury and whom the States was created to serve. Petitioners' argument apparently also would characterize as 'protectionist' rules restricting to state residents the enjoyment of state educational institutions . . . police and fire protection . . . Such policies, while perhaps 'protectionistic' in a loose sense, reflect the essential and patently unobjectionable purpose of state government—to serve the citizens of the state.'[97]

The Supreme Court has never developed a coherent set of rules for judging the constitutionality of residence requirements for access to public services, but in the literature it has been argued that the basic assumptions in judging the

[95] Ch 2, s 8.6.1.

[96] *Supreme Court of New Hampshire v Kathryn Piper*, 470 U.S. 274 (1985) 284 and *Barnard v Thorstenn*, 489 U.S. 546 (1989) 552–3.

[97] *Reeves, Inc v State*, 447 U.S. 429 (1980) 443. By comparison, Justice Brennan held in *Zobel v Williams* (1982) that permitting states to offer benefits and services to their citizens 'inheres in the very idea of maintaining the States as independent sovereigns'. *Zobel v Williams*, 457 U.S. 55 (1982) 2317.

constitutionality of discrimination in the private and public sectors are, or at least ought to be, reverse.[98] The constitutional aim of economic integration would indeed demand that discrimination against non-resident traders must be outlawed unless a substantial interest dictates otherwise. Above all, however, the Constitution sets out the framework for a political Union based on a federal system of government. Individual States were not intended to be convenient 'local administrative departments of the national government designed to assist in the implementation of national policy.' Rather, they were perceived as governmental entities holding independent lawmaking powers aimed at the provision of public benefits and services within their territory. This power, so it has been argued, would not only provide the basis for the right of States to exclude non-residents from public services when, or in as far as, this is necessary for upholding these services. The range of lawmaking powers would go even further to provide the rule that States can in principle preserve public benefits for their residents:

> 'Like other groups free to combine their members' efforts to produce collective benefits to be shared among the group, political communities, including states, have a prima facie justification for limiting distribution of their public goods to those who combined to provide them.'[99]

The correlation between residence and payment of taxes is not perfect. Not all residents pay taxes whilst some non-residents may pay taxes. Yet, when a State uses revenues

> 'to create public goods and services, it has a prima facie justification for allocating . . . resources to State residents .. simply because residents as a class combined to establish them, and non-residents as a class did not.'[100]

This does not necessarily imply that non-residents' claims for public services must always yield. Non-residents do have a right to equal treatment which may prevail in particular cases or when particular circumstances so require. The appeal of non-residents' claim to public services would vary depending on the burden which might be imposed on the State if services must be provided and the burden on the non-residents if access to benefits is denied. The 'less non-resident access interferes with state ability to serve residents, or the greater the harm that would be inflicted on the non-resident by denying access, the stronger the nonresident claim' would be.[101]

Some factors may strengthen non-residents' claims. A first one concerns a possible abundance of public services. Where 'the supply of a public good seems

---

[98] Varat, "State Citizenship' and Interstate Equality' (1981) *UChicLRev* 487–571.

[99] *Ibid*, 523.

[100] *Ibid*, 529–30. The 'reality of the existence of states qua states, rather than as departments of a national government, requires a conception that the state's citizens own state-owned resources, and that a state is not required to share its treasury with the nation at large'. Cohen, 'Equal Treatment for Newcomers: The Core Meaning of National and State Citizenship' (1984) *ConstComm* 9–19, 17.

[101] Varat (1981) n 99 above, 530–1.

ample enough to satisfy both resident and non-resident demand,' the non-residents' claim of access will be strong. Another factor involves the need of non-residents for certain services. Thus, the claim for medical emergency, police or fire protection would be much stronger than claims for gaining access to public golf and tennis facilities. Further, some public services may be necessary for the exercise of constitutional rights. For instance, if States were free to close their public roads, airports or transport facilities, constitutional rights such as freedom of trade and the right to travel would be curtailed. Lastly, in assessing the claims of non-residents one may have to include the (im)possibility of obtaining benefits elsewhere. Claims of non-residents would be weaker where they can also obtain the services from private actors or where they can do so in their home State. Non-residents' claim to obtain medical treatment which is not available in their home State is stronger than if the treatment in question can be received in the home State. There might still be persuasive arguments for denying non-residents access, but the State's 'creation of unique resources imposes greater equality obligations than its creation of resources also found in other States.'[102]

When in a fully-fledged federal union like the United States, where freedom of movement and equality of treatment are firmly protected values, States hold a *prima facie* justification for denying non-residents access to public services, then it would seem only logical to assume that the same premise applies in the European Community, which does not even seek to become a federation. Nonetheless, the above analysis and arguments do not compel the conclusion that Community law is, or must be, based on the premise that Member States have a *prima facie* justification for denying non-residents access to public services.

Constitutional charters of federal(-like) entities such as the United States Constitution and the EC Treaty safeguard a multiplicity of values which include, besides the preservation of locally provided welfare state services, a common citizenship and rights to freedom of movement and equality of treatment. These constitutional values may conflict and, when they do, one value may have to be given priority over another. Arguably, however, the sole premise following from the choice for a federal system of government, is that rights to freedom of movement and nondiscrimination should not be construed so broadly as to affect the States' capacity to uphold public services. In order to avoid that from happening there is no absolute need for a *prima facie* justification in denying non-residents access to public services. The funding and infrastructure of such services could just as well be protected by accepting the rule that non-residents are entitled to get access to public benefits, unless the State in question can demonstrate that non-residents' access would affect their public services. The taxpayer argument does not command the suggested *prima facie* justification. From the fact that only residents are fully taxable, and that

---

[102] *Ibid*, 540.

only residents can be required to contribute to the funding of public services, it only follows that States have no valid claim to deny residents access to these services. The argument that non-residents cannot be required to make their equal contributions to the funding of public services and that they therefore in principle can be denied access to public services, is based on a subjective weighing of the competing constitutional values of preserving local public benefits and the non-residents' right to equal treatment in other States. Different federal(-like) entities can make different choices as to how they wish to combine these values and each can alter its choice for one constitutional value whenever the need is felt to strengthen another. Because the United States has matured into a true federation and because constitutional values of a common citizenship, freedom of movement and equal treatment are already firmly protected by the American Constitution, there might indeed be scope for stressing the need to preserve local welfare state services[103] and for accepting the premise that States have a *prima facie* justification for denying such services to non-residents. The European Community, however, could very well decide to make another choice. Precisely because the notions of Union citizenship, freedom of movement and equality of treatment are still not fully developed, the Community could opt for the premise that its citizens have a *prima facie* entitlement to gain access to public benefits in States other than the one in which they reside and that Member States can only rebut this presumption when they can demonstrate to have compelling reasons for denying non-residents access to their public services.

The European Community's institutional structure does not dictate the premise that Community law is based on the premise that citizens have a *prima facie* entitlement to gain access to all public benefits in States. The above is just to say that the Community can choose to protect public services of the Member States either by recognising a *prima facie* entitlement for non-residents to gain access to public services or by accepting a *prima facie* justification for States to exclude non-residents. Nonetheless, much can be said for choosing the suggested *prima facie* entitlement. If taken seriously, the constitutionally protected values of Union citizenship, freedom of movement and equality of treatment would seem to require that Community citizens are entitled to travel to other States for whatever purpose and that they are under no obligation to explain, or to submit any specific reason as to their need to be treated equally. Further, the premise in favour of Union citizens does not have to affect or undermine Member States' capacity to uphold these systems and it does not necessarily have to lead to legal uncertainty. The premise is not absolute. It merely implies a *prima facie* entitlement to gain access to public services; Member States are still entitled to impose restrictions or to deny access to public benefits whenever these are necessary for safeguarding the funding and/or organisation of their systems. Due regard can be given to the Member States' interests by giving them

---

[103] Cp Varat, 'Economic Integration and Interregional Migration in the United States Federal System' in Tushnet (ed), *Comparative Constitutional Federalism* (1990) 21–61, 49.

room to rebut the *prima facie* entitlement of non-residents to gain access to public services and to develop a clear and coherent set of criteria determining when, or what kind of, limitations on non-residents' access are permissible.

3.3.2.2.3 Justification of Residence Requirements

A *prima facie* entitlement of non-residents to gain access to public benefit systems in other Member States implies that residence requirements are to be regarded as being incompatible with Article 12(1) EC unless the States in question can demonstrate that the requirements are necessary to uphold the systems. This indirect discrimination test implies a limited balancing act. It is a balancing act in that Member States' claims for maintaining their public services are to be weighed against the constitutional values of Union citizenship, free movement and equal treatment. The test, however, entails only a limited balancing act because it only requires a weighing of the States' need to exclude from, or to impose additional conditions on non-residents seeking access to, public services. The right to equal treatment is a given and fixed value, which does not have to be supported by any additional arguments. The strength of the claim of the individual Community citizen seeking access to public services does not vary according to the importance of the desired benefit or the degree to which the benefit is needed. The burden of proof is not on the non-residents, but on the Member State that wishes to deny access to public services. The weight to be given to States' claims varies from benefit to benefit. A (rough) distinction can be made between three types of public services.

The first category comprises services which can be attributed to the classical 'night watch State' and the 'industrial welfare state.'[104] It concerns benefits such as police and fire protection, court systems, public roads, transport facilities, and benefits for victims of crime. Such services are not likely to be affected by non-residents' access. The magnetic effect of such services on non-residents is minimal. The number of Community citizens who would move to other States in order to gain access to such services is minimal. Further, spillover effects are basically absent. These services are only effective at the place where they are consumed.[105] For business or touristic reasons, some countries may receive comparatively large numbers of non-residents, and thus potential users of such services, but these numbers are not likely to be so high as to cause serious difficulties in maintaining such services. States may be entitled to charge certain fees for the use of these services when these reflect the true costs involved and are fixed at a nondiscriminatory rate,[106] but they should not be entitled to

---

[104] Ch 1, s 2.1.

[105] Cp von Wilmowsky (1991) n 76 above, 272–3.

[106] See, eg: Dir 93/89 on the application of taxes to certain vehicles used for the carriage of goods by road and tolls and charges for the use of infrastructures (OJ 1993 L 279) which states in Art 7 that tolls and user charges may not discriminate, directly or indirectly, on grounds of nationality of the haulier or of origin of the vehicle and that toll rates shall be related to the costs of constructing, operating and developing the infrastructure net work concerned. On this Dir see also Case C–205/98 *Commission v Austria* ('Brenner Motorway') [2000] ECR I–0000.

impose tolls or user fees on non-residents for the sole reason that they, unlike residents, are as a rule not taxable. Arguments in favour of compensatory fees could possibly be made if the premise of a *prima facie* justification for States to exclude non-residents were applicable, but such fees are not needed in order to protect the quality of public roads, public parks, etc. In fact, such fees would seem to constitute wholly gratuitous discrimination against non-residents and, arguably, this is one of the reasons why one should reject the general premise that States have a *prima facie* justification for preserving public benefits to their residents.

The second group of public services consists of social assistance benefits, maintenance grants and other tax-funded benefits which seek to offer beneficiaries a 'minimum income' for meeting basic costs of living. The magnetic effect of such benefit systems is strong and spillover effects would occur if non-residents were to be awarded such benefits. Budgets available for such benefit schemes are scarce and the grant of any additional benefit leads to an increase in costs. The claims of States to deny residents such benefits are so strong that the *prima facie* entitlement of non-residents to obtain such benefits is in fact automatically reversed in a blanket permission for States to deny benefits to all non-residents. As regards such tax-funded 'income benefits,' Community law is based on the assumption that benefits can be obtained in one Member State only and that it is in principle the State of (habitual) residence which is responsible for paying benefits.

The third group of benefits consists of welfare state services that are offered in kind such as education and health care. The legality of residence requirements for entitlement to such benefits is far more difficult to predict than in the case of the other two groups of benefits. The weight to be given to States' interests and claims may vary and is often quite difficult to establish. Such social benefit-in-kind systems have a much bigger magnetic effect on residents of other Member States, and they are more likely to be affected by non-residents' access, than the first group of benefits discussed above. At the same time, benefit-in-kind systems are not as 'fragile' as the cash income benefits of the second group. Any additional grant of the latter benefits implies an increase in costs, but this is not necessarily the case with benefits offered in kind. Further, the impact of non-residents' access may differ for the various benefits in kind. For instance, the claim of Member States to exclude non-residents from primary schools or general practitioner services does not seem as strong as their claim to refuse non-residents access to intramural health services such as heart transplants or hip replacements for which waiting lists may exist.

On the basis of existing case law, one cannot conclude much more than that Member States can make entitlement to such benefits conditional upon residence within the national territory where they can demonstrate that this is necessary for, and proportional to, the legitimate interests of maintaining the 'financial stability' and/or protecting the 'infrastructure' of such benefit-in-kind systems. In two respects the test to be applied is not clear.

First, the interests which may constitute a ground for justification are not clearly defined. For instance, it could be argued that any increase in costs or expenditure caused by non-residents affects the equilibrium between expenditure and revenue and that non-residents can be denied access whenever the (marginal) costs are not compensated for. It could also be argued, however, that the financial stability is only affected where the additional cost of non-residents' access forces the host State to increase its budgets for the services in question or to compromise the quality of the services. What, then, is precisely meant by the financial stability of welfare state services? Comparable issues arise as regards the protection of the organisation or infrastructure of welfare state services. In deciding on the provision of education and health care facilities, States will have to make a certain assessment about the expected demand for such services. Thus, States, on a long-term basis, will have to consider how many students are likely to attend schools or universities and, subsequently, will have to decide on the number of teachers to be appointed, the types of courses that will be offered and what housing or other facilities for students are required. Further, access by non-resident pupils or students could impact on the size of classes or tutorial groups. Where the size of classes is increased by 2 or 3 students or pupils the quality of education would not seem to be affected, but this, so it might be argued, could very well happen with increases of 10 pupils or students. At what point could the educational infrastructure possibly justify restrictions on non-residents' access?

Secondly, it is uncertain how strictly necessity and proportionality requirements must be applied under Article 12(1) EC. A case like *Bickel* demonstrates that the Court is willing to strike down residence requirements where the maintenance or quality of public services is unlikely to be affected by access by non-residents. This would seem to imply, for instance, that the Court will not allow Member States to rely on the financial stability ground for justification where they are entitled to have the costs reimbursed by other States or 'other' social security institutions or when the non-resident is willing to pay the costs. In other cases, however, it is far more difficult to predict how the Court would rule. The proportionality requirement imposes on Member States a duty to seek the least restrictive means for protecting their systems, but is not always easy to determine what the least restrictive means are. For instance, it could be argued that Member States that are net-importers of students have no strong claim to limit the number of non-residents to be admitted to their universities when they can also protect their interests by imposing on these students a duty to pay additional tuition fees. Yet, tuition fees may have a much more restrictive effect on student mobility than quotas when the fees are set at a high rate. Answering the question as to which means are the least restrictive may require such a detailed examination of the pros and cons of the various alternatives, that a strict application of the proportionality test would lead to a serious intrusion upon the States' autonomy in the fields of education and health care. In judging the compatibility of national rules with common market freedoms the Court has applied the proportionality requirements so strictly, and it has scrutinised national rules so thoroughly, that it has often actually substituted Member States' views on the need to apply a certain rule for its own view. However, because the European Community lacks the power to harmonise the national health care and educational systems and because it is bound to respect the autonomy of the States to organise such systems in the way they deem appropriate, the Court may, and indeed it would seem desirable if it were to, show some restraint in applying the proportionality test under Article 12(1) EC.

4 THIRD COUNTRY NATIONALS

One of the conclusions drawn in this book is that Member States are no longer entitled to safeguard the funding and organisation of their welfare state services by means of nationality requirements. Union citizenship requires, as the Court put it in *Grzelczyk*, that all 'those who find themselves in the same situation' must 'enjoy the same treatment in law irrespective of their nationality.'[107] Unfortunately, however, the prohibition of nationality requirements is still limited in scope. It only applies to Union citizens, not to the majority of third country nationals residing within the Community. The latter may enjoy certain rights as family members of Community citizens who have moved to other Member States or under one of cooperation or association agreements which the Community and its Member States have concluded with third countries, but, as a group, third country nationals are excluded from the main Community provisions on freedom of movement and nondiscrimination.[108] From a social, economic and political perspective the weak status of third country nationals under Community law is, to put it mildly, problematic. There is no need to go into the question whether it is necessary to improve that status. The sole question to be addressed is how that status must be strengthened.

The Community institutions and the Member States have recognised the need to improve the status of third country nationals. Being aware of the institutional flaws of the extra-communautarian framework of the Schengen Treaty and the intergovernmental framework of the European Union's third pillar on Home Affairs and Justice, the Member States agreed in 1997 at the summit in Amsterdam to include in the EC Treaty a new Title on visas, asylum, immigration and other policies related to the free movement of persons.[109] The new title,

---

[107] Case C–184/99 *Grzelczyk* [2001] ECR I–6193, 31.

[108] For an extensive overview of the legal status of third country nationals under Community see, eg: Staples, *The Legal Status of Third Country Nationals Resident in the European Union* (1999).

[109] On the new title see, eg: Guild, 'European Community Law from a Migrant's Perspective' (2000) ch 9; O'Keeffe, 'Can the Leopard Change its Spots? Visas, Immigration and Asylum—Following Amsterdam' in O'Keeffe and Twomey, *Legal Issues of the Amsterdam Treaty* (1999) 271–88 and the various contributions in Guild and Harlow, *Implementing Amsterdam—Immigration and Asylum Rights in EC Law* (2001).

which aims to achieve an 'area of freedom, security and justice,' is an institutional title in the sense that it only provides the legal framework and the powers for the development of common policies in these fields. The title does not contain detailed substantive rules prescribing what the various common policies concerning third country nationals should consist of. Looking at the goals that have been set, the powers that have been attributed and the various proposals for legislative measures that the European Commission has already sent to the other institutions, however, a rough sketch of the future policies can be detected. Leaving aside asylum seekers and refugees, it would seem that the common European policies, just like the American immigration policies, will focus on three distinct categories of persons: permanent residents, non-immigrants and visitors, and undocumented aliens.

Article 63 confers upon the Council the power to adopt measures regarding entry and residence, and standards on procedures for the issue by Member States of long term visas and residence permits (paragraph 3) and measures defining the rights and conditions under which nationals of third countries who are legally resident in a Member State may reside in other Member States (paragraph 4). On the basis of these provisions the European Commission has recently submitted to the Council a proposal for a Council Directive concerning the status of third country nationals who are long-term residents.[110] The Commission proposes a common status for third country nationals who have resided legally and continuously for five years in one of the Member States and who are, when asked, able to provide evidence that they have 'stable resources corresponding to the level of resources below which social assistance may be granted.' These long-term residents are given a right to equal treatment in the State of residence, the right to move to and reside in other Member States and a right to equal treatment in those other Member States. The rights accorded to long-term residents largely resemble the rights enjoyed by Community citizens residing in another Member State. In the State where they have obtained their status long-term residents enjoy a virtually unlimited right to equal treatment in social-economic matters including work and related issues, education, student grants, social security and social assistance, tax benefits and housing. The same rights can be enjoyed by long-residents status who have moved to another Member State, with the notable exception of social assistance and study grants.

In comparison with Community law governing the status of third country nationals as it stands at present, the Commission's proposal implies a significant step forward. Third country nationals are promised a status which largely resembles the constitutional status of permanent residents under American law and which does justice to the fact that they have lived, worked and paid taxes in the Community for a significant number of years under the same conditions as nationals of the Member States. The Commission's proposal, however, is not wholly free from criticism. Besides the fact that there does not seem to be a

---

[110] COM(2001) 127 final.

compelling reason for wholly denying long-term residents social assistance and study grant in Member States other than the one in which they acquired their status, the main point of the critique is that the proposal still subjects third country nationals to a different set of rules. Special rules for the grant of long-term resident status are needed, but would it not have been possible to insert a single provision stating that long-term residents are granted all rights that Community law confers upon Union citizens residing in the territory of another Member State? In fact, it would seem inevitable that one day the issue will arise whether distinctions made between Union citizens and long-term residents are compatible with Article 12(1) EC. Indeed, one could very well argue that third country nationals who have lawfully resided within the Community for a given number of years, should not be granted long-term resident status but Union citizenship.[111]

As regards the other categories, ie, short-term residents, and undocumented third country nationals living in the Community, it is much less clear whether or to what extent they will be able to claim access to public services. Article 62 only speaks of immigration issues in the strict sense. It confers upon the Community powers to adopt measures on the crossing of the external borders, the internal abolition of border controls and the conditions under which third country nationals shall be entitled to travel to and stay in other Member States for a period of no more than three months. No mention is made of the extent to which 'third country travellers' must be awarded equality of treatment as regards welfare state services and benefits. When the measures just mentioned have actually been taken, many questions will arise on this point. Most important, will third country nationals be entitled to rely on Article 49 EC in order to travel to and receive services in other Member States? Will third country travellers be entitled to invoke Article 12(1) EC in order to challenge national rules denying them rights or benefits for reasons of their nationality or place or residence?

Article 63(3)a empowers the Council to adopt measures in the areas of illegal immigration and illegal residence. In earlier policy documents the European Commission seemed to favour a dual approach focussing, on the one hand, on preventing illegal or irregular migration and, on the other hand, the need to pro-

---

[111] See, eg: Staples (2000) n 109 above, at 354–5; Castro Oliveira, 'The Position of Resident Third Country Nationals: Is it Too Early to Grant Them Union Citizenship?' in La Torre (ed), *European Citizenship: An Institutional Challenge* (1998) 185–99; Rubio Marín, 'Equal Citizenship and the Difference that Residence Makes' in La Torre (1998) above, 210–27; Sørensen, *The Exclusive European Citizenship—The Case for Refugees and Immigrants in the European Union* (1996) 170–1 and Dummett, 'The Acquisition of British Citizenship. From Imperial Traditions to National Definitions' in Baubök (ed), *From Aliens to Citizens: Redefining the Status of Immigrants in Europe* (1994) 75–84. See also: Hansen, 'A European Citizenship or a Europe of Citizens?—Third Country Nationals in the EU' (1998) *JEMS* 751–68 and Sørensen (1996),at 169–70 above, who claim that the status of third country nationals could be strengthened by encouraging Member States offer long-term residents national citizenship. This objective is supported by the European Council. COM(2001) 127 final.

[112] See, eg: COM(94) final, 27–8.

tect the rights of undocumented third country nationals.[112] The measures that so far have actually been taken, however, almost exclusively deal with the former objective such as measures to strengthen external border controls, penalties for illegal entry and detention of illegal migrants and sanctions against carriers, employers, migrant smugglers and traffickers.[113] Difficult questions concerning undocumented aliens are likely to arise. In the fields of social and educational policies, is it wholly up to the Member States to regulate the status of undocumented third country nationals or is there a role for the Community to play? Do undocumented third country nationals fall within the scope of Community law and, if so, can they benefit from Article 12(1) EC? To what extent can the rights of undocumented be restricted on the ground that they lack legal immigration status? Is a violation of immigration laws a sufficient ground for denying undocumented third country nationals rights in other policy areas? In answering these questions, should any distinction be made between undocumented third country nationals and their children who, as a rule, are not accountable for their unlawful residence status?

More issues could be addressed but the above may suffice to demonstrate that in the course of the development of a common visa and immigration policy the Community institutions will be faced with, and will have to address, numerous questions regarding the rights of the various categories of third categories in the fields of social, educational and health policy. It is submitted that in handling these issues the institutions should always start from the presumption that third country nationals in principle must be offered the same rights as Community citizens finding themselves in a comparable situation. In essence, the discussions in this chapter and book have demonstrated that for the purposes of cross-border access to public services nationality is wholly irrelevant factor. It is not imposed as a condition for payment of taxes or social security premiums and there is no need to impose nationality as a condition for entitlement to welfare state services. Distinctions between Union citizens and third country nationals must be viewed and treated as 'suspect' and only be accepted when necessary for compelling or weighty governmental interests.

5 CONCLUSIONS

Lurking beneath the numerous questions concerning cross-border access to public services which have been discussed in this book lies a potential conflict between, on the one hand, the goals of realising freedom of movement and securing equality of treatment and, on the other hand, the need to develop and maintain adequate public services. Initially, the conflict was decided in favour of Member States. Community law hardly imposed any limits on States' power

---

[113] For an overview see Cholewinski, 'The EU *Acquis* on Irregular Migration: Reinforcing Security at the Expense of Rights' (2000) *EJML* 361–405.

to control immigration and to determine whether, when and the conditions under which, nationals and/or residents of other Member States were accorded access to their public services. Over the years, however, Community law has limited Member States' powers and significantly extended the possibilities for European (Union) citizens to move to other Member States and to get access there to public benefits.

This particularly holds true for Union citizens who have decided to establish residence in other Member States. Today, Community law can be interpreted to confer upon all Union citizens a right to equal treatment as regards access to (virtually all) welfare state services from the moment they establish lawful residence in the territory of another Member State on the basis of Community law, international law or national law until the moment they voluntarily give up, or involuntarily lose, their lawful resident status. Community law allows the Member States to deny lawful residence status to nationals of other Member States who do not perform 'effective and genuine' work and who are not able to provide for themselves, but they can no longer protect their welfare state interests by making distinctions between nationals and non-nationals or 'recently arrived' and 'long-term' residents. Union citizens lawfully residing in the territory of a Member State other than the one(s) of which they hold the nationality must be treated as equal members of the welfare state.

Community law governing the legal status of Community citizens who are merely visiting other Member States is still less well developed. The case law demonstrates that all Union citizens enjoy the right to travel to other Member States and to claim access to public benefits there under the same conditions as nationals of the host State. Member States are no longer entitled to protect their welfare state regimes against an influx of residents of other States who may be in need, or come for the sole purpose, of obtaining public benefits by refusing them entry to the national territory or by denying them benefits on grounds of their nationality. Member States can only protect their interests by applying residence requirements. So far, however, Community law has not provided a clear and coherent set of criteria for determining the legality of residence requirements for entitlement to public services. It is submitted, however, that Community law should be based on the premise of a *prima facie* entitlement for Community citizens to gain access to public services in State other than the one in which they reside. Without necessarily undermining the ability of Member States to maintain their public services, recognition of such a *prima facie* entitlement could contribute to a more efficient use of public services and provide the basis for strengthening the currently still underdeveloped notion of Union citizenship.

Bibliography

ABEL-SMITH and MAYNARD, *De Organisatie, Financiering en Kosten van de Gezondheidszorg in de Europese Gemeenschap* (Brussel, Commissie van de Europese Gemeenschappen, 1978).

ABRIEL, 'Rethinking Preemption for Purposes of Aliens and Public Benefits'(1995) *UCLA Law Review* 1597–630.

ADAMS, 'State Control of Interstate Migration of Indigents'(1942) *Michigan Law Review* 711–33.

ADLER, 'The "Habitual Residence Test" in the UK' in Eichenhofer (ed), *Social Security of Migrants in the European Union of Tomorrow* (Osnabrück, Rasch, 1997) 53–9.

ALANAT, 'Freizügigkeit als Prüfstein der Assoziation EWG-Türkei—General Framework of the Association' in Lichtenberg *et al* (eds), *Gastarbeiter—Einwanderer—Bürger? Die Rechtstellung der Türkischen Arbeitnehmer in der Europäischen Union* (Baden-Baden, Nomos, 1996) 17–26.

ALEXANDER, 'Free Movement of Non-EC Nationals: A Review of the Case Law of the Court of Justice' in Schermers *et al* (eds), *Free Movement of Persons in Europe* (Dordrecht, Martinus Nijhoff Publishers, 1993) 485–502.

ALLARD, 'Revisiting Shapiro: Welfare Magnets and State Residency Requirements in the 1990s' (1998) *Publius* 45–66.

ALLEN, 'Equal Treatment, Social Advantages and Obstacles: In Search of Coherence in Freedom and Dignity' in Guild (ed), *The Legal Framework and Social Consequences of Free Movement of Persons in the European Union* (The Hague, Kluwer Law International, 1999) 31–48.

ALSTON (ed), *The EU and Human Rights* (Oxford, Oxford University Press, 1999).

ALTMAIER, 'Europäisches Koordinierendes Sozialrecht—Ende des Territorialitätsprinzip?' in Eichenhofer and Zuleeg (eds), *Die Rechtsprechung des Europäischen Gerichtshof zum Arbeits- und Sozialrecht im Streit* (Köln, Bundesanzeiger, 1995) 71–91.

ALTMAIER and VERSCHUEREN, 'The Extension of the Scope of Regulation 1408/71 to Nationals of Non-Member Countries' in *Commission of the European Communities/Departemento de Relações Internaçionais e Convenções de Segurança Social, Social Security in Europe—Equality Between Nationals and Non-Nationals* (Lisbon, 1995) 245–61.

ALTMEYER, 'People on the Move: Effect of Residence Requirements for Public Assistance' (1946) *Social Security Bulletin* 4.

ANDERSON and LUTES, 'The Demise of the Durational Residence Requirement' (1972) *Southwestern Law Journal* 538–68.

ANDRÉ DE LA PORTE and ZEGVELD, *Mobiliteit van Studenten binnen de Europese Unie* (Amsterdam, Nuffic, 1996).

—— and ——, 'Het Europa van de Student—Studentenmobiliteit binnen de Europese Unie' (1995) *AA* 685–93.

ANTIEAU, 'Pauls's Perverted Privileges or the True Meaning of the Privileges and Immunities Clause of Article IV' (1967) *William and Mary Law Review* 1–38.

ARNULL, *The European Union and its Court of Justice* (Oxford, Oxford University Press, 1999).

——, *The General Principles of EEC Law and the Individual* (London, Leicester University Press, 1990).

——, 'Of Strip Cartoonists, Vets and Gunsmiths' (1988) *European Law Review* 260–7.

AVENARIUS, 'Zugangsrecht von EG-Ausländern im Bildungswesen der Bundesrepublik Deutschland' (1988) *NZfV* 385–93.

BADOUX, 'Dertig Jaar Vrij Verkeer van Personen' in Fernhout (ed), *Dertig Jaar Vrij Verkeer van Werknemers* (Nijmegen, 1999).

BAEYENS, 'Free Movement of Goods and Services in Health Care: A Comment on the Cases Decker and Kohll from a Belgian Point of View' (1999) *EJHL* 373–83.

BALLON and PIETERS, *Het Europese Kartelrecht en de Ziekenfondsen* (Antwerpen, Maklu, 1997).

BALTHASAR, 'Inländerdiskriminierung in der EU nach dem EWG-Vertrag und aus Öster-reicher Sicht' *ZföR* (1988) 143–216.

BANTING, 'Looking in Three Directions: Migration and the European Welfare State in Comparative Perspective' in Bommes and Geddes (eds), *Immigration and Welfare—Challenging the Borders of the Welfare State* (London, Routledge, 2000) 13–33.

BARENTS, *De Communautaire Rechtsorde* (Deventer, Kluwer, 2000).

——, 'De Tabaksrichtlijn in Rook Opgegaan' (2000) *NTER* 327–31.

——, *Het Verdrag van Amsterdam in Werking* (Deventer, Kluwer, 1999).

——, *Het Verdrag van Amsterdam* (Deventer, Kluwer, 1997).

BARNARD, 'Fitting the Remaining Pieces into Goods and Persons Jigsaw?' (2001) *European Law Review* 35–59.

——, *EC Employment Law* (Oxford, Oxford University Press, 2000).

——, 'Regulating Competitive Federalism in the European Union? The Case of EC Social Policy' in Shaw (ed), *Social Law and Policy in an Evolving European Union* (Oxford, Hart Publishing, 2000) 49–69.

——, 'Social Dumping and Race to the Bottom: Some Lessons for the EU from Delaware?' (2000) *European Law Review* 57.

——, 'Article 13: Through the Looking Glass of Union Citizenship' in O'Keeffe and Twomey (eds), *Legal Issues of the Amsterdam Treaty* (Oxford, Hart Publishing, 1999) 375–94.

BARR, *The Economics of the Welfare State* (London, Weidenfeld and Nicolson, 3rd edn, 1998).

——, *The Economics of the Welfare State* (London, Weidenfeld and Nicolson, 2nd edn, 1993).

BARRY, 'Self-Government Revisited' in Miller and Siedentrop, *The Nature of Political Theory* (Oxford, Clarendon Press, 1983).

BAUBÖCK, *Transnational Citizenship—Membership and Rights in International Migration* (Aldershot, Edward Elgar, 1994).

BEAN *et al*, *Social Europe: One for All* (London, CEPR, 1998).

BECKEDORF AND HENZE, 'Neuere Entwicklungen in der Bildungspolitik der Europäischen Gemeinschaft' (1993) *NVwZ* 125–30.

BECKER, 'Freizügigkeit in der EU—Auf dem Weg vom Begleitrecht zur Bürgerfreiheit' (1999) *EuR* 522–33.

BEENEN, *Citizenship, Nationality and Access to Public Services Employment—The Impact of European Community Law* (Groningen, European Law Publishers, 2001).

BEHRENS, 'Die Konvergenz der Wirtschaftlichen Freiheiten im Europäischen Gemeinschaftsrecht' (1990) *EuR* 145 *et seq.*

BELCHER, *The Role of the European Union in Healthcare* (Zoetermeer, Council for Health and Social Service, 1999).

BELL, 'Equality and Diversity: Anti-Discrimination Law after Amsterdam' in Shaw (ed), *Social Law and Policy in an Evolving European Union* (Oxford, Hart Publishing, 2000) 157–70.

——, 'The New Article 13 EC Treaty: A Sound Basis for European Anti-Discrimination Law?' (1999) *Maastricht Journal J* 5–23.

BELL and WADDINGTON, 'The 1996 Intergovernmental Conference and the Prospects of a Non-Discrimination Treaty Article' (1996) *Indiana Law Journal* 320–26.

BENDER, 'Die Sozialhilfe im System Ausländerrechts' (1974) *DuR* 36–42.

BENNET, 'The Threat of the Wandering Poor: Welfare Parochialism and its Impact on the Use of Housing Mobility as an Anti-Poverty Strategy' (1995) *Fordham Law Journal* 1207.

BENNET and SULLIVAN, 'Disentitling the Poor: Waivers and Welfare "Reform"' (1993) *UMJLR* 741–84.

BERCUSSON, *European Labour Law* (London, Butterworths, 1996).

BERG, *Gesundheitsschutz als Aufgabe der EU—Entwicklung, Kompetenzen, Perspektiven* (Baden-Baden, Nomos, 1997).

BERGREEN, 'Das Bildungswesen nach Maastricht—Auswirkungen der Beschlüsse von Maastricht auf den Bildungsföderalismus' (1992) *RJB* 436.

BERNARD, 'Discrimination and Free Movement in EC Law' (1996) *International and Comparative Law Quarterly* 82–108.

BERTOLA *et al*, 'EU Welfare Systems and Labor Markets: Diverse in the Past, Integrated in the Future?' in Bertola *et al*, *Welfare and Employment in a United Europe* (Cambridge, Mass, MIT Press, 2000) 23–122.

BETTEN and GRIEF, *EU Law and Human Rights* (London, Longman, 1999).

BIEBACK, 'Krankheit und Mutterschaft' in Eichenhofer (ed), *Reform des Europäischen Koordinierenden Sozialrechts* (Köln, Heymann, 1993) 55–73.

——, 'Soziale Sicherung für den Fall der Krankheit und Mutterschaft' in *Europäisches Sozialrecht—Bundestagung des Deutschen Sozialrechtverbandes e.V. 9. bis 11. Oktober 1991* (1992) 51–69.

BIGO, 'Frontiers and Security in the European Union: The Illusion of Migration Control' in Anderson and Bort (eds), *The Frontiers of Europe* (London, Pinter, 1998) 148–64.

BIJZONDERE, *Bijzondere Euregionale Commissie Grensoverschrijdende Zorg, Zorg Dichtbij oòk over de Grens—Advies over Grensoverschrijdende Zorg in de Euregio Maas-Rijn* (Maastricht, 1994).

BLAKE, 'Family Life in Community Law: The Limits of Freedom and Dignity' in Guild, *The Legal Framework and Social Consequences of Free Movement of Persons in the European Union* (The Hague, Kluwer Law International, 1999) 7–17.

BLASI, 'Constitutional Limitations on the Power of States to Regulate the Movement of Goods in Interstate Commerce' in Sandalow and Stein (eds), *Courts and Free Markets: Perspectives from the United States and Europe* (Oxford, Clarendon Press, 1982). 174–221.

BLOCH, 'Auswirkungen des Europäischen Binnenmarktes auf die Gesetzliche Krankenversicherung' (1989) *BB* 2405–10.

BLOIS, 'De Blois, Europees Gemeenschapsrecht en Onderwijs' (1991) *SEW* 513–37.

BOBINSKI, 'Unhealthy Federalism: Barriers to Increasing Health Care Access for the Uninsured' (1990) *UCD Law Review* 255–348.

BOGEN, 'Privileges and Immunities Clause of Article IV, (1987) Case *Western Law Review* 794–861

BÖHNING, 'The Scope of the EEC System of Free Movement of Workers—A Rejoinder' (1973) *Common Market Law Review* 81–6.

——, *The Migration of Workers in the United Kingdom and the European Community* (London, Oxford University Press, 1972).

BOKELOH, *Export von Pflegeleistungen innerhalb der Europäischen Union, in: Zentrum für Europäischen Wirtschaftsrecht, Die Krankenversicherung in der Europäischen Union* (Bonn, 1997) 115–62.

BOLLY, 'Droit d'Entrée et de Sejour des Ressortissants Communautaire: Développements Récents' (1990) *Act du Dr* 735–48.

BOMMES and GEDDES, 'Introduction: Immigration and the Welfare State' in Bommes andGeddes (eds), *Immigration and the Welfare State—Challenging the Borders of the Welfare State* (London, Routledge, 2000).

BONGEN, *Schranken der Freizügigkeit aus Gründen der Öffentlichen Ordnung und Sicherheit im Recht der Europäischen Wirtschaftsgemeinschaft* (Berlin, Duncker & Humblot, 1975).

BONI, *Freizügigkeit und Integration. Struktur und integrationspolitike Bedeutung der Arbeitsmarktverflechtung zwischen den Mitgliedstaaten der Europäischen Wirtschaftsgemeinschaft* (Frankfurt am Main, Lang, 1976).

BOONK, *Openbare Orde als Grens aan het Vrij Verkeer van Goederen, Personen en Diensten in de E.E.G.* (Alphen aan de Rijn, Tjeenk Willink, 1977).

BORK, 'The Impossibility of Finding Welfare Rights in the Constitution' (1979) *Washington University Law Review* 695.

BOSCO, *Are National Social Protection Systems under Threat? Observations on the Recent Case Law of the Court of Justice* (Groupement d'Etudes et de Recherches Notre Europe, 2000).

BOSNIAK, 'Exclusion and Membership: The Dual Identity of the Undocumented Worker under United States Law' (1988) *Wisconsin Law Review* 955–1042.

BOVBJERG and KOPIT, 'Coverage and Care for the Medically Indigent: Public and Private Options' (1986) *Indiana Law Review* 857.

BRAEUTIGAM, *Das Problem des "Gemeinsamen" Marktes unter Sozialem Aspekt,* (1956) *Aussenwirtschaft* 170–89.

BRINKAC, 'Should Undocumented Aliens be Eligible for Resident Tuition Status at State Universities' (1986) *San Diego Law Review* 467–84.

BROEKMANS *et al*, 'Europees Geneesmiddelenbeleid in Ontwikkeling' in Roscam Abbing and van Berkestijn, *Gezondheidsbeleid in Europa* (Houten, Bohn Stafleu van Loghum, 1995) 109–27.

BROUWER, *Het Nederlandse Gezondheidszorgstelsel in Europa—Een Economische Verkenning* (Zoetermeer, Raad voor de Volksgezondheid en Zorg, 1999).

BROUWER, *De Europese Gemeenschap en Onderwijs: Geschiedenis van de Samenwerking en het Communautair Beleid op Onderwijsterrein* (Baar, BKE, 1996).

BRUBAKER, 'Membership without Citizenship: The Economic and Social Rights of Non-Citizens' in Brubaker (ed), *Immigration and the Politics of Citizenship in Europe and North America* (Lanham, University Press of America, 1989).

——, 'Citizenship and Naturalization: Policies and Politics' in Brubaker (ed), *Immigration and the Politics of Citizenship in Europe and North America* (Lanham, University Press of America, 1989) 99–125.

BRÜGGEMANN, *Die Freizügigkeit der Arbeitnehmer im Bereich der Europäischen Gemeinschaften* (Würzburg, 1973).

BUCHANAN, 'Who Should Distribute What in a Federal System' in Hochman and Peterson (eds), *Redistribution Through Public Choice* (New York, Columbia University Press, 1974).

BULTERMAN, 'Annotation *Bicke*' (1999) *Common Market Law Review* 1325–34.

——, 'Annotation *El-Yassini*' (1999) *Common Market Law Review* 1357–64.

BURNHAM, *Introduction to the Law and Legal System of the United States* (St Paul, West Publishing, 1995).

BUSQUIN, 'De Sociale Slang en het Europees Programma ter Bestrijding van Armoede' (1990) *BTSZ* 557.

BUYS, *Met het EG-Recht Strijdige Belastingstelsels en de Rechtsbescherming van de Burger* (Arnhem, Gouda Quint, 1994).

BUYSER, 'De Buyser, Grensoverschrijdende Gezondheidszorg', in *Jorens Grensarbeid* (Brugge, Die Keure, 1997) 129–60.

CABRAL, 'Cross-Border Medical Care in the European Union—Bringing Down a First Wall' (1999) *European Law Review* 387–95.

CALABRESI, 'A Government of Limited and Enumerated Powers': In Defense of *United States v. Lopez*' (1995) *Michigan Law Review* 752–831.

CALLENS, 'De Arresten Kohll en Decker: Implicaties voor Grensoverschrijdende Zorg' in Essers *et al* (eds), *Grensoverschrijdende Zorg—Marktwerking vs. National Zorgbewaking* (Lelystad, Koninklijke Vermande, 2000) 11–13.

CAMISSA, *From Rhetoric to Reform?—Welfare Policy in American Politics* (Boulder, Westview Press, 1998).

CAPRON, United States of America'in Fuenzalida-Puelma and Scholle Connor (eds), *The Right to Health in the Americas* (Washington, World Health Organisation, 1989) 498–520.

CARENS, 'Immigration and the Welfare State' in Gutmann (ed), *Democracy and the Welfare State* (Princeton, Princeton University Press, 1988) 207–30.

CARLIER, 'Proportionality and Citizenship in Relation to the Free Movement of Persons' in Carlier and Verwilghen, *Thirty Years of Free Movement of Workers in Europe* (Luxembourg, Office for Official Publications of the European Communities, 2000) 41–57.

CASPARIE *et al*, *Competitive Health Care in Europe—Future Prospects* (Aldershot, Dartmouth, (1990).

CASSESE *et al*, *European Union—The Human Rights Challenge* (Baden-Baden, Nomos, 1991).

CASTRO OLIVEIRA, 'The Position of Resident Third Country Nationals: Is it Too Early to Grant Them Union Citizenship?' in La Torre (ed), *European Citizenship: An Institutional Challenge* (The Hague, Kluwer Law International, 1998) 185–99.

CATH, 'Blijft het Tobben of Onstaat er Iets Moois? Decker en Kohll Spoken door Europa (2)' (1999) *MC* 468–71.

——, 'Europa en Vrij Verkeer—Consequenties voor de Zorgsector' (1999) *PhW* 1779–80.

——, 'Vuurwerk of Veenbrand? Decker en Kohll Spoken door Europa (1)' (1999) *MC* 466–7.

CENTEL, 'The Social Security of the Turkish Workers in Europe within the Framework of the Association Agreement' in Jorens and Schulte (eds), *European Social Security Law and Third Country Nationals* (Bruxelles, Die Keure, 1998) 281–197.

Center on Social Welfare Policy and Law, *Living at the Bottom: An Analysis of AFDC Benefits Levels* (New York, 1993).

CHAFEE, *Three Human Rights in the Constitution of 1787* (Lawrence, University Press of Kansas, 1956).

CHAMBERS, 'Residence Requirements for Welfare Benefits: The Consequences of their Unconstitutionality' (1969) *SW* 29–37.

CHANG, 'Immigrants under the New Welfare Law: A Call for Uniformity, a Call for Justice' (1997) *UCLA Law Review* 205–80.

CHARALAMBIS, *Die Arbeitnehmer im EWG-Recht* (Nürnberg, 1970).

CHARDON, 'Principles of Co-ordination', in Jorens and Schulte (eds), *Coordination of Social Security Schemes in Connection of the Accession of Central and Eastern European States: "the Riga Conference"* (Brugge, Die Keure, 1999) 43–79.

CHOLEWINSKI, 'The EU *Acquis* on Irregular Migration: Reinforcing Security at the Expense of Rights' (2000) *EJML* 361–405.

——, *Migrant Workers in International Human Rights Law—Their Protection in Countries of Employment* (Oxford, Clarendon Press, 1997).

CHRISTENSEN and MALMSTEDT, 'Lex Loci Laboris versus Lex Loci Domicilii—An Inquiry into the Normative Foundations of European Social Security Law' (2000) *EJSS* 69.

CLAPHAM, 'Human Rights and the European Community: A Critical Overview' in Cassese *et al* (eds), *European Union—The Human Rights Challenge* (Baden-Baden, Nomos, 1991) 29–61.

CLARK, *Does Welfare Affect Migration?* (Washington, Urban Institute, 1990).

CLARKE, 'State Legislation Denying Subsistence Benefits to Undocumented Aliens: An Equal Protection Approach' (1983) *Texas Law Review* 859–92.

CLARKE, 'Validity of Discriminatory Nonresident Tuition Charges in Public Higher Education under the Privileges and Immunities Clause' (1971) *Nebraska Law Review* 31–64.

CLASSEN, 'Bildungspolitische Forderprogramme der EG—Eine kritische Untersuchung der Vertragsrechtligen Grundlagen' (1990) *EuR* 10–19.

CLERMONTS *et al*, *Verblijfsrecht en Gebruik van Collectieve Voorzieningen door Immigranten* (Nijmegen, Katholieke Universiteit, 1991).

CLOSA, 'Citizenship of the Union and Nationality of the Member States' (1995) *Common Market Law Review* 487–519.

——, 'The Concept of Citizenship in the European Union' (1992) *Common Market Law Review* 1137–70.

CLOSON *et al*, 'Public Health Policy in the European Community' in Holland and Mossialos (eds) *Public Health in the European Union* (Aldershot, Ashgate, 1999) 49–67.

COENEN, 'State User Fees and the Dormant Commerce Clause' (1997) *Vanderbilt Law Review* 795–844.

COHEN, 'Discrimination Against New State Citizens: An Update' (1994) *Const Comm* 73.

——, 'Equal Treatment for Newcomers: The Core Meaning of National and State Citizenship' (1984) *Const Comm* 9–19.

COHEN, 'Europa en het Onderwijs(recht)' in Postma (ed), *Europa en het Onderwijs* (Voorburg, Stichting Bijzondere Leerstoelen Onderwijsrecht, 1993) 21–42.

CONRAD, 'Die Rechtsprechung des Gerichtshofs der Europaeischen Gmeinschaften auf dem Gebiet des Bildungswesen' (1989) *Wiss R* 97–116.

CONSTANTINESCO, 'La Citoyennette de l'Union', in Scharze (ed), *Vom Binnenmarkt zur Europaeische Union—Beitraege zur Aktuellen Entwicklung des Gemeinschaftsrecht* (Baden-Baden, Nomos, 1993) 25.

COOMANS, 'Recht op Onderwijs, Ook voor "Illegale" Vreemdelingen' (1996) *MR* 57–60.

——, *De Internationale Bescherming van het Recht op Onderwijs* (Leiden, Stichting NJCM-Boekerij, 1992).

CORNELISSEN, 'The Principle of Territoriality and the Community Regulations on Social Security (Regulations 1408/71 and 574/72)' (1996) *Common Market Law Review* 439.

CORNETT, *The Treaty of Maastricht: From Conception to Ratification* (Harlow, Longman, 1993).

CORSON, 'Reform of Domicile Law for Application to Transients, Temporary Residents and Multi-Based Persons' (1981) *Col J L S P* 327–64.

COUSSINS, 'The EC Recommendations on Social Protection: A Case Study in EC Social Policy' (1993) *SPA* 286.

COUGHLIN *et al*, *Medicaid since 1980: Costs, Coverage and the Shifting Alliance between the Federal Government and the States* (Washington, Urban Institute Press, 1994).

COVAR and SIMON, 'La Citoyennete de l'Union' (1993) *CDE* 285–316.

CRAIG and de BURCA, *EU Law: Text, Cases & Materials* (Oxford, Oxford University Press, 1998).

CREMONA, 'Citizens of Third Countries: Movement and Employment of Migrant Workers within the European Union' (1996) *LIEI* 87–113.

CREUTZ, 'Accord européen Concernant l'Octroi des Soins médicaux aux Personnes en Séjour temporaire' (1985) *RISS* 42–9.

——, 'The European Agreement Concerning the Provision of Medical Care during Temporary Residence' (1985) *ISS Rev* 38–45.

CRIJNS, 'EG-Recht en Onderwijs' (1989) *NTOR* 23–41.

CULLEN, 'From Migrants to Citizens European Community Policy on Intercultural Education' (1996) *EJFL* 109–29.

CURALL, 'Bildung und Ausbildung im Recht der Europaeischen Gemeinschaft' (1991) *RJB* 139–61.

——, 'Education Rights under the EC Treaty' in X, *Mobility of People in the European Community* (Dublin, Irish Centre for Law, Trinity College, 1990) 13–32.

CURTIN *et al*, *Free Movement for non-EC-Workers within the European Community* (Utrecht, Nederlands Centrum voor Buitenlanders (1997).

DAHLBERG, 'The E.E.C. Commission and the Politics of the Free Movement of Labour' (1968) *JCMS* 310–22.

DALICHOW, 'Academic Recognition within the European Community' (1987) *EJE* 39-58

DAVIES, *The EU Higher Education Exchange and Mobility Programmes* (London, University of North London, 1997).

DAVIS, 'The Evolving Right to Travel: *Saenz v Roe*' (1999) *Publius* 95–110.

DEFALQUE, 'Annotation *Echternach*' (1989) *JT* 426 *et seq*.

DE GANS, 'Annotatie Molenaar' (1999) *RZA* 252–60.

——, 'Kroniek: Persoonsgebonden Budget' (1998) *RZA* 15.

DE GROOT, 'The Relationship between the Nationality Legislation of the Member States of the European Union and European Citizenship' in La Torre, *European Citizenship—An Institutional Challenge* (The Hague, Kluwer Law International, 1998) 115–47.

DE GROOT, *Staatsangehörigkeitrecht im Wandel—Eine rechtsvergleichende Studie zu den Erwerb- und Verlustgründen der Staatsangehörigkeit* (Köln, Heymann, 1989).

DE GROOT, *De Wettelijke Verzekering van Geneeskundige Verzorging en Ziekengeld binnen het Kader van de EEG-Verordeningen, in: Boot et al, Europees Sociaal Verzekeringsrecht* (Deventer, Kluwer, 1978) 91–110.

DE WITTE, 'The Influence of European Community Law on National Systems of Higher Education' in Pertek (ed), *General Recognition of Diplomas and Free Movement of Professional* (1992) 73–88.

——, 'The Past and Future Role of the European Court of Justice in the Protection of Human Rights' in Alston (ed), *EU and Human Rights* (Oxford, Oxford University Press, 1999) 859–97.

——, 'The Scope of Community Powers in Education and Culture in the Light of Subsequent Practice' in Bieber and Ress (eds), *Die Dynamik des Europäischen Gemeinschaftsrechts—Die Auslegung des Europäischen Gemeinschaftsrechts im Licht nachfolgender Praxis der Mitgliedstaaten und EG-Organ* (Baden-Baden, Nomos, 1987) 261–181.

——, 'Equivalentie van Studieperiodes en Erkenning van Diploma's' (1992–1993) *TOO* 290–6.

——, 'Higher Education and the Constitution of the European Community' in Gellert (ed), *Higher Education in Europe* (London, Jessica Kingsley Publishers, 1993) 186–202.

——, *Het Europees Onderwijsrecht, in: Europa en het Onderwijs* (1992) 13–44.

——, 'Recht op Onderwijs zonder Grenzen?' (1990) *JF* 535–49.

—— (ed), *European Community Law of Education* (Baden-Baden, Nomos, 1989).

DEGEN, 'Die Unionsbürgerschaft nach dem Vertrag über die Europäische Union unter besonderer Berücksichtigung des Wahlrechts' (1993) *DöV* 749–58.

DELPEREE, 'De Gemeenschappelijke Arbeidsmarkt en het Vrije Arbeidskrachtenverkeer' (1956) *Arbbl* 177–205.

DENYS, 'Het Burgerschap: Meer dan een Schim?' (1998) *NTER* 210–13.

——, 'Grote Schoonmaak in de Overheidssector' (1996) *NTER* 221–4.

——, 'Het Begrip Kind' (1995) *NTER* 115–16.

DIMAKOPOULOS, 'Wanderarbeitnehmer aus der Türkei in der Europäischen Gemeinschaft— Zur Zukunft der Gastarbeiderfrage in Europa' (1988) *InfAuslR* 309–15.

DI STEFANO, *La Libre Circulation des Travailleurs dans la Communauté Économique Européenne* (Toulouse, 1968).

DOHMS, 'Die Kompetenz der EG im Bildungsbereich der algemeinen Bildung nach Artikel 126 EGV' (1992) *RJB* 451 *et seq*.

DOLLAT, *Libre Circulation des Personnes et Citoyenneté européenne: Enjeux et Perspectives* (Bruxelles, Bruylant, 1998).

DOMHOF, 'Untersuchung zur Entstehung der Richtlinie des Rates der Europäischen Gemeinschaften von 25.7.1977 über die schulische Betreuung der Kinder von Wanderarbeitnehmern' (1979).X (source unknown)

DOMMERS, 'An Introduction to European Union Health Law' (1997) *EJHL* 19–41.

DONNER, 'De Ontwikkeling van het Vrije Verkeer van Personen binnen de Europese Gemeenschappen en de Overeenkomst ter Uitvoering van het Akkoord van Schengen' (1990) *SEW* 766 *et seq*.

DOWELL, 'State and Local Government Responsibilities to Provide Medical Care for the Poor' (1988–89) *JLH* 1–45.

DRIJBER, 'Gelijke Behandeling van Studenten uit de EEG—Zijn er nog Grenzen?' (1988) *NJB* 22–9.

DRIVER, *Die Integration des europäischen Arbeitsmarktes* (Köln, Photostelle Universität Köln, 1962).

DRUESNE, 'Remarques sur le Champ d'Application personnel du Droit Communautaire: des "Discriminations à Rebours" Peuvent-elles Tenir en Echec la Liberté de Circulation des Personnes' (1979) *RTDE* 429–39.

DUMMETT, 'The Acquisition of British Citizenship. From Imperial Traditions to National Definitions' in Bauböck (ed), *From Aliens to Citizens: Redefining the Status of Immigrants in Europe* (Aldershot, Avebury, 1994) 75–84.

DYE, 'The Policy Consequences of Intergovernmental Competition' (1990) *CatoJ* 59–73.

DAVIS and ROWLAND, 'Uninsured and UndeservedL Inequities in Health Care in the United States' (1983) *MMF Quart* 157 et seq.

DE GROOF and FRIESS, 'Opportunities for a European Educational Policy' (1997) *EJELP* 9–17.

DE JONGHE and DILLO, *Access to Higher Education* (Brussels, Commission of the European Communities, 1991).

DEVROE and WOUTERS, *De Europese Unie* (Leuven, Peeters, 1995).

DITTMANN and FEHRENBACHER, 'Die Bildungdrechtliche Harmonisierungsverbote (Art.126 Abs.4 EGV, Art.127 Abs.4 EGV) und ihre Bedeutung für die nationale Bildungshoheit' (1992) *RJB* 478.

DOUGLAS-SCOTT and KIMBELL, 'The Adams Exclusion Order Case: New Enforcable Civil Rights in the post-Maastricht European Union?' (1995) *Public Law* 516–25.

DWORKIN and STEYGER, 'Aids Victims in the European Community and the United States: Are They Protected from Unjustified Discrimination?' (1989) *Texas International Law Journal* 295–329.

DUE and FRIEDLÄNDER, *Government Finance—Economics of the Public Sector* (Georgetown, Irwin-Dorsey, 1977).

EARDLEY *et al, Social Assistance in OECD Countries: Country Reports* (London, HSMO, Department of Social Security Research, 1996).

——, *Social Assistance in OECD Countries: Synthesis Report* (London, HSMO, Department of Social Security Research, 1996).

EICHENHOFER, 'How to Simplify the Co-ordination of Social Security' (2000) *EJSS* 231.

——, *Dienstleistungsfreiheit und Freier Warenverkehr als Rechtsgrundlagen für Grenzüberschreitenden Behandlungsleistungen, in: Zentrum für Europäisches Wirtschaftsrecht, Grenzüberschreitenden Behandlungsleistungen im Binnenmarkt* (Bonn, 1998) 1–20.

EICKE, 'The Third Country Agreements: The Right to Work and Reside in the First Generation Agreements' in Guild (ed), *The Legal Framework and Social Consequences of Free Movement of Persons in the European Union* (The Hague, Kluwer Law International, 1999) 89–103.

EINERHAND, 'Bijstand een Internationale Vergelijking' (1997) *SMA* 207–20.

——, 'Sociale Zekerheid: Een Europese Vergelijking' (1997) *TvA* 5–20.

——, *Sociale Zekerheid: Stelsels en Regelingen in Europese Landen* ('s Gravenhage, VUGA, 1995).

ELMAN, 'The Limits of Citizenship: Migration, Sex Discrimination, and Same-Sex Partners in EU Law' (2000) *JCMS* 729–49.

ENTZINGER, 'De Andere Grenzen van de Verzorgingsstaat—Migratiestromen en Migratiebeleid' in Engbersen *et al* (eds), *Zorgen in het Europese Huis—De Grenzen van Nationale Verzorgingsstaaten* (Amsterdam, Boom, 1994) 142–72.

ESCHMANN, *Die Freizügigkeit der EG-Bürger und der Zugang zur öffentlichen Verwaltung—Eine Untersuchung zur gemeinschafts- und verfassungsrechtlichen Stellung der EG-Bürger im öffentlichen Dienst der Bundesrepublik Deutschland* (Baden-Baden, Nomos, 1992).

ESPING-ANDERSEN, 'Comment' in Bertola *et al EU Welfare Systems and Labor Markets: Diverse in the Past, Integrated in the Future?* in Bertola *et al Welfare and Employment in a United Europe* (Cambridge, Mass, MIT, Press, 2000) 127–43.

——, *Three Worlds of Welfare Capitalism* (Princeton, Princeton University Press, 1990).

EUZEBY, 'Financement de la Protection sociale, Efficacité économique et Justice sociale' (1997) *RMCU* 253.

——, 'Le Financement de la Protection sociale dans les Pays de la CEE: Problèmes et Perspectives' in X, *Quel Avenir pour l'Europe sociale: 1992 et Après* (Bruxelles, 1990).

EVANS, 'Union Citizenship and the Constitutionalization of Equality in EU Law' in *La Torre, European Citizenship: An Institutional Challenge* (The Hague, Kluwer Law International, 1998) 267–91.

——, 'Third Country Nationals and the Treaty on European Union' (1994) *European Journal of International Law* 199.

——, 'Nationality Law and European Integration' (1992) *European Law Review* 190–215.

——, 'European Citizenship' (1982) *Modern Law Review* 497–515.

EVANS and JESSERUN D'OLIVEIRA, 'Nationality and Citizenship' in Cassesse *et al* (eds), *Human Rights and the European Community: Methods of Protection* (Baden-Baden, Nomos, 1991) 298–345.

EVERLING, 'Das Niederlassungsrecht in der Europäischen Gemeimschaft' (1990) *DB* 1853–59.

——, 'Von der Freizügigkeit der Arbeitnehmer zum Europäisches Bürgerrecht?' (1990) *EuR Beiheft I* 81–103.

——, 'Zur Rechtsprechung des Europäischen Gerichtshofs über die Beschäftigung von EG-Ausländern in der öffentlichen Verwaltung' (1990) *DVBl* 225–31.

——, 'Vertragsverhandlungen 1957 und Vertragspraxis 1987 dargestellt an den Kapiteln Niederlassungsrecht und Dienstleistungen des EWG-Vertrages' in Mestmäcker *et al* (eds), *Eine Ordnungspolitik für Europa—Festschrift für von der Groeben* (Baden-Baden, Nomos, 1987) 111–30.

EVERSON, 'The Legacy of the Market Citizen' in Shaw and More (eds), *New Legal Dynamics of European Union* (Oxford, Clarendon Press, 1995) 73–90.

FARBER, 'National Security, the Right to Travel, and the Court' (1981) *SCRev* 263–90.

FELMER, 'Gemeinschaftsrecht und Nationales (Aus-)bildungsrecht' (1989) *RJB* 175.

FERNHOUT (ed), *Dertig Jaar Vrij Verkeer van Werknemers* (Nijmegen, Reeks Recht & Samenleving, 1999).

——, 'De Verenigde Staten van Europa zijn Begonnen', Maar voor Wie (Zwolle, Tjeenk Willink, 1992).

FEUCHTHOFER, 'Europäische Förderprogramme in Bildungswesen' (1992) *RJB* 180–92.

FIELD, *European Dimensions—Education, Training and the European Union* (London, Jessica Kingsley Publishers, 1998).

FIERSTRA, 'Annotatie *Vlassopoulou*' (1992) *SEW* 640–9.

FLATH, 'Noch Einmal: Freizügigkeit in der EWG' (1968) *der Landskreis* 342–4.

FLYNN, 'Gravier: Suite de Feuilleton' in De Witte (ed), *European Community Law of Education* (Baden-Baden, Nomos, 1989) 95–112.

——, 'Vocational Training in Community Law and Practice' (1989) *YEL* 59–85.

FOBLETS, 'Extra-Collegegeld voor Buitenlandse Studenten aan Belgische Universiteiten?' (1985) *JF* 535–44.

FORDE, 'Social Assistance and the EEC's Regulations' (1978) *LIEI* 9–28.

FOX PIVEN, 'The Race Among the States in Welfare Benefits: A Comment' (1998) *Publius* 39–43.

FRAZIER, 'L'Education et L'Union Européenne' (1997) *RMC* 476–91.

——, 'L'Education et la Communauté Européenne' (1995)

FREEMAN, 'Migration and the Political Economy of the Welfare State' (1986) *Annals AAPSS* 51–63.

FUCHS, 'Bildung ohne Grenzen' (1990) *DV* 245–6.

FRIES and SHAW, 'Citizenship of the Union: First Steps in the European Court of Justice' (1998) *European Public Law* 533–59.

FURROW *et al, Health Law* (St Paul, West Publishing, 1991).

GACON-ESTRADA, 'The Co-operation Agreements Concluded between the European Community and the Maghreb Countries' in Jorens and Schulte, *European Social Security Law and Third Country Nationals* (Bruxelles, Die Keure, 1998) 323–31.

GARDNER, 'The European Agency for the Evaluation of Medicines and European Regulation of Pharmaceuticals' (1996) *European Law Journal* 48–82.

GAROT, 'A New Basis for European Citizenship: Residence?' in La Torre (ed), *European Citizenship: An Institutional Challenge* (The Hague, Kluwer Law International, 1998) 229–48.

GARRONE, *La Libre Circulation des Personnes—Liberté de Mouvement, Egalité, Liberté Économique—Etude de Droit Communautaire et Suisse* (Zürich, Schulthess, 1995).

——, 'La Discrimination Indirecte en Droit Communautaire: Vers une Théorie Générale' (1994) *RTDE* 425–49.

GARTH, 'Migrant Workers and Rights of Mobility in the European Community and the United States: A Study of Law, Community and Citizenship in the Welfare State' in Cappelletti *et al Integration Through Law—Europe and the American Federal Experience* (Vol I, Baden-Baden, Nomos, 1986) 85–163.

GASSNER, 'Pflegeversicherung und Arbeitnehmerfreizügigkeit' (1998) *NZS* 313–18.

GAZAN and OOMEN, 'Internationaliseringsprogramma's en het Nederlandse Hoger Onderwijs—van Erasmus naar Socrates in de Europese Unie' (1995) *IS* 155 *et seq.*

GEDDES, 'Thin Europeanisation: The Social Rights of Migrants in an Integrating Europe' in Bommes and Geddes (eds), *Immigration and Welfare—Challenging the Borders of the Welfare State* (London, Routledge, 2000) 209–26.

——, 'Free Movement of Pharmaceuticals within the Community: The Remaining Barriers' (1991) *European Law Review* 295,

GERGEN, 'The Selfish State and the Market' (1988) *Texas Law Review* 1099–153.

GILLIAMS, 'Van "Gravier" tot "Erasmus": Over de Bijdrage van het Hof van Justitie tot de Uitbouw van een Europees Onderwijsbeleid' (1989–1990) *RW* 494–504.

GOBRECHT, 'National Reactions to Kohll and Decker' (1998) *Eurohealth* 16–17.

GODRY, 'Krankenbehandlung ohne Grenzen—Anmerkungen zu einem Modellprojekt im Nederländischen-deutschen Grenzgebiet' (1997) *ZFSH/SGB* 416 *et seq.*

GONZALEZ, 'The Interstate Privileges and Immunities: Fundamental Rights or Federalism' (1986) *CapULRev* 493–513.

GOODWIN-GILL, *International Law and the Movement of Persons Between States* (Oxford, Clarendon Press, 1978).

GORDON and JALLADE, 'Spontaneous Student Mobility in the European Union: A Statistical Survey' (1996) *EJE* 133–51.

—— and ——, 'Student Mobility within the European Union: A Statistical Analysis' (http://europa.eu.int/comm/education/socrates/erasmus/statisti/index.html, 1995).

GORI, 'External Relations in Community Education and Vocational Training Policies' (1998) *Maastricht Journal* 25–51.

GOULD, 'Equality of Access to Education' (1989) *Modern Law Review* 497.

GOULOUSSIS, 'Equality of Treatment and the Relationship between Regulations 1612/68 and 1408/71' in *Commission of the European Communities/Departemento de Relações Internacionais e Convenções de Segurança Social, Social Security in Europe—Equality between Nationals and Non-Nationals* (1995) 75–88.

GRABITZ, *Europäisches Bürgerrecht zwischen Marktbürgerschaft und Staatsbürgerschaft* (Köln, Europa Union Verlag GmbH, 1970).

GRAMLICH and LAREN, 'Migration and Income Redistribution Responsibilities' (1984) *JHR* 489–511.

GREENWOOD, 'Nationality and the Limits of the Free Movement of Persons in Community Law' (1987) *Yearbook of European Law* 7

——, 'Limits on the Free Movement of Persons in EEC Law' (1987/1988) *Yearbook European Law* 185–210.

GREWAL, 'Economic Criteria for the Assignment of Functions in a Federal System' in *Advisory Council for Inter-Governmental Relations—Towards Adaptive Federalism* (1981) 27.

GROENENDIJK, 'Security of Residence and Access to Free Movement for Settled Third Country Nationals under Community Law' in Guild and Harlow (eds), *Implementing Amsterdam—Immigration and Asylum Rights in EC Law* (Oxford, Hart Publishing, 2001) 225–40.

——, 'The Growing Relevance of Article 39 (ex 48) EC Treaty for Third Country Nationals' in: Carlier and Verwilghen, *Thirty Years of Free Movement of Workers in Europe* (Luxembourg, Office for Official Publications of the European Communities, 2000) 207–23.

——, 'De Betekenis van Artikel 39 EG-Verdrag voor Werknemers uit Landen buiten de Europese Unie' in Fernhout (ed), *Dertig Jaar Vrij Verkeer van Werknemers* (Nijmegen, Reeks Recht & Samenleving, 1999) 35–49.

GROENENDIJK and GUILD, 'Converging Criteria: Creating an Area of Security of Residence for Europe's Third Country Nationals' (2001) *EJML* 37–59.

GRUNWALD and SMIT, *Grensoverschrijdende Zorg—Zorg op Maat in de Euregio Maas-Rijn; Evaluatie van een Experiment* (Utrecht, Nzi, 1999).

GUENDELSBERGER, 'Equal Protection and Resident Aliens Access to Public Benefits in France and the United States' (1993) *Tulane Law Review* 631–76.

GUILD, *European Community Law from a Migrant's Perspective* (Nijmegen, 1999).

——, 'Primary Immigration: The Great Myths' in Guild and Harlow (eds), *Implementing Amsterdam—Immigration and Asylum Rights in EC Law* (Oxford, Hart Publishing, 2001) 65–94.

GUILD and HARLOW (eds), *Implementing Amsterdam—Immigration and Asylum Rights in EC Law* (Oxford, Hart Publishing, 2001).

GUILD and NIESEN, *The Developing Immigration and Asylum Policies of the European Union—Adopted Conventions, Resolutions, Decisions and Resolutions* (The Hague, Kluwer Law International, 1996).

GUILD and PEERS, 'Deference or Defiance? The Court of Justice's Jurisdiction over Immigration and Asylum' in Guild and Harlow (eds), *Implementing Amsterdam—Immigration and Asylum Rights in EC Law* (Oxford, Hart Publishing, 2000) 267–89.

GÜMRÜKCÜ, 'EU-Türkei-Beziehungen im Spannungsfeld zwischen Assoziation und Vollmitgliedschaft—Werdegang einer Ungleichen Partnerschaft' in Lichtenberg *et al* (eds) *Gastarbeiter—Einwanderer—Bürger? Die Rechtstellung der Türkischen Arbeitnehmer in der Europäischen Union* (Baden-Baden, Nomos, 1996) 27–60.

GUTTMANN, *Die Assoziationsfreizügigkeit Türkischer Angehöriger* (Baden-Baden, Nomos, 1999).

GUNTHER, *Constitutional Law* (Mineola, Foundation Press, 1985).

——, 'The Supreme Court 1971 Term—Foreword: In Search of Evolving Doctrine on a Changing Court: A Model for a Newer Equal Protection' (1972) *Harvard Law Review* 1–48.

GYSELEN, 'Annotation *Albany*' (2000) *Common Market Law Review* 425–48.

HAGEN, 'University Co-operation and Academic Recognition in Europe: The Council of Europe and the Communities'(1987) *EJE* 77–83.

HAILBRONNER, 'Die Entscheidung des EuGH zur Freizügigkeit Türkischer Arbeitnehmer' (1988) *NVwZ* 220–4.

——, 'Die Neuere Rechtsprechung zum EG-Freizügigkeitsrecht' (1988) *ZAR* 3–13.

——, 'Aufenthaltbeschränkungen gegenüber EG-Angehörigen und Neuere Entwicklungen im EG-Aufenthaltsrech' (1985) *ZAR* 108–16.

HAILBRONNER and POLAKIEWICZ, 'Non-EC Nationals in the European Community: The Need for a Coordinated Approach' (1992) *Duke Journal ICLaw* 49.

HALL, *Nationality, Migration and Citizenship of the Union* (Dordrecht, Nijhoff, 1995).

——, 'The ECHR and Public Policy Exceptions to the Free Movement of Workers under the EEC Treaty' (1991) *European Law Review* 466 *et seq*.

HAMILTON, 'Interne Markt en (Aanvullende) Ziektekostenverzekeringen' (2001) *NTG* 37–48.

——, 'Annotatie *Decker-Kohll*' (1998) *TvG* 394–7.

HAMMAR, 'Legal Time of Residence and the Status of Immigrants' in Bauböck, *From Aliens to Citizens—Redefining the Status of Immigrants in Europe* (Aldershot, Avebury, 1994) 187–97.

——, *Democracy and the Nation State: Aliens, Denizens and Citizens in a World of International Migration* (Aldershot, Avebury, 1990).

HAMMERSTROM, 'Constitutional Law—Equal Protection—Residency Requirements' (1970) *CaseWRLRev*.

HAMPEL, *Einwanderungsgesetzgebung und Innereuropäische Wanderung—Die Rechtlichen Regelungen der Zulassung Ausländischer Arbeitnehmer in FünfzehnEeuropäischen Staaten* (Kiel, Institut für Weltwirtschaft Universität Kiel, 1957).

HANCHER, 'Creating the Internal Market for Pharmaceutical Medicines—An Echternach Jumping Procession' (1991) *Common Market Law Review* 821.

——, 'The European Pharmaceutical Market: Problems of Harmonization' (1990) *European Law Review* 9.

HANDOLL, *Free Movement of Persons in the EU* (Chicester, Wiley, 1995).

——, 'Article 48(4) and Non-National Access to Public Employment' (1988) *European Law Review* 223–42.

HANEKUIJCK, *Het Recht op Vrijheid van Migratie* (Leiden, Sijthoff, 1957).

HÄNLEIN, 'Problems Concerning Decision No 3/80 of the Council of Association—A Point of View from a EU Perspective' in Jorens and Schulte (eds), *European Social Security Law and Third Country Nationals* (Bruxelles, Die Keure, 1998) 299–322.

——, 'Fehlende Unmittelbare Wirkung der Bestimmungen des Assoziationsratsbeschlusses EWG-Türkei über Invalidität und Renten bei Alter und Tot' (1997) *EASr* 21–3.

HANSEN, 'A European Citizenship or a Europe of Citizens?—Third Country Nationals in the EU' (1998) *JEMS* 751–68.

HARTLEY, 'Free Movement of Persons' in Green *et al The Legal Foundations of the Single European Market* (Oxford, Oxford University Press, 1991).

——, 'La Libre Circulation des Etudiants en Droit Communautaire' (1989) *CDE* 325.

——, *EEC Immigration Law* (Amsterdam, North-Holland Publishing Company, 1978) 77–80.

——,'The International Scope of the Community Provisions Concerning Free Movement of Workers' in Jacobs (ed), *European Law and the Individual* (Amsterdam, North-Holland Publishing Company, 1976) 19–37.

HARMAECKERS, 'Fiscal Sovereignty and Tax Harmonization in the EC' (1991) *EurTax* 173.

HARVITH, 'The Constitutionality of Residence Tests for General and Categorical Assistance Programs' in tenBroek (ed), *The Law of the Poor* (San Francisco, Chandler, 1966) 243–317.

HATZOPOULOS, 'Recent Developments of the Case Law of the ECJ in the Field of Services' (2000) *Common Market Law Review* 43–82.

——, 'Annotation *Svensson*' (1996) *Common Market Law Review* 569.

HEDEMANN-ROBINSON, 'An Overview of Recent Developments at Community Level in Relation to Third Country Nationals within the European Union, with Particular Reference to the Case of the Euroepan Court of Justice' (2001) *Common Market Law Review* 525–86.

——, 'From Object to Subject?: Non-EC Nationals and the Draft Proposal of the Commission for a Council Act Establishing Rules for the Admission of Third Country Nationals to the Member States' (1998) *Yearbook of European Law* 289–335.

——, 'Third Country Nationals, European Union Citizenship and Free Movement of Persons: A Time for Bridges Rather than Division' (1997) *Yearbook of European Law* 321–62.

HEISE, 'Les Possibilités d'une Harmonisation Social des Régimes d'Assurance Sociale dans les Etats Membres de la Communauté Economique Européenne' (1966) *DS* 580–9.

HELLMUTH, *Residency for Tuition Purposes: A Study of the Rules in Use at the Fifty State Universities* (Madison, working paper, University of Michigan, 1981).

HENDRIKS, 'The Right to Freedom of Movement and the (Un)Lawfulness of Aids/HIV Specific Travel Restrictions from a European Perspective' (1990) *NJIL* 86.

HENNIS, 'Access to Education in the European Communities' (1990) *LJIL* 35–44.

HEPPLE, 'Welfare Legislation and Wage Labour' in Hepple (ed), *The Making of Labour Law in Europe—A Comparative Study of Nine Countries up to 1945* (London, Mansell, 1986) 115–53.

HERMANS, 'The Socrates Programme: From Negotiation to Implementation' (1997) *EJELP* 19–39.

HERMANS, 'Access to Health Care and Health Services in the European Union: Regulation 1408/71 and the E 111 Process' in Leidl (ed), *Health Care and its Financing in the Single European Market* (Amsterdam, IOS Press, 1998) 324–43.

——, 'Patients' Rights in the European Union—Cross-Border Care as an Example of the Right to Health Care' (1997) *EJPH* 11–17.

——, 'Gezondheidszorg bij Tijdelijk Verblijf over de Grens: Toepassing Verordening 1408/71 (E111) in de Europese Praktijk' (1996) *SR* 343–8.

——, *Europese Unie en de Gezondheidszorg—De Gevolgen van de Eenwording voor de Nederlandse Gezondheidszorg* (Deventer, Kluwer, 1994).

HERMANS and BUIJSEN, 'Aanbesteden van Medisch-Specialistische Zorg' (2000) *SR* 282–92.

HERMANS and DEN EXTER, 'Cross-border Alliances in Health Care: International Co-operation between Health Insurers and Providers in the Euregio Meuse-Rhine' (1999) *CMJ* <http://www.mefst.hr/cmj/1999/4002/400219.htm>.

HERMANS *et al*, 'Zorg in het Buitenland: Gevolgen voor Patiënten en Zorgverzekeraars' (1998) *Staatscourant 5*.

HERMANS *et al*, 'Zorgverzekeraars en Uitvoeringsorganen Sociale Zekerheid: Ondernemingen in het Licht van het EG-Recht' (1996) *SMA* 227–38.

HERMANS *et al*, *Health Care in Europe after 1992* (Aldershot, Dartmouth Publishing Company, 1992).

HERMESSE, 'Opening Up the National Borders to Patients—The Economic Consequences' in *Association Internationale de la Mutualité/ European Institute of Social Security, Health Care without Frontiers within the European Union—Free Movement of Goods and Services in the Health Care Sector* (Luxembourg, AIM, 1999) 49–58.

HERMESSE and LEWALLE, *L'Accès aux Soins en Europe—Quelle Mobilité du patient?* (Bruxelles, Academia, 1993).

HERMESSE *et al*, 'Patient Mobility within the European Union' (1997) *EJPH* 4–10.

HERMESSE *et al*, *Gezondheidsbescherming in de Europese Gemeenschap* (Brussel, Sauer, 1991).

HERSHKOFF, 'Positive Rights and State Constitutions: The Limits of Federal Rationality Review' (1999) *HarvLRev* 1131–96.

HERVEY, 'Up in Smoke? Community (Anti-)Tobacco Law and Policy' (2001) *European Law Review* 101–25.

——, 'Social Solidarity: A Buttress Against Internal Market Law?'in Shaw (ed), *Social Law and Policy in an Evolving European Union* (Oxford, Hart Publishing, 2000) 31–47.

HEYNIG, 'Freizügigkeit in der Europäischen Wirtschaftgemeinschaft Endgültig Hergestellt' (1968) *BB* 337–9.

HILF, 'Europäisches Gemeinschaftsrecht und Drittstaatsangehörige' in Hailbronner *et al* (eds), *Staat und Völkerrechtordnung—Festschrift für Karl Doehring* (Berlin, Springer-Verlag, 1989) 339–64.

HILSON, 'Discrimination in Community Free Movement Law' (1999) *European Law Review* 445–62.

HINNEKENS, 'Compatibility of Bilateral Tax Treaties with European Community Law—The Rules' (1994) *EC Tax Review* 146–146.

HIRSCH, 'Europäische Sozialunion durch Richterrecht?' (1998) *FAZ* 18.

HOCHBAUM, 'The Federal Structure of Member States as a Limit to Common Educational Policy: The Case of Germany'in De Witte (ed), *European Community Law of Education* (Baden-Baden, Nomos, 1989) 145.

——, 'Politik and Kompetenzen der Europäischen Gemeinschaften im Bildungswesen' (1987) *BayV* 481–90.

HOEPELMAN, 'Het Verblijfsrecht van Studenten uit EU-Staten: De Praktijk aan een Nederlandse Universiteit' in Fernhout (ed), *Dertig Jaar Vrij Verkeer van Werknemers* (Nijmegen, Reeks Recht & Samenleving, 1999) 103–16.

HOFMANN and KOCKS, 'Freier Zugang zu Gesundheitsleistungen im Grenzgebieten—Grenzübershreitendes Projekt in der Euregio Maas/Rhein' (1998) *ZFSH/SGB 306*

HOLLMANN, 'Der Einfluss der EG auf das Gesundheitswesen der Mitgliedstaaten' i (1998) *ZIAS* 180–214.

HOLLOWAY, *Social Policy Harmonization in the European Community* (Farnborough, 1981).

HOOGENBOOM, 'Free Movement and Integration of Non-EC Nationals and the Logic of the Internal Market' Schermers *et al* (eds), *Free Movement of Persons in Europe* (Dordrecht, Martinus Nijhoff Publishers, 1993) 497–511.

——, 'Integration into Society and Free Movement of Non-EC Nationals' *European Journal of International Law* (1992) 36.

'HOUSE OF LORDS, Select Committee on European Communities, 27th Report on Student Mobility in the European Community' (1998).

HULL, 'Undocumented Alien Children and Free Public Education: An Analysis of *Plyler v Doe*' (1983) *University of Pittsburgh Law Review* 431.

——, 'Resident Aliens and the Equal Protection Clause: The Burger Court's Retreat From *Graham v Richardson*' (1980) *Brook Law Review* 1–42.

——, *Without Justice for All—The Constitutional Rights of Aliens* (Westport, Greenwood Press, 1980).

HULST, *Studiefinanciering in Zes Europese Landen* (Zoetermeer, Ministerie van Onderwijs en Wetenschappen, 1995).

——, 'Reforming Health Care in Seven European Nations' (1991) *HA* 1–10.

HURWITZ, *The Free Circulation of Physicians within the European Communities* (Aldershot, Avebury, 1990).

HYMAN, *Public Finance—A Contemporary Application of Theory to Policy* (Fort Worth, The Dryden Press, 1999).

International Labour Office (ILO), *Analysis of the Immigration laws and Regulations of Selected Countries* (Geneva, International Labour Office, 1954).

INGELSE, 'Verplichting tot Vergoeding van in Andere Lid-Staten Gemaakte Ziektekosten: Decker en Kohll in Nederland' (2000) *SMA* 208–11.

IPSEN, 'Europäisches Gemeinschaftsrecht' (1964) *NJW* 340.

ISAAC, 'L'Enseignement supérieur et le Champt d'apllication du Traité CEE' in Philip (ed), *L'Enseignement Supérieur et la Dimension Européenne* (Paris, Economica, 1989) 11–18.

JACKSON, 'Persons of Equal Worth: Romer v Evans and the Politics of Equal Protection' (1997) *University of California Law Review* 453–501.

JACOBS and GODDARD, *Social Health Insurance Systems in European Countries—The Role of the Insurer in the Health Care System: A Comparative Study of Four European Countries* (York, Centre for Health Economics, 2000).

JAKUBOWSKI and BUSSE, *Health Care Systems in the EU—A Comparative Study* (Luxembourg, European Parliament—Directorate General for Research, 1998).

JANSEN, 'Vrij Verkeer van Turkse Werknemers in de EG?' (1986) *MR* 261–3.

JARVIS, *The Application of EC Law on the Free Movement of Goods by National Courts of the Member States* (Oxford, Clarendon Press, 1997).

JESSERUN D'OLIVEIRA, 'Vrij Verkeer voor Geregistreerde Partners in de Europese Unie' (2001) *NJB* 205–10.

——, 'Nationality and the European Union after Amsterdam' in O'Keeffe and Twomey, *Legal Issues of the Amsterdam Treaty* (Oxford, Hart Publishing, 1999).

——, 'Is Reverse Discrimination still Permissible under the Single European Act' in de Boer *et al* (eds), *Forty Years On: The Evolution of Postwar Private International Law in Europe* (Deventer, Kluwer, 1990) 71–86.

JOHNSON and O'KEEFFE, 'From Non-Discrimination to Obstacles to Free Movement: Recent Developments Concerning Free Movement of Workers' (1994) *Common Market Law Review* 1313–46.

JORENS, 'Annotatie *Decker-Kohll*' (1998) *RZA* 303–9.

——, 'Non-European Union Nationals and the Co-ordination of European Social Security Law: The International Agreements Concluded by the European Union with Third Countries and Conflict Rules in European Social Security Law' in Jorens and Schulte (eds), *European Social Security Law and Third Country Nationals* (Bruxelles, Die Keure, 1998) 1–110.

——, *De Rechtspositie van Niet-EU-Onderdanen in het Europees Socialezekerheidsrecht* (Brugge, Die Keure, 1997).

——, *Wegwijs in het Europees Sociaal Zekerheidsrecht* (Brugge, Die Keure, 1995).

JØRGENSEN, *Union Citizens—Free Movement and Non-Discrimination* (Denmark, Jurist—og Okonomforbundets Forlag, 1996).

JORIS, 'Het Hof van Justitie van de Europese Gemeenschappen en het Vrije verkeer van Turkse Werknemers: De Zaak Demirel' (1988) *TvV* 3–20.

JORIS and VENY, 'Bijkomende Inschrijvingsgelden voor Buitenlandse Studenten—Welke Wetgeving is van Toepassing?' (1988) *RW* 735–40.

KAISER *et al, Public Expenditure on Higher Education—A Comparative Study in the Member States of the European Community* (London, Jessica Kingsley, (1992).

KALEN, 'Durational Residency Requirements and the Equal Protection Clause: Zobel v Williams' (1983) *Journal of Urban and Contemporary Law* 329–59.

KAMOIE, 'EMTALA: Reaching Beyond the Emergency Room to Expand Hospital Liability' (2000) *JHL* 25–55.

KAMP, 'Die "Richtige" Rechtsgrundlage der Richtlinie über das Aufenthaltsrecht der Studenten' (1990) *EuR* 397–404.

KAMPF, 'La Directive 90/366/Cee Relative au Droit de Séjour des Etudiants Communautaires: sa Transposition en France' (1992) *RMCE* 303–17.

KANAVOS, 'Cross Border Health Care in Europe—European Court Rulings Have Made Governments Worried' (1999) *British Medical Journal* 1157–8.

KAPTEYN and VERLOREN VAN THEMAAT, *Introduction to the Law of the European Communities* (London, Kluwer Law International, 1998).

KARST, 'The Supreme Court 1976 Term—Foreword: Equal Citizenship under the Fourteenth Amendment' (1977) *Harvard Law Review* 1.

KATZ, 'More Equal than Others, The Burger Court and the Newly Arrived State Resident' (1989) *New Mexico Law Review* 329–76.

KESTELOOT *et al,* 'The Reimbursement of the Expenses for Medical Treatment Received by Transnational Patients in EU-countries' (1995) *HP* 43.

KETELSEN, 'Einreise, Aufenthalt und Ausweisung von Ausländern aus Drittstaaten' (1991) *ZfRV* 115–27.

KEUNEN, 'Annotation *Jauch*' (2001) *RSV* 671–74.

——, *Schets van het Europese Socialezekerheidsrecht—Europese Coordinatieregels inzake Sociale Zekerheid* (Lelystad, Koninklijke Vermande, 2001).

KIRKMAN and LIFF, 'Stelselwijzigingen in Enkele Andere Landen' in Elsinga and van Kemenade, *Van Revolutie naar Evolutie—Tien Jaar Stelselwijziging inde Nederlandse Gezondheidszorg* (Utrecht, De Tijdstroom, 1997).

KLARMAN, 'An Interpretive History of the Modern Equal Protection' (1991) *Michigan Law Review* 213–316.

KLEINMAN and PIACHAUD, 'European Social Policy—Conception and Choices' (1993) *JESP* 1–19.

KNOBBE-KEUK, 'Niederlassungsfreiheit: Diskriminierungs- or Beschränkungsverbot?—Zur Dogmatik des Art.52 EWG-Vertrag—am Beispiel einiger Gesellschaftsrechtlicher Beschränkungen' (1990) *DB* 2573–84.

KNOLLE, 'Freizügigkeit der Arbeitnehmer—Zur Verordnung Nr.15 der Europäischen Wirtschaftgemeinschaft' (1961) *BArbBl* 674–79.

KOCH, 'Die Entscheidung des EuGH zum Leistungsexport des Pflegegeldes vom 5. März 1998 (Rs C-160/96)' (1998) *ZFSH* 451–4.

KOENIG and PECHSTEIN, *Die Europäische Union—Der Vertrag von Maastricht* (Tübingen, Mohr, 1995).

KOKKINI-IATRIDOU *et al, Een Inleiding tot het Rechtsvergelijkende Onderzoek* (Deventer, Kluwer, 1988).

KON, 'Aspects of Reverse Discrimination in Community Law' (1981) *European Law Review* 75–101.

KOMMERS and WAELBROECK, 'Legal Integration and the Free Movement of Goods: The American and the European Experience' in Cappelletti *et al Integration through Law—Europe and the American Federal Experience* (Berlin, De Gruyter, 1985) 165–227.

KONRAD, *Die Internationale Arbeitsmobilität in der Europäischen Wirtschaftsgemein-schaft* (Würzburg, PUBLISHER,1969).

KRAUS, *Niederlassungsfreiheit der Freien Berufe in der Europäischen Gemeinschaft unter Besonderer Berücksichtigung der Apotheker* (Würzburg, 1989).

LAFRANCE, *Welfare Law: Structure and Entitlement in a Nutshell* (St Paul, West Publishing, 1979).

LANE, 'New Community Competences under the Maastricht Treaty' (1993) *Common Market Law Review* 939–79.

LANFRANCHI, *Droit communautaire et Travailleurs Migrants des Etats Tiers—Entrée et Circulation dans la Communauté Européenne* (Paris, Economica, 1994).

LANGER, 'Probleme der Koordinierung beim Public/Privat-Mix von Gesundheitsleist-ungen' (1999) *ZSR* 716–34.

——, 'Künftliche Rechtliche Koordinierung der Pflegeversicherung in Europa' in Sieveking (ed), *Soziale Sicherung bei Pflegebedürftigkeit in der Europäischen Union* (Baden-Baden, Nomos, 1998) 251–72.

LANNES, 'International Mobility of Manpower in Western Europe: II' (1956) *International Law Review* 135–49.

LASHBROOK, 'Back from a Long Vacation: The Privileges and Immunities Clause of the Fourteenth Amendment in *Saenz v. Roe*' (2001) *CapULRev* 481–512.

LASKE, 'The Impact of the Single European Market on Social Protection for Migrant Workers' (1993) *Common Market Law Review* 515–40.

LASLETT, 'The Mutual Recognition of Diplomas, Certificates and Other Evidence of Formal Qualifications in the European Community' (1990) *LIEI* 1–66.

LAURSEN, 'Constitutional Protection of Foreign Travel' (1981) *Col Law Review* 902–31.

LAYCOCK, 'Equal Citizens of Equal and Territorial States: The Constitutional Foundations of Choice of Law' (1992) *Col Law Review* 249–337.

LAYTON-HENRY, 'Citizenship or Denizenship for Migrant Workers' in Layton-Henry (ed), *The Political Rights of Migrant Workers in Western Europe* (London, Sage, 1990) 186–95.

LEENKNEGT, *Vrijheid van Onderwijs in Vijf Europese Landen—Een Rechtsvergelijkend Onderzoek naar de Gemeenschappelijke Beginselen op het Gebied van Onderwijs in België, Duitsland, Engeland, Frankrijk en Nederland* (Deventer, Tjeenk Willink, 1997).

——, 'Onderwijs en Europese Integratie' (1993) *S&W* 50–5.

LEENEN *et al, Trends in Health Legislation in Europe* (Paris, Masson, 1986).

LEGOMSKY, 'Immigration, Federalism and the Welfare State' (1995) *UCLA Law Review* 1453–74.

LE GRAND *et al, The Economics of Social Problems* (Basingstoke, MacMillan, 1993).

LEIBFRIED, 'Multitiered Institutions and the Making of Social Policy' in Leibfried and Pierson (eds), *European Social Policy—Between Fragmentation and Integration* (Washington DC, The Brookings Institution, 1995) 1–40.

——, 'Semisovereign Welfare States: Social Policy in a Multitiered Europe' in Leibfried and Pierson (eds), *European Social Policy—Between Fragmentation and Integration* (Washington DC, The Brookings Institution, 1995) 43–77.

LEIBFRIED and PIERSON, 'Halbsouveräne Wohlfahrtsstaaten—Soziale Sicherung in der Europäischen Mehrebenen-Politik' 1997) *BDIP* 45.

LEINGÄRTNER, 'Diskussionsbeitrag zur Kritik and der Rechtsprechung des EuGH in den Rechtsachen C–160/96, C–120/95, C–158/96, Molenaar, Decker u. Kohll aus der Sicht der Lesitungsberechtigten' in Schulte and Barwig (eds), *Freizügigkeit und Soziale Sicherheit—Die Durchführung der Verordnung Nr.1408/71 über die Soziale Sicherheit der Wanderarbeitnehmer in Deutschland* (Baden-Baden, Nomos, 1999) 117–21.

LENAERTS, 'Education in European Community Law' (1994) *Common Market Law Review* 7–41.

——, 'Het Onderwijs in het Europees Recht na "Maastricht"' (1992–1993) *TOO* 264–81.

——, 'Erasmus: Legal Basis and Implementation' in De Witte (ed) *European Community Law of Education* (Baden-Baden, Nomos, 1989) 113–26.

LENGAUER, 'Drittwirkung von Grundfreiheiten—Eine Besprechung der RS C–281/98 *Angonese*' (2001) *ZfRV* 57–65.

LENZ, 'Zuständigkeiten und Initiativen der Europäischen Gemeinschaft im Bereich des Bildungswesen' (1990) *EG-Forum, Beilage zu IBW-Heft* 183–208.

——, 'Die Rechtsprechung des Europäischen Gerichtshofs im Bereich des Bildungswesen' (1989) *EA* 125–34.

——, 'The Public Service in Article 48(4) EEC with Special Reference to the Law in England and the Federal Republic of Germany' (1989) *LIEI* 75–122.

LEVI, 'The Equal Treatment of Aliens: Preemption or Equal Protection?' (1979) *Stanford Law Review* 1069–91.

LEVI-SANDRI, 'Free Movement of Workers in the European Community' (1968) *EC Bulletin 5*.

LEVMORE, 'Interstate Exploitation and Judicial Intervention' (1983) *Virginia Law Review* 563–630.

LHERNOULD, 'Avantages Sociaux et Egalité de Traitement—Une nouvelle Etape dans la Jurisprudence de la CJCE' (1999) *DS* 938–9.

LHOEST, 'Annotation *Boukhalfa*' (1998) *Common Market Law Review* 247–67.

LICHTENBERG, 'Freizügigkeit und Bildungswesen in der Europäischen Gemeinschaft an der Schwelle zum Gemeinsamen Binnenmarktes' in Baur *et al* (eds) *Festschrift für Ernst Steindorff zum 70. Geburtstag am 13. März 1990* (Berlin, De Gruyter, 1990) 1269–86.

LINDERS, 'De Arresten Kohll en Decker: Impact op de Tariefstelling in de Gezondheidszorg' in Essers *et al* (eds), *Grensoverschrijdende Zorg—Marktwerking vs. National Zorgbewaking* (Lelystad, Koninklijke Vermande, 2000) 14–18.

LIPPERT, *Gleichbehandlung bei Sozialen Vergünstigungen und Arbeitnehmerfreizügigkeit in der Europäischen Gemeinschaft—Eine Analyse von Art.7 II (EWG) Nr.1612/68 auf der Basis der Rechtsprechung des Europäischen Gerichtshofes* (Augsburg, Heuser, 1993).

LOENEN, *Verschil in Gelijkheid—De Conceptualisering van het Juridische Gelijkheidsbeginsel met Betrekking tot Mannen en Vrouwen in Nederland en de Verenigde Staten* (Zwolle, Tjeenk Willink, 1992).

LOFFREDO, 'If You Ain't Got the Do, Re, Mi, The Commerce Clause and State Residence Restrictions on Welfare' (1993) *Yale L P R* 147–202.

——, 'Poverty, Democracy and Constitutional Law' (1993) *University of Pennsylvania Law Review* 1277.

LOGATTO, 'Residence Laws—A Step Forward or Backward?' (1961) *Catholic Law* 101.

LONBAY, 'Picking over the Bones: Rights of Establishment Revisted'(1991) *European Law Review* 507–20.

——, 'Education and Law: The Community Context' (1989) *European Law Review* 363–87.

LONG, 'Poverty States and Receipt of of Welfare Among Migrants and Nonmigrants in Large Cities' (1974) *ASRev* 46–56.

LOOZEN, 'CAO's, Bedrijfspensioenen en het EG-Mededingingsrecht' (1999) *NTER* 274–84.

LOTTMAN AND VAN DER WILT, *Eindrapportage Project Grensoverschrijdende Zorg in de EU-Region* (Rijn and Waal, 1999).

LOUE, 'Access to Health Care and the Undocumented Alien' (1992) *JLM* 271–332.

LUCASSEN, 'The Great War and the Origins of Migration Control in Western Europe and the United States (1880–1920)' Bocker *et al* (eds), *Regulation of Migration—International Experiences* (Amsterdam, Het Spinhuis, 1998) 45–72.

LUNDSTRÖM, 'Family Life and the Freedom of Movement of Workers in the European Union' (1996) *IJLP Family* 250–80.

LYON-CAEN, 'Social Security and the Principle of Equal Treatment in the EC Treaty and Regulation No.1408/71' in *Commission of the European Communities/Departemento de Relações Internacionais e Convenções de Segurança Social, Social Security in Europe—Equality Between Nationals and Non-Nationals* (1995) 45–73.

——, 'La Libre Circulation des Travailleurs (Règlement et Directive des Communautés européennes du 15 Octobre 1969)' (1969) *Juris-Classeur Periodique* 2222.

MACHERET, *L'Immigration Étrangère en Suisse a l'Heure de l'Integration Européenne* (Genève, Georg, 1969).

MADRA, *Migrant Workers and International Law* (Nijmegen, Ars Aequi Libri, 1986).

MADURO, 'Europe's Social Self: The Sickness unto Death' in Shaw (ed), *Social Law and Policy in an Evolving European Union* (Oxford, Hart Publishing, 2000) 325–49.

——, 'Striking the Elusive Balance Between Economic Freedom and Social Rights in the EU' in Alston (ed), *The EU and Human Rights* (Oxford, Oxford University Press, 1999) 449–72.

——, *We the Court: The European Court of Justice & the European Economic Constitution* (Oxford, Hart Publishing, 1998).

MAERTENS, *De Geografische Mobiliteit van Werknemers in de Europese Gemeenschap* (Antwerpen, 1969).

MANCINI, 'The Free Movement of Workers in the Case-Law of the European Court of Justice' in Curtin and O'Keeffe (eds), *Constitutional Adjudication in European Community and National Law: Essays for the Hon Mr TF O'Higgins* (Dublin, Butterworths, 1992) 67–77.

MANDELKER, 'Exclusion and Removal Legislation' (1956) *W Law Review* 57.

——, 'The Settlement Requirement in General Assistance' (1955) *Washington University Law Quarterly* 355–77.

MARENCO, The Notion of Restriction on the Freedom of Establishment and the Provision of Services in the Case-Law of the Court' (1992) *Yearbook of European Law* 111–50.

MARESCEAU, 'Komt Toegang tot het Onderwijs ook Binnen de Werkingssfeer van het EEG-Verdrag?' in Van den Bogaert *et al* (eds), *Beschouwingen Rond het Project "Versterking Integrale Planning"—Liber Amicorum Van Den Bogaert* (1989) 165–85.

MARIAS, 'European Citizenship in Action: From Maastricht to the Intergovernmental Conference' in La Torre (ed), *European Citizenship—An Institutional Challenge* (The Hague, Kluwer Law International, 1998) 293–316.

——, 'From Market Citizen to Union Citizen' in *Marias, European Citizenship* (Maastricht, European Institute of Public Administration, 1994) 1–23.

MARINER, 'Access to Health Care and Equal Protection of the Law: The Need for Heightened Scrutiny'(1987) *AJLM* 345–80.

MARMOR, *Understanding Health Care Reform* (New Haven, Yale University Press, 1994).

MARTIN, 'Comments on *Angonese*' (2000) *EJML* 431–44.

——, 'Comments on *Ferlini*' (2001) *EJML* 257–70.

——, 'Discriminations, Entraves et Raisons Impérieur' (1998) *CDE* 561.

MASSART-PIERARD, 'Vers une Politique Commune de la Sante?' in Massart-Pierard (eds), *L'Europe de la Santé. Hasard et/ou Nécessité?* (Louvain-la-Neuve, Academia, 1988) 27.

MASTERS, 'Comment—Nonresident Tuition Charged By State Universities in Review' (1970) *UMKC Law Review* 341–54.

MAVRIDIS, 'La Fin des Doubles Cotisations en Europe?' (2000) *DS* 1104–13.

——, 'Une Libéralisation des Soins de Santé—Un premier Diagnostic après les Arrêts CJCE Kohll et Decker' (1999) *DS* 172–5.

——, 'Le Citoyen Européen Peut-il se Faire Soigner dans l'Etat de son Choix?' (1996) *DS* 1086–94.

MAXWELL, 'An Alien's Constitutional Right to Loan, Scholarship and Tuition Benefits at State Supported Colleges and Universities' *CalWLRev* (1979) 514–62.

McCONN, 'Round Table: Positions and Reactions of the Public Actors' in Association Internationale de la Mutualité/ European Institute of Social Security, *Health Care without Frontiers within the European Union—Free Movement of Goods and Services in the Health Care Sector* (1999) 39–40.

McCOY, 'Recent Equal Protection Decisions—Fundamental Right to Travel or "Newcomers" as a Suspect Class' (1975) *Vanderbilt Law Review* 987–1023.

McGINNIS, 'Undocumented Aliens' Right To Medicaid after *Plyler v. Doe*' (1984) *Fordham International Law Journal* 83–117.

McMAHON, *Education and Culture in European Community Law* (London, The Athlone Press, 1995).

MEADE, 'Free Movement of Students: Access to Higher Education in another Member State' (1988) *MR* 260–3.

MEINHOLD, 'Notwendigkeit und Möglichkeit der Harmonisierung von Sozialleistungen im EWG-Raum' (1964) *DVZ* 1–4.

MENDELSOHN, 'The European Court of Justice and Human Rights' (1981) *Yearbook of European Law* 125.

MILLER, 'Freizügigkeit in der EWG' (1968) *der Landskreis* 56–8.

——, 'Völlige Freizügigkeit der Arbeitskräfte in den Europäischen Gemeinschaften' (1968) *BArbBl* 590–4.

MINDERHOUD, 'Regulation of Migration: Introduction' in Bocker *et al* (eds), *Regulation of Migration—International Experiences* (Amsterdam, Het Spinhuis, 1998) 7–24.

MINISTERIE, *Ministerie van Volksgezondheid, Welzijn en Sport, De Gevolgen van de Arresten Kohll en Decker voor het Nederlandse Stelsel van Ziektekostenverzekeringen* (Den Haag, 1998).

MISSON, 'The Sporting Side of Community Law' Carlier and Verwilghen, *Thirty Years of Free Movement of Workers in Europe* (Luxembourg, Office for Official Publications of the European Communities, 2000) 79–87.

MITCHELL, 'EU Cooperation in Higher Education and Training: New Challenges and Recent Progress' (1996) *EJVT* 43–54.

MOHR, *Studentenhandboek* (Luxemburg, Bureau voor Officiële Publikaties der Europese Gemeenschappen, 1990).

MOOR, 'Article 7 of the Treaty of Rome Bites' (1985) *Maastricht Law Review* 452–9.

MOORE, 'Annotation *Cabanis-Issarte*' (1997) *Common Market Law Review* 727–39.

MORE, 'The Principle of Equal Treatment: From Market Unifier to Fundamental Right?' in Craig and de Búrca (eds), *The Evolution of EU Law* (Oxford, Oxford University Press, 1999) 517–51.

MORTELMANS, 'Annotation *Groener*' (1989) *AA* 736–47.

——, 'Omgekeerde Discriminatie en het Gemeenschapsrecht' (1979) *SEW* 654–74.

MÜLLER-SOLGER, *Bildung und Europa—Die EG-Förderungsmassnahmen* (Bonn, Economica-Verlag, 1993).

MÜNNICH, 'Art 7 EWGV und Inländerdiskriminierung' (1992) *ZfRV* 92–100.

MUUS, *Internationale Migratie naar Europa: Een Analyse van Internationale Migratie, Migratiebeleid en Mogelijkheden tot Sturing van Immigratie, met Bijzondere Aandacht voor de Europese Gemeenschap en Nederland* (Amsterdam, SUA, 1993).

MARTIN and GUILD, *Free Movement of Persons* (London, Butterworths, 1996).

MÉGRET *et al* (eds), *Commentaire Mégret Le Droit de la CEE* (Bruxelles, Université de Bruxelles, 1992) 60.

MEIJERS *et al* (eds), *Schengen—Internationalisation of Central Chapters of the Law on Aliens, Refugees Privacy, Security and Police* (Leiden, Stichting NJCM-Boekerij, 1992).

MORTELMANS and TEMMINK, 'Het Vrije Personenverkeer Tussen de Nederlandse Antillen en Aruba en de Europese Gemeenschap' (1992) *Justicia—TvAR* Vol 1.

MORTELMANS and VAN OOIK,'Het Europese Verbod op Tabaksreclame: Verbetering van de Interne Markt of Bescherming van de Volksgezondheid' (2001) *AA* 114–30.

MUSGRAVE and MUSGRAVE, *Public Finance in Theory and Practice* (Tokyo, McGraw-Hill—Kogakusha, 1976).

NACHBAUER, 'Art.52 EWGV—Mehr als nur ein Diskriminierungsverbot?' (1991) *EuZW* 470–2.

NATIONAAL ZIEKENHUISINSTITUUT and DEUTSCHE KRANKENHAUSINSTITUT, *Grensoverschrijdende Gezondheidszorg—Duits-Nederlandse Samenwerking in de Gezondheidszorg in de Euregio Rijn-Waal* ('sHeerenberg, Euregio Ryh-Waal, 1995).

NATIONAL, *National Travellers Aid Ass'n, One Manner of Law—A Handbook on Residence Requirements in Public Assistance* (1961).

NEAVE, 'The Role of Education in European Integration' (1986) *IP* 277–84.

——, *The EEC and Education* (Trentham–Stoke-on-Trent, Trentham Books for the European Institute on Education and Social Policy, 1984).

NEIPP, *Das Gesundheitswesen der USA: Ein Vorbild für die Gesetzliche Krankenversicherung?* (Baden-Baden, Nomos, 1988).

NELSON, 'Unanswered Questions: The Implications of *Saenz v. Roe* for Durational Residency Requirements' (2000) *Kansas Law Review* 193–220.

NEUMAN, 'Aliens as Outlaws: Government Services, Proposition 187, and the Structure of Equal Protection Doctrine' (1995) *UCLA Law Review* 1425–52.

——, 'Territorial Discrimination, Equal Protection and Self-Determination' (1987) *University of Pennsylvania Law Review* 261–382.

NEUMAN-DUESBERG, 'Defizite, Probleme und Perspektiven bei der Umsetzung des Europäischen Koordinierenden Sozialrechts—Verordnungen Nr. 1408/71 und Nr.574/72—Leistungen bei Krankheit und Pflegebedürftigkeit' in Schulte and Barwig, *Freizügigkeit und Soziale Sicherheit—Die Durchführung der Verordnung Nr.1408/71 über die Soziale Sicherheit der Wanderarbeitnehmer in Deutschland* (Baden-Baden, Nomos, 1999) 89–108.

——, 'Grenzüberschreitenden Behandlungsleistungen—Die Praxis der Gesetzlichen Krankenversicherung' in *Zentrum für Europäisches Wirtschaftsrecht, Grenzüberschreitende Behandleistungen im Binnenmarkt* (Bonn, Zentrum für Euro-päisches Wirtschaftsrecht, 1998).

——, 'Kohll-Decker-Urteile "Die EuGH-Position ist Angreifbar"' (1998) *GuG* 22–7.

——, 'Krankenversicherung' in Schulte and Zacher, *Wechselwirkungen Zwischen dem Europäischen Sozialrecht und dem Sozialrecht der Bundesrepublik Deutschland* (Berlin, Duncker & Humblot, 1991) 83–109.

NEUWAHL, 'The Treaty on European Union: A Step Forward in the Protection of Human Rights?' in Neuwahl and Rosas (eds), *The European Union and Human Rights* (The Hague, Nijhoff, 1995) 1.

NICKLESS, 'Kohll and Decker: A New Hope for Third Country Nationals' (1999) *Eurohealth* 20–2.

NIHOUL, 'Le Minerval Réclamé aux Etudiants Communautaires en Belgique' (1994) *JdT* 705–12.

NIXON, '"Rational Basis with a Bite": A Retreat from the Constitutional Right to Travel' (2000) *Law and Equality* 209–42.

NORBERG, 'The Agreement on a EEA' (1992) *Common Market Law Review* 1171.

NOTE, 'Welfare Reform: Treatment of Legal Immigrants' (1997) *Harvard Law Review* 1191.

NOTE, 'Devolving Welfare Programs to the States: A Public Choice Perspective' (1996) *Harvard Law Review* 1984–2001.

NOTE, 'State Burdens on Residents Aliens: A New Preemption Analysis' (1980) *Yale Law Journal* 940–61.

NOTE, 'A Dual Standard for State Discrimination Against Aliens' (1979) *Harvard Law Review* 1516.

NOTE, 'Durational Residence Requirements From *Shapiro* through *Sosna*: The Right to Travel Takes a New Turn' (1979) *NYU Law Review* 622.

NOTE, 'Durational Residence Requirements From Shapiro through Sosna: The Right to Travel Takes a New Turn' (1975) *NYU Law Review* 622–80.

NOTE, 'The Right to Travel—Quest for A Constitutional Source' (1974) *RutgCLJ* 122–43.

NOTE, 'Residence Requirements for Tuition: An Unresolved Dilemma' (1972) *Indiana Law Review* 283.

NOTE, 'State University's One-Year Waiting Period Requirement to Attain Resident Status for Tuition Payment does not Violate Fourteenth Amendment' (1971) *Ala Law Review* 147–62.

NOTE, 'The Constitutionality of Nonresident Tuition' (1971) *Minn Law Review* 1139–62.

NOTE, 'Shapiro v. Thompson: Travel, Welfare and the Constitution' (1969) *NYULRev* 989–1013.

NOTE, 'Residence Requirement for Public Relief: An Arbitrary Prerequisite' (1966) *ColJLSP* 133–43.

NOTE, 'Residence Requirements in State Public Welfare Statutes-I' (1966) *IowaLRev* 1080–95.

NOURISSAT, 'Quand Panacée Rejoint Europe ou Comment la Cour de Justice Consacre la Liberté des Soins dans la Communauté' (1999) *SJ* 10002.

NOVAK, 'EG-Grundfreiheiten und Europäisches Sozialrecht' (1998) *EuZW* 366–9.

NOWAK, 'Realizing the Standards of Review under the Equal Protection Guarantee—Prohibited, Neutral and Permissive Classifications' (1974) *GeorgeLJ* 1071 *et seq.*

NYBORG, 'International Student Mobility: The Nordic Experience' (1996) *EJE* 193–203.

NYS, *Patiënt in Europa—Op Zoek naar een Europees Geneeskundig Dienstverlening-srecht* (Maastricht, Universitaire Pers, 2000).

NIELSEN and SZYSZCZAK, *The Social Dimension of the European Union* (Copenhagen, Handelshojskolens Forlag, 1997).

OATES, *Fiscal Federalism* (New York, Harcourt, 1972).

OERTZEN, *Bildung und Berufsausbildung in den Europäischen Gemeinschaften—Eine Analyse der Kompetenzgrundlagen und der Subjecktiven Rechte im Rahmen des EWG-Vertrages* (München, Verlag V. Florentz GmbH, 1992).

O'KEEFFE, 'Recasting the Third Pillar' (1995) *CMLRev* 893–920.

——, 'Annotation *Raulin*' (1992) *CMLRev* 1215–28.

——, 'Union Citizenship' in O'Keeffe andTwomey (eds), *Legal Issues of the Maastricht Treaty* (London, Wiley Chancery Law, 1994) 87–107.

——, 'Judicial Interpretation of the Public Service Exception to the Free Movement of Workers' in Curtin and O'Keeffe (eds), *Constitutional Adjudication in European Community and National Law—Essays for the Hon Mr Justice TF O'Higgins* (Dublin, Butterworth, 1992) 89 *et seq.*

——, 'The Agreement on the European Economic Area' (1992) *LIEI* 1 *et seq.*

——, 'The Schengen Convention: A Suitable Model for European Integration' (1991) *YEL* 185 *et seq.*

——, 'Equal Rights for Migrants: The Concept of Social Advantages in Article 7(2), Regulation 1612/68' (1986) *YEL* 93–123.

——, 'Practical Difficulties in the Application of Article 48 of the EEC Treaty' (1982) *CMLRev* 35–60.

O'LEARY, 'Putting Flesh on the Bones of European Union Citizenship' (1999) *European Law Review* 68–79.

——, 'The Free Movement of Persons and Services' in Craig and de Búrca, *The Evolution of EU Law* (Oxford, Oxford University Press, 1999) 377–415.

——, 'Employment and Residence for Turkish Workers and their Families: Analogies with the Case Law of the Court of Justice on Article 48 EC' Scritti in Onore do Giuseppe Federico Mancini (1998).

——, 'The Principle of Equal treatment on Grounds of Nationality in Article 6 EC—A Lucrative Source for Member State Nationals?' in O'Leary and Tiilikainen (eds), *Citizenship and Nationality Status in the New Europe* (London, Sweet & Maxwell, 1998) 105–36.

——, *European Union Citizenship—Options for Reform* (London, Institute for Public Policy Research, 1996).

——, *The Evolving Concept of Community Citizenship—From the Free Movement of Persons to Union Citizenship* (The Hague, Kluwer Law International, 1996).

——, 'The Social Dimension of Community Citizenship' in: Rosas and Antola, *A Citizens' Europe—In Search of a New Order* (London, Sage, 1995) 156–81.

——, 'Annotation Case C–295/90 *Parliament v Council*' (1993) *CMLRev* 639–51.

——, 'Nationality Law and Community Citizenship: A Tale of Two Uneasy Bedfellows' (1992) *YEL* 353 *et seq.*

OLIVAS, '*Plyler v. Doe, Toll v. Moreno*, and Postsecondary Admissions: Undocumented Adults and "Enduring Disability"' (1986) *JLE* 19–55.

OLIVER, 'Some Further Reflections on the Scope of Art.28–30 (30–6) EC' (1999) *CMLRev* 783–806.

——, *Free Movement of Goods in the European Community* (London, Sweet & Maxwell, 1996).

OLIVER, 'Non-Community Nationals and the Treaty of Rome' (1985) *YEL* 57–92.

OLSSEN, 'Welfare State Research Inc—The Growth of a Crises Industry' (1987) *AS* 371–8.

ONSLOW-COLE, 'The Right of Establishment and Provision of Services: Community Employers and Third Country Nationals' in Guild (ed), *The Legal Framework and Social Consequences of Free Movement of Persons in the European Union* (The Hague, Kluwer Law International, 1999) 63–71.

OOSTERBEEK, 'An Economic Analysis of Student Financial Aid Schemes' (1998) *EJE* 21–9.

OOSTERMAN-MEULENBELD, 'Quality Regulation on Professional Health Care Practitioners in the European Community' (1993) *LIEI* 61 *et seq.*

OPPERMANN, Von der EG-Freizügigkeit zur Gemeinsamen Europäischen Ausbildungspolitik? Die "Gravier"-Doktrin des Gerichtshofs der Europäischen Gemeinschaften (Berlin, De Gruyter, 1988).

——, Europäisches Gemeinschaftsrecht und Deutsche Bildungsordnung—Gravier und die Folgen (Bad Honnef, Bock, 1987).

OIJEN et al, International Comparative Study of Financial Assistance to Students in Higher Education (Zoetermeer, Ministerie van Onderwijs en Wetenschappen, 1990).

PABON, 'Het Vrije Verkeer van Werknemers' (1969) SMA 83–95.

PAIS MACEDO VAN OVERBEEK, 'AIDS/HIV Infection and the Free Movement of Persons within the European Community' (1990) CMLRev 791–824.

PAPASTAMKOS, Die Erweiterung der EG-Freizügigkeit auf Griechische Arbeitnehmer (Berlin, Duncker & Humblot, 1983).

PARENT, 'Tuition Residence Requirements: A Second Look in Light of Zobel and Martinez' (1986) IndLJ 287–314.

PARMET, 'Regulation and Federalism: Legal Impediments to State Health Care Reform' (1993) AJLM 121–44.

PARRET, 'EG-Recht en Sport: Is Sport Anders' (2001) SEW 53–61.

PEERS, 'The EC-Switzerland Agreement on Free Movement of Persons: Overview and Analysis' (2000) EJML 127–42.

——, 'Dazed and Confused: Family Members' Residence Rights and the Court of Justice' (2001) European Law Review 76–83.

——, 'Aliens, Workers, Citizens or Humans? Models for Community Immigration Law' in Guild and Harlow (eds), Implementing Amsterdam—Immigration and Asylum Rights in EC Law (Oxford, Hart Publishing, 2000) 291–308.

——, 'Annotation Akman' (1999) CMLRev 1027–42.

——, 'Annotation Sürül' (1999) European Law Review 627–37.

——, 'Building Fortress Europe: The Development of EU Migration Law' (1999) CMLRev 1235–77.

——, Justice and Home Affairs in Europe (Harlow, Longman, 1999).

——, 'Raising Minimum Standards, or Racing to the Bottom?—The Commission's Proposed Migration Convention' in Guild (ed), The Legal Framework and Social Consequences of Free Movement of Persons in the European Union (The Hague, Kluwer Law International, 1999) 149–66.

——, 'Equality, Free Movement and Social Security' (1997) European Law Review 342–51.

——, 'Towards Equality: Actual and Potential Rights of Third-Country Nationals in the European Union' (1996) CMLRev 7–50.

PENNINGS, Grondslagen van het Europese Socialezekerheidsrecht (Deventer, Kluwer, 2000).

——, 'Het Einde van de Exporteerbaarheid van Wajong-uitkeringen?' (2000) MR 71–4.

——, 'Het Arrest Sürül: Een Arrest dat Knaagt aan de Koppelingswet' (1999) SMA 442–50.

——, Introduction to European Social Security Law (The Hague, Kluwer Law International, 1998).

——, '"Bijstandsuitkeringen" en het Recht op Vrij Verkeer van Werknemers' (1992) MR 146–55.

PERRIN, 'Les Prestations non Contributive et la Sécurité Sociale' (1961) DS 179–88.

PERRY, 'Modern Equal Protection: A Conceptualization and Appraisal' (1979) *ColLRev* 1023–84.

——, 'Equal Protection, Judicial Activism, and the Intellectual Agenda of Constitutional Theory: Reflections on, and Beyond, Plyler v Doe' (1983) *UpittLRev* 329–51.

PERTEK, *L'Europe des Diplomes et des Professions* (Bruxelles, Bruylant, 1994).

——, 'Free Movement of Professionals' (1992) *YEL* 293–324.

PICKUP, 'Reverse Discrimination and Freedom of Movement for Workers' (1986) *CMLRev* 135–56.

PIETERS, *De Nederlandse Zorgverzekering in het Licht van het Recht van de EG— Onderzoek naar de Verenigbaarheid van het Nederlandse Zorgstelsel met het Recht op Vrij Dienstenverkeer en het Europese Mededingingsrecht* (Raad voor de Volksgezondheid en Zorg, 1999).

——, 'Enquiry into the Legal Foundations of a Possible Extension of Community Provisions on Social Security to Third Country Nationals Legally Residing and/or Working in the EU' in *Commission of the European Communities/Departemento de Relações Internacionais e Convenções de Segurança Social, Social Security in Europe—Equality Between Nationals and Non-Nationals* (Lisbon, 1995) 189–243.

——, 'Brengt "1992" Coördinatie en Harmonisatie van de Sociale Zekerheid?' (1989) *NJB* 831 *et seq.*

——, *Sociale Zekerheid na 1992: Eén over Twaalf* (Katholieke Universiteit Brabant, Tilburg, 1989).

POPPE, 'Defining the Scope of the Equal Protection Clause with Respect to Welfare Waiting Periods' (1994) *ChicLRev* 291–323.

PLENDER, 'Competence, European Community Law and Nationals of Non-Member States' (1990) *ICLQ* 599–610.

——, *International Migration Law* (Dordrecht, Nijhoff, 1988).

——, 'An Incipient Form of European Citizenship' in Jacobs (ed), *European Law and the Individual* (Amsterdam, North-Holland Publishing Company, 1976) 39–53.

PORTER, 'Comment: A Constitutional Analysis of the Right to Travel Intra-State' (1992) *NorthwULRev* 820–57.

PALM *et al*, *Implications de la Jurisprudence Récente Concernant la Coordination des Systèmes de Protection Contre Le Risque de Maladie* (Bruxelles, AIM, 2000).

PARMET and O'CONNELL, 'Rehnquist's Road to Serfdom: The Ominous Message from *Rust v Sullivan*' (1992) *AP* 94 *et seq.*

PENNINGS and ESSERS, 'Het Voorstel van de Europese Commissie tot Vereenvoudiging van Verordening 1408/71' (2000) *SMA* 512–25.

PENNINX and MUUS, 'No Limits for Migration after 1992?—The Lessons of the Past and a Reconnaisance of the Future' (1989) *IMp*373–88.

PIETERS *et al*, *Inleiding to het Sociale Zekerheidsrecht van de Landen van de Europese Gemeenschap* (Ministerie van Sociale Zaken en Werkgelegenheid, Den Haag, 1990).

PIETERS and VANSTEENKISTE, *The Thirteenth State—Towards a European Community Social Insurance Scheme for Intra-Community Migrants* (Leuven, 1993).

PIETERS AND VAN DEN BOGAERT, *The Consequences of European Competition Law for National Health Policies* (Antwerpen, Maklu, 1997).

RAAD VOOR DE VOLKSGEZONDHEID, *Europa en de Gezondheidszorg* (Zoetermeer, Raad voor de Volksgezondheid en Zorg, 1999).

RAMBAGS, 'Samenloop Ziekenfondsverzekering (EG-verordeningen 1408/71 en 574/72) en Reisverzekering' (1988) *De Beursbengel* p.448 *et seq.*

REICH, *Bürgerrechte in der Europäische Union* (Baden-Baden, Nomos, 1999).

REISNER, 'National Regulation of the Movement of Workers in the European Community' (1964) *AJCL* 360–84.

RENARDEL DE LAVALETTE, 'Facetten van het Vrij Verkeer van Werknemers in de Europese Gemeenschappen' (1983) *SMA* 213–27.

RIESENFELD, 'The Formative Era of American Public Assistance Law' (1955) *CalLRev* 175 *et seq.*

ROBERTS, *The Rulings of the European Court of Justice on the Association and Co-operation Agreements in Matters Concerning Social Security, in: Jorens/Schulte, European Social Security Law and Third Country Nationals* (Bruxelles, Die Keure, 1998) 209–34.

ROMBOUTS, *Grensoverschrijdende Gezondheidszorg? Een Onderzoek naar de Huidige en Toekomstige Mogelijkheden en Knelpunten van Grensoverschrijdende Gezondheidszorg* (1990).

ROMERO, 'Migration as an Issue in European Interdependence and Integration: The Case of Italy' in Milward *et al* (eds), *The Frontier of National Sovereignty 1945–1992: History and Theory* (London, Routledge, 1993) 33–58.

ROORDA, 'Het Vormgeven van de Rust; of: De Teloorgang van de Wet op de Studiefinanciering' (1994) *NTOR* 2–16.

ROSBERG, 'Discrimination Against the "Nonresident" Alien' (1983) *UPittLRev* 399 *et seq.*

——, 'Free Movement of Persons in the United States' Sandalow and Stein (eds), *Courts and Free Markets—Perspectives from the United States and Europe* (Oxford, Clarendon Press, 1982) 275–362.

ROSBERG, 'The Protection of Aliens from Discriminatory Treatment by the National Government' (1977) *SCRev* 275–339.

ROSCAM ABBING, 'Editorial: Public Health Insurance and Freedom of Movement within the European Union (Cases Kohll and Decker)' (1999) *EJHL* 1–6.

——, 'Volksgezondheid in het Verdrag van Amsterdam—Een Beknopte Analyse' (1998) *TvG* 75–80.

——, 'Quality of Medical Practice and Professional Misconduct in the European Union' (1997) *EJHL* 273–8.

——, 'The Right of the Patient to Quality of Medical Practice and the Position of Migrant Doctors Within the EU' (1997) *EJHL* 347–60.

——, *Patiënt en Gezondheidszorg in het Recht van de Europese Gemeenschap* (Utrecht, Vereniging voor Gezondheidsrecht, 1993).

——, *International Organizations in Europe and the Right to Health Care* (Deventer, Kluwer, 1979).

ROSEN, *Public Finance* (Homewood, Irwin, 1985).

ROSENBLATT, 'Health Care Reform and Administrative Law: A Structural Approach' (1978) *Yale LJ* 243 *et seq.*

ROSENHEIM, 'Shapiro v Thompson "The Beggars are Coming to Town"' (1969) *SCRev* 303–46.

ROSSI, 'The Taxation Aspects of the Free Movement of Persons' in Carlier and Verwilghen, *Thirty Years of Free Movement of Workers in Europe (Luxembourg, Office for Official Publications of the European Communities, 2000) 127–42.

RÖTTINGER, 'Bedeutung der Rechtsgrundlage einer EG-Richtlinie und Folgen einer Nichtigkeit' (1993) *EuZW* 117–21.

RUBIO MARIN, *Stranger in Your Own Home—The Incorporation of Resident Aliens into the Political Community: Theory and Constitutional Practice in Germany and the United States* (Florence, EUI, 1997).

——, 'Equal Citizenship and the Difference that Residence Makes' in La Torre, *European Citizenship: An Institutional Challenge* (The Hague, Kluwer Law International, 1998) 210–27.

RUTTEN, 'Elasticity in Constitutional Review: *Adarand Constructors, Inc v Pena* and Continuing Uncertainty in the Supreme Court's Equal Protection Jurisprudence' (1997) *SouthCalLRev* 591–642.

REESE and GREEN, 'That Elusive Word, "Residence"' (1953) *VdBiltLRev* 561 *et seq.*

REDISH and NUGENT, 'The Dormant Commerce Clause and the Constitutional Balance of Federalism' (1987) *Duke LJ* 569 *et seq.*

RIBAS *et al*, *Traité de Droi Social Européen* (Paris, Presses Universitaires de France, 1978).

ROS and VAN DER ZEE, *Grensoverschrijdende Zorg—Vooronderzoek naar de Haalbaarheid van een Experiment in een Grensgebied betreffende Verruiming van Mogelijkheden voor Grensoverschrijdend Zorgverkeer—Uitgevoerd door het NIVEL in opdracht van de Ziekenfondsraad* (Utrecht, Nivel, 1996).

ROTUNDA and NOWAK, *Treatise on Constitutional Law* (St.Paul, West Publishing, 1992).

SAKSLIN, 'The Concept of Residence and Social Security: Reflections on Finnish, Swedish and European Legislation' (2000) *EJML* 157–83.

——, 'Social Security Co-ordination—Adapting to Chance' (2000) *EJSS* 168–87.

——, 'The Agreements on the European Economic Area' in Jorens and Schulte (eds), *European Social Security Law and Third Country Nationals* (Bruxelles, Die Keure, 1998) 1–110.

SAYARI, 'Migration Policies of Sending Countries: Perspectives on the Turkish Experience' in Heisler and Schmitter-Heisler (eds), *From Foreign Workers to Settlers? Transnational Migration and the Emergence of New Minorities—The Annals of the American Academy of Political and Social Science* (1986) 86–97.

SHAH, 'British Nationals and Community Law: The Kaur Case' (2001) *EJML* 271–8.

SHANKS, *European Social Policy, Today and Tomorrow* (Oxford, Pergamon Press, 1977).

SCHECHNER, 'Constitutional Law—Equal Protection—Shapiro v. Thompson, 394 U.S. 618 (1969)' (1969) *SuffULRev* 572–85.

SCHEIFFERS, 'Openbare Aanbesteding van Zorgcontracten'in Essers *et al* (ed), *Grensoverschrijdende Zorg—Marktwerking vs. National Zorgbewaking* (Lelystad, Koninklijke Vermande, 2000) 33–8.

SCHERMERS, 'De Minerval voor Buitenlanders' (1986) *AA* 37–40.

SCHIEFFER, *De Europese Arbeidsmarkt. Het Vrije Verkeer en de Migratie van Werknemers* (Leiden, Stenfert Kroese, 1961).

SCHINK, *Kompetenzweiterung im Handlungssystem der Europäischen Gemeinschaft: Eigendynamik und Policy Entrepreneurs* (Baden-Baden, Nomos, 1993).

SCHLACHTER, *Discrimination à Rebours—Die Inländerdiskriminierung nach der Rechtsprechung des EuGH und des französischen Conseil d'Etat* (Frankfurt, Fischer, 1984).

SCHLOSBERG, *Not-Qualified Immigrants' Access to Public Health and Emergency Services After the Welfare Law* <http://www.healthlaw.org/pubs/19980112immigrant.html)>

SCHMIDT, *Die Arbeitsrechtliche und Sozialversicherungsrechtliche Stellung der Europäischen Wanderarbeiter im Rahmen der Europäischen Wirtschaftsgemeinschaft* (Würzburg, 1963).

SCHMIDT-RÄNTSCH, 'Erlass von Förderprogrammen durch den Rat der EG Aufgrund Art.128 EWGV' (1989) *NJW* 3071–2.

SCHNEIDER, 'The Impact of Welfare Reform on Medicaid' (1998) *Publius* 161–74.

SCHNEIDER, *Die Anerkennung von Diplomen in der Europäischen Gemeinschaft* (Antwerpen, Maklu, 1995).

SCHOCKWEILER, 'La Portée du Principle de Non-Discrimination del'Article 7 du Traité CEE' (1991) *RDE* pp3 *et seq.*

SCHOLSEM, 'A Propos de la Circulation des Etudiants: Vers un Federalisme Financier Européen?' (1989) *CDE* 306–23.

SCHOUKENS, *Coördinatiebepalingen linzake Gezondheidszorg: het Overige Europees Recht* (Antwerpen, Maklu, 1993).

——, *Coördinatiebepalingen Inzake Gezondheidszorg: het Communautaire Recht* (Antwerpen, Maklu, 1992).

SCHRAUWEN, 'Sink or Swim Together? Developments in European Citizenship' (2000) *FordILJ* 778–94.

SCHRAUWEN, 'Annotatie *Martínez Sala*' (1999) *SEW* 426–30.

SCHREIBER, 'Europese Overeenkomst Betreffende het Verlenen van Geneeskundige Verzorging bij Tijdelijk Verblijf' (1981) *Info RIZIV* 199–203.

SCHULER, *Das Internationale Sozialrecht der Bundesrepublik Deutschland* (Baden-Baden, Nomos, 1988).

SCHULER, 'Equal Protection and the Undocumented Immigrant: California's Proposition 187' (1996) *BostCTWLJ* 275–312.

SCHULTE, 'Pflegeleistungen Zwischen Sozialer Sicherheit und Sozialer Hilfe—Aspekte der Europarechtlichen Abgrenzung' in Sieveking (ed), *Soziale Sicherung bei Pflegebedürftigkeit in der Europäischen Union* (Baden-Baden, Nomos, 1998) 143–59.

——, 'Social Security Legislation in the European Communities: Co-ordination, Harmonization and Convergence' in Pieters, *Social Security in Europe* (Antwerpen, Maklu, 1991) 153–68.

SCHULZ, *Freizügigkeit für Unionsbürger* (Frankfurt am Main, Peter Lang, 1997).

SCHULZ, *Freier Arbeitsmarkt und Niederlassungsfreiheit in der Europäischen Wirtschaftsgemeinschaft—Unter besonderer Berücksichtigung der Grenz- und Gastarbeitnehmer* (Würzburg, 1967).

SCHULZ-WEIDNER, 'Rechtliche Entwicklungen bei Krankenkassenleistungen im Ausland' (1998) *KrV* 241–5.

SCHUTTE, 'Schengen: Its Meaning for the Free Movement of Persons in Europe' (1991) CMLRev 549 *et seq.*

SCHUTYSER, '"Round Table: Positions and Reactions of the Private Actors"' in *Association Internationale de la Mutualité/ European Institute of Social Security, Health Care without Frontiers within the European Union—Free Movement of Goods and Services in the Health Care Sector* (1999) 63–5.

SCHUYT, 'Het Rechtskarakter van de Verzorgingsstaat' in Van Doorn and Schuyt, *De Stagnerende Verzorgingsstaat* (Meppel, Boom, 1982) 73–96.

SCHWARTZ, *Super Chief—Earl Warren and his Supreme Court—A Judicial Bibliography* (New York, University Press, 1983).

SCHWEITZER, 'Bildungspolitik und EWG-Vertrag—Eine Bestandsaufnahme' (1991) *ZfRV* 14–25.

SEGAL, 'Residency, Tuition and the Twelve Month Dilemma' (1969) *HoustLRev* 241–56.

SELMER, 'Die Öffentlichen Sicherheit und Ordnung als Schranke der Arbeitnehmer-Freizügigkeit Gemäss Art 48 Abs 3 EWG-Vertrag' (1967) *DöV* 328–34.

SEWANDONO, 'Het Commissievoorstel tot Wijziging van Verordening (EEG) nr.1612/68: Meer Bescherming van Familie- en Gezinsleven en Meer Gelijke Behandeling' (1999) *SEW* 284–90.

SEWANDONO, *Werknemersverkeer en Gezinsleven* (Deventer, Kluwer, 1998).

SHANKS, *European Social Policy, Today and Tomorrow* (Oxford, Pergamon Press, 1977).

SHAW, 'From the Margins to the Centre: Education and Training Law and Policy' in Craig and De Búrca, *The Evolution of EU Law* (Oxford, Oxford University Press, 1999) 555–95.

SHAW, 'The Nature and Extent of Educational Rights under EC Law' (1998) *JSWFL* 203 *et seq.*

——, 'Vocational Training and Education in the European Community' (1991) *EBLRev* 279–82.

SHI and SINGH, *Delivering Health Services in America—A Systems Approach* (Gaithersburg, Aspen Publishers, 1998).

SIEVEKING, 'Bildung im Europäischen Gemeinschaftsrecht' (1990) *KritV* 344–73.

——, 'Europäisierung der Bildungspolitik?' (1987) *ZAR* 99–108.

SIMM, *Der Gerichtshof der Europäischen Gemeinschaften im Föderalen Kompetenz Konflikt—Kontinuität und Neubesinnung in der Rechtssprechung vor und nach 'Maastricht'* (Baden-Baden, Nomos, 1998).

SIMSON, 'Discrimination Against Nonresidents and the Privileges and Immunities Clause of Article IV' (1979) *UPennLRev* 379–401.

SINGER, 'Free Movement of Workers in the European Economic Community: The Public Policy Exception' (1977) *StanfLRev* 1283–97.

SØRENSEN, *The Exclusive European Citizenship—The Case for Refugees and Immigrants in the European Union* (Aldershot, Avebury, 1996).

SPIEGEL, 'Der EuGH Als (Wiederentdecktes) Feindbild' (1998) *SS* 665–8.

STAPLE, 'Vrij Verkeer van Personen—Wie is Burger van de Unie' (2001) *NTER* 109–11.

STAPLES, 'De Associatieovereenkomst EEG-Turkije—Een Leidraad voor de Rechtshulp' (1999) *MR* 179–88.

——, *The Legal Status of Third Country Nationals Resident in the European Union* (the Hague, Kluwer Law International, 1999).

STARKLE, 'Extension du Principe de Non-Discrimination en Droit Communautaire au Ressortissant d'un Etat Membre Licitement Installé dans un autre Etat Membre' (1984) *CDE* 672 *et seq.*

STEIN, 'Annotation *Vlassopoulou*' (1992) *CMLRev* 625–36.

STEINBACH, 'Constitutional Protection for Freedom of Movement: A Time for Decision' (1968–69) *KentLJ* 417–38.

STEINDORFF, 'Ausbildungsrechte im EG-Recht' (1983) *NJW* 1231–3.

——, 'Dienstleistungsfreiheit im EG-Recht' (1983) *RIW* 831–9.

STEINER, 'The Right to Welfare: Equality and Equity under Community Law' (1987) *ELR* 477 *et seq.*

——, 'Annotation *Gravier*' (1985) *CMLRev* 348–52.

——, 'Recipients of Services—Some More Equal than Others' (1985) *European Law Review* 348 *et seq.*

STEINMEYER, 'Familienleistungen und Ausbildungsförderung' in *Deutschen Sozialrechtsverbandes, Europäisches Sozialrecht* (Wiesbaden, Verlag Chmielorz, 1992) 169–92.

STEYGER, 'De Neveneffecten van het Vrij Verkeer op Specifiek Nationale Beleidsterreinen' (1999) *SEW* 226–33.

——, 'Het Europees Recht en Stelsels van Sociale Zekerheid' (1994) *SMA* 8–19, 71–8.

STIEMER, 'Sickness Insurance—Viewpoint from the EU-Member States' in Jorens and Schulte (eds), *Coordination of Social Security Schemes in Connection of the Accession of Central and Eastern European States: "the Riga Conference"* (Brugge, Die Keure, 1999) 225–53.

——, *Ziekte en Moederschap—Arbeidsongevallen en Beroepsziekten, in: Pieters, Europees Sociale Zekerheidsrecht—Commentaar* (Apeldoorn, Maklu, 1988) 69–88.

STONE, 'Why States Can't Solve the Health Care Crisis' (1992) *American Prospect* 51 *et seq.*

SWART, *De Toelating and Uitzetting van Vreemdelingen* (Deventer, Kluwer, 1978).

SZCZEKALLA, 'EuGH: Begriff des "Kindes" in Art.12 Verordnung (EWG) Nr.1612/68' (1995) *EuZW* 670–2.

SCHELL and PIETERS, *De Middelentoets in Rechtsvergelijkend Perspectief* (Den Haag, Ministerie van Sociale Zaken en Werkgelegenheid, 1989).

SCHNEIDER *et al*, *Gesundheitssysteme im Internationalen Vergleich* (Augsburg, Basys, 1989).

SCHULTE and TRENK HINTERBERGER, *Sozialhilfe, eine Einführung* (Heidelberg, Müller Juristischer Verlag, 1986).

STONE *et al*, *Constitutional Law* (Boston, Little Brown & Co., 1986).

STUIJCK and LOOIJETIJN-CLEARIE (eds), *The European Economic Area EC-EFTA: Institutional Aspects and Financial Services* (Deventer, Kluwer Law and Taxation Publishers, 1993).

TASCHNER, 'Free Movement of Students, Retired Persons and other European Citizens— A Difficult Legislative Process' in Schermers *et al* (eds), *Free Movement of Persons in Europe* (Dordrecht, Martinus Nijhof Publishers, 1993) 427–36.

TEICHLER, *Europäische Hochschulsysteme. Die Beharrlichkeit Vielfältiger Modelle* (Frankfurt, Campus, 1990).

TENBROEK, 'California's Dual System of Family Law: Its Origin, Development and Present Status' (1964) *StanfLRev* 257 *et seq.*

——, *The Constitution and the Right to Free Movement* (New York, National Travelers Aid Association, 1955).

THIELE, 'Die Rechtssprechung des Gerichtshofs der Europäischen Gemeinschaften zum Recht auf Gleichbehandlung von EG-Ausländern beim Zugang zu Bildungseinrichtungen und auf Studiefinanzierung' (1993) *ZfRV* 185–97.

THOMAS, 'Summing Up and Points of Comparison' in Thomas (ed), *Immigrant Workers in Europe: Their Legal Status, A Comparative Study* (Paris, UNESCO Press, 1982) 211 *et seq.*

THOMSON, 'The Right to Travel—Its Protection and Application Under the Constitution' (1971–1972) *UMKCLRev* 66–96.

TIEBOUT, 'A Pure Theory of Local Expenditures' (1956) *JPolEc* 416 *et seq.*

TIMMERMANS, 'Free Movement of Persons and the Division of Powers between the Community and its Member States—Why Do It the Intergovernmental Way?' in Schermers *et al* (eds), *Free Movement of Persons in Europe* (Dordrecht, Martnus Nijhof Publishers, 1993) 352–88.

——, 'Annotatie *Gravier*' (1986) *SEW* 86–94.

——, 'Annotation *Luisi and Carbone*' (1984) *SEW* 753–9.

Titmuss, *Social Policy, an Introduction* (London, Allen and Unwin, 1974).

T.M.C. Asser Instituut, *Studiefinanciering Buiten Nederland in het Licht van de Europese Jurisprudentie* ('s Gravenhage, 2000).

Toebes, *The Right to Health as a Human Right in International Law* (Antwerpen, Intersentia Hart, 1999).

Tomscheid, 'EG-Binnenmarkt Rüttelt an den Nationalen Sozialversicherungssystemen' (1998) *KrV* 246–50.

Tomuschat, 'Annotation *Martínez Sala*' (2000) *CMLRev* 449–57.

Toner, 'Judicial Interpretation of European Union Citizenship—Transformation or Consolidation?' (2000) *MJ* 158–82.

——, 'Passport Controls at Borders between Member States' (2000) *European Law Review* 415–24.

Trattner, *From Poor Law to Welfare State—A History of Social Welfare Law in America* (London, Collier MacMillan, 1984).

Traversa, 'L'Interdiction de Discrimination en Raison de la Nationalité en Matière d'Accès à l'Enseignement' (1989) *RTDE* 45–69.

Tribe *American Constitutional Law* (Mineola, Foundation Press, 1988).

Troclet, *Europees Sociaal Recht—Institutioneel Kader, Rechtsinstrumenten, Sociale Problemen en hun Oplossing* (Amsterdam, Scheltema & Holkema, 1971).

Tushnet, 'Rethinking the Dormant Commerce Clause' (1979) *WisLRev* 125–65.

Teichler and Maiworm, *The Erasmus Experience—Major Findings of the Erasmus Evaluation Research Project* (Luxembourg, Office for Official Publications of the European Communities, 1997).

Tusman and ten Broek, 'The Equal Protection of the Laws' (1949) *CalLRev* 341–81.

Ulleroe, *Le Budget de l'Etudiant et son Financement en Europe* (Amsterdam, European Association for Education, 1994).

Union, *Union des Caisses de Maladie, Avis officiel aux Assurés des Caisses de Maladie* (Luxembourg, 1998).

Van den Bogaert, 'The Consequences of the Gaygusuz Judgement for Belgian Social Security' in Van den Bogaert (ed), *Social Security, Non-Discrimination and Property* (Antwerpen, Maklu, 1997) 123–48.

Van der Bend, 'Aanbestedingsrecht in de Gezondheidszorgsector—Verdient het Aanbestedingsrecht in de Gezondheidszorgsector meer Zorg?' (1999) *NTG* 359–69.

Van den Bossche, 'Elders Gaan Studeren op Andermans Kosten?' (1992) *NJB* 792–7.

Van Crayenest, 'La Nature juridique des Resolutions sur la Cooperation en Matiere d'Education' in: De Witte (ed), *European Community Law of Education* (Baden-Baden, Nomos, 1989). 127 *et seq*.

Van der Hurk, 'The European Court of Justice Knows its Limits' (1999) *ECTax Rev* 211–23.

Van Look, 'Het Vrije Verkeer van Werknemers in de EEG nu een Realiteit' *SEW* (1969) 274–88.

Van der Mei, 'Freedom of Movement and Financial Aid for Students: Some Reflections on *Grzelczyck* and *Fahmi and Esmoris-Cerdeiro Pinedo Amoris*' *EJSS* (2001) 181–207.

——, 'Zorg over de Grens: Het Arrest *Geraets-Smits en Peerbooms*' (2001) *USZ* 852 *et seq*.

——, 'Vrij Verkeer van Studenten en Export van Studiefinanciering' (2001) *USZ* 606–11.

——, 'Annotation *Meeusen*' (1999) *USZ* 687–8.

VAN DER MEI, 'De Rechtmatigheid van Woonplaatsvereisten voor Bestaansminimumuit-keringen onder het EG-Recht' (1999) *SMA* 451–9.

——, 'The European Court of Justice and the Co-ordination of Health Insurance Schemes' in *Association Internationale de la Mutualité/ European Institute of Social Security, Health Care without Frontiers within the European Union—Free Movement of Goods and Services in the Health Care Sector* (1999) 18–25.

——, 'Cross-Border Access to Medical Care Within the European Union: Some Reflections on the Judgments in *Decker* and *Kohll*' (1998) *MJ* 277–97.

——, '*Decker* and *Kohll*: Op Weg Naar een Vrij Verkeer voor Patiënten in de Europese Gemeenschap?' (1998) *SR* 187–96.

——, 'The Kohll and Decker Rulings: Revolution or Evolution?' (1999) *Eurohealth* 14 *et seq.*

——, 'Grensoverschrijdende Toegang tot de Gezondheidszorg in de Europese Gemeenschap' (1998) *USZ* 462–71.

——, 'Het Arrest Molenaar: Export van het Persoonsgebonden Budget?' (1998) *USZ* 407–12.

——, 'The Elusive and Exclusive Concept of Union Citizenship, A Review Essay' (1998) *MJ* 391–402.

——, 'Het Vrij Verkeer van Personen binnen de Europese Gemeenschap en de (Niet-)Exporteerbaarheid van Gemengde estaansminimumuitkeringen' (1997) *USZ* 895–902.

——, 'Patients' Access to Cross-Border Care and Insurance Cover' in *Alliance Nationale des Mutualités Chrétiennes/Association Internationale de la Mutualité, Competition and Solidarity—Can They Co-exist in Europe's Health Care Systems?* (1997) 68–75.

——, 'Artikel 118A EG-Verdrag en Arbeidstijden in Europa' (1997) *Sociaal Recht* 108–15.

——, 'The Bosman Case and the Legal Status of Third Country Nationals under European Community Law' (1996) *ASICLaw, Proceedings of the 8th Annual Conference* 144–58.

——, 'EG-recht en Onderwijs' (1995–1996) *Jaarboek voor Onderwijsrecht en Onderwijsbeleid* 17–26.

——, 'Kinderen van EG-Werknemers: Het Recht op Onderwijs en Studiefinanciering' (1995) *NTOR* 211–17.

——, 'Nogmaals: Inschrijvingsgelden voor EG-Studenten' (1995) *NTOR* 202–8.

——, 'Vrij Dienstenverkeer in de EG en Toegang tot het Onderwijs' (1994) *NTOR* 102–7.

——, 'EG-recht en Onderwijs' (1993–1994) *Jaarboek voor Onderwijsrecht en Onderwijsbeleid* 17–26.

VAN DER MIJN, 'Kansen en Bedreigingen voor Beroepsbeoefenaren bij een Vrije Europese Markt' (1989) *TvG* 305–15.

VAN DER STEEN, 'Horizontale Werking van de Vier Vrijheden en van het Discriminatieverbod van Artikel 12 EG' (2001) *NTER* 4–9.

——, 'Studiefinanciering ook voor Kinderen van Grensarbeiders' (1999) *NTER* 210–15.

——, 'Verbod van Nationaliteitsdiscriminatie op het Gebied van Arbeidsvoorwaarden: Gevolgen voor het Verblijfsrecht' (1999) *NTER* 137–9.

——, 'De Europese Burger Krijgt Handen en Voeten' (1998) *NTER* 163–6.

——, 'Vergoeding van Medische Zorg over de Grens: Alleen bij Toestemming Vooraf?' (1998) *NTER* 159–63.

——, 'Vrij Verkeer van Overheidswerknemers en CAO's in de Publieke Sector' (1998) *SMA* 484–6.

——, 'Annotatie *Cabanis*' (1997) *SEW* 207 *et seq.*

——, 'Controle bij Ziekte in het Buitenland' (1996) *NTER* 176–8.

——, 'Vrij Verkeer en Sociale Zekerheid van Ambtenaren' (1996) *NTER* 53–6.

——, 'Medische Zorg voor Gezinsleden van Grensarbeiders' (1995) *NTER* 121–2.

VAN DER VALK, *Van Pauperszorg tot Bestaanszekerheid—Een Onderzoek naar de Ontwikkeling van Armenzorg in Nederland tegen de Achtergrond van de Overgang naar de Algemene Bijstandswet 1912–1965* (Delft, Eburon, 1986).

VAN OOIK, 'Omgekeerde Discriminatie van EEG-Onderdanen' (1990) *MR* 83–6.

VANISTENDAEL, 'Annotation *Gilly*' (2000) *CMLRev* 167–79.

——, 'The Consequences of Schumacker and Wielockx: The Steps Forward in the Tax Procession of Echternach' (1996) *CMLRev* 255–69.

VANSTEENKISTE, 'The Idea of the Thirteenth State System: Towards a Competition between a Federal Social Insurance System and the National Social Security System' in *Colloqui International Sobre Seguretat Social. Cap a la Competencia entre Sistemes de Proteccio Social* (Escaldes-Engordany, Caixa Andorrana de Seguretat social, 1991).

VARAT, 'Economic Integration and Interregional Migration in the United States Federal System' in Tushnet (ed), *Comparative Constitutional Federalism—Europe and America* (New York, Greenwood Press, 1990) 21–66.

——, '"State Citizenship" and Interstate Equality' (1981) *ChicLRev* 487 *et seq.*

VAN DER VEN, 'De Europese Unie en de Nederlandse Studiefinanciering' in *De Staat van de Studiefinanciering* ('s Gravenhage, OCenW, 1999) 37–61.

VAN DER VEN, *Onderwijsrecht en Onderwijsbeleid in Nederland en de Europese Unie— Ontwikkelingen voor Hoger Onderwijs na Maastricht* (Den Haag, Nuffic, 1996).

——, 'Europees Onderwijsrecht na Maastricht' (1994) *NTOR* 140–52.

——, 'Naar een Europese Studiefinanciering?' (1992) *NTOR* 156–66.

VAN DER VEEN, 'De Wankele Verzorgingsstaat—Een Vergelijkende Analyse van Verzorgingsstaten in het Licht van Internationaliseringsprocessen' in Engbersen *et al* (eds), *Zorgen in het Europese Huis—De Grenzen van Nationale Verzorgingsstaaten* (Amsterdam, Boom, 1994) 59–88.

VAN DER WOUDE, *Belastingen Begrensd: De Doorwerking van het Discriminatieverbod en de Richtlijnen van de EG op Nationale Belastingen* (Delft, Eburon, 2000).

VAN RAEPENBUSCH, 'La Libre Choix par les Citoyens Européens des Produits Médicaux et des Prestataires de Soins, Conséquence Sociale de Marché Interieur' (1998) *CDE* 683–97.

——, *La Securité Sociale des Personnes qui Circulent a l'Intérieur de la Communauté économique Européenne* (Gent, Story-Scientia, 1991).

VAN THIEL, *Free Movement of Persons and Income Tax Law: The European Court in Search of Principles—An Investigation into the Constitutionality of Income Tax Laws and Treaties of the Member States and the Potential Consequences of the Court's Income Tax Case Law* (Rotterdam, 2001).

VERBELEN, *The United States' Health Care System. Invisible Hand, Visible Effects* (Antwerpen, Maklu, 1995).

VEIL, *Report of the High Level Panel on the Free Movement of Persons* (Luxembourg, Office for Offical Publications of the European Communities, 1998).

VERBRUGGEN, 'The Commission's Green Paper "Education, Training, Research: The Obstacles to Transnational Mobility": Content and Comment' (1997) *EJELP* 41–8.

VERBRUGGEN, 'Toegang tot het Onderwijs en Studiefinanciering' (1992–1993) *TOO* 282–90.

VERLI-WALLACE, 'Le nouveau Programme communautaire "Socrates"' (1995) *RMCUE* 517–20.

VERMEYLEN, 'Elementen van het Juridisch Statuut van de Vreemdeling in Europa' in Deslé *et al* (eds), *Denken over Migranten in Europa* (Brussel, VUBPress, 1983) 211–28.

VERSCHUEREN, 'The Sürül Judgment: Equal Treatment for Turkish Workers in Matters of Social Security' (1999) *EJML* 371 *et seq.*

——, 'The Commission's Proposal to Extend Regulation (EEC) No 1408/71 to Third Country Nationals' in Jorens and Schulte (eds), *European Social Security Law and Third Country Nationals* (Bruxelles, Die Keure, 1998) 187–208.

——, 'EC Social Security Coordination Excluding Third Country Nationals: Still in Line with Fundamental Rights after the *Gaygusuz* Judgment?' (1997) *CMLRev* 991–1017.

——, Na het Arrest Taflan-Met: Is er Leven na de Dood?—Besluit 3/80 (Sociale Zekerheid) van de Associatieraad EEG-Turkije Bestudeerd, in: MR (1997) pp29–34.

——, 'Libre Circulation des Personnes et Protection Sociale Minimale' (1996) *RMUE* 83–105.

——,, 'Les Prestation Spéciales à Caractère non Contributif et le Règlement Communautaire' (1995) *DS* 921–30.

——, 'Het Arrest Taghavi en de Tegemoetkoming aan niet-EG-familieleden van EG-werknemers' (1993) *MR* 74–5.

——, 'Vrij Verkeer van Werkzoekenden' (1992) *MR* 15–19.

——, 'De Toegang tot de Openbare Dienst voor EG-onderdanen—Macht en Onmacht van het Europese Gemeenschapsrecht' (1991) *MR* 211–20.

——, 'De Buitenlandse Student' in van Hoestenberghe (ed), *Studentenrecht—De Sociale en Juridische Gids voor de Sudent Hoger Onderwijs* (Leuven, Acco, 1991) 259–72.

——, *Internationale Arbeidsmigratie* (Lelystad, die Keure, 1990).

VERWERS, 'Towards a New EC Health Policy?' in *European Public Health Association Uniting Public Health in Europe* (1992) 11–14.

VILA COSTA, 'The Quest for a Consistent Set of Rules Governing the Status of Non-Community Nationals' in Alston (ed), *The EU and Human Rights* (Oxford, Oxford University Press, 1999) 411–46.

VILARAS, 'Freedom of Movement in the Public Sector—Developments and Prospects' in Carlier and Verwilghen, *Thirty Years of Free Movement of Workers in Europe* (Luxembourg, Office for Official Publications of the European Communities, 2000) 89–104.

VÖLKER, *Passive Dienstleistungsfreiheit im Europäischen Gemeinschaftsrecht* (Berlin, Duncker & Humblot, 1990).

VON MAYDELL, 'Wenn Schutzzäune Fallen Das Kohll-Decker-Urteil des Europäischen Gerichtshofes (EuGH) hat Fragen Aufgeworfen: Gefährdet die Grenzöffnung die Deutschen Krankenversicherung? Oder verheisst der Richterspruch mehr Markt im Gesundheitswesen?' *GuG* (1998) 3.

——, 'Treatment of Third Country Nationals in the Member States of the European Union and the European Economic Area in Terms of Social Law' in *Commission of the European Communities/Departemento de Relações Internacionais e Convenções de Segurança Social, Social Security in Europe—Equality Between Nationals and Non-Nationals* (Lisbon, 1995) 137–54.

Von Wilmowsky, 'Zugang zu Öffentlichen Leistungen anderer Mitgliedstaaten—Das Integrationskonzept des EWG-Vertrages in der Leistungsverwaltung' (1990) *ZfaöR* 231–81.

Von Wittkowski, *Die Rechtsprechung des Europäischen Gerichtshofs zur Freizügigkeit und Gleichbehandlung von Angehörigen der EG-Mitgliedstaaten hinsichtlich des Besuchs von Ausbildungsstätten und deren Auswirkung für die Bundesrepublik Deutschland* (Frankfurt am Main, Lang, 1991).

Vonk, 'Conflicterend Conflictenrecht' (2001) *SMA* 150–61.

——, *Overijverige Rechter of Tekortschietende Wetgever?—De Rol van de Rechter en Wetgever bij het Proces van Doorwerking van Internationale Normen in het Socialezekerheidsrecht* (Deventer, Kluwer, 1999).

——, *De Coördinatie van Bestaansminimumuitkeringen in de Europese Gemeenschap* (Deventer, Kluwer, 1991).

——, 'Het HvJEG-arrest in de Zaak Kziber—Een Levenskus voor de Slapende Paragrafen in de EG-samenwerkingsovereenkomsten' (1991) *MR* 149–51.

Voogsgeerd, *Interstatelijkheid—De Aard en de Intensiteit van het Grensoverschrijdend Element in de Rechtspraak van het Hof van Justitie van de EG met Betrekking tot de Vier Vrijheden* (Groningen, 2000).

——, *Vrij Verkeer en Sociale Zekerheid* (Deventer, Kluwer, 1999).

——, 'Aspecten van Grensoverschrijdende Tewerkstelling' in Pennings, *Tewerkstelling over de Grenzen* (Deventer, Kluwer, 1996) 129–63.

Vossensteyn, *Mobiliteit en Studiefinanciering—Studiefinancieringsarrangementen van 16 West-Europese Landen voor het Volgen van een Volledig Hogerwijsprogramma in het Buitenland* (Cheps, 2000).

——, *Access: Selection and Affordability—A Comparative Analysis of the Barriers for Entrance in Higher Education in Nine Western European Countries* (Zoetermeer, Ministerie voor Onderwijs, Cultuur en Wetenschap, 1997).

——, 'Studiefinanciering in Internationaal Perspectief' (1996) *THOM* 5.

Van Vught and Vossensteyn, 'De Toekomst van het Nederlandse Stelsel van Studiefinanciering in Europees Perspectief' in Cohen *et al*, *Expertbijdragen, Scenario's en Achtergondinformatie—Een Bundeling Bijdragen ten Behoeve van het College Toekomst Studiefinanciering* (Zoetermeer, College Toekomst Studiefinanciering, 1997) 31–44.

Vreugdenhil and De Bruine, *Gezondheidszorg in Europa—Structuur en Financiering van de Gezondheidszorg in Enkele Europese Landen* (Rotterdam, Erasmus Universiteit, 1992).

Van Gerven *et al*, *Kartelrecht—Europese Gemeenschap* (Kluwer, 1997).

Van Gerven and Van den Bossche, 'Freedom of Movement and Equal Treatment for Students in Europe: An Emerging Principle?' in Schermers *et al* (eds), *Free Movement of Persons in Europe: Problems and Experiences* (Dordrecht, Martinus Nijhoff Publishers, 1993) 405–26.

Van der Mei and Waddington, 'Public Health and the Treaty of Amsterdam' (1998) *EJPH* 129–54.

Van Tits and Gemmel, *Haalbaarheidsonderzoek Samenwerkingsnetwerk Ziekenhuizen in de Euregio Scheldemond* (Tilburg, 1995).

——, *Een Grensoverschrijdende Verkenning van Belangen. Ziekenhuiszorg in Zeeuwsch-Vlaanderen en Belgisch Vlaanderen* (Tilburg, 1995).

Vermeulen and Kuijer, *Toegang tot het Onderwijs Binnen de Europese Unie—Juridische Aspecten van de Toegang tot Onderwijsvoorzieningen voor Middelbaar en Hoger*

Onderwijs voor EG-migranten en Derdelanders Binnen de Europese Unie in een Drietal Lidstaten (Utrecht, Nederlands Centrum Buitenlanders, 1997).

VON DER GROEBEN et al (eds), *Kommentar zum EWG-Vertrag* (Baden-Baden, Nomos, 1997).

——, et al (eds), *Kommentar zum EWG-Vertrag* (Baden-Baden, Nomos, 1991).

WADDINGTON, 'Testing the Limits of the EC Treaty Article on Non-Discrimination' (1999) *IndLJ* 133–51.

WÄGENBAUER, 'L'Europe des Vétérinaires' (1979) *RTDE* 653–63.

WÄGENBAUER, 'La libre Circulation des Médicins dans la Communauté Européenne— Problèmes Actuels' (1976) *CDE* 707–35.

——, 'Die Einbeziehung der Hochschulen in den Europäischen Integrationsprozess' (1990) *ER* 135–42.

WALZER, *Spheres of Justice—A Defense of Pluralism and Equality* (New York, Basic Books, 1983).

WAPENAAR, *Personenverkeer binnen de Europese Unie—Het Communautaire Recht inzake Personenverkeer, met Bijzondere Aandacht voor de Positie van Derdelanders* (Utrecht, Nederlands Centrum Buitenlanders, 1997).

WATSON, 'Wandering Students: Their Rights under Community law' in Curtin and O'Keeffe, *Constitutional Adjudication in European Community and National Law— Essays for the Hon Mr TF O'Higgins* (Dublin, Butterworths, 1992) 79–88.

——, 'Annotation Gravier' (1987) *CMLRev* 89–97.

——, *Social Security Law of the European Communities* (London, Mansell, 1980).

WEATHERILL, 'After *Keck*: Some Thoughts on How to Clarify the Clarification' (1995) *CMLRev* 991 et seq.

——, 'Annotation *Cowan*' (1989) *CMLRev* 563–88.

WEBER, 'Die Rechtsprechung des EuGH zum Vorbehalt der öffentlichen Ordnung und Sicherheit im Bereich der Freizügigkeit' (1978) *EuGRZ* 157–60.

WEILER, '"Thou Shall Not Oppress a Stranger" (Ex 23:9): On the Judicial Protection of Human Rights of Non-EC Nationals' in Schermers et al (eds), *Free Movement of Persons in Europe* (Dordrecht, Martnus Nijhoff Publishers, 1993) 248–71.

——, 'Methods of Protection: Towards a Second and Third Generation of Protection' in Cassese et al (eds), *Human Rights and the European Community—Methods of Protection* (Baden-Baden, Nomos, 1991) 575–620.

——, 'The Transformation of Europe' (1991) *YaleLJ* 2403–83.

WEISS, 'Inländerdiskriminierung zwischen Gemeinschaftsrecht und Nationalem Verfassungsrecht' (1983) *NJW* 2721–6.

WERNER, 'Post-war Migration in Western Europe' (1986) *IM* 543–57.

WHITE, *EC Social Security Law* (Harlow, Longman, 1999).

——, 'Children and Right to Education under Article 12 of Regulation 1612/68' (1995) *European Law Review* 501–7.

——, *Competing Solutions—American Health Care Proposals and International Experience* (Washington, Brookings Institution, 1995).

WIENK, *Europese Coördinatie van Aanvullende Pensioenen* (Deventer, Kluwer, 1999).

WILDENTHAL, 'State Parochialism, the Right to Travel, and the Privileges and Immunities Clause of Article IV' (1989) *StanfLRev* 1557–95.

WILENSKY, *The Welfare State and Equality: Structural and Ideological Roots of Public Expenditures* (Berkeley, University of California Press, 1975).

WIMMER, 'Freedom of Movement for Students under Community Law' (1992) *ELSA* 53–68.

WITTEK, 'Eine Europäische Dimension von Ausländerpolitik—Zur Richtlinie der EG vom 25.7.1977' (1982) *RJB* 40–50.

WOLFF, 'Right Road, Wrong Vehicle?: Rethinking Thirty Years of Right to Travel Doctrine: *Saenz v . Roe*, 119 S.Ct.1518 (1999)' (2000) *UdayLRev* 307–35.

WOOD, 'Public Policy, Discrimination in the EEC: A Proposal for Assuring the Free Movement of Workers' (1985) *FordILJ* 447–78.

WOUTERS, 'The Principle of Non-Discrimination in European Community Law' (1999) *EC Tax Review* 98–106.

——, 'European Citizenship and the Case-Law of the Court of Justice of the European Communities on the Free Movement of Persons' in Marias (ed), *European Citizenship* (Maastricht, European Institute of Public Administration, 1994) 25 *et seq*.

——, 'The Case-Law of the European Court of Justice on Direct Taxes: Variations Upon a Theme' (1994) *MJ* 179–220.

WEDEMEYER and MOORE, 'The American Welfare System' in tenBroek (ed), *The Law of the Poor* (San Francisco, Chandler Pub Co, 1966) 2–33.

WELLS and HELLERSTEIN, 'The Governmental Proprietary Distinction in Constitutional Law' (1980) *VirgLRev* 1073 *et seq*.

WILLIAMS and TORRENS, *Introduction to Health Services* (New York, Chicester, 1984).

WISMAR and BUSSE, 'Freedom of Movement Challenges European Health Care Scenery' (1998) *Eurohealth* 13–15.

WOHLFARTH *et al, Die Europäische Wirtschaftsgemeinschaft—Kommentar zum Vertrag* (Berlin, Vahlen, 1960).

X, 'Unenforced Boundaries: Illegal Immigration and the Limits of Judicial Federalism' (1995) *HarvLRev* 1643–60.

X, 'Developments in Law—Immigration Policy and the Rights of Aliens' (1983) *HarvLRev* 1286–465.

ZILIOLI, 'The Recognition of Diplomas and its Impact on Educational Policies' in De Witte, *European Community Law of Education* (Baden-Baden, Nomos, 1989) 51–70.

ZOLBERG, 'Contemporary Transnational Migrations in Historical Perspective: Patterns and Dilemmas' in:Kritz (ed), *US Immigration and Refugee Policy* (1983) 36 *et seq*.

ZUBLER, 'The Right to Migrate and Welfare Reform: Time for Shapiro v. Thompson to Take a Hike' (1997) *ValpULRev* 893–950.

ZULEEG, 'Das Urteil Taflan-Met des Europäischen Gerichtshofs' (1997) *ZASR* 170 *et seq*.

——, 'International Instruments on Equal Treatment in Social Security Matters', in *Commission of the European Communities/Departemento de Relações Internaçionais e Convenções de Segurança Social, Social Security in Europe—Equality between Nationals and Non-Nationals* (1995) 89–101.

ZWICKER, 'Equal Protection III: Non-Resident Discrimination' (1986) *ASAL* 469–94.

Index